W9-CTA-778

Learning Group Leadership

Third Edition

Learning Group Leadership

Third Edition

An Experiential Approach

Jeffrey A. Kottler
California State University, Fullerton

Matt Englar-Carlson
California State University, Fullerton

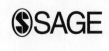

Los Angeles | London | New Delhi
Singapore | Washington DC

SAGE

Los Angeles | London | New Delhi
Singapore | Washington DC

FOR INFORMATION:

SAGE Publications, Inc.
2455 Teller Road
Thousand Oaks, California 91320
E-mail: order@sagepub.com

SAGE Publications Ltd.
1 Oliver's Yard
55 City Road
London, EC1Y 1SP
United Kingdom

SAGE Publications India Pvt. Ltd.
B 1/I 1 Mohan Cooperative Industrial Area
Mathura Road, New Delhi 110 044
India

SAGE Publications Asia-Pacific Pte. Ltd.
3 Church Street
#10-04 Samsung Hub
Singapore 049483

Copyright © 2015 by SAGE Publications, Inc.

All rights reserved. No part of this book may be reproduced or utilized in any form or by any means, electronic or mechanical, including photocopying, recording, or by any information storage and retrieval system, without permission in writing from the publisher.

Printed in the United States of America

Library of Congress Cataloging-in-Publication Data

Kottler, Jeffrey A.

Learning group leadership: an experiential approach / Jeffrey A. Kottler, California State University, Fullerton, Matt Englar-Carlson, California State University, Fullerton. — Third Edition.

pages cm
Includes bibliographical references and index.

ISBN 978-1-4522-5668-9 (pbk.: alk. paper) 1. Group relations training. 2. Social group work—Study and teaching. 3. Leadership—Study and teaching. I. Englar-Carlson, Matt. II. Title.

HM1086.K67 2014
302'.14—dc23   2014002907

This book is printed on acid-free paper.

All photos appear courtesy of Jeffrey A. Kottler.

Acquisitions Editor: Kassie Graves
Production Editor: Olivia Weber-Stenis
Copy Editor: Megan Granger
Typesetter: C&M Digitals Ltd.
Proofreader: Susan Schon
Indexer: Scott Smiley
Cover Designer: Scott Van Atta
Marketing Manager: Shari Countryman

SUSTAINABLE FORESTRY INITIATIVE
Certified Chain of Custody
Promoting Sustainable Forestry
www.sfiprogram.org
SFI-01268
SFI label applies to text stock

14 15 16 17 18 10 9 8 7 6 5 4 3 2 1

Contents

Acknowledgments

As we have just finished our own journey of completing the revision of this book, we would like to take stock of the wonderful people along the way who made this journey attainable, pleasant, and memorable. We are thankful to have worked on this project again with Kassie Graves, one of the best editors in the world. She has the uncanny ability to balance gentle encouragement, patience, and understanding. We are also grateful to our former students Kim Jackson, Larissa Patton, and Christine Tomasello for their research assistance with the previous edition. For this revision, we appreciate the research assistance and contributions from Brooke Constable, Desiree Rausch, Curtis Thompson, and Tamy Maxwell. We would also like to acknowledge the hundreds of students we have taught in group counseling classes for their feedback on effective teaching methods and clarification of group leadership concepts. Specifically, we would like to acknowledge the graduate students in counseling at California State University, Fullerton, who have been enrolled in our group courses. Many of these students contributed excerpts from their personal journals describing the joys and challenges of group leadership. Their voices and experiences serve as the background for much of this book.

I (Jeffrey) wish to acknowledge the support, caring, and cohesive group functioning of the Department of Counseling at CSUF. I have spent most of my professional life searching for a team of colleagues who not only challenge and sustain me but who can also "walk the talk" of being models of competence and integrity in their own group membership and leadership. Thank you, Alison, Leah, Skip, Jose, Sapna, Mary, Olga, and Rebekah. And Matt, my cycling partner, coauthor, coleader, trusted confidante, partner in mischief, and one of my closest friends—thank you for challenging me, pushing me, supporting me, and listening to me, helping me understand so much better what I do that matters most. I also wish to acknowledge the support of Ellen, Cary, Aliya, and Meredith, who form the primary family group in my life.

I (Matt) would like to begin by thanking my friend, colleague, and coauthor, Jeffrey Kottler. It is a joy to be around someone who loves group work as much as I do. So much of our lives are intertwined, and having you by my side has been invaluable. I continue to cherish every bike ride, coffee stop, donut experience, improvisational group performance, and moment with you. Together we have created a solid family, and I look forward to new adventures. I would also like to thank our editor at SAGE, Kassie Graves, for being the supportive and brilliant editor she is. Over my professional career, my many teachers and co-group leaders got me to this point, and I universally recall the kindness offered to me along the way. I can clearly trace my development as a group leader, from my very first group, where I struggled to say just three words, to today, when I am so excited about facilitating that I struggle to keep my mouth closed. My growth as a group leader is a direct result of thoughtful feedback and mentoring. In particular, my appreciation goes to Mark Stevens for our many years of friendship and time leading groups together. Our work at Esalen Institute is a professional highpoint in so many ways, and I am fortunate to share that time with you. My final acknowledgments are to my wife and children. Alison, you are the love of my life and my closest friend, and you make me the person I am. To my children, Jackson and Beatrix, you are the grounding force in my life, and I continue to view each of you with wonderment.

SAGE Publications would like to thank the following reviewers: Mikaela Albrecht, St Helens College; Eric Chen, Fordham University; Corinne Hutt Greenyer, University of Southampton; Marilyn MacGregor, Western New Mexico University; Marla Muxen, South Dakota State University; and Joel Muro, Texas Woman's University.

Introduction

I f you are reading this book, then you have at least a passing interest in group leadership, if not a passion for this amazing helping structure. We are really excited for you and what will likely unfold in the coming weeks. Take a deep breath, and get ready for something truly remarkable that will likely occur, an experience that will challenge and test you, that will force you to look more deeply at your own behavior as well as the complex and fascinating process of what happens when people get together in a healing environment.

We find group work to be absolutely amazing. Quite simply, there is no professional helping activity that is more fun, stimulating, and challenging than group work. No matter how much you learn or how many books you read, classes you take, workshops you attend, supervision you receive, and groups you lead, you will still find that every experience is distinctly different from any others you have witnessed previously. We have been doing this work for a lot of years, and yet we are still surprised by how much we learn in every session.

Unlike individual sessions, group work is a form of chaos in action. But there is order, pattern, and ways to navigate what appears to be both puzzling and inscrutable. In any given moment when you are attending to a single event or a client's needs, there are a hundred other things going on at the same time. As a leader, there is rarely one clear direction to take. Imagine this moment taken from the perspective of a group leader: You see group members signaling one another, smirking or frowning, shaking their heads in astonishment or perhaps confusion. Two of the group members are whispering to each other. What is that all about, you wonder, but then something else catches your attention. It appears that the group member across from you is crying. There is little time to ponder what just happened because, before you know it, there is something else going on. Then another distraction. By the time the group is over, you will likely walk out feeling energized, overwhelmed, exhausted, and confused—all at the same time. You could spend a lifetime trying to make sense of a single session and still never get a complete handle on all that transpired and what it all means. For some, the sheer volume of activity occurring in group work may be too much. For others, including us, the constant stimulation and uncertainty are what make group work the most exhilarating aspect of our work. But it is not just enjoyable for the leaders, as we also know that group operates powerfully for the group members as well.

There is something poetic and beautiful about seeing group process in action. In an appropriately led group with active and engaged members, the therapeutic process is akin to a well-oiled machine. Each group member plays a role that leads to the shared attainment of insight and connection that comes from a common bond emanating from being the only witnesses to transformative actions and relationships. And what about the poorly led group? As easy as it is to imagine the well-oiled machine, you can also imagine one broken down and burning by the side of the road. It is easy to conjure up images of awkward interactions that leave group members confused and struggling with questions of how to get help. These groups can be boring or even harmful to their members. Our hope is that this book will inspire you to create group sessions akin to the poetic experience where group members come to gain strength and encouragement.

What This Book Will Do and What It Will Not Do

Group work is a specialty area that requires a different sort of mind-set than other helping procedures. In addition to everything else you have learned about helping people change during individual or couple sessions, group work involves a whole host of additional skills, interventions, knowledge, and research. It also requires a new vision in terms of how one views interaction. Because it is far more complex and challenging than sessions with a single person, additional training is needed. That is why you have at least one course in group work. And that is why you are reading this text.

Whether your goal is to run therapy or counseling groups, lead discussion groups, introduce guidance activities, use process activities in the classroom, direct meetings or task groups, or even coach a soccer team, this book contains all the basic information, theory, concepts, research, interventions, and guidelines you will need to get started. It is not intended to provide you with everything you would want to feel completely prepared for any group situation; that is beyond the scope of any course. There are many other resources available for specific populations and settings. This book is focused on teaching you the competencies needed to actually be a leader across many types of grounds. Yet it also provides advanced skills and training for those of you who feel ready to move beyond the basics. This includes not only mastering the core process interventions, leadership behaviors, and other skills but also learning how to function in a coleadership role and make the best use of adjuncts, metaphors, and risk-taking exercises. The book also provides an understanding of the theory and research that guide clinical action. Finally, we also want to inspire you to understand the power of groups in contributing to meaningful change.

Taking an Experiential Journey

This text is a bit unusual in that it takes an *experiential approach* to the subject. What this means is that every effort has been made to help you *apply* what you are learning to real-life situations in class, your work, and your life. We want you to filter what you are reading through your own life and allow your own experiences in class to provide real-life, contextual examples. The helping professions are one of the few professional endeavors in which you have the opportunity to apply everything you are learning in your training to your personal life. This is no less true with respect to group work. As you become more skilled and perceptive about group behavior and its management, you will find yourself fostering far more confidence in any social situation. You will become more aware of what people are doing around you and what their actions mean. You will develop greater sensitivity to nuances in human behavior, even being able to "read minds" by decoding what others are thinking and feeling. You will also acquire expertise in guiding others' behavior, reducing interpersonal conflicts, working toward a consensus, and helping others feel understood. While this background helps tremendously during group sessions, such skills are just as useful in your personal life.

To master the intricacies of group leadership, you must experience the things we are writing about in this book. It is not nearly enough to merely read about group dynamics, hear a lecture about group stages, discuss ethical issues, watch videos of group sessions, or observe groups in action—you must *experience* the power of these ideas, firsthand, to learn ways to lead groups. Until you experience the feeling of being in a group, what you read is just words on the page, devoid of context.

That is why a significant portion of your time in this class is devoted to applying what you have read and heard about. This not only brings the theory and dynamics alive but also helps you find out for yourself what group members experience when they talk about their reluctance to reveal themselves and allow themselves to be known.

Some Legitimate Concerns

You may feel some legitimate apprehensions about the prospect of participating in any academic class that requires a degree of self-disclosure, or reading any text that encourages you to apply what is presented to your personal life. That is why there are ethical guidelines developed to protect you from the potential harm of dual relationships in which you might be graded not on your professional development but on who you are as a person. You will be relieved to know that instructors who teach group work are extremely sensitive to these issues; that is why they will do everything they can to protect your rights, safeguard your dignity, and provide informed consent so you know what you are doing and why.

Between us, we have more than 50 years' experience facilitating groups and teaching various group classes (Group Dynamics, Group Process and Practice, Group Experience and Applications, Group Counseling, Group Counseling Practicum, Group Techniques and Procedures, and Advanced Group Leadership, as well as Doctoral Seminar in Group); frankly, we do not know any other way to help you develop as a group leader without your (1) *experiencing* groups as a member, (2) *practicing* concepts and skills in simulations and role plays, (3) *personalizing* the content in such a way that it becomes real for you, (4) *engaging in structured opportunities* to practice leadership behaviors, and (5) *receiving constructive feedback* for improving your skills. Though being in groups (friendship groups, workplace groups, cohort groups, sports teams, etc.) is a universal experience, exploring oneself within that context is the road less traveled. We legitimately ask you, "How can you effectively and empathically ask group members to risk, reveal, and share themselves in a group setting if you have not taken those risks yourself at some point?"

So our goals for you are centered on having you experience the world of group interaction in a genuine and meaningful manner. There are challenges in meeting these goals for both the instructor and the student. Teaching group leadership in such a way that it truly comes alive is a difficult proposition that comes down to two things: patience and practice. Being fully open to a group experience will not happen overnight; rather, it will develop and deepen over the course—this patience is required. Further, it is not enough for you to learn the theory unless you can apply it to actual group situations. Test performances, term papers, and essays mean little if you cannot demonstrate leadership skills where they count the most: in the real world.

Your instructor must balance the need for realistic, experientially based activities with protecting your safety and rights against coercion, dual relationships, and casualties. Every effort will be made to inform you of risks involved, safeguards in place, and rules that protect you against harm. In that sense, the principle of *informed consent* will be followed to ensure that you know exactly what you are doing and why you are doing it—that is, how such activities are directly related to making you a skilled group leader. Ultimately, you will be given some degree of latitude in how much of yourself you choose to reveal and how much personal risk you take in venturing outside your comfort zone. Let us remind you, however, of something you are likely to say to your own group members again and again: Comfort is not associated with change. The more constructive risks you take, the more you venture into the unknown, the more you push yourself to try new behaviors and experiment with alternative roles, the more likely you will be to experience lasting change. After all, what kind of leader would you be if you asked people to do things that you were unwilling to do?

Throughout the book we offer "Student Voices," which are reflections from actual group leadership students. These voices have experienced group and have agreed to share their reactions.

Student Voice

Taking the Plunge

At the beginning of group I remember telling myself that I am not one to reveal deep and personal feelings, and I sure as heck don't do it in front of others. So I held back. After a few weeks I found myself wanting to share more but feeling a little afraid of what to talk about and how to do it. Some of the other group members seemed so skilled at revealing personal stuff, and I thought I might not be able to do it like them. But I soon came to the realization that this is part of the process of group. If I did not share I would only feel on the outside looking in. I took a small plunge after a few weeks and then a bigger one a week later. It was tough, but I felt like people listened to me, and I honestly felt different after. These people in group were strangers a few weeks ago, but after I shared, I felt closer to them. After all, they knew some things about me now that my best friends don't even know. So I learned that this was part of the bonding process that all participants must go through. There is no pressure to contribute, but there is no gain without giving it a shot and taking a risk.

You will definitely be challenged in this class. The ultimate goal is to learn enough about groups, the theory, research, and basic concepts that you can actually lead groups effectively. It will do you little good to recite facts, spout relevant theories, or choose correct answers on examinations if you cannot apply what you have learned to help others. That is why an experiential approach to this subject is so crucial. It is akin to painting: You can know all there is to know about paint, brushes, and canvases, but unless you have actually dipped the paintbrush into the paint and moved it across the canvas, your knowledge is purely academic. So we encourage you to be a painter in this course—mess around, take some risks, and see what you come up with.

In most groups, the greatest challenge each person faces is allowing yourself to be *truly* known. For you, this challenge can be seen as the opportunity to reveal yourself in the class—but not so much that you have regrets or compromise yourself in ways you would rather not. Of course, it is impossible not to reveal yourself, even if you decide to "play" the role of someone else. In everything you do and say, even when you pretend to be someone else, you are sharing a part of yourself. In any case, you want to find a balance between presenting yourself as authentically and honestly as you can and sharing more than feels comfortable. Much will depend, of course, on how much you trust your instructor and classmates and how safe the environment feels. Our belief is that, as the course progresses, you will face choice points where you will have the opportunity to share about yourself, and we encourage you to take small steps in this endeavor.

You may notice a paradoxical facet of our advice to you. On the one hand, we are saying, "Take care of yourself—don't reveal more than feels comfortable." On the other hand, we are also telling you that being uncomfortable is necessary for significant learning and change to take place. So you might legitimately ask, "What's with you guys? Are you telling me to play it safe or to stick my neck out?" Like true counselors, we are telling you to do both. Ultimately, you have to decide how much you want to learn and what you are willing to do to reach those goals. A good guide to follow is to *lean into discomfort* and risk, rather than blindly leaping into it.

A Structure That Goes Beyond Basics

This text provides the content needed to develop a working knowledge of the field's basic theoretical foundation. This will help guide your leadership behaviors, assist you in making sound ethical and clinical decisions, and, more pragmatically, support your efforts to pass any certification, licensing, or comprehensive exams. This text, moreover, will help you go far beyond those basics to where you can understand what it is like to be in the leader's chair.

As an experiential learning structure, each chapter will introduce important conceptual and practical information, and then help you apply these ideas to your work and life. As noted previously, we have included student voices, but also leader voices throughout the chapters to provide reality-based descriptions of experiences. *Reflective activities* will guide you to think about material in a particular way, considering how it might be useful in your unique situation. *Personal applications* will demonstrate how you can take what has been learned and adapt it to situations in your personal and professional life. We recommend *field studies* to help you gain valuable experience as you observe what you have read about in the real world. There are photographs (many taken by Jeffrey) that represent critical concepts. Finally, suggested class activities provide structures to practice new skills. The overall goal of all these assignments is to personalize your learning and make it come alive.

Student Voice

Dealing With Apprehensions

At the beginning of group I felt anxious and nervous. I did not know what to expect, not only from others, but from myself as well. As I trace my feelings throughout the class, I see that I gradually became more and more comfortable in the group. However, I did not truly give up my feelings of anxiety until the first time I shared deeply about myself and my experiences. Prior to sharing my story, I carried with me a certain nervousness, as I knew I was going to share more deeply at some point, but was afraid of my own feelings and the reactions of others. By sharing, I lost that fear because I realized I could handle my own feelings and the reactions of the group. Not only could I handle these things, I could learn from them and grow emotionally and interpersonally.

New to the Third Edition

Over many years and across many group courses, students have told us how much they enjoy the style of this book and its approach to teaching group leadership. Our intention in revising this book is to maintain that student-focused tone while updating the content to reflect changes in the field and current trends. There are many substantial differences in the third edition, including the following:

- More than 200 updated and new references have been added to reflect current concepts and recent evidence on group work. While our emphasis in this book is on experiential group leadership and learning, we also want the content to reflect the growing evidence base that supports group work.
- One of more exciting trends in group leadership is the focus on social justice and client advocacy. Throughout the entire book we have addressed and integrated social justice concerns, and, notably, Chapter 16 (Group Leadership Applied to Social Justice and Social Action) has been completely rewritten. This chapter reflects the wealth of scholarly work published since the second edition of this book, in particular the Association for Specialists in Group Work's Multicultural and Social Justice Competence Principles for Group Workers (Singh, Merchant, Skudrzyk, & Ingene, 2012). Further, it reflects our own experiences engaged in social justice group leadership in our community.
- We added a new Chapter 17 (The End of Our Journey: Where to Go Next?) as a final chapter to the book.
- A focus on multicultural and diversity issues remains a priority throughout all the chapters in the book. Student voices and group case examples reflect the broadest range of cultural identities.
- More than 30 new photos have been added, replacing older photos. Many of these images reflect group leadership in action.
- A new DVD accompanies the third edition. This DVD focuses on conceptualizing group process, seeing a real group in action, and emphasizes group leader intervention. Group participants in the DVD are graduate students in experiential training groups exploring their own actual concerns. We have created an exciting way to see many of the concepts from the text come alive.

Meet Your Authors

We have written about this book as a journey you are about to undertake, and it is reasonable to wonder about your guides who are leading the way. We met years ago out jogging in the streets of New Orleans (where we were attending a conference) on the morning after Halloween. In that context, we started our first conversation about group work. Over the following years, we made plans to run together when we were both at the same professional conferences, and naturally our conversations always shifted to group work and the exciting experiences we were having. As it tends to do in life, serendipity happened; life took an interesting, yet unexpected twist. At one of our professional conferences we found ourselves as members in a makeshift experiential group for male counselor educators. Naturally, as the group began, some concerns were raised about vulnerability and confidentiality—namely, how could the group members be vulnerable when it was quite likely that future contact outside the group would occur? We might engage in future scholarly projects, work in the same place or clinical setting, or even be in the position of hiring each other somewhere down the road (which might be a concern you are having right now, as you begin the process of joining an experiential group with your classmates). Those concerns seemed to bring the group process to a halt, as it appeared few group members wanted to take risks. Throwing caution to the wind, we (Jeffrey and Matt) saw each other in the room and just began to share about valuing vulnerability and revealing parts of ourselves. A few others followed, but there was not enough momentum and this was not a terribly successful group. Oddly enough, 7 months later, Matt found himself interviewing for a faculty position at California State University, Fullerton, and the search committee contained two people who had been in that group. Later, we talked about how that small group experience had brought us closer together and how, rather than hindering future contact, being vulnerable had enhanced our desire for a deeper relationship.

Over the years we have become much closer. We have spent many hours together in shared activities such as surfing, running, and cycling. We have joined in the celebrations of marriages and births with our collective families and also consoled and supported each other through grief and loss. We have taught internationally in Australia and engaged in social justice work in Nepal. In short, we have known each other in a variety of contextual groups, both professionally and personally. Given this inside knowledge, we thought it might be useful for us to introduce each other, beginning with Matt reflecting on Jeffrey.

Matt: Jeffrey is a deeply loving and caring person. What is remarkable is that his intentions to connect with and better the world around him remain consistent in his public persona as a successful writer, teacher, and scholar, and in his more private persona as a loving husband, father, grandfather, colleague, and friend. What you see is what you get—and that can be both wildly attractive and scary at times. Jeffrey is driven in ways I do not fully understand, but most of this drive relates to experiencing the full richness of life with all his senses. He is game to try just about anything and open himself up to the full experience (physical, emotional, or psychological), even when the outcome is uncertain. That is a rare quality. I have seen Jeffrey climb Himalayan peaks, attempt to surf huge waves, be driven to tears by a beautiful story, finish monumental bike rides, tackle completely new classes and writing projects, and struggle to reveal painful parts of who he is in the midst of personal difficulties. In all these experiences, he is a seeker of new knowledge and experience. He is figuratively allergic to being bored—his impatience stems from a desire to avoid the mundane and engage solely in deepening experiences. Carpe diem, indeed. This is not an act or a performance; it is who he is. In group settings, Jeffrey always has an eye for facilitating growth experiences for others by encouraging people to take just one more step farther than they expected. Again, he looks to move people toward the ambiguous and unexplored parts of who they are. Importantly, he is not afraid to take the first risk and model for others. In that sense, he can be unpredictable and spontaneous, but he does not suffer fools or psychological defenses all that well. Rather, he wants his group members, students, and friends to come along for the *whole* ride.

Jeffrey: In many ways, Matt is my role model even though he is 20 years younger than I am. He introduced me to coffee, to biking, and to one of my best friends—his son, who plays with me when he is not otherwise occupied. Matt and I are opposites in a lot of ways, which I suppose makes us very compatible as coleaders. Whereas I am inclined toward impulsivity, Matt is reflective, deliberate, and moves at his own pace. I envy Matt because of his (seemingly) effortless grace—whether riding a bike, playing sports, or operating in groups. I can be overly blunt and direct (sometimes insensitive), yet Matt responds in our faculty meetings, classes, and groups with incredible sensitivity and patience. Sometimes I stand (or sit) in awe of Matt and his wisdom so far beyond his years, how he manages to say things to others that I could never get away with because of his wit and caring. When we colead, I defer to him when a confrontation is required because he can accomplish this without others even realizing they have been challenged.

Since I used to be chair of our department, one of my tasks was to review instructor evaluations, which in Matt's case are as close to perfection as one can get. If Matt has one major struggle that I have noticed, it is trying to resolve the conflict between his ambition and desire to be productive and the time his work takes away from his family, friendships, sports, and cycling. He struggles sometimes with appreciating what he's got, rather than dwelling on dreams and fantasies of what else might be possible. And who among us is immune to that?

In these brief introductions, we've presented ourselves to you in much the same way we might if we were coleading a group. A critical aspect of leading groups involves modeling for your group members the ways you wish them to be, meaning the embodiment of openness, authenticity, warmth, courage, and essential kindness.

What You Can Expect

This text is divided into three main parts. The first section, Foundations of Group Work, covers basic concepts and introduces you to the field of group leadership. Chapter 1 discusses the strengths and weaknesses of a group approach, as well as the types of groups you might lead. Chapter 2 puts the focus on your own group behavior throughout your lifetime. What are the roles you usually play in groups? What are your personal strengths and weaknesses as a potential group leader? What are the ways you can develop yourself, as a person, to become a more influential and effective helper?

Chapters 3 and 4 cover the basic theory of group dynamics and group behavior in such a way that you will understand the ways people typically act. Chapter 3 explores why group leadership requires a more "systemic" approach to assessment and diagnosis. This means you must look at the circular dynamics that occur between people, in which every action affects and is in turn affected by whatever else occurs. Furthermore, like any living organism, a group has a developmental cycle that is rather predictable. Chapter 4 reviews the stages of group development and looks at the techniques and perspectives group leaders use at each stage.

Chapter 5 examines the sort of individual and cultural differences associated with one identity that occur among people, and how they intersect in a group setting. You have probably already learned something about the importance of exploring the cultural background and salient identity of each group member and tailoring interventions in line with one's worldview and identity. This can be much more difficult in group settings, with the endless cultural identities represented in the various group members. Furthermore, peer pressure is often rampant in group settings, and coercion often forces conformity toward the majority viewpoint. This chapter explores how leaders can use group work to engage diverse cultural identities.

Chapter 6 closes the conceptual material by reviewing the theoretical approaches to group leadership. Just as in individual or family interventions, there are dozens of excellent theoretical frameworks for guiding your professional actions. You must learn about these various paradigms even though you are likely to stick with only one or a few of them. We will review some of the traditional frameworks and also some new, innovative theoretical models.

The second part of the book, Skills of the Group Leader, covers practical considerations. This begins with Chapter 7, which explores diagnostic processes. Whereas in an individual setting, concentration is often focused on a single person's dysfunctions, personality, and presenting complaints, in a group you must do all this plus attend to the larger phenomena that are unfolding. The conceptual background you developed in the early chapters will equip you with what you need to recognize significant patterns.

Chapters 8, 9, and 10 are among the most practical in the text. They cover the specific skills and interventions needed to lead a group effectively. We will look at pragmatic interventions for creating healthy groups and then explore how to work with specific concerns and interactions.

The third part of the book, Applications and Significant Issues, looks at some of the core themes and reoccurring issues that arise in group settings. Chapter 11 introduces a model for coleading groups with colleagues so you might gain valuable experience under safe and constructive conditions. Most novice group leaders will start coleading groups, and this chapter addresses the benefits and difficulties associated with this model of leadership.

Chapter 12 reviews challenges, obstacles, and critical issues you will face. We try to illustrate common real-life situations that you will encounter as a leader. The chapter is meant to encourage you to understand effective ways of meeting these challenges before you experience them for the first time.

Chapter 13 considers ethical issues and how the group setting presents unique dilemmas and expectations. You will learn how to prepare yourself for these inevitable challenges in such a way that you can respond appropriately.

The final section of the book, Advanced Group Structures, explores some of the skills, interventions, and adjuncts to group work that are available to group leaders. Chapter 14 addresses advanced group leadership by reviewing the use of interventions and metaphors, and how to work with difficult group members. Chapter 15 looks at additional interventions and support structures available to group leaders and members. Chapter 16 focuses on the ways you can apply what you have learned in the larger community to promote social justice and social action. This is a significant aspect of group work, and this chapter provides practical guidelines and reflection on what you can expect. In closing the book, Chapter 17 offers some final thoughts on where you can go next to continue your leadership training.

Some Final Advice

As you prepare for this long journey, we want to offer you encouragement and support. We wholeheartedly welcome you to the wonderful world of group work, but we also caution that this can be a trip with ups and downs. Keep an open mind, and approach the subject with a mixture of excitement and apprehension.

Become reflective about your own behavior and its impact on others, and in doing so learn to be responsible for yourself. Confront your excuses for avoiding action. Work to do your part to create a supportive climate and atmosphere of trust in your class. Take some constructive risks by pushing yourself to go beyond what is familiar and comfortable. After all, isn't this what you intend to ask of others? If you can do that with good faith and effort, we have little doubt that your world is about to change. Buckle up, take a deep cleansing breath, and let the adventure begin. . . .

Part I

Foundations of Group Work

The World of Groups 1

There was a noticeable buzz in the room when the group leader walked in and took her customary seat. Clearly, the dozen or so adolescents in attendance were excited about the scheduled session, yet there was also a hint of apprehension in the air. The leader felt a little anxious as well: No matter how many groups she ran, or how much time she spent at the helm, she still felt uncertain about what would unfold. Would the group members be in a mood to disclose themselves in any sort of authentic and honest way? What if they wouldn't talk at all? Or worse yet, what if someone shared a problem so serious that everyone else was scared off?

The leader took a deep breath and went through a mental checklist of things to consider before she called the group to order. Remember to talk to them about confidentiality and how impossible it is to guarantee it. Discuss boundaries and ground rules. Warn them about the ways people can get hurt, and tell them that they always have the right to pass. Mention the problem of having limited time to divide equitably among all the participants. Oh yeah—most important of all—inspire them to take risks so the work of building cohesion and intimacy can begin. And through it all, try to normalize the anxiety and curiosity that accompanies the first session. Remember to pace things in a way that keeps everyone engaged but doesn't scare anyone away. And remember to breathe.

This group hasn't even started yet, she thought to herself with a shake of her head, *and already I feel a headache coming on . . . but I also feel the rush of adrenaline.*

For Reflection

Take a moment to think back to the feelings and thoughts you experience when you come to a group for the first time. What are you excited about? What is most scary? What are the first things you notice when you come into a new group? What are the things you typically do to help yourself feel more comfortable and less anxious?

The Challenge of Leading Groups

Welcome to the world of group leadership, a helping activity that is among the most powerful structures available to promote lasting changes in behavior. This is a therapeutic environment that is so fertile, enriched, stimulating, and laden with learning opportunities that often people can make dramatic progress within relatively short periods of time. This potent atmosphere, however, does not come without certain risks (Argyrakouli & Zafiropoulou, 2007; DeLucia-Waack & Donigian, 2004; Moreno, 2007; Rapin, 2014; Sadr, 2006). Some of these risks are as follows:

1. Casualties can occur far more easily in group sessions than in individual sessions, because the leader has considerably less control over the proceedings.

2. Peer pressure increases the likelihood that participants may be coerced to do or say things for which they do not yet feel ready.

3. Confidentiality cannot be guaranteed, and so personal disclosures could be compromised.

4. One member who demands disproportionate attention, or who exhibits a highly manipulative or abusive behavior, can cloud the whole experience for others.

5. It is difficult to monitor closely how each participant is responding to circumstances during any given moment.

6. Safety is more difficult to maintain. Scapegoating can easily occur.

7. It is easier for someone to hide and not be helped. Quieter members may be shortchanged.

8. Members of minority cultural groups may be forced to conform to majority values that are dominant in the group.

Whereas there is most likely an appropriate group for almost everyone, it just might not be the one you are leading. That is our way of saying that there are some people for whom groups may not be the best fit at that time; rather, they may benefit from individual treatment. Thus, providing appropriate referrals to help people find the best setting and screening group members for goodness of fit becomes paramount (Rapin, 2014; Riva, Wachtel, & Lasky, 2004). Those coping with acute distress, feeling actively suicidal, and/or with narcissistic or psychotic features may not be the best candidates for a community-based group experience, but they might find a better fit with another form of group, such as those offered in an inpatient setting (Emer, 2004; Yalom & Leszcz, 2005). Furthermore, groups are often not the best setting for certain people, especially those who are interpersonally prone to manipulation, control, dominance, intellectualizing, or game playing. Others who are unusually vulnerable or shy may feel too inhibited to use the structure effectively (Table 1.1). Of course, those with low motivation and an inability to follow group rules may also find groups difficult (MacNair-Semands, 2002).

Table 1.1 Avoiding Casualties in Groups

Think of a time you participated in a group experience in which you or someone else felt hurt. What happened in that encounter that most contributed to the negative effects? Protecting members is an ethical obligation, a part of the ethical codes of all helping professions. This often means discussing the impact of exploring concerns in a group setting and assessing one's ability to cope with new changes. Safeguards can be used to protect clients from potential negative effects:

1. Adequately prepare all group members before the first session so that they understand the expectations of the group and the advantages and disadvantages of the group setting.

2. Don't pressure anyone to do anything for which he or she does not feel ready.

3. Don't allow anyone in the group to speak or act disrespectfully toward others.

4. Check in frequently with each member to see how interactions and events are being interpreted and experienced.

5. Make sure that permission is secured before anyone is invited or encouraged to reveal himself or herself.

6. Emphasize collective responsibility for taking care of one another.

7. Stress the importance of confidentiality, and talk about how to handle transgressions.

8. Negotiate clear ground rules of appropriate behavior; enforce these boundaries consistently.

9. Note that confrontation is a natural interpersonal process and a useful tool in a group, but not if it is used to harm or attack another group member. Group leaders can model appropriate ways to confront others and can look to focus on specific behaviors rather than making complete judgments about another group member.

10. Don't attempt any intervention unless you have a clear, defensible rationale for what you wish to accomplish.

11. Work under the supervision of or in collaboration with a more experienced colleague.

The Joys of Leading Groups

We don't wish to begin our journey together by instilling in your mind a great fear for all the harm you might inadvertently cause through your inexperience, neglect, misjudgments, or mistakes. It is a good thing to have a healthy respect, even awe, for the potential power of therapeutic groups. However, it is also important to keep the cautions in mind so you proceed carefully and sensitively in your leadership efforts.

> **Student Voice**
>
> ### I Love Group
>
> *I entered the graduate program just to learn about leading groups. Without a doubt, the most significant events in my life have happened in groups, and I want to be a part of that. Even at work, I tend to always feel better in group settings. Maybe it is because culturally I am used to working with others like my family and neighborhood to get things done. Usually, I am a rather cautious and reserved person, but something feels right in group settings to the point where I thrive in the unpredictability and crave the immediate real interactions. The other part that I absolutely love is the live emotions that are so raw and real.*

In spite of the limitations and side effects previously mentioned (or possibly because of them), groups are also ideal places for change to take place (Kottler, 2014).

1. Perhaps more than ever, people hunger for intimacy and closeness with others. Groups provide a surrogate family of support and nurturance.

2. Groups provide simulated experiences for participants to practice new behaviors in safe settings and then receive constructive feedback that can be incorporated into future efforts.

3. Not only do group members receive help in groups, but they also have the chance to help other group members. In that sense, people can feel as though the group environment allows opportunities to provide for the social welfare of others.

4. Vicarious learning, modeling, and observational learning occur readily in groups where members can grow as a result of witnessing others do work.

5. Participants learn leadership and helping skills at the same time as they work on their own personal issues. They are able to practice helping others.

6. Groups tend to be emotionally charged environments, sparking the kind of arousal that often leads to change if processed constructively.

7. After experimenting with new ways of thinking, feeling, or behaving in the group, participants receive feedback and suggestions for improvement.

8. Groups are often the most efficient use of available resources and tend to be cost-effective.

9. Groups can provide one of the rare situations in life where members can ask for and receive honest and truthful feedback on how others see and experience them.

10. Group settings provide for a diversity of viewpoints and maximum resources that may be harnessed during the process of helping people develop new alternatives.

For a Class Activity

With several partners, talk to one another about the best group experience you ever had. Each of you should take a few minutes to describe what happened and what effects you experienced in that group and afterward. As with any group exercise, make sure that each person gets a fair share of time and that no one person dominates the discussion.

Make a list of the variables and characteristics that appear commonly throughout all your stories. What was it about these groups that seemed to provoke the most constructive changes? Be prepared to talk to the larger group about what you discovered as the most important ingredients of effective group experiences.

The World of Groups

Although so far we have been looking at particular kinds of groups that are designed, by their very nature, to be educational or therapeutic for participants, human beings experience group structures on a daily basis. The moment we are born, we enter a family group that is designed to offer protection and safety and to teach us the skills we need to survive in the world. Our species is often described as "social organisms," meaning that we are actually built to function as part of tribal units (Glantz & Pearce, 1989). At least historically, our very survival has depended on the strength of our kinship bonds (Wright, 1994). Evolutionary science confirms that interpersonal relationships are adaptive and necessary. Without deep, reciprocal bonds with others, human beings would not survive. Similar to ants, termites, and herd animals, humans cannot live very well on their own; we have evolved as group creatures whose well-being depends on cooperation, division of labor, and reciprocal favors (Buss, 2011; Dugatkin, 1999). In this regard, we cannot really understand an individual person without taking the time to consider how that person functions within a matrix of interpersonal relationships.

Social cooperation is certainly a part of the different ways people earn a living and contribute to the gross national product. Almost all our work is connected to the activities of others; all our efforts are synchronized within the context of a larger group system that has its own hierarchy of authority and control.

Just imagine what we would look like to aliens observing our actions from above. We commute to work in "herds," congregate together in meetings and consultations, and go out to lunch or for coffee in small units. Even when we appear to be alone, we are actually connected to others through computer or television screens, telephones, faxes, and even our fantasies.

Not only do we spend most of our lives working in groups, but we also choose to spend as much discretionary time as possible in the company of others. We live with families, composed of immediate kin or perhaps chosen as roommates. Depending on cultural background, some individuals live as part of larger extended families, sometimes in the same home but often in the same vicinity. Neighborhoods become the next level of tribal affiliation, as do memberships in clubs and organizations, churches, temples, and synagogues.

It is important also to note that group and communal interaction is a long-standing form of healing and surviving that has been a critical part of numerous indigenous cultures. As opposed to the more individually focused cultural identities, many cultures have more of a communal or group-focused orientation to life and mental health. During healing rituals, not only is the whole community present for support but so, too, are all the ancestral spirits, who are invited to lend their guidance and the wisdom of the ages (Kottler, Carlson, & Keeney, 2004).

Humans join dozens of groups as part of their work, social, or leisure activities. Take an inventory of your own group memberships and you will notice that you are part of various teams, committees, and clubs. You go to parties for fun.

Even now, as part of your commitment to learn group leadership skills, you are part of a community setting, a group that exists to promote learning.

The inescapable conclusion here is that most people are dependent on groups. We often learn best in groups, especially through direct experiences in which we can (1) interact with others, (2) observe others modeling new behaviors, (3) find support and encouragement, (4) take risks and receive constructive feedback, and (5) feel a sense of cohesion, intimacy, and strong connection to others. If you think about it, those are exactly the conditions that ideally will operate in this group class.

For a Field Study

Look at the ways you spend a typical day. Keep a log of how much time you spend in the company of others—as part of a group. Note the roles you play in these various groups. Monitor how others' behavior affects your moods, choices, and actions.

Observe others you know going about their daily business, functioning as part of many different groups. Initiate discussions with family members, classmates, and friends about the ways their lives are controlled by various groups.

Kinds of Groups

Although the generic term *group work* describes the therapeutic process of helping people learn about themselves for the purpose of making constructive behavioral and life changes, some specific varieties of group treatment are uniquely geared toward special goals, situations, and client populations. If many different kinds of groups are part of daily existence, the same is true for the variety of groups for which you may someday serve in a leadership role. Depending on your career goals, desired work setting, and preferred specialty, you may be required to lead any of the following groups.

EXPERIENTIAL GROUPS

In the history of the group movement, the discipline developed primarily from two main sources: vocational-guidance groups that were begun in schools by pioneers such as Jesse Davis and Frank Parsons and personal-growth groups that emerged in the 1940s from the work of Kurt Lewin, Wilfred Bion, and Carl Rogers (Barlow, 2014; Gladding, 2012). It is this second force that spawned the concept of growth groups, or experiential groups, that became so popular in the 1960s. Images might immediately come to mind of a bunch of hippies sitting around in an encounter group, spilling their deepest secrets, confronting one another, and perhaps even ending up in a hot tub together.

Historically, growth groups were divided into three main types: training, encounter, and marathon. Used primarily in business and educational settings, the training groups were designed to develop greater interpersonal sensitivity and skills in participants. Encounter groups were developed as an extension of Rogers's person-centered theory and evolved from a training format to include growth opportunities for people in all settings. Rather than concentrating on skill development, the goal was to increase genuineness and authenticity. These groups are often called personal-growth groups. In the marathon structure, prolonged time periods (over a weekend) permitted more intense, in-depth interactions that broke down defenses and promoted greater intimacy (Stanger & Harris, 2005; Weigel, 2002).

In one sense, all groups are experiential in that they provide participants with direct experience—hence the focus of this text. That is why the group course is often taught in such a way that you can (1) study the ways groups operate, (2) increase awareness of your own reactions to various incidents and interventions, (3) analyze and make sense of experiences in light of the theory and research presented, and (4) increase the resources available for later learning. In other words, you find out what works and what does not work based on your own personal observations and experiences. While these data are certainly limited, biased, and prone to "sampling error," they provide a legitimate source of information to complement what you read, study, and hear in lectures and discussions.

Since the encounter group movement in the 1960s and 1970s, experiential or growth groups have gained a degree of respectability even for mainstream settings (Barlow, 2014). Many members of the clergy, for example, lead growth groups in their churches and temples to build greater cohesion and intimacy among congregants.

If guidance/educational groups are on one end of a continuum that concentrates on content and intellect, then experiential groups are on the other end, emphasizing affect and interpersonal engagement. They stress (1) learning through doing instead of merely talking about issues, (2) role-playing and rehearsal of new skills, (3) the primacy of direct experience that comes from increased awareness and action, and (4) structured practice until new skills become part of one's normal functioning (Johnson & Johnson, 2012).

Much of the negative publicity surrounding this type of group during the encounter group era was attributed to casualties that occurred as a result of poorly trained leaders, little screening of participants, and unchecked coercion of members (Stanger & Harris, 2005; Yalom & Leszcz, 2005). Nowadays, in any group, efforts are made to safeguard members through appropriate screening, informed consent (letting members know the risks involved), defining clear boundaries, preventing dual relationships, and protecting the rights of individuals to pass.

Experiential types of growth groups tend to have certain characteristics that distinguish them from others. They are more focused on the present than the past. Members tend to be reasonably well-adjusted and working on general growth issues rather than specific problems. The focus is on interaction among members, providing opportunities for feedback and practice of new behaviors. Members are invited to concentrate on self-disclosure, risk taking, and being as authentic and genuine as possible with one another. The emphasis in the group is often on "processing," which is the action of group members examining and reflecting on their own behavior and the behavior of the group as a whole to finding meaning, knowledge, and awareness about what is happening and why (Brown, 2009; Ward, 2014).

One experiential growth group might look something like this:

Leader: We were talking earlier about our fears of being closer to one another and how this pattern plays itself out in other relationships.

Tomas: Yeah. Well, it's just not part of my culture for men to be that intimate, if you know what I mean.

Carole: [Laughs] Yeah, that's our loss.

Tomas: Hey, back off!

Leader: Tomas, talk to Carole about how you're feeling right now after that comment.

Tomas: It's just that she always jumps on me . . .

Leader: [Pointing] Tell Carole.

Tomas: Why are you digging at men like that? I never did anything to you before.

Carole: No, you misunderstand, Tomas. I like you. I really like you. I'm just frustrated because you won't let me get close to you.

Leader: Kia, I noticed you nodding your head while Carole was talking to Tomas. Perhaps you could talk to Tomas as well about how you see him.

You can see quite readily that the emphasis in this type of group is helping participants learn more about themselves and about the ways they interact with others. In this interaction, group members are encouraged to speak directly to each other about their experience with each other in the present moment. While the interaction above could easily have occurred in other types of groups we will discuss, it illustrates the main ingredients of an experiential growth group in which members work on becoming aware of issues in themselves, others, and their interactions.

TASK GROUPS

Just like it sounds, some groups come together to accomplish rather specific goals. Such groups include staff meetings, task forces, committees, community organizations, and similar structures that are designed to complete mutually determined tasks. They also involve the sort of informal study groups you might organize to prepare for class projects or exams.

In task groups, while attention may be paid to member needs and the process developing among participants, the main focus is on completing some assignment or objective that is related to the world outside of the group. In effect, the main goal is getting down to the business at hand (Levi, 2011). This could involve solving a problem, reaching a consensus, or developing a plan to be implemented.

For a Classroom Activity

Try completing some complicated, stressful, and challenging assignment in which there is diversity of opinion about the best way to proceed. For example, meet in groups of six to eight to determine a new procedure for assigning grades in the class. With a volunteer leader, take about 10 or 15 minutes to discuss various options.

Debrief one another afterward, talking not just about your relative effectiveness in completing your assigned task but also about how members felt during the experience. Did each person feel heard, acknowledged, and understood? How satisfying was the experience for each member? It is not only what you do that is important but also how you do it.

Now reconvene your group to continue your discussion for another 15 minutes. This time, however, identify two individuals to serve as coleaders. While one leader will perform the task of the facilitation role attempted earlier, making sure that people stay focused on the assignment, the other leader will closely monitor the extent to which members are being heard and understood.

Discuss the differences between the two group experiences.

The percentage of task groups in the workplace has been increasing over time (Levi, 2011). More and more often, companies and organizations are interested in hiring group leaders or "process consultants" who can help various work groups function more effectively, not only developing better "products" but also helping participants feel more valued and supported. One of the main reasons for the rise in workplace task groups is the increasing complexity of work tasks and uses of technology to form online communities. Since product development or process improvement is increasingly requiring more knowledge and skill than what one can handle on one's own, most work tasks are being undertaken by teams. Collaboration and effective communication between employees and managers is essential and often requires effective group membership and leadership skills (Wheelan, 2004b).

The most common interventions used to help task groups become more effective and productive involve team-building strategies (Burke et al., 2009). This involves trust building, communication, decision making, and other aspects of effective group dynamics. Leaders who work with task groups tend to be skilled not only in therapeutic-type skills designed to help members develop trust, cohesion, and close affiliations but also in those interventions needed to keep the group productive to reach the stated objectives (Komives, Lucas, & McMahon, 2013). Traditionally, leaders work to balance between traditionally male-gendered activities that are focused on content, goals, objectivity, and measured performance, and traditionally female-gendered values that emphasize process, feelings, communication, and quality of experience. The best task-group leaders borrow the strengths of each approach so the team members develop characteristics demonstrating commitment to the group goals, involvement in and support of the process, a sense of pride and recognition in the contributions, and a feeling of personal satisfaction in the efforts. Other innovative leadership models with task groups involve the use of emotional intelligence, which is the ability to recognize and understand emotions and the skill to use this awareness to manage self and relationships with others, as a means of creating a cooperative and effective group (Blattner & Bacigalupo, 2007).

EDUCATIONAL GROUPS

The purpose of an educational or psychoeducational group is often to disseminate specific information to participants (Rath, Bertisch, & Elliot, 2014). You are most likely in this type of group right now. Similar to task groups, there tends to be a balance between content and process (Brown, 2011). In other words, your job in this classroom group is not only to learn the theory, research, and skills of group leadership but also to experience the process of constructive groups. Your attitudes, thoughts, feelings, interactions, and very personal reactions to the content of the course (and this text) are just as important as the material. The objective of educational groups is to help participants meet desired learning objectives, while also addressing distinctly emotional/social needs.

Almost every helping professional leads some group in this category. Social workers, psychologists, addiction counselors, and mental health counselors run groups designed to inform participants about the dangers of alcohol and drugs. People court-ordered due to engaging in spousal or child abuse, as well as convicted drunk drivers, are often mandated to participate in groups that are structured to educate them about the consequences of their behavior. Private practitioners and other psychological educators offer courses for the public on themes related to self-esteem, assertiveness, weight loss, and eating disorders. Elementary school counselors run a whole curriculum of guidance/educational groups for younger children, covering themes of conflict, sharing, self-confidence, and values clarification. High school counselors organize similar groups structured around career guidance, college planning, study skills, sexually transmitted diseases, decision making, relationship skills, and divorce adjustment. College counselors offer dozens of educational groups as well, customizing the themes to their audience. Family counselors might present short courses on effective negotiating skills, marital satisfaction, parenting, or sex education.

Regardless of the setting and specialty area, educational/guidance groups tend to be rather content oriented, with specific lesson plans and learning objectives. They rely on questionnaires, multimedia presentations, group discussions, role-playing, panel presentations, mini-lectures, and other strategies that combine the delivery of information with opportunities to personalize the content. Education groups also allow members to learn in a group environment and receive some emotional support, and this often occurs in a cost-effective manner (Rath et al., 2014).

For Reflection or a Classroom Activity

Pick some topic that you know quite a bit about. It should be a subject that has an emotional component, as well as a content area.

Design a short course that you could teach to a group of people. Include a specific outline and lesson plans to cover eight sessions.

Build into your structure not only the information that you want to impart but also how you intend to help participants personalize and integrate the material in their lives. You might want to consider including focused discussions, reflective activities, skills practice, role plays, small-group exercises, and similar structures.

If possible, present a part of your unit (5 minutes) to your class or work group. Solicit feedback from the participants on how you could improve your program.

PROCESS GROUPS

If the emphasis of some educational groups is on content, another type stresses the process of learning. In a process group, the focus is rarely on the educational content germane to the topic, although this content is important. Rather, the focus is more on the psychological and social issues that are generated around the content or topic (Rath et al., 2014). A commonality among these groups is their emphasis on processing, which helps participants reflect on their behavior and that of other members present. Processing can be defined as an "activity in which individuals and groups regularly examine and reflect upon their behavior in order to extract meaning, integrate the resulting knowledge, and thereby improve functioning and outcome" (Ward & Litchy, 2004, p. 104). Not only can such a focus address underlying issues, and increase productivity and outcomes, but it can also help people feel heard and validated (Ward, 2014). In running effective meetings, for example, it is necessary that leaders understand and focus not only on the content (e.g., agenda, goals, discussion topics) but also on the interpersonal process components. This might involve asking questions such as, "What is going on right now?" "What is the meaning of the long silences?" "How can more people become actively engaged?"

As another example, imagine that a teacher is introducing to a group of ninth-graders a unit on the American Civil War. The content of this presentation would, of course, be on the facts of the historical record as they are currently known: What precipitated the conflict? What were the turning points in the war? Who were the notable protagonists in the struggle? Which battles were most significant, and what were their outcomes? This is the traditional introduction of content material that is deemed important.

For Reflection

For new group leaders, getting an understanding of process can often be tricky. As noted above, in group interactions, there are two major ingredients: content and process. The first deals with subject matter or the task on which the group is working. In most interactions, the focus of attention of all persons is on the content. The second ingredient, process, is concerned with what is happening among and to the group members while the group is working. Group process deals with items such as morale, feeling, tone, atmosphere, influences, participation, styles of influence, leadership struggles, conflict, competition, cooperation, and so on. These can often be sensed in an emotional moment. The process component of any interaction can often be understood as what is not being said or conveyed in the content. In that sense, it communicates the true nature of the relationship among those involved.

In most of the usual interactions in life, very little attention is paid to process, even when it is the major cause of ineffective group action or the very thing that makes you feel uncomfortable. In many cultures, drawing attention to the process is viewed as rude or socially inappropriate behavior. However, in group settings, being able to detect and being sensitive to group processes will better enable you to diagnose group problems early and deal with them effectively. Since these processes are present in all groups, awareness of them will enhance your worth to a group and enable you to be a more effective group leader. Below are some guidelines to help you observe and analyze group process. At the group level, which is looking at the unit as a whole, consider the following:

- What are the themes that have emerged?
- What is the energy in the group like?
- Where are there tensions in the group?
- When do the group members seem particularly tense?
- What precedes tense moments?
- What are the repetitive patterns of behavior in the group (e.g., what is the order of speaking, what members always support/attack each other, who breaks the silences, who takes risks, who rescues the group)?
- What is the emotional tone of the group?
- How do members react to distressed members?
- How do members respond to one another's self-disclosure? The leader's self-disclosure?
- What are the incongruences between verbal and nonverbal messages?
- What is the body language of the members? Are they excited, bored, agitated?
- What is the tone of voice being used? Focus less on *what* is being said and more on *how* things are being said.
- What did group members carefully avoid talking about? In short, what things were *not* said?
- What does the group look to the leader for? Direction? Affection? Answers?

Whether you ever work as a teacher or become responsible for introducing some sort of content material to group members, another facet of the learning includes attention to process dimensions in addition to cognitive mastery. In the preceding example discussing the Civil War, for instance, the teacher might direct attention in quite a different direction from the original lesson plan on the causes of the war.

Teacher: Megan, I notice you seem a little bored during this talk on the causes of the Civil War.

Megan: No, it's not that . . .

Teacher: That's okay. Some of this material can be boring if you don't see how it means something to your life.

Timmy: [Blurts out] You mean like sex?

Teacher: Exactly. So let's think of a way that what we've been doing can be related to what's important to you.

Megan: But how could this history stuff . . . ? You know.

Teacher: Well, let's all think of a time when each of us got into a huge fight with someone over something that started out seemingly small and, over time, became a very big deal.

The teacher moves the discussion from one level of engagement to quite another that involves the students' own experiences, feelings, and values. It takes the engagement from a discussion of facts and content from the past to a present encounter of how the content is being experienced at the moment. One could say that this is what all good teaching is about, regardless of the setting and context. We would have to agree. In fact, both of us overwhelmingly teach our courses from a process perspective.

Student Voice

Learning About Process

Without a doubt the best lesson I learned about groups was understanding the process level of interaction. It was hard to figure out, but I remember my light bulb moment. During an early group I was feeling and appearing rather anxious and frightened, but nobody was saying anything about it. At that point, the group leader made a joke about how he believed that at this point everyone must have memorized what shoes others were wearing. This was a time when all of us were quiet and looking down at the floor. At first, I was taken aback, then I laughed because he was right, I could name the shoes each person was wearing since I was trying so hard not to make eye contact with anyone. And in fact, each group member was doing the same thing to hide his or her anxiety and tension. This is when it all started to make sense to me as the leader was speaking about what was not being said but was fully present in the room. The group chuckled and then got into the felt pressure and fear that was alive in the group at that time.

Traditional classroom groups become process oriented when the leader takes the following steps (Kottler & Kottler, 2006).

1. The focus changes from specific information to an exploration of underlying processes that are experienced. Let's stop for a moment and look at what has been happening these past few minutes. What have we really been talking about?

2. The learning environment changes from a focus on correct answers to an expression of opinions, feelings, and beliefs. "I know that's why the battle

started," the teacher might say, "but how do you feel about people trying to kill one another over their disputes?"

3. Participants are urged to own their personal reactions. "I know that's what the book says, but what do *you* think is going on?"

4. Small talk and rambling are reined in more than ever. Don't let the participants digress, intellectualize, or ramble. Keep them focused on their own internal processes, as well as those of the group. Anticipate that there will be some resistance to this; what you are asking people to do is not only difficult and strange but also threatening.

5. Structure discussions to be member rather than leader centered. In traditional learning environments, most communication is filtered through the teacher. If the room has been arranged in a circle, if members are directed to speak to one another, if the leader downplays authority functions and instead encourages people to talk to one another, the atmosphere becomes more open and egalitarian.

6. As the leader, attend to the dynamics and process of the group. The specifics of what this means will be discussed in the following chapters. For now, understand that you will be looking closely at the underlying meanings of behavior and the interactive patterns that emerge.

If you could listen in to the internal dialogue of a leader who is thinking in this way, you might hear the following reflections:

- Interesting that most of the boys are hanging back and the girls are more actively involved.
- I wonder what we are *not* talking about right now that is important in the discussion.
- The coalitions that have formed seem to discourage some people from talking. I've got to figure out a way to get more students involved.
- They seem to be staying with safe comments, afraid of revealing too much of themselves.
- There's a lot of approval seeking going on right now, not just toward me but toward those who are perceived as the leaders.

SELF-HELP/MUTUAL-HELP GROUPS

While, strictly speaking, you won't be leading this type of group, it is still important to know how they work so you can make use of their resources. This is particularly the case considering that more than half a million such groups are currently operating in North America alone. There are more than 800 self-help organizations that focus on almost every major chronic condition and leading cause of mortality. Some estimates indicate that 7% of adults in America participate in some sort of self-help group (Klaw & Humphreys, 2004). In fact, visits to self-help groups represent the majority of group help seeking.

Perhaps the most well-known of all such groups are Alcoholics Anonymous (AA) and Narcotics Anonymous (NA). Capitalizing on the same powerful factors that operate in any group—sense of belonging, mutual support, altruism, and sharing—self-help groups are blossoming in almost every community and setting. There are groups for the recently divorced, frustrated parents, those suffering from cancer or HIV, people learning to express emotions, people learning not to horde things, and people trying to lose weight, to mention just a few.

Self-help groups do not have professional leaders present, although they may rotate the leadership role. In addition, they differ significantly from other, therapeutic kinds of groups that you will most likely be leading. Highlighted in Table 1.2 are several distinctions to remember (Corey, 2013).

Table 1.2   Distinctions Between Self-Help and Therapeutic Groups

Self-Help Groups	Therapeutic Groups
Rotated leadership among members	Professional leaders
Leader role as peer facilitator	Leader role as consultant and expert
Single issue as focus (addictions, divorce, etc.)	Multiple issues are addressed
Homogeneous membership with shared problem	Heterogeneous membership
Emphasize inspiration and support	Emphasize understanding and action
Function as surrogate family and support	Function as catalyst for change
Tend to be open-ended and ongoing	Tend to be time limited
Accepting and supportive climate	Climate parallels real world

If you are ever called on to help guide some kind of self-help group or train others to do so, you might wish to keep the following guidelines in mind:

1. Determine what the group norms are, specifically focusing on the expectations of member participants and observing how, or if, the group members speak directly to each other during the meeting.

2. Balance the amount of structure so everyone participates constructively, but without ignoring the powerful moments.

3. Review the concept of safety so that everyone is respectful of one another and no one is cut off. Likewise, distribute the time equitably among each of the participants so no one feels cheated.

4. From the onset, use your own tone of voice and attending behaviors to model the kinds of disclosures and behaviors you want others to follow.

5. Most self-help groups are powered by members' own stories; so offer support, connection, and help from your own experiences rather than from a position of authority or expertise.

6. Be sure to explore how the members are applying what they are learning in their day-to-day lives.

For Personal Application

Attend a self-help group in some area of interest or need to you. This could be related to lifestyle (Weight Watchers), addictions (AA, NA), behavior (hoarding, Clutterers Anonymous), support (Al-Anon), grief and loss, or even leisure and entertainment (book club).

During your visits, examine the ways the effective members make the most of the experience. See if you can answer the seemingly simple yet complex question: What brings the members back each week?

COUNSELING GROUPS

There is considerable debate in the field as to whether there are meaningful differences between counseling and psychotherapy. With respect to group work, it is generally accepted that counseling groups tend to be relatively short-term, focused on adjustment issues, and designed for relatively normal-functioning individuals, whereas therapy groups are suited for inpatient settings or more severely disturbed populations that require long-term care. Historically, counseling groups tended to focus on development, enhancement, prevention, self-awareness, and growth, whereas group psychotherapy appeared more clinical and focused on reeducation through insight and a focus on the past and present (Corey, 2013). These distinctions become quite complex when you consider the varied professional training of the group leaders, who may come from social work, psychology, nursing, counseling, family therapy, psychiatry, human services, organizational development, or education and, thus, may have preferences for what they call their work. That is one reason why in this text we have been using the term *group leader* (rather than *group therapist* or *counselor*) so as to be inclusive of different fields. Furthermore, regardless of whether the activity is called *counseling* or *therapy*, virtually identical processes are usually going on within them.

Counseling groups (and most therapy groups as well) create an environment that is designed to simulate the real world as much as possible. Members work on specific problems they are experiencing, often in concert with others who may be experiencing similar difficulties. Counseling groups are aimed not only at "fixing" current problems but also preventing others in the future.

As far as what you might expect in such a group, the experiences often begin with a "check-in," in which each member briefly talks about what has transpired during the preceding week and reports on the progress made, keeping in mind the previous sessions. Depending on the length of the sessions (40 to 50 minutes in a school, 1 hour in some community agencies, or 90 minutes to 3 hours in other settings), several members receive specific help in the group working on their identified difficulties. Typically, groups are co-led by two trained leaders, but in some settings members act as coleaders, being guided by the leader to the appropriate behaviors that are most useful. Often, members identify strongly with the person receiving attention and may choose to share their own experiences or reflections related to the theme. Sometimes, a core theme may evolve in a given session, and many individuals may talk about their issues related to love, rejection, failure, or a similar subject. The session usually ends with members doing a "go-around," taking turns talking about what they are leaving with and what they intend to do during the next week to apply what they have learned.

Ideally, counseling groups are designed to be as heterogeneous as possible, with the greatest possible diversity in cultural background and experience so that more varied resources are available for members. Screening is usually done to make sure that each member is suitable for the group and will be a compatible team member. Such groups are often limited to a specified period of time—for example, 10 weeks, one semester, or 6 months.

Peering into a counseling group in action, we join them during the fifth session, smack in the middle of the "working stage."

Myra:	My father doesn't listen to me at all. My mother . . . I wish she didn't listen at all, 'cause she's just a pain in the butt.
Cal:	[Laughs] Hey, I know what you mean. My ol' man . . .
Leader:	Wait a sec, Cal. I don't think Myra was finished yet.

Myra: That's okay. I was pretty much done. It's just that . . . I don't know . . . it's
            just that I was thinking about maybe leaving home.

Midge: Way to go, girl! Don't take any crap from them!

Leader: Myra, you're getting a lot of support from Midge and Cal and others. If you
            look around the room, you'll see almost everyone is with you right now. I
            guess my concern for you is what the consequences will be if you move
            out of the house right now. Maybe we could spend a few minutes looking
            at that. Anyone have some input for Myra?

It appears as if this group is problem solving on behalf of one member who
apparently is prepared to leave home without much of a plan. But there is actually far more than that going on in the group. Almost all the adolescents in
attendance can relate to Myra's problems with her parents. Even those who are
getting along with family at home can still identify with the experience of not
feeling understood and valued. While they are helping Myra sort out her problem at home, they are looking at their own lives and thinking about what they
can do to make things better for themselves. Furthermore, they are developing a
level of trust and intimacy with one another that feels wonderful during these
times when they often feel so alone.

For a Field Study

Interview several different people who have participated in counseling or other
therapeutic/growth groups. Find out what it was about the experience that made the
maximum difference to them. Why did they go, and what did they gain? Ask them to
describe in detail some of the most memorable moments of the time they spent with
the group.

INPATIENT THERAPY GROUPS

Therapy groups, whether led in outpatient or inpatient settings, are usually suited
for those with more severe disorders. In some cases, the members may have essentially the same problems as those in the counseling groups (e.g., depression, anger,
anxiety, physical complaints), only the severity of their symptoms is more pronounced and their duration may be more chronic (Emond & Rasmussen, 2012).

Therapy groups are longer-term treatments than the other groups that have
been presented here, often lasting several months, if not longer. They are generally led by professionals who have more advanced training, since they often deal
with disorders that may require medication, hospitalization, or other medical

interventions. In more remote settings, sometimes those with paraprofessional training are called on to lead groups with the most disturbed populations.

Inpatient groups are an integral part of most mental health programs, whether for those patients with mental disorders, chronic addictions, or other severe emotional disturbances (Emond & Rasmussen, 2012). The groups are often structured so as to provide support daily (or at least a few times per week) and to complement the work being done during the individual sessions.

Just as in other forms of group work, many different models are employed in inpatient groups. Some approaches help participants learn coping or interpersonal skills; others attempt to create a surrogate family to work through issues from the past; still others teach problem-solving strategies (Brabender, Fallon, & Smolar, 2004; Emer, 2004). Others work to engage group members, reduce their sense of isolation, help address anxiety caused by being in an inpatient setting, and provide the experience of universality and of being helpful to others (Hajek, 2007).

When working with members who are diagnosed with "personality disorders" or "psychotic symptoms," it is more important than ever to enforce firm boundaries and limits to make sure that things remain under control. While most texts advise against group therapy as the treatment of choice for those who act out in dramatic ways, the reality is that many institutions use these structures because of a staff shortage and cost-effectiveness. It is possible, however, to accomplish a number of limited goals with this population, as illustrated below:

Leader:	Who would like to tell us about something you did since our last meeting that made you feel really good?
Kimba:	I whacked off.
Tanya:	Gross!
Michael:	Whacka . . . whacka . . . whacka . . .
Leader:	Okay, guys. Enough of that.
Tanya:	But that idiot . . .
Leader:	Remember our rules about no name-calling and no sex talk just to shock people?
Kimba:	But it did feel pretty good. And that's what you asked us.
Leader:	All right. Listen up, everyone. One person talks at a time. Kimba, you volunteered first so you get to tell us about one thing you accomplished since our last session.
Kimba:	[Sulks and looks down]
Leader:	Your feelings are hurt now. Say what you're feeling like we practiced earlier.

While this might seem like a scene out of a situation comedy, leading therapy groups with more disturbed populations does present some volatile, unpredictable, and chaotic situations. In fact, many of the popular motion picture depictions of group work are of inpatient groups (e.g., *The Dream Team; Girl, Interrupted; One Flew Over the Cuckoo's Nest*). Goals are kept modest. Lots of structure is introduced. Members are held accountable for their behavior. Lots of work is done on social skills and learning more appropriate ways of communicating (Emond & Rasmussen, 2012).

> **For Reflection**
>
> Before reading the next section, consider on your own what you believe are the most important elements in life-changing groups. Based on your own experiences during which you have made the most transformative changes, as well as based on the observations you have made about others, what factors concerning group experiences do you think contribute to life changes in people?

Universal Therapeutic Factors in Groups

Before you start to feel overwhelmed with all the types of groups, theories, and styles of group leadership, you should know that efforts have been made to look at some of the common factors that operate in groups to understand how group works. Among all the various formats just reviewed, there are some obvious differences in their intent, structure, process, and leadership style, yet almost all groups contain similar ingredients. In fact, the most effective groups have a common identity and sense of shared purpose. This research has explored the factors that group leaders and members have identified as important (Barlow, Burlingame, & Fuhriman, 2000; Burlingame, McClendon, & Alonso, 2011a, 2011b; Lau, Ogrodniczuk, Joyce, & Sochting, 2010). Yalom and Leszcz (2005) outlined therapeutic factors that warranted attention: cohesion, altruism, catharsis, family reenactment, hope, universality/identification, imparting information, developing socializing techniques, vicarious learning/modeling, and interpersonal learning. Barlow et al. (2000) noted additional factors as feedback, reality testing, and role flexibility. Research has found a link between group-related therapeutic factors and outcomes (Cheung & Sun, 2001; Johnson, Burlingame, Davies, & Olsen, 2002; Kivlighan & Kivlighan, 2014; Ogrodniczuk & Piper, 2003; Robbins, 2003; Shechtman & Gluk, 2005). Further, Lemmens, Eisler, Dierick, Lietaer, and Demyttenaere (2009) found that therapeutic factors increased as the groups developed over time. Below, we examine some of these factors and add a few of our own:

Photo 1.1   Among most mammals, belonging to a "herd" or "tribe" is what protects us against predators, as well as what increases resources, division of labor, and support. In modern times, alienation and loneliness have intensified, in large part, because people feel so disconnected and hunger for greater intimacy. An important therapeutic ingredient of groups is to provide this sense of belonging and collective identification.

• *Cohesion:* A foundation of group work is the notion that the process of the group is not the sum of its parts but that, instead, it has properties of its own. This supports the idea that it is not the individual members of a group but, rather, the connection among the members that forms a crucial therapeutic factor (Lepper & Mergenthaler, 2005). Yalom was one of the first to examine group cohesion, and he compared it to the concept of the therapeutic alliance in individual treatment (Yalom & Leszcz, 2005). In many ways, cohesion speaks to all the relationship constructs in a group (e.g., alliance, group climate, group atmosphere, etc.), and it tends to be one of the most predictive variables in terms of good outcome across multiple settings (Burlingame et al., 2011a; Joyce, Piper, & Ogrodniczuk, 2007), meaning that cohesive groups fare better than disjointed ones (Burlingame, Fuhriman, & Johnson, 2001, 2011). Cohesion often occurs on three different levels: member to member, member to leader, and member to group (Burlingame et al., 2011b). Practically speaking, cohesion is about members being drawn to group to accomplish a given goal or task, or feeling connected to one another due to emotional support of the group. Cohesion is more prominent in groups that encourage member interaction (Burlingame et al., 2011a).

- *Support:* Above all else, groups make it possible for people to explore the unknown. There is a feeling that even if you fall flat on your face, there will be others to break the fall and help you recover. Since many people come into groups having recently suffered a decline in self-esteem, the presence of support within a group allows the members to maintain a more positive outlook about the group's involvement (Brabender et al., 2004). Support is a crucial component of interpersonal relationships and has significant impact on both physical and mental health (Sarason & Sarason, 2009). Group members report that support is one of the most helpful experiences in a group, as far as good outcomes (Boutin, 2007; Cheung & Sun, 2001; Lieberman & Golant, 2002). In a supportive group, negative behaviors can be reduced (Harel, Shechtman, & Cutrona, 2012). Support in a group helps reduce the level of initial anxiety for participants, maintains the smooth development of the group process and group cohesion, and lays the groundwork for constructive feedback exchanges among members (Bernard et al., 2008; Burlingame, Whitcomb, & Woodland, 2014). A crucial aspect of support is the instillation of hope, which conveys to group members that being in the group will enhance their sense of well-being. A clear example of this can be found in AA groups, where veteran members receive chips that delineate the length of their sobriety. For a new member, witnessing someone receive a 10-year sobriety chip conveys the understanding that this group can support his or her recovery.

- *Sense of belonging:* Most people feel very alone with their situations and the corresponding feelings, especially when they are experiencing personal difficulties. Groups create a sense of cohesion and trust that make it much easier to feel safe. Cohesiveness has been described as one of the key foundational qualities of a good group experience (Burlingame et al., 2011a). Whereas there is little consensus on what exactly cohesiveness is, it is often described as feeling an attraction to the group, with a notion of identifying with the group or group members (Hornsey, Dwyer, & Oei, 2007). A key aspect of this is the feeling of universality in a group, where a group member recognizes that he or she is not alone with personal difficulties. Universality is a component of almost every group setting and is understood as one of the more important therapeutic factors (Argyrakouli & Zafiropoulou, 2007; Kivlighan & Holmes, 2004; Kivlighan & Kivlighan, 2014).

- *Catharsis:* Groups create a degree of emotional intensity, a condition that is often associated with positive changes (Cheung & Sun, 2001) if the arousal leads to some sort of resolution. Catharsis is a release of feeling that brings with it a sense of relief (Brabender et al., 2004). Often, the emotions have been pent up for some time. But catharsis can have a double-edged quality to it; in spite of what was once theorized, it does little good (and some harm) to stir up feelings just for the sake of expressing them. In that sense, the release followed by validation from the group tends to lead to a better outcome. However, an unexpected emotional release of intensity may surprise or even frighten group members if a frame is not provided. In that situation, group members may not know how to respond, and the end result may be increased distress.

- *Vicarious learning and modeling:* Unlike other helping relationships, group members learn not just from direct experience but also from observation. The leader models effective behavior, and in groups that are co-led, the leaders demonstrate with each other effective ways to communicate and resolve conflicts (Lanza, 2007). At the same time, group members identify strongly with themes that others explore. Every time anyone in the group speaks, works, or is addressed, others take in what is happening, adapting the lessons for their own use. Modeling occurs in groups when members directly copy a particular behavior or set of behaviors. Group leaders might specifically supply behaviors to model (Gladding, 2012). Vicarious learning occurs when a group member privately applies the knowledge gained from seeing another's behavior in group or from seeing other group members interact (Brabender et al., 2004).

- *Mutual influence:* Beyond observing other members, it is reasonable to assume that the outcome for the other members of a group will also be related to an individual member's outcome (Lau et al., 2010; Paquin, Kivlighan, & Drogosz, 2013). This indicates the power of mutual influence between group members—namely, that the success of people making positive changes will rub off on those around them. Thus, as particular group members improve, the whole group benefits. The core of Yalom and Leszcz's (2005) model is that group members have a direct effect on others; seeing other people's progress helps group members realize that they, too, can feel better and change. Vicarious learning and modeling can occur only in the presence of others, and hope has to be instilled by others who are actually improving. Namely, mutual influence shows that successful groups are like a rolling snowball, gaining momentum and bringing all the members along with it.

- *Awareness:* Group experiences help participants become more aware of their behavior and the impact it has on others. Moreover, they also become far more sensitive to nuances in others' behavior. Although such awareness is not enough, in itself, to promote lasting change, it does get people's attention in such a way that they increase motivation to grow and learn.

- *Family reenactment*: Groups provide an interpersonal context that is reminiscent of a family, complete with parental figures, sibling rivalries, and struggles for power and control. This environment makes it possible for participants to work through family issues, both past and present.

- *Public commitment*: There is nothing like telling a bunch of people, out loud, what you intend to do to increase the likelihood of your following through with your plans. It is so much harder to back down knowing that you have committed yourself in front of others. Some people elect not to return to the group because they are so ashamed by their failure to complete their self-declared tasks, and that should be avoided. Effective group leaders help members set and declare realistic goals, and still make it possible for them to return to the group without "losing face" should they not do what they said they would.

- *Task facilitation*: Because people receive less individual attention and time in a group, it is critical to help them translate new insights into constructive plans. It is not enough to talk about problems unless members do something to act on what they have learned. That is why many groups end with a final "go-around," in which members declare aloud what they will do during the next week and begin by reporting on what they have done. This mutual accountability is what facilitates continued completion of therapeutic tasks that bring the participants closer to their desired goals.

- *Risk taking*: Various kinds of risking take place in group, all of which get the heart pumping at high volume. Imagine what is involved in revealing out loud one of your deepest, darkest secrets, something you have never told another human being. Picture the courage it takes to tell someone in the group how much you like him or her . . . or how irritating you find his or her behavior. Consider the level of risk involved in revealing yourself to others in the most authentic, honest, and genuine way possible. Feel your heart beating harder as you contemplate telling group members that you intend to go out during the next week and make some startling changes in the way you conduct your life. Risk taking is at the heart of group work.

- *Rehearsal*: One of the unique advantages of group work is that it acts as a real-life laboratory for practicing new behaviors. It is possible to experiment with new behavioral options, new ways of relating to other people, and then to get feedback on the impact of this action. Role-playing and other psychodramatic strategies also make it possible to rehearse confrontations in a reasonably safe setting and then refine the strategies in light of suggestions made by others.

- *Confrontation and feedback*: In a high-functioning group, it is safe to speak the truth. Groups are one of the few places where it is okay to be yourself and then hear how others honestly respond to you. You do not have to wonder how others react: You can ask. You do not have to second-guess what others might be thinking: You simply ask. You do not have to hold back your own thoughts, feelings, and reactions to what is going on (assuming they are communicated sensitively and respectfully): You can say what you want. This is probably the most powerful learning tool of all in groups—the gift of others' honesty.

- *Magic:* That's right. Magic! This is one of our additions to the list. Amazing things happen in groups, some of which defy description, much less explanation. In a matter of weeks, participants can dramatically change their lives in ways that would never have been possible in any other setting. The feeling of camaraderie and caring—yes, the feeling of love—becomes intrinsically healing. For the first time in people's lives, many participants feel heard and understood. They realize that they are not so alone after all. They learn things about themselves that they never believed possible. The hard part, of course, is making the changes last once the group ends.

Therapeutic factors play a critical role in successful group outcomes. Whereas the factors listed above are important, they may not be present in the same degree in all groups. Kivlighan and Kivlighan (2014) suggest that group leaders often decide which therapeutic factors to emphasize in their group. The emphasized factors may relate to the type of group offered and the goals inherent. For example, a support group would emphasize cohesion, support, sense of belonging, and catharsis, whereas an interpersonal-insight–focused group would additionally emphasize awareness, risk taking, confrontation, and feedback. Further, one's leadership style, the group climate, and the group structure can also be manipulated to emphasize specific factors.

Student Voice

My Family Coming Alive in Group

Being a part of a group allowed me to experience and work through some of my own family concerns and issues. I tend to worry over my adult children, and when I entered the group, right away I found myself worrying over a few men and women who were the same ages as my children. I found myself protecting and worrying about them. But then something happened. These same group members showed me something. I experienced the courage, intellect, tenacity, kindness, and a sense of purpose of fellow group members who are the same age as my own children. They appreciated my protecting and worrying, but also taught me that it was not necessary. As a result, I found myself able to let go of the worry and doubt that I had not prepared my adult children well enough to grapple with the volatile, harsh world that they are now a part of. I realized the capacity and competence of my children as a fact gained through interaction with their contemporaries in my group. I was given the opportunity to see my adult children as the world must see them.

> **For Reflection**
>
> The previous section explores the curative factors in therapeutic groups that lead to growth and change. If you trace your own development from birth until the present moment, you will find that many of these variables have been major influences in your own growth. What are some of these dimensions that have been most influential in helping shape who you have become and even why you are taking this course right now? It is absolutely critical that you understand those factors that have been most significant in your own evolution as a group member and leader. In the next chapter, we look more deeply at your behavior in groups, with particular attention to the development of those personal qualities that would make you an optimal group leader.

Do Groups Work?

It is fitting that we end the first chapter of this book by addressing a question that is most likely on your minds: All this stuff about groups sounds good, but at the end of the day, do we know if groups actually work to help people? Early investigations into the effectiveness of group counseling concluded in the 1960s that group counseling was an effective adjunct to treatment but that its utility as a stand-alone intervention was not supported by existing empirical research (Burlingame et al., 2014). However, over the past 50 years, those who work in groups have intuitively perceived the benefits of groups, and recent efforts have empirically shown that group work is effective for general and specific factors (Barlow, 2012; Burlingame, Fuhriman, & Johnson, 2011; Burlingame, Fuhriman, & Mosier, 2003; Burlingame et al., 2011b; Burlingame, Strauss, & Joyce, 2013; Burlingame et al., 2014; Guimón, 2004; McDermut, Miller, & Brown, 2001; Stout & Hayes, 2005; Ward, 2004) and for a wide range of presenting concerns (e.g., eating disorders, social phobia, panic disorder, mood disorders, substance abuse; see Burlingame et al., 2014, for more information).

In terms of understanding which types of groups may show better outcomes, Burlingame et al. (2003) noted that those in groups of a homogeneous nature tend to be better off than those in groups whose members have mixed concerns. Furthermore, groups with a behavioral orientation in which the acquisition of information and practice of behaviors is a main goal tend to show more improvement than groups with a more eclectic orientation. The effectiveness of inpatient counseling groups has also been shown to be robust (Emond & Rasmussen, 2012; Kösters, Burlingame, Nachtigall, & Strauss, 2006); however, outpatient counseling groups tend to show more improvement than inpatient groups (Burlingame et al., 2003). Some research has indicated that the longer the duration of the group, the better the outcomes (Tschushke, Anbeh, & Kiencke, 2007).

In terms of comparing the differences between individual and group treatments, it is important to note that group and individual treatments have demonstrated equivalent outcomes (Burlingame & Krogel, 2005; McRoberts, Burlingame, & Hoag, 1998). Yet some have questioned whether there are any real differences between individual and group modalities in terms of their underlying processes. It does seem clear that there are at least some *apparent* differences. It is obvious, for example, that additional competencies are required of group leaders in general and of advanced practitioners in particular, in much the same way as there are differences between tutoring and classroom instruction. In terms of the underlying processes that contribute to change, Holmes and Kivlighan (2000) found that the relational nature of group counseling—namely, the influence of others—helped create change. Furthermore, they noted that the focus on others that is inherent in groups, highlighted by the therapeutic factors of universality, altruism, and vicarious learning, also set the group outcomes apart from individual treatments. Even in self-help groups such as AA, it often is not the 12-step practices or content that most help people recover but, rather, the therapeutic elements: instillation of hope, interpersonal learning, universality, and altruism, to name a few (Kelly, Magill, & Stout, 2009). Yet, like individual counseling settings, positive ratings of the therapeutic alliance (i.e., relationship between group members and their group leader) are predictive of good outcome (Burlingame et al., 2011a, 2011b; Joyce et al., 2007; Piper, Ogrodniczuk, Lamarche, Hilscher, & Joyce, 2005). Furthermore, even children in groups have identified the relationship aspects of the group as the most useful (Shechtman & Gluk, 2005).

Group work has its own identity even though it does share a number of similarities with individual treatment—especially with family therapy (except that all members are related; Brabender et al., 2004). And although group work has a number of contextual and process similarities to family therapy, there are also some notable differences. For instance, whereas a family is a kind of group, it is also made up of people who have a long history together and who will be going home together after the session ends. There are also differences between the modalities in requirements for inclusion, degree of enmeshment, structural hierarchies, norm establishment, and ways therapists and counselors relate to members (Nichols & Schwartz, 2012). Nevertheless, systemic thinking and family theory have had a tremendous impact on group work, just as the notions of group dynamics and coalitions have influenced the work of family practitioners.

Review of What You Learned

- You cannot learn about group leadership merely by reading about it; you must find ways to personalize the content and apply the concepts to your daily life.
- People can change faster, but can also be hurt more readily, in group settings because of the enriched atmosphere.
- Many of the risks associated with group experiences can be minimized through protecting member rights, providing informed consent, and not pressuring people to do things for which they are not yet ready.
- Although there are many different kinds of groups—task groups, self-help groups, counseling and therapy groups, and others—they all share similar dynamics, processes, and stages. Although their intent and clientele are distinctly different, you can adapt sound leadership principles to any of these settings.
- The most important part of learning to be a group leader is not what you do in class or with the text but what you do in your own life to integrate the useful concepts.

Your Behavior in Groups 2

Group leadership is not just about theory, research, strategies, and interventions, but also about the personal characteristics of the leaders. To what extent can you model what you expect of others? How much of your own passion, compassion, and caring come through in your interactions with others? In this chapter, you will examine your own behavior in groups throughout your life and understand the meaning of these characteristic roles. Being a group leader does not only involve what you *do* but also *who you are* as a person. Without a doubt, who you are personally in group settings will influence who you are when leading a group.

If you will ask people to examine their behavior in various groups in their lives, then you must be prepared to do the same. It is pretty remarkable to reflect on the number of groups you have been a member of over your lifetime. Your membership in your family of origin, play groups, athletic teams, work groups, and so on all represent the array of groups in which you have taken part and played a role. There are likely consistent patterns in the roles you have played, from your earliest childhood play groups up to the present classroom group you are part of. Equally interesting are the different ways people in various groups perceive you. In some groups, you act in a leadership role; in others, you are a follower. Some groups find you as a serious taskmaster, while others spark a silly, irreverent part of you. You may feel valued in some groups but not in others. Generally, however, you have a preferred interpersonal style that you adopt consistently.

The beauty of group leadership, just as in all forms of counseling, is that no single style is necessarily best. It is possible to be a quiet, reflective leader, or one who is charged with energy. You can be soft or hard, calm or dramatic, serious or fun-loving, probing or cautious, patient or proactive. And in the situation of coleading a group, it is often good to have two different types of interpersonal styles. Of course, ideally, it is desirable to have a number of different leadership options to choose from depending on (1) the kind and composition of the group, (2) what is happening in the group at any moment in time, and (3) what is precisely needed by group members in that particular situation. In that sense, group leaders need to be flexible enough to adapt their interpersonal styles based on what the situation requires (Galanes, 2003; Luke, 2014).

A Lifetime of Group Skills: The Good News

As you arrive at this professional juncture in your life, prepared to learn group leadership skills, you are not without some experience in this arena. You already have some background that will aid you in reading group behavior, responding in constructive ways, and even guiding others in helpful directions. We do not mean to imply that group leadership is naturally developed, because it often is not. Consistent, helpful leadership requires intensive study, much observation, active participation in groups, good role models, diligent practice, risk taking, and lots of supervision (Riva, 2014; Stockton, Morran, & Chang, 2014). Most of all, it involves the experience of group participation. As you can clearly see, we believe that the crux of becoming an effective group leader is consistent and purposeful time spent in group settings.

For Reflection

Bring to mind the most satisfying, productive group you have ever had the privilege to participate in. This was not only a group in which you were very successful in accomplishing meaningful things, getting work done, or meeting desired objectives but also one in which people enjoyed themselves tremendously during the process. It may have been difficult, but at the end you could say you all learned a lot. What were the ingredients of that group that created your positive outcome? What was happening in the group? What did the leader or leaders do? Construct a list of the characteristics of this group experience that made it so satisfying and effective.

The good news is that you already have a lifetime of experience in groups, some of them quite inspirational and memorable; yet we are sure you can also remember more than a few group experiences that were downright awful, dysfunctional, and potentially damaging. Based on your own experience (which may not be representative of others'), you know what makes a group fun and satisfying, as well as what causes one to be tedious or destructive. Before we present what research tells us about what makes for the most effective type of high-functioning group, first try to figure it out for yourself.

For a Class Activity

In small groups, each of you take a few minutes to tell your story of the most effective group you were ever part of. One person in your group, acting as scribe, will write down all the qualities and variables that were part of these best group experiences. After everyone has had a chance to tell his or her group story, brainstorm a list of all those factors that you believe were common among your experiences. In brainstorming exercises such as this, it is best to come up with as many ideas as possible, even if some sound a little outlandish. Make your list as exhaustive as you can.

In the next step, organize all your variables of effective groups into several categories that make intuitive sense to you. Put each of your factors into one of the categories. Give the groupings names based on a word that captures the essence of these characteristics. Be prepared to share what you developed with the rest of the class. Look for the commonalities.

In reviewing your own positive group experiences, you may be interested to learn that whether we are talking about productive task groups, growth groups, therapeutic groups, or even business meetings, some similar characteristics distinguish them from less productive and satisfying experiences (Hornsey, Dwyer, & Oei, 2007; Jacobs, Masson, & Harvill, 2012; Joyce, Piper, & Ogrodniczuk, 2007; Kivlighan & Kivlighan, 2014; Logan, King, & Fischer-Wright, 2011; Miles & Paquin, 2014; Yalom & Leszcz, 2005).

Following are some of the signs and symptoms that tell you a group is functioning at optimal levels. Compare these ingredients with those that match your own experience.

• *High levels of trust and safety are established.* People feel supported by the leader and other group members. People are willing to make mistakes without fear of censure or ridicule. They are inclined to take risks, saying and doing things that may involve venturing into new territory, because they trust that it will be helpful in the short and long term. Furthermore, the group leader promotes safety and trust by protecting members from taking unnecessary risks (Barlow, 2013; Luke, 2014).

- *Individual and cultural differences are valued and respected.* Even with all the peer pressure, cohesion, and conformity that are common to groups, cultural differences are recognized and respected. Biased, racist, and culturally derogatory remarks are not allowed to take root. There is an interesting relationship between trust and safety (which allows people to honestly express themselves and discuss racial/cultural issues) and the understanding that cultural conversations in a group setting will occur in a respectful manner. Members are allowed to be different, their cultural, gender, and individual backgrounds welcomed and appreciated, and find that they can be honest with other group members about their cultural identities. Further, group leaders facilitate the empowerment of those individuals marginalized in the greater society (Singh, Merchant, Skudrzyk, & Ingene, 2012).

Student Voice

Supporting Me and My Religious Faith

I wouldn't have taken any risks if I hadn't felt connected to someone in the group at some point. One day I had chatted a little before the session started with the person sitting to my left. We got into a conversation about our shared religion and some of the frustrations I was having at work, and also in life, because of my faith. I didn't say a word in group that day. However, as I was walking out of the class that evening, that member told me that they could tell that I was holding a lot of hurt inside, that he hoped I was okay, and that he felt that the group was there to support me. That evening when I got into my car for the drive home I burst into tears. Next week, I shared my experience and openly wondered if the group would be able to support me and my faith-based identity. People were honest, they said that they would try and remain open, but what I really felt was support from the group and the group leaders. I got the message not to hide myself and my faith but, instead, to let the true me come out.

- *Clear boundaries and rules about appropriate conduct are established.* Few groups are more frustrating than those that are chaotic, disorganized, and without structure or rules about what is acceptable and what is not. In good group experiences, you know what is expected and are confident that the leaders will enforce group norms and expectations (Barlow, 2013).

- *Conflict is acknowledged and worked through.* Ironically, the best groups are not those without any conflict. There is always tension and disagreement whenever more than two people get together. The danger is in ignoring or minimizing these conflicts, as the natural inclination for many people is to repress them (Barlow, 2014). Solid groups are those that have developed constructive means for members to disagree with one another, making room for those disagreements to be processed within the group (Ward, 2014). Conflict is conceived as helpful when it is initiated from a position of good faith in which participants in the struggle want to resolve their differences. Conflicts might not always be resolved in the group, but acceptance of conflict and an understanding that the group will attempt to work through conflict creates groups that are alive and honest.

• *Information and resources are shared efficiently.* You have been in groups before where everyone talks but nobody listens. Effective groups are those that have developed ways to pool their experiences. Members link their statements to what others have said. Whatever products are developed result from maximum input from all participants. In that sense, each group member is a resource to tap and feels important.

• *Everyone participates.* In every group, there is a tendency for some people to hang back and others to dominate and control things. The best groups are those that feature shared participation and responsibility. Nobody is allowed to dominate, and nobody is marginalized. Everyone gets a say.

• *Acting out is blocked.* Every group has members who are distracting or dysfunctional. Such members can include those who attempt to be manipulative, monopolizing, distracting, rambling, abusive, disrespectful, and so on. The problem is not in having such members in a group (since this kind of behavior is often the reason they are in group setting to begin with) but in allowing their behavior to flourish. In the best groups, everyone takes responsibility for confronting destructive behavior, but they also take responsibility for working through the behavior and processing it together (Ward, 2014).

• *The group is efficient.* People can have a good time in a group and feel cared for and supported, but unless the group accomplishes its objectives, it has not done its job. The best groups are not only fun and satisfying but also productive. All members, not just the leader, feel responsible for making certain that the planned agenda is completed (Levi, 2011).

• *Nonverbal behavior is consistent with what is communicated aloud.* There is an essential congruence between what people are saying and what they are thinking and feeling. There is an absence of covert cynicism, criticism, scorn, and ridicule.

• *Continuity and follow-up from session to session are an integral part of the experience.* Groups are most productive when they do not have to start over each session, when efforts can be continued from prior meetings. All members, not just the leader, make certain that participants report on progress, assignments, and goals. Building on this is the understanding among members that attending groups on time and not missing meetings are a must. Consistent attendance allows a group to naturally evolve through developmental stages (Forsyth & Diederich, 2014).

• *A healthy culture in the group has been developed.* Every group develops certain norms, or established behavioral codes, that guide how people act. Effective groups are those that have developed a positive culture that reinforces caring, productive contributions. There is an even balance of work and play. Participants feel good about being part of the experience, and they share ownership of the group and its identity. Members begin to use "my" to describe their group.

• *Ideas result in some form of action.* You have been in groups before where people talk about things but nothing much ever changes. People do not act on what they claim they believe or have learned. In excellent groups, members invest time and energy outside the group to work on issues raised. The most effective groups are those in which whatever is done has lasting, significant effects on the participants' lives.

As you compare each of these characteristics with your own experiences in groups, we hope you are nodding your head in agreement, thinking to yourself: *Yes! This is exactly the sort of group I would like to be part of.*

We want you to remember your own best experiences throughout your training in group leadership. You know what it feels like to be part of a group that is destructive, boring, or useless. You also know how great it feels to be part of a group that is transformative. What you are learning in this course, and from this text, will only help you supplement and strengthen your existing interpersonal skills.

For a Field Study

Interview several people who know you best, including classmates, coworkers, friends, and family members. Ask them to be as honest and constructive as they can in telling you about what they see as your major strengths and weaknesses as a communicator and group member. This will be a difficult assignment, doubly so because it is challenging to get people to be honest and really tell you what they think. Nevertheless, it is invaluable—make that critical—to have accurate feedback about how you are perceived by others and how they react to your behavior. You might prompt them by starting out with a few strengths and weaknesses you already know about. For example,

Matt might start with, *"I have an assignment for class, in which I need to find out as much as I can about my interpersonal strengths and weaknesses."* Then explain about the class, what you are learning, and why you must have solid feedback from others who know you best and have observed you in a variety of situations.

I already know, for instance, that I really like being in groups, but I am not very good at keeping quiet. I tend to talk too much, and get a little antsy when there is something that I want to say. I also have a tendency to talk really fast, hence my childhood nickname of Motormouth. My head is often racing so fast that at times I lose people because my thoughts are jumpy. On the other hand, I think I'm pretty good at conveying safety and respect. So what else can you tell me that I might not already know?

By all means, do not think of the preceding example as a script. Rather, it is an illustration of the way you might approach people to solicit useful information. When you are done with your study, you may be asked to write about what you learned in a reaction paper or to report to classmates on themes that emerged.

More Good News: Group Leadership Training and Personal Growth

One of the truly amazing things about learning to be a group leader is that the more you learn about professional issues and intervention skills that will make you effective in your work, the more powerful and influential you will become as a person. Just consider some of the things you will learn in this class (and in the rest of your training):

- How to read people's behavior to make sense of their innermost desires and needs
- How to figure out what people are really saying beneath the surface
- How to determine who is working behind the scenes, and through hidden agendas, to sabotage group progress
- How to build trusting relationships in very short periods of time
- How to express yourself clearly and effectively, explaining complex phenomena in terms that are more understandable
- How to communicate effectively to help people take risks that they are afraid to attempt
- How to mediate conflicts between people and work through them in a positive manner
- How to confront people sensitively and effectively
- How to validate people's experiences in a way that becomes healing and helpful

- How to help people get along better with one another
- How to honor and respect the wide range of identities in a group setting
- How to make sense of complex group interactions so you can actually be a leader

These are only a few of the skills you will learn. There are actually so many more that it takes a whole book to cover just the basics. Now imagine all the ways you could apply these same skills to your personal life. Picture how much deeper, more intimate, and satisfying you could make your most significant relationships. Imagine how much better you would be at getting your needs met. Think about all the ways you could use your group leadership skills to influence people in positive directions. We tell our classes that there is a plus/minus effect of learning group leadership and in being able to assess and understand group dynamics. The plus is that you will never see a group setting the same way again. Honest. You will learn to see through group interactions to what is happening behind the scenes. You will gain insight to what is not being verbally expressed but is most likely driving the group interaction. Now here comes the minus: Once you gain this vision and way of viewing group interactions, it will most likely be hard for you to be quiet about it. You can't avoid it anymore and remain in a state of ignorant bliss. You will learn to speak the truth and illuminate these dynamics. That will make you a leader, and it might make others a little bit uncomfortable since they can't fake it with you around.

Now the Bad News

Whereas the good news is that much of what you will learn is applicable to every facet of your life, this learning will not come without a certain amount of pain and discomfort. Could you really expect anything else considering that what you already know about significant change is that it involves some degree of personal sacrifice?

If it is your desire to get through your training unscathed and unmarked, you can probably do so. Just avoid taking risks at all costs. Don't reveal yourself in an honest and vulnerable way. Keep your defenses at a high level of readiness. Intellectualize whenever you can. Stay as superficial as possible. Don't think about anything significant, and heaven forbid, don't personalize anything. In this way, you just might escape without suffering pain, or without feeling anything much at all. Remember, however, if that is your goal, then you will be selling to your group members the idea that they should do things you were unable or afraid to do yourself. If you can live with yourself under these circumstances, give it a

Photo 2.1 Much of your life is dominated by group interactions, whether with family members, friends, coworkers, or as part of your work and leisure activities. The skills you learn to make you a skilled group leader will be invaluable in enriching *all* your relationships.

shot. We doubt very much, however, that you can truly hide in a group class that is taught experientially. At some point, you will feel the pain of something, even if it is only the fear of being discovered. And not only that, just ask yourself if you would rather have a group leader who is unwilling to experience risk or one who has truly experienced the power of being vulnerable in a group setting.

For Personal Application

Take a moment to reflect on some of the greatest sources of ongoing pain in your life. Take a brief inventory of the places you hurt the most, including the following areas:

- Failures and disappointments that still linger
- Times when you were rejected or ignored
- Grief and loss over a loved one
- Situations that still make you feel nervous and anxious
- Traumas you have suffered

- Conflicted relationships that bother you
- Periods of intense moodiness, loneliness, or sadness
- Ways you "medicate" yourself with drugs, alcohol, exercise, or escape

In reviewing the sources of pain in your life, which are the ones you might bring up to work through in a group? What would keep you from bringing them up? What would you be afraid of revealing in front of others?

Practicing What You Preach

Whether in groups, classes, or workshops, self-disclosures are most useful when they are concise and illustrate a particular point. The idea is that by modeling what you want others to do—practicing what you preach—you make it easier for others to follow your lead (Frank, 1991; Johnson, Burlingame, Olsen, Davies, & Gleave, 2005; Kottler & Carlson, 2014; Lanza, 2007; Luke, 2014). Also, it sends a message that you are willing and able to do what you are asking the group members to do. When group leaders or counselors self-disclose, it can build a relationship bridge that indicates that you are engaged in a real relationship with the group. When such modeling works best, participants feel inspired to imitate what was demonstrated by taking risks and revealing themselves in authentic ways.

We can certainly see a number of reasons why participants in a workshop or class would not wish to be very open in groups. Maybe they do not feel as though it is a safe place. Perhaps they do not want to risk jeopardizing their reputation among peers by appearing as anything other than perfectly in control. It is also possible that they do not want to stir things up without adequate time to complete the process. We are sure that you can relate to their concerns, as you might struggle with a similar dilemma about how much of yourself to reveal to your classmates and instructor. It is probably pretty easy to think of all the reasons not to speak up or allow yourself to be truly known. But now try comparing those fears with the opposite scenario: How would it feel to be truly known and supported by your peers and those around you? What if you did not need to be so careful all the time about what you shared? How could your relationships with others flourish and grow if you were able to simply be you?

What strikes us about the resistance of some group leaders to participating in an experiential group is the inconsistency and hypocrisy evident in the assumption that "groups are for everyone else but not for me." We wonder how it is possible to operate in good faith when you are not willing to do what you ask of others. Furthermore, how do we face our clients, urge them to take risks and disclose their innermost thoughts and feelings, and push them to do what is most difficult when we are not willing to do the same?

Being a group leader actually affords you the opportunity to work constantly on your own personal functioning so you may live your life with the degree of passion, commitment, and courage you want for those you help. It allows you to learn consistently from your clients and group members (Kottler & Carlson, 2005, 2009, 2014). We love this about our work, although it also terrifies us. There are so many times, often every week, when we confront a situation we would rather avoid. Just when the urge to escape takes over, we think: *Now, what would my clients or students say if they saw me in this situation? They would expect me to practice in my life what I tell them to do.* That is usually all that is needed to choose to lean into the situation and confront it with a sense of purpose and courage.

For a Class Activity

In small groups of three or four, make a list of all the reasons why you would and would not want to disclose in this group class something very personal about yourself. Be sure not to reveal what the personal thing is, but instead stay focused on the reasons to speak about it or to remain quiet. Make sure your list has an equal number of items on each side. Take some time to review and discuss each of these.

Now that you understand some of the major concerns of your small group, you also have a sample of the reasons to disclose and not disclose information. Now imagine that each of you will be the leader of a subgroup of classmates. Your job will be to help them experience what a group is like so they will be better prepared to address the resistance and reluctance of their own clients. Plan several strategies together for how you might (1) relieve some of the group's apprehension, (2) protect the safety of participants, and (3) ultimately encourage deep-level disclosure.

For a Field Study

If you have not yet participated in a therapeutic or growth group, make plans to do so as soon as you can. Join a group at the local counseling center or a community agency, or a support group in some area of interest. Go for yourself and make it personal, rather than viewing it as an assignment. As we review our own training as group leaders, with all the courses we took at the undergraduate, master's, and doctoral levels, all the workshops we attended, all the books we read, all the supervision we received, and all the experience we logged as coleaders, both of us still believe that we learned the most being members of a group for a year. The best way to learn is to actually experience it—all the highs and lows—so you can empathize with group members and also understand the complex relationship between group leaders and members by being fully engrossed in that relationship.

The Personal Qualities of Group Leaders

It should now be apparent that being an effective group leader is not just about what you can do but also about who you are. Knowledge about theory, solid intervention skills, past experiences to draw on, a bag of tricks you can pull from—these are all important. But so is who you are as a person (Wojciszke, 2005). In fact, in making a good impression, people's judgments of your warmth (e.g., friendliness, kindness, trustworthiness) are often more important than your competence (e.g., efficiency and capability; Brambilla, Sacchi, Rusconi, Cherubini, & Yzerbyt, 2012).

In the area of psychotherapy outcome studies, the personal qualities that counselors bring to each session to assist clients are called therapist factors, and they are associated with the variance in outcome (Baldwin, Wampold, & Imel, 2007; Huppert, Fabbro, & Barlow, 2006; Kim, Wampold, & Bolt, 2006; Wampold, 2010). So what do you bring to groups that would motivate people? What personal qualities do you model that others would be wise to imitate? What do you demonstrate in your life that will act as an inspiration for others to follow? Which personal characteristics do you have that you feel most proud of?

We find these questions so important to answer. If it is true that who you are is as important as what you do as a group leader (see Kottler, 2010; Kottler & Carlson, 2008, 2009, 2014; Kottler & Marriner, 2009; Kottler & Shepard, 2011), then the interesting question is, "What are you doing to develop yourself as a person as well as a professional?" Your training program will likely spend lots of time filling you up with content; teaching you skills, techniques, and methodologies; having you memorize ideas and master theories, analyze cases, write papers, and take examinations. What program are you following, however, to develop yourself as a more powerful, inspirational human being—someone who leads by example? This is the stuff you cannot fake or learn solely from a book. You have to grow as a person to lead others (Komives, Lucas, & McMahon, 2013). This has been the hallmark of some of the most charismatic and influential leaders in history; from Mahatma Gandhi and Martin Luther King to Winston Churchill and Golda Meir, these leaders were continually reinventing themselves while remaining true to their deepest convictions. You may not aspire to political or social activism, but the same principles apply, in that part of your job is to inspire and motivate people to do things they don't believe they are capable of doing.

Following is a list of characteristics most often associated with effective group leaders, whether they operate in the arena of therapeutic groups, the business world, politics, or the media (Komives et al., 2013; Kouzes & Posner,

2013; Luke, 2014; Northouse, 2013; Riva, Wachtel, & Lasky, 2004; Stockton et al., 2014; Wageman, Nunes, Burruss, & Hackman, 2008). As you review these personal qualities, consider the ways you demonstrate each characteristic in your own style.

TRUSTWORTHINESS

The first and foremost goal of any group leader is to create an atmosphere in which members feel safe enough to reveal themselves in authentic ways (Luke, 2014). This also means making group members feel valued and appreciated in the group (Galanes, 2003). Creating an atmosphere where group members feel wanted often starts with the leaders revealing themselves as utterly truthful, maintaining integrity, and doing everything they say they will do. Professionalism as a group leader is essential (Barlow, 2013). For many group leaders who live and work in small communities, it is not enough to exhibit dependability and trustworthiness only while the group is in session; wherever the leaders go, people are watching to see if they are among those "crazy shrinks" who do not practice what they preach. If you are a leader, people watch your children for signs of instability. They scrutinize every move you make and wonder if it is evidence that you are not what you pretend to be. Obviously, this puts tremendous pressure on you to "walk the walk." Part of the walk, however, is accepting yourself as imperfect, fallible, and prone to mistakes. Nobody is perfect; one of the more trustworthy things a group leader can do is be honest about times when he or she makes mistakes or poor interventions (Kottler & Carlson, 2014).

SELF-ACCEPTANCE

A turning point in every group is often the moment when the group leader is caught doing or saying something that is less than perfect. An error in judgment, an insensitive remark, a miscalculation or lapse—any of these will bring a gasp to the mouths of members who put you high on a pedestal, beyond mortal beings. Yet these instances are often pivotal points, not because you made a mistake but more because of how you deal with the repercussions (Kulp, Ladany, & Klinger, 2012).

Mistakes are made all the time, and some are bigger than others. When I (Matt) am aware of missing a client, making an error, or just saying something inappropriate, the first thing I try to do is acknowledge and own the misstep. On the outside, that may mean apologizing or simply noting aloud that what I did was not ideal and was wrong. Humility often goes a long way with a group. Rather than viewing this as a problem, most group members will see a moment when the group leader was more "real" and human, and that often strengthens cohesion and connectedness. However, early in group work, group members often prefer the illusion that their leader is beyond mere mortal flaws, since it establishes more confidence that the leader can help them. Group members desperately want to believe that leaders are omnipotent and omniscient so that they might be perfectly prepared to protect members from harm (and, ultimately, perfectly equipped to make them feel better).

CHARISMA

Charisma comes in many different forms of passion and enthusiasm. Depending on your personality and interpersonal style, you can either be loud or soft, dramatic or understated. The key, however, is to radiate power to the extent that people are inclined to listen to you. You must be persuasive and influential. You must command attention. And, simply put, group members who have a favorable view of their leaders are more likely to make progress. So in that sense, it helps to be warm, likeable, supportive, and genuinely interested in group members (Luke, 2014).

Some time ago, social learning theorists such as Bandura (1969) discovered that there were many ways models could stimulate enough interest in people that they would likely be influenced by a group leader's behavior. Research on small groups indicates that leaders who display confidence and self-efficacy with the group task create high self-efficacy for group members to meet the task (Hoyt, Murphy, Halverson, & Watson, 2003). This in turn leads to better group outcomes. Being perceived as an expert and capable certainly works well, but so does appearing to others as nurturing, prestigious, attractive, or even physically imposing. The common denominator is that for people to be persuaded by what you have to say, or disposed to imitate what you do, they must be interested in you (Kottler & Carlson, 2014). Whether you call this charisma, power, charm, passion, enthusiasm, or attractiveness, you must use your personal attributes to your advantage.

For Reflection or a Class Activity

Think about leaders who inspire you in your life. What is it about them that you find so attractive or inspiring? Write in your journal, or talk to classmates in a small group, about personal qualities you might develop into a base for charismatic leadership. It is important to be extremely honest with yourself at this juncture. If there is no way you can ever imagine yourself as the Oprah, Barack Obama, Steve Jobs, or Nelson Mandela type of leader, then look at other personal strengths you have that could be harnessed in such a way as to communicate your passion and commitment to others.

Since one of the overriding beliefs of group leadership is that people can change who they are and become quite different people if they so choose, talk (to yourself or classmates) about the kind of person you would someday like to become. One student expressed this as follows:

You probably look at me now and see a pretty shy and quiet girl. And I know I look so young that I appear as a girl, not a woman. That's okay, though. People tend to underestimate me. But I know I have within me the capacity to be much more assertive and forceful. You haven't seen me when I'm with my brothers, but believe me when I tell you that I don't take any crap from them at all! I want to be tougher. I want to be taken more seriously. I don't want to be seen anymore like this innocent girl. I intend to be a wise, worldly woman. Just watch me!

SENSE OF HUMOR

Group work can be very grim and depressing business. After all, most people come to group because their lives are not very good, and they are not all that happy. On top of that, most are interpersonally difficult and have a hard time communicating with others. Despite the serious nature of group work, group participants want to have fun and enjoy their time in group settings. Laughing, joking, showing a good sense of humor, and remembering to celebrate accomplishments in the group are all qualities and actions that lead to desirable groups. It is often up to the leader to determine the balance between seriousness and humor. Humor and fun can satisfy members' need for intimacy and connection, and leaders are often the ones who can set the tone and make enjoyment a part of a group setting (Galanes, 2003).

Humor and playfulness are an integral part of the group experience. They are used for a variety of purposes, such as to reduce tension, loosen people up, deal with forbidden subjects, build shared experiences, express creativity, and spice things up. There is a long history of exploring the role of humor in developing relationships and in the helping professions (Goldin et al., 2006; Vereen, Butler, Williams, Darg, & Downing, 2006; Vereen, Hill, & Butler, 2013). Of course, humor can also be abused, especially if members are scapegoated or ridiculed (Gladding, 2011a, 2011b), or if its tone is overly hostile, mocking, aggressive, or defensive (Maples et al., 2001).

In the group context, the use of humor can be a technique or intervention, but we are trying to draw more attention to the quality of humor as a personal characteristic in the group leader. You could certainly make a case that there are many excellent group leaders who would never be described as humorous or playful. Nevertheless, playful group leaders do have an advantage over their chronically serious brethren by having at their disposal the means to change the tone of a group as needed. Besides, leading groups can at times be so stressful, draining, and futile that you must have some way to build in comic relief.

FLEXIBILITY

Adaptability and flexibility are probably the most important characteristics of all for a group leader (Galanes, 2003; Luke, 2014). You certainly should go into every group with a plan or agenda, a set of goals, or at least an expectation for what you think and hope might happen. In fact, a large body of research indicates that, especially during the early stages of group, group leaders' providing structure is associated with good group outcomes (Miles & Paquin, 2014; Riva et al., 2004).

More often than not, however, events will not unfold as expected. For example, imagine that in the preceding week's group session, you talked about a theme related to fears of mediocrity. A number of group members spent time interacting about the messages they received as children that they would never amount to much. Almost everyone got involved, sharing personal examples of times when parents or teachers betrayed them. As an assignment for the next session, most of the group declared a personal goal they intended to work on, related to doing something they felt skilled at doing. The session ended with people excited about future possibilities and a plan for each person to report his or her progress the next week.

Now you have your plan for the upcoming session: Check in with the participants on how their homework proceeded. Follow up with Karin, who said she wanted some time. Make sure that Ben gets some attention, because he was so quiet last time. Then return to the mediocrity theme and see what each group member did over the previous week. You think this is a brilliant plan, and you should have just enough time to get through everything on your agenda. Then the group members arrive, take their seats, and before you can even open your mouth, Kali starts sobbing hysterically because her mother was hospitalized after a serious car wreck. Your plan goes out the window, and your focus moves to the most pressing issue in the group. So much for your agenda.

Flexibility is not only important in the way you structure group sessions but also as a personal trait. Being flexible means being a creative problem solver (Gladding, 2011a). It means being able to respond instantly to the most subtle nuances in human behavior. One moment, you are about to intervene to stop a member from rambling, and then because of something you see out of the corner of your eye (or maybe a tiny sound you hear), you sense that an opportunity has opened to cue a chronically silent member.

One of the reasons leading groups is so exhausting is that every second, not just every minute, the atmosphere and circumstances of a group change. There is never one clear way to proceed, but, rather, hundreds of options arise over a group period. You have to track continuously not only what the person in focus is saying but also how everyone else in the group is reacting, both internally and externally. So in a group with eight members, you could go in one of eight directions at any given time. As if that were not daunting enough, consider that the whole is even greater than the individual parts—meaning that the interactive behavior among participants, their meaningful looks, whispers, nonverbal behavior, connections, and interactions with one another, must also be attended to.

We do not mean to frighten you unnecessarily if you are telling yourself at this point that maybe you no longer want to do this sort of work. Once you have completed this course, studied hard, and practiced diligently, you will be able to do this stuff (awkwardly at first) under the supervision of a more experienced coleader. One thing that will make things go much easier for you is if you develop greater flexibility so you can go with the flow of whatever is occurring in the moment. Go ahead and make your plans, if that makes you feel better, but be prepared to throw away your agenda so you can track and respond to whatever arises.

For Reflection

Consider the ways you are overstructured, rigid, and controlling in your life. Think of a recent time when you were unusually reluctant to give up your commitment to a particular way of doing things, even though there may have been several other better courses of action (at least, that is what other people suggested). What would it have taken for you to stop the direction you were heading, consider other options, and perhaps take a different path or action?

What are some ways you could develop greater flexibility in the ways you respond to situations in your life? What kinds of tips might you give to a group member who is controlling and inflexible?

HONESTY

Be who you want your group members to be. If you value sincerity, authenticity, and genuineness in your groups (and in the world), then demonstrate these qualities in your own behavior—and not just while you are working. Authenticity is at the core of leading by example (Komives et al., 2013). Many group norms and guidelines are not explicitly discussed but are modeled by the leader (Galanes, 2003). Remember, group members will watch you very closely to see if you are able to deliver what you promise. Furthermore, they will check up on you as much as possible to find out if you are really the compassionate, caring person you appear to be. After all, would you trust a leader just because he or she said you should? In so many groups, participants are hardly volunteers; many have been referred by the courts, are mandated to attend by authorities, or are being blackmailed by relatives ("Either you go, or I'm walking out"). Other members have long-standing trust issues (or, rather, mistrust issues) and tend to be very suspicious of anyone such as yourself who seems so helpful. As you can imagine, the notion of being an authentic leader is quite important.

You are likely to be tested. Group members will watch for the slightest inconsistency between what you say and what you do, or what you say now and what you have said before. If you walk through life with a commitment toward honesty and authenticity, you are much more likely to earn the respect and trust of people who have some very good reasons for being cautious. In fact, cross-cultural research indicates that people tend to reward honesty and be more upset with deception (Wang & Leung, 2010).

COMPASSION

We could use other words here to describe the essential caring that must be communicated to group members—*loving, respectful, empathic, nonjudgmental, warm, kind, supportive*—but what all these characteristics mean is that you are someone who is really invested in others' welfare and that, as a leader, you create a consistent, positive relationship with group members. Compassion is essential to all schools of helping and has been viewed by many throughout time to be a profound agent of healing (Armstrong, 2011). Yalom and Leszcz (2005) noted that "nothing, no technical consideration, takes precedence over this attitude" (p. 117).

We hope that you are doing this work in the first place because you want to make a difference in people's lives and you recognize that group work is the most ideal environment to make these changes possible. In your search for techniques, interventions, and skills that will make you optimally effective, do not underestimate the power of your own compassion. While it is often not enough simply to care for people (if this were true, we would not need professionals), the relationships you develop with group members are at least as important as anything else you do. Relationships are, in fact, the core of all professional helping efforts (see Kottler & Shepard, 2011; Rogers, 1980; Wampold, 2007). Komives et al.

(2013) added, "Leadership has to do with relationships, the role of which cannot be overstated. Leadership is inherently a relational, communal process" (p. 95).

CLEARHEADEDNESS

Group members depend on you to be fair, honorable, equitable, and free of biases, prejudices, and other oppressive attitudes. They also need you to be somewhat logical and analytical—a steady hand at the helm of the group, navigating members through both calm and stormy waters. Not only that, but being clearheaded means being based in reality, aware of yourself and others, and able to rise above the fray.

Our own relational blocks, biases, and countertransference issues—those distorted reactions leaders have toward particular members—must be resolved fully, or people may be harmed. As you look around any group, you are likely to have strong reactions to everyone present. Some participants will seem attractive to you; others may elicit strong negative reactions. Although some of your personal feelings may certainly be a logical response to provocative behavior, at other times, you may indeed be overreacting based on your own distortions and failure to address your own unresolved issues.

For Reflection

Make a list of all the excuses you have for not seeking the guidance of a counselor or therapist at this time in your life. Make sure to include the old standbys: (1) you can't afford it; (2) you don't have time; (3) even if you did have the money and time, you don't really need the help; and (4) it would be too embarrassing if others found out. This, of course, is exactly what your group members will say!

Knowing that you have some excuses for not seeking professional help, if you were going to consult with a professional (for the experience, if nothing else), what are some of the personal issues you could work on? What would you like to be different in your life? How could your personal relationship be better? Keep in mind the sorts of problems and struggles people are likely to bring to your groups and what that might trigger for you.

Many of the dangers associated with exaggerated personal reactions can be checked when you are working with a coleader (DeLucia-Waack & Fauth, 2004). Unfortunately, that option is not always available because of strained resources and overscheduled case loads. As nice as it might be to depend on an experienced colleague or supervisor to keep you continuously clearheaded (Riva, 2014), rarely will you receive all the feedback and help you need. That is why experiencing group and individual counseling is so useful for beginning practitioners: Not only are you able to reduce personal conflict and stress during a difficult time of transition, but you are also able to learn what it is like to be in the client's chair.

Being clearheaded is closely related to being levelheaded in times of stress. Group members often want to explore scary and painful stuff, but they will do it only if they believe that the group leader will be able to guide them.

For a Class Activity

Talk to a group of peers about the ways you might profit from a group counseling/ therapy experience. Share with one another some of the personal buttons that might be pushed inadvertently by group members. Common areas to explore might include fear of intimacy, fear of failure, perfectionism, recurrent conflicts, addictions, poor self-esteem, childhood trauma, grief reactions, chronic depression or anxiety, family difficulties, loneliness, or career confusion. In other words, we all suffer from the same kinds of issues that bring people to our offices.

For a Field Study

Now the hard part: Make an appointment to attend a few sessions in a group or individual counseling experience. Pay attention to all the ideas you have been reading and learning about to see how they arise in your own experience.

Guidelines for Group Membership and Participation

You have probably noticed that we hold a very strong belief that to be an effective group leader, you must first know how to function optimally as a member. You must know what it's like to sit in the group member's chair, to know what works and what doesn't, to feel the dread and reluctance when you are pressured to reveal more about yourself than you feel comfortable revealing. Of course, you are actually living that role as we speak: You are now a member of a class group devoted to learning leadership skills.

One of your first jobs as a group leader is to teach members how to get the most from the experience. They neither know the rules nor understand what is expected. They will do their best to cooperate, but many of their assumptions about what you are looking for may not be valid. For instance, some members will talk too much because they think they are pleasing you. Others will stir up conflicts because they once saw that on television. It is your first objective to provide members with ground rules and guidance for how to behave in the group and how to get the most from the experience.

Student Voice

Learning the Rules

The importance of honoring confidentiality was impressed on us as being key in developing trust needed for group members to feel safe enough to reveal personal and important issues in group. At first, I was wondering why the group leader was spending so much time talking about the rules. But then I immediately became nervous. The leader was creating a foundation so that we could share personal things. At that moment I felt like the last thing I wanted to do was tear down carefully crafted walls, which hid from others the part of myself I felt was deeply flawed and lacking. I noticed everyone else nodding and agreeing to the expectations, and so it hit me that I was going to take some risks, and I also really needed the comfort and boundaries that these ground rules were establishing.

Some leaders distribute handouts that review ground rules and suggestions for how to behave (Yalom & Leszcz, 2005). Others handle this orientation during screening interviews or the first group meeting, or they cover it in both meetings (Miles & Paquin, 2014). Still others devote the first session solely to helping members create their own rules, knowing that people are far more committed to obeying norms they have had a role in creating. When we begin a counseling group, we make sure to cover these points:

- *What do we do in group?* Many people are not sure what happens in a group setting, or their ideas of group are purely related to depictions (often grossly inaccurate) from television and movies. It is important to give group members an honest picture of what happens in the group you are leading. Group settings have many benefits that are exclusive in many people's lives. Ultimately, group settings can allow the chance to receive and offer feedback in an honest manner—and that can be a rare thing. For example, you can't walk up to a random person on the street and ask, "What do you think of me?" and assume that you will get an honest answer you can believe, but in group you can. Furthermore, groups give you the chance to improve interpersonal relationships and communication; try new behaviors; talk honestly and directly about feelings; gain insight into motivation about your own thoughts, feelings, and behaviors by looking at relationship patterns; and improve self-esteem and confidence. Yet one of the greatest possibilities of a group setting is the chance to allow oneself to be known in a true and genuine manner.

- *What is essential in group work?* Confidentiality is essential in group work. Members are asked not to discuss anything that is said in group or anyone in the group with people outside of the group. Even contact between members outside of the group sessions is discouraged. To facilitate group effectiveness, group members should discuss their group experiences and other group members only during group time.

- *What do we talk about?* People are often unsure what is okay to bring up in group; without guidance, they tend to err on the side of caution and keep risky topics to themselves. I like to tell the group that we can talk about anything, but the caveat is that it should be important to them *right now* and should be *about them.* Group is a special and unique time each week, and so members should use that time accordingly not to talk about chitchat or surface stuff that can be discussed anywhere but, rather, to talk about the stuff they *don't* talk about elsewhere.

- *How do we decide what to talk about?* Members work together to determine what is discussed. Often these are concerns that all the members share, such as interacting with others, taking social risks, disclosing feelings, listening, working with issues as they arise in the group, and trying new behaviors. Usually, groups start with a check-in, during which each person gets a turn saying how he or she is doing and noting if he or she wants to bring anything to the group to discuss. After the check-in, the group has a good idea about where to go.

- *How does group counseling work?* Group counseling works by establishing a safe and trusting environment and a sense of "cohesiveness"—the feeling of being a part of a group with a shared purpose. This takes a few sessions to establish; so give yourself some time to feel connected to the group. Cohesiveness allows members to share themselves and be "real," confront others as appropriate, and learn to resolve conflicts. Members learn by both speaking and observing, and they develop awareness about their impact on others and learn to change the behaviors that create interpersonal problems. Self-esteem is also enhanced as members encourage, support, and offer suggestions to others.

You can go into more or less detail on these points depending on the group context and composition. Further, depending on the group you are leading, more specific information will need to be discussed and shared. Yet you can't have a high-functioning group without basic rules for timely arrival, expected attendance, and respect for boundaries. These are the macro rules that define each group meeting. From your own experiences in group situations, you know how distracting it can be if people come and go whenever they want. One way or another, you must indoctrinate members into the most healthy norms possible for group behavior.

For a Group Activity

Meet in groups of six, and pretend that this is your first session. Create a list of ground rules and guidelines for members that would ensure the experience would be safe and productive.

Compare your rules with those of others in your class to reach a consensus.

If you were going to construct a list of guidelines for members, it might include some of the following:

1. Speak only for yourself in the group. Use "I" rather than "we."
2. Racist, sexist, or otherwise disrespectful language will not be tolerated.
3. All members take responsibility for making sure that they get their own needs met in the group.
4. Nobody will be coerced or pressured into doing something for which he or she does not feel ready.
5. What is said in this group is considered privileged information. Everyone is responsible for maintaining confidentiality.
6. Time must be equitably distributed among all members.
7. Any member who is late more than three times or misses more than three sessions will be asked to leave the group.
8. If you are going to be late or miss a group, contact the group leader or tell the group the prior week.
9. No writing or note taking during sessions. Furthermore, no cell phones or other communication devices.
10. Timely payment for group sessions is expected.

If not all ground rules are established ahead of time, sometimes they can be defined as things proceed:

Leader: Caroline, I see you couldn't get here on time again.

Caroline: Sorry about that. It's just . . .

Leader: I didn't mean to make you feel defensive. I just wanted to bring up the issue here in the group to see how people wanted to handle late-arriving members. What do you all want to do in the future?

Kim: It's no big deal to me.

Sam: Well, it is to me. I was in the middle of something when Caroline came in late today. I don't like to be interrupted like that.

Kim: That's your problem then.

Lucy: Well, I don't like it either. I drive 45 minutes to get here, and I plan ahead so that I am not late because group is important to me.

Leader: Okay, so there are some reactions to this. Let's allow others to have their say as well. Is it okay for people to come late? Or leave early? If so, how do you want to handle this?

These are just a few examples of what might be included in a list of guidelines. To develop the most useful and comprehensive list possible, you will not only wish to consult numerous published sources but also want to draw on your own experiences as a group member. Whether you know it or not, you are already becoming an expert on being a group member, even if you haven't functioned as optimally as you would like to. You know what makes you bored, frightens you, and drives you crazy. You also have some idea of what others respond best to (Shakoor, 2010). This limited sample of experience is hardly enough, but it is a great start.

Learning to be a skilled and competent group leader results not only from serious study and supervised practice but also from your personal experiences—both good and bad—in the role of consumer. Next, we broaden your perspective, moving from your own behavior to that of a larger perspective of how group dynamics typically unfold.

Review of What You Learned

- Group leadership involves far more than what you do—it also involves who you are as a person.
- Certain personal qualities are associated with effective leaders. You do not need to be born with these characteristics—you can develop them through hard work and commitment. The key is taking the risks to learn about yourself in a group setting.
- High-functioning groups, whether designed around content or process, have similar structures that balance attention to agendas as well as participant reactions.
- Group leaders must be as committed to their own growth as they are to the development of their clients.
- Much of what you learn as a group leader will help you function as a more powerful and effective human being.
- There are universal guidelines and expectations for working in group settings. You will need to recognize what these are and learn how to convey them in a clear manner to your future groups. There will also be expectations that are unique to each group setting.

Understanding Group Dynamics and Systems 3

What is going on? Meghan has been so open and responsive in the past, but now she seems shut down. Folded arms. She hasn't said a word today. Should I say something to her, or would that just push her deeper into with-drawal? Wait a minute. I'm missing something. Dana is staring at her, frowning. So is Chet. Something's going on between them. It seems like Meghan's quietness is reflecting some hesitance on the part of others, almost as if she is "speaking" for them. If so, I'd be better off not focusing on Meghan but instead encouraging others to draw her out.

In this chapter, you will learn to think in new ways about human behavior, attending not only to the individual but, more important, to the larger systemic and interactive dynamics among people. Working in groups requires a whole different set of perceptual filters through which to make sense of what is going on. Rather than focusing on one person, you must be aware of multiple people, various interactions, and all the process events happening in between, just as illustrated in the reflections of the group leader above. It is enough to make your head spin.

If all you did as a group leader was constantly follow the main speaker or inter-action, group sessions would be rather tiring, potentially boring, and most likely not terribly effective. Worse yet, you would also be missing out on all the potential collective energy and interactions that group work can offer. Even though you use many of your individual therapeutic skills, they are applied quite differently in a group setting. For this reason, experienced group leaders leave linear thinking behind and learn to think recursively (circularly) and systemically, taking into account group dynamics among people. This means learning to look at the bigger picture of how each person's actions fit within the larger context of that person's world, as well as that of the group. You will not only diagnose individual difficulties but also assess interpersonal patterns, group stages, systemic functioning, coalitional alliances, and other dynamics that are important to understand. In a sense, effective group leaders learn to see the forest and the trees.

Many of the models and theories about group dynamics are focused on interpersonal interaction and are drawn from interpersonal theory, systems theory, social psychology, and research on collective behavior (Day, 2014). The interpersonal focus is useful since it draws attention to exchanges and behavior not only in the present but also from the past. It also regards all behavior as a sequence of ongoing, interactional, recursive, or reoccurring events with no beginning or end (Teyber & Faith, 2011). The focus on systems allows group leaders to expand their vision of a group and see how it evolves over time. Furthermore, it brings attention to the communication patterns and interpersonal patterns that emerge among group members as the group organizes as a whole. Essentially, it deepens the understanding of group dynamics and reminds group leaders that group work is not individual counseling in a group setting but, rather, group counseling in a systemic setting (Barlow, 2013; Connors & Caple, 2005).

Linear and Circular Causality

The strange thing about leading groups is that you are attending not only to group members as individuals but also to the interactive effects of how each person's behavior influences, and is in turn affected by, everyone else's actions. Look at your own classroom as one example. The instructor does and says things that have a huge impact on what happens in the room. It would appear as if you and your classmates react in a linear way to the stimulus of a statement such as, "Okay, count off by fives and organize yourselves into small groups." As students begin to organize, some students look annoyed and others seem bored. Others eagerly comply, excited that they do not have to sit quietly for the period and hear a lecture. You might feel both apprehensive and interested about what will occur next. As students around you respond in a variety of ways, others behave according to these reactions.

According to one model, favored by traditional behavioral theorists over the years, human reactions occur either as a stimulus-response, *classical conditioning* (à la Ivan Pavlov) process, or as a response-stimulus, *operant* (à la B. F. Skinner) mode. In the former, the instructor's directions elicit an automatic response in class members that has been conditioned over time; in the latter case, a particular response—the instructor's observation that the energy level is low in the room—is conditioned by a stimulus designed to alter current conditions. In both examples, behavior is viewed as linear in nature: One action affects the other in a direct line.

Even contemporary behaviorists now see this as a gross simplification of what happens during complex human interactions (Spiegler & Guevremont, 2010). Not only are there internal, cognitive, and affective processes going on within each person that influence how the world is perceived, but behavior in groups follows a much more circular rather than linear path. In circular causality, group members' behavior is simultaneously moving in all directions at once, "a continuous series of circular loops or recurring chains of influence" (Goldenberg & Goldenberg, 2013, p. 22). In a sense, this speaks to different forces moving in multiple directions—not influenced by one action but, rather, by ongoing, mutually influencing processes. Any action (verbal or nonverbal) by a group member influences all other members of the group and the group as a whole; group members' responses influence other responses and the group, and so on. Building on the example above, the instructor's asking the class to break into small groups is really just one of many processes happening at that moment.

For a Class Activity

In groups of three, identify one critical incident or dramatic moment that recently occurred in class and affected many people. Go back and try to re-create what might have led up to the culminating event, as well as its aftermath. Rather than relying on *linear causality,* employ a model of *circular causality* (reciprocal influences, causes, and effects) in which you examine how each person's behavior was both a trigger and an effect on others' actions.

As one example, linear causality might lead one to say that a student asked a "dumb" question at the end of class, eliciting groans from classmates, frustration in the instructor, and then shame and regret in that student for opening his mouth. If you look at that same incident from a circular perspective, you identify that many more complex processes were occurring. The student asked the question in the first place because he read a look in the instructor's eye that seemed to invite such an inquiry. The instructor was actually trying to encourage more student participation because he interpreted that this particular student was bored when he was really confused and so had checked out for a while. The groans from the class may have to do with some students wanting to leave early, another being annoyed by the question, and yet another who was not even paying attention in class but was looking at his iPhone and saw that his favorite team had lost. Once you bring in the contributory influences and effects of others in the room, you have quite a complex situation—far more so than you ever imagined.

Whether trying to make sense of what is going on in a classroom or what started a fight among a group of people, it is virtually impossible to identify who caused what. And finding the cause is not really all that important. All group behavior occurs within a context that includes the individual's perception of reality, as well as the interactions taking place, both consciously and unconsciously, among all people present. That process itself becomes the area of intervention and change.

Systems Theory

The concept of circular causality is only one of many ideas spawned from what has become known as "systems theory." Developed by biologist Ludwig von Bertalanffy (1968), this approach to understanding behavior was designed to make sense of the way that all living creatures organize themselves and act in predictable patterns. Furthermore, he was instrumental in getting others to consider the whole as greater than the sum of its parts, which is called *holism*. Since he was a biologist, and also fond of physics metaphors, many of the terms he introduced to describe the way groups of people behave sound more appropriate for a science class: *homeostasis, morphogenesis,* and *feedback loops.*

Until group leaders had a framework in which to look at systemic behavior—that is, the interactive patterns and subsystems of a group—there was a tendency to treat group work like doing individual counseling or therapy, but with an audience present (Barlow, 2014). There are still some group structures that operate that way, just as there are some group leaders who are essentially doing individual therapy in a group setting with witnesses. Obviously, this does not capitalize on many of the powerful therapeutic ingredients that are present in a community healing environment.

In the helping professions, the family therapy movement (with figures such as Murray Bowen, Jay Haley, and Virginia Satir, to mention a few) has been instrumental in introducing systemic thinking as a means to assess the ways groups of relatives organize themselves over time, creating stable patterns (homeostasis) that are inclined to return to familiar states (equilibrium). In this sense, one of the beliefs is that systems tend to be self-correcting based on feedback, either positive or negative, and that systems maintain stability (Goldenberg & Goldenberg, 2013).

For Personal Application

Think of a time in your family when someone created a problem or conflict to "help" everyone else resume a familiar, stable pattern. For instance, your parents were having a disagreement and you or your siblings distracted them by acting out. Consider the ways your family of origin organized itself consistently into the same, familiar ordered system. Whenever things became destabilized or chaotic, what roles did you and others play to bring things back to equilibrium?

Most family therapists, who are also group specialists, favor a whole glossary of terms that are used to describe the way family systems tend to operate. Many of these ideas are quite useful in understanding behavior in all groups, not just family systems (Bitter, 2013). As an example of this, imagine that a group member claims that another participant hurt him deeply by confronting him about his tendency to ramble. The confronting group member defends herself by saying that the rambler drives her crazy with his tendency to talk all the time. Each believes that the other is causing him or her to act the way he or she does (e.g., A $\rightarrow$ B, or B $\rightarrow$ A), even though each is actually both the cause and the effect of the other's behavior (e.g., A $\longleftrightarrow$ B). We simplified this interaction considerably, of course. Remember that they are both part of a larger group in which other members are also covertly involved in this interaction, rooting for one person or the other depending on their loyalties.

Group coalitions, or subsystems, are also important phenomena to observe and identify. All groups organize themselves into smaller units, each with its own set of rules or norms that regulate behavior (remember that homeostasis is the key in this model). Each of these smaller coalitional groups has certain boundaries that control who can say what to whom. In a family, this phenomenon might be readily observed as a father–mother subsystem; another between two of the three siblings; and another composed of the mother, her mother, and the third child (Goldenberg & Goldenberg, 2013). In a group, you might see this when there is a popular and powerful subgroup—a couple of members who have become close compared with those who are shy and not too confident. You can therefore appreciate that these coalitions are organized around mutual needs, loyalties, and control of power. When these subsystems are dysfunctional and destructive, such as when a parent is aligned with a child against his spouse or a child is in coalition with a grandparent against her parents, the family therapist's job is to initiate realignments in the structure and power, creating a new set of subsystems that are more functional. In a group setting, imagine a dysfunctional subsystem of three group members, in which they always protect one another and work to deflect any attempts to provide constructive feedback. In this situation the group leader's job is to intervene, to help realign the group so that subsystem has less power and the group as a whole can begin to interact more honestly with one another without loyalties and coalitions getting in the way.

In groups, as well, you will observe that members will align themselves with allies according to shared values and what is in their best interest. Different group members find ways to stick together. For example, we have seen male group members align together, Muslim or fundamental Christian group members form coalitions, and gay and lesbian group members pull together in a subgroup against other group members who may appear threatening or aligned against them. Of course, people do tend to be drawn to those who are like them, so it is quite normal for these coalitions to form. You will notice this most dramatically when members form a coalition against you as the leader, a common dynamic that can be therapeutic if handled constructively. This recently happened to Matt in a group he was leading.

A group member, Jillian, who was usually active and emotionally available, alluded to a troubling event but then said, "I don't want to get into it right now." After saying that, she looked directly at me (Matt), as if beckoning me to respond, and I followed up by asking, "What makes it hard to talk about it right now?"

Jillian paused, explained a little bit about her fears of being vulnerable and of being judged, and then spent the next 5 minutes revealing the event and her response to the group. She was tearful and sad throughout. When she finished, I noticed that a few group members began to make eyes at me as though they were upset. I inquired about this, and three group members talked about how inappropriate I had been by pushing Jillian to talk when she clearly did not want to. These three group members had spent most of the first 4 weeks in group remaining relatively quiet, alluding to some distress in their lives but always created a boundary from the group by saying that they felt anxious in the room and were not sure if the group was a good fit for them. They had created a coalition around the issue of remaining hidden since it seemed they all feared revealing their own inner worlds. They added that they did not feel safe in the group and that I ought to apologize to the group member, Jillian.

I attempted to validate their observations and concerns, and noted that it may have appeared as though I was pushing or bullying Jillian to speak. At this point, I asked the three members if they might be willing to explore their reactions with the group, and why they had such a strong reaction (when the other group members did not). Jillian noted that she did not feel pushed to speak and was actually proud of herself for speaking up, but that in previous groups she had often wanted to push these three group members to open up more about their lives. For the rest of the group, we explored hesitancy and safety in the group with these three members and found that by the end of the night, the group had grown closer to these three and they indicated feeling less anxiety about being in the group.

Photo 3.1   Rather than functioning as a cohesive team, working together for common goals, group members sometimes become competitive toward one another. They vie for attention, compete for leader approval, sabotage one another—as if trying to win a race. This dynamic can begin easily enough, apparently as a form of linear causality in which one person's behavior seems to trigger someone else to respond. Yet each member's behavior becomes both a cause and an effect, sparking a form of circular causality in which things can spin out of control.

You can apply family systems ideas to look at not only the *structure* of a group but also its *patterns of communication.* A number of group theorists (Agazarian, 2011; Connors & Caple, 2005; Donigian & Malnati, 2005; Gantt & Agazarian, 2011) have adapted systems thinking to all group settings in which you can observe and label the characteristic ways that members relate to one another. Group systems theory helps clarify group processes that are occurring and provides interventions to move the group dynamics in more productive directions (Agazarian, 2011; Connors & Caple, 2005). In fact, you can step back from any group you are part of and ask yourself a number of questions about the systemic functioning, and see many group systems concepts come to life:

- *What roles are various individuals playing in the group?* Who is placating whom? Who has the power in the group? These questions speak to the notion of each group having a control and power structure. This is also indicated by the following questions: How do decisions get made in the group? Who gets time, and how is that negotiated among members? Other than the leader's direction, how is it decided who talks and what is discussed?
- *Which coalitions have formed?* Who is aligned with whom? Which alliances have formed temporarily and permanently? Which members are in conflict with one another?
- *Are the boundaries within a group open enough to allow new information to enter the group?* Boundaries can be tight or loose, depending on the needs of the group. An example of boundaries is the admission criteria for a group setting. Who gets into your group? What are the criteria? An open 12-step group may have a loose set of criteria, whereas an intensive psychotherapy group for depression may have a strict set of entrance criteria.
- *How do members communicate with one another?* Are the lines of communication clear and direct? Where do members focus their attention when they speak?
- *Do group interactions tend to move in patterns that contribute to keeping the system stable?* Repetitive patterns tend to maintain safety and regularity. What norms have developed in the group that regulate behavior? Which rules were established by the leader and which emerged covertly among members? What are the meta-rules (the rules about rules) in the group? One such rule might be, "Make sure you don't say anything about bald people or it will piss the leader off."
- *How is information exchanged among group members?* How do people share what they know with one another? Who is excluded or ignored? Which data are accepted and rejected? What critical information is neglected? How is the information synthesized?
- *Did change in a system occur via the use of positive and negative feedback?* Rather than a value judgment, positive feedback tends to create change, whereas negative feedback tends to support the current system. Conflict can be an example of positive feedback that provokes change. How are conflicts resolved? Who doesn't like whom? What are the ways members

try to sabotage or undermine one another or the leader? How do members show their disagreement with what is going on? At the same time, during conflict there will be group members who try to downplay or squash the conflict. This can be viewed as negative or change-resistant feedback. So who tries to make things better? Who squelches the conflict? Who tries to create distractions?

- *What was the holistic outcome of the group?* Rather than group members acting as solitary agents, each is interdependent on the others, meaning that the whole is greater than the sum of its parts (von Bertalanffy, 1968). While new group leaders may evaluate a group based on how some of the members did, holism instructs group leaders to ask, "How did the group do today?"

This is just a sample of questions that could emerge from systemic thinking applied to groups. So far, we have been looking at group systems as they are contained within a closed unit. Of course, each individual, and each group system, is part of an interconnected series of other, larger systems that convey sociopolitical and cultural forces (Burnes & Ross, 2010). Further, an individual's behavior in a group is influenced not only by what others are doing in that system but also by significant others in the outside world, as well as by the person's family of origin.

For Personal Application

Pick a group system you would like to understand better. This could be your own family, a social group, or perhaps the class. Apply the principles introduced in this chapter to analyze the structural and communicational patterns of this system. You might find it helpful to use a sociogram (a tool used by social psychologists and sociologists) to plot out the various subsystems in your group. Use a graphical drawing to display the coalitions, communication patterns, control and power issues, and boundaries in place. You can either make up your own method for plotting and illustrating patterns, consult standard manuals that teach family systems specialists how to diagram structural and communication patterns (see McGoldrick, Gerson, & Petry, 2008; Tomlinson, 2009), or try some Internet-based applications for constructing sociograms (see www.phenotyping.com/sociogram).

In addition to illustrating the group dynamics you observe, answer the questions listed above to sort out the roles played by various members—who controls power, what the norms (and unstated rules) are, and your final assessment about the relative strengths and weaknesses of this group system.

Family of Origin and Interpersonal Issues

One of our major operating assumptions is that the way people act in group is representative of how they tend to act in any group throughout their lives. Of course, there are exceptions to this, but generally speaking, people often re-create the same patterns and behavior in group that they have established as templates from their early years. This means that people will create a social microcosm (Yalom & Leszcz, 2005), an extended reality of what they are used to in the outside world. They will negotiate with others in the group for comfort zones that are familiar. They will engage in the same dysfunctional patterns that get them in trouble elsewhere. And they will respond to people not just as they really are but as they imagine them to be. Simply put, one's interpersonal style and maladaptive patterns that are present in every other facet of life ultimately will appear in group, too. Despite attempts to hide or change normal behavior, the "real" group member's true self will emerge. In reality, then, there is really no need to describe one's interpersonal problems or difficulties in life, as they will eventually come to life in the group. Though that may sound scary, or even improbable, the fact that each group member's true self will be revealed is one of the bedrock reasons why group can be particularly helpful. If the behaviors, beliefs, or feelings that cause distress or get people into trouble emerge in the group, then the group will get a true sense of what is happening (rather than having it described verbally), group members can use their own reactions to give honest feedback, and they can display their true selves in a supportive space where change is possible.

For Personal Application

When we talk about the concept of social microcosm with our students and group members, it often creates some personal anxiety. The premise of this idea is that regardless of your efforts to hide, appear different, or present a different version of yourself in group, the true you will ultimately be revealed. That can be scary simply because of the notion that one cannot hide in group. Putting your anxiety aside, what might that mean for you in a group setting? What parts of yourself, either your personality or interpersonal behavior, do you like to hide or keep hidden from people when you first meet them? What are your fears around having these parts of yourself revealed? How do you think people respond to these parts of you?

This phenomenon in which people's unresolved issues with members of their original family and other significant people play themselves out in a group presents some difficult challenges and wonderful therapeutic opportunities. Under the right circumstances and leadership, the group environment can be used to produce a "corrective emotional experience" (Frank & Ascher, 1951), which can lead to real change. The premise of the corrective emotional experience is to expose the group member to emotional stimulation he or she could not handle in the past. Often people could not handle past experiences because their settings were threatening or anxiety provoking. However, in a supportive and effective group setting, the group member can work through this experience in a more productive manner, essentially healing the wounds of the past.

Student Voice

The Social Microcosm

In my group's course, I learned about the social microcosm and thought it just seemed like psychobabble. This was a different setting than my work or my family at home. After a few weeks, however, this strange feeling seemed to come over me as I realized that people were saying things to me that was almost verbatim to what I hear at work and at home. People experienced me as defensive and aloof—that was my main piece of feedback from my last evaluation at work! Then some of the female members of the group gave me feedback that I seemed distracted and not fully engaged with them—that is exactly what my wife tells me! After I heard that I said, "Time-out, something freaky is happening here." Then it hit me that maybe the true me was coming through in group, and I really could not hide from it. That actually freaked me out more but after a while that ended up being the insight that helped me the most.

Yalom and Leszcz (2005) provide a thorough overview of the corrective emotional experience in group settings. This sort of critical incident occurs once it is recognized that someone is experiencing a strong emotional reaction to someone or something occurring in the group, often way out of proportion to what would be expected. This is often seen when a group member experiences strong anger or dislike toward another member, when a self-disclosure deepens one's connection with the group, or when one has strong positive affect toward a group member yet this is experienced as odd or unique since one expected feelings of rejection. For the corrective experience to occur, the group must be safe and supportive enough so that sensitive and risky interpersonal emotions can be honestly expressed, and there must be enough engagement and honest feedback among group members to permit effective reality testing so the group members can explore the situation with consensual validation from others. As this occurs, one can gain increased awareness and recognition of entrenched patterns and inappropriateness of some interpersonal feelings and behaviors. An individual can also use the group to interact more deeply and honestly to try new behaviors and work through destructive patterns. Such an interaction might look something like this:

Dorothy: When I was your age, I never . . .

Nevin: What is this crap about when you were my age? You were NEVER my age! I'm so sick of hearing old people like you judge me when you don't even . . .

Leader: Hey, Nevin, calm down. I can see you're upset with what Dorothy said, but you need . . .

Nevin: You're another one! Always telling me what I need to do. You know what? Y'all can just kiss my ass. I've had just about enough of this.

Monty: Nevin, man, hey, the guy's just trying to help. Tranquillo, buddy. He don't mean anything. He's just trying to help.

Nevin: Stay out of it, Monty. This ain't your business either. This is between me and Dorothy. She's been on my back since this group started.

Leader: Okay, Nevin, let's stop for a minute and look at what's going on.

Nevin: What's the point?

Leader: I know that the two of you have not been getting along since the group began. It may be hard to understand right now, but I believe there's a good chance you'll learn from each other and ultimately be important to each other over the course of this group.

Nevin: What do you mean?

Leader: Even though I know this is uncomfortable for Dorothy and Monty, I can see that your feelings are hurt, too. I think this is important stuff. In all the time we've been together, Nevin, this is the first time you've really spoken from your heart.

Nevin: Damn right! I am pissed off.

Leader: And that's good. And while I applaud your courage to finally say out loud what you've been feeling—including confronting me, too—I can't help but think there's something else going on here as well.

Nevin: Whaddaya mean?

Leader: Anyone want to help Nevin with the question?

You can see how the leader is trying to get other group members involved in sorting out why Nevin reacted so emotionally to Dorothy's offer of help and then reacted rather strongly to his friend Monty's support. The leader hypothesizes that what is going on right now has little to do with the present members; rather, it is actually a reenactment of previous interactions that Nevin has experienced with older authority figures. With further exploration and prompting, it is discovered that Dorothy reminds Nevin of his fifth-grade teacher, the one who beat him with a set of extra-long rosary beads for no reason he could ever understand. Furthermore, the whole group reminded him of situations he had faced over and over again in his life—a bunch of do-gooder White folks pretending to care but secretly harboring beliefs that he is not capable and is inferior.

It turned out that this interaction was a very familiar one to Nevin, and so he began to unconsciously respond in the same way he had always responded in the past. He got angry as a way to push people away in an attempt to protect himself. This time, however, after the intervention by the group and the group leader, events unfolded much differently than in the past. Once what was occurring was recognized, the dynamic could be labeled and the alternative responses could be developed.

Reviewing the process that was just described, there will be times when you are sitting in groups and you notice that people seem to be reacting not only to what is actually occurring in the room but also to some perception they have that is more influenced by their past experiences than by present circumstances. In the psychological literature, this is often called transference, yet psychoanalytic/interpersonal theorist Harry Stack Sullivan called it *parataxic distortion* (Sullivan, 1953). This describes the tendency in group not to see others for who they are but, rather, to distort them into who they represent or who we expect them to be based on our own past experiences. So this means that we (group members and even the group leaders) often are not relating to others in reality but instead relating to internal ideas and fantasies of what certain people represent. For example, a group member with an abusive father may relate to older, male authority figures as if they were his father. You may notice this phenomenon in your own interactions with authority figures (teachers, supervisors) who remind you of your parents in some way. When you become aware that such a reaction might be occurring, ask yourself the following questions:

- What is this emotional outburst really about?
- What is this person seeing, feeling, and experiencing that I am missing?
- What is it about this person's cultural, ethnic, and gender background that would explain his or her unique experience?
- How does this fit with what else I know about this person?

- To what extent is this person distorting or exaggerating what is going on?
- How are others in the group reacting to what is happening?
- What does my intuition tell me is going on?
- What can I do to help this person become more aware of his or her behavior and find connections to the past?
- Who might this group member represent?
- What are the intrapersonal needs that are trying to be met through the distorted relationship?
- What do I need to do to work this through toward closure in the group?
- What object lessons can be generalized from this single episode to other group members' experiences?

One of the exciting things about a group setting is the chance to discover and work through some of the distortions. Often the best way to address this is to use other group members to test your assumptions. This is often achieved by consensual validation from other group members by comparing one's interpersonal validations with those of others in the group. So if Willie sees Franklin, an older man in the group, as harsh and rejecting (much the same as Willie experienced his own father), then the group setting allows Willie the chance to see if other group members see and experience Franklin in the same way. When the other group members disagree, then Willie can explore what gets activated intra- and interpersonally with Franklin, and he can gain some insight and potential healing on this issue.

For a Class Activity

Groups are powerful means for solving problems and completing tasks, given the right atmosphere and structure. The type of leadership and members who participate also play a significant role in group productivity.

This activity has two main goals:

1. To practice the art of compromise and consensus seeking

2. To witness group dynamics in action

The first step involves taking about 10 minutes to make a list of what you consider to be the ideal characteristics of a good group member.

Get together in groups of about eight members. Two of you will serve as observers of group dynamics. Your job is to watch how the group shares information, makes decisions, and works toward consensus. You will take notes on what you observe and then lead a discussion afterward about what transpired, sharing your perceptions as well as eliciting reactions from participants.

All the members of your assigned group must come to an agreement over the best qualities in your team members. You have 20 minutes to identify what you consider to be the 10 most important member attributes. During this process, it would be good to view differences of opinion as helpful rather than harmful in your consensus seeking. Just make sure that you budget your time so you are able to complete the task in the allotted 20 minutes.

Under the leadership of the observers, take another 10 minutes afterward to talk about the dynamics of your groups, especially with regard to (a) how you organized yourselves, (b) how you shared ideas, (c) how you achieved consensus, and (d) what sort of climate emerged.

For Personal Application

Think of a time recently when you were especially puzzled by the way someone reacted in a group or social situation. The person's behavior struck you as so inappropriate or strange that you could not fathom what was going on. You may have felt annoyed, frustrated, or even angered by this incident.

Attempt to review this incident again, but this time leave your own frame of reference and view the incident from the perspective of this person whose behavior you did not understand. Try to use pure empathy and compassion to get inside the other person's skin and imagine what it must be like to experience the world through this other's senses and background. Take into consideration the person's unique cultural, religious, family, educational, and historical background. As much as you can, try to be this person, seeing the world through his or her eyes.

Of course, you can never really know another's experience, but using your empathic skills, intuition, and some logical hypothesis based on the limited information available, reconstruct the meaning of this outburst in light of this person's background. Remember, this person likely felt misunderstood, so make sure you describe this situation the way he or she would.

Now, talk to yourself (or to others) about how you could use this methodology, as a group leader or in your personal life, whenever you confront behavior that appears incomprehensible to you.

Interaction Patterns

In groups you will be observing not just how members speak to one another but also how they behave. This includes their facial expressions, body posture, special positioning, and anything else that provides clues about internal states. It should come as no surprise to you to learn that people do not always say out loud what they are thinking or tell the truth all the time. Sometimes people don't even know what they are feeling inside. During those times when group members know what they want to say and intend to be utterly honest in their disclosures, they still can't communicate as fully as they would like. With words, much gets lost in the translation.

As a group leader, you will not only be listening very closely to what partici- pants say, but you will also be observing very carefully how they are behaving. Listen inside the mind of a group leader during a typical moment in a session when she is processing the interaction patterns she observes:

> *Cynthia is saying that she is upset by what happened in her life this week, but she looks like she is almost proud of the attention she is getting. And notice the way her eyes keep flitting over toward Kevin, as if she is looking for his sympathy. But he is ignoring her, turning his body toward Carlos: I wonder if they know some secret about Cynthia?*
>
> *Trina, over there on the other side, is not even listening to Cynthia; she seems to have something else on her mind altogether. It looks to me like she is waiting for a pause so she can say something. That certainly isn't the case with Mai today. Look, she has her chair pulled back, as if she wants to be closer to the door. Candy looks worried about her, too; she keeps trying to get Mai's attention, but Mai is ignoring her, ignoring everyone, as if she is in her own world.*
>
> *The whole energy of the group seems restrained today, as if there is some collective conspiracy not to get into too much. I wonder who has been talking to whom, outside the group this week. I've got to get a more accurate picture of what is going on behind the scenes. . . .*
>
> *Hey, what's that? Is it my imagination, or is Megan finally going to say something? Look, her foot is fidgeting and she's playing with her hair. I know she needs an invitation to talk, but I wonder if this might be the moment when she will jump in all on her own. Should I cue her or not? Wait. I have a better idea. Paul appears to see the same thing I do. He is looking at me, as if to tell me that I should do something to invite Megan to talk. That's what I always do, though.*
>
> *This time I think I'll let Paul do the work. Maybe it will help wean Megan off the notion that she needs to be invited to talk before she can say something. I know this is the way she has been treated her whole life. Her family never lets her talk at home, so why should she be any different here? But she can be different, starting right now! The first thing I've got to do, though, is switch direction from Cynthia (who is rambling now and seems to have lost the interest of the other group members) to cue Paul so he will bring out Megan.*

The remarkable thing about this whole internal dialogue is that in the 1 min- ute this took place (Yes, that was only 1 minute in the mind of a group leader!

Are you already exhausted?), all these assumptions, hypotheses, and observations were based completely on nonverbal behavior. It is certainly possible that if you train yourself to notice nuances in behavior, to watch behavioral cues, to decode underlying meanings that are just beneath the surface, you will mine a rich source of data that can be used to make accurate assessments about what is happening, and then make informed choices about which interventions to choose.

For a Field Study

One of the best ways to learn about group dynamics and leadership is to familiarize yourself with the journals in the field that are devoted to group work. Spend some time in the library perusing the literature so you can identify those sources that will be most valuable to you in the future. Many times you will find yourself confused and hungry for information about a particular problem.

There are hundreds of such journals that include articles about group leadership. Following are some of the specialized group sources you will wish to consult:

Group
Group Analysis
Group Dynamics: Theory, Research, and Practice
Group Facilitation
Group and Organization Management
Group Processes and Intergroup Relations
International Journal of Group Psychotherapy
Journal of Child and Adolescent Group Therapy
Journal of Group Psychotherapy, Psychodrama, and Sociometry
Journal of Social and Personal Relationships
Journal for Specialists in Group Work
Leadership Quarterly
Small Group Behavior
Small Group Research
Social Work in Groups

What to Look For

All groups organize themselves in particular ways, with or without designated leaders. You could spend a whole lifetime trying to familiarize yourself with all the literature and research that has been accumulated on this subject. At some point you may wish to review a basic text on group dynamics (see Beebe &

Masterson, 2011; Forsyth, 2013; Levi, 2011) that outlines the science of group behavior, including topics such as interpersonal attraction, conflict, performance, decision making, problem solving, power, influence, team building, and so on. Here is an overview of some basic ideas.

PROXEMICS

Proxemics is a term introduced by anthropologist Edward T. Hall (1966) to describe the set measurable distances between people as they interact. Proxemics specifically describes the social use of space in the physical world, and personal space in particular. Personal space can be understood as the area, marked by invisible boundaries, surrounding an individual's body. This area functions as a comfort zone during interpersonal communication (Nova, 2005). It disappears in some environments, such as a full elevator or crowd, but can often be managed in a group setting. As you surely know from your own life and interactions with others, people adjust their physical distance from one another according to the degree of attraction or tension they feel. There have been studies that actually measure the number of inches people stand from one another when they talk and how that is correlated with physical attraction. Obviously, friends stand closer than strangers, women tend to be more comfortable than men with intimate space, and when you like someone you are inclined to approach that person more closely. Further, there are cross-cultural differences regarding what is considered appropriate space (Hogh-Olesen, 2008).

In a group, you will want to watch the ways members seat themselves—who they prefer to sit next to and who they position themselves opposite from. Watch not only for where people choose to sit and how close they sit to one another, but also notice the body positioning and other clues that may reveal inner states. See if people move their chairs out of the group or how they adjust them. Who always sits next to the leader? Who is closest to the exit? It is surprising how much you can learn from simple observations of space. Furthermore, people tend to engage in rather predictable patterns that are often unconscious to them, so pointing these patterns out can provide a portal to exploring how one is relating to the group on a conscious and unconscious level. Many of your observations will lead to theories about what is happening between people. Rather than laying out such a theory in a group, the group leader usually just needs to offer the observation and let the group members make sense of why they do what they do.

Student Voice

Sitting Next to the Leader

One of my big insights in group came from understanding why I always sat right next to the leader. Of course that also translated into my life where I often stand with those people who can protect me. This may sound obvious now, but I was terrified of group for months. I did not want to join it since it was so scary. Based on my past, I found it hard to trust people, and I thought people simply wouldn't be kind to me. Furthermore, I felt they would attack me if I talked. So I sat next to the leader seeking protection, with the feeling and belief that he would keep me safe. And he did, and it led me to actually take the risk to expose my fears to the group and allowed them to support me. It was better than I expected, and I did feel safe, but I saw that most of the safety came from the other group members. Oddly enough, but not so odd now, it was after finally taking the risk and being accepted that I started sitting away from the leader. I did not need him to protect me anymore, and I began to figure out that maybe I did not need protection in my life.

Of course, the structure of how and where people sit has major significance for how you decide to arrange the room. You would be amazed at how often leaders fail to organize the room in a way that is conducive to open communication, shared responsibility for the meeting, and constructive interaction. In a typical classroom, for example, chairs are arranged so they all face the front. Besides the instructor, the only things you can see are the backs of classmates' heads. This works well if you believe that all learning emanates from the mouth of the instructor and that nothing valuable happens as a result of group interaction (it also is the most efficient use of space when resources are limited). If your goal, however, is to encourage group members to interact with one another, then a far better arrangement is one in which people sit in a circle, in such a way that every person can directly see the others and nobody has to twist around to catch someone's eye. Of course, there are many ways to set up the physical structure of any group. Though circles are most popular, you can also use a chain (people sitting in a line or half circle based on some ranking or order), a wheel (one person sitting in the middle, acting as the hub through which all messages go, and others surrounding in a circle), or one of our favorites, the fishbowl (a circle of group members facing one another, with other group members on the outside of this circle, often silently observing the process of the inner circle). In any groups you lead, make certain that you arrange the room so the seating is most conducive to the structure and atmosphere you wish to create. When you want some changes, simply ask people to move in or move back. If the leader states that this is important, the group will also learn it is important.

NONVERBAL BEHAVIOR

When observing members in your group, you will want to monitor not only their body positioning but also other nonverbal states (Brown, 2011). In a previous section, we looked at the interactive patterns among members; you will also want to examine behavioral cues that let you know what people are thinking and feeling. People say a lot with their body language and posture (are they leaning in, slouched over and tired, agitated with their arms crossed, etc.); their movements (nervous twitch, tapping of the foot, wringing of the hands, etc.); and the direction of their gaze and attention. Of all the possible nonverbal behaviors—such as body movements, posture, gaze, voice—facial expression is probably the most commanding and complicated, and perhaps the most confusing (Cohn & Ekman, 2005; Ekman, 2007). The face is commanding because it is always visible and always communicating something. The face really cannot hide, as there is no facial equivalent to concealing one's hands in one's pockets. Whereas sounds and the body movements that illustrate speech are intermittent, the face, even in repose, may provide information about some emotion or mood state.

You notice, for instance, that one group member is smiling a lot, but this expression is incongruent with the serious nature of what he is saying. Another participant sits quietly, seemingly without a care in the world, but every time a particular subject comes up, you notice a short tensing around the eyes. All these cues are fair game for a group leader to call out and draw attention to. We tend to keep our observations rather direct and to-the-point with group members. If Alec is tapping his foot, we might say, "Alec, I notice that your foot keeps tapping." If Bea is rolling her eyes, we might say, "Bea, what is happening with your eyes right now?" If Cole is clinching his fists, we might say, "Cole, what are doing with your hands?" All these simple statements are meant to allow the group member to become more aware of the behavior and then give that person a chance to talk about it, or verbally communicate what the behavior is trying to say. Often, we find that group members say, "Oh, it is nothing. I do that all the time." When that happens, we tend to withdraw and say, "Okay, but if I see it again I will mention it." The key here is drawing attention to patterns and essentially putting words to what the nonverbal behavior is trying to say. Behavioral patterns tend to repeat themselves, and they will likely appear again in the group.

For Reflection

Professional poker players watch one another carefully for "tells" that give away clues about how an opponent is feeling at any given moment—nervousness, jubilation, caution, frustration. By watching nonverbal behavior, they hope to identify whether someone is bluffing or not by noting consistent patterns. Since poker is shown on television all the time, take a moment to watch the nonverbal communication that is happening during a game.

Closer to home, look around your class to identify the "tells" of classmates, as well as the instructor. How do particular individuals act when they are excited or frightened? How can you tell when your instructor is disappointed or frustrated? How can you determine when he or she is greatly satisfied with what is happening?

One of the most difficult challenges of leading groups, distinguishing it from individual sessions, is trying to monitor the way a dozen or more different individuals are reacting to what is happening at any given moment. That job becomes so much easier if you teach the group members to monitor their own behavior, as well as that of the others, so you do not have to be continuously responsible for knowing what is going on every second.

SILENCES

It is not just what people say that matters but also what they do not say, and how they choose not to say it. It is impossible not to speak; sometimes the "loudest" members of the group will be screaming silently through their dramatic withdrawal. We recall one memorable group in which, during the go-around, one member, with arms crossed and chair pulled back, announced that he had nothing to say. This was unusual behavior because it had become a norm for everyone to check in briefly to start the group. If someone really did not want any attention, all that person would need to do is make up some report or give a perfunctory statement such as, "Well, not much going on this week. I'm doing well and feeling fine."

When pressed by other members as to what was going on, the group member insisted that nothing was happening; he just had nothing to say. Throughout the rest of the session, he sat with his arms crossed, scowling and looking bored. He never said another word to the group (and dropped out the next session), but he completely dominated the meeting with his dramatic silence.

Silence is often a normal, natural, useful part of any group session. It gives members time to think, reflect, formulate or process ideas, bear witness to others, take a breath, or just relax a little between intense intervals (Bunkers, 2013). It is rather important during group sessions to establish norms reinforcing that it is okay to be quiet for a while; otherwise, people will continuously chatter even when they have nothing to say, as a way to keep the conversation flowing and to reduce awkward feelings. Steady conversations often help create social validation and belonging, and many people experience silences as a disruption of those perceived connections (Koudenburg, Postmes, & Gordijn, 2011). Yet group work is generally not focused on creating consistent social ease in the group, and silence can allow for other factors to enter the group that may not often arise.

Kurzon (2007) outlined five functions of silence. The first function is *linking*, when silence binds people together—such as in a "moment of silence," a silence during prayer, or a silence after someone makes an inappropriate remark. The second function is *affecting*, when the silence has an effect on the others in the room that might communicate indifference, dislike, or coldness. A third function of silence is *revelational*, when silence shows people don't know what to say or cannot provide an appropriate response. A fourth function of silence is *judgmental*, when silence may indicate approval or disapproval of what has been said. In group settings, this can be seen as "silence as admission" or as a type of silent protest. The fifth function of silence is *activation*, when silence may mean a group member is choosing words before speaking. The impression might be that a group member is quiet and doing nothing, but in reality that person is pondering what to say and how to respond. If silence is being perceived as troubling to the group process or the group itself, it is necessary to intervene (Brown, 2008).

For Reflection

You are leading a group in which you just summarized what you believe has been happening the past few minutes. You intended this as a transition to the next segment, whatever that might be. After your brief reflection on the events that have transpired, there is a long silence. You look around the room and see people looking down, shuffling their feet, but nobody looks ready to speak any time soon. What should you do?

The correct answer to this question (and you should commit it to memory) is, "IT DEPENDS."

What you do as a leader in *any* situation depends on your reading of what is going on. How can you determine what you should do in any clinical situation until you have first formed a hypothesis about what is going on and, based on that assessment, figured out what is needed to move things along in a constructive manner?

What you do with silence, any silence, depends on your interpretation of what is really going on.

Is this silence thoughtful and reflective, a result of members' musing about what they want to say? If so, then wait.

Is this silence indicating confusion because members don't know what you want from them? In that case, you'll need to clarify further.

Or perhaps there is some collective resistance going on. Maybe members resent the interpretation you offered, so they are punishing you by remaining quiet.

Another possibility might be that they are hiding, afraid to speak because they don't feel safe.

In each case, depending on what you assess is going on, the circumstances would dictate a different sort of intervention.

Beginning group leaders view silence among their most dreaded critical incidents. What you do in such situations depends very much on what you believe the silence means. If silence marks productive time for reflection, then you might let it go for a while. But if people are confused, looking for direction, feeling unduly anxious or uncomfortable, you might need to do something. Our favorite option, by the way, in this or any other situation, is to cue members to do the work rather than taking the lead ourselves: "I'm curious, Jackson, about what you think the silence means right now."

For a Field Study

Try out this method on your own. Next time you are in a group situation in which you become aware that you are having a strong reaction (boredom, anxiety, frustration, anger, amusement), look at the others carefully until you find someone you are pretty certain is feeling the same way you are. As you are probably well aware, some people show what they are feeling so readily that you can read them instantly.

Cue this person to speak out loud what you sense is being felt by you and others. Validate this person's experience by sharing your own reactions as well.

We might notice, for instance, that we are feeling bored in the group and interpret the silence to mean that there is a marked lack of motivation and energy on that day. The increasing quiet times do not appear to be useful; they are making the session seem interminable. Rather than confronting this situation ourselves, and risking the usual strong reactions to leader behavior, we can scan the group and notice someone else who appears to feel the same way. That is a possible signal to cue that member to do the work for us: "Arthur, I notice that you are looking bored by what's been happening in the group today. When Kara was speaking earlier, you seemed particularly distracted. Maybe you could talk about what's going on for you today?"

It is also useful to determine the role that silence is serving in the group. In the early stages of a group, extended silences may be creating unnecessary anxiety in group members, so we might break the silence to move the group along. Later on, however, we might explore what silence means for group members. In established groups, we rarely break silences but might make process observations such as, "I notice it is quiet today."

The important thing to remember about silence is that it can be extraordinarily useful, a waste of valuable time, or even destructive. Are members being resistant or defensive? Are they punishing you or others through withdrawal? Perhaps members do not understand what you want. Maybe they are afraid of saying the wrong thing—this could be evidence that trust levels are not yet sufficient to do what you expect. You have to read what exactly the silence means and then respond accordingly.

For a Field Study

Find a place where you can unobtrusively watch a group of people interact with one another. This can be at a playground, a party, a dinner, or even in a class. Pretend you are an expert in interpersonal behavior, whose job it is to make inferences and predictions about how people are likely to act in the future. Like any respectable anthropologist or social scientist, make field notes about what you observe. Try to uncover clues as to what people are really saying to one another and what they really feel and think inside.

Try to identify sources of tension and conflict. Figure out who is most attracted to whom. What are people feeling and thinking but not saying out loud?

Member Roles

In a group setting, not every group member does the same thing. Like every other group you have been a part of in your lifetime (such as your family, sports team, friendship group, or work group), you know that people take on different roles and tasks, some of which are stable and ingrained (such as always needing to be the center of attention) and others of which are situational and contextual (such as being quiet around older people). Each group contains a degree of differentiation of roles and tasks among group members. In that sorting out, you can see that people do different things in a group setting that lead to different outcomes. People adopt particular roles in groups depending on (a) what they have done in the past, (b) the composition of the group, and (c) what gets triggered by the unique dynamics of the situation. These characteristic roles can be seen as basically facilitative, as a maintenance function, or as obstructive to the process and goals of the groups. When someone takes the lead in supporting others, as well as in offering encouragement, this role is often helpful. But another variation of this theme can be dysfunctional—when an overly supportive member, because of that member's own fears of intimacy, continuously rescues people when things get intense.

Another common dynamic has to do with *scapegoating*, in which some members disown or project unacceptable parts of themselves onto others. When it appears as if one designated person is the only one to exhibit strong feelings of guilt, anger, or shame, this person is actually serving as the "lightning rod" for others' uncomfortable feelings (Johnson & Johnson, 2012). This could easily happen, for example, when tension is high and one member takes the risk of talking about what is going on. This person can end up being the scapegoat, not only for that interaction but also for others in the future. Just as that one member is often repeatedly attacked as a scapegoat for the group's disowned feelings, another might very well be designated the "holy cow" (Schoenwolf, 1998). This person is idealized in the group as a sacred object, or the favorite child, just as so often happens in a family. That person can do no wrong in the group; the feedback from that person is highly valued, and other group members always respond in a pleasing manner. These are just a few of the dynamics that often develop with respect to designated roles.

A number of writers have catalogued the typical roles people play in groups. In families, Satir (1972) classically identified four different roles that block good communication among members: (a) *The placater* appears to be accommodating and cooperative ("I'll do whatever you want") but actually sabotages things by refusing to say what is really thought and felt; (b) *the blamer* plays the opposite role ("This is all your fault"), using criticism and aggressive tactics to put others on the defensive; (c) *the irrelevant member* is distracting and annoying ("That reminds me of a story"), to the point that it is difficult to work cooperatively; and (d) *the super-reasonable member* appears at first to be very helpful ("Logically, this all comes down to basic needs") but actually prevents any deep-level intimacy from occurring.

These typical dysfunctional roles in families often occur in groups, in addition to others that have been identified. *The aggressor* keeps everyone off balance by trying to control others. *The monopolist* attempts control by filibuster—talking often and at length so that nobody else has a chance to contribute. For *the rescuer*, who keeps things from getting too deep, or *the withdrawn member* who says nothing at all, the object is to hide as long as possible.

For Personal Reflection

Think about your behavior and roles, past and present, as a member of important groups throughout your life, which should include but not be limited to the following:

- Family of origin
- Social groups or organizations
- Friendship groups

- Work groups
- Other significant groups in your life (such as sports teams, military experience, other group therapy experiences, other cohorts)

What roles do you play in groups? Why do you play these roles? What are the behaviors associated with these roles? Consider what you felt able to say/do/feel in this role and what was limited. As you look at your roles over time, consider any patterns that emerge or significant changes in your role. Try to explain why your roles have changed.

In addition to the various dysfunctional roles, there are also constructive roles that members play to advance process and task goals (Gladding, 2012). *The facilitator* works as a host to make people feel welcome and comfortable. *The gatekeeper* keeps people on task, making sure that established norms are honored. *The compromiser* acts as a mediator during conflicts. *The energizer* motivates people during times of boredom or when some action is needed. *Information seekers* work to collect relevant data and help members share information. *The evaluator* lets the group know how things are going, encouraging adjustments for greater efficiency. A nonproductive role is a *blocker*, which is someone who basically is against the group and gets in the way of progress. This role is focused on disruption and moving attention away from the group's task.

As we have listed the numerous types of group roles that have appeared in the scholarly and popular literature, we have to admit feeling a bit uncomfortable with these ways of categorizing people. In one sense, knowing that there are common roles people take on is helpful in terms of recognizing patterns that may require intervention to help members get out of their established ruts. Yet there is also a coercive, "colonizing" effect of labeling people and placing them into preexisting schemas. People are complex and rarely fulfill one pure role. Postmodern and narrative frameworks propose that many roles are put on us by the environment, culture, and media and do not truly represent who we are or who we would like to be in group settings. Group roles can define people in negative ways and present little evidence for alternative roles. We bring this up as a caution for group leaders to understand group roles as being more fluid than concrete, and as a reminder that many of the roles group members adopt are ones they have been taught, influenced toward, or forced to adopt. This can be particularly true for members of oppressed or marginalized groups, who are often put into specific roles based on stereotypes. For group work to be truly liberating and freeing for group members, effort must be taken to see beyond roles and fixed identities that keep people stuck (Hays, Arredondo, Gladding, & Toporek, 2010).

Relational–cultural theorists such as Judy Jordan and Jean Baker Miller have advocated that roles are not only indoctrinated into historically marginalized group members but also almost always take place within a relational field (Jordan, 2010). The connections between and among people are considered the greatest healing forces, but it is within these very connections where roles are formed and stabilized. Many women thus learn to be passive, deferential, and accommodating in groups because of the interpersonal context that is so much a part of early training. In contrast, many men learn to be dominant, competitive, and task oriented in groups. This offers a warning to be careful of the ways we view client roles that can be limiting and one-dimensional.

The important point to recognize here is that all groups naturally (and with prodding from the leader) create a division of labor. Evolutionary biologists (Buss, 2011; Dugatkin, 1999) have argued that one of the attributes that makes us so successful as a species is our tendency to specialize in various functions within groups. One person in a tribe hunts, while another skins and cleans, another cooks, and another cleans up. In groups, as well, members will organize themselves into different roles that are needed for activities to proceed in an orderly manner (unless the goal is to keep others from getting too close). This is both natural and highly efficient—it is inborn for us to function as part of a collective tribe.

Regardless of the roles various group members play, or those you feel are important for participants to adopt to be facilitative, your job as leader is to teach everyone to serve several important functions for one another, and for themselves, to get the most from the experience. These roles can include, but are not limited to, the following suggested by Berg, Landreth, and Fall (2012):

1. Group members will be valued and, in turn, encouraged to value one another. If nothing else is accomplished, or no specific goals are identified, at the very least all members should be helped to feel validated and supported.

2. Group members will feel understood. The leader will model appropriate listening and responding behavior, but beyond these fundamental skills, an essential value that develops in the group is that everyone should play a role in helping others feel they have been heard.

3. Group members will work collaboratively, sharing in decision making and owning responsibility for the outcome. You must make it clear that this is their group, not yours. Your job is to act as the facilitator, but their job is to make sure that the group meets their own needs.

For a Class Activity or a Field Study

Find a group of about six members, either among classmates or friends. Explain that this is a fantasy exercise, but for it to work, you all have to pretend that it is real, that you are all really in this predicament. Unless everyone is prepared to take the task seriously, you will not experience a meaningful demonstration of group dynamics and roles.

You are all traveling together via a small cruise ship that encounters an unexpected storm. The ship sinks, and you are the only survivors, washed ashore on a deserted island. You have an unlimited supply of fresh water but limited food supplies on the island, enough to last everyone just a few weeks.

After having rested and recovered, you meet together to decide your fate and make some preliminary decisions about how you will live, how you will govern yourselves, and what you will do to survive.

The particular content of your group discussions is relatively unimportant. This is merely a vehicle by which you can observe and experience various group roles and dynamics you have read about.

After spending about 20 or 30 minutes in your survival simulation, debrief one another by talking about how you functioned together, the roles each of you played in the group, and the aspects of your behavior that were effective and dysfunctional. Talk about what you learned from this exercise and what you can use from it in your life.

High- and Low-Functioning Groups

When you put together what you now understand, you will see an image emerging of groups that work well, and others that do not. The following are the characteristics of the best and most effective groups (Johnson & Johnson, 2012).

1. Participants know what is expected of them. Their individual goals are consistent with those of the group.

2. Decision-making procedures are matched with the situation so that different methods are used at different times. Healthy norms are established that permit a balance between structure and spontaneity.

3. There is a high degree of trust, safety, and cohesion in the group. There is a high level of honesty and openness in the group so that constructive feedback is shared.

4. Information and experiences are shared readily among participants.

5. The style of leadership is described as democratic, with shared responsibility, rather than authoritarian or laissez faire (passive). Goal accomplishment, internal maintenance, and developmental change are underscored.

6. Conflict and disagreement are viewed as constructive and seen as the key to high-quality and creative decision making and problem solving. Conflicts are worked through rather than ignored.

7. Conflicts of interest are resolved through negotiation and mediation so that agreements are reached that maximize outcomes and leave all members satisfied.

8. Communication flows in multiple directions so that the open and accurate expression of feelings is emphasized.

9. There is an equitable distribution of power, control, and contributions. Ability and information determine influence and power.

10. There is consistent observable growth and change among the members, not just in the group but also in their day-to-day lives.

Keep in mind that the dynamics described in this chapter represent general principles, especially as applied to groups in mainstream North American populations. You have learned previously that members of various cultural groups may behave according to different norms and have different expectations (Chung & Bemak, 2014; D'Andrea, 2014; McWhirter & Robbins, 2014; Rivera, Fernandez, & Hendricks, 2014; Steen, Shi, & Hockersmith, 2014). For example, dimensions of power and prestige develop in different ways among group members of some cultural groups compared with others. What this means is that with all the concepts contained in this chapter and book about group dynamics and processes, you must make adjustments according to the unique backgrounds of the people you help, and based on the dynamics that develop from the interactions among group members.

Review of What You Learned

- Working in groups is inherently different from working with individuals. The shift from linear to circular causality underscores the influence group members have on one another at all times.
- Systems theory contributes the idea of conceptualizing a group as one large entity that constantly reorganizes itself as it tries to maintain a sense of

balance (homeostasis). Groups usually are inclined to return to familiar states (equilibrium). Group coalitions, or subsystems, work to achieve balance in a group. Each smaller group coalition has specific boundaries that control who can join and what can be said to whom.

- The idea of group settings as a "social microcosm" suggests that one's interpersonal style and maladaptive patterns that are present in everyday life will ultimately appear in a group setting, regardless of attempts to hide patterns or behave in a new way. Ultimately, the member's true interpersonal self will appear.

- Family-of-origin issues constantly appear in group settings as people respond to people and situations in maladaptive ways that are reminiscent of their past experiences. Effective groups provide the opportunity for a "corrective emotional experience" to work through these past difficulties via honest feedback and support.

- Proxemics, nonverbal behavior, and silence are all ways group members communicate in group settings. Effective leaders call attention to what members are trying to communicate nonverbally.

- Group members often play roles in a group setting that represent familiar and reoccurring roles from their past experiences in other groups. These roles can either facilitate or hinder effective group communication.

Stages of Group Development 4

For many new students and group leaders, there is a lot of apprehension associated with leading groups. As we have said before, it is quite normal to feel overwhelmed with making sense of what is going on at any given moment in a group, as well as anticipating what might happen next. There is so much going on simultaneously that it is difficult to track each member's reactions and behavior as well as the group processes and dynamics. It would be easier if group work were more predictable, such that you had a rough idea of what was happening in the context of usual developmental stages. What you need is a road map to follow—a rough plan of the territory, so to speak. Such a conception would allow you to understand current behavior in light of its evolutionary sequence. It would also permit you to make some reasonable assumptions about where things are heading and what you might do to nudge them along in desired directions. In a sense, such a road map would allow you to make sense of what is happening and why at a given moment in time.

We are pleased to inform you that researchers and scholars of group work have provided such an itinerary. It is generally understood that every group follows a similar path in which participants struggle to know and trust one another, reach some sort of accommodation, complete their work with different degrees of satisfaction, and then disband with the hope of applying what they've learned to other areas of their lives (Forsyth & Diederich, 2014). This same developmental sequence has been applied to so many other facets of human behavior, including psychosexual development (Freud), psychosocial development

(Erikson), cognitive development (Piaget), moral development (Kohlberg), gender identity (Gilligan), and cultural identity (Cross, Helms).

What You Should Know About Developmental Theory and Groups

Certainly you have had some previous experience with developmental stage theory. Consider the ways so many of your relationships have evolved over time. First, you meet someone and become superficially acquainted. You engage in small talk and test each other to see if you share interests and values. If this appears mutually satisfying, you spend more time together, taking things to the next level and revealing more of yourself. If you stick with it long enough, trust develops and so also does deeper intimacy.

You probably didn't set out to develop a relationship according to formal rules; they just unfolded naturally over time. These "norms" were negotiated for how you would behave with each other and how decisions would be made. You may, for example, join someone in a business partnership and over time see that partnership grow along predictable lines. Romantic relationships may bloom into marriage with children, careers, and community roots. And yet, at some point, many relationships end, sometimes due to a fierce conflict, as in divorce; sometimes because one person moves far away from the other; and sometimes because those mutual interests evolved in different directions.

Whether we are talking about physical maturation, emotional development, family evolution, cultural or gender identity, or almost any other facet of growth, developmental theories proceed according to certain principles that operate in groups as well:

1. Development often occurs in an orderly progression of stages.

2. Generally, the sequence of stages cannot be skipped.

3. If you know what stage people are currently operating within, you can usually predict where they are going next.

4. Each stage often has a set of tasks or challenges that need to be mastered.

5. Developmental evolution can be encouraged and facilitated by helping people move to the next level.

For Personal Application

Learning to be a group leader involves going through a series of progressive stages that began when you first decided to seek additional training. For instance, most counseling and therapy practitioners go through stages that look something like this:

Training:	What if I don't have what it takes?
Hero worship:	If only I could be like you.
Enchantment:	I can't believe I get paid for this!
Golden years:	Hey, I'm really good at this!
Midcareer doubt:	What if I'm not really doing anything?
Pre-burnout:	Another day, another dollar.
Revitalization:	What in me is getting in the way?
Mentorship:	You want to be like ME?

Consider your journey as a group leader of the future. Make up names for the sequential transitions you think might take place as a group leader grows in experience and expertise. Start by looking back at where you were before this class even began. What stage are you in now? As you imagine your fantasy of being a model group leader, what stage will you be in when that time comes?

The previous chapter mentioned that groups may be thought of as a dynamic social system, analogous to any other living system that exists in the world. This particular conception has formed the basis for much of what we understand about the ways families evolve (Bitter, 2013), as well as groups. Metaphorically, then, groups are formed and pass through periods of "childhood," where they learn how to get needs met, and then "adolescence," where authority is tested, boundaries are pushed, and the group forms an identity. Later, groups mature into "adulthood," where productive work is accomplished and contributions are made. Finally, groups, like families, settle into quiet reflection and poignant reckoning of what has been gained and what must eventually end.

The concept of group stages or development is crucial for group leaders. Group dynamics, member and leader behaviors, and focal issues change over the life of a group. Knowing about the general parameters of group stages provides leaders with a compass that helps them steer the group in the best direction. It helps leaders keep their bearings when the group enters uncharted, stormy waters. It enables leaders to sequence their interventions in a timely and effective manner, as many interventions are more typical or better suited during some group stages than others. Effective group leaders assess where the group and the group members are, and select appropriate interventions that match their level of readiness (Forsyth & Diederich, 2014; Morran, Stockton, & Whittingham, 2004). Finally, knowledge about group stages can provide valuable benchmarks to support a leader's intuition about group processes. For example, let's draw a parallel between human development and group development. Without a conceptual scheme of human development, many of the typical characteristics of an adolescent male (e.g., risky health behaviors, emotional outbursts or withdrawal, rapid body changes, moodiness, physical awkwardness, believing that friends mean everything, constant striving for peer approval) might seem really odd. Yet when a developmental model about male adolescence is applied, all those characteristics make sense (Robertson & Shepard, 2008). For a group, without a conceptual scheme of development, the characteristics associated with the first few group meetings (e.g., nervousness and anxiety, acting superficially, being overly nice and never hostile, following others' lead to try to act appropriately, waiting for the leader to delegate responsibility and structure) might appear to be quite dysfunctional and insincere. Yet when this behavior is understood within the context of the beginning stages of group work, such observations become understandable and expected.

One benefit of knowing group stages is that it helps organize the timing of interventions. For example, in the early stages of group development, the group leader will often need to be more active, model effective disclosure and feedback, and take risks to show how risk taking can happen in a group setting. A group leader might break awkward silences and use humor and playfulness to reduce anxiety among members. All these actions are developmentally appropriate and consistent with the experiences of the early/induction stage of group. As the group evolves, however, the group leader can become less active and more supportive in encouraging group members to speak to one another directly.

In the previous chapter, we examined the ways groups, as living systems, seek some sort of balance and equilibrium and yet also move toward increasing levels of complexity that make room for interpersonal and individual growth. This tug-of-war between safety and risk taking weaves throughout the group's life and assumes different forms and levels of intensity as the group develops.

For Personal Application

Work with a partner to flesh out your own ambivalence and conflict regarding safety versus risk taking in this group class. Arrange yourselves so you have some privacy and bring an extra chair if one is available (if not, you will take turns vacating one chair).

With prodding from your partner, you will imagine that one chair contains the part of you that wants to take greater risks in the class and reveal more of yourself, and the other chair contains the part of you that would rather play it safe and protect yourself.

Stage a dialogue between the two different parts of yourself, changing chairs as you switch roles.

Such an enactment might look something like this:

Risky Self: I guess I'd like to show more of myself in class, but . . .

Safe Self: You're damn right, BUT! I mean, what's the point? These people will judge you. And it won't be pretty. It will be really hard to be in class with them for the rest of the year.

Risky Self: I know that's possible. Some people will pass judgment, but then some won't. Plus, it might be interesting to understand what they see in me.

Safe Self: Yeah, but what about the instructor, though? She will be grading you!

Risky Self: I am pretty sure my instructor really values risk taking and self-reflection. If she did not, I really doubt she would be teaching class in an experiential way.

After you have completed the exercise, give your partner a chance to try it out. When you are both finished, talk to each other about what themes emerged for you and what you resolve to do based on this awareness.

Donigian and Malnati (2005) address the intrinsic conflict in groups. Essentially, they contend that members are motivated to express wishes, desires, and needs that will move them forward, but inner fears of rejection, humiliation, and punishment argue against the expression of these motives. This inner clash or conflict creates anxiety, a signal either to find a workable solution or to fall back on failed but familiar defensive maneuvers. The purpose of group work, from this prospective, is to activate group processes that trigger self-exploration of conflicted issues so that members can acquire more adaptive solutions to interpersonal living. Growth occurs when fears are faced, thus enabling motives and needs to surface in a context where more adaptive solutions can be tried and supported (Forsyth & Diederich, 2014).

These dynamics apply equally to the group as a whole and to the individual members and leader. Developmental stages provide a useful framework for viewing these dynamics at work over the life of a group.

So Many Group Stages

Research and theorizing about group development has been a core of group work. Seminal figures such as Bales (1950) and Bion (1948, 1961) were some of the first to observe that various groups experienced similar issues. They theorized that basic issues facing groups move in temporal order, with resolution of these issues following a predictable sequence (Forsyth & Diederich, 2014). Out of this early theorizing came a host of models and stage theories to describe the growth of groups over time. Alas, as in so many other aspects of this profession, there are many different perspectives and models. Some authors (Brabender & Fallon, 2009; Corey, Corey, & Corey, 2014; Gladding, 2012; Jacobs, Masson, & Harvill, 2012; Napier & Gershenfeld, 2004; Tuckman, 1965; Tuckman & Jensen, 1977) conceive of group stages as unfolding along a sequential path, similar to developmental theories in other domains. This development can be viewed as linear and, for the most part, outlines group development as small, gradual, and path dependent (Chang, Duck, & Bordia, 2006). This model fits particularly well with relatively short-term groups.

Donigian and Malnati (2005) discuss an alternate perspective that views longer-term groups as moving through a cyclical rather than linear process. It is helpful to keep in mind that these stages would also vary according to the type of group, experiential and therapy groups evolving in a slightly different form than task groups (Wheelan, 2004b). Regardless of the type of group or length of time it meets, there are many similarities in the processes that characterize group stages.

Perhaps a caveat to any generalizations about the ways groups are supposed to evolve is that believing in stage theory, or any theory for that matter, may create its own reality (Becvar, Canfield, & Becvar, 1997). Thus, postmodern or social constructivist theorists caution against prejudging how groups might develop, because such filters might lead you to see something that is in your own mind rather than actually in the group (Dickerson, 2007). This is often referred to as theory countertransference (Duncan, Hubble, & Miller, 1997) and speaks of the idea of seeing more what a theory indicates one ought to see than what is actually happening. The same can occur in a group (or any helping setting) in which you "force" what is happening to fit into an idea or schema in your head, rather than remaining open to seeing (or experiencing) something quite new and different. This is one of the hardest tasks, as well, for those doing qualitative research in that they have to suspend preconceptions and expectations about what they are observing or hearing so they can remain open to what is new and fresh.

As an example of this phenomenon in groups, imagine that in a second session, one group member appears reluctant to share very much. You tell yourself that this behavior is "stage appropriate," given how early it is in the life of the group. You fully expect any group member to be reluctant and cautious until cohesion and trust are established. Operating from that assumption, you don't encourage this member with a follow-up probe to explore further. But what may be going on with this member is that he feels more than enough safety to talk in the group; in fact, he *wants* to open up but is just waiting for a more explicit invitation from the leader because that is what he is used to within his culture.

With this caution about not being too rigid in the way you conceptualize development, group stages have been described as including somewhere from 3 to 10 distinct stages, with 5 being the most popular. Table 4.1 summarizes how several writers over time have labeled and characterized group stages.

It may strike you as somewhat confusing and arbitrary that stages can be divided into so many different units. Before we get into more detail in the next section, we'd like to simplify this discussion by saying that basically the stages of group development are quite logical. There is a "beginning stage" characterized

Table 4.1 Summary of Group Stages

Authors	Number of Stages	Labels/Descriptions
Bennis and Shepard (1956)	Two	Authority and structure; intimacy and interdependence
Schutz (1958)	Five	Inclusion; control; openness; mutual trust; letting go
Tuckman (1965)	Five	Forming; norming; storming; performing; adjourning
Fisher (1970)	Four	Orientation; conflict; emergence; reinforcement
La Coursiere (1980)	Five	Orientation; dissatisfaction; resolution; production; termination
Vander Kolk (1985)	Four	Beginning; conflict and dominance; cohesiveness and productivity; completion
Wheelan (2004a)	Five	Dependency and inclusion; counterdependency and fight; trust and structure; work; termination
Yalom and Leszcz (2005)	Three	Orientation and search for meaning; conflict, dominance, and rebellion; cohesiveness
Donigian and Malnati (2005)	Five	Orientation; conflict and confrontation; cohesiveness; work; termination
Corey et al. (2014)	Five	Pregroup; initial; transition; working; final
Jacobs et al. (2012)	Three	Beginning; middle/working; ending/closing

by a certain caution and testing, a "middle stage" when trust and cohesion are established and most of the work gets done, and an "ending stage" when members solidify gains and draw closure from the experience.

Stages of Group Evolution

When you examine all these different descriptions of group stages, it is clear that some solid themes emerge. We have considerably simplified the stages of group development and synthesized the features we find most important into four distinct segments that will make immediate, intuitive sense. These four stages are *induction* (beginning stage), *experimental engagement* (middle stage, Part I), *cohesive engagement* (middle stage, Part II), and *disengagement* (ending stage). We feel that these four stages are easy enough to remember when you are in the midst of panic, trying to figure out which stage you are in and which one comes next. In the later chapters of this book, we will cover some of the specific skills and interventions (e.g., pregroup screening, ending a group) that are associated with many of these stages. At this point, however, we tend to focus more on what is happening with group members as they grow and evolve as the group develops.

STAGE I: INDUCTION

Members first enter a group needing considerable orientation. This is a type of induction stage wherein members lean heavily on the leader for guidance and direction. The group setting is new and foreign, and often the rules and norms are not very clear. It is not uncommon for people to respond to a new group in the same way they would respond in any other uncertain situation. For many, that results in a blend of confusion, curiosity, and personal protectiveness. Members are asking themselves questions such as these:

- What the heck is going on here?
- Who are these people?
- How am I supposed to act?
- Is this the right place for me?
- What do they want from me?
- How much am I willing to share?
- What are we actually going to do?
- Where do I fit in with these people?

Most often, members are prepared for participation in the group through some induction or screening procedures that inform them about rules, rights, consent, policies, and goals. They may be asked to fill out background questionnaires, write an autobiography, or disclose facts from their personal history in an interview (this will be discussed more in later chapters). Yet even though most members have been screened and provided information about the group, once the group has begun, most of that information goes out the window as the current reality of actually being in the group clouds one's thoughts and feelings.

Student Voice

Coming Into Group

I enjoy attending groups, but I always experience anxiety coming into the group about what others will think of me. I wonder what impressions others have of me coming in, what knowledge they have of me beforehand from other places and how those perceptions will change as the group goes on. I try to convince myself that it does not matter what other people think of me, but I always come back to wondering about that. I started the group assuming that I have been in a group before and knew what it was all about, but I sat in a group for the first time and again felt afraid—just another rude awakening for me that I had some stuff to deal with in the group.

Emotionally, this first stage is one of tentativeness and guardedness, because group members' safety is in question. Closely related to safety, members wonder if they will be accepted and valued by other group members and the leader. They feel insecure and disoriented, which can lead to a mild to moderate sense of fear, if not panic. Consider the way you feel in a new group, or even in a class such as this one, in which you want people to respect and like you but are fearful if they find out what you're *really* like, you may be rejected. On the one hand, you want to be honest and authentic, but on the other, you want to make a good first impression. Even though it is usually not the case, most people mistakenly believe that these two goals are at odds.

Although most group members have chosen to attend because it is something they *ought* to do (as is often the case with counseling), being in the actual group can activate worries that have kept members from making progress in the past. In that sense, the fear and uncertainty can fuel doubts as to whether the group will measure up to their expectations and fantasies.

You can expect a high degree of defensiveness and resistance at the beginning of a group (but be pleasantly surprised when this is not the case). This is not only normal but a healthy way to deal with an environment that may be dangerous. Obviously, during this period, trust is one of the biggest issues in the room.

The work of this stage is to find constructive ways to be with one another. Members don't know the rules. They don't know how to be "good" group participants. It is your job to model productive ways to be in the group and effective ways to communicate with one another. This is where you set the stage, explain what is expected, introduce what roles will be played, and provide the initial structure that is needed to move to the next level of minimal cohesion and intimacy. Your job is also to facilitate a period of introduction in which group members reveal who they are and why they are in the group. This can be done by members' sharing their individual goals for being in the group, or in a task or psychoeducational group, this can be accomplished when the leader talks about expected outcomes of the group. You are also looking to connect group members by highlighting moments of universality so they begin to feel less alone in the group. Of course, since all this happens in the critical window of first contact, it is also important to provide reassurance during those times when a member departs from what you had in mind.

In one recent group class, a student talked at length about his plans for the future even though participants had been asked to talk about the present. The interaction developed in this way:

Kirk: So if I could just find a way to relocate, I think that it would . . .

Leader: Excuse me, Kirk?

Kirk: Uh, yeah?

Leader: I couldn't help but notice that you were speaking primarily about the future rather than how you are feeling and thinking in this group right now.

Kirk: Oh gosh! I'm SO sorry. I heard what you asked us to do, but I guess I got carried away. I suppose the future is just weighing heavily on me right now, so that's what I wanted to talk about.

Leader: You're absolutely right. And you didn't do anything wrong. When you're being a member in this group, your job is to go after what it is you need most. You are allowed to be selfish to get your needs addressed, and I encouraged each of you to work to meet your own needs. It is MY job to make sure that we follow a particular agenda or balance the participation so that we all get involved.

Kirk: But I feel so stupid . . .

Leader: I actually appreciate that you were being so proactive in letting us know what you wanted to talk about. And we will get back to that again shortly. For now, though, let's finish talking about what you are experiencing right now, even in response to this interaction. You said that you were feeling kind of stupid . . .

During this dialogue, the leader was trying to do two things simultaneously: first, teach Kirk and other members about norms related to following instructions and, second, demonstrate that even when they violate those rules, they will not be censured but instead gently guided back on track. Both messages are critical because during this early stage, members need to be reassured that a structure will be enforced and yet departures from that agenda will not cause them to be ridiculed or censured. Rather, deviations will be met with gentle reminders to keep on task. With enough of these reminders, you will find that group members will learn to catch themselves when they fall back into familiar patterns not associated with group.

How do you know when a group is ready to move from the induction stage to the next stage? Look for evidence of the following:

- Ground rules have been internalized, accepted, and are followed consistently.
- At least moderate levels of trust have been established.
- The group is perceived as moderately safe by almost everyone.
- Facilitative communication patterns have been established in which members appear respectful and caring, yet open.

For a Class Activity

In small groups, make a list of all the norms that have been established in your class. Review how you were inducted into your assigned (or self-adopted) roles. How is it that you learned the appropriate ways to be viewed as an able student and constructive group member? What are some of the unstated, subtle, or "secret" rules of the class that are not talked about overtly?

STAGE II: EXPERIMENTAL ENGAGEMENT

Groups usually move to the experimental engagement stage by the second to fourth meeting, though this can vary considerably based on what happens in the initial group meetings. This is the time when members naturally want to stretch themselves, the leaders, and the group itself to new levels. In a sense, members are moving from initial feelings of awkwardness with themselves to feelings of awkwardness with the others in the group. Members want to test the group to determine how it responds to bids for power and to deeper levels of self-disclosure. They have their eye on the leaders, wondering if they can maintain the group's safety while allowing for more direct challenges. Members may send out test balloons by disclosing something dearer to their being but more controversial in meaning. At this stage, group members are competing to find their place in the group and are beginning to test the limits of what the group can do and hold.

The following statements are examples of what members often say at this stage:

- "We don't seem to be getting anywhere. Shouldn't we have an agenda?"
- "I'm not sure I want to bare my soul any more because some of you have barely opened up."
- "I sense that it is wrong to be deeply religious here. I feel judged about my faith in God."
- "This group doesn't seem real to me—the real world is dog eat dog, and people here are too nice."
- "We don't seem to talk about real issues. I was hoping we would discuss how to deal with a mean boss, but we seem to dance around important stuff."

There is typically great variability in members' readiness levels to engage with one another. Some participants are impatient, more than willing to get involved as deeply as possible. Others feel suspicious, cautious, and even hostile. These members may have become disenchanted because the leader failed to offer the structure and wisdom they had expected. Still other members are satisfied to dance to any tune, so long as they feel safe. Group leaders should expect anxiety, resistance, defensiveness, conflict, and some confrontation. All these reactions are useful in that they reflect members' efforts to engage in the group setting. In terms of resistance, it is not uncommon to see it expressed by certain members through intellectualization, constant questioning of other members, advice giving, and monopolizing the direction of the group.

The best descriptor of behavior in this stage would be "tentative," as all actions become experimental, testing the waters to see if it is safe. Tension, jealousy, conflict, power struggles, and coalitional battles are common in this stage as members fight for influence and personal agendas. Some members are experiencing rather strong "transference reactions" (those that represent distortions) toward the leader, just as the leader may also be transferring personal feelings toward certain members.

Student Voice

Are People Really Being Honest?

As I experienced the first couple of groups I was wondering if this was truly real. Were the members really being honest about what they were sharing and with their feedback with each other? Group members were responding with what seemed to be genuine concern. Support came in the form of listening and validating other's feelings, and through the sharing of similar experiences, but that seemed foreign to me so I doubted it. Then one member shared that she had been recently assaulted. After this group session, I knew this was for real. I felt so uncomfortable and inadequate, not knowing what to say. But that is like me in real life. Yet others stepped up—the support the group members gave made me feel that this was a safe place to share, safe enough that I, being so introverted, actually shared with the group the following week about an issue I was having. I guess that was when I really joined the group.

Direct confrontation is usually avoided during this stage, but that does not mean there isn't a high degree of conflict. Compared with the alternative, when members pretend that everything is perfect, disagreement and tension at this stage are not a bad state of affairs and can often provoke constructive engagement. Group leaders will have multiple opportunities to demonstrate how the group can grow through conflict. The greatest problems you may face occur when certain members begin to act out, and so you will have to reel them in by being validating, kind, but clear in honoring the group norms and expectations.

Many, if not most, groups never get beyond this stage. Members remain in a state of superficial, cautious, minimal engagement with one another. They get some work done, but the quantity and quality is limited, if not mediocre. Some group members never feel very safe but tell themselves that this tension is acceptable, especially considering that any additional gains don't feel worth the risks. So they are aware of risks they could take in revealing personal information or sharing direct feedback with other group members, but they teeter over the decision to take the chance and risk it. Knowing that this happens at this stage, conscious group leaders emphasize validating the fears around taking the risk rather than the risk itself. If fears and anxiety are noticed and reduced, risk taking will naturally follow and group will continue to develop.

The following tasks face group members during the experimental engagement stage:

- Finding the courage to surface their lingering concerns about safety
- Testing the leader's ability to manage member-to-member conflicts
- Establishing a means of feeling empowered and valued
- Testing the leader's ability to receive confrontation nondefensively
- Moving toward higher levels of emotional expression
- Gaining insight into their interpersonal issues
- Learning how to use conflict as an instigator of interpersonal and personal growth

Your job during this stage is to manage your own anxiety level in the face of increasing group tension. People are watching you very carefully to see how you handle yourself and deal with conflicts that emerge. More than anything else, you model ways of supporting and confronting that you want others to adopt. As a leader, some skills and interventions are effective during this stage and help create more contact and effective communication among members. These simple interventions help establish group norms that value direct communication. These interventions include the following:

- *Conflict resolution versus conflict management.* Leaders are often less focused on trying to resolve all the conflicts than on facilitating and managing conflict. This is done to model a process of working with conflict, but also to show that disagreements can exist in the room in a way that does not signal an end to the group's engagement. Groups will end with conflicts unresolved. Though that can be extremely uncomfortable for group members (and even the leader), group leaders can reframe this as an evolving process that group members can learn from during their time away from the group, knowing that the group can reengage in the next meeting.
- *Use of "I" statements (general to the personal).* Leaders encourage members to speak in the first-person singular, rather than using the more general *you* or *we.* For example, when a group member says, "We all feel anxious when we are confronted" or "You feel anxious when confronted," the leader may ask, "Can you say that again using 'I'? Try saying, 'I feel anxious when I am confronted.'"
- *Point out when advice is being given.* Ask for the intent or feeling behind the advice. When one member offers advice to another, the leader may say: "It sounds like you really want to help. Can you say that directly to Tammi?"
- *Encourage eye contact and talking to one another.* It is common for members to speak to the group leader even though they are really saying something

meant for another member. A simple intervention is to say, "Bob, rather than looking at me, can you say that directly to Hanna?"

- *Point out monopolizing and intellectualizing when it occurs.* In every group, some people talk too much and others too little. It is your job to manage the interaction so everyone has a voice and contributions are equitable and balanced. This means that at times you will have to "block" certain excessively verbal members and actively invite the quieter ones to talk: "I am wondering if we can hear from other voices that have not spoken yet today."

- *Personalize what is happening.* Look for places where you can direct concerns about the group or the leadership directly to yourself. Though it may encourage conflict or dissatisfaction with the group, this provides a modeling opportunity for the leader to nondefensively validate the concern and work through it. "Milo, it sounds like you often feel like people at work don't really listen to you or feign interest, and that is upsetting. I am wondering when that has happened in our group?"

- *Highlight constructive risk taking.* Point out and reinforce those times when group members extend themselves, revealing themselves in deep, vulnerable ways. This can be done at the end of group by saying, "I am aware that there were a lot of risks taken tonight by group members. Some of the risks have been obvious to the group, but I suspect there are other risks taken today that are a bit more hidden and possibly only known to individual members. So I wanted to acknowledge the work of everyone tonight."

When is it time to move to the next stage? Actually, the progression will happen so slowly that you will barely know you are there until you have arrived. You will notice that people seem closer to one another after a critical incident. Trust and risk taking have increased. More and more, members spend as much time taking care of one another as they do addressing their own interests. It begins to come out through feelings of *we-ness* among group members as they talk and view themselves as one unit. The emergence of group identity and cohesiveness signal that members are thinking and feeling that they belong together.

For Personal Application

If you think about it, most of the groups you have experienced in your life—at work, in class, at social gatherings, and in organized activities—remain in this stage of tentative, safe, experimental engagement. Yet there are possibly others that moved beyond that level to a more cohesive place. How did that leap occur? How did you know the group was different?

Now, think of one group in your current life that feels unsatisfying, or at least less productive and joyful than you would prefer. This could involve a family coalition, roommates, neighbors, friends, a social organization, or a class. It could be a long-term group you are part of that has remained superficial, or it could be a group that is just beginning. What if you wanted to initiate a movement to the next level of cohesion, intimacy, and productivity? What would you need to do?

Take the risk to bring to this group your awareness of the stage in which you have been operating and what this means for your relationships. Initiate a discussion among members about what it would take to move to the next level.

STAGE III: COHESIVE ENGAGEMENT

If groups grow beyond the experimental stage—many do not, and some should not—a cohesive engagement stage is entered. This is what is ordinarily described as the "working stage," which means that sufficient trust and accommodation have been reached to enable productive activities to take place. Group members identify with one another. They come in each week having thought about the group, group members, and what they want to do each meeting. There is a sense of cooperation and collaboration, as well as hope and positive expectations for what is happening. Whether your groups ever reach this stage depends on several prerequisite conditions:

- First of all, it takes time. The longer the group meets, the more likely that it will reach an advanced stage of engagement.
- Homogeneous group composition leads more quickly to cohesive functioning.
- A stable setting for the group helps members feel safe.
- The atmosphere in the group should be conducive to individual self-expression.
- Taking on the leader, and resolving this rebellion successfully, can be very constructive in moving toward mature group development.
- A democratic rather than authoritarian leadership style is preferred for preventing dependency and destructive coalitions. So the group leader has to be okay with ceding power and air time to group members. The leader is still present and active, but the group members at this stage should be more vocal and capable of moving the group along.

In this stage, people know what is expected from being in the group. The group has transitioned from forming itself and resolving basic conflicts to the point where group norms are established. Members know how to behave most constructively with one another. Furthermore, the leader no longer has to do all the work. Because the members have learned appropriate facilitative behavior, the leader plays mostly a supporting role in this stage, cuing members as needed, monitoring safety and progress, but pretty much allowing things to proceed according to the needs of the participants. This stage is dominated by addressing the initial and continually revised goals of the group members.

> ## Student Voice
>
> ### Taking the "Big" Risk
>
> *My goal in a group was to be more opinionated and assertive, often feeling discounted because of my inexperience with life issues. So I took a big risk and disclosed being sexually abused as a child, yet I quickly regressed back to my former ways of communication. My anxiety level heightened as to divulging too much, too fast and how others would perceive my family and me. This is exactly why our family, especially my father, was so fearful of letting anyone know about what had happened for fear of "losing face." Then I had a "light bulb" moment when I finally felt how group is a microcosm of how I interact in the outside world. The group reached out to me. I felt that I was comforted, not alone, relieved to finally divulge a secret and received so much information that I had not previously known. What was also endearing for me personally was seeing others share their painful experiences, knowing how much it would hurt them to share, in order to relate to me. It was as if a floodgate had been opened and an outpouring of emotion came out for me, which was followed by the floodgates of other group members sharing their experiences as well. It seemed that after this, the group was never the same.*

Cohesiveness has been noted as one of the most important therapeutic elements in group work (Argyrakouli & Zafiropoulou, 2007), and it is just as important in moving groups through developmental stages (Forsyth & Diederich, 2014). Group cohesion refers to the bond between the members and the leader, the relationship among group members, and the bond between the members and the group as a whole (Joyce, Piper, & Ogrodniczuk, 2007). What *cohesive* means is that members are sensitive and responsive to one another's needs, often without being told, but in a much more natural manner. Members feel an emotional attachment to one another, as well as a high degree of trust. Self-disclosures occur at very intimate, revealing levels. In that sense, members are taking the risk to allow themselves to be truly known to the group. Members take risks in their behavior in terms of what they reveal but also in what they say to one another via feedback. In a cohesive group, feedback is more direct, considerably more risky, and often more accurate since members have been with one another long enough to have a sense of interpersonal history. Of course, not everyone will feel this way or take the same risks. You will still encounter bumps, distractions, and challenges along the way, but you will no longer be solely responsible for managing these difficulties. In a group that has attained cohesive engagement, most participants monitor their own behavior and are willing to engage with one another. Yalom and Leszcz (2005) noted that cohesion may not be a sufficient condition for effective groups but that it might be a necessary one. And it is hard to imagine any group advancing into cohesive engagement without significant unity, solidarity, and cohesiveness.

In a sense, the group has become a high-functioning family—in some cases, the healthy family members have never experienced before. People are caring and compassionate toward one another, but they are also very honest and direct. If work is truly taking place, then people also feel free to disagree and confront one another.

Other things you will notice during this stage are that participants spend more time centered in the present. They talk to one another about how they feel. They ask spontaneously about previous homework assignments. They bring in material from previous sessions.

Here are some statements that illustrate what members might say in this stage:

- "Jill, I have been reviewing what I said to you last week. I want to add something very important that I failed to mention: I appreciate your courage to confront, even though it scares me when directed my way. I was not aware of how scared I was to talk to you, and I realized that part of my fear is because you are not afraid to respond."
- "I thought of a name for our group—The Magnificent Eight—because we all seem to rally behind the underdog."
- "Ralph, I have wondered all week, did you ask her out?"
- "Margo, all week I thought about you and your mom. I prayed for you each night, and it is so good to see you here tonight."
- "I want to take up where we left off last week, Kim, if we might start with you."
- "Paul, could you personalize that? I get the idea of the situation but not your part in it."

Leaders wrestle with several temptations during this stage. The members have reached a level of autonomy that can beguile leaders into believing that their input is no longer needed. Members may collude in this belief for what has been termed a *flight to health*. Some leaders may abdicate their role and attempt to become members. Others may miss the limelight and resort to structured exercises that are rarely needed or useful at this point. Experienced leaders monitor the group's dynamics, gently urging members to go deeper, however slightly. This can be a seductive stage for leaders, as members are really working together, but they still do need help to explore deeper, core concerns. As the group progresses, there is a greater likelihood that a group member may actually reveal and explore core issues. The common reaction is to pull away and experience some resistance and fear. When the group seems to be running smoothly, it is easy to overlook subtle resistance, and so the group leader needs to remain steadfast in facilitating and deepening the work of the group. Furthermore, since the group members are cohesive and tend to be fonder of one another at this stage, there can be group collusion driven by a protective instinct to avoid concerns that are too painful or hurtful. As you can see, the leader has a different and somewhat more complex role at this stage. The following statements illustrate what leaders might say:

- "Barbara, you have shared much, but I have yet to hear where you are in this story. Where are your feelings?"
- "Fred, you haven't really answered Gloria's concern. Would you try again, or talk about what makes it hard to tell her?"
- "Maria, I think your observations are important. Who in particular are you addressing with your observations?"
- "Patsy, when you're ready, put words to your tears."
- "I'm enjoying our lighthearted mood, but I am wondering if that is all you want from today."
- "Mike, you have sought input from Barbara, Sandy, and Jill each week, but never from Troy, Jerry, or Arturo. Any hunches about what this is about?"
- "The group has been working hard the past few weeks, and we have reached the halfway point of our time together. I am wondering if you can remember what brought you into group and then assess your progress on these goals."
- "Felix, are you getting what you need from this group? You seem silently satisfied at the end of session, yet you continually open each group by downplaying your progress and accomplishments. What keeps you from getting your needs met?"
- "Tammi, you mentioned that at work you often feel that people don't listen to you or take your opinions very seriously. When does that happen in our group?"
- "What Julio is describing seems similar to what Aaron brought into group on the first day. How can the two of you help each other?"

Members are thus challenged with several tasks during this stage to develop more intimate connections with others, to take greater risks in what they say and do, to go deeper in what they reveal about themselves, and to take more responsibility for their own changes, as well as the direction the group takes next. Group leaders here become more precise in deepening the connections between members.

STAGE IV: DISENGAGEMENT

Groups enter their final stage as the end draws near, usually when only a few sessions remain. As a way of previewing this stage, we will say that we have been struck by how many students share that what they will miss most after graduation is belonging to "their" interpersonal growth group, a regular feature of many training programs. Our response is often to reassure them that groups exist in most cities and that wherever their career takes them, they can join another group. The look in their eyes expresses their doubt that this will come to pass, and indeed, on reflection, we realize how rare it is for any of us to be a part of a group that feels truly safe and secure, yet encourages us to be as honest, genuine, and open as possible.

Most groups exist not only for the pure pleasure, support, caring, and entertainment they provide but also for the changes they promote in the outside world. Ultimately, the true test of a group's functioning is not how well members are getting along when they are together but how they are performing in their lives. The questions you must ask members at this stage, and encourage them to ask one another, include the following:

- To what extent have you reached your stated goals?
- In what specific ways have you changed as a result of this experience?
- Where are you now in relation to where you would like to be?
- What is left to do before the group ends?

For many people, the final stage is often the trickiest of all. Many people do not say goodbye very well, and they often find themselves let down, frustrated, or left with a sense of regret about what they did not do in group when they had the chance. Ending a group raises issues of grief and loss, illuminating the process of letting go and moving on in the here and now. Given that members have experienced such a high level of caring and support, they often feel tremendous ambivalence at the prospect of ending the group. On the one hand, members are

Photo 4.1   It is challenging to help a group end in such a way that members can let go of their close relationships and yet continue the momentum after the session. Your job is to help people say goodbye effectively, acknowledging their sadness and pride, and help them continue making progress toward their goals without the support they have become used to.

excited about their freedom; on the other hand, they are sad to say goodbye. Group members make real connections, sometimes for the first time, and saying goodbye is often quite painful and sad.

It is not uncommon to experience resistance from group members during this stage. For many, there is a deeply ingrained tendency to avoid endings, or at least to minimize the impact of closure. We believe a critical function at this stage is to keep people engaged in the process so that the end of the group does justice to the amount of work that has been accomplished. In a sense, the disengagement stage provides another opportunity for interpersonal and group learning, yet the lesson learned is how to say goodbye well. The ultimate goal of successfully ending a group is that each person can leave with few regrets and little is left unsaid among members.

Student Voice

Ending Is Hard to Do

During the last day of group, I felt very similar feelings to what I had felt on the first day together. Though I did not feel as anxious or panicked, I experienced a great sense of sadness. However, in addition to the sadness, I also felt a sense of accomplishment and a strong connection to the other group members. I felt a strong sense of unity and comfort among the group and I felt like one with everyone else. Though I had yet to achieve my goals, I was much closer to my destination than I have ever been or imagined. I was very proud of myself, for I had grown so much on this journey and achieved many other goals that I had not anticipated. Yet I did not want the group to end, I wanted it to continue. I had grown so fond of people who I did not know existed 5 months ago. I was filled with joy and sadness at the same time, knowing that I had made strong connections like never in the past, but I was still sad because I knew it had come to an end. Ending was bittersweet.

Disengagement is a transition out of the group experience, yet it begins well before the last session. Effective endings are planned and executed rather than random occurrences. The leader is responsible for reminding members how many group meetings are left and when the last session will be held. One of the greatest challenges you will face is helping members continue their progress after the group ends. It is not unreasonable to fear that people will experience setbacks, or even regress to dysfunctional patterns. That is why it is so critical at this stage to help group members express their fears, work through their apprehensions, and plan for the inevitable challenges they will face. Many of these concerns are reasonable and realistic considering how rarely the effects of any learning experience are long-lasting. Just consider how often in your own life you have attended a class or workshop, been fired up about what happened there, but then "forgot" to apply the new knowledge or skills once the group was no longer meeting on a regular basis. That is why it is so important that you have an open and honest conversation with group members about what they will need to do to ensure that their changes stick once the group ends.

A part of this last stage is really a final chapter called "follow-up," in which you may, at some point in the future, call for a reunion, or at the very least engage in some sort of post-group checkup to see how members are progressing. This not only keeps people accountable for their behavior after the group ends but also allows you to monitor their progress and recommend additional treatment if needed.

Personal Reflection

We made the observation that ending is often one of the hardest tasks in a group. Facilitating good endings for others necessitates that you have reflected on your own tendencies when it comes to ending and saying goodbye. Without such personal reflection, it is likely that your entire group will end the same way you tend to end in your life.

What are the patterns in how you generally end relationships or say goodbye to others? Consider your personal relationships and groups you have been a part of. How do you feel when ending? Do you take endings head-on, do you tend to avoid them, or do you do something else? What types of changes do you need to make to feel more satisfied with how you end?

Group Stages in Action

So far, this stage business sounds pretty theoretical; so let's apply the concepts to an actual group that was experiencing a kind of "civil war." The group was composed of eight students, four men and four women, who were participating in an experience to satisfy the requirements of the group leadership course. Although the group had not been proceeding altogether smoothly, the critical incident occurred during the fifth meeting.

Halfway through the session, Janice interrupted one of her counterparts (Bethany) and angrily charged her with wanton, seductive, and compulsive pursuit of the attention of male group members. Two other women quickly joined the fray, angrily adding similar accusations. Sensing imminent bloodshed, the male group members avoided the conflict as they inspected the floor for minute traces of some unidentified substance. The group leader, as well, was caught in the grips of inaction, fearful of doing anything to make matters worse. It was a pretty tense situation.

After a few deep breaths, the group leader intervened by directing the members to focus on their own behavior rather than that of others: "How is this also about you and your own needs?" As their stories unfolded, it was clear that the three women who were accusing Bethany wanted desperately to feel more comfortable with their own sexuality. They each noted seeing in Bethany a quality and comfort with her own sexuality that they admired. As is often the case, Janice's preemptive attack was not really about Bethany's behavior but, rather, about what it sparked in her accusers.

Bethany was initially defensive and a little bit confused by all this. She felt attacked, a bit angry, but also wounded at being confronted by women in the group whom she was feeling close to. Once she regained her sense of balance and was able to talk through the range of her feelings, Bethany revealed that she was all too aware that she depended on her sexuality to gain attention and approval from men, and that she had done this most of her adult life. She suspected that much of the conflict with other women in her life stemmed from this attention-seeking behavior. Bethany further shared that she hated this about herself and wanted to change.

When the group leader debriefed the incident with his supervisor, he was first asked why he had failed to see the growing tension among these members. Surely, this conflict had been brewing for some time. His supervisor worked with him to explore what made it hard to see this coming. One reason, he admitted reluctantly, was that Bethany was indeed strikingly attractive and seductive. The leader had been so uncomfortable with his own attraction toward this woman that he completely denied what was going on. He neither recognized what was inappropriate about her behavior in terms of creating the type of connection she desired nor realized how others were reacting. Typical of this experimental engagement stage, one member's behavior became the focus, the scapegoat, of others' strong feelings.

For Personal Reflection

Applying the various stages of group development to your classroom, where do you believe your class is currently operating? Identify evidence to support this assumption by thinking about specific behaviors that are representative of this stage.

If you were the instructor and wanted to move things to the next level, how would you do so?

Like so many critical incidents in a group, this one became a catalyst for members to become more cohesive and less competitive, but it came out of conflict expressed honestly. Bethany changed dramatically after this session, not only in appearance but also in behavior. The men in the group, including the leader, seemed to wake up a bit more in terms of Bethany and engaged her in a manner that was less directed by sexuality and attraction, and more by seeing her as another person in the group trying to work through some serious concerns. Over time, the group came to value her wit and perceptiveness, abilities she yearned to express that had previously been kept under wraps. Similarly, two of the confronting members unveiled a vivaciousness that seemed to energize the entire group.

The transition from experimental to cohesive engagement, also referred to as moving from "storming" to "norming," often occurs as a result of some incident that brings people closer. After finally recognizing what might have been happening in the group and within himself, the group leader was first able to support and protect the confronted group member. Yet it was critical that he did not collude in denial of an issue so rich in meaning for all members. It was essential that the here-and-now exchanges become a normative feature of the group's culture.

What to Look for Over Time

It is highly likely, in any debriefing or supervision session you have, that some discussion will take place about the stage in which the group is presently working. Generally, the following patterns will be observed as the group develops:

- Communication becomes less leader centered and more member centered.
- Self-disclosures change from being impersonal and in the past to being more present oriented and personally revealing.
- Instead of being minimized, or avoided altogether, conflicts are acknowledged and worked through.
- Norms change from being imposed (via ground rules) to being developed specifically for the group's culture.
- Boundaries among members move from rigid to more flexible.
- Individual and cultural differences become increasingly respected, understood, and cherished rather than feared and resented. They are also discussed in an honest manner so that one's full identity is fully revealed.
- Feedback moves from a global level ("You are a nice person") to a more specific recognition of when a quality is felt or a behavior is observed ("When you ask me how I am doing today after having such a rough day last week, I can sense your caring nature").
- Rather than fearing honest feedback, members become hungrier for direct input.

As a beginning group leader you would be well-advised to develop skills in the following areas:

1. Identifying the major characteristics of each stage

2. Recognizing the needed therapeutic tasks for each stage

3. Applying specific interventions that are best for each stage

As an example, imagine a group you are leading that has just gotten started (third session) and whose members appear reluctant to confront one another even about the most obvious transgressions. When a person rambles, people make faces but don't say a word of protest. When someone feels hurt, he suffers silently. Some members come late, but their behavior is ignored.

Before you decide how to handle these matters, you must first assess how these dynamics represent the current stage of development, in which trust and cohesion are typically minimal. You wouldn't want to force progress before participants are ready, or they may shut down even further, perhaps even flee. Neither can you ignore the covert avoidance of honest interaction that is typical of a group that has yet to really get going. What you do at this time is very different from how you might handle this situation once the group is in the cohesive engagement stage.

As you develop more confidence, you will learn to use your knowledge of group stages in more effective ways. A group leader who is developmentally astute can facilitate, hasten, slow down, or draw out the process at each stage to the group's benefit (Ward, 2014). Over time, you can learn to let a group follow the developmental course it requires to be a supportive and change-focused environment. You can learn to be confident that a group will grow through a conflict, and group members can be eased by your belief. Further, you can use knowledge about group stages to help conceptualize and understand unexpected events in a group (Forsyth & Diederich, 2014).

For a Class Activity

Meet with several partners to discuss alternative intervention options for how you might address the avoidance of direct communication in the illustrative example. Based on what you know about this group's current stage of development, what might you do next?

We have presented a general framework for understanding the progressive stages of a group in such a way that you can construct a clearer idea of what is going on during any session in light of developmentally appropriate behavior. Actions take place in a context that is not only influenced by the individual backgrounds of members, group dynamics, and processes but also related to where things stand along a time continuum. Yet we have also cautioned against becoming too dependent on what is "supposed" to occur at each stage in the process, lest you impose a vision that doesn't accurately reflect what is occurring. Just as there is a wide range of individual differences in group behavior, each group also "behaves" in a variety of ways. After leading hundreds of groups, we are continually amazed by the ways each experience is unique. Some groups move quickly into cohesion and action, whereas others struggle to develop trust and connection. The important point to keep in mind is that a developmental progression of stages is linked with group tasks that support the foundation of the group. Thus, even though some groups in the early stages may behave in a manner that mirrors cohesive engagement, effective leaders are fully aware that the group foundation will still need to develop the support that comes from experiencing the tasks of induction and experiential engagement.

Review of What You Learned

- Group stages are naturally occurring phenomena. Like any other living system, they are progressive, sequential, and often accompanied by predictable behaviors.
- Knowledge about stages helps the leader assess what might be happening and predict future patterns. Stages provide direction for group leader intervention.
- Stages follow different progressions in some groups; so use the theory as a rough guide rather than a final blueprint.
- There is an ongoing struggle in every group between playing it safe and taking risks. Your job is to shepherd the process along from the early stages of reluctance to greater sharing and experimentation. Each group stage has its own levels of risk taking.
- Groups have a beginning, middle, and end, each stage of which has its own developmental obstacles and challenges. Over time, you are helping people develop sufficient safety, trust, and intimacy to accomplish individual and group goals.

Multicultural Dimensions of Group Work 5

The group had been going extraordinarily well thus far, which was somewhat surprising to the leader given the diversity represented. Among the 14 participants, there were at least 8 different racial/ethnic/religious/cultural backgrounds, and that didn't include the differences in age (spanning 22 to 65 years), sexual orientation (including a gay man and a bisexual woman), occupation, and presenting problems. Perhaps the leader was feeling a little too confident, or he could have misread the readiness level of some members to go deeper, but he decided to push things a bit by asking members what they were avoiding. "Let's go around the group and have each person share something that you have been holding back," he said, with as much enthusiasm as he could muster.

If he had been paying closer attention, the leader would have noticed the look of horror on the young Vietnamese American woman's face as she covered her mouth and scooted back her chair. She was from a culture and household in which women defer to older men and in which it is also considered highly inappropriate to speak so frankly about personal matters. There were others as well—a gay man who had yet to come out in the group, a Persian woman who had experienced repeated verbal violence from White males who resembled the group leader, an African American woman and a Mexican American man who had clashed previously—who were horrified at the prospect of being "forced" to go way beyond their comfort levels. Up until this point the group had been active, but it was not safe enough for some to take bigger risks.

On some level, the leader realized that he had his hands full managing such a diverse group of individuals, all of whom brought their own cultural values and expectations to the experience, but he had neglected to exercise the caution and empathy required to keep the group safe for the members. Early on in the group, he had acknowledged the range of diversity, but he had yet to facilitate any exploration of how those differences and identities were alive in the room. Mentioning the diversity was not enough. The leader had excellent therapeutic skills, and his choice of this intervention could have worked quite well in a more homogeneous group in which trust and cohesion had been established and stabilized. But, in this case, his misjudgment and cultural insensitivity—or, rather, lack of awareness—contributed to the group's taking a huge step backward in terms of the leader's functionality. Many of the members afterward reported that they didn't feel safe after that incident, and it took several weeks before they even felt ready to talk about these concerns openly.

What could—and should—the leader have done differently?

That is just one of the questions we will be addressing in this chapter to help you become more skilled at adapting the theory and skills you've already learned to a variety of group contexts and cultural settings. This is often talked about as multicultural competence, but far more than that, it is developing a degree of self-awareness, knowledge, sensitivity, skills, and responsiveness to people that validates and honors their characteristics, background, identity, and experience (Metzger, Nadkarni, & Cornish, 2010).

Helping Everyone Who Needs Help

Surely, you have been exposed at some point in your study to the necessity of being able to help people from diverse cultural backgrounds. We are speaking here not only of diversity in the strict sense of ethnicity but also of culture, broadly defined to include others who have experienced oppression and discrimination. In fact, it is almost impossible to lead any group and not come into contact with a wide range of cultural identities that are different from your own. Whereas contact and exposure to diversity is a certainty, effective facilitation of multicultural group interactions takes specific attention and skills beyond a group leader's general abilities (Ridley, Mollen, & Kelly, 2011). Being a multiculturally competent group leader is widely recognized as not just good practice (Sehgal et al., 2011) but also an ethical imperative and an expectation for all professionals engaged in group work (Association for Specialists in Group Work, 1998, 2012; Corey, Corey, Corey, & Callanan, 2015; D'Andrea, 2014; Debiak, 2007).

Group leaders have been particularly concerned with developing structures that can be adapted to the unique needs of specific populations, as well as with

Photo 5.1   Throughout most of the world, indigenous cultures use group interventions to promote healing as well as a sense of community. The Bushmen of Southern Africa practice the oldest known healing rituals exactly as they have been doing for tens of thousands of years. In this women's ceremony, the group process makes use of chanting, drumming, shaking, and dancing to evoke the ancestral spirits to lend support and guidance to those experiencing medical or psychological problems. The group leader is an expert at capitalizing on many of the same principles operative in Western group therapy, such as cohesion, intimacy, and support, to build a sense of community.

creating an atmosphere in heterogeneous (mixed) groups that makes it possible for everyone to feel welcome. Some have suggested that heterogeneity in groups is particularly useful in helping group members see problems and solutions from different perspectives (Anderson, 2007; Yalom & Leszcz, 2005).

As you are no doubt aware, members of historically underrepresented groups are more likely to avoid therapeutic experiences, whether in individual, family, or group therapy; they are more likely to drop out of treatment prematurely; and, when they do participate in group counseling, they are far more likely to leave with unsuccessful outcomes (American Psychological Association, 2003; Casas, Raley, & Vasquez, 2008; Zane, Hall, Sue, Young, & Nunez, 2004). One specific reason for these difficulties in group work is that the setting has origins in a particular cultural context that traditionally has supported Eurocentric assumptions related to autonomy, independence, and assertiveness (Taha, Mahfouz, & Arafa, 2008; Toseland, Jones, & Gellis, 2004). These assumptions tend to value thoughts and thinking, verbalization and self-disclosure, unstructured and unscripted interactions between members, taking risks and trying new behaviors, public confrontation and feedback, and the display of emotion (D'Andrea, 2014; DeLucia-Waack & Donigian, 2004).

Ironically, most indigenous healing traditions around the world, from those of Australian aboriginals and Native Americans to those of Zulus and Bushmen from Southern Africa, incorporate group rituals into their "treatments" and have been doing so for tens of thousands of years. Group work promotes spiritual and social relatedness among people while highlighting the awareness of the interconnectedness of all things. Yet such therapeutic community interventions integrate the particular values of a culture to draw on the collective resources of everyone present, as well as ancestral spirits of the past. Such groups bring together spiritual (prayer), psychological (storytelling), physical (dance and music), and medicinal elements to capitalize on every dimension of human experience (Keeney & Connor, 2008; Kottler, Carlson, & Keeney, 2004; McWhirter & Robbins, 2014).

It is clear that, in the past, group leaders have not been particularly responsive, or effective, in addressing the needs of those who have experienced discrimination and are especially mistrustful of coercive groups. This applies to members of ethnic minority groups (e.g., Native Americans, Latino/as, African Americans, Asian Americans), those with disabilities (physical, mental, and emotional), those who historically have been without voice or power (the poor, the disadvantaged), and those who have experienced discrimination based on sexual orientation, gender, age, religion, or other human characteristics.

If you hope to serve those people who need your help the most, you must devote considerable time, energy, and commitment to learning ways to adapt your leadership skills to fit the unique needs of different cultural groups (Ibrahim, 2010; Metzger et al., 2010). Training requires intentional planning to learn strategies to examine culture and privilege in group work (Ibrahim, 2010). This is not an easy challenge. Many people have experienced the pain of discrimination in group settings or at the hands of a group. Obviously, anyone who has felt harmed, disrespected, or marginalized in the past may very well be cynical, pessimistic, and suspicious regarding what it is you hope to offer. It is, therefore, the group leader's task to create group cohesion around feelings of respect for cultural identities.

This chapter will begin by looking at some of the factors that are unique to exploring diversity in groups. We present narratives that will highlight some of the special challenges you will face. We also discuss some of the concerns that culturally diverse clients wrestle with when they participate in groups, as well as some of the common mistakes leaders make. It is our intent to help you understand how experiences of racism, prejudices, and oppression can affect someone's current perceptions and behavior in a group setting. This will allow you to create more culturally sensitive and responsive interventions, regardless of the people you are helping.

What Is a Multiculturally Competent Group Leader?

The characteristics and qualities of multiculturally competent group leaders must match the expectations and needs of their diverse clients. Anderson (2007) defined the practice of such leaders as being informed by multicultural knowledge, skills, and abilities, with the goal of promoting client development, health, autonomy, and liberty within a sociocultural context. Brinson and Lee (2005) added that multiculturally focused groups share a common goal: to raise the cultural consciousness level of participants and provide a degree of social support. You can see that these expectations go beyond stated group goals and speak to the need for felt experiences of respect, acceptance, and validation on a cultural level within the group.

Meeting these goals requires that group leaders develop an awareness of their own biases and prejudices, as these may affect their judgments, perceptions, and behavior. And, make no mistake, each one of us holds certain assumptions and biases—that is, prejudgments—about people we encounter, based on our prior experiences with those whom they appear to resemble (Metzger et al., 2010). Even if this does not involve full-blown racism, homophobia, or religious prejudice, there is little doubt that everyone harbors certain beliefs about others based on their physical characteristics, behavior, or labels. It is highly likely that unintentional biases, attitudes, and behaviors will extend to the process of group work, where you will encounter a vast array of cultures and worldviews.

Multiculturally competent clinicians are most likely to display certain characteristics, including openness to others who are different, awareness of their own internal reactions, and a functional knowledge of a variety of cultural groups (Caldwell et al., 2008). This means that prospective leaders must be more than well intentioned about attending to diversity in groups. They must be proactive and aware that they are likely to make mistakes and, at times, appear insensitive, no matter how well prepared they might be. The good news, however, is that group members are often forgiving of leaders who are willing to acknowledge their errors and failures, apologize when they are off base, and demonstrate a willingness to learn from the experience. If one's intention was not to offend, then that is likely to show through an apology or admission of a mistake.

For a Field Study

You must develop awareness and knowledge of all the various cultural groups with whom you expect to work. Start out by identifying three or four of the most prominent cultural groups that are likely to show strong representation in the groups you will lead, and focus particularly on those you know the least about.

Interview several members of each of these groups to find out what their concerns would be in participating in a group you would lead. Ask them to educate you about the main cultural values you would need to understand to be able to help them. Find out the reasons why they would feel reluctant to participate in a group that was not led by a member of their own culture. What could you do to create a climate that would be optimal for them?

Your job, in this field study, is to gain a working knowledge of the cultural backgrounds you are most likely to see in your work on a daily basis. Each week or month, you can make it a priority to learn about another cultural group that is beyond your experience.

The key to developing cultural empathy involves understanding how people's values and backgrounds are integrally connected to the relationships they develop with you and with other group members (Pedersen, Crethar, & Carlson, 2008). As you have already learned, empathy is absolutely central to everything you do in your work. Given the mistrust, uncertainty, hesitance, and fear that many clients feel at the beginning of a group, it is critical that each person feel honored, respected, and understood. Empathy means understanding others by entering their worlds and placing yourself inside their frame of reference, and also being able to effectively communicate your understanding of that world. Group leaders who are culturally empathic not only retain their separate cultural identities but also are simultaneously aware of and accept the group members' cultural values and beliefs.

Building Strong Multicultural Alliances

You have most likely heard more than a few times already that one of the strongest outcome factors in creating change is the alliance between clients and their therapists (Vasquez, 2007). Regardless of the theory and techniques used in a group, success often depends on each member's sense of alliance with the leader and other members (Arnd-Caddigan, 2012; Carter, 2006; Norcross, 2011). This is particularly important for clients from historically marginalized groups or those groups that have faced pervasive discrimination (Smith, Rodríguez, & Bernal, 2011). Be aware that all people want to experience some sense of belonging in a group setting. Markin and Marmarosh (2010) found that regardless of whether individuals come from individualistic or collectivistic cultures, we all have a fundamental need to belong to various groups; however, we are likely to express the need differently depending on our cultural backgrounds.

Attention to the relationship between leaders and cultural minority group members may require special considerations because of previous historical misunderstandings and miscommunications. Imagine the added difficulties of trusting a helper when that person resembles those you have always viewed or experienced as oppressors. To add to the challenges you will face, many group members may hide their apprehensions out of fear of rejection and in deference to the leader's authority. Thus, as a leader, you may not even be aware of cracks in the therapeutic relationship. Concealment of negative reactions is a normal human process, yet people of color experience slights and offenses so consistently that they tend to "edit" their responses on a regular basis (Sue, 2010; Vasquez, 2007). Thus, leaders must create safe opportunities to express negative affect and connections to the group, as illustrated in the example below:

Diego: I'd rather not talk about that.

Leader: Diego, I want to honor and respect your choice not to go further, and yet . . .

Kyle: Hey, why does he get let off the hook? You guys were all over me when . . .

Diego: *No me chingues, chico.*

Kyle: Who you callin' boy, boy?

Leader: Okay, guys, that's enough! We are moving away from what is happening in the room. Before you were interrupted, Diego, you were saying you didn't want to talk any more about your family situation.

Diego: That's right. Especially now.

Leader: It seems like you don't feel that much trust in here. Even before Kyle con-
               fronted you a bit, you seemed cautious and careful in what you said and
               how you said it.

Diego: Yeah. So?

Leader: Well, I think you have a good reason to feel that way. And if you'd be will-
               ing to do so, I'd like to invite you to talk about why you don't feel safe. No
               pressure at all to talk about your family stuff, but it might be useful for us
               to hear more about the mistrust you feel and why you don't like being here.

The leader is validating Diego's right to feel reluctant and even to have quite
negative feelings about the group experience. Realistically, it is highly likely that
others in the group feel the same way but don't have the courage yet to talk about
that openly. If the leader can encourage Diego to express his doubts and hesita-
tions, this can lead to major breakthroughs in building greater trust for the future.

Group leaders need to pay close attention to cultural factors present in the
group by tailoring relationships to each group member's interpersonal, developmental, and cultural needs (Asnaani & Hofmann, 2012; Comas-Díaz, 2006). We
think of this in terms of "taking the pulse" of each member, asking ourselves at
any given moment how each person is doing and what each of them needs most.
This involves adapting your style, tone, and approach to the situation and the
individual based on what you know and understand about their backgrounds
and preferences.

We have mentioned previously how one of the core assumptions of group
work is that the same interpersonal dynamics that occur in everyday life will be
re-created in the group setting. Even though group leaders try to intervene and
create supportive settings, potentially harmful interactions steeped in prejudice
and bias can easily occur and, in many ways, should be expected. Remember that
in groups you have much less control than in individual/one-on-one settings.
Not only might you say and do things that can be misinterpreted, but other
members can cause casualties through their insensitivity and prejudices. Before
you even know what's happening, irreparable damage can be done. Sometimes
you won't even know it until a member, feeling wounded, fails to return the following week.

Microaggression is a term used to describe power dynamics in cross-cultural
encounters that convey attitudes of dominance, superiority, and denigration:
when people of privilege communicate that they are better than people of color,
who may be seen as less intelligent, capable, worthy, and so on (Fouad & Arren-
dondo, 2007; Sue, 2010; Sue, Capodilupo, & Holder, 2008; Sue et al., 2007). This
can occur not only with issues of race and ethnicity but also with differences in

gender, age, sexual orientation, socioeconomic status, religious affiliation, and disability status. In the group setting, microaggressions often occur with well-meaning group members who hold egalitarian beliefs but who have not become aware of their negative attitudes and stereotypes about people of color due to limited contact with people different from themselves (Fouad & Arredondo, 2007). Participants in groups may not always know when they convey negative judgments. Racism among Whites is often subtle, often unintentional and unconscious, but is transmitted through negative body language (less eye contact, less warm or natural voice tone, particular facial expressions) in response to those different from themselves (Dovidio, Gaertner, Kawakami, & Hodson, 2002). Most Whites report not being aware of this negativity, yet members of ethnic minority groups usually pick up negative attitudes toward them (Sue, 2010; Vasquez, 2007).

Of course, leaders are not immune to these harmful interactions. Being a group leader carries with it a sense of power that can be both helpful and harmful in facilitating change (Sue & Sue, 2013). When a group leader asks a group member to perform a task or respond in the group, that directive carries a weight that must be acknowledged. For members of traditionally underrepresented groups, saying no can be challenging (Asnaani & Hofmann, 2012; Taber, Leibert, & Agaskar, 2011). Because of a history of oppressive and rejecting experiences, many ethnic minorities are easily shamed or feel anxious about underperforming in the group (Furukawa & Hunt, 2011). Practitioners must be careful to understand and remember this power and take care not to abuse it. Rather, group leaders can use that power to model openness, sensitivity, and respect for exploring issues of discrimination, oppression, and bias in groups. This is a case where self-disclosure can be especially useful in modeling for other members the importance of owning up to biases and insensitivity.

For instance, your coauthors are both educated White males who hold power and privilege. In addition to our status as members of the majority culture, our ages, socioeconomic status, and professional positions and achievements may lead you to defer to us even when your own experience tells you something quite different. We are certain that you have already encountered more than a dozen instances when your internal voice was responding to something we said with, "No way!" Perhaps in some instances, you were misinformed or unaware of research that supports the position we were offering, or perhaps our perspectives and examples are rooted in experiences of power and privilege that cloud us to experiences we have not encountered. We are just as positive that there have been instances (with more to follow) when you mistrusted your own wisdom because you felt marginalized as "only a student."

For Reflection

No matter what your race, religion, socioeconomic status, gender, or sexual orientation, it is quite likely that you have been marginalized or even abused (physically, emotionally, psychologically, verbally, or sexually) by someone in a position of power and authority. In that situation, you felt helpless as a victim, fearful of striking back or defending yourself out of concern for retribution. You may have acted out in self-destructive ways. You may have withdrawn to protect yourself. In some cases, you may have tried to fight back, with limited success.

Now imagine what it will be like for group members to sit in your group and feel that *you* are the person of privilege and power because of your position. Consider the ways they might fear and resent you.

For group leaders, it is not so much *whether* you will step over a line but *how often* that will occur and what you will do about it when it does (Owen et al., 2011). Cross-cultural encounters are loaded with missed empathetic opportunities (Comas-Díaz, 2006). How you handle these interactions creates a template for how diversity and culture will be addressed in the group. No matter how well prepared you are and how hard you try, some group members will inevitably feel disrespected, neglected, and even abused by you—and they will attribute this to perceptions that you are biased, racist, homophobic, insensitive, or power hungry. Whether justified or not from your perspective, if a group member perceives this as reality, then it is true for that group member. To further complicate things, if you bring up the possible cultural lapse in a way that puts the person on the defensive, this can actually exacerbate the problem. It is critical for group leaders to bring up and address cultural issues in the group and to create a group where culture is invited, yet equally important for them to attend to the relationships in the group when talking about culture and to avoid putting people on the defensive (Owen et al., 2011).

Until You Have Walked in My Shoes: Exploring Discrimination in Group Settings

Imagine being in a room with a group of people who appear to be neither physically, spiritually, culturally, nor emotionally similar to you. They talk differently than you do; they even think differently. You see some people who remind you of other people you have learned to question or distrust over the course of your life—and for good reason. You have heard stories from friends and family about what they will do to you if you let your guard down, and you also have your own personal experiences of discrimination, personal slights, and micro- and macroaggressions. You have been warned repeatedly that although they may pretend to like you, secretly they despise you and think you are inferior. At the very least, these are people who don't understand, honor, or respect your culture or experience.

For a Class Activity

In small groups, tell a story about a time when you were, or felt you were, marginalized or oppressed. This experience could have involved a minor transgression or a significant one, but pick an instance when you were treated disrespectfully, or even abusively, because of your gender, religion, race, sexual orientation, social class, disability, or some other factor.

After each person has mentioned a particular oppressive incident, talk about what it would feel like for you to be in a group with members or even a leader who resembles those who have hurt you.

Now, imagine that you are asked to share or disclose your most intimate thoughts and feelings with these people in a group. You are expected to be vulnerable, to say what you really think and feel, even though you have some very good evidence to support that doing so may be incredibly stupid and self-destructive. The following scenarios are from group members from diverse backgrounds who decided to trust the group process and ended up having negative experiences. Each story is told in the person's own words.

SCENARIO 1: UNDERSTANDING THE BLOOD

The first thing I noticed was that they had a nurse and someone who wasn't licensed leading the group. This really upset me, but it was one of the things that was like, "Oh." I was actually surprised that they did a fairly good job.

There were about six different families in the group. We were there because of problems my husband and I were having with my stepdaughter. What got me was—and it didn't dawn on me until I left—that the problem was a cultural one. Because what was happening was that people were saying to me that she, my stepdaughter, was my daughter and that I should treat her as my daughter.

Her mother and stepfather were sitting in the room, too. I told them she already has a mother. I would do what I can, but she is not my child by blood. I am Native American, and that is important to us. I could tell that the people in the group just didn't understand the concept of bloodline. This was frustrating, that the other people, and the leaders, didn't understand what I was talking about, but my husband did. After that, I just didn't trust the atmosphere that much.

They asked my stepdaughter if I ever hugged her or anything like that. But I'm not a hugging, touching person. I am just not that way, and we didn't do that in my family. They asked my stepdaughter about that, but it wasn't an issue for her; it was an issue for them. They made me feel like something was wrong with me. This was very frustrating. It was a very negative experience. I did not want to go to groups ever again.

For Personal Application

Think of a time when you were in a group or social situation in which people tried to pressure you to be or act in a particular way that was in direct conflict with your values and beliefs. If a leader had been present, what would you have liked the leader to say on your behalf to protect your rights and help you feel understood?

In this first example, the Native American participant never felt accepted in the group; she never felt as though she belonged there. Moreover, she felt judged harshly by others regarding norms she did not share. She was convinced that there was nothing she could do to change their minds. This was unfortunate because she desperately needed help in her relationship with her stepdaughter.

SCENARIO 2: YOU GOT TO STAND UP

The group didn't work for me because of the way I was brought up in a Mexican American family. My mom did basically everything for my dad and the household. When I got married, though, my wife wanted a more equal relationship. I was troubled by that, since part of me wanted her to have my supper ready when I came home from work, wash and iron my clothes, and things like that. She was saying, "Hey, I work, too!" Part of me loved her because of her desire for an egalitarian marriage—because I want that, too.

I don't remember if it was the leader or a group member who said, "You got to stand up! If you are not getting what you want out of this relationship, then get out of it." So I went home and told my wife, "If you are not going to do those kinds of things, then we can go our separate ways." I told her that I was going to move out, and then I packed my things. I wasn't gone for more than 24 hours when she came by and talked to me and we cried together and we talked about it.

I started thinking, "Why am I doing this? What's wrong with changing my ways? Why do I have to be like my dad was?" So I asked her for forgiveness, and we got back together, and we started doing things together. Now we do a lot of stuff together, and I do my share of the chores.

That group almost ruined things for me. I still think that the group wanted to support me and all, but they didn't take the time to get to really know my situation or where I was coming from. The group got all into action and telling me things without ever really knowing me and some of my own stuff around this issue. What I was really struggling with was machismo and the traditional ideas of being a Mexican American man that I saw from my dad. That is what the group could have supported me on.

For Reflection

If we interviewed the group leader, or other members, we might hear a very different version of this story. Perhaps this man was not really told to go home and lay down the law to his wife—maybe that's just what he heard. The critical error may not have been with this ill-advised suggestion but, rather, the leader's failure to check out what this participant heard and understood and what he was going to do. Of course, we are giving the leader the benefit of the doubt.

Assuming that a situation such as this arose in a group you were leading, what steps would you take to make sure that miscommunications and cultural misunderstandings were minimized?

In this situation, a member from an ethnic minority group felt misunderstood by others. In this case, he genuinely felt the concern of group members, but the help they offered was misguided because neither the leader nor the members had the appropriate background to understand the context of his situation. Furthermore, they never got into his identity or struggled to work with cultural and gender-bound expectations.

SCENARIO 3: GROUP CLASS

I was required to be in a group as part of my training. When I first entered the room, I felt a sinking feeling at the pit of my stomach, closely followed by dread. I felt trapped. As I looked at all the White faces, I felt like I was in an enemy camp.

I slowly pulled out a chair and joined the others sitting in a circle: One African American clustered with 12 White group members. Our ultimate purpose, as explained by Mac [the leader], was to learn how to become effective group leaders. Mac was a 60ish, long-legged, physically fit, White gentleman who was always casually and neatly dressed. Both his nonverbals and verbals epitomized the

Rogerian therapist: active listening and reflecting, sitting squarely, open, leaning forward, and very attentive and relaxed. His voice was soft, and his eyes were warm.

Mac was charming, suave, and soft-spoken. He had spent previous class sessions discussing theory, techniques, and the characteristics of an effective group leader. This group was to be experiential, and we were to find out what it was like to be members in the sort of groups we would someday be leading.

I liked Mac, and I think my liking him led me to think that he saw my vulnerability as the only person of color in the room. In spite of the best of intentions, this group was a nightmare to me. I always felt alone, and that was never acknowledged. How hard was that to do? I felt attacked and that my thoughts and feelings weren't understood, respected, or validated. I don't recall the exact context or details of the group, but even after so many years I am still plagued by that awful, depressing, horrible group-training experience and that overwhelming feeling of powerlessness. I kept getting overrun, and my voice was nonexistent. I felt like an "other."

For a Class Activity

The previous narrative is, of course, your own worst group-leadership nightmare. Whether as a group leader trying to prevent casualties or a participant trying to protect your own safety, you are extremely concerned with people being hurt as a result of incompetence, neglect, or insensitivity. Although the details of the preceding story are sketchy, it is clear that this group member felt powerless. She also mentions feeling like an outsider, being the only Black member of an otherwise White group. Her identity and cultural background were not acknowledged, and her voice was not supported.

Talk as a class or in small groups about what this story triggers for you. Consider what you could have done as a group leader to create a different outcome.

This group member describes with vivid language the kind of casualty that can result from groups—even with well-meaning and highly skilled leaders. As long as one or more participants feel like outsiders in the midst of others who appear to share a common bond, feelings of alienation will often result. The significance of this group's demographics seems obvious, yet they were never addressed in an overt way, and this member did not feel cultural empathy from the leader. As can be observed in this example, sometimes the negative effects are so enduring that the person becomes reluctant ever to join another group.

SCENARIO 4: IGNORING THE OBVIOUS

I would like to relate an incident that happened in a group situation, which I found to be very demeaning. I knew from the beginning that the facilitator was not comfortable with me being in the group. I knew it was because I was blind. I tried to be positive. Yet I was virtually ignored.

Before the session began, I let the leader know about me, but the leader seemed surprised that I wanted to be in the group and seemed put out at the idea of being accommodating to me. At first I thought that maybe the leader was a little uncertain or overwhelmed with working with a blind person, since I get that a lot. So I gave the leader the benefit of the doubt, thinking that the leader might fumble in attempts to include me, but I could at least value the attempt. Boy, I was wrong! Throughout that first group session, I felt isolated, unwelcome, and pretty much ignored. I was not encouraged to participate in exercises that were part of the group session. It was like the leader never even considered how I could be included. The hurt, the anger, and feeling of isolation are still with me today.

I left the group after the second session. I left feeling that my time had been wasted and my efforts to continue with the group had been thwarted. Normally, I would have assertively confronted the facilitator on a one-to-one basis at a later time. However, this time I didn't have the energy or the desire. I felt that the leader's perceptions were more than I wanted to deal with.

This case illustrates an unfortunately common experience: Some members never return to group, and you may never learn exactly why or what happened. It is one of the most frustrating and confusing aspects of leading groups, in that you are often quite unsure why some group members don't come back. Were they hurt by the experience? Are they feeling lingering negative effects? Maybe they just didn't feel it was a good match? Or perhaps they got what they wanted and don't need any more? Wishful thinking.

The client in this scenario was understanding of how others are often uncomfortable with his sightlessness. He was prepared to be forgiving and patient. But when his unique situation was never addressed, never even mentioned, and he was actually ignored and not accommodated, it seemed as though this group was not going to be very genuine and honest. If the group leader was not even able to acknowledge the obvious, how could other issues be addressed?

SCENARIO 5: SEXISM IN THE LEADER'S CHAIR

My group experience as student coleader with a male partner was absolutely horrible. As a single parent in school I was also juggling work and home, often rushing to go from one thing to another. I showed up huffing and puffing for group, often right as things began.

Throughout the group, I noticed my male coleader often dominating the conversation and behaving as if he knew it all. He would cut me off and interrupt constantly. I often felt that he was attempting to control the group, and I didn't think we were working well as a team. I mentioned this during our supervision with our professor, but he seemed to think it was my problem of needing to speak up more. I suggested that he needed to speak less in order to provide some space for me. He did not agree with that idea. It seemed to me that we were just acting out sim- ilar issues of oppression that our group members were also struggling with. He also did not agree with that assessment. And the group never got any better for me.

At the end of the group experience that semester, one of the female group mem- bers pulled me aside and told me that she felt it only fair that I be told that during the previous meeting the male coleader and the male professor had conspired. They had plans to ask me in front of everyone what I had given to the group process. In her mind, she felt that they were sexist and controlling, unwilling or unable to relin- quish typically male patterns of dominance. I had to agree with her.

This example contains lots of complicated issues. First of all, it demonstrates the ways cultural conflicts and misunderstandings occur between leaders as well as members. Second, it shows the way tension between leaders plays out in the group, with other members taking sides and becoming triangulated in the con- flict. Third, it illustrates the ways gender roles related to power and control can become toxic and hurtful.

SCENARIO 6: CAN I SHARE MYSELF?

My goal in group seemed rather simple—to be honest and share with others. I told the group my goal the first day, but what I left out was that I was gay and that only a few people knew that about me. So my secret goal was to come out in the group as a way of taking a risk that might boil over to my actual life. I guess what I really wanted was to gain the courage to come out to my family, and coming out to the group would be a trial run. I knew that was going to be tough because my parents aren't exactly, well, they would probably freak out.

I liked the group members; but about half of the group was pretty conservative, and I doubted they would understand. There was nothing overt ever said, but there were a few little digs and admissions about gays and lesbians that seemed to fly under the radar. It was around an election period, so I had a pretty good sense where many of the group members were on issues like same-sex marriage. Around these issues, it seemed like the leader was pretty neutral. I didn't know what she believed, but she didn't exactly do much to pave the way for me.

After a few months, I got feedback that I wasn't sharing enough, but I struggled with what to do. I mentioned it was hard to share and that there was something I was hoping to reveal, but I struggled with how I would be accepted. I revealed that over the years I felt discrimination over it. The group kept pressuring me to open up, but to tell you the truth, it felt like I was being coerced. Finally, I gave in and told the group I was gay, and rather than feeling supported, I felt minimized. I heard comments like, "Is that all?" and "Your fears in here were unfounded." It seemed like they heard the words but missed the entire message of my struggle and how my history has been one of feeling stepped on. My experience in life had taught me to fear many straight people, and now it was happening again. So now I was out, exposed, and more terrified than before. I came back a few times, staying really quiet, and then just dropped out.

This group member experienced one of the hazards of groups that we discussed previously—that is, when people are pressured to do or say things for which they don't feel ready. Coercion, especially with members who have been victims of discrimination, can be very hurtful. A compounding factor is that he felt pressured to share a protected part of his identity. Not only was that disclosure not supported, but his worldview of experiencing marginalization was dismissed.

We don't wish to leave you with the impression that all members of historically underrepresented and marginalized groups have unsatisfactory group experiences. Quite the opposite is true: When efforts are made to help people feel included, to respect their differences, and to help them feel heard and understood, groups are the perfect place for positive change to occur. The problem has been, at least historically, that leaders have not been well-informed and prepared to work with diverse cultures and identities. Group leaders wishing to create multiculturally effective groups can provide respect to meet group member goals collaboratively. This means allowing group members to fully express their individual stories and to explain how their cultural beliefs have been uniquely part of this story and their experiences (Asnaani & Hofmann, 2012; Pedersen et al., 2008). This can happen only with group leaders who are multiculturally competent.

Start With Yourself

You are, of course, a member of a variety of cultures related to your ethnicity, age, religion, gender, sexual orientation, and even family background. Whether you identify strongly with one culture or another, others will perceive you as a member of various groups. Of course, you have your own cultural identity shaped by the salient cultural variables you value most.

As addressed above, you bring your own biases and prejudices to any group, based on your previous experiences. You form first impressions of people after observing their physical or behavioral characteristics. This is nothing to feel ashamed of necessarily; it is actually adaptive behavior for humans and other animals to form instant assessments of others as to whether they might represent danger. We tend to view "those like us" as safe and "those not like us" as being a potential risk. These initial impressions are often reformed quickly in light of new information, but it does not change the fact that we are all prone to making impulsive judgments about strangers based on our previous experiences with those who resemble them.

Whether you are Latino, White, African American, Asian, or biracial; whether you were born on this continent or another; whether your native language is English, Hungarian, or Spanish; or whether you hold membership in some other aspects of the majority or minority culture, you still have some strong attitudes and values that you bring to the group. These include what you think is good for people and what you think they should do to get the most out of life.

For Personal Application

All of us have a rather long list of values and beliefs regarding what we think is healthy for people. For example, you might think that people are much better off if they are involved in a romantic relationship, if they have lots of friends, if they know how to enjoy their own company, if they are resourceful, if they have lots of choices, if they are assertive and responsible, if they are educated, and so on. Now, take some time to make a list of those strong ideas you have about what is good for almost all people. Think about what you really believe to be true. After you have compiled your list, analyze it by considering where these ideas came from. How might your beliefs, which are embedded in your own cultural values, clash with those of people who come from different cultural groups? Have you experienced that clash before in your life? You might choose to take this a step further and share your list with someone in the class who you believe might see the world differently. Compare your lists, and talk about the differences in your beliefs. Where do those differences come from?

Common Themes to Consider in Multicultural Group Work

The big question for you as a beginning group leader is, How do you adapt what you have learned (and are learning) about general principles of group dynamics, development, and growth to the varying needs and expectations of each participant, along the lines of diverse multiple identities? Each group member possesses a unique identity in which certain values and beliefs significantly shape perceptions, values, and behavior. Those with a history of discrimination have also suffered their share of abuse from group leaders in positions of power and control. Below we look at some common themes and experiences that deserve attention in group settings.

CAUTION

The first principle to keep in mind is that people from underrepresented cultural groups are often more likely to be suspicious and tentative in their participation due to traditional lack of power and voice in Eurocentric spaces (Taha et al., 2008; Toseland et al., 2004). Furthermore, overt and covert prejudices are a way of life that contributes to experiences of discrimination (Sue, 2010). We offer this cautionary advice with a degree of hesitance, since any generalizations we make are, in themselves, contributing to stereotypical views. One of the truths about human diversity in general is that the variations within any given culture are often greater than those between cultures. What this means is that there are often greater differences in basic values within groups of African Americans or Native Americans or Mexican Americans than there are among these groups.

Keeping this warning in mind, it is safe to recommend that you proceed carefully, sensitively, and cautiously when dealing with any person who has previously suffered discrimination or oppression—but you should proceed nonetheless. If it turns out that such caution is unnecessary, you can always accelerate your efforts. Yet the practice of being sensitive and supportive of the voices of all group members will send a message that everyone in group is a valued member. Remember, as well, that it is an absolute myth that you must tread lightly in discussions of cultural or racial differences. An open forum for talking about such diversity can actually promote even greater closeness and cohesion (D'Andrea, 2014; DeLucia-Waack & Donigian, 2004). Furthermore, most group members will look to the leader to initiate cultural discussions, to signify that this is an appropriate topic for the group. If you fail to do that, the opposite message will be sent—that culture is not very important.

COURAGE

Group work around cultural issues can be one of the most potent forms of therapeutic intervention; yet it certainly can also be one of the most affectively volatile and challenging (Anderson, 2007). Entering into interactions around cultural concerns and identity can often create feelings of trepidation. That is particularly true for group members who have identities that hold a privileged status in North America, since issues of guilt may be pervasive and the fear of being culturally insensitive or offensive may be overwhelming (Spanierman, Todd, & Anderson, 2009). There can also be a belief that discussing cultural issues will naturally lead to conflict and disconnection. Thus, some group members (and leaders) can be avoidant of wading too deep into the cultural waters. In this situation, groups really do need a courageous leader who will not shy away from cultural concerns or from recognizing the differences within the group. That can mean bringing up issues of discrimination and marginalization within the group even though the group is avoiding these issues or does not want to talk about them. It can mean taking the risk of shattering a (false, of course) sense of cohesion and togetherness by shining a light on what is hard to talk about. Modeling courage in the face of uncertainty sends the message that your group can talk about the issues that are relevant to each group member's core identity. Further, understand that not speaking up is the easier thing to do, as you are often supporting the majority position or viewpoint in doing so, and not speaking up or naming discrimination or marginalization is the enactment of privilege (Hays, Chang, & Havice, 2008; Pinterits, Poteat, & Spanierman, 2009). The harder task, and the one the leader should be undertaking, is speaking out about the tougher things in group and supporting those who need it.

LABELING

How you identify a person is an important part of a culture and identity. This is especially true with those who have experienced oppression. It is important for group leaders to be sensitive to how people want to be identified and the language used to describe cultural phenomenon. When in doubt, always ask or model each person's own language. Furthermore, use the words a group member uses in communication with the whole group as a way to develop a new dialogue in the room (Vasquez, 2007). Spend some time in the group discussing cultural issues openly so that everyone understands what is preferred and a shared, respectful language develops. Such an interaction might sound something like this:

Leader: I noticed that you just referred to yourself as Indian, rather than Native American. I wonder if you wouldn't mind saying more about what that means to you.

Sally: In my family we are proud of being American Indians. Native Americans is just a name that Whites have given to us. But I am part Paiute, part Ute, and I have Irish blood, too. But I am Indian through and through.

Leader: So what you are saying is that you would be comfortable if we talked about your Indian heritage. It also sounds like if we are to understand and really know you, then we need to learn more about your identity. If you feel ready to do so, tell us more about your background that you think would be important for us to know.

The leader is showing as much respect and courtesy as possible while demonstrating interest in Sally's cultural background. Permission is secured for eliciting more information. Requests are worded tentatively, giving Sally a way to decline if she prefers. The leader is also modeling the way the group will explore and honor the cultures of each member.

For Personal Application

Everyone has an identified culture (or many cultures) that includes their core values and beliefs. These can encompass your ethnic background, your ancestral blood, your geographical location, your religion, your profession, your sexual orientation, your gender, or your recreational pursuits. It is not only a matter of being African American, Muslim, gay, or Italian American but also of being a marathon runner, a rural Nevadan, a feminist, or an engineer. In each case, you may identify strongly with the values, interests, and beliefs of your group membership. Taken together, these multiple identities form your cultural identity.

If you were going to educate a group about the basic things members need to know about you to understand your background and help you, which would be your strongest cultural identifications? Within those cultures, what are the basic ideas you think others should know to understand your origins?

If time permits, talk to classmates in a small or large group about what they would most need to understand. After you have each had a chance to share your cultural backgrounds, talk about what you learned from the experience.

Self-Disclosure

As you are probably well aware, personal disclosure is treated in various ways across cultures (Adams, 2005; Sehgal et al., 2011). Of course, self-disclosure of personal or family information or dynamics in a group setting carries an additional layer of complexity. For many people, it is a completely foreign concept to tell those outside their family anything personal. This disclosure may be viewed as a form of weakness or betrayal. Thus, cultural differences are found in the content as well as the amount of what is verbalized.

Anything that has been said previously about the importance of trust in a group to encourage sharing and risk taking includes an additional layer formed by the cultural ramifications or risks. Most leaders are trained to attend to personal reactions or responses to self-disclosure, yet it is also critical to attend to the *cultural* connotations that go with such disclosures. An example of this is below:

Leader: Connie, over the past 10 minutes you've shared a lot about your relationship with your family. You've mentioned previously that your parents are immigrants from Japan, and I was wondering about the cultural context around your sharing today.

Connie: Well, that is the real issue that I am dealing with right now. I feel good about talking about my stuff from my family, but I felt this blanket of shame and guilt coming over me like I have wronged my parents and family. It is pretty heavy right now.

Leader: So stay with that a moment. You are feeling like you crossed a cultural barrier that is forbidden?

Connie: Exactly, and so now I'm struggling with a way to tell everyone here that my parents are not that bad and that we are a normal family. Gosh, even saying that feels like I am channeling my father! I also want to suck all of those tears back up and act like they did not come out.

LEVEL OF CULTURAL IDENTIFICATION AND ACCULTURATION

Obviously, not everyone who says they are Latino, Filipino, Baptist, or feminist means the same thing. Since there are degrees of commitment and attachment to particular cultures, you want to be careful about making assumptions without first checking things out. When someone says he is Jewish, is he Reform, Conservative, Orthodox, or nonpracticing? When someone says she is Catholic, does it mean she honors all the proclamations of the Pope, attending church every week, or does she attend only Easter Mass? When someone says he is Cuban American, does he speak Spanish at home? When someone says she is Asian American, which one of the hundreds of Asian cultures is she a member of? How long ago did her family immigrate? How important is it for her to be seen and understood as Chinese, Korean, or Cambodian?

We are speaking here about two concepts you will likely learn about in more specialized study of multicultural issues (Schwartz, Unger, Zamboanga, &

Szapocznik, 2010). *Acculturation* refers to changes that take place as a result of contact with culturally dissimilar people, groups, and social influences. Acculturation is most often studied in individuals living in countries or regions other than those where they were born—that is, immigrants, refugees, asylum seekers, and sojourners (Inman & Tummala-Narra, 2010). Cultural identity refers to our sense of belonging to a particular cultural or ethnic group and embracing the particular core values and beliefs of that group. Assessing these two factors in group members is especially critical, considering that they are often related to dropout rates, attitudes toward the group, and the kinds of problems that will be presented (Pedersen et al., 2008).

One of the valuable roles groups can play is in helping group members deal with the acculturation process by learning ways they can preserve their own heritage at the same time as they adopt the language and customs of their new home (Schwartz et al., 2010). The group becomes a sort of surrogate family, but one with diverse perspectives about preferred strategies.

For a Field Study

Identify several types of groups that you might like to lead with relatively homogeneous populations that have been marginalized. Read articles written by group leaders who have specialized in work with these populations. You will be relieved to learn that considerable work has been done on this subject, specifying the unique ways groups can be adapted to particular cultures. Classified by ethnicity, specialized group structures have been developed for these populations: Native Americans (Garrett, 2004; McWhirter & Robbins, 2014; Rivera, Garrett, & Crutchfield, 2004), Asian Americans (Chung & Bemak, 2014; Liu, Tsong, & Hayashino, 2007; Singh & Hayes, 2008), Latinos (Rayle, Sand, Brucato, & Ortega, 2006; Rivera, Fernandez, & Hendricks, 2014), and African Americans (Greer & White, 2008; Steen, Shi, & Hockersmith, 2014; White & Rayle, 2007). In addition, methods have been developed for use with gay, lesbian, bisexual, transgender, queer, and questioning people (Horne, Levitt, Reeves, & Wheeler, 2014); women (Kees & Leech, 2014); men (Rabinowitz, 2014); immigrants and refugees (Ringel, 2005); older adults (Vacha-Haase, 2014); and adults with disabilities (Ellis, Simpson, Rose, & Plotner, 2014). This is a good way to get some preliminary background on the populations you intend to work with and how you could tailor your group.

Second, go to some original sources. Talk to members of the target culture. Find out what their previous experiences in groups have been like, what they liked best and least. If they had negative outcomes, what could have been done differently? What advice do they have for you in reaching out to this population?

Finally, interview group leaders who already work with your identified populations. Pick their brains about the mistakes they have made and the things they have learned over the years.

POWER

Because of many clients' experiences of oppression along the lines of cultural identity, the process of empowerment is important when leading groups. Empowerment means that powerless people are made aware of the debilitating power dynamics in their lives and are helped to regain and exercise control. Certainly, you can appreciate that a group is an ideal setting in which to deal with these issues, given that so many interactions are really about dominance and control as members attempt to get their needs met and influence others according to their preferred way of thinking. Furthermore, many people have actually been silenced within group settings in the past as power hierarchies have been established. Thus, the group setting can provide an opportunity to explore power dynamics within the group and develop ways to help all members gain a voice.

VALIDATION

Groups are ideal settings to validate the experiences of cultural groups and provide a corrective experience in relation to previous experiences that may have led to mistrust of institutionalized systems, such as mental health services. Most, if not all, marginalized and discriminated-against populations (including women) focus on the group or tribe or self-in-relation, not on the individual, as the most salient element of existence (Jordan, 2010). This is in direct conflict with the predominant Western values of autonomy, independence, privacy, competition, individual power, and control (Ruiz, 2012).

Yet groups are actually a perfect place to practice those values that are so much a part of cultures that value collective or communal interaction. For a group to operate effectively, cooperation is stressed over competition, trust and intimacy over privacy, relationships over self-sufficiency, and interdependence over autonomy. Groups function as a tribal system, in ways very similar to those of indigenous cultures or those most familiar to people of Latino, Asian, and African origins (McWhirter & Robbins, 2014). In group work, we return to the roots of human culture, stressing the importance of collective rather than individual actions. To the extent that we can build a climate that respects the cultural diversity and identities of all members, that is so inclusive that nobody feels marginalized, we begin to heal the rifts and conflicts that have been so prominent in our larger society.

Review of What You Learned

- All group work is considered multicultural group work, due to the wide range of cultural identities.
- Be careful not to make gross generalizations about people based on their apparent or even espoused cultural identity. There are wide individual differences that may not be apparent.
- Dropout rates and unsatisfactory outcomes are more frequent among group members from historically underrepresented and marginalized groups, unless special efforts are made to help them feel validated, understood, and valued.
- Your own cultural identity, including values and biases, influences the way you lead a group. Thus, the task for all group leaders is to maintain self-awareness of cultural issues. Cultural competence is achieved by developing knowledge, beliefs, and skills about the diverse populations you serve in your role as group leader.
- Culturally diverse groups provide more opportunities for all members to confront issues related to powerlessness and oppression. Yet the leader often needs to model that exploring cultural issues and identities in the group is welcomed and appropriate.
- Helping each participant inform all others about important cultural beliefs provides a context for understanding current concerns.
- Specific considerations are necessary around issues of self-disclosure, cultural identification, and acculturation, validation, and power.

Theories of Group Intervention 6

I f there is ever a time when an experiential approach to the subject is needed, surely it is in this chapter on theory applied to groups. Never in so short a space will you be exposed to so many new terms and confusing ideas that either seem so alike that you can't tell much difference between them or seem so different that you can't imagine how it's possible to lead groups in such opposing ways. We will give you a hint, though: These different theories of group work are far more alike than you imagine, and also more different than they seem. Confused already? Not surprising, considering the complex nature of this subject.

Naturally, there are whole books devoted to the theories of group work (see Corey, 2013; Gladding, 2012). You are probably aware that entire semester- or even year-long classes focus exclusively on theories related to counseling, family therapy, consultation, or intervention. Perhaps you can therefore appreciate that if you ever hope to learn even the most rudimentary overview of these various theories and approaches, you must find a way to personalize and integrate them into your life.

The goal of this chapter is not to help you master the various approaches to group work; there will be plenty of time for that later. As a beginner, your job is to familiarize yourself with the very basic theoretical ideas and concepts, at least to the point where you can recognize many of them, even if you are not able to distinguish them clearly. Another preliminary goal is to search through these conceptual options to identify those that seem most appealing to you, most compatible with your values and personal style, and most applicable to the setting in which you hope to practice. Adopting and using a theoretical model is often a process of discovering which model aligns with your own worldview and ideas about why people are the way they are, who they are, and how change best occurs. Finally, another goal is to understand how that theoretical model can be applied in a group setting that values interaction and experience with others in relationships often distinct from those in one's everyday world (Day, 2014).

Keep in mind that the theories we will review are not limited to group settings; most of them were originally designed for individual sessions and later adapted for group leadership. Once you have narrowed down the work settings in which you hope to practice, as well as the styles that seem most appealing, you will be able to concentrate further study on those few approaches that seem most suitable. You will most likely not limit your exploration to how a theory is applied to group settings but will also extend your focus to how it is employed with families, individuals, or even organizations.

Obviously, one chapter on theory provides limited space to cover all the theoretical approaches to group leadership (nevertheless, this is still the longest chapter in the book). We anticipate, however, that you will integrate what you learn here with other theory courses or studies you will undertake.

For Reflection

Review in your own mind what you already know about theories of helping. You might, for example, recall the names of certain approaches that have historical significance—Freudian or psychoanalytic, for instance. Consider what you already understand about the ways these theories are organized. For example, you might remember that a behavioral approach helps people set specific goals or that a humanistic approach concentrates on the quality of relationships. If you have had little background or training in theory thus far, then make your own guesses about how they are constructed.

Now, before you read about theories of group leadership, make some inferences and predictions about how various approaches you already know about would be adapted for groups.

Theories and Group Leadership

You already have your own ideas about the best way to help people in groups. You might not have a well-articulated theory, or one grounded in systematic research and field tested across multiple populations, but you do have some notions about the best ways to use groups for constructive purposes.

Your whole life, you have been watching people and observing how they behave at family gatherings, at meetings, and in social groups. These observations have provided some rough notions about how to liven up a party, how to restrain someone who is being distracting at a dinner, or how to ease the discomfort for people who are meeting for the first time. Although it may seem to you that these techniques represent a mere collection of "best practices," tested and tried through experience, you may be surprised to realize that you already have a well-developed conceptual paradigm that guides your behavior. You have preferred explanations to account for why people act the way they do. You have hypotheses that lead you to behave in certain group situations in ways you believe will produce desired outcomes. In some cases, you may have even spent the time organizing what you know and understand into a coherent framework. This is not unlike the theories you will study—each represents an attempt on the part of an individual, or team, to make sense of why people act the way they do in groups and what can be done to organize circumstances in such a way that growth and change are maximized.

For Group Discussion

In small groups, reflect on your instructor's behavior so far with respect to the theory or theories you believe are guiding his or her choices in leading your class group. Your instructor has probably already given you clues (or made explicit statements) about which theories he or she favors, but keep in mind that what people espouse is not necessarily what they end up doing in practice.

Make a list of all the statements, disclosures, and evidence that support a particular theory your instructor may be following. For instance, he or she seems to like demonstrations and role plays a lot, believes the past is important in understanding the present, or says that people learn leadership through direct experience and immediate feedback. Don't worry about giving a name to the theory (you may not have learned that yet); just try to identify consistent patterns you have observed.

Exchange your analysis with other small groups to note the different perceptions.

A theory helps you organize what you know, in addition to providing a structure for explaining or predicting behavior (Day, 2014; Wampold, 2010). Rather than a single entity that remains constant over time, your theories constantly evolve with your exposure to new experiences, your understanding of how you fit with the theories presented, and your own development as a leader and practitioner (Frew & Spiegler, 2013).

Keep in mind that although we will be looking at different approaches to group work that appear to follow unique lines of inquiry and apply radically divergent methodologies, they all actually share the same basic operating principles. Even if the theories in their raw form strike you as completely at odds with each other (one may say you should remain in the present, while another insists that you dig into the past), most group leaders tend toward a degree of pragmatism in their styles. This means that regardless of their espoused theories, they do what works according to what a given situation demands. In regard to the use of theories, a popular misconception is that those aligned with a particular theory are unwilling to adapt their practices to the demands of the group members and the group. Rather, effective practitioners are flexible, and useful theories are widely applicable across situations (Wampold, 2010). Furthermore, a preference for one type of theory or way of seeing the group does not somehow preclude the use of concepts, interventions, or techniques from another theory (Prochaska & Norcross, 2010). The contemporary norm in clinical practice has moved away from staunchly following or adhering to one model or theory and toward integrating multiple theories to provide more adaptive services (Stricker, 2010). The key in using integrated theories is having a rough conceptual scheme that keeps you grounded but allows the use of multiple interventions to help people attain their desired changes in life.

The reason this chapter follows others that were about group dynamics, stages, and processes is that most group practitioners, in spite of their ideological differences, share similar ideas about the ways groups organize themselves. For example, in their treatise on the psychoanalytic group approach (to be covered shortly), Rutan, Stone, and Shay (2007) describe the use of leader interventions that almost all professionals employ, such as confronting inappropriate behaviors and clarifying member statements.

For a Field Study

Interview several experienced group leaders to find out which theories they subscribe to in their work. Ask them about the journey they followed to arrive at their particular set of operating assumptions. Ask them to describe their process of theory development, from the moment they began their training and up to the present time. What advice do they have for you, just starting out in the field, about the best way to learn and apply the theories you are reading about?

Before moving more deeply into understanding and reviewing group theories, it is important to take a step back and understand the context in which most theories reside. Most of the theoretical models of group work are reflective of the settings in which they were developed. Thus, most models reflect a Western European, male, middle- to upper-class perspective that is filtered through the North American dominant culture where the theories evolved and group counseling was practiced (Frew & Spiegler, 2013). Therefore, most models stress individuality, freedom, personal choice, and autonomy, which are a big part of many Western cultures. Imagine, however, how inappropriate these models are for other cultures with very different value systems that stress cooperation, codependence, and subjugation of individual needs over those of the larger community (e.g., Native American, Latino/a, African, Asian). In such cultures, issues such as personal responsibility are less meaningful than collective responsibility. For this reason, all the previous theories must be adapted to the specific population you are working with and the special culture of the group's members.

In contemporary practice, most theories have undergone some type of revision or adaptation to reveal some of the biases and to acknowledge how the models can be tailored to work with people representing a wide range of cultural identities. Granted, some theories (e.g., relational–cultural theory, narrative theory) were developed as alternatives to traditional approaches. Regardless of whether the theory itself has been adapted, it is the group leader who uses the theory to make sense of the group and then applies interventions to create change. Importantly, best practices in group work note that group leaders are able to articulate a conceptual framework to guide their practice and techniques (Thomas & Pender, 2008). Further, as we previously mentioned, the group leader must be culturally aware of personal biases and theoretical biases to enact the theory in a culturally responsive manner (Singh, Merchant, Skudrzyk, & Ingene, 2012).

Why Bother With Theories?

If it is true (don't take our word for it—ask group leaders in the field) that most group practitioners do not practice theories in their pure form, and if the approaches are often diluted, adapted, and integrated into others, why do you need to bother to learn this stuff at all?

As a result of your thoughtful reflection on and discussion of this matter, you likely realize that a theoretical grounding in the major approaches gives you some options for the ways you can proceed in any situation. Knowledge of the main theories provides a compass for understanding what could be happening with group members, and, importantly, theories provide a map or direction to help members meet their goals. Once you understand the history of the field, the ways various ideas and leadership styles evolved, then you can make some informed choices about which approaches might be best for which clients and contexts. Moreover, before you can integrate the best parts of theories into an organized framework you can follow, you must first be aware of which options are available.

As a beginning group leader, you would be well advised to stick with the basics about group dynamics/group development presented in the earlier chapters, plus the selection of one theoretical model to follow. As for which theory you should select, that often depends on the following:

1. *Your professional identity:* Some professions are more closely identified with particular models. Social workers leading hospital inpatient groups will choose a different approach than will family therapists doing couple enrichment groups.

2. *The needs of your clients:* Elementary school students, adults suffering from chronic pain, or those experiencing alcohol and drug problems will respond better to some approaches than to others.

3. *The guidance of your instructors and supervisors:* Your teachers and mentors will help you narrow the choices down to those they think are most appropriate for your situation. You may find that your instructors and supervisors are good models for practice, and so, initially, you may want to be like them. Because your instructors and supervisors are your introduction into the field of group work, they will offer you a good starting point.

4. *Your own felt sense:* Pay attention to which theories seem most attractive to you and which seem less interesting. Each theory has its own philosophy, values, goals, and strategies that will strike you as more or less compatible with your own beliefs. Also, be well aware that you will most likely change your preferred theory or model as your experience grows and you learn more about yourself as a group leader or helping professional. Your decision now is not set in stone.

For a Class Activity

In general, study groups are excellent structures to help you master complex ideas. Each participant takes responsibility for providing expertise in a particular area. Peer support provides needed encouragement. All members are able to pitch in to help one another understand difficult concepts. Most of all, study groups make learning fun!

If you have not already done so, it would be a good idea to team up with several classmates to learn the theory basics contained in this chapter. There is just not enough time in class, or space in this text, to cover all the material you will need to know. We are not talking about stuff you should know for any exam; far more important, you must understand these theories to function effectively in your leadership efforts.

Even if time is limited and you are overloaded with other commitments, it would be worthwhile to form a study group for a short time to talk about the theories in this chapter. Even if you can meet only a few times, you could still talk to one another about points of confusion, areas of interest, and personal applications. Ideally, each of you could take responsibility for summarizing a few of the theories, directing others to additional sources for further study.

In the following sections, you will be introduced to the basic concepts of several major theoretical approaches to group leadership. Concentrate on the "broad strokes" rather than the finer details you can pick up through more intensive study.

The Psychoanalytic Approach

Like most of the theories you will read about, the psychoanalytic or psychody-namic approach (so named because of its attention to *intrapsychic* or internal struggles) evolved originally as a form of individual therapy. We are covering this theory first because it has had such a powerful influence on all the other approaches.

REVIEW OF BASIC ASSUMPTIONS

You will recall that Sigmund Freud and his followers developed a theory that helped people investigate past experiences that continue to exert an influence over present behavior. For example, if someone is inappropriately hostile toward a teacher, it might be theorized that some sort of "transference" is going on in which injustices inflicted on this individual by authority figures in the past are clouding current perceptions (Jacobs, 2010; Safran, 2012). Perhaps you can imagine how easily a dynamic such as this might play itself out in a group in which people are constantly responding to one another not as they really are but as they imagine one another to be.

For Reflection or a Class Activity

Record the names of your classmates in a column down the side of a page. Next to each of their names, write how that person reminds you of someone else you have known (maybe this classmate looks, acts, or talks a bit the same). If you find yourself drawing a blank for someone, just skip that person; alternately, you can take a wild guess and list someone who bears a passing similarity in some trait.

During private reflection, or a discussion with others, explore the challenges of developing relationships with people when there is so much distortion going on. What are some ways you can see people more clearly as they present themselves, rather than as you perceive them through your perceptual filters?

You have probably had some exposure to other Freudian ideas that are important in therapeutic relationships. In this type of group, attention is directed toward deeper processes, exploring underlying needs and desires rather than surface-expressed goals and presented symptoms. Rather than solving immediate problems, there is more emphasis on making the unconscious conscious and changing one's personality and character (Rutan et al., 2007). There is also an interest in uncovering core issues of abandonment, emptiness, intimacy, and achievement that are grounded in early experiences.

The unconscious is an area of considerable focus in this theory. The unconscious represents the part of the mind that is out of awareness but that was classically theorized to serve as the driving force of repressed impulses. Contemporary psychoanalytic theory views the unconscious as being a repository of unformulated expectations of other people (Altman, 2013; Safran, 2012). Regardless of these two ideas, people are motivated not only by conscious intentions but also by forces beyond their awareness that are most likely associated with infant or childhood needs, drives, and desires. This means that group members will do and say things that, at first, appear to make little sense in light of their stated desires. A woman proclaims, for instance, that what she wants more than anything is a lasting, intimate relationship. It has been apparent to everyone, however, that when she is presented with viable opportunities to realize this goal, she inadvertently sabotages the relationship and chases the person away. Unconscious influences may be operating here in which, beneath her awareness, she is so terrified of intimacy that she is actually seeking to protect herself.

In the previous example, we see a manifestation of something psychodynamic theorists call *defense mechanisms*, which is a term you surely have heard before. According to this approach, core threats are kept at bay through the use of characteristic strategies that act as buffers to ward off perceived attacks. Defense mechanisms, when working well, protect people and can be understood as functional. However, defense mechanisms break down at times and become overwhelmed due to anxiety and stress, and in these situations they can do more harm than good (Jacobs, 2010; Safran, 2012). You will see the following defenses in action many times in groups (or in any social situation):

- *Denial:* A group member has been told repeatedly that every time there is conflict in the group, he works to diffuse it, acting as a rescuer. He vehemently denies that this is his intent, claiming he is just trying to help others. What you know about his past, however, is that he came from a home where there was a high degree of conflict that he found so intolerable he ran away as a teenager.

- *Projection:* "You seem so angry today. Must have had a tough day, huh?" Actually, the person being addressed is quite puzzled since she did not have a difficult day; on the contrary, she had a pretty good day. Furthermore, she does not feel so much angry as misunderstood. After exploring the situation further, we find that the first speaker is the one who is feeling upset about something that happened at work, and he projected those unacceptable feelings onto someone else.

- *Rationalization:* "It's really no big deal. I decided a while ago that I wouldn't even want to go to college. I don't know why we are even talking about this." It hurts too much, of course, to admit to failure. An alternative defense that employs a type of intellectualizing denial is one in which the person seeks to disown the hurt by explaining things away.

- *Reaction formation:* You happen to know for a fact that one group member absolutely despises everything that another member stands for in terms of lifestyle and basic values. Yet in the group, you notice that he goes to extreme lengths to appear overly conciliatory and cooperative with this person. As in the previous defenses, a person may push down threatening feelings by overcompensating in opposite ways to those expected.

Given more space, we could review other defenses, as well as other important psychodynamic concepts. But you can get a taste for how this sort of group would operate from the following principles:

1. The focus of attention is on understanding how past experiences affect current behavior.

2. Under the leader's guidance, members seek to increase awareness of their characteristic defenses and unconscious motives.

3. Dreams and other unconscious material are used to access feelings and experiences beyond awareness.

4. Groups are of a relatively long duration, helping members develop the degree of safety and support required to explore long-standing patterns.

5. Intrapsychic (internal) and interpersonal tensions play a large role in the group as members attempt to sort out their reactions to past experiences and one another's behavior.

6. Insight plays a huge role. The focus is much more on understanding oneself, and one's interactions with others, than on translating this awareness into action.

WHAT DO YOU DO WITH THIS STUFF?

Assuming that you see some validity in these ideas, you might wonder how to use them in practice. As with most groups, the leader's job is to create a safe and supportive climate that makes it possible to explore frightening ideas and experiment with risky behavior. Since these types of groups aspire to go deeper than most others, cohesion is even more important.

Psychodynamic groups are often designed as relatively long-term—lasting more than a few months and sometimes even years. As you can imagine, it takes quite a while to develop the level of trust needed for people to willingly explore their deepest, most repressed issues. Also, because these groups are after characterological changes rather than only symptomatic relief, considerable time is needed to produce this sort of transformation.

Group leaders often endeavor to present themselves as "neutral" and objective so as to maximize transference opportunities that could be worked through when members "project" their authority issues onto the leader. Exploring transference becomes a focal point of group intervention (Rutan et al., 2007). In line with the concept of the social microcosm (Yalom & Leszcz, 2005), group members re-create their social interactions in the group, thus providing an in vivo experience of how they relive past relationships (often with parents and siblings) unconsciously in the present. Exploring transference allows group members to see how their past relationships come alive in the present and often obstruct their well-being (Jacobs, 2010). Needless to say, it is also critical for group leaders to monitor their own "countertransference" reactions (those personal reactions directed toward members) that might distort or impede therapeutic work. The leader works to project a positive and warm model as a way to create a supportive atmosphere within the group.

Interpretation of individual as well as group behavior is often used in group to bring repressed material into awareness and to support the creation of insight. It was observed in one group, for instance, that rather lengthy silences occurred after one member, Kathryn, confronted another, Toby, about behavior she found irritating. Rather than responding, Toby withdrew (his normal defense). Other group members brought this to Toby's attention as characteristic of what he had previously recalled doing in childhood when his parents censured him. Couldn't it be possible, they ventured, that he was responding to Kathryn the way he had to his mother?

To complicate matters further, Kathryn had her own issues brought into play. Her reaction to Toby seemed way out of proportion to his alleged transgression. Group members went to work on her as well, until the leader intervened and offered this observation:

It seems to me that many of you are working very hard to keep the focus on this disagreement between Toby and Kathryn as a way to prevent any attention being directed toward yourselves. Mandy, is this not the exact scenario you said used to happen at your dinner table all the time? You mentioned how you would keep everyone from getting into your stuff by keeping the focus on others.

These interpretations, by members and the leader, are typical of a group that sees its primary mission as increasing awareness of self and others by addressing unresolved past issues. While traditionally such a group structure would take many months or years to operate effectively, more recent psychodynamic group structures have been designed to work more efficiently (Rutan et al., 2007).

It could be said that almost all other theories are offshoots of psychoanalytic thinking, because it really was the first therapeutic approach. There are several distinct models, however, that are now becoming far more popular than traditional psychoanalytic groups because of their greater responsiveness to contemporary life. Object relations groups represent one such approach, originally developed by Heinz Kohut (1971) and Otto Kernberg (1975) to work with those manifesting extreme personality disorders. One of the core goals is helping members learn other ways to respond to primitive fears (Ganzarain, 2008). These groups were designed to maintain strict boundaries, consistent norms, and a "holding environment" conducive to feeling safe. Object relations theory has been applied in group settings for complicated grief (Piper, Ogrodniczuk, & Sierra-Hernandez, 2014) and trauma (Klein & Schermer, 2000).

Given more space, Adlerian group therapy would be at least as deserving as others of more detailed treatment. It is not strictly a psychodynamic approach even though its inventor, Alfred Adler, was once a colleague of Freud's—the one, in fact, who most adapted the theory for group situations. In fact, Adler was one of the first to run therapeutic counseling groups (Hoffman, 1994). Whereas Freud looked primarily at the biological basis for human behavior, Adler examined social roots.

Like other approaches we will cover later, the Adlerian group is viewed as a psychoeducational environment in which members examine the ways their early family experiences are affecting their current relationships. Adlerian theory focuses on relationships, and the concept of social embeddedness is central to understanding why people do what they do. The group setting just extends the natural experiences that happen in the family environment, among peers, and in the larger community. The benefit of Adlerian groups is seeing that social embeddedness in the here and now, among other group members. Sonstegard, Bitter, and Pelonis (2004) outlined a four-stage model (forming, psychological investigation, psychological disclosure, and reorientation) for group development that mirrors the traditional Adlerian model of therapeutic work.

In contrast to the psychoanalytic approach, however, this model is concerned far more with the present than with the past, an emphasis on action over insight alone, being integrative rather than exclusive in its selection of techniques, and feeling a sense of belonging in the group (Carlson & Englar-Carlson, 2013). Furthermore, Adlerian group work encourages group members to grow by providing concrete strategies to cope with problem situations.

The Person-Centered Approach

With all his contributions to therapy and counseling, Carl Rogers was first and foremost a group specialist. He believed that group settings, with their climate of support, cohesiveness, acceptance, and caring, were the perfect environment for change to take place (Rogers, 1970). Rogers believed that if a group leader could create a place of safety for participants where an atmosphere of genuineness and empathy prevailed, members would grow and learn at their maximum potential. Furthermore, Rogers believed that people could learn from organizing themselves rather than being organized (Cain, 2010).

Certainly you have heard about (or can remember) the encounter group movement of the 1960s. The idea was that groups could be structured for almost everyone such that they could encounter one another in honest and authentic ways. In that protected space, group members could relate to one another in real ways that would help them cultivate their actualizing tendencies toward differentiation, growth, and autonomy. Unfortunately, because little was known at that time about how to prevent casualties and because little training was available for leaders, many people were wounded by these experiences. Nowadays, person-centered groups are designed according to the same guidelines as any other professional group experience that fosters growth; that is, the protection of people from coercion and harm is a foremost concern.

BASIC PRINCIPLES

Person-centered groups are probably more familiar to you than you imagine, because they have been depicted in films and television as the classic group experience in which people sit around a circle and share their feelings with one another. In reality, this limited vision simplifies a complex model. There is much more at work during these groups. Some of the guiding concepts of a person-centered group are listed below:

1. *Feelings are the core focus.* The previous group models we examined place a great emphasis on the intellect and reasoning powers. The person-centered approach, in contrast, sees the understanding and expression of feelings as the most legitimate focus of work. If an individual were to say, "My best friend ignored me," the psychoanalytic group would explore the deeper meaning in this statement with regard to past issues, fears of abandonment, family-of-origin issues, and so on. In a person-centered group, however, members would instead help the person explore more deeply his sense of hurt, anger, betrayal, and confusion as a way to become more congruent with his inner self and his experience of being ignored (Cain, 2010, 2013). They would help him feel heard and understood. They would validate those feelings, resonate with his experience, and perhaps join him in his struggle by sharing similar examples from their own lives. Most important, they would let him know that he is not alone.

2. *Relationships are everything.* It is through the relationships among members that growth, learning, and healing take place. The content about which people speak, the issues they raise, and the subjects they discuss are far less important than the bonding that takes place among members. The leader models this type of connection as much as possible by demonstrating in his or her own relationships with participants the same qualities that he or she would like to see others develop. Person-centered leaders are thus warm and accessible, as opposed to the more objective, detached posture of a psychoanalytic leader. They present themselves as authentic, transparent, honest, and genuine as much as possible, hoping that these qualities will become contagious in the group (Mearns, Thorne, & McLeod, 2013).

3. *Growth is as important as remediation.* Although many other models concentrate their efforts on fixing problems and alleviating symptoms, the person-centered theory is growth oriented. It seeks to help anyone, regardless of present functioning, reach greater potential.

4. *It is all about trust.* The conditions of high-functioning groups are designed to encourage a degree of openness and honesty not possible in other settings. Imagine there is a place where you can say whatever you want without fear of being judged or criticized. In a person-centered group, trust and openness create a setting where members can move

their locus of evaluation within the self so that they learn to value themselves rather than looking toward others to gauge their value. When the locus of evaluation rests within the self, one's personal experience becomes the criterion on which one assesses personal value (Cain, 2010, 2013).

5. *Being real is a must.* The hallmark of a person-centered group is the attention to immediacy. This means being aware of what you are feeling in the present moment and being willing to express those genuine feelings aloud. Obviously, it takes a lot of courage and trust to do such a thing.

6. *Active listening and responding are emphasized.* The person-centered approach to helping is most known for its skills geared to reflect others' feelings. The group leader models this behavior as much as possible, letting group members know that they are being heard and understood at the deepest possible level. It might sound something like this:

Sueanne: I can't seem to figure out what's wrong exactly. It's all kinda muddled in my head, like it's . . . I don't know.

Leader: You're feeling so confused about everything you've been saying that it's hard to sort out what is most important. It's also really scary for you that you don't feel in control.

Simon: Yeah! That's it for me, too, Sueanne. I mean, as I was listening to you talk and all, I was feeling confused, too. Not about what you were saying so much, but about something that has been going on in my life as well that I don't understand.

Leader: Simon, you're feeling relieved in a way to know that you aren't the only one who is so confused. And, Sueanne, I can see by your face that something that Simon said really hit home with you. I wonder if you could talk to him about what is happening for you right now.

You can see quite easily how this person-centered leader is trying to keep members in the present, focused on their feelings, and is facilitating their deep communication with one another. The leader is using active listening, or reflection of feeling, to encourage this process.

7. *Facilitation is the focus.* Rogers believed that anything worth learning cannot be taught. Whether in the role of therapist, counselor, teacher, or parent, he felt strongly that our job is to help people teach themselves. As such, the leader's role is seen as "nondirective," which really means subtle

rather than controlling. A core concept behind this is promoting the freedom of group members to choose what will be addressed, how it will be addressed, and when and how members will make decisions to change.

8. *Members explore conditions of worth.* People may engage in certain behaviors depending on whether they result in regard from another person or a group. Rogers believed that seeking the approval of others resulted in learning that one's value is associated with the attainment of regard from others, to the point that one learns to disregard whether or not the behavior is healthy or beneficial. Group settings provide constant situations where approval seeking from others is present. This allows the group members to explore how and why they seek approval from others, and how it may lead them further away from self-directed needs and growth.

For a Class Activity

This is among the most challenging and risky of all experiential activities in this book. It is not for the timid, and it is not for anyone who does not feel ready for such an intense, authentic encounter with others. Keep in mind, however, that you do not want to ask others to do anything that you are not willing to try yourself. If you are not yet willing to "volunteer" to be open and honest with others, consider what it would take for you to arrive at that point.

Arrange yourselves in small groups with your chairs pressed together as close as you can. Take a few minutes and make eye contact with everyone in the group. Do not speak. Resist the urge to laugh. Do not whisper. Keep your attention focused completely on the eyes of each member in your group.

As you make contact with each person, note how you feel inside. Pay attention to the various reactions you have to each person, the complexity of sensations and awarenesses. Tune into the dialogue inside your head as well, but concentrate mostly on your primary feelings.

After everyone has had a chance to connect with eyes alone, begin speaking to one another about your feelings and reactions. You must follow these rules: (1) Preface what you say with the stem, "I feel . . ." or "I am aware of . . ."; (2) do not talk about what is happening, only what you are experiencing in the moment; (3) be respectful, caring, and sensitive in what you communicate; and (4) be real and genuine.

After several minutes of this encounter, talk about what it was like for you. Mention the aspects you found most uncomfortable, as well as the parts you enjoyed. Talk about how you can incorporate this "way of being" into your life.

You may have your doubts whether such behavior in the group necessarily leads to permanent change outside the group, and this skepticism is a reasonable caution. A person-centered group (or any group, for that matter) is most effective when the leader does make sure that participants generalize what they are learning in group to their lives in the outside world. Furthermore, many of the theoretical underpinnings of the person-centered approach (e.g., development of the therapeutic relationship, promoting client recourses, unconditional positive regard, therapeutic empathy) have been empirically supported as the components of effective psychotherapy (Wampold, 2010). Furthermore, these concepts also form the core of effective work with diverse populations.

The Existential Approach

The person-centered approach, the existential approach, and the Gestalt approach (to be covered next) are all considered to be part of the larger family of existential–humanistic theories. These models are primarily concerned with helping people find meaning in their lives and with making their internal worlds consistent with their experiences of the outside world. Of course, in one sense, *every* group is existential to the extent that it helps its members explore issues related to personal responsibility, isolation, meaninglessness, and mortality. Furthermore, most groups focus on members' relating to one another in the moment. Yet the existential approach specifically focuses on a healthy awareness of life goals and a clear understanding of meaning in life (Schneider & Krug, 2010).

BASIC PHILOSOPHY

Perhaps more than any other theorist, Viktor Frankl (1963) embodied existential philosophy when he wrote about the survival strategies employed in Nazi concentration camps. Here was a group environment so toxic, so filled with hopelessness that people literally died of despair; they simply gave up. Frankl tried to create some meaning in his experience, some reason to live, even if it was only to tell the world about what he witnessed. He constructed a form of therapy that attempted a similar path—to help people find meaning in their suffering.

Borrowing from the work of existential philosophers and building on the early work of existential therapists, Bugental (1978, 1990), Yalom (1980), and Yalom and Leszcz (2005) have been among the most responsible for translating existential ideas to the practice of group work. Many of the core group texts in the field (including this one) are existentially based as well, helping students develop an appreciation for complex issues related to finding personal meaning. One of the reasons so many groups adopt this model is its emphasis on providing group members with conditions that maximize self-awareness and reduce blocks to personal growth. Furthermore, a core tenet of existential therapy is working in the present moment, or the here and now, and group work provides a perfect setting for that type of goal.

USES OF THE EXISTENTIAL APPROACH

Group members will often come to the group setting with specific symptoms or problems in need of attention, be they in the form of addictions, failed relationships, anxiety, or other dysfunctional behaviors. Others will present issues that do not lend themselves to easy resolution, or they may have complaints you cannot do much about. Imagine, for instance, individuals who have a terminal or chronic disease. An existential group focus seems especially appropriate when the members can profit from making sense of their existence rather than necessarily initiating specific courses of action. In that sense, the focus moves to *being* among group members and being aware of the present, rather than being told to just do something different. Like the person-centered or psychoanalytic approach, this is an insight theory, one that follows the premise that people should be challenged to reflect on their lives, where they have been, where they are headed, and, most of all, where they are now (Yalom & Leszcz, 2005).

The existential approach often focuses on certain core themes. As a leader, when you hear the group talking about, or around, these issues, you can be relatively certain that existential themes are at work (Schneider & Krug, 2010; Yalom, 1980):

- *Self-awareness*: Being aware of the present, noting that nothing exists except the now, to the extent that when you are living the past or future you are not fully alive. Group members may talk about trying to become more aware of the here and now.
- *Isolation:* Being alone is terrifying for most people, and thus they crave connections with others; yet many people cannot create satisfying relationships. Learning self-awareness helps people get in touch with the self and who they are, which ultimately lays the foundation for better relationships. Most people spend their lives seeking intimacy and trying to connect, but we all must ultimately confront our aloneness. It is that

confrontation and acknowledgment that enables us to create more meaningful relationships.

- *Meaninglessness:* Meaning is often pursued indirectly in life. It is a by-product of life, love, and general engagement with others, but it must also be sought specifically throughout one's lifetime in light of new experiences and making sense of the world. Many people fear looking within for meaning and finding nothing. A crucial aspect of the existential approach is not describing meaning but, rather, the process of courageously seeking to make sense of the universe and one's place in it. One of the paradoxes of meaninglessness is the question, "How does a being who requires meaning find meaning in a universe that has no meaning?"
- *Freedom:* Each person must make choices each day. Making decisions can be terrifying, and many people fear making bad decisions and, thus, choose not to choose. In that situation, people turn their backs on freedom and the need to lead a purposeful life. Choosing not to choose is often a source of anxiety.
- *Angst and anxiety:* Angst and anxiety are often the consequence of dealing with existential issues. Because many of these themes are scary and force us to face our life and existence head-on, it is not surprising that we do not address them.
- *Personal responsibility:* Existential theory promotes the notion that we are not victims in life but, rather, responsible for the choices we make and don't make. We are therefore responsible for our lives and for making decisions.
- *Death:* One certainty about living is dying—each of us will die. Existentialists note that when one thinks about death, one must also think about living and life. Death is often terrifying to confront, yet the process of exploring death is often what makes us most alive in the present.

When can participants profit from greater self-awareness? It is often when they are struggling to find some purpose in their lives, when they must create some meaning from their suffering, when they are perhaps unable to change conditions outside their control (e.g., disease, poverty, oppression, age) that existential issues come to the forefront. Group members are also thrust into the existential realm when they have *boundary experiences* (e.g., losses, traumas, close calls).

The concept of self-awareness is as true for the group leader as it is for the participants, because this is an approach that requires a high degree of authenticity and humanness on the part of the helper. This means being aware of your own struggles and exploring them as they arise.

Student Voice

Exploring Death and Loss

Early on in group, one of the group members lost her aunt and talked about being at her death bed and then attending the funeral. I felt sad for her, but beyond the feeling, I basically had a sense of paralysis. I have not experienced death in my life and have been relatively shielded from thinking about it. We spent the whole group time talking about death, and it freaked me out! The leader kept us focused on the topic, and many members talked about losing their parents and friends and how it changed their lives. But not me—I was quiet and withdrawn from the group that day, but inside I was churning. I was really unsettled that whole week, and next week one of the group members checked in by stating that he was worried about me last week. So I faced some of my fears and began to talk about how scary death is to me. I cried a lot that day but felt really supported. I was not alone in the room—others admitted also to being scared, and by the end I was actually feeling a bit more energized. That night I called my parents and for the first time spoke about being afraid of them dying. That was a tough, but amazing, phone call. Next time I saw my mom I hugged her like never before.

EXISTENTIAL GROUP IN ACTION

Groups become existential when members explore core issues of personal meaning. Almost anything can push conversation down such a path—loss of control, restriction of personal freedom, reluctance to accept responsibility, feelings of isolation, or the recent death of a close friend.

Aron: I don't know. It's just so hard to accept the idea that he's gone. And it was all so sudden. It could happen to any of us at any time.

Ned: [Laughs] Not me. I'm going to live forever!

Carole: Hey, if you're talking immortality, don't forget to include me, too.

Leader: I notice that it's hard to stay with Aron and his grief, not to mention the issues he's raised. Anyone notice something interesting that just happened?

Pam: Sure. As soon as Aron reminded us that we could all die at any moment, Ned and Carole started joking around, trying to defuse the subject because it's so scary.

Leader: What about that, guys? [Long silence.]

Aron: I don't mean to bum y'all out or anything by talking about this stuff. It's just that I'm kind of blown away. This friend of mine had so much to look forward to, and then . . . wham! . . . snatched just like that. It's really got me thinking about my own priorities. I'm wondering about whether I want to keep doing the things I'm doing with my life. Is that all really that important? Maybe I ought to be doing things a bit differently.

Leader: How about the rest of you? What has this stirred up in you?

When groups take an existential turn, members become reflective and deeply personal. They talk about the directions their lives have taken and what they can do to make different choices.

For Personal Application

Imagine that you have just been told you have a terminal illness and only a few months left to live. What will you do differently with the time you have left? What unfinished business do you need to complete before you die? What choices will you make to live your life more fully, to experience more love and excitement and tranquility? What will you do to extract every precious moment from your limited time left on this planet?

In fact, you do have a terminal illness. And you are dying this moment as your heart and body slowly wear out. You may not die in a few months, or even a few years, but each second is taking you closer and closer to your own mortality. What do you resolve to do in light of this fact?

Talk to others about your resolutions, committing yourself to more intense engagement with your own existence.

The Gestalt Approach

Like the person-centered approach, Gestalt counseling was seemingly born for group settings. Like the existential approach, Gestalt groups are concerned with issues related to freedom and responsibility, especially in the present moment. Yet, whereas in the previous theories members often talk about their concerns, Gestalt groups are specifically, intensely action oriented around experiencing freedom and responsibility (Wheeler & Axelsson, 2015).

Fritz Perls, the founder of the Gestalt approach, was vigorously anti-intellectual. Like most therapists of his day, he was trained as a psychoanalyst. And like so many of his brethren, he found this theory to be restrictive and not at all suited to his personality and style. Perls enjoyed being dramatic and provocative, and he often found group settings to be the ideal stage to perform. He was not as concerned with the past as with the present. An existentialist at heart, he cared deeply about the ways people attempted to escape the present.

Over the past 30 years, group work has remained a constant for many Gestalt group practitioners. However, the practice has seen less of an emphasis on some of the radical experiential techniques and more use of blended approaches that draw on intrapersonal, interpersonal, and systems-level interventions. Gestalt group practitioners continue to see group support as the most important curative factor in current Gestalt therapy (Feder, Frew, & Burley, 2006). Yet the main focus of Gestalt work is noticing and developing opportunities for greater awareness and change for group members (Schoenberg, Feder, Frew, & Gadol, 2005).

GESTALT PRINCIPLES

Gestalt means a sense of wholeness, an integration of the various parts of self (Wheeler & Axelsson, 2015). According to the theory, people become fragmented in contemporary life, pulled in so many different directions that they lose their sense of being grounded. They escape the present with forms of self-medication, avoid responsibility for their lives, become cut off from their essential wants and needs, and feel disconnected from the community of others. Gestalt group work is then focused on putting meaning back into life and becoming more whole by bringing to awareness the shadow or hidden side of each person.

Gestalt practitioners follow several basic procedures:

1. They keep the focus of the group in the present.

2. Instead of delving into why people do the things they do (most people don't know, and this keeps them in the past), attention is directed to "how" and "what" questions.

3. Self-awareness is paramount. This is the most experiential of all groups in that participants are urged to become actively involved in interactions and "experiments" and then report on what they sense and feel (but not think).

4. Enactments and role-playing help members become more aware of their inconsistencies and unfinished business.

5. Certain language patterns that reflect avoidance of responsibility are confronted. Members are asked to substitute "I won't" for "I can't," "I choose to" for "I should," and "I" for "you." In each case, the emphasis is on personal responsibility.

GESTALT TECHNIQUES

Compared with other group approaches, Gestalt therapy comes loaded with a bigger bag of tricks, filled with clever and powerful exercises designed to help members experience themselves and others more fully. Various exercises are introduced that help group members explore their fantasies, speak to their opposite selves, act spontaneously, increase awareness, work through dreams, and develop greater intimacy. For example, the technique of the empty chair is designed to help members work through unfinished business. In this technique, a member uses an empty chair to approximate the person with whom the unfinished business exists. The group member then speaks to the chair or sits opposite the chair to role-play an interaction with that person. With all techniques, but especially Gestalt techniques that are focused on revealing hidden parts, group leaders do need experience in applying skills of timely and intentional choices, and of creative, yet appropriate, interventions (Schoenberg et al., 2005).

Because it is somewhat incongruent to talk about Gestalt theory instead of experiencing it firsthand (remember, its essence is primary experience), the best way to learn about it is to try out some of the techniques yourself.

For a Class Activity or Field Study

One favorite Gestalt method is called the "hot seat," so named because it turns up the heat for those who are willing to risk being completely honest with themselves and others. This is also an exercise useful for those who are first learning to use open-ended questions—those that require elaboration about deeply personal issues.

The rules are deceptively simple. Each group member takes a turn, on a volunteer basis, to answer any question that others might ask. The intent is to build intimacy and cohesion rather rapidly by moving beyond small talk to the most personal aspects of human experience. The other group members construct questions that are designed to facilitate deep exploration. We like to introduce it this way: Imagine that you can ask this person only one question, and based on the answer you hear, you must give a 20-minute talk on the essence of who this person is.

Whether at a family gathering or social situation or in any group, you can imagine how quickly intimacy and trust will develop. Try it for yourself. Here are a few of our favorite questions to get you started:

1. What are you most proud of in your life?

2. What are you most ashamed of?

3. When was the last time you cried? Describe what happened and how you felt afterward.

4. When was the last time you felt out of control?

5. What is something that nobody in the world knows about you?

6. Which question are you most afraid I might ask? (Answer it.)

The object of this exercise is not to be intrusive or nosy. It is designed to help you practice getting to know someone in an efficient period of time, and it helps the volunteers work on issues related to self-acceptance.

We have observed that students tend to either love the Gestalt approach or hate it; it is hard to feel neutral about a method that is so provocative, so dedicated to stirring things up to work through them. It is likely that even if you do not find the theory suitable for the type of work you intend to do, you will still use a lot of its techniques in whichever groups you lead.

The Cognitive Behavioral Approach

Over the past three decades, cognitive behavioral therapy (CBT) has become a widely used and effective treatment for a variety of different concerns that can be addressed in a group setting. This theory is far more action oriented, more logical and analytic, more focused on problem solving, and more geared toward teaching specific, adaptive skills. This may very well appeal to those group leaders who will be doing relatively short-term groups in a psychoeducational format, such as the kind favored by school counselors and substance abuse therapists. Among some of the strengths of CBT in group are a well-developed theoretical model, a strong research base for clinical effectiveness, and the availability of many treatment manuals that provide structures for problem-focused groups (Bieling, McCabe, & Antony, 2006). Cognitive behavioral groups have specifically been applied to a wide range of problems and situations, such as early psychosis (Chung, Yoon, Park, Yang, & Oh, 2013), hoarding disorder (Gilliam et al., 2011), social anxiety disorder (Hope, Burns, Hayes, Herbert, & Warner, 2010), insomnia (Castronovo et al., 2011), menopausal symptoms (Green, Haber, McCabe, & Soares, 2013), breast cancer (Cohen & Fried, 2007), posttraumatic stress disorder (Sloan, Bovin, & Schnurr, 2012), helping spouses of stroke patients develop coping skills (Wilz & Barskova, 2007), panic disorder (Wesner et al., 2014), social phobia (McEvoy, Nathan, Rapee, & Campbell, 2012), and depression in adolescents (Hunter, Witkiewitz, Watkins, Paddock, & Hepner, 2012) and adults (Sudak, 2012).

Rather than a single intervention, CBT is a combination of behavioral interventions that stem from learning theory and a set of behavioral and cognitive interventions that stem from cognitive theory. Whereas several of the previous theories have valued feelings and experience as the most legitimate sources for group attention, this approach works on underlying thinking and behavioral patterns. CBT recognizes both the effects of learned associations among stimuli and reinforcement contingencies (i.e., the behavioral side) and the effects on functioning of cognition and styles of information processing (i.e., the cognitive side). The interventions that form CBT share the common aim of replacing maladaptive with more adaptive patterns of behaving, thinking, and emoting. This is achieved, in essence, by creating new learning experiences and by teaching coping skills (Craske, 2010). One of the foundational assumptions from this theory is that people experience emotional suffering not because of what happens to them but because of how they choose to interpret those events. Of course our choices are influenced by deep-seated cognitive structures and core beliefs that construct our filters for seeing the world. It is our thinking patterns that determine how we feel rather than the event itself.

UNDERLYING ASSUMPTIONS

Rather than speaking about one approach, this section refers to a family of theories that share similar underlying assumptions. Whether they are called rational emotive behavior groups (Dryden & Neenan, 2002; Ellis & Ellis, 2011) or cognitive behavioral groups (Bieling et al., 2006; Christner, Stewart, & Freeman, 2007; Craske, 2010; McEvoy, 2007), the intent is essentially the same: Teach group members to become more aware of their dysfunctional thinking and how to substitute alternative strategies that produce more desirable outcomes and behaviors.

In this approach, it is believed that if people learn to think differently, they will feel and behave differently. If, for instance, a group member thinks to himself, "I've been disrespected by this guy in the group," he will likely feel angry and upset and may then act aggressively toward that other guy. If, on the other hand, he thinks, "I've been misunderstood," then he will feel only mildly annoyed, and he may then try to clarify the misunderstanding. The goal of this approach is to help people choose the way they want to feel, which is a powerful enticement for most people.

BASIC STRUCTURE

CBT assumes that patterns of cognitive, behavioral, and emotional responding can be modified through the principles of reinforcement, weakening of conditioned associations between stimuli, self-efficacy, and cognitive reappraisal.

Emphasis given to specific mechanisms varies, highlighting primarily changes in patterns of reinforcement and learned associations, or changes in appraisals. This variation influences subtleties in the ways cognitive and behavioral intervention strategies are implemented. For example, a more behaviorally oriented clinician will view exposure therapy as a primary vehicle for extinction of associations, whereas a more cognitively oriented clinician will view exposure therapy as a vehicle for providing information that disconfirms misappraisals (Craske, 2010). Cognitive-behaviorally oriented groups are often structured around a teaching model in which participants learn sound principles of working through emotional struggles and then applying the concepts to specific problems in their lives as a way to modify their behavior and emotional reactions. The leader acts as a teacher who, after introducing basic ideas, coaches group members to help one another dispute their irrational beliefs and reason through alternative ways of thinking about their situations.

IRRATIONAL BELIEFS

According to CBT, people get in trouble when they adopt certain thinking patterns that are not considered a part of reality. These patterns represent distortions, exaggerations, and faulty logic (Ellis & Ellis, 2011). Here are several of the most common ones:

1. *Life is not fair.* This is irrational because the world clearly is not a fair place where everyone gets exactly what they deserve.

2. *This is terrible.* People tend to exaggerate what they have experienced, believing it is truly awful, rather than annoying or disappointing, that they did not get what they wanted or expected.

3. *I can't stand it.* A corollary to the previous irrational belief, this one represents the idea that your situation is far worse than it really is. It may seem so bad that you cannot stand it, but, actually, you can tolerate anything except death.

4. *I must do well.* People also make absolute demands of themselves (and others) that cannot possibly be attained. Nobody can do as well as he or she expects in every situation.

Whether operating in individual, family, or group settings, as the leader, you would sensitize yourself to recognize these signs of underlying distorted thinking, bring them to the client's attention, and help challenge their validity.

DISPUTING BELIEFS

Cognitive behavioral groups tend to be fairly confrontational settings in which members are challenged by the leader and others to examine what they are saying to themselves internally and then to learn alternative interpretations of their situation. This process can unfold in a somewhat unstructured manner in which members bring up issues and then learn the method as it is applied to the situation, or they can follow a far more structured program. Group members are taught to identify their own irrational beliefs and actively dispute them through strategies such as asking what the evidence is for a particular belief (e.g., "What is the evidence that one must be perfect?"). In addition, they are taught logical disputation (e.g., "Does it follow that if I want to do well, I *have* to do well?"); pragmatic or heuristic disputing (e.g., "Where will it get me if I keep demanding that others do what I want instead of just preferring that they do?"); changing *musts, oughts,* and *shoulds* to preferences; and setting goals without raising them to unattainable and illogical demands (Craske, 2010; Ellis & Ellis, 2011).

Some cognitive behavioral groups proceed according to a series of "lesson plans" in which the first few sessions are devoted to exploring the presenting problems, the next three sessions to learning how to identify and challenge the dysfunctional or irrational thoughts, the next sessions to systematic problem solving, and the final few sessions to other applications and generalization of learning (Scott & Stradling, 1998). Throughout this process, members receive specific, written homework assignments to complete. Other strategies that may be used include rational coping statements, positive visualization, cost–benefit analyses, modeling, unconditional self-acceptance, and practical problem solving.

A CBT GROUP IN ACTION

What would it sound like to listen in on a group that places such an emphasis on teaching thinking and problem-solving strategies? In the following dialogue that takes place during the fourth session, after members have already learned the basic ideas, one person is struggling to digest the notion that she is creating her own problem.

Chris: I tell you, he really does make me so angry.

Leader: Yeah? How does he do that? How does he get inside your head and trigger your emotions? I thought only you had the power to do that.

Chris: Oh, you know what I mean. It's just that he can be so mean . . .

Don: So because he acts cruel, that means you have to get all bent out of shape over it?

Leader: And it is just your perception that he is mean. I don't imagine that he would agree with you.

Chris: No, he'd say he is just trying to help me.

Morgan: [To leader] Is this the time when I ask her to look at what she's telling herself about his behavior?

Leader: [Nodding] Go for it.

If this sounds like individual therapy in a group setting in which everyone takes turns to get help, that is often what occurs. Since this is an educational model, the focus is more on meeting individual member goals than on facilitating group dynamics and processes. Of course, cohesion and trust are still important but only to the extent that they create a climate useful for the learning.

The Reality Therapy Approach

This is another action-focused model of group work that helps people be more reality based in their perceptions and behavior. Originated by William Glasser (1965, 1985) and further developed for group work in a variety of settings (see, e.g., Kim, 2007; Suh & Lee, 2006; Wubbolding, 2007, 2011), this approach bears a similarity to the cognitive behavioral models we have just reviewed. It is educationally based and seeks to persuade people to choose different ways of behaving to meet their self-declared goals. In fact, the whole theory is all about making choices, which is why Glasser (1998) later called his approach "choice theory."

SOME BASIC PREMISES

Reality therapy comes from the premise that regardless of what has "happened" or what people have done in the past, we can choose behaviors that will help us meet our needs more effectively in the future. Behavior is viewed as purposeful and as one's best attempt to satisfy one or more of five basic needs: love/belonging, freedom, fun, power, and survival. Each person is unique and highly motivated to reach personal desires. Yet people become frustrated when what they are getting out of life is less than what they want or perceive they need (Wubbolding, 2011). A few basic questions are asked of people in reality therapy, whether in groups or individual sessions: What are you doing now? Is it getting you what you want? If not, what could you do differently?

For Personal Reflection

Identify one area of your life right now where you are experiencing difficulty as a direct or indirect result of the strategy you have currently adopted. Ask yourself the reality therapy questions and answer them.

1. What are you doing now to solve your problem?
2. What are the effects and consequences of this behavior?
3. Is this getting you what you want?
4. What could you do differently to produce a different outcome?
5. What is stopping you from doing what you claim you want?
6. What will you do in the future?

Gets right to the point, doesn't it? Group members are challenged to examine the choices they make every day, with every decision they make and every action they take. They are forced to look at what works in their lives and what does not work. Finally, they are encouraged to make a plan for being more effective in meeting their needs.

The leader takes a highly directive, active, and confrontational role in the process, teaching group members to challenge one another, asking the difficult question, "Is what you are doing getting you what you want?" Because the answer is inevitably in the negative, the group is used as a brainstorming session to consider other options and what their likely consequences would be. Needless to say, this type of group becomes problem centered and is especially well suited to participants such as addicts, offenders, and delinquents who have not been acting responsibly.

As with some of the other approaches we have examined (cognitive, person-centered, Gestalt, existential), the emphasis is on the present rather than the past. No excuses are accepted for failing to do what one said one would do. That is not to say that people are blamed or shamed for not following through; rather, they are simply confronted to examine what got in the way, which choices they made, and what they would like to do instead as a means of creating some action toward creating a new outcome.

Relational-Cultural Theory

Relational-cultural theory (RCT) arose from an effort to better understand the importance of growth-fostering relationships in people's lives. The founding scholars of RCT (Judith Jordan, Jean Baker Miller, Irene Stiver, and Janet Surrey) were all trained in psychoanalytically oriented models. Many concepts from those earlier models are incorporated or adapted into RCT.

Whereas most of the traditional psychological theories emphasize development as a trajectory from dependence to independence, RCT is built on the premise that throughout the life span human beings grow through—and toward—connection. A core assumption of RCT is that humans require this intimacy to flourish; likewise, isolation is a source of considerable suffering for people on both a personal level and a cultural level (Jordan, 2010). The notion of seeing connection as the primary organizer and source of motivation for people has a specific meaning for group work because it promotes the goals of developing relational skills and creating mutuality in relationships (Comstock, Duffey, & St. George, 2002). Furthermore, RCT explores the sociopolitical forces of disconnection that create significant pain for people (Frey, 2013). With a clear objective of social change, RCT provides a model for doing group work that emphasizes movement out of isolation. RCT challenges not only the prevailing developmental theories, which frame independence as the hallmark of mature development, but also some of the basic tenets of 21st century Western culture that celebrate autonomy, self-interest, competition, and strength in isolation (Jordan, 2010).

The effects of privilege, marginalization, and cultural forces are seen as central to psychological development. The tenet that relational development is always completely connected with social and cultural identities is critical to the development and practice of RCT. Though primarily conceptualized for working with women, RCT has increasingly been applied to working with men (Duffey & Haberstroh, 2014).

The core concepts of RCT include the following (Comstock et al., 2008; Frey, 2013; Jordan, 2010):

1. People grow through and toward relationship throughout the life span.

2. Movement toward mutuality rather than separation characterizes mature functioning.

3. Relationship differentiation and elaboration characterize growth.

4. Mutual empathy and mutual empowerment are at the core of growth-fostering relationships. Mutual empathy suggests that for empathy to facilitate change, each person must see, know, and feel the responsiveness of the other person. Mutual empathy involves mutual impact, mutual care, and mutual responsiveness. It contributes to repair of empathic failures and alters relational expectations created in early formative relationships.

5. Authenticity is necessary for real engagement and full participation in growth-fostering relationships. In these relationships, people are able to bring themselves most fully and authentically into connection. These relationships have five outcomes: (1) a sense of zest; (2) a better understanding of self, other, and the relationship (clarity); (3) a sense of worth; (4) an enhanced capacity to act or be productive; and (5) an increased desire for more connection (Miller & Stiver, 1997).

6. In growth-fostering relationships, all people contribute and grow or benefit. Development is not a one-way street.

7. One of the goals of development from a relational perspective is increased relational competence and capacities over the life span.

Rather than moving toward greater separateness and independence, the goal of RCT is to increase the capacity for relational resilience, mutual empathy, and mutual empowerment. Mutual empathy is the process that allows for growth in a relationship. In a dyad, it involves the responsiveness of two people, but it can occur within a group when all are responsive to one another. In this view of recursive empathy, with every person affected by and seeing their impact on others, everyone sees the possibility for change and connection. Thus, aspects of one's experience that have been split off and seen as unacceptable or threatening begin to come back into a relationship. When protective strategies of disconnection are operating, people remain stuck in old patterns of disconnection. Under these conditions, there is not enough room for growth. In mutual empathy, people begin to see that they can bring more and more of themselves into a relationship. In this process, they become more present, more open to change and learning.

In group settings, Comstock et al. (2002) outlined a five-step process of relational movement grounded in RCT:

1. *Supported vulnerability:* This is the step of establishing safety. Group leaders can develop this by helping all group members commit to the process of working through disconnections. During this step, group members may express their emotions related to difficult relationships and disconnection while working to identify their own relational patterns.

2. *Flexibility:* As the group grows more cohesive around trust and shared history together, group members begin to develop the capacity for healthier choices regarding whom to build relationships with. This also means learning how to make choices regarding the degrees of engagement and the level of vulnerability extended into nonmutual relationships.

3. *Empowerment and conflict:* As group members become closer, conflict naturally occurs. "Good conflict" is necessary for change and growth, and people often undergo profound changes and grow most deeply when they encounter differences and work on conflict or differences in connection. In this setting, conflict is not defined by dominance, violence, or aggression; rather, these modes of interaction are seen as maneuvers to avoid conflict and change. Working with conflict and difference in groups becomes crucial.

4. *Relational confidence:* As the relational capacities of group members grow, it is natural that they become more confident and comfortable in allowing others to truly know them.

5. *Relational awareness:* When group members learn how to rework disconnection and empathic failures, they also learn how to manage and become aware of disconnections.

RCT groups are appropriate for a broad range of populations presenting concerns that are associated with the need for a relational analysis. The model has been used in personal growth groups for men and women, grief, sexual abuse/assault recovery, relationship violence, divorce, and eating disorders. As each of these issues often has a component of disconnection, the goals of RCT around fostering growth-focused relationships are appropriate. Furthermore, the relational model has been applied to ethnic-minority populations (Frey, 2013; Ruiz, 2012) and populations affected by trauma, oppression, and loss (Duffey & Somody, 2011; Schiller, 2007).

For Personal Application

Take some time to consider your own relationships and your relational style. RCT theorists suggest that although individuals yearn for connections with others, they often develop a wide-ranging repertoire of strategies to block this goal. This is referred to as the *central relationship paradox.* Such strategies include withholding love, affection, and approval; withdrawing from others; criticizing others; and hiding one's authentic self and true emotions.

What are the ways you sabotage your own yearning for greater intimacy and connection with others? As you examine these issues, consider the familial, cultural, and gender influences that have established these patterns. What would it take for you to reach beyond your isolation and fears of rejection to create closer relationships with loved ones, as well as others with whom you want connections?

The Narrative Approach

Constructivist approaches emphasize the ways individuals construct their own perceptions of reality through their language, culture, background, and creations of meaning (Avdi & Georgaca, 2007; Raskin & Bridges, 2008). Narrative therapy was originally designed for family settings because of its sensitivity to the stories people learn about who they are and the ways their particular experiences are framed within a unique cultural context (Freedman & Combs, 2012; Madigan, 2011; White & Epston, 1990).

Constructivist (also called *social constructionist,* with some subtle differences) approaches to individual or group work are incredibly complex and intellectually challenging. What they offer is a model for explaining how people co-construct a shared reality of their group experiences. Narrative approaches are among the most well developed, or at least more clearly described, theories that can be adapted for your purposes as beginning group leaders. Actually, only in the past few years has a well-articulated model of narrative group work been developed (Brown & Augusta-Scott, 2007; Monk, Drewery, & Winslade, 2005), although this is an approach that lends itself particularly well to group settings because of the ways it acknowledges individual and cultural differences among participants. It has been applied in group settings to work with older adults (Poole, Gardner, Flower, & Cooper, 2009), men who have exhibited abusive behaviors (Beres & Nichols, 2010), people with HIV/AIDS (Garte-Wolf, 2011), and women with body dissatisfaction (Duba, Kindsvatter, & Priddy, 2010).

Like many of the other approaches, narrative therapy has been adapted from individual interview settings to a group format. It has evolved in a professional and cultural climate very different from what many North Americans find familiar, because its first proponents worked mostly in Australia and New Zealand. It is within this context that narrative group work is especially responsive to the gender and cultural backgrounds of participants. It has been described as both a feminist theory and one especially well suited to work with indigenous peoples (Freedman & Combs, 2012; Madigan, 2011).

NARRATIVE ASSUMPTIONS

A narrative approach to group work subscribes to certain beliefs that may strike you as very different from others you will study. In a narrative approach, difficulties are seen to reflect situations where one's self-narratives do not sufficiently represent vital aspects of lived experience. The treatment then becomes one of story repair where problematic self-narratives are reconstructed to become more coherent, complex, and inclusive (Madigan, 2011). Accordingly, the group leader's role is changed to more of a witness to the client's storytelling, as well as a coeditor of the unfolding narrative. What the group leader is not, however, is a superior or arbitrator of adequacy or the "right" responses (Monk et al., 2005).

1. *The group member's presenting problem is the issue to be addressed.* Whereas some approaches see the problem as symptomatic of underlying deeper issues, or perhaps as a manifestation of a disease, family dysfunction, early trauma, or weak spirit, narrative group work treats the symptoms as the most legitimate focus of attention.

2. *Personal experience is treated as the ultimate authority.* Reality is constructed from the stories one has heard (from the media, parents, books, and so on), as well as those one creates about one's life.

3. *Human beings tend to "story" their lives.* Our brains appear to be wired in such a way that we feel a natural affinity for the narrative to provide a coherent record of what we experience. These stories are our reality.

4. *Behavior is not viewed as abnormal or pathological but, rather, as a functional adaptation to unique circumstances.* Rather than using a medical model to diagnose problems, the narrative approach favors one that uses the group member's own language and metaphors.

5. *The group leader takes on the role of a guide rather than an expert.* A position of "not knowing" or "curious questioning" is adopted, in which the group leader attempts to model for participants a respectful, persistent, and probing style of exploring the dominant narrative.

NARRATIVE GROUP TECHNIQUES

Narrative therapy introduces a whole new vocabulary of terms to describe the novel techniques and interventions (Freedman & Combs, 2012). Many of these have been adapted for group settings (Monk et al., 2005).

Genuine Curiosity. Narrative group leaders work from a position of "not knowing" into a place of being a naïve inquirer with true curiosity. The stance creates the space for group members to bring forth their own private stories and meanings in an environment in which they are experts on their own lives rather than others. This position also keeps at bay dominant stories that would usually overwhelm or blanket one's experiences, allowing one to give one's own private account.

Narrative Metaphors. In the process of constructing meaning from life experiences, people tend to use particular words and metaphors to represent their narratives. For example, in telling a group about her life as the child of a neglectful father and abusive mother, Kristen described herself as worthless: "I'm like the recycled trash that people put in front of their houses when they've emptied the receptacles. That's why I've been in three marriages. I get used up and then thrown away."

Is this really what's happening in Kristen's life? From a narrative perspective, this is her "constructed reality," pieced together from the "dominant story" she has subscribed to. It is the job of the group leader to help Kristen, with the aid of other group members, refashion a quite different story in which she feels empowered rather than victimized. Eventually, a new narrative will become internalized, not just by Kristen but by others in the group who can relate to her problem. That, of course, is one of the beauties of group work: It may appear as though you are helping only one person at a time, when actually many others are identifying with the narrative, personalizing the issues, and working through parallel processes.

Externalizing the Problem. It is a very peculiar idea that instead of getting group members to accept responsibility for their difficulties, the way other approaches proceed, the narrative group leader gets people to *disown* their problems as a way to reduce scapegoating and self-blame, and to help people not see themselves as problems (or problem-saturated people; Madigan, 2011). Contrast, for example, the way different group leaders would address the same issue:

- Cognitive behavioral group leader: "How are you making yourself depressed?"
- Reality group leader: "What are the consequences of choosing to be depressed?"
- Existential group leader: "How are you using your depression as a way to avoid responsibility for your freedom?"
- Narrative group leader: "How has depression ruined your life?"

In the last case, the tone and syntax imply that depression is not a choice, or even an internal condition, but an externalized problem that is creating misery. This clever strategy allows group members to work together to defeat the externalized problem.

Deconstruction. How are your dominant narratives influenced by the ways your culture has taught you what it means to be a member of your gender, sexual orientation, ethnicity, religion, and geographical identity? Group members work together to "deconstruct" the ways roles and stories have been learned. This is especially the case when group members have been taught to "pathologize" their experiences. Kristen, for instance, learned from a child psychologist when she was younger that she had a "conduct disorder" because she tried to stand up to her abusive mother. Group members can help her understand that an alternative version of those events is that she was appropriately assertive in the face of attempts to enslave her. One outcome of this exercise is that group members learn to question continuously the origins of their beliefs and how they have been shaped by forces representing the majority culture.

Relative Influence Questions. Typical of many "brief" therapies, narrative group work helps participants sort out the consequences of their behavior by looking at how the problem-based story is affecting their lives and what the likely outcome is if the story continues in the same fashion. Examples of these questions include the following:

- What are the effects of continuing to act the way you do?
- What is the likely outcome if you continue in this way?

These types of questions help members learn the extent of the problem and their own role as agents within the problem-based story. They also tend to invite initiative and action around getting one to engage in a more purposeful way to create a new story. As members begin to make changes, other questions can begin to illuminate the ways the new story can start to take hold, gain some life, and make changes in one's life:

- What are some instances when you have not felt controlled by your problem?
- How have you managed to keep the problem from disrupting your life at various times?

These questions tend to indicate ways one is taking action and to remind one of the recourses and competencies one possesses.

Other brief therapies might call this "looking for exceptions," but in the narrative approach, you are trying to do more than just balance the negative with some instances of success; you are also learning a process for tracking the effects of maintaining the current narrative.

For a Class Activity

Narrative group leaders adopt a stance of "curious questioning" when they explore issues with participants. They demonstrate a respectful, naïve, but intensely interested attitude that says, "Help me understand your story. More than that, tell me about your experiences that are outside your dominant story." This strategy is intended to help people bring out new ways of viewing their life narratives.

In a group of three or four, take turns telling a story that represents an important lesson in life. Use a stance of curious questioning to help the person find exceptions to this dominant narrative. In other words, ask the person to tell alternative stories in which he or she was able to overcome the problem or ignore it.

Afterward, talk about the effects of this exercise and what you learned.

Brief Group Structures

Although not strictly a theory as much as an abbreviated approach to doing groups, brief methods have evolved in recent years in response to the demands of managed care in the mental health and medical systems, as well as pragmatic concerns in schools, agencies, and other settings. Essentially, any of the preceding theories may be shortened in their scope as long as more modest goals are defined, time-limited sessions are negotiated (usually 3 to 10 meetings), presenting problems are addressed (rather than deeper issues), careful screening is undertaken to include only good candidates, and follow-up evaluations are conducted (Piper & Ogrodniczuk, 2004).

PLANNING A BRIEF GROUP

If you find yourself in a work situation where you have far too many people to help and too little time available to do your job, you may very well design brief group experiences. In such structures, you will want to take the following guidelines into consideration:

1. Set a definite time limit as to how long your groups will run.

2. During prescreening interviews, help group members get a running start by identifying problems to work on. Remember that group work begins not with the first session but with the first decision to seek help.

3. Establish a thematic focus to your group, one that all your group members can relate to. For this reason, it is often better in short-term groups to work with a central issue (divorce, anger, depression, weight loss, etc.).

4. Remain solution focused rather than explanation oriented. Include structured homework assignments that help members work on problems between sessions.

5. Don't get fancy. Stick with a basic group process that keeps things in the present rather than the past and addresses specific problems.

6. Work efficiently to establish trust and cohesion as quickly as possible so you can move the group into the working stage.

7. Monitor closely those participants who may need longer, more intensive treatment, individual sessions, or more support than can be provided in briefer groups. Make referrals accordingly.

8. Remind participants that the clock is running, that time is limited and must not be wasted. Make group members responsible for using the group time in the most efficient manner possible.

For Reflection and a Field Study

Think of a time in your life when you made a dramatic change in a relatively short period of time. Write about this experience, including what happened, why you were ready to change at that critical juncture, and what you believe was responsible for such a rapid shift.

Talk to other people about the times in their lives when they transformed themselves within a very short period of time as a result of some supportive or confrontational group experience. Compare your experiences with those of others you interview.

Based on what you learned, what would you do in brief groups to capitalize on those forces that you believe are most responsible for rapid, potent changes?

Other Theories We Did Not Review

In the limited space available, we could survey only several of the most popular approaches to group work currently in practice. Depending on your interests, desired work setting, and type of group you wish to lead, you may wish to investigate other theories that might be of relevance to your work.

- Transpersonal group work has a spiritual, mystical flavor that is missing from the others we have reviewed (McClure, 2005; Shorrock, 2008).
- Feminist group work is especially sensitive to issues of power and oppression that are so much a part of the dominant culture (Brown, 2010; Kees & Leech, 2014; Lubin & Johnson, 2008).

- Social work practice groups emerged as integrated and specialized applications of this discipline (Hepworth, Rooney, Rooney, Strom-Gottfried, & Larsen, 2010; Jacobson & Rugeley, 2007).
- Dialectical behavior therapy (DBT) combines behavioral theory, dialectics, cognitive therapy, and mindfulness to treat specific behaviors and disorders. DBT has two components: an individual component that explores issues from the previous week and a skills group that meets to explore specific skills such as core mindfulness, emotion regulation skills, interpersonal effectiveness skills, and distress tolerance skills (Linehan, Ward-Ciesielski, & Neacsiu, 2012; Rizvi, Steffel, & Carson-Wong, 2013).

An Integrative Model

Although we have introduced you to a sample of theoretical models favored by group leaders, many practitioners use a variety of approaches in their work. They may prefer one theory over others because of its compatibility with their style, yet may borrow techniques and structures from a variety of approaches, depending on the situations they face. In fact, many group leaders follow an integrative model that combines the best features of several theories (Caplan, 2006; Cook & Tedeschi, 2007; Day, 2014; Jacobs, Masson, & Harvill, 2012; Stricker, 2010; Yalom & Leszcz, 2005).

Perhaps later in your career you will choose to specialize in a particular theoretical orientation to group work, one that fits your unique style, client population, and work setting. As a beginner, it makes more sense for you to learn the basics of group leadership by following a fairly generic, universal model, one that can be adapted to a number of situations. Throughout this book you will learn the means by which to make assessments and diagnostic decisions in groups; to read accurately the stage, dynamics, and processes that are operating; to apply basic leadership skills; to select appropriate interventions; and to function effectively with a coleader. Most of this content will serve you well regardless of which kind of group you wish to lead.

For a Group Activity and Field Study

We have just covered an extraordinary amount of material in a ridiculously short period of time. You could spend a whole lifetime studying any one of these group theories, so you can appreciate the depth of your challenge in trying to make sense of a dozen or more.

Form a study group with several classmates to review the various theories and talk about the features you like best and least. Based on your limited exposure, talk to one another about what draws you to a few of these models and what you find distasteful about others.

Make a commitment to investigate a few of these theories in greater detail. Read original sources written by the developers (Freud, Rogers, Perls, Ellis, Glasser, Adler, White and Epston, etc.). Also read secondary sources by group leaders who have adapted the theories to various group formats. Peruse journals devoted to the particular theory of interest (e.g., *Psychoanalytic Psychotherapy, Journal of Humanistic Education and Development, Journal of Rational Emotive and Cognitive Behavior Therapy, Journal of Reality Therapy*). Finally, interview group practitioners in the field to find out which theories they follow. Ask them to tell you about how they settled on those particular models.

Photo 6.1   It is not usual or customary for group leaders to follow one theoretical approach exclusively. More likely, they will take a little from one theory, a little from another, and still more from others, weaving them together into an approach that fits their own style, not to mention the needs of their clients. As a beginner, you will likely stick to one model (usually the one introduced by your instructor or supervisor), but over time, you will find yourself developing a unique approach that reflects your personality, interests, style, values, strengths, weaknesses, and work context.

Review of What You Learned

- Theories of group intervention provide guidance and organization for leaders to supply a rationale for why group members are experiencing difficulties and to suggest an intervention model for creating change.
- Various group theories share a number of similarities in spite of their apparent differences. It is useful to search for common elements that can be integrated into your own leadership style.
- Group approaches differ in their focus on such variables as past versus present, symptoms versus underlying issues, cognitive versus affective versus behavioral dimensions, insight versus action-oriented focus, individual versus family structures, group versus individual goals, process versus task completion, and the role of the group leader.
- Most group leaders are flexible and pragmatic, borrowing concepts and interventions from a multitude of theories, depending on what the group or individual member needs. They tend to be grounded conceptually in a theory to make sense of the group and group members' behavior, yet eclectic in intervening.
- Some leadership approaches are best suited for certain settings, client populations, and presenting concerns.
- Regardless of the theory preferred, group leaders blend their approach with a foundation in group dynamics and group stages to acknowledge the influence of the group on each group member.

Part II

Skills of
the Group Leader

Assessment and Group Diagnostics

7

Each of the theoretical approaches reviewed in Chapter 5 provides a framework for making sense of what is going on in a group and with individual group members. Depending on its underlying philosophy, the theory may focus on assessing individual member issues or larger group dynamics. This is not really an either/or proposition: As a group leader, you are responsible for closely monitoring what is happening with each participant, including presenting problems, interpersonal style, unique needs and goals, and progress toward identified objectives. Depending on the group you lead, you may also be required to consult and assess the performance of the group in a work setting (Barlow, 2013; London, 2007). Being able to assess a group is a foundational leadership skill.

Not only are you collecting and organizing information for each member, but you must also keep track of what is happening in the group at any moment in time. Much of that is related to assessing the process variables such as group climate, group dynamics, and therapeutic factors. Related to the group process factors is the evaluation of how group members are responding to the group (Luke, 2014). Group leaders are constantly questioning: Who is bored? Who is anxious? Who is about to bolt? Which member should receive the attention next? Should I change directions or keep going with present flow? These are just a few of the questions you will consider during every minute of your leadership responsibility.

Knowing Where to Hit the Pipe

There is a story about a billion-dollar luxury liner, outfitted with every possible appointment, convenience, and necessity, and designed to gratify every decadent demand that could possibly be of interest or use to its several thousand prominent passengers. This floating Taj Mahal, booked solid for months by wealthy citizens and cargo exporters, exhibited a phenomenally delicate profit margin in which time was equivalent to money. For this great ship to sit idle for even an hour, much less for a day or a week, would cost the company millions in delays, late penalties, and inconvenience for everyone concerned.

Every effort had been made to ensure that the ship would operate at peak efficiency. The engine room had as many backup systems and fail-safe mechanisms as an Apollo rocket. No quality had been overlooked in building the most reliable, durable mechanical equipment money could buy. The engine room was staffed by officers, experts, and mechanics from around the world. Each stood vigil in a gleaming white uniform looped with gold braid and brass buttons. Computer systems, draped in pastel plastics and steel, lined the walls. Nothing could possibly go wrong.

Except that the ship's engines would not start. The crew had tried everything to remedy the situation as the passengers paced restlessly for an hour, then two. The captain frantically wired around the world for advice, getting nothing in return but sympathy. So the great ship stood idle in its berth. Experts and engineers were at a loss as to what to do next. Finally, an officer recalled hearing about a mechanic who could fix anything. For 60 years, he had repaired broken engines of every sort, although his methods were alleged to be somewhat unorthodox.

After scouring the dockside streets, the crew finally located the weathered old man in a bar. Creaking slowly to his feet, he agreed to help solve their problem and shuffled to the scene, pushing a wheelbarrow full of greasy tools. He entered the engine room, surveyed the scene, and ordered everyone to give him room. Like a rat, he scurried from one end of the room to the other, feeling parts, smelling the air, nodding absently to himself.

After several tense minutes, the observers grew restless. The old man's staccato grunts became more urgent as he settled into a corner of the room with hundreds of color-coded pipes traveling in every direction. Selecting an obscure pipe, he studied its shape and form for a moment and then returned to his wheelbarrow to search for the correct tool. Selecting an immense monkey wrench, he strolled over to the pipes, reared back with his wrench, and, to the astonishment of everyone, gave one of the pipes a great whack. The shudder reverberated along the gleaming metal until, a minute later, the engines sputtered, hiccupped a few times, and then settled into a gentle purr.

The other engineers embraced the old man, and the captain solemnly approached him to offer his gratitude. As the ship prepared to embark, the captain took out the company checkbook to pay the mechanic. "How much do we owe you?" he asked. "$50,000," replied the old mechanic. The captain sputtered: "You old crook, how dare you overcharge us for the little you did. For an expenditure this large I must clear the amount with the owners. You'll have to submit an itemized statement."

The mechanic nodded, found an old scrap of an envelope in his pocket, and scribbled his bill:

Mechanic's Bill for Fixing the Ship	
Hitting the pipe	$10.00
Knowing where to hit the pipe	$49,990.00
Total	$50,000.00

Philosophers, engineers, surgeons, mechanics, plumbers, and group leaders are all skilled diagnosticians who find out exactly what is wrong, how it happened, and what needs to be done to put it right. But all the skills of a mechanic or techniques of a group leader are useless without the knowledge of precisely where and how to "hit the pipe." In the case of group leadership, assessment and diagnosis have a special value in identifying individual (microlevel) as well as collective/group (macrolevel) behavior patterns. Economists, too, think in terms of macro- and microlevel concepts—respectively, that which affects a whole system and that which affects any component of the universe (McConnell & Brue, 2011).

Whereas microdiagnostics deals with labeling and naming individual client actions, macrodiagnostics is concerned with the larger processes that help the leader assess what is going on in the group. What can the heavy silence mean? What effects are minicoalitions having on total group functioning? Why can't things seem to get started? These and similar critical questions permit the group leader to think macrodiagnostically while analyzing significant themes as they arise.

What Is Assessment and Diagnosis in Groups?

All helping professionals, group leaders included, increasingly use differential therapeutics (Clarkin, 2005; Hoffman & Rosman, 2003) and technical eclecticism (Carter, 2006; Gold & Stricker, 2006) as a way to conceptualize what people bring into sessions. These models stress the importance of accurately assessing the specific needs of each group member and delivering specialized treatments to address particular problems. Although this concept is better suited to individual formats, the idea behind this thinking is that different modalities (such as group, family, individual) are best for certain clients; different kinds of groups (such as experiential, goal oriented) are best for certain client needs; and even within the same group, particular members require different kinds of interventions (such as confrontationist, supportive) to benefit the most.

Group leaders engage in three parallel assessment processes (i.e., individual, group, and self) occurring in a group at any given time. This creates some unusual challenges in that you must split your attention among these domains at all times. For many new group leaders, the switching back and forth between domains tends to be one of the hardest tasks associated with leading. Since there is so much happening in a group and because interactions often move at a rapid pace, many new leaders feel as though their heads are spinning trying to make sense of what is happening. Of course, just when you think it is all figured out, new dynamics are at work that require more assessment.

There is no easy solution for developing individual and group self-assessment skills, other than simply leading groups, learning to be at ease in group settings, and then processing your reactions with your coleader or group supervisor after each meeting. Over time you will gain an appreciation for what group factors need attention and how to make sense of what is happening.

INDIVIDUAL ASSESSMENT

Individual assessment refers to the monitoring and observing of individual group members *while the group* is in action. Remember that group members are often privy to knowledge about others that was revealed between sessions or during informal conversations (often in the parking lot). Likewise, the leader has access to information contained in clients' charts or shared during individual sessions. For example, imagine that during a pregroup screening you learned that Edward identifies as gay, but you know that he has yet to come out to his friends and family and that he is uncertain about coming out to the group. When another group member starts to talk about his own experiences with his boss who is gay, you can assume that this topic might be of interest to Edward, as he may be trying to gauge the group's reaction to this information to determine how safe it is to come out to the group.

A group leader is constantly shuffling members internally, closely watching each person's behavior. You will have formulated some sort of working diagnosis for each person, including presenting problems and treatment goals. Furthermore, you develop a sense of how each person communicates and connects with other group members. You will often examine each person's behavior in terms of that person's relative contribution to the overall group objectives and to the group as a whole. Examples of what this might sound like inside the leader's head include the following:

- For some reason, Jay is being very quiet today. I wonder if something happened at home that he is not talking about.
- Elke has chosen not to report on what she did last week. She may have forgotten, but I doubt it. I think she is hoping to avoid the issue altogether.
- I've just got to help Kirk become more concise, as people are not connecting with him. He has been talking for the last few minutes, but nobody, including me, is even listening.
- Carrie seems to lose track of what she has said previously, almost as if there are some memory deficits. I may need to refer her for a neurological exam.
- Melissa seems less than her usual lucid self. That could mean she has started drinking again.
- Charlie just moved his chair farther out of the circle, and he looks rather upset. I need to check in with him to see what is going on.

For Reflection

Review each of the members of your class, identifying some of their most characteristic patterns that have been displayed consistently. Some of these patterns bring you closer, whereas others may push you away. What patterns do you imagine might come out in a group setting that each of them would most need to work on (in your humble opinion)? What are some things about each person that puzzle you?

Now, since everyone else in the class is looking at you the same way you have been looking at them, what are some of the things they probably identified about you?

GROUP ASSESSMENT

In addition to the individual assessment, you are watching very carefully what is happening in the group, especially with regard to dynamics, stage development, and ongoing processes. In many ways, assessing the group is the default focus, as both the individual group members and the group leader are encapsulated within the group and this serves as the focal point of intervention (Barlow, 2013). You are looking at the flow of information (verbal and nonverbal), the level of engagement and connection, the balance and contribution of each group member, the intensity of the interactions, the presence or absence of therapeutic factors, and so on. Many questions will come to mind as you watch things unfold, as illustrated in the internal comments of a group leader:

- I thought we were moving into a stage of cohesive engagement, but now it seems like more induction needs to take place first. I am wondering, what is keeping us apart?
- What would it take to develop more cohesiveness among the three different factions? The group feels divided and fragmented.
- Fred seems to be designated as a scapegoat by some of the others, yet he also seems to welcome the role.
- I see some collusion going on whenever attempts are made to get into risky areas. The group wants to stay friendly with any conflict, but they are becoming less authentic.
- There have been numerous moments of silence today during which members seem distracted rather than thoughtful.
- What is a metaphor to describe what is happening right now?
- The underlying conflict from last week between Eric and Warren does not seem over even though they are saying it is. Other group members seem to be walking on egg shells. I need to explore this more.

SELF-ASSESSMENT

Finally, you are continually assessing what is going on inside of you throughout the experience. This internal monitoring will become a source of intuition and a "felt sense" about what is happening in the group. Far more than that, however, you must be especially careful to watch out for signs of countertransference toward particular members. Identifying and working with your own internal reactions can be among your most effective clinical tools (Hopper, 2006; Markin, 2009). Reading one's own reactions can help a leader enter the interpersonal world of a group member and understand how others respond and react (Markin & Kivlighan, 2007). You will learn to read your own body and hear what it is telling you. Look for areas of tension within, and note where the tension is located and how it feels. You may also look for the following symptoms:

- The arousal of guilt from your own unresolved personal struggles that parallel those impulses and emotions of a member
- Impaired empathy, making it difficult to feel love and respect toward a member

- Awareness that you are distorting a person's behavior, perhaps based on your own unresolved issues
- Inaccurate interpretations of a member's feelings due to your own distortions
- Feeling generally blocked, helpless, and frustrated with a particular group member
- Evidence of boredom or impatience when working with some members
- Unusual memory lapses regarding the details of a group member's life
- A tendency to speak about a client in derogatory terms
- An awareness that you are working harder than a member

For Personal Application

Again review each of the individuals in your class, including your instructor. This time, however, concentrate on your personal reactions, noting those people you have a strong attraction to, as well as those who rub you the wrong way.

Rather than concentrating on what others do that provokes, stimulates, or irritates you, look at what you are doing inside that prevents greater compassion, empathy, and understanding on your part. In particular, note the ways you are critical of people who are most different from you, who engage in behavior you don't understand, or who are more like you than you would prefer to admit. Or see if those people you are critical of tend to remind you of someone from your past with whom you had a difficult relationship.

Obviously, you have considerable work cut out for you, simultaneously assessing yourself, individual members, and the group as a whole. That is one reason why it is so helpful to work with a coleader to divide the diagnostic responsibilities. When that isn't feasible, you will need to consult with a supervisor frequently to check your impressions.

Student Voice

Too Much Assessment!

By far, the hardest thing for me when I started leading groups was trying to figure out what to focus on and how to make sense of everything that was happening in the group. I was trained at first in individual settings, so that seemed natural, but in group I needed to look at the whole group picture, not just the individual people. Then there was all my own reactions to individual group members that kept clouding my vision. I think that for the first 6 months I was just a group leading mess, and I was never sure what to do. Over time, I began to figure some things out, such as looking at how each member's own concern would then contribute to the group dynamic. I also began to learn how to use my own reactions to help make sense of people rather than having these reactions bog me down.

An Example of Diagnosis in Action

Some may ask why a group leader diagnoses group members. A couple of simple responses are that labeling and diagnosing is a convenient way to make sense of a situation, and it is aesthetically pleasing to have people grouped in neat little categories. Yet, from a working perspective, diagnosis is the process of understanding a group member using a system of classification that can help the leader establish goals and select the most advantageous base for promoting learning (Morrison, 2014). Furthermore, diagnosis can serve several functions:

- Making predictions about group member behavior so a plan can be formulated that will fit with the anticipated outcomes
- Summarizing group members' issues, their causes, and abnormal features based on observable characteristics
- Determining the unique personality dynamics of each group member
- Identifying skill deficiencies in group member functioning
- Understanding the significance of group member behavior
- Creating working hypotheses that can aid this understanding of group members

Thus, diagnostic thinking is the culmination of deductive reasoning to reach conclusions that guide leader behavior. Therapeutic diagnosis is essentially a process of problem formation in which the group member's concerns are simplified to manageable levels by reducing the significant variables to their lowest common denominator, without sacrificing their essential qualities.

Here is an example of diagnosis in action. During an 8-week period in the group, Martha displays the following behavioral symptoms:

1. Has a compulsive drive to achieve straight As in school

2. Feels pressure to meet perfectionist standards and expectations from friends and lovers

3. Experiences bouts of depression after events that should have been exciting (such as exams, dates, new experiences)

4. Is reluctant to cooperate with early helping efforts of others, although she verbalizes a great desire for help

5. Has very few friends and, although lonely, does not approach interesting strangers

6. Feels trapped living at home; quarrels with family but can't find affordable housing

7. Is almost always in control of social conversation, leading the discussion and introducing the topics

8. Is extremely skilled at communication and extraordinarily perceptive of others' feelings

9. Engages in a lot of approval seeking with group leader, showing off superior mind

10. Acts condescendingly toward a group member of the opposite sex

11. Is the only group member who preferred not to receive feedback in the introduction exercise

12. Acts moody in the group whenever another person reports substantial progress

13. Is fantastically insightful in understanding the origins and payoffs of the presenting concerns but balks at the prospect of talking in terms of goals

14. Refuses to do any psychological homework between sessions

15. Is extremely supportive, caring, and helpful to group members perceived as less intelligent or less capable

16. Withdraws when faced with confrontation; will not fight back

Now, this is only a sampling of the possible cues indicative of Martha's characteristic behavior. We could also mention a variety of other data, which may or may not be relevant, such as how other group members react to the group or what Martha has done previously to cope with difficulties. But let us assume that these 16 behavioral symptoms are those most important to the situation (an invalid assumption in reality since we never know whether we have accumulated enough background). We must now decide which symptoms are the most significant in terms of helping us understand the best way to assist Martha. Based on the available evidence, what might we logically conclude is the most reasonable diagnosis of this client's principal problem? We don't care to categorize or classify; we wish only to label the main concern in need of resolution.

Themes of approval seeking, psychological dependence, and externally controlled thinking are all prevalent here, as are attitudes of perfectionism and a fear of failure. As we think more about Martha, the diagnostic arrow eventually points toward her reluctance to take risks of any kind, both in life and also in the group setting. She has programmed her life and relationships to maximize security and predictability, preferring to remain alone rather than risk feeling vulnerable. She works methodically in school, not because she enjoys learning or wants good grades but because she needs the structure and routine of compulsive studying. She avoids parties or any social setting where she has to relinquish total control. In the group, she resents anyone who is willing to take risks, because risk taking reminds her of her own inadequacies.

The group leader is in the position of playing detective to determine which pieces of evidence are important, which symptoms need further investigation, what variables are confounding the picture or masking actual circumstances, and what causal relationships are involved in the situation. In this problem formation, the group leader can as easily complicate the existing difficulties by misjudgment, oversimplification, and illogical thinking as reconcile the conflicts.

One of the more difficult aspects of trying to determine what is going on in a group at any particular moment is that the process is affected by what each member is thinking, feeling, and doing—whether these reactions are a result of what just took place or reverberations of some personal factors. Any group event can be interpreted in many different ways, depending on the stage of group development, content of discussion, quality of interaction, meaning ascribed to each action by each member, and psychological distance between and among participants, as well as a host of personal variables such as individual perceptions, attitudes, and values.

As group leaders, we attempt to sort out this maze of confusing stimuli and find or create some meaning to the action. The degree to which our inferences are accurate is based on our ability to know what is going on inside each participant. Freeze a moment, any moment, in a group session and there will be an assortment of individual reactions to what is going on. For example, in one moment in a group, this could be happening:

- Lamar is speaking about his problem of talking too much.
- Jeanne is trying to get Deana's attention, rolling her eyes skyward in exasperation.
- The leader notes this reaction but misreads Deana's blank response as agreement, when, in fact, she is rehearsing something else she wants to say later.
- In her absentmindedness, Deana leans too far forward, completely enthralling James with a forbidden view down her blouse.
- James is now lost in his own world of attraction and embarrassment for seeing what he saw.

- Renee is listening carefully to Lamar's monologue, nodding compassionately as he speaks.
- Ray sighs in frustration, disgusted with how Renee is encouraging Lamar to keep talking.

Photo 7.1 As you monitor the behavior of each person in the group, you are conducting ongoing assessments on multiple levels and dimensions. You are observing their individual patterns and behavior in light of their primary issues and presenting complaints. You are checking on interpersonal and systemic dynamics in terms of how individuals relate to one another, coalitions that are formed, and other group processes. In addition, you are carefully monitoring your own reactions to everything that is happening.

If this is the reality of what is taking place inside each participant's head during one frozen moment, the leader's view of events (or any other outside observer's) bears a rough but incomplete approximation of phenomenological accuracy. The leader can see the general boredom and malaise among the members, and may even catch James peeking down Deana's blouse. But nothing indicates either the extent to which Deana is distracted or the fact that Ray is becoming increasingly agitated. This represents the unfortunate diagnostic limitations that a group leader must contend with in trying to infer what is happening at any given moment. Since we can neither read minds nor be expected to interpret behavior accurately all the time, it is crucial that we understand the boundaries of what we can assess and work to enlist the help of group members to be responsible for "diagnosing" and expressing their own internal processes.

Models of Individual Assessment and Diagnosis

Group leaders use methods of reliable individual diagnosis in a much different way than those operating from a hospital staff approach. It is crucial for group leaders to be able to label client self-defeating behaviors, not for the sake of pigeonholing a person into a discrete category but to get a handle on specific problem areas as a prerequisite for systematic change efforts. This process of microdiagnostics gives the group leader a much more comprehensive framework for understanding and practicing effective therapeutic observations.

Several different diagnostic models are currently in use by practitioners of various specialties and professional identities (Morrison, 2014). You are probably familiar with the "medical model," for example, and the two main classifications in mental health diagnostics: the fifth edition of the *Diagnostic and Statistical Manual of Mental Disorders* (DSM-5; American Psychiatric Association, 2013) and the *International Classification of Diseases* (National Center for Health Statistics, 2014; World Health Organization, 1992). These manuals are not limited to psychiatrists or medical doctors, as psychologists, nurses, social workers, counselors, family therapists, and other mental health professionals must also refer to the diagnostic terms contained therein.

We also believe that a good assessment must suggest hypotheses for intervention and not merely result in categorization or labeling. Therefore, when assessing and developing a diagnosis, we encourage group leaders to consider the following questions:

- How and why did the group member decide to seek help?
- What has the group member already attempted to do to resolve the problem?
- What are the group member's expectations for treatment, including leader and group member roles?

- What is the group member doing that she or he should not be doing because it is disturbing others?
- What is the group member doing that is disturbing to self?
- Is the presenting concern interactive in nature? Who else is involved?
- How often, when, and where does the presenting concern arise?
- What events and experiences in the group member's past are relevant to the current problem?
- What are the group member's characteristic functioning levels in life skills (e.g., sleeping, eating, loving, sex, integration skills, appearance, moods, and energy level)?
- What are the group member's behavioral assets, deficiencies, and abilities?

DIAGNOSTIC MODELS AND THEIR USE IN GROUPS

The medical model is, naturally, disease based, and for the most part disregards group dynamics. This means that various emotional disorders are classified in the same way as are physical maladies. In the case of mental health problems, however, a complicated system has been developed that examines a given person's functioning in a number of areas. Although this method was not intended for group settings, per se, you will still observe that diagnostic manuals such as DSM-5 can provide some useful guidance. Furthermore, because of the widespread use of DSM-5, the knowledge and experience of popular diagnoses (e.g., depression, anxiety, panic disorder) are common, and so you will find that many group members will come into group and announce their given DSM-5 diagnosis.

Basically, DSM-5 looks at several features of a person's functioning, including personality characteristics, symptomatic behaviors, biological conditions, coping levels in the present and past, and other such variables. You will often overhear group leaders talking in this DSM-5 language: "I've got this guy with borderline features who is wreaking havoc in the group," or "I'm not sure if this guy's depression is reactive to his recent loss or if there is preexisting dysthymia." In the first case, the leader is describing a member with features of a manipulative personality disorder. In the second example, the leader is trying to differentiate between a form of acute depression that is a normal adjustment reaction and a chronic, low-grade form of depression that may have been present before the crisis.

The most traditional type of diagnosis is one in which the group leader is required to develop a diagnosis for each member of the group, including present complaints, preexisting conditions, precipitating events, and a specific treatment plan. Insurance companies routinely require this sort of information before they will process claims, and many agencies also see it as sound clinical practice. These diagnostic models have limited utility in group settings outside of understanding and diagnosing individual group members. The problem is that only part of the work in groups has to do with individual issues; the rest involves interactive and interpersonal contacts that do not lend themselves cleanly to individual diagnostic classification (Barlow, 2013). It is also likely that you will make your initial impression and diagnosis of a group member during the pre-group screening to see if the person is a good fit for the group. This is particularly important for experiential and process groups, where the emphasis in the assessment is on how the presenting concern or diagnosis presents interpersonally (e.g., among other people; Gladding, 2012; Yalom & Leszcz, 2005), as that is the area of focus in those settings.

PROGRESS NOTES

You may very well be required to keep records and update charts on each participant in your group, a challenging task that requires time-consuming paperwork. For each member, you often need to formulate a DSM-5 diagnosis, develop an individual treatment plan, justify group work as the preferred modality to reach identified objectives, and then include progress notes documenting which interventions led to which outcomes that furthered the treatment plan identified earlier. If this sounds as though it requires a large amount of writing, you are probably not far from the truth. Nevertheless, it is an essential exercise to make notes after each group session, recording the progress of each group member and where you intend to go next.

As a beginner, you will most likely be required to keep detailed treatment plans and progress notes for each group member as a way to learn about group dynamics; however, the task of keeping good progress notes is one all group leaders must tackle. This practice of recording progress notes not only helps you develop sound clinical habits but also provides valuable notes for supervision. After group sessions, it is a good idea to jot down notes for yourself, including what each group member worked on, what goals or homework members have declared, and which directions seem viable for next time (see Table 7.1).

It might take a half-hour, at most, to write out these notes, but you should find that they help you evaluate and organize the previous group. Notes provide an ongoing record of the experience, suggesting possible treatment options for the future, and help remind you of group process. In many groups, members are urged to keep their own progress notes in the form of a journal, sometimes even exchanging their writing with the leader or with one another. The object is to

Table 7.1   Partial Group Progress Note

Sharon:	Quiet today, seemed withdrawn but denied there was anything going on. Noted that her feelings of anxiety in group have slightly improved. Was she looking for an invitation to talk more? If things don't change next time, I'll draw her out. Reported that she was making good progress on her relationship with her husband because she has observed other group members taking risks with their partners and sharing their concerns. She may want to role-play how she might do this with her husband.
Sam:	Seemed like a breakthrough for him today. For the first time he neither appeared defensive nor tried to keep the focus off himself. Depression seems to be under better control with cognitive restructuring, so medical evaluation for medication may not be indicated at this time. Agreed to talk to his wife about their lack of intimacy. We role-played this scenario and gave him feedback. He left feeling optimistic that he could change the way things have been going.
Mandy:	No significant progress on her issues related to being more assertive either in the group or outside. Still engages in approval seeking with me and other males in group. Reports she is doing well, but there is no evidence to support that. When confronted, she tends to acquiesce. Would be interesting to try getting her to exaggerate her behavior next time. Need to get her honest feedback from the group members about how they perceive her.

help all participants become more reflective about what is going on in the group. Other groups have used process notes as a strategy to enhance the group process. Falco and Bauman (2004) provide an example of this in a group-counseling course in which the process notes were written by the group leaders and then distributed to each group member just before the next group began. The leaders found that sharing the process notes helped clarify the group process and improved the integration of the group leader's tasks with the experience of group members. Furthermore, the group members found that the process notes enhanced their experience by refreshing their memory, providing continuity to group meetings, and helping members focus on salient group issues. Yalom and Leszcz (2005) note using a similar format in some of their groups to help absent members catch up on what they missed, but also to help group members focus on the group-level process occurring.

Others have used interactive process notes to exchange written feedback regarding group process and individual insights from group members and written responses from the group leaders (Hall & Hawley, 2004). Similar to interactive journaling, this approach creates a record of group member progress but adds the interactive and learning component through which group members get additional feedback from the group leaders.

Alternative Diagnostic Models

Almost all mental health professionals must use DSM-5 language in their work, even if they do not subscribe to the underlying assumptions of a medical model in which people are labeled with emotional disorders. Even those who do groups in inpatient settings, inheriting terminology such as "the bipolar," "the borderline," and "the dual diagnosed" (sounds like a movie title), do not necessarily think in terms of this diagnostic schema that often reduces people to labels.

Although you will use DSM-5 concepts and language in your assessment of individual group members, you may also wish to employ other diagnostic models that are more consistent with group methodology and a different philosophy. If you are leading a group that is working primarily on adjustment reactions to life stress, developmental adjustments, and growth issues, a medical model seems highly inappropriate. Even if you are working with more severe kinds of problems in your group, you and your group members may still profit from employing alternative assessment models.

DEVELOPMENTAL ASSESSMENT

In a *developmental assessment process,* you are not looking at pathology, disorders, or problems but, rather, at current developmental functioning compared with what would be expected for a given person's age, culture, gender, life situation, and stated goals. You may recall from psychology courses that human growth and development is segmented into several broad areas, including physical maturation. Certain "developmental tasks" are considered age appropriate—mastering scissors for a preschooler or driving a car without bumping into things for a 16-year-old. How are your group members functioning with respect to their developmental progress? Are they where they are supposed to be in relation to their peers?

In a developmental assessment model, the question you are asking is not whether people are dysfunctional but, rather, how they can be encouraged and stimulated to move to the next levels of maturation. This is seen as a natural process that unfolds under the right circumstances. Your job as a group leader is to create the kind of climate that is most conducive to fostering developmental growth.

Imagine that you observe a 30-year-old male group member whose life is dominated by playing video games, as well as chatting online with others who favor his preferred fantasy domains. He has not been able to hold a regular job, cannot relate well to others in the group, and has never been involved in a sustained romantic relationship. He also hasn't ever bothered to get a driver's license, claiming that it's just easier to walk or ride his bike. Whereas you could easily select half a dozen different pathological labels to describe his psychological state and life context, instead you choose to assess his behavior in developmental terms. This allows you to set incremental, realistic, sequential goals that will help him grow psychologically, interpersonally, emotionally, and socially.

> **For Reflection**
>
> Consider the case described above of the young man whose life is focused on video games, to the exclusion of productive work, intimacy, and other developmentally appropriate life skills. Describe the different ways you might use the group to help him mature. What structures or interventions might you introduce to help him grow? Would the group be ideal for fostering this kind of development?

BEHAVIORAL ASSESSMENT

Ironically, humanistic and behavioral theories share something in common when it comes to diagnosis: Both frameworks believe that it is not useful to label people but, rather, better to describe their behavior. Though the developmental model is concerned specifically with normative behavior, the behavioral model is focused instead on particular maladaptive behaviors in need of change.

Regardless of what each group member presents as their main concerns, the important questions in behavioral assessment are which target behaviors can be changed and how that might best occur (Spiegler, 2013). Consistent with a theory that values specificity, objectivity, and measurability, the group leader operating from this framework would think in terms of which specific goals can be worked on for each member during the session and in between sessions.

A strict behavioral model would not be the only one that might adopt an assessment strategy like this; other approaches we have covered, such as cognitive behavioral, reality therapy, and brief therapy, also make use of procedures that identify specific behaviors in need of upgrading. Whether the focus is on observable behavior (assertiveness), verbalizations (shoulds, musts), cognitions (exaggerations), or other internal processes, the key is to describe specifically what is to be changed and how this will take place. The group leader would thus help members formulate what they intend to change about themselves during a given period of time. These goals would be created according to the following criteria:

1. Specific, targeted behavior

2. Observable behavior

3. Measurable outcomes

4. Mutually negotiated contracts

5. Realistic, attainable objectives

6. Useful plans that are relevant to the main problem

This means that you would not ask group members to conduct self-assessments in a general way. Instead, you would help them develop specific assignments that they could work on during each group session and between each meeting that would get them closer to their desired goals. This process in a group develops as follows:

Mandy: I'm just so tired of getting in trouble in class. I do want to stop that, but I just don't know how.

Jose: Why don't you just keep your mouth shut? That's what I try to do. [Laughs]

Leader: Well, that's one solution, Mandy. What else could you work on this week that would help you make progress toward avoiding trouble and improving your grades?

Mandy: I don't know. That's why I'm here, right? Why don't you tell me?

Leader: Let's all figure this out together. What could Mandy do to work on her problem?

Stephan: Aren't we supposed to build on what we've done before? Last week, Mandy, you tried to do your homework every day, but then you got frustrated because that wasn't realistic for you. You don't go from not doing any homework at all to then doing it every day. Maybe you could start off doing just 10 minutes a few times.

Mandy: So I could start by doing 10 minutes of homework each night? That is doable. But I may need to do more than that to stop getting in trouble.

So goes the discussion and negotiation among group members who assess for themselves what they need to do and then are helped to translate their goals into specific plans they can complete. This may not sound like diagnosis in the traditional sense, but the behavioral model does get you to assess behavior instead of diagnosing people.

For a Class Activity

In small groups, take the case of Mandy described in the preceding dialogue as a starting point. She is a 14-year-old girl who repeatedly gets in trouble because she rarely turns in assignments and talks to friends in class when she is supposed to be paying attention.

One of you play the role of Mandy in the group while everyone else works together to help her identify what specific behaviors she wants to change and how she might do that. Help her set short-term goals for the next session that meet the criteria given below:

1. Specific, targeted behavior

2. Observable behavior

3. Measurable outcomes

4. Mutually negotiated contracts

5. Realistic, attainable objectives

6. Useful plans that are relevant to the main problem

After you are done, talk with your group about the process of assessment and setting goals. What seemed easier, and what seemed more difficult?

INTERPERSONAL ASSESSMENT

One of the shortcomings of DSM-5 is its almost total disregard for interpersonal behavior and social–psychological variables. Since group leaders are largely concerned with interpersonal behavior, the psychiatric classification system is virtually useless as a functional tool. Many of the classic interpersonal approaches to diagnosis, such as those of Horney (1945), Berne (1966), and Sullivan (1947), have been ignored in the current system, leaving group leaders to fend for themselves. However, clearly the interpersonal realm is where many of the reactions of group leaders are the most vivid, as this is the realm of actually experiencing a group member's presenting concerns and ways of being with other people.

Teyber and Faith (2011) outlined an interpersonal model that takes into account the client's functioning within a social context by focusing on the here-and-now interaction. Specifically, Teyber suggests initially working to identify recurrent themes to help the members make sense of their experiences and to gain a better understanding of what is important or central to everything a member talks about. Moving to the interpersonal realm, the next step is focusing on members' repetitive, self-defeating relational patterns. Crucial to this assessment is identification of the main, recurrent themes that are acted out, subtly structuring alternative ways of experiencing and relating to others. The interpersonal model assumes, just like the idea of the social microcosm, that the self-defeating interpersonal relational patterns a group member enacts in real life will come to life in the group, in the interactions with the group leader and other members.

One of the advantages of interpersonal assessment is that because it focuses on social behavior (most likely alive in the room already) rather than on a disease, it often has less of a stigma associated with it. And the here-and-now aspect is often more reliable and consistent in the group since the group member will be experiencing the pattern and other group members have been observing it, and clearly the group setting itself provides a tailored forum to address these concerns.

Below, we have compiled a list of behavioral labels that represent a meaningful selection of common self-defeating interpersonal patterns found among group members. Only after these difficulties are clearly and specifically identified, with the group member involved in the self-diagnostic process, can the group leader hope to go to work on them. This summary of dysfunctional behaviors is therefore converted into the labels to which group members can most easily relate.

- *Approval seeking:* Deliberately or unconsciously speaking or acting to win the leader's or other members' good opinion, even at the expense of one's personal convictions. This could occur so that whenever a client speaks, he makes eye contact only with the leader.
- *Mothering:* Acting as a rescuer and nurturing figure to reduce one's personal level of discomfort over conflict. For example, a member jumps in and says, "I wish you'd stay off Michael's back. Can't you see he's had enough?"
- *Politicking:* Speaking for others in the group without their consent. As an example, a member says, "*We* don't like the way things have been going."
- *Boring:* Speaks in a monotone with little animation; prone to rambling about inappropriate irrelevancies. For example, a group member who rarely speaks says, "I guess—I don't—have—much—to say."

- *Jesting:* Inappropriately making jokes and clowning to win attention, disrupt group focus, or shrug off a painful confrontation. For example, a client starts laughing hysterically, making funny faces of rejection right after receiving direct confrontation.
- *Withdrawal:* Passive behavior characterized by silence, blank expression, and escape defenses. Throughout a session, one client scoots to the back, stares out the window, and doodles on paper.
- *Martyrizing:* Taking on the image of a sufferer who has no choice but to shoulder the burdens of the world. One member repeatedly complains about how miserable life is but does nothing to change the situation.
- *Interrogating:* Excessive aggressive questioning with an implied demand for the "right" answers. A group member challenges another by saying, "Why, are you so weak that you can't face up to me?"
- *Monopolizing:* Self-centered rambling, storytelling, and talking to the point where it is difficult for others to have group time when they want it. A group member may repeat herself and engage in "filibuster"—that is, keep talking so nobody else can get a word in.
- *Shrinking:* Playing pseudo-leader by dispensing advice or over-intellectualizing. A group member explains, "I think my problem is just a manifestation of the unresolved hostility I feel toward my father."
- *Evasiveness:* Watering down the truth out of a fear of hurting others' feelings or because of vulnerability. "You want feedback?" a group member asks. "I think you're a pretty nice guy."

SYSTEMIC ASSESSMENT

Another method of diagnosis is one that does not look at individual behavior at all but, rather, at interactive patterns among group members. You learned earlier about the systemic, interactive view of cause–effect relationships that contrast with the more linear, traditional perspective of most individual therapists and counselors. Group leaders must actually apply both assessment methodologies, thinking in terms of individual disorders and dysfunctions à la DSM-5 plus the systemic patterns evident in group behavior (Barlow, 2013). This is a diagnostic model also favored by family therapists because it examines the systemic context for any problem (Bitter, 2013). The problem in a dysfunctional family (or group) is rarely one person, or even a particular behavior, but rather the larger system that makes someone into a scapegoat. To apply systems theory to group work, the group leader must attend to a number of processes, specifically, identifying structures and subsystems that evolve among members. Just as the family therapist looks carefully at boundaries, coalitions, and power hierarchies within the family system, the group leader explores various group structures and processes, including but not limited to the following:

- How group members make decisions
- How information is processed
- What boundaries are in place that divide, filter, and restrict information
- How subsystems function in relation to one another
- Communication patterns
- Cultural/ethnic values in place
- Assigned or adopted roles
- Controls and sanctions to pressure conformity
- Equity of need satisfaction
- Balance between individual and group goals
- Developmental evolution of individual and group stages
- Conflict resolution
- Metaphoric/symbolic messages

In each of these areas, the group leader continually makes diagnoses and reassessments regarding the current level of group member functioning. This labeling process helps the group leader make adjustments in methodology to reach desired goals more effectively. Crawl inside a group leader's head once again during a session, and you are likely to hear something like the following:

Gee, Carole seems unusually timid and cautious today. I wonder if she is getting enough sleep. Her depression sometimes keeps her up at night worrying about things. I must check out her thinking these days.

Why does she keep looking at Iris? Now that I think about it, she's real quiet today as well. I wonder if they have had some sort of fight. They used to be so close, but today, and last week, they barely spoke to one another.

I notice that every time Steve talks he makes a point to look at one or the other of them. The guy has such an incredible need for attention, big-time attention seeking going on. He could be playing them against each other.

You will have noticed that there are two parallel assessment processes going on. The group leader is carefully scrutinizing each member's individual behavior, especially in light of what is already known. In addition, the group leader is looking at the ways each member's behavior is both the cause and effect of others' actions. Just as an economist looks at the scope on a micro and macro level, so, too, does a group leader assess individual and group behavior.

THEORETICAL MODELS OF ASSESSMENT

All the theories we reviewed in Chapter 6 also come with their own assessment strategies and methods of diagnosis. In summarizing many of these approaches (see Table 7.2), the intent is not to overwhelm you with choices but, instead, to get you thinking flexibly and creatively about all the ways you can make sense of what is happening in groups and all the various facets you can attend to.

Picture a group in which several different individuals are talking about their difficulties in finding meaningful work. They all feel stuck in dead-end jobs and see few possibilities of things changing in the future. This is a common topic in the group and has been a core theme for a few weeks. In the group today, the conversation has been going on for long enough that you know you need to do something to intervene in some way, but you are not sure which direction to go. Some of the possible avenues you could take are given below:

- Interrupt the conversation and refocus on a subject that is more optimistic.
- Get other group members involved who have been left out.
- Help them see some possibility of hope in the future.
- Confront their excuses.
- Reflect their feelings.
- Interpret the underlying despair.
- Connect their experiences to other things you know about their past.
- Discuss with them options such as where to go and what to do.

To make any sort of informed decision about what action you should take, you must first form some diagnostic impressions of what you believe is going on with each group member (this is something you began doing upon first contact with each group member, and you continually revise this impression based on new information). There are so many dimensions of this brief interaction that you could attend to, and you will most likely make sense of it based on (a) how you conceptualize each group member and (b) how that relates to group process occurring in the present. If you look at Table 7.2, you can generate a thousand different possible questions and more than a dozen different hypotheses about what might be going on and which might be the best course of action.

Table 7.2   Assessment Models of Selected Group Theories

Theory	Assessment Strategy
Adlerian	Look for personal strengths that provide leverage for change; recognize patterns of early family dynamics in present interactions; conduct thorough lifestyle assessment of family constellation; identify faulty perceptions.
Narrative	Name the problem in the person's own language; identify the themes in personal narratives; deconstruct the ways the dominant narrative evolved; externalize the problem; find out when the problem does not exert control.
Gestalt	Examine experiences in the present moment; recognize disowned or fragmented parts of members; label unfinished business; recognize when enactments might be useful; listen for distorted language; monitor awareness of own experience in group.
Existential	Observe avoidance of responsibility and freedom; recognize times of inauthenticity and avoidance of intimacy; look for themes that are related to meaninglessness, isolation, angst (generalized anxiety), death.
Cognitive	Recognize irrational beliefs evident in member thinking; listen for exaggerations, overgeneralizations, and overpersonalization in member speech patterns.
Reality	Recognize member needs; label irresponsible behavior; find excuses for inaction; assess consequences of behavior.
Psychoanalytic	Look for unconscious motives in behavior; label defense mechanisms; find sources of present difficulties in past traumas; diagnose projections and transferences; monitor own countertransference reactions.
Behavioral	Define specific behaviors to be changed; recognize skill and information deficiencies; identify reinforcers of dysfunctional behavior; delineate specific, measurable goals; follow up on previous assignments and evaluate progress.
Person-centered	Decode underlying feelings; look for blocks to intimacy and trust; recognize when people are being judgmental, disrespectful, dishonest, inauthentic, or uncaring; identify areas for people to grow rather than problems to fix; monitor own feelings during process.
Brief	Define the problem; reframe the problem in such a way that it may more easily be solved; look for exceptions when the person is problem-free; specify solutions already tried that do not work.

For a Class Activity

It's time to apply what you learned in the previous chapter based on theories and in this chapter based on an actual situation. Divide the members into two groups: One group of 10 (two leaders and eight group members) will role-play a group setting that builds on the group example presented above. The role-play group will focus on work concerns, and the leaders will facilitate the interaction. The other group will create a fishbowl outside of the role-play group. Each member of the outside group will pick a theory from Table 7.1 and try to make sense of the group process and the group members from that theory.

Let the role play go on for about 20 to 25 minutes, and let the group members either present their own issues with work or role-play someone with a work problem. After the role play, give each person in the outside group a chance to form a diagnostic impression of what they think might be going on and to suggest a treatment plan using their specific model. After each person has gone, poll the class to see what everyone views as the best direction to proceed. If you have time, see if the two leaders can move the group in that direction for the remaining time in class.

A sound and thorough cultural assessment of the group member and the presenting concern would encompass all the previous areas of assessment. Group leaders will want to know how much of the presenting concern is associated with the group member's cultural identity (Asnaani & Hofmann, 2012). Rather than assuming that visual cultural identifiers are salient to a group member, it is good to regard each person as a unique individual on a spectrum of cultural identifications (Sue & Zane, 2009). To understand group members, the group leader will have to gather information directly or by watching group interactions closely. This type of assessment will allow the group leader to be more sensitive in intervening and to show more cultural empathy to group members (Pedersen, Crethar, & Carlson, 2008).

Review of What You Learned

- Assessment activities are divided among diagnostic impressions of each group member, readings on group dynamics, and close self-monitoring of one's own personal reactions. All three of these assessment levels exert mutual influence on one other.
- Group diagnosis can function to predict group member behavior and create treatment plans, to determine the unique personality dynamics of each group member, to identify skill deficiencies in group member functioning, to understand the significance of group member behavior, and to create working hypotheses that aid this understanding of group members.
- Several different assessment models (DSM-5, developmental, behavioral, interpersonal, systemic) allow you to focus on those aspects of group behavior that are most relevant.

- It is sound practice to get in the habit of keeping progress notes for every member at each session, as well as observations about group stages and issues. In your notes, include critical issues to follow up on, such as future goals, declared homework assignments, and unfinished business.
- Assessment strategies are also linked to the theoretical model one is choosing. These models provide a specific focus for assessment and then provide model-specific strategies for intervention.

Specialized Leadership Skills 8

It is clear that leading groups is quite similar to other forms of helping, yet also somewhat different. The same skills that might be used during individual sessions would also be entirely appropriate during groups. If you have learned about active listening skills, for example, then you must realize that in group settings you can also easily reflect the content and underlying feelings that you hear. Likewise, all the other skills that would be commonly employed during interviews can be adapted for group settings as well (see Brew & Kottler, 2008; Conyne, Crowell, & Newmeyer, 2008; Corey, Corey, Callanan, & Russell, 2015; Kottler, 2008; Nelson-Jones, 2012; Shulman, 2011). Just as you might interpret, confront, summarize, or clarify with a single person present, you would apply these same skills when people talk in groups. In fact, one of the most amazing benefits of participation in a group is that members will learn to apply these same skills by watching and imitating the leader. Thus, modeling occurs in which group members learn to communicate better in all their relationships.

Group leaders must not only learn to adapt their usual helping skills to the requirements of a larger setting; they must also master a set of unique interventions that often have the goal of creating and maintaining group cohesion. Group leadership skills are unique because they spur interaction within and among group members, as well as promoting therapeutic factors and the development of the group (Luke, 2014). In this chapter, we will review how you can take what you already know and make needed adjustments for groups, and we will also cover additional skills that will be useful to you.

Helping Skills in Groups

If you compiled a list of all the things that make a group leader effective, you might come up with a number of broad areas. Certainly, what group leaders know is important—their knowledge of theory and human behavior, their understanding of what gets people in trouble and what gets them out, their familiarity with research that guides professional behavior, their ability to create group cohesion, and their skill in appropriate preparations for creating effective group interactions. You would also likely mention several personal characteristics of the leader—integrity, responsibility, dependability, charisma, and so on. You would also list the ability to build positive leader/group-member relationships and the exhibition of Carl Rogers's classic core person-centered skills: empathy, warmth, and unconditional positive regard (Barlow, 2013). No doubt, experts will also have logged a lot of experience in groups, feel comfortable in those settings, recognize important signs during group meetings, and feel confident negotiating through difficult passageways. After all, a guide should be familiar with the territory and how to travel through it.

Knowledge, background, and experience are indeed important for group leaders. In addition, the skills needed to communicate effectively, clarify issues, mediate conflicts, and negotiate through the various stages in the group journey are also required (Brown, 2011).

When participants in groups are asked to contribute to this discussion by listing those skills and behaviors *they* most appreciate in their leaders, they mention such things as a leader who:

- has a clear vision for the group,
- demonstrates caring and compassion,
- teaches new skills,
- listens and responds to issues,
- helps everyone work together as a team, and
- makes everyone feel valued. (Ray & Raiche, 2006)

Although this survey is related primarily to work groups in organizations, the same set of skills would also apply in any context or setting. Assuming that you agree with this assessment, the question now becomes, How do you propose to learn these skills?

For a Class Activity

Conduct your own piece of research with classmates. In small groups, each person shares an experience describing the best group leader ever encountered. This could have been in a therapeutic type of group but may also have been in a class, a business setting, or any other group.

Talk to one another about the skills this leader demonstrated, rather than about any personal qualities or other dimensions that were present. In other words, what was this person able to do that made him or her so effective? How did that influence you in the group?

You can read books and journal articles to learn the conceptual background of what works in groups. You can talk to more experienced group leaders and supervisors to find out about the stuff you need to make sense of groups. All these ideas will give you insight into being an effective group leader, but we strongly believe that to master the skills of group leadership, actual structured experience is a requirement. You must find ways to practice new skills, receive constructive feedback on your progress, and then make appropriate adjustments.

One of our favorite skills in groups is called *immediacy*. This is when you access what you are experiencing in the moment and then communicate aloud what you sense and feel. It is an especially potent intervention to use when someone is talking in a detached way. For instance, imagine that you are leading a group in which one of the members, Owen, presents himself in a robotic, monotone voice. You want to help him be more expressive because you can tell that others are starting to disengage. In this situation, you might use immediacy to say something like this:

Leader: Owen, I'm aware that right this moment, as you talk about your strong desire for closeness, I don't feel close to you. Rather, it seems like you are doing a lot to put distance between yourself and the rest of us.

Owen: [Shrugs] I don't know. Maybe. I guess so.

It is apparent that this intervention, however accurate, was a bit premature, since Owen now seems defensive and even more withdrawn. He actually pulled his chair back and crossed his arms. The leader again tries to use immediacy to address this.

Leader: I just noted that as I gave you feedback, you moved your chair back a bit. I wonder if what I said came across as threatening in a way that pushed you away from me. I did not mean to push you away; rather, I was trying to feel closer to you.

You can imagine the intensity of the encounter, the realness of the feedback that forces a person to confront behavior—that is, if the time is right. In this case, because the leader was not paying close attention to Owen's reactions, the use of immediacy was not initially useful.

Now, if you had been sitting in that group, closely watching the interaction, perhaps you could have pointed this out to the leader, suggesting that Owen wasn't ready to hear what was being offered. One of the best things about groups is that even when the leader is off-base, other members can jump in to save the day and talk about what is happening in the room. Indeed, in the example above, another person did intervene and let the leader know that what he was saying did not appear to be helping. It takes this kind of feedback to get better at your leadership skills. For that to happen, however, you are going to have to solicit ways to get supervised experience and practice.

For Personal Application

Immediacy is a core helping skill in group because it brings the attention of the group to the present moment, also known as the "here and now." Here-and-now interactions in group are so powerful because they refer to experiences and events that every person in the room can relate to—the experience is unfolding before everyone's eyes, and each person is intimately involved. Generally, people spend little time in the here and now; we tend to relate to past events or talk about the future, but the experience in the present is often dismissed or disregarded. One reason for that is that being in tune with the present often carries a feeling of risk, especially when relating to another person. So we are asking you to take a risk and try being in the here and now with another person by practicing immediacy. Find a person whom you trust, and go to a private place that is quiet. Stand close to that person so you can clearly see each other. Now, look at each other and speak only about your immediate reactions to each other, what you are feeling, and what you are aware of. See how long you can do this. At first, most people go for only a short time before a defense mechanism kicks in, such as laughing or being silly, since it feels vulnerable and threatening to be so close to someone and reveal your present experience. Yet, after a few times trying this, you will find it easier and much more rewarding to be with that person.

Soliciting Honest Feedback

It is not as easy as it sounds to receive honest feedback from others—that is, to find out what people really think of what you are doing and how you present yourself. Furthermore, it is a rare occurrence to ask for someone's impression of you and then get truly honest feedback you can use. More often than not, when you ask for input from others, you will get "yearbook feedback," the kinds of platitudes people write in high school yearbooks, such as the following:

- "You're so sweet. Don't ever change."
- "You're really nice, and I like you a lot."
- "I just think you're the best, and I'm glad you're here."

Now, all that may be true, but that type of feedback is easy to dismiss since it can appear as a throwaway line. And if the feedback is perceived as negative and you don't like it, you can also dismiss it with a simple response: "Well, you don't really know me, because if you did you wouldn't say that."

For Personal Application

Select three people whom you trust to be completely open and honest with you. Although these could include family members, it would be better to pick classmates, acquaintances, or others whose thoughts and opinions you don't normally hear.

Tell these individuals that you need to collect feedback as part of a school project. Impress on them how important it is that they be as honest and forthright as possible. Explain, as well, that the best feedback is specific, with supporting examples. If needed, provide a few examples.

Ask each person to tell you three things you might not already know about yourself that could be considered strengths and then three things that could be viewed as areas in need of growth. The strengths will most likely be easy to obtain, but most people will struggle with telling you the growth areas for a number of reasons. For one, it is really hard to be honest. Second, it is difficult to tell people things they might not want to hear, and they might not be sure what you are really looking for. That's okay, though. Whatever you hear from others gives you some notion of the challenges involved in giving and receiving feedback.

Our bet is that, in the past, when you have asked someone to review your clinical training tapes (if you are in the helping professions) or to observe you leading a group in action, more often than not you have heard that you are doing a fabulous job. Trust us: They were lying, or at least not telling you the whole story. Even though you may be talented and gifted, there are plenty of areas for growth and improvement, since you likely have limited skills and experience. But the truth is, everyone can get better and find places to improve. Even after all our years of leading groups, we leave every session with our heads hurting over all the things we wish had gone differently, all the things we could have done instead, all the gaffes and mistakes we made, and all the different courses of action we wish we had considered. After we talk to colleagues about the session, we find out about dozens of other things we missed.

Of course, it is important to be forgiving of mistakes, especially if you hope to learn from them. A nice thing about group work is that for the most part, despite the mistakes or missteps leaders make, the group itself often does okay and still evolves. In that sense, groups are pretty resilient. So at the end of a group, if you can say that the group did okay, it evolved, or took a step forward, then you should be happy with that, since that is the most important thing. However, you can still look at your performance and search for areas of growth. What we enjoy so much about leading groups is that there is always so much to learn. No matter what you do or how you do it, there are other things you could have done that might have worked better. The point we are making is that you must get lots of honest feedback from peers and supervisors if you are ever to improve your skill levels. One useful practice is to purge from your vocabulary the words *positive* and *negative* in reference to the activity of receiving feedback. After all, is it "positive" when someone tells you that you did a good job? What can you learn from that statement? And is it "negative" when someone tells you that you raise your voice at the end of statements, communicating doubt and undermining your persuasive influence? Rather than using those labels, it is better to think in terms of "supportive" and "constructive" feedback and to consider using the term *areas of growth*. We think that each group leader, whether a novice or an expert, should carry an imaginary "Work in Progress" sign over his or her head to acknowledge that we are always in the process of improving.

For a Class Activity

It's time to practice giving and receiving feedback regarding your basic skills. In groups of four, divide the roles as follows: One of you will be a client and talk about some issue (real or imagined), another will be the helper, and the other two will be observers who take detailed notes on the proceedings. You are to conduct a 5-minute interview in which you practice helping skills you have already learned. You might want to stick with the basics: open-ended questions (those that can't be answered with "yes" or "no"), rephrasing (reflecting content), and reflecting feelings. At the end of the 5 minutes, close the brief session with a summary statement.

The observers have the toughest job. Your role is to write down at least three things your partner did that you thought were especially good and three things you think might be useful to work on. Your feedback here must follow the cardinal rule of being direct, concise, and to the point. You are not responsible for being "right" or seeing the "truth." Your job is simply to express your opinion about what you observed. There will be two of you to compare notes, and your partner can decide whether what you offer fits. If this is the first time this particular feedback was heard, maybe it is more about the observers' perceptions (or experience level) than about the helper's behavior. End the round by giving the observers feedback on their feedback. Remember, this is really an exercise in the importance of being honest and constructive.

Switch roles after each round so each partner gets a chance to give and receive feedback.

Sample Observer Notes

Supportive feedback:

1. Good eye contact and attending behavior, communicating intense interest.

2. Good rapport established early when you told her what you understood.

3. Restatements were clear and concise, natural rhythm and flow to the conversation.

Constructive feedback:

1. Vocabulary of "feeling" words too limited. Kept saying *sad*, *mad*, and *frustrated*.

2. Waited too long to insert comments. Let client ramble too much. Seemed reluctant to say the "wrong" thing.

3. Try not to ask so many questions. At times you seemed impatient. Rather than waiting for her to think, you'd ask another question before she had a chance to answer the previous one.

Skills Adapted for Groups

It is assumed that you are not experiencing this course in isolation—that you have taken, or will at some point take, a class on basic helping skills. It might be useful for you to review or familiarize yourself with these skills as you prepare for working in group settings.

One of the challenges of groups compared with individual sessions is that customizing your skills and interventions to the special needs of your clients is so much more difficult. Remember that each of the group members comes from a unique background, through which the things you do and say will be interpreted differently. Thus, acquiring competence in these skills is one thing;

it is quite another to become sufficiently sensitive in their application that you can make adjustments according to the group members you are working with at any given moment (Ivey, Ivey, & Zalaquett, 2014). Thus, not only do you have to work on communicating effectively, but you also have to be concerned with how what you communicate will be received and interpreted by group members depending on their cultural identities as influenced by gender, culture, race, socioeconomic background, sexual orientation, religion, age, and other factors (Singh, Merchant, Skudrzyk, & Ingene, 2012). Rarely will you lead a group in which homogeneity is the prevailing characteristic. Rather, you will find that every group you lead is populated by a veritable United Nations of cultural backgrounds and ethnicities. Even though the struggles and personal issues of group members may be very similar, you must be extremely flexible in choosing your skills wisely and employing them with appropriate sensitivity. Below, we review some of the core helping skills and how they are used in a group setting.

REPHRASING

Also known as *paraphrasing, restating,* or *reflecting content,* this is probably the most common and benign helping skill, used to confirm what was heard. In groups, the leader uses this behavior to model how important it is to listen carefully and respond sensitively to what is said. Ideally, group members catch on to this interpersonal style and begin using it naturally.

Don:	I'd like to try to do more with my life, but I'm so afraid that I'll just be disappointed again. Like always.
Leader:	It'll be another time in your life that you put yourself out there and set yourself up for disappointment.
Don:	Yeah. What's the point? If I'm just going to end up stuck where I am, maybe I shouldn't even try anymore.
Marsha:	So you don't even want to try anymore?

The leader is trying to demonstrate attentive listening and responding behavior, letting Don know that he has been heard. Marsha tries to follow his lead, but as you would expect from a beginner just learning this skill, she turns it into a closed-ended question. Nevertheless, the intention is good. Members are learning how to listen and respond appropriately. The leader is showing that he cares and understands.

REFLECTING FEELINGS

A companion to rephrasing, this skill also reflects back what was heard, but on a deeper level. This is infinitely more difficult to do, because you must listen not only to what was said but also to what is felt beneath the surface. When group leaders employ this skill, they are not only taking the discussion to a deeper, more emotional level, but they are again showing group members how to listen, respond to emotion, and convey empathy. As with all behaviors used in group, there is a parallel process going on in which members learn their own helping skills by observation and personal experience at the same time as they are working on their personal issues.

Don: Well, I don't want to give up completely. It's just that . . . I don't know . . . it's just really tough for me.

Leader: You really do have some hope; you're just so frustrated and tired of being let down.

Marsha: I sure know what that's like, too. I remember when . . .

Leader: So, Marsha, you're really relating easily to what Don is going through. Maybe you can talk directly to him [looking at Marsha and gesturing toward Don] and tell him what you sense he's feeling.

Notice the way the leader uses the reflection to interrupt Marsha's digression: She was about to go into her own stuff, which would have taken the focus away from Don. The leader is prompting Marsha to use her own reflections to communicate that she understands. Notice, as well, how the leader directs Marsha to talk directly to Don rather than to the group. That is a way of increasing the intimacy between group members and gently teaching them to direct their comments to other members rather than to the group leader. And you can see how the leader keeps the discussion on a more emotional level, rather than just talking about the content.

INTERPRETING

This is still another way to listen carefully to the communication, decode underlying meaning, and offer that interpretation back to the group member to promote greater self-understanding. In group settings, interpretations can take place on an individual level in which you venture a hypothesis about what might be going on for one person, or such explanations can be offered about group dynamics and process. Since this is potentially a threatening intervention, you want to make sure that the timing is appropriate; otherwise, people may become defensive or shut down.

Don:	Marsha, I appreciate sincerely what you are saying. And I know that you have had some tough times as well, but it's just not the same.
Leader:	Don, Marsha was trying to make contact with you, to show you that she cares, and now it seems that you are negating her experience and pushing her away. You've reported that you do this with others when you feel vulnerable or threatened.
Don:	No, it's not that exactly. I mean, you're right, of course, that I have a hard time letting people get close to me. It kinda freaks me out since I don't trust most people.
Kena:	I have that same problem, Don. Don't feel too bad about it.
Nancy:	Hey, you aren't the only ones! You remember I told you . . .
Leader:	I think that's great that you are all jumping in to give Don some support and that you can relate to his problem. I wonder, though, if what might be going on is that many of you are feeling uncomfortable with this issue yourselves, you sense Don's vulnerability, and so you are trying to distract the focus away from Don.

In this scenario, the leader interprets both Don's statement and the group's behavior. Since such skills are based on assumptions and limited data, you want to phrase them tentatively and sensitively. Notice the way the leader offered the interpretations as "wonderings" and didn't ask them as closed questions ("Are you feeling uncomfortable?"), which often invite a denial.

QUESTIONING

Often, the previous skills are effective in eliciting all the information you might need in working with group members. Sometimes, however, you must resort to more direct inquiries. Here are three guidelines for asking questions:

1. Use them only when indirect means do not work, or you may come across as interrogating.

2. Structure them in an "open" versus "closed" manner so the answers require elaboration.

3. Avoid "why" questions (people usually don't know), and instead ask about "what," "where," and "how."

Remember, it is not just *what* you ask but *how* you ask it that is important. Compare the ways the following questions might be directed toward Don.

Closed-Ended Questions	Open-Ended Questions
Have you always had this problem?	When did you first become aware that you had this problem?
Are you feeling upset with us for intruding so much?	How are you feeling right now?
Do you have brothers and sisters in your family?	Who is in your family?
Do you feel fearful in here?	When do you feel fearful in this group?

Notice that open-ended questions facilitate a much greater level of elaboration and collect more information. In group settings, you will likely do some tutoring with members, teaching them how to ask good questions. For example, if a participant were to ask one of the closed questions just illustrated, you might say, "I wonder how you could frame that question in a slightly different way to get more information."

You will also notice that during the early stages of group development, members will ask a lot of questions as a way of gathering more information about a topic. This may be indicative of members' natural curiosity about one another, but there is usually much more behind the questions, which the group leader can help reveal.

Miles: This has been a really tough day today, and I wasn't sure if I would come to group. I got laid off from my job today and it's pretty rough. I mean, I didn't really even like the job and I have been thinking of quitting for months, but right now I've got tons of bills to pay and the economy isn't good. I don't really know what I'm going to do.

Elvin: Man, that's rough. What kind of job was it?

Miles: Well, I was working as a shipping manager for a local company.

Elvin: So do you have unemployment benefits? Maybe I know someone who could hire you. I can make some calls and . . .

Leader: Elvin, let me stop you for a second. You seem really concerned about Miles.

Elvin: Well, yeah. I mean, I was laid off last year. I am worried about him.

Leader: Elvin, talk to Miles directly about your concern for him.

The group leader blocks the excessive questioning and instead directs Elvin to talk about the thoughts and feelings underlying them. For beginners, it often feels awkward and intrusive to interrupt people in this way, but it is absolutely imperative that you stop counterproductive behavior and teach group members alternative ways of expressing themselves more effectively. Elvin is not asking offensive questions, but the process message behind the questions is that he feels for Miles and wants to help. In a group setting, that can be conveyed directly, and this often strengthens connections and intimacy among group members.

REFRAMING

Many of these skills originated with particular theoretical orientations. You might have recognized, for example, that interpretations evolved from psychoanalytic theory or reflections of feeling from the person-centered approach. In the same vein, reframing is a skill that was once part of brief and family therapy, although it is now as "generic" as the others (Bitter, 2013). The object of this more advanced intervention is to help group members change the way they view their situations or their problems.

Reframing is a form of reauthoring between the group leader and a group member (Luke, 2014). Within a group, reframing is when a group leader supports and affirms part of what is said while offering a new perspective or twist on the rest of the behavior or thought (Corey, Corey, Callanan, & Russell, 2015). This usually means an invitation by the group leader to view the experience, behavior, or thought in a different way. One benefit of reframing is that it helps integrate and make sense of the group experience, and may lower defensiveness. When it is used optimally, reframing creates a perceptual shift that makes it much easier to work with an issue. It is as if you are taking a painting, removing it from an ugly frame, and putting it into a new frame that reveals it in the best possible light. This is something you might want to do in a group when you are aware that you cannot do much with the present issue as it is conceived. Importantly, reframing is often a skill that group members integrate into their own interactions with others, including other group members (Gillies & Haynes, 2011).

In our previous group example, Don says, "I've got a problem with intimacy. Everyone in my family does. It's just in our family genes."

What would you do with a situation like that? As long as Don believes that he has "poor intimacy genes," there is very little you can do for him, short of genetic engineering.

If you attempt to disagree with him or argue with his interpretation directly, he may become defensive. In reframing, you take his conception of the problem and put a slightly different cast on it: "What you are saying, Don, is that many members of your family have shared your fears about getting close to others."

Notice that in this "rephrasing" of Don's statement, some subtle differences work to create openings. The leader uses *many* instead of *all*, implying that there are exceptions to his family disorder. Second, the problem is changed from a genetic predisposition toward lack of intimacy, which cannot be overcome or controlled, to a learned fear of intimacy that might require some new teaching to correct. This is a problem that could actually be worked on in the group, whereas the previous one is not.

For a Class Activity

Work with a partner to devise several ways to reframe each of the following presentations of a problem by a group member:

1. "I guess I'm kind of promiscuous. At least that's what my parents say. I've only had sex with three different people, but I didn't really date them very long before we slept together."

2. "I'm stupid. I've always been stupid. I mean, how else can I explain my inability to get a decent grade in this class?"

3. "It isn't my fault that things keep going wrong. It's this damn system that is so screwed up."

CONFRONTING

Confrontation has a bad reputation. That is because most people conjure the images of arguing, fighting, and chaos often depicted on rambunctious afternoon talk shows. Yet within group settings, the best confrontations do not require raised voices or chairs flying through the air but, rather, subtle comments the person doesn't even recognize as confrontation. In the working stage of a group, there will be many confrontations, since the reality of any group is that each person is different and sees the world and others in unique ways. It is often in the working stage when honesty prevails and these differences come into the open. Furthermore, group members are usually not very good at either confronting one another or responding to these honest statements. That is why the leader models this behavior as much as possible to point out discrepancies among words, body language, and behavior, either in the present or between what was said or done earlier and what is happening now.

Kena: Don, I think you're just saying that stuff about your family as an excuse so you don't have to change. It is so much more convenient to claim that it's in your makeup rather than facing that you own part of that issue.

Don: That's not helpful or true!

Leader: Okay, let's slow this down for a second. Kena, as you can tell, Don is feeling angry and put off about what you've just said, so most likely he's not hearing the message you're trying to give him. Perhaps you could try that again, but this time say it in a way that Don can hear what you're trying to convey to him.

Kena: Okay, that's cool, 'cause I'm not trying to tick him off. Let's try this again. Sorry, Don. Okay, so some of this is my stuff. I've dated too many guys who just say they can't get closer to me because it's not part of their makeup. So hearing that come from you upset me since I experience you so differently and can see each week how much you're trying to change. So when you keep saying "it is not possible," it negates what I see in you each week. So what I meant to say to you is that maybe you have your own fears of getting close to others and getting close to me, but don't turn off and say you *can't* change, because each week I see what's happening to you.

Don: Um, okay . . . wow, Kena! I am a bit speechless, and that's a little hard for me to hear because it's new to me, but thanks for saying that.

The leader has obviously been working in this group to help members learn to confront one another effectively. Since this is one of the hardest skills to learn, it takes considerable practice to find a balance. Otherwise, group members will either "make nice" and avoid confrontations altogether (a conspiracy to avoid deep, threatening work) or become too aggressive and combative.

Student Voice
Learning to Confront Others

By far the best skill I learned in group is the semantics of how to confront people on their behaviors. During this group, I have confronted so many people on their behaviors (and they have confronted me as well) and so far no one has cut ties with me or punched me in the face. I still struggle with how I want to say it, but at least now I know how to start with, "I am aware" or "I have noticed." This is a huge skill for me to have as a counselor because it will allow me to challenge my clients. It is also a very important skill for me to have in my personal life. I have not been able to be as assertive as I have always wanted and as a result I have allowed people to take advantage of me. Every time it happened, I lost a bit of my self-esteem and my self-worth. However, now with this skill, I have some tools to stop my self-defeating cycle. Based on the feedback a group member gave me, I realized I have become more assertive in my life and I am not the shy, quiet girl who always got stomped on. I was not aware of this part of my growth until this person's feedback (and then four other group members' feedback) pointed it out to me. This validation was reassuring. Certainly, it has given me the confidence to continue working on this area of my life. It is so fascinating how another person's perspective of me dramatically changes the way I see myself.

For a Class Activity

Form small groups, choose a topic of discussion, and practice basic listening and responding skills with one another. As each person speaks, rephrase the content of what was said or reflect the underlying feeling being expressed. Do not attempt to ask questions yet or engage in any "fix-it" behavior; just practice listening and responding with reflections of content and feeling.

SELF-DISCLOSING

Among all the basic skills, self-disclosure or leader transparency is often the most important one for the leader to demonstrate. The object is to make it safe for group members to reveal themselves in an honest, open way. If the leader, who has power and status, can show members how attractive it is to be open and vulnerable, then others will follow. The leader often reveals personal, here-and-now reactions to what is happening in the group (Luke, 2014). In doing so, the leader shows genuineness, authenticity, and aspects of his or her true life and personality. The leader must be careful, though, as leader self-disclosure can be easily abused since it takes the focus off the members.

In our illustrative group, the leader might address Don's reluctance to talk about his intimacy issues in the following way:

Don, I can see that you're feeling uncomfortable with all this attention and even getting into this issue. I once had similar difficulties, especially in groups. Yes, I can see you're surprised, but I came from a very challenging family in which the only way my parents showed intimacy was to scream at each other, or at me. I decided that I'd never trust anyone to the point they could hurt me. What made the difference for me was realizing that although there are risks involved in trusting people, letting them get close, the alternative is far worse. Now, it took some time and some very caring people to help me learn that, but ultimately I feel like I did. I don't know about you, but I often felt very lonely relying only on myself all the time.

It is hoped that Don will feel encouraged by this disclosure. If this successful leader, who obviously is now quite skilled at intimacy, can overcome this problem, maybe Don can, too. Such a disclosure gives members explicit permission to be vulnerable and afraid. It also shows that the problem can be overcome through commitment, hard work, and allowing others to help.

Self-disclosure is a skill that can easily be overused and abused. It carries with it certain dangers because it takes the focus off clients and puts it on the leader. You've probably encountered people in powerful positions (supervisors, teachers, professors, etc.) who talked way too much about themselves, leaving you to feel overburdened or bored. When using self-disclosure, you will want to be brief and focused, making certain not to lapse into self-indulgence.

Before using self-disclosure, you should always ask yourself the following questions:

1. Is there another way I can do this without putting the focus on me?

2. Will a group member say the same thing? If so, better for the group member to say it.

3. How can I say this in the most efficient way so as not to keep members' attention for very long?

4. How will this help the group and the group members?

5. Am I balanced in who I am choosing to self-disclose with?

SUGGESTING

As we mentioned in the very first chapter, giving people advice is generally not a good idea. For one thing, people hardly ever listen to advice; for another, if what you tell group members to do does not work out as they hoped, *you* will be the one blamed. Even worse than giving bad advice, if what you suggest does turn out well, then you have inadvertently reinforced the idea that they should come back to you for advice in the future.

Just as you must be mindful of the unforeseen side effects of self-disclosure, confrontation, and other skills, you must be careful whenever making suggestions. Ideally, such guidance should be framed tentatively, so as to get group members to think creatively and perhaps come up with their own specific course of action. Such a skill might be used whenever someone is about to do something you know is unsound or unsafe (possibly reacting in haste or in the heat of the moment), or whenever you believe that others may profit from a gentle probe in a particular direction. You can also see that we have reframed the notion of *advice* by using the term *suggestion,* which is a bit more subtle and indirect.

Even if you refrain from advice giving as a policy, you are going to find that group members rely on this strategy as their favorite method of being helpful to other members, especially in early stages of the group (Brown, 2011; Forsyth & Diederich, 2014). The responsibility will fall on you to interrupt these well-meaning attempts gently and lead participants to find more suitable and effective means to reach desired goals.

Don:	I'm hearing what everyone is saying, and it's really given me a good idea. Remember that woman I've been talking about? The one from work who I had coffee with a few times? So, I was thinking that maybe I'd approach her and tell her I want to be close to her.
Leader:	If I might make a suggestion, Don?
Don:	Sure, I'll take all the advice I can get.
Leader:	Well, this isn't so much advice as an observation or suggestion. In the past, you have managed to scare people away in various ways, usually by withdrawing.
Don:	Yeah. So? This time I'm doing the opposite and trying to get closer.
Leader:	Exactly! And that shift in your stance toward staying engaged is a big step in the direction you want to go. But in this situation, can someone help Don understand what might happen?
Kena:	Hey, Don, you know that I love you, but man, all I can tell you is that if you came on to me like that and I barely knew you, I'd run so fast you wouldn't even find my trail. It would freak me out just a little too much.
Sabine:	Yeah, I'd have to agree. Kinda creepy. Seriously, dude.
Don:	I'm confused. So, are you saying I shouldn't tell her how I feel? I thought that was the point of all this.
Marsha:	No. I agree with Kena. Just tone it down a bit, find the middle ground. It's just that you gotta be a bit more subtle.
Kena:	Okay, Don, here's how I see it. Stick with wanting to be close to her and others. But don't tell her that yet. Not everyone is in a group like us, and other people might not get it like we do.

In groups, it is so much more challenging for the leader to get the members to do the work, rather than doing it all oneself. That means you have to thoroughly master these skills before you can ever hope to teach them to others. Your job is to get the ball rolling, to recognize that a suggestion is indicated, and then to cue members to do what needs to be done. You can always fill in whatever they miss. But a key point here is that if the group members can actually do the work, let them do it so they gain confidence and skills and feel more capable and cohesive as a group.

SUMMARIZING

Just as in individual sessions, there are opportune times in groups when it is helpful to review what has just been covered. This can bring together disparate themes, connect related elements, link several issues that have been discussed, or bring some sort of closure to a topic as a transition into a new area (Corey, Corey, Callanan, & Russell, 2015).

Summaries should generally be initiated anytime you are about to leave one topic or subject and move to another, when discussions are disjointed and chaotic, or when a transition is needed. Most of the time, sessions will end with some sort of summary statement. Don't make it a monologue; rather, try to be concise and to the point. Even better, ask group members to summarize what they thought the main issues or themes were, beginning with the one(s) who received the focus. Then you can fill in important issues that were missed.

Leader: Don, you've heard a lot of feedback today, and it really seemed valuable. You've thought about a number of things related to your fears of getting close to people and letting them get close to you. I wonder if you wouldn't mind summarizing what you think this was all about for you.

Don: We were talking a lot about the things I learned growing up in my family about not trusting people. I had a lot of excuses for using that stuff as a reason for not having many good relationships now. That's about it, I guess.

Leader: As you finished speaking, I saw a few members smile and shake their heads like there is a bit more to add.

Nancy: Hey, Don, don't forget the part about the uncertainty you still feel about changing this pattern.

Sabine: Donnie, don't forget the observations from people in here that we're seeing you make changes in group and that people are feeling close to you and you are feeling close to them. You are doing the work. We see it.

Kena: Yeah, and remember about being cool and finding the middle ground and not coming on too strong to people you like.

Leader: Thanks. Okay, that's helpful. In addition, Don, you talked a lot about the closeness you felt to others in this group, how this felt like a good beginning for the kinds of relationships you want in your life. You got excited about possibilities and even identified one woman who you wanted to get closer to. We talked about ways you could make that happen and how you might sabotage things. Finally, you declared that you wanted to try some new things and report back to us. Maybe you could tell us some more about exactly what you intend to do?

Notice the way this summary naturally leads into a homework assignment that Don can complete between group sessions. It also sets the stage for the next group, when Don can update the group on how he used this information over the week. Not all group leaders structure the group in this way, but generally speaking, it is agreed that unless members work on issues between sessions, lasting change is not very likely (Corey, Corey, Callanan, & Russell, 2015; Morgan & Flora, 2002; Prochaska & Norcross, 2010; Viers, 2007).

For a Class Activity or Field Study

For several minutes, participate in a group discussion about some topic of mutual interest. If you are doing this with classmates, you could take turns talking about your strengths and weaknesses in various skill areas, including what you think you do best and where you feel less prepared. After each person speaks, spend another few minutes giving that person feedback based on what you have observed. Remember to include both supportive and constructive comments.

Before each person begins, select someone else in the group to act as a scribe. The scribe will take detailed notes on what you say about yourself and what others tell you in the way of feedback.

Once a person has heard the feedback, he or she must summarize what was said, highlighting the most important areas and commenting on new things learned. Afterward, the scribe will fill in anything you missed by referring to the notes taken.

Group Skills

The previous section reviewed skills that are common to all helping encounters, although they were demonstrated to show how they might be adapted to group settings. This next set of skills is somewhat unique to the practice of group leadership.

LINKING

Linking involves building as many bridges and connections as you can between members, joining their issues and fostering direct interaction. It also involves creativity and insightfulness to relate what one person says to another person's concerns. You will do this in many ways. One challenge in leading a group is that people will be all over the place with their comments and input. One person will talk about some poignant moment, and before she can even finish, someone else will say, "That reminds me of a story . . . ." Then another group member will make a comment about something else that seems completely unrelated. It is the leader's task to look for common themes and to link group members together. One way of doing this is by observing aloud a common experience or theme that connects members' stories or behavior. It could sound like this: "Something I am hearing in many of your experiences is this idea of feeling invisible, as if people see you but not enough to notice that you are in pain or needing some attention; so many of you are feeling alone with this sadness."

Another form of linking involves a type of summary in which you connect several comments together:

> Carole, when you were talking about how it's hard for you to sleep at night, I noticed that both you, Jamie, and you, Ronnie, were nodding your heads. Earlier, you both were talking about how you get stressed out as well, but in different ways. It seems to me that this is also related to what Megan was talking about earlier when she said she doesn't like to go to parties because she gets all jittery and then drinks too much. It seems that one theme that's emerging has to do with managing stress in new situations.

A more active and present form of linking is facilitating an interaction among group members in the here and now. This is a way of directly connecting group members' intrapersonal experiences. This type of linking is more elegant, since you get the group members to do the work in the here and now:

Jamie: [Talking to leader] I know just what Carole is going through 'cause I also get . . .

Leader: [Pointing to Carole] Talk to Carole. Tell her what you are telling me.

Jamie: [Turning to Carole] Yeah. Well, it's just that I get pretty upset about things, too. It's not my sleep that gets disrupted so much as I start eating too much.

Leader: Ronnie, I noticed you were nodding your head when Jamie and Carole were talking, as if you can relate to what they're saying. Talk to them about your experience.

The interaction above highlights another challenge you will face in that group members will initially direct all their comments to you, ignoring everyone else. It is as if you are the hub of a wheel and they are linking to you; everyone talks and looks to you even though they are talking about someone else. At the beginning of groups, most members don't know what to do, and so they seek the leader's approval and validation. If these tendencies are left unchecked, you will end up with a "leader-centered" group in which all communications are filtered through you. The best intervention is simply to ask, "Can you say that directly to Bob [or to whomever the comments are directed]?"

The leader is building cohesion and trust in the group by joining group members in their common experiences. Every time a communication is directed to the leader, a gentle reminder is given to speak directly to the other members. In some cases, the group leader will refuse to make eye contact with the speaker, which often forces the speaker to find a more attentive audience. In such instances, we prefer to explain what we are doing so as not to appear rude. After a few times doing this, the group members will automatically switch their focus from the leader to other members. Of course, the added benefit is that most group members will also begin to do this in their lives outside of the group.

CUING

You already witnessed a bit of cuing in the preceding example. This skill involves scanning the group very carefully every minute or so, watching for the slightest nuance in nonverbal behavior. It is like taking the pulse of each group member, checking to see how each person is reacting to everything that is happening. You would be amazed how much you can read in people's expressions, body posture, and nonverbal behavior. Most group members are not very good at bluffing—they give away all their reactions nonverbally.

One of our favorite interventions is to become aware when we are having a strong reaction to something going on in the group. Maybe we are bored or frustrated or just having a hard time connecting with what is being said—but we are reacting to the group process and looking for a way to draw attention to that process. Perhaps someone said something that seemed unusually insensitive or misinformed. Generally, there are negative side effects to the leader being the one to say something in such instances, since the leader has a lot of power and should wield it carefully. Leader comments are often taken as a censure or as critical, and often as the ultimate truth. It is usually far better to get others to communicate aloud what you think needs to be said or what you perceive to be happening in the group. One way to do this is by inviting members to say what you think they are feeling, based on the nonverbal cues you observe.

I (Matt) can remember an example that has often played out in groups I have run. A Caucasian male group member (Carter) was talking about how easy his job was and how he never had any problems. I had heard this before from Carter and others like him, and it was a little hard to listen to since Carter tended to depersonalize his comments so that others were the ones with the problems and never him. Carter had led a rather privileged life, yet many others in the group had come from much more modest backgrounds and had encountered numerous struggles along the way. I noticed some glazed eyes in the group and thought to myself, "Man, this guy has no idea how he sounds!" Yet I knew from previous interactions with Carter that if I said something to him, he would likely feel hurt, sense my disapproval, and immediately become defensive and pout. So I scanned the group to see who else might be feeling the same way I was. I noticed that among the several members who appeared bored, there was one group member who was particularly tactful and sensitive in the way she gave feedback to other members. "Samantha," I said to her, startling her out of a fantasy, "I noticed that as Carter was talking, you seemed to be somewhere else, as if you were not very connected with what he was saying. Perhaps you could tell Carter what was going on for you."

Cuing is used whenever you believe someone needs an invitation to speak, or when you want to redirect the discussion to another area, such as the present group process. It is a way to control the flow of the group, to cut off rambling, and to get maximum participation from the widest number of members.

New group leaders often question if it is okay to cue someone who has not verbally stated an intention to speak or even raised a hand. Maybe people are still reeling from early school experiences of being called on to solve a math problem on the board. But remember that cuing is not random and that people constantly signal (consciously and unconsciously) that they have something to say about what is happening. Leaders should feel free to cue others; some will refuse, and that is fine, but most of the time, you will be bringing people into the group and helping them speak about their current impressions or experiences.

BLOCKING

If cuing is an invitational skill, then its counterpart involves stopping those member actions that are deemed inappropriate, insensitive, or unnecessary. That often means cutting off a member from talking or continuing to talk. There are many ways to do this, most directly by saying, "I'm going to stop you right now." This might be accompanied by raising a hand, palm turned outward to create a visual "stop sign." This is not done in an obnoxious or in-your-face kind of way but, rather, in a subtle gesture that is the universal sign for stopping—what kids do when they are playing traffic cop.

Photo 8.1 It is challenging, yet absolutely critical, for skilled group leaders to be prepared to intervene when someone is rambling, dominating time, playing games, being disrespectful, or otherwise acting inappropriately. This may be uncomfortable for you, at first, but you must learn to block a group member without shutting that person down and then to draw out others to balance the interactions.

When might blocking be indicated? Here are several clear examples:

- When someone is being pressured to do or say something that he or she does not feel ready for
- When someone is talking way off-topic or storytelling too much
- When someone is being ridiculed or picked on
- When someone is rambling or being distracting
- When someone uses intellectualizing as a defense
- When someone starts making excuses
- When someone is disrespectful or abusive toward others
- When someone uses an insensitive or offensive slur
- When someone is doing anything that is interfering with the productive flow of the group
- When someone is talking about events and persons outside the group that can't be controlled
- When you just need to stop the group for any reason to process something that is happening

Note in the example below the ways the group leader tries several different blocking strategies before one of them is successful.

Murray: So I was thinking maybe that it wasn't that important after all. I mean . . .

Leader: What you're saying, Murray, is that . . .

The leader first attempts to interject a summary statement as a way to help this member stop rambling and be more precise, but that doesn't work.

Murray: What I was trying to say is that . . . I don't know. It's just hard to put it into words.

Leader: Maybe it would be best if you stopped for a moment and gathered your thoughts, and then we can come back to you later.

This intervention is a lot more direct, but Murray is persistent and doesn't like to be sidetracked. Ordinarily, you might let him go on a bit longer, but you are trying to model for other group members ways they can engage one another directly. In addition, time is running short, which is often the case. Whereas in individual sessions you might allow clients to take their time getting to the point, in group you are required to intervene much more quickly because you are attempting to meet so many different needs simultaneously.

Murray: No, that's okay. I'd rather finish now.

Leader: Before you continue, Murray, I couldn't help but notice that some other things seemed to be going on while you were talking. Kammy, you seemed to be feeling impatient while Murray was talking. Your foot was moving up and down. You kept squirming in your chair. And at one point, you even started snorting. Perhaps you could tell Murray what has been going on for you?

In this case, rather than confronting Murray directly and risking that he might feel further censured by an authority figure, the leader instead scans the group to see who else is having a similar reaction. The leader cues Kammy to do the confronting work because she is known to be direct and honest, yet diplomatic and sensitive. The particulars of what you try in your efforts to block inappropriate or counterproductive behavior are less important than the realization that some intervention is called for. Trust us: You will know when this is happening, because you will be bored and wondering how to stop what is going on, and/or you will notice group members intently staring at you or sending a very clear nonverbal message in your direction that basically says, "You are the leader. Do something!"

Blocking can be a tough group leader intervention to learn, and some feel ambivalent about it because it may seem socially inappropriate or against what they have been taught. But it is important to remember that leading a group is not a social outing or interaction. Leaders often have to block to protect group members or to keep the group process relevant to the task of the group (Luke, 2014).

SUPPORTING

When you work with one person at a time, it is relatively easy to monitor closely how the person is doing throughout the experience. You are constantly observing the person's every movement, gesture, and verbalization—checking for understanding, responsiveness, defensiveness, readiness, openness, and a host of other things. In a group setting, however, you have a dozen or more different individuals who are all responding to what is happening in their own unique ways. It is not unusual for some people to inadvertently get in over their heads, either because they have gone too far or because they find themselves surprised by the intensity of their reactions.

In the example from the previous section, Kammy confronted Murray and then felt remorse afterward. You were actually quite proud of her courage in demonstrating honesty, so it is important that she feel supported in her efforts.

Kammy: I'm sorry, Murray. I didn't mean to hurt your feelings like that. I guess I should learn to be more patient.

Murray: Yeah. Well. That's okay. But what I was trying to say earlier . . .

Leader: Wait a moment, Murray. [Notice more blocking here on the leader's part.] It seems important to stay here with Kammy. She seems to be struggling with her decision to be honest with you in saying that she finds it hard to listen to you when you take so much time to repeat yourself. In fact, I notice you are about to do it again.

Murray: Yeah. I guess so.

Leader: So let's take a moment to work with Kammy on this. I'm wondering how the rest of the group feels about Kammy's attempt to give Murray feedback. Do you think she was out of line? You can tell she is beating herself up pretty good right now.

Fred: I don't know about the rest of you, but I'm in awe of her. I think . . .

Leader: [Pointing toward Kammy] Fred, tell Kammy.

Photo 8.2 There are times when a group member can profit from honest and direct feedback and other times when support is needed. Reading this person's nonverbal behavior, you can see that she is either pouting or withdrawn (other factors may also be at play). In any case, other group members have been encouraged by the leader to offer caring and support until such time as she feels ready to continue.

Notice the leader's attempt to recruit support for Kammy by encouraging members to talk directly to her. The leader wants to make sure that Kammy ends up feeling supported and reinforced for her courage. When group members take risks, they need to be validated and supported for doing so. In the example above, this was a critical moment in the group—the first time a member confronted another member. Even though the leader initiated the action, it is crucial that this behavior be rewarded as much as possible so that others will follow the lead. While the leader is working to support Kammy, getting additional support for Murray is also important. That may not be the immediate focus, but it is important to remember that he may also need support.

For Personal Application

Experiment with using support as a helpful skill during your time in this class or in others (or in online discussions). Whenever someone says something that you especially appreciate or that you believe took courage to initiate, show the kind of encouragement to others that you would most appreciate if roles were reversed. Now, take this experience out of the classroom. Choose one day when you are going to focus on supporting anyone you encounter who does something that you appreciate or who has the courage to take a risk. Evaluate the experience when you are done. What happened? How did people respond? How do you feel about it?

Group members need support when they become overemotional, when they do or say something they are unsure about, or when they are feeling mistrustful. At the most basic level, you should support group members anytime they do something you want them to continue doing. This could occur in situations when someone:

- says something kind or caring to another,
- discloses something very personal,
- takes a significant risk,
- confronts another appropriately,
- uses the language of self-responsibility,
- ceases doing something inappropriate or distracting,
- completes an assignment or keeps a promise of forgiving a mistake or failure,
- shows unusual sensitivity toward others' cultural or personal differences, or
- facilitates the process and progress of the group.

In other words, every time a behavior you like occurs in the group, you will want to support that behavior. One of the most common forms of leader support is attentiveness to group members (Harel, Shechtman, & Cutrona, 2012). Remember that you have an audience watching, so vicarious reinforcement is occurring at all times. When you communicate that you like a particular member's contribution, most everyone thinks, consciously or unconsciously, "Hey, I want the leader to like what I'm doing, too!" Yet, at a more basic and caring level, when you see someone who is dangling out there and needing support, and for some reason is not getting it, look for ways to make sure that member gets some support before the group ends.

Importantly, providing support to group members is effective modeling of how they can interact with one another in a prosocial manner. When group members reveal their pain or risk sharing intimate details of their lives, they are requesting support for their stressful experiences and, in doing so, hoping to reciprocate later in providing support to others. Getting support and giving it to others feels good. Modeling and creating a supportive group matters, as supportive behavior can have the strongest positive impact on members' behavior in the group (Shechtman & Toren, 2010). Conversely, nonsupportive group leader behavior is associated with negative outcomes and group dropout (Bernard et al., 2008).

For Reflection

Think of a time in class when your instructor used overt support to reinforce desirable behavior. Recall the effects of that intervention not only on the target person's behavior but also on your own inclinations to do something similar in the future.

Make a list of all the specific behaviors, actions, and contributions that are consistently supported by your instructor in class. Make a separate list of specific behaviors that your instructor has tried to extinguish or discourage. Try to trace how the norms were established that certain behaviors are supported and others are blocked.

ENERGIZING

If group members are not fully engaged in the experience, they will not learn much. Even worse, if they are bored, they will not return. Groups are special, unique places that value engagement and connection. Yet, when that is not being achieved, you can be sure that something is happening at a group process level that requires your attention. You will often be the one who has to note the lack of energy, bring people into focus, and help remind group members about why they are there.

During a session, you are taking continual readings of the group energy level. Are people paying attention to what is going on? Who has checked out? What is the intensity level in the group? Essentially, you are trying to maintain an optimal level of engagement in which people are fully present, thoroughly enamored with what is happening, but not overstimulated to the point where they feel threatened and shut down.

You can assess the group's energy level in two ways. First, you can check your own internal reactions to what is happening. This can be a very useful tool since, presumably, you have full access to what is going on inside you. The only problem with this measure is that your reactions may not be representative of what others are feeling, especially if you have a lot of experience in groups. Jeffrey becomes bored very easily, for instance, not only because he has been leading groups for so long but because, generally, he has a high threshold for stimulation. This is an issue he is constantly working on. It also explains why he enjoys groups so much: They have much higher energy levels than do individual sessions. Matt, however, can sometimes engage so intensely with a group member that he is not bored when others in the room are yawning or planning their grocery lists. In either circumstance, we have to work consciously to correct for our own inclinations when trying to determine the group energy level.

Student Voice

Gaining Support

I came in pretty excited, but I was a little unsure about sharing in a group. I am great sharing one-on-one, but I get nervous in groups and tend to keep myself quiet and have others talk. In my group, I quickly learned that by opening up, I was able to connect more deeply with other people in the group and strengthen interpersonal bonds. Sharing became a powerful interpersonal tool rather than an intrapersonal weakness. Before this particular group experience, I believed the best and only way to strengthen bonds with other people was to constantly be supportive of them, to help them through their trials, and to sacrifice my own need for support. I had done that my whole life! This group experience showed me another way to strengthen bonds with other people by being open and honest and asking for the support I need. I learned on a personal level the power of group work.

The second, and probably more reliable, way to detect current levels of engagement is to scan members for nonverbal cues. Is anyone yawning? Who appears to be lost in fantasy? Who seems antsy and impatient? What about voice tone and sense of drama? Where is the eye contact? Are people checking the clock or their watches? Are they sending the leader the message that a blocking intervention is desperately required?

Now, you might think the most direct method is to ask group members if they are engaged in the group or with a speaker, but we caution you (even though you will not believe us and will therefore learn for yourself) that this will not work. Telling someone they are boring or revealing that you are not engaged in the group can be viewed as a risky thing to say, and so our experience, especially with groups in the induction phase, is that group members will lie. They will yawn one moment and the next say how interesting the speaker was, when asked. So just don't ask; rather, go off the clues and cues in the room that indicate that group members are checking out, and intervene.

It does take real skill not only to read this mood accurately (you can easily misinterpret what you see) but to do something effective to change the energy level. One thing you can always do is simply bring what you observe to the attention of the group and let them deal with it. Another favorite method is to use self-disclosure to talk about your own low energy level or, better yet, to cue someone else to do the same. Finally, I (Matt) often use centering techniques to bring group members together in the present moment when I sense that their minds might be elsewhere. Using a calm pace but a deliberate tone, I might say something like,

> I notice that there seems to be low energy today, as if people are elsewhere in their minds. So let's bring it back to the group. Let's take a moment together and take a deep breath or two . . . . Now look around the room, reacquaint yourself with everyone in the room, see their faces, the people you know in this room . . . okay. We are all here and ready to go . . . .

Groups are about entertainment as much as learning and growth. If participants are not having fun, laughing as well as crying, then they will not be fully engaged in the experience. As much as it is within your control, you want to do everything you can to keep group members engaged and stimulated by what is going on.

For a Field Study

Find a group you can observe that is being led by an experienced leader. Just as useful would be to watch a video of a group in session. Your department or library probably has several videos demonstrating expert group leaders in action. A third option is to complete this exercise anytime there is a demonstration group in class.

It is important to increase your awareness of leadership skills. Using the checklist below as a guide, make a notation every time the leader employs a particular skill. If the leader does something you do not recognize, make a note to yourself so you can check later to find out what it was. Do not focus on the "interventions" or "techniques" that are used (these are more complex), since we have not covered most of those yet. The emphasis here should be only on the leader's skills, meaning those specific, simple behaviors that respond to individual and group actions.

A warning: The action is likely to happen so quickly in places that you may not have time to make sense of what the leader did, much less figure out which of these skills were selected. The object of this exercise is just to get you in the habit of watching what various leadership skills look like when they are used in groups.

Skills checklist:

- Rephrasing
- Reflecting feelings
- Interpreting
- Questioning
- Reframing
- Confronting
- Disclosing
- Suggesting
- Summarizing
- Linking
- Cuing
- Blocking
- Supporting
- Energizing

Review of What You Learned

- Although there are similarities between helping skills used in groups and those used during individual sessions or meetings, some adaptations must be made to acknowledge that a group is present and to let the group members do most of the work.
- One of the main differences is that group helping skills tap into the group process and work to bring together group members so their own reactions to one another are noted and used as group assets.
- Group members especially appreciate leaders who have the skills to listen and respond sensitively, demonstrate respect and fairness, protect member safety, teach new ideas, provide appropriate structure, and help interactions progress smoothly.
- One of the main processes of change in groups occurs through the soliciting and processing of feedback. Since the group setting is one of the rare places where feedback can be obtained from multiple sources, many groups use feedback as one of the key mechanisms of change.
- Skill proficiency is developed only through practice. To master leadership skills, you must find opportunities to demonstrate what you can do and then receive feedback from others about what worked best and ways you can improve.

When to Intervene in Groups 9

With basic theory and skills now in hand, the next challenge is what to do in specific group situations you will face. As a beginner, you will likely be concerned (maybe even obsessed) with doing or saying the "right" thing. You may even have the notion, albeit mistaken, that there is a single correct intervention for any given situation that will arise. Although it is true that there are best practices (Miles & Paquin, 2014), some rudimentary actions you would or would not wish to take, at this point we are more concerned with your knowing that *something* has to be done. There will be times when you are sitting in group, things pleasantly humming along, and you are thinking to yourself, *Gee, this isn't so bad after all. I've really got the hang of this.* Then—wham!—out of nowhere it seems (there were probably warning signs, but you missed them), you are faced with a dilemma and you have to do something.

Maybe someone said something incredibly stupid or insensitive and everyone is looking at you to make it right. Perhaps you notice that nobody seems to be saying much, no matter what you do to prompt them. Maybe there is a proverbial elephant in the room and nobody will talk about it. Or maybe there are long periods of silence, without any indication of stopping. Worst of all, maybe one of the members starts freaking out, right before your eyes, making the rest of the group nervous.

Student Voice

When the Group Needs Me

The first time I led a group, it was a nightmare. First of all, I was too nervous. Maybe I put too much pressure on myself to achieve success. I seemed to lose my grasp on language; I couldn't find the proper words to give feedback and communicate effectively. I also became an overly anxious leader and failed to include all members in the process. I blamed myself for not knowing enough, not having the necessary skills, not being sensitive enough, and not being able to emphasize my thoughts more. I felt as if I behaved like a nervous, inexperienced, and unorganized group leader struggling the whole night to try to hide her anxiety and ineffectiveness. So from my perspective it was a train wreck, yet the group seemed to do okay that night. And me, 1 year later, I am out in the community leading support groups. Thinking back, I probably learned the most from my mistakes, which is exactly how I reframed the whole experience. Now I have a much better sense of when to intervene in my groups—I still am not sure exactly what to do, but I have a good ability of communicating to my group members that I am able to do something to help the group be successful. I used to be so concerned about needing to do the perfect thing, but now I am more focused on just intervening when the group needs me.

Believe it or not, at this juncture it is not that important that you know what to do, as long as you know that you must do something. Your instructor or others might disagree with this point, with the justifiably good reason that you are supposed to know what to do in most situations you face, but the reality is that it is not that easy. Our true confession is that even after so many years of leading and teaching about groups, there are many times when we don't know exactly what to do. That is not to say that, with a minute's consideration or a slight pause, we will not find a route of action and come up with something suitably appropriate; it is just that when we face unforeseen events, our first reaction is usually some anxiety around the realization that we have to do something. A good thing to keep in mind is that if you sense as a leader that you must do something, chances are the group members also sense the need for you to intervene; so most group members will give you a break, since they just want you to take control of the situation.

Much of the time, when you lead groups or do any kind of counseling, the first thing you try will not work anyway. It often takes several different attempts before we stumble on the right combination of skills and interventions to deal with a situation. It may sound odd, but we have learned over time that often the best response to a situation such as this is the same response the fire marshal gives to anyone in a scary situation: Take a deep breath, and try not to panic. Slow down the process, work with the group to state the obvious ("Clearly, something is happening that we need to address . . ."), and then determine an appropriate direction (and if stuck, you can even say, "I am wondering where the group wants to go . . .").

For Personal Application

Think of a time recently when you were sitting in a group situation—in class, at a social gathering, in a meeting—and it was clear to you that some intervention was needed to keep people on task, or to stop them from rambling or hurting one another.

Although in this particular episode nobody did intervene, review in your mind all the things you could have done that would have made things better. Think of at least three different options that could have been used.

Consider each of the alternatives you could have employed, reasoning through what the advantages, disadvantages, and likely consequences would have been. Based on this assessment, select what you think might have been the best choice.

This process is exactly what you do in group leadership situations every time it occurs to you that something might need to be done. The only difference is that instead of having a few minutes to consider your intervention options, you have a few seconds!

It Is Not Always What You Do but When and How You Do It

If it sounds as though we are trying to let you off the hook, take some pressure off, you are right. You have enough to worry about without having to second-guess yourself constantly about choosing the most appropriate intervention. With experience, supervision, and lots of practice, you will become better and better at choosing the most effective response.

Certainly, you have no business leading groups if you do not have a good idea about what to do in various circumstances you will face. And that is exactly what we are saying: You should have a good idea but not necessarily a rigid agenda. It is very important to remain flexible, to read and respond to how members are acting and reacting (Corey, Corey, Callanan, & Russell, 2015). If the first thing you try does not work, it is usually no big deal—you have time and the opportunity to try something else. That is why in this chapter, we care less that you do exactly what you should and more that you do something that is based on sound clinical judgment and common sense.

Differences of Opinion

You will find that if half a dozen different group leaders were faced with an identical situation, even if they all perceived the incident the same way (which of course is very doubtful), they would not necessarily take the same action. Group leaders are all unique in the way they see the work, based on a unique vision and perspective (Nitza, 2014; Stockton, Morran, & Chang, 2014). These individual differences can be influenced from a variety of sources, such as cultural background, theoretical orientation, training and supervision experiences, and so on.

Let's take as an example a situation in which a group has been merrily going about its business when, all of a sudden, with about 25 minutes left in the session, one member announces that he will not be returning again. Members register their surprise. They attempt to explore with this person why he is leaving, but he is evasive and seems as though he does not really want to talk about it. Some group members become angry, feeling manipulated. Others feel hurt and abandoned. This whole episode has lasted all of 4 minutes.

Experienced group leaders would agree that this clearly calls for an intervention. But what exactly needs to be done? Here is a sampling from our experts:

Leader A: I see this as an attempt to control the group and get attention. With the limited information I have, it seems as though he needs to be confronted about more appropriate ways to get his needs met. Even if he does desire to leave the group, this is probably not the most responsible way to do so.

Leader B: Granted, the guy is awkward in announcing his decision. His timing is also a bit strange. Still, I'd take him at face value and applaud his courage in doing what he needs to do to take care of himself. I would respect his right not to disclose any further, but I would ask his permission to have members say goodbye by offering him some final reactions. This closure would be critical.

Leader C: I would ignore the guy for the moment and go with the intense feelings he has stirred up, the anger and the hurt. This is not really about his announcement but about his own issues around saying goodbye. Everything that happens in a group represents an opportunity for growth and work. I would reframe the situation as that. Only after that would I return to the guy who said he is leaving and explore the meaning of this for him and for others.

Leader D: I see the struggle here between exploring the reason for wanting to leave and looking at how the group members are experiencing this moment. There is clearly a concern about the amount of time left in the group and an understanding that this will most likely not get resolved. Rather than press the guy about why he wants to leave, I would instead work with the group members about their reactions, with the belief that this will lead the guy to reveal what is happening for him. If that does not happen, then I would shift to letting the guy say goodbye to the group in the best possible way, knowing that the other group members can process this unscheduled ending next week.

We could go on with other possibilities, but you get the point. There are really a number of viable intervention options, all of which are legitimate, professional responses to the situation. If we surveyed enough experts, surely we would find some sort of consensus about what the best course of action might be. With experience, you will have faced this situation enough times that you will be able to pick what you believe is the best option. Of course, if that option does not work as you hoped, you can then try something else the next time or even come back to it the next week and repair what has happened.

Perhaps we are belaboring the point. We just want you to concentrate on knowing the specific situations when you must intervene in a group. This will form the framework for the various therapeutic options you collect.

For a Field Study

Imagine a difficult scenario in a group you are leading. This could involve a group member challenging your authority and saying aloud that you do not know what you are doing, a hostile conflict between two group members, or your having to confront a group member who consistently arrives late to group but always has a good reason. Or maybe it is something simpler than that, such as a long period of silence lasting for minutes, continuing no matter what you do. It does not matter which challenge you pick as long as it is a very specific situation.

Now, present this scenario to half a dozen people who have led groups. Ask them how they would handle this situation and their reasons for doing so. Compare the answers to see if there is a consensus among all their various opinions.

When You Must Do Something

How do you know when to intervene in groups? Jeffrey notes hearing little bells ringing in his head when he leads a group. No, he's not hallucinating, but rather, he has trained himself to "hardwire" warning signals in his brain when he faces various situations that require some intervention. When something happens in a group that requires immediate attention, the jangling starts, first as a little tinkle, then building to a gigantic gong if he ignores it too long. That is the reminder to act.

For a Class Activity

Your instructor, or an experienced group leader, will conduct a group session in a "fishbowl" in front of your class. This means that the members of the active group sit in the middle of the room in a circle, and the other people sit on the outside of the group "looking in" at what is happening in the active group. This group should be composed only of volunteers who are willing to talk about a particular theme that is introduced, or perhaps simply what it is like to be part of this group. The leader's role will be to employ as many group interventions as can be reasonably inserted in this limited format.

Observers on the outside of the group will serve as process consultants. Your job is to take notes on what you see unfolding in the session. Pay particular attention to the following:

1. What specific interventions, techniques, and strategies do you see the leader using?

2. Applying concepts you have read about or learned in class, which dynamics and processes do you observe in the group?

3. Who in the group most closely speaks for you, expressing your own personal reactions to what occurs?

After the session is completed, the observers will take center stage by forming their own group in the middle of the class. Talk to one another, as if you were alone, about what you observed and experienced during the group session.

After sufficient time, the leader and group members will join the discussion talking about not only how they experienced the group but also their reactions to the observers' comments.

Compile a list of all the group interventions that were witnessed. Discuss alternative strategies that could have been employed as well.

So far in your training you have been exposed to considerable disagreement among researchers, theoreticians, and practitioners about the best way to proceed in your work. Rest assured, however, that there are not only generic skills that almost everyone agrees are useful but also certain predictable situations that will crop up that require an intervention. There may be some debate about the most effective course of action, but almost everyone agrees that bells should be ringing in your ears if you face any of the following situations.

LACK OF GROUP COHESION, TRUST, AND INTIMACY

You should by now be thoroughly convinced that not much constructive work will take place in the groups you lead unless you are able to build collaborative relationships among participants. Cohesion, trust, and good group relationships are among the most important building blocks for any therapeutic activities that take place (Burlingame, McClendon, & Alonso, 2011a; Burlingame, Whitcomb, & Woodland, 2014; Joyce, Piper, & Ogrodniczuk, 2007).

How do you know when you have a problem in this area? Bells and whistles should sound in your head whenever you see evidence of the following:

1. Remarks made in group are consistently superficial and safe.
2. Self-disclosures are minimal and forced.
3. Members come late, leave early, or skip sessions.
4. More than one participant says the group does not feel safe.
5. Risks and honesty seem to be avoided.
6. Confidentiality has been breached.
7. Ground rules and established norms are not respected.
8. People seem to get offended easily.
9. Members are not caring and respectful in their communications.

The preceding symptoms could mean that something else is going on in addition to mistrust issues that are not being talked about. It is generally a good idea to return to basics when the group is not proceeding as expected, and in that sense the leader needs to intervene directly. Ask yourself what you have needed to do in other situations to build closer trust and intimacy. In the group setting, rather than talk around the concern, specifically look for ways to address what makes it hard to form connections and establish trust. One thing to remember is that it is common in a group to have some members who feel connected and safe and others who do not. Rather than making a blanket statement that the "group is not safe" and solely focusing on what is not working for some members, try to explore what is working for others.

For a Class Activity

1. In small groups, share a time when you did not feel safe in a group. Discuss what about the experience made it difficult for you to trust others.
2. After each person speaks, summarize the main barriers to cohesion and collaborative relationships.
3. Apply the variables you identify to your own group experiences in class.
4. Brainstorm ways you could develop more closeness and trust in your class so you would be more inclined to work at a deeper level.

DISRESPECT AND ABUSIVE BEHAVIOR

This should be an easy one to detect. And the direction we offer will be unequivocal and definitive: Do not allow anyone to speak or act disrespectfully toward anyone else. No matter how heated things become, how emotional and passionate the interaction, it is never permissible for people to become abusive. Further, negative behaviors toward group members (e.g., expressed in sarcasm, criticism, strong disagreement, interruption, complaint, refusals to help), though unavoidable, cannot be tolerated, as they lead to disruption and disrespect (Harel, Shechtman, & Cutrona, 2012). When you experience this happening in group, your alarm bell should be loud and persistent, telling you to intervene immediately.

Remember that people come from varied family and cultural backgrounds with different tolerances and definitions for what is considered inappropriate communication. For one person, "asshole" is an affectionate term; for another, screaming at the top of his lungs is simply a way of saying he loves you. In other cases, making aggressive eye contact, interrupting people before they are finished, or even using a nickname may be interpreted as disrespectful. Since you will miss many of these slights, and perhaps commit a few yourself, you must make group members responsible for telling others when a line has been crossed. If you can succeed in facilitating this interaction, in which one member effectively communicates about a perceived offense, then you have gone a long way in modeling that disagreements and conflicts can be worked out.

In general, there are some fairly obvious signs when a group member is being abusive enough to require intervention:

- Someone physically or verbally attacks another.
- Someone shows a marked insensitivity toward others.
- Someone makes a racist or gender-biased remark.
- Someone makes inappropriate nonverbal gestures, for example, with the hands or face.
- A participant becomes so out of control that he or she does not notice the resulting negative effects.
- You notice that someone appears offended or withdrawn as a result of some comment or action.

What all this means is that you have to watch and listen very carefully to make sure that nobody is harmed. In some ways, you are like a playground monitor, but your job goal corresponds to the most fundamental guideline of helping others: Do no harm. Your job is to make sure that while everyone is interacting, learning, and having fun, nobody gets so careless that others are hurt.

For Reflection

Think of a time when someone in a group said or did something—toward you or someone else—that you found extraordinarily hurtful. What happened inside you as a result of this disrespect or insensitivity? How did your behavior change in the future as a result?

RAMBLING

Nothing can kill the energy of a group quicker than one member who talks and talks and talks, not saying much in the process. Others become bored. They check out. Time becomes so squandered by the filibuster that you are unable to address other issues that need attention. Unless some intervention takes place, the whole session can be lost.

Before you go and blame the talker for being boring or so clueless about group interaction, remember that, for all you know, the person who is rambling might think this is what you want. If you were to ask her why she is talking so much, she might say, "Well, heck, nobody else was talking so I thought I might as well use the time."

There are a lot of reasons why people ramble—but usually it comes down to the fact that they do not know better or are not aware of what they are doing. And that simple realization can provide the empathy and understanding to address this with sensitivity and an eye toward positive change and learning. Also, in group settings where others do not want to talk, ramblers could even be unconsciously encouraged to do so by others in the group who want to avoid attention. Rambling can also mean that the person talking is trying to push others away, keeping people from getting too close.

The first signs that you need to do something are when you notice that (1) you are bored and impatient with someone who is speaking or (2) you observe other members showing nonverbal signs of restlessness and boredom. You are most likely aware when you are bored—and, trust us, when you lead groups it will happen. The important thing to consider here is whether your boredom is about you or about the person and the interaction in the room. If the latter, then you will need to look for a way to intervene. In the situation where other group members are bored, rest assured that you will be getting clear signals from them about how they are feeling.

Usually, you will get what we like to call "The Look," which is when group members stare intently in your direction and nonverbally communicate to you, "This person is driving me crazy. You're the leader. Do something!"

The most direct intervention is one in which you stop the person who is rambling, saying something such as this:

- "Let me stop you for a moment. I notice that you have a lot to say about this. I wonder if you could summarize this concisely."
- "Susan, let's stop for a second. You have been speaking a lot about this, and I want to make sure that we are able to assist you. It seems important that we understand your situation. So what exactly do you want us to know?"
- "Let's take a time-out. Bradley, this seems very important, and I can see there are a lot of details to this story, but I am concerned that as you talk more about people and situations not in this group, we might get a little lost and further away from you."
- "Franco, this is a very involved story, and it makes me think that it is very important for you that we understand what has happened. What, specifically, do you want us to know?"

Depending on whether this is a chronic problem or a single episode, you may wish to use the opportunity to elicit feedback for the person: "Candy, if I could interrupt you for a second, I noticed while you were talking that several others seemed to be restless. Clyde's foot is moving a mile a minute. Nigel is yawning. And Lauren is looking off into space. One reason might be because you are taking a long time to get to your point, and I think you have lost people in the details. Before you continue with what you wanted to say, it might be helpful to hear how others are reacting to you."

An intervention such as this accomplishes several things at the same time. First, and often rather importantly, it stops the rambling behavior. Second, and equally important, it gives people valuable feedback on how they are being experienced and perceived; this could change characteristic patterns not only within the group but outside it as well. Finally, it demonstrates ways group members can confront one another effectively during appropriate times. It sends the message to the group that experiences that occur among group members (i.e., feedback and interpersonal relationships in the group) are often more interesting and dynamic since everyone in the room can attest to the experience.

For a Class Activity

In small groups, take turns playing the role of a rambler who takes far too long to make a point. Talk to one another about the power and other benefits that are enjoyed as a result of dominating the group time and avoiding deeper issues.

Practice different ways of getting the rambler to stop the self-defeating behavior, but without wounding the person to the point that he or she withdraws, pouts, or feels defensive. How might you stop and intervene? How would you reframe this intervention as an opportunity to gain feedback rather than stopping someone and shutting that person down?

WITHDRAWAL AND PASSIVITY

It is often difficult to tell when someone has withdrawn in group for some reason that needs attention. Withdrawal is often a conscious attempt to stay out of the spotlight. Furthermore, some members are naturally quiet, so you have to examine behavior in a normative context. At the same time, withdrawal can also be an unconscious behavior used to protect oneself from a perceived threat. Regardless of the reason behind the withdrawal, group leaders need to constantly be on the lookout for such behavior.

Withdrawal often occurs after someone receives feedback that has been filtered in a negative light. Immediately after someone is addressed in this way, watch carefully to see how that person processes the comments. If the person pulls their chair back, refuses to respond, or folds their arms and pouts, then you can tell that something is obviously wrong. But what about other members in the group who may be having their own strong reactions to what happened?

Since passivity or withdrawal represents an absence of participation, it is important to monitor carefully how each person is doing (Ward, 2014). We think of it a little like periodically taking the pulse of each member, checking in by sight if not direct inquiry: "I notice you are unusually quiet today. What's going on with you?" At other times you can do quick verbal check-ins to assess member engagement. If someone does appear to be withdrawn, you have the choice of ignoring the behavior if you think it is intended as attention seeking and manipulative, or calling on the person to talk about what nonverbal messages are being communicated to the group.

APPREHENSION AND ANXIETY

As part of your responsibility to monitor each member's current condition, you will at times notice that some people show overt signs of intense agitation and activation. They may be upset about something that has been triggered internally as a result of group interaction, or they might be feeling extremely uncomfortable about someone else's disclosures.

Imagine a group session in which one member starts speaking about some sexual difficulties she is having in her current relationship. In the course of her disclosure, she alludes rather casually to the sexual abuse she suffered as a child. It is apparent from the way this person is talking that many of the issues related to that experience have already been addressed and resolved. She has done the work on her past and can confidently talk about it. But as you scan the group, you can see that another woman is fidgeting. Her foot is tapping nervously. Her hands are wringing. Her eyes are darting around the room but refusing to remain settled on any one spot. Obviously, she is upset about something and it seems to be escalating. But she is not bringing it up on her own.

Now you must decide what to do. You have a responsibility not only to this person who is anxious but also to the woman who is speaking, not to mention to everyone else in the group. Anything you do or say to help the apprehensive group member is likely to affect everyone else as well. What do you do?

The first thing you try to figure out is whether this group member is merely embarrassed about the explicit, casual talk about sex or whether she might be identifying strongly with the disclosure about being sexually abused. Naturally, you might wonder if she was sexually abused as well but has not yet dealt with this trauma, or is uncertain if she wants to process this with the group at this time.

There are actually a hundred possible reasons for her behavior, including that she just has to go to the bathroom. Since we are not mind readers, there is no way you can know what is really going on and choose an appropriate intervention until you collect more information. The simplest way to do this is to call attention to what you observe: "Nancy, I noticed that while Frieda was talking about her past sexual abuse, you seemed uncomfortable. I wonder if you might want to talk about what is going on for you."

Notice that the punctuation in the wording above does not include a question mark. This is because the intervention is offered as a statement in a neutral tone of voice, rather than as a direct question. Nancy is given the opportunity to go as deeply as she wants at that moment. If she is ready to pursue this topic, she can do so; if she would rather pass, that option is available as well. Everyone who is watching this intervention will observe: *Gee, our leader is watching us very closely to see how we're doing. I didn't even notice that Nancy was upset, but the leader did. I like the way Nancy was invited but not pressured to talk.*

In all groups, some members are pouting and do not feel ready to talk yet. Others are too threatened or scared to take the plunge. And some just need a little attention and invitation to join in the group. Even if the invitation to speak is declined, the group members get the clear message that all behavior, even withdrawal, is subject to scrutiny and accountability.

FEEDBACK

There are various times throughout the group when members could profit from feedback on how they are being perceived and experienced by others. This could take place after someone discloses something personal, after an issue is worked on, or whenever someone is doing something that appears especially counterproductive.

For the most part, we find that people usually do not know how to give feedback effectively. People often mix up feedback with evaluation or judgment they received elsewhere, so the group leader may need to clarify the difference (Luke, 2014). Some people are too harsh and critical, whereas others are just too nice and so become evasive, too general, or even dishonest. It is your job to teach group members how to give feedback to one another. One way you do this is by modeling the behavior you would like others to practice.

Using feedback as an intervention accomplishes two goals: It lets someone know about the effects of some aspect of their behavior, and it shows everyone else how important it is to tell people what you observe.

There are lots of ways to offer feedback, whether in the form of self-disclosure, confrontation, or immediacy. Basically, what you are doing is telling someone how they come across to you. When it comes to giving feedback, there are a few simple guidelines:

- *Use "I" statements.* This means that the person giving the feedback owns it. Rather than saying something such as, "*We* all find you a little hard to follow," you might more accurately say, "*I* find you hard to follow right now."
- *Speak directly to the person.* Often, members will avoid looking directly at the subject of the statement when giving feedback, regardless of whether it is positive or negative in nature. Rather, members will say things to the group leader that are really meant for another member. As a leader, encourage members to speak directly to each other when giving feedback, as it creates a more intimate and complete interaction.
- *Relate the feedback to a specific example.* Rather than general feedback, such as, "You are kind and friendly," encourage members to provide specific examples for what they are offering: "When you just offered support to Kat, I could see how kind you are." That type of feedback is hard to dismiss, since it is tied to a specific event in the group.
- *Keep it short and to the point.* The key here is brevity, as many people will talk too much when giving feedback. This often waters down the message and lessens the impact.

Feedback is one of the most powerful exchanges in group and has the ability to deepen any encounter immediately. It can be something as simple as asking group members to share their observations by asking, for example, "What did you sense a moment ago when Byron spoke?" "How did you experience that interaction?" Furthermore, it allows group members to have here-and-now interactions rather than just sharing past stories. One of the wonderful things about group settings is that members do not have to take your word for it; they can check with others.

Byron:	It's just so hard to get anything done when everyone else doesn't keep up their end of things. I don't mean to . . .
Leader:	Let me interrupt you for a minute, Byron. You've been talking about what everyone else is doing and not doing for some time. I was thinking to myself as you were talking that you sounded like a child who is whining. I was finding it difficult to listen anymore. If you're interested, you could ask others how they were reacting as well.

While this intervention may come across as direct, and perhaps too honest, the group leader was watching Byron's reactions closely while giving him this feedback. It was offered in the spirit of pointing out what was observed, which may or may not be valid in light of how others react. Sometimes the best outcome from such a discussion is a promise on the part of the member receiving feedback to check with others in his life to see if they have similar perceptions. In the example above, Byron will report to the group the following week on what he learned from his family and friends about his perceived whining.

THREAT TO HARM

The ethical codes of all helping professions mandate clearly that if someone is a danger to self or others, you *must* do something to protect the safety of all concerned (Rapin, 2014). In groups, just as in individual sessions, people will occasionally reveal—directly or implicitly—that they are thinking about hurting themselves or someone else. This could involve any of the following:

- Suicidal ideation or recurrent thoughts, often with a specific plan
- Threats of homicide or physical assault
- Past or ongoing child or spousal abuse
- An HIV-infected individual's continuing to have unprotected sex with strangers
- Engaging in criminal acts that may lead to harming others

What do you do in situations such as this? Presumably, you have included a statement of informed consent as part of your intake procedures, so group members are well aware of your responsibility to protect others' welfare. When group members reveal threats to harm in group, often they are asking for help and intervention, since they are well aware of what you must do. Group settings are often not the ideal place for addressing acute stress and crisis situations, since the focus is usually on group care rather than the provision of individual care. Most group members in these situations will cede control of the group to the leader to take charge and offer support. A key here is that the group leader does act in an obvious way that shows the other members that the leader is taking specific action.

This situation requires definite action by the group leader. As with most critical incidents that occur, the best course of action is often to bring the issue up for everyone to discuss in an effort to provide support and feedback. Yet it is often beyond the scope of the group members to resolve such a situation, even though they can provide a large degree of assistance. So use the power that lies within the group to help, remembering that you are not absolved of your responsibility to report suspected abusive or criminal acts or to protect others' welfare but knowing that it does demonstrate the kind of collective decision making that is so important for promoting continued mutual responsibility and accountability in the group.

BOREDOM

At some point, many groups become predictable and stale. You can tell that you have reached this point when you find yourself unable to maintain focus and notice others showing restlessness as well. People start yawning and looking at their watches, and all sense of interest and urgency has left the group. If left unaddressed, this marked lack of energy will encourage members to slip into complacency. You must do something to stoke the energy level.

As for what you can do, the sky is the limit. This is a time to be creative, dramatic, and provocative. Boredom stems from predictable routines, so you must do what you can to shake these up. Matt notes that he cannot see how any group setting could ever really be boring when there are so many possibilities and so much potential in a group. Therefore, he views boredom as symbolic of some other process occurring within the group that needs to be addressed. The key is just finding the right combination to reengage group members so they talk about whatever they are not talking about.

Photo 9.1   Nothing kills a group faster than prolonged boredom. You must continually assess energy levels of group members, monitoring nonverbal cues (yawns, restlessness, fidgeting, etc.), to determine their degree of engagement. When momentum flags, you must intervene to reignite passion and excitement, even if it involves simply naming what you observe: "I notice that some people are checking out right now, and I wonder what's going on."

Here are just a few things group leaders have been known to do during times of boredom:

- "I am really bored! I don't know about the rest of you, but I've been sitting here for the last few minutes looking at the clock, just counting the minutes until we get out of here. Anyone else feeling the same way? So what is happening in here?" In this first example, the leader says out loud what he or she senses the others are feeling. This gives permission for group members to talk about the low energy and then brainstorm things they can do to change it.
- "Okay, everybody stand up. Time to stretch." In this case, the leader changes the level of engagement from passive to active mode. Rather than allowing members to sit quietly, the leader stirs them up.

- "So what are we *not* talking about right now?" This is a strategic question that assumes there is something in the room not being addressed or that group members have been hesitant to bring up.
- "Let's stop for a moment and reflect on what's going on right now." Rather than doing the work, the leader simply takes a time-out and invites participants to label and describe what is happening. This reinforces the idea that they are responsible for what happens or does not happen. It also notes that something is occurring at the process level that needs attention. This can often be the proverbial "elephant in the room" scenario, where the elephant is actually boredom and disinterest.
- "If I were a member of this group, I sure would be feeling cheated about now. I mean, taking all the time to come here, to say that I want to change and become involved, and then sitting around waiting for someone else to take the lead." Rather than a scolding, the group leader is actually creating a scene. He is trying to provoke some reaction from members and is likely to get one.
- "Time to do something different. Count off by threes. I want you to talk to one another as consultants about what could be done to make this group more inspiring and responsive to your needs." A change in structure and atmosphere is initiated. With this change in scene and dynamics and with a specific, structured task to complete, group members are likely to venture into new territory.

This is just a sampling of possible interventions. The key here is recognizing that there is a problem that must be addressed. When boredom takes hold, when routines become entrenched, when energy runs low, it often takes a major effort to change the atmosphere. Just keep in mind, and remind members as well, that it is their group, not yours. They are the ones responsible for keeping the group responsive to their needs. If they are bored, then they are also responsible for taking care of their own problems. Furthermore, if they are bored, maybe each person needs to take the responsibility and start talking about what is truly important to them. Of course, it does not hurt to remind the group of this.

LACK OF DIRECTION

As a beginner, this may be the problem you face the most. If not, you are likely to encounter the opposite: too much structure. It is often difficult to create a balance between sufficient structure, in which people know what is expected, what their roles are, and what they can do to make good things happen, versus so much control that every minute is scripted.

When groups are overstructured, members feel stifled. The leader is firmly in control but also totally responsible for what happens. Participants are along for the ride. Yet when groups lack structure, members do not know what to do or how to do it. They are grasping for some direction and often stumble down ineffective paths because they are trying to figure it out.

How do you know that your groups lack direction? For one thing, ask the participants. Pay attention to the bottom line: Are group members meeting their stated goals? You will also notice long silences, as if members are waiting for you to tell them what to do next. You may want to ask for a progress report on each person's goals as a way of resetting the bearings for the correct course. You might say something such as this: "I want to go around and have each person talk about his or her progress toward his or her goals. If you are hitting them, then how is that happening? If not, then what are you going to start doing today to create some progress?"

Another key sign that direction is lacking is that movement is all over the place. There appears to be little continuity, as is evident in the following exchange:

Margaret: I've had this problem for, I don't know, maybe a year or more.

Simon: Yeah. That's a bitch when you can't get what you want. Like Mick and the Stones sang, though, you can get what you need.

Tamar: Simon, what the heck are you talking about? Who are Mick and the Stones? I don't know what you're talking about half the time.

Nigel: Come on, Tamar, leave Simon alone. He doesn't know any better. He's just trying . . .

Margaret: Do y'all mind? I think I was talking about something that was . . .

Simon: Yeah. I mind. We heard that story before. Besides, I thought we were supposed to be talking to each other, not telling stories. And you never heard of the Rolling Stones? I could talk about them forever . . .

Obviously, without leader direction and intervention, this group loses control quickly. Members are not listening to one another. They are not responding well, either. They seem lost, moving from one topic or person to another. Unless the leader jumps in to mediate, to direct the flow of traffic, there are likely to be some casualties.

LIGHTS. CAMERA. ACTION.

People can talk and talk in groups without doing much to make changes. Talking is usually not enough to create meaningful movement. There often comes a point when it becomes necessary to move an individual member, or the group, from talk to action: "Now that we understand what is going on—what the problem probably stems from and what you'd like to do about it—what do you intend to do?"

Moving into this action phase can take a number of forms:

- Declaring a goal to work on
- Agreeing to let the group comment and offer feedback on your observed progress toward your goals
- Committing oneself to some specific course of action over the next week
- Rehearsing, practicing, or role-playing new behaviors
- Agreeing to complete a homework assignment before the next session

The transition from insight to action might look something like this, with one group member, Jon, who has been talking at length about his struggle to control his temper:

Jon: It's not like I enjoy having everyone I love scared of me all the time or anything.

Leader: What about right now?

Jon: Excuse me?

Leader: Right now. You say you don't like having a bad temper, but I've noticed lots of ways you have used that threat to get what you want in this group. So how do you feel in here about having people fearful of your temper?

Jon: That does not happen in here.

Leader: Are you sure?

Midge: [Taking a deep breath] Jon, it does happen in here, at least for me. I am not sure what else to say . . .

Leader: Jon, listen to Midge for a moment. Midge, tell him more about it so he can understand how it happens in the group.

So far, the leader has started to prepare Jon for taking action with his anger problem instead of just talking about it, which he has done several times before with no discernible change. Next, the leader and the group members would help Jon rehearse alternative ways he could get his needs met in group other than resorting to tantrums. Group members could offer him feedback on the side effects of his current patterns. Next, he would be encouraged to declare something he would be prepared to work on during the week that would demonstrate significant progress. Finally, other group members would be urged to talk about ways they can also relate to this issue and what they would like to work on.

For a Class Activity

Write down some relatively minor concern in your life that you are facing right now. It could be something related to a primary relationship, your eating or exercise habits, or schoolwork.

Think of a goal you would be able to complete within the next week. Keep in mind the criteria for an effective goal: (1) It should be as specific as possible, (2) it must be realistic so you are absolutely certain you can do it (no excuses), and (3) it should represent a baby step toward where you eventually want to be.

Take turns declaring out loud to members of your group what you intend to do. Make an agreement to check in with one another next week so you are held accountable for what you said you would do.

MANIPULATION AND ATTENTION SEEKING

Manipulative and attention-seeking behaviors come in two basic kinds: situational and chronic. In the first case, the person might normally be reasonably cooperative, either in the group or in life. There is something about the group environment, or perhaps a given situation, that encourages the person to engage in self-protective behavior that involves a hidden agenda. In the second case, however, the person's manipulative tendencies are "characterological," meaning they are part of the individual's personality. You have probably heard of diagnostic labels such as *borderline, hysterical,* and *sociopathic,* all of which have highly manipulative features. Keep in mind, as well, that often these labels are used by therapists to externalize their own frustration, blaming clients for not cooperating the way they would prefer (Kottler, 1992). In other words, group members who are acting in ways that appear counterproductive may actually be trying to protect themselves against perceived threats, perhaps because they were pushed faster and further than they were prepared to handle at the time.

Whether the group member acts manipulatively because of a particular situation or as a typical interpersonal style, you must intervene to stop this behavior or at least draw attention to it in a way that indicates other methods to connect more effectively. Otherwise, you may lose control of the group.

We are certain that you can recall any number of instances when you have seen a whole class disrupted because of the persistent efforts of students who keep asking annoying questions, who try to show the instructor how brilliant they are, or who operate behind the scenes to sabotage progress. In spite of your best efforts, lots of damage can be done if you do not confront those with hidden agendas or manipulative mind-sets.

Here are just a few examples of what you can expect to encounter:

- *Excessive approval seeking:* "Thank you so much for your help. This is just the best group I've ever been in. You are just so good at what you do."
- *Attention seeking:* "No. I don't have anything to say and nothing is going on with me," folding arms and sulking.
- *Power struggles:* "You say that this is our group, but you keep telling us what we can and can't do."
- *Boundary testing:* "Can't we stay a little later tonight? What I have to say is really important and can't wait until next week."

There are whole books written on how to handle situations such as these (Kottler, 1992; Kottler & Kottler, 2009; Mitchell, 2007; Wofford, 2012), as well as several excellent sources for group leaders (Rutan, Stone, & Shay, 2007). All the advanced training in the world will not prepare you for the myriad ways group members can act manipulatively. At first, you may attempt to stifle this behavior by confronting it in group. If that does not work, a second option is to arrange for a consultation or individual session with the individual to deal with the issue. This usually focuses on ways to manage the behavior or some pointers and coaching on how to engage in more interpersonally effective interventions. If that does not produce a change, sometimes you might have to ask the person to leave (which will create another set of problems).

COERCION AND PEER PRESSURE

Tommy: I'm not sure if I want to get into this or not right now.

Alice: Come on! We've all said stuff. It's your turn now.

Jean: Yeah, it's only fair.

Tommy: Well, I'm not sure . . .

Mickey: Look, I spilled my guts and you just sat there and watched the show. Now when it's your turn, you skip out. Man, you've got no guts.

This is not only a common scenario in group settings but a predictable one. Sometimes the coercion is overt, but at other times it is more covert and is relayed in subtle ways. If you recall the dynamics of groups moving toward cohesion and intimacy, then you know that there are strong—intensely powerful—forces that act to pressure people into revealing themselves. Sometimes this occurs before they are ready. Remember that there is no universal timeline or expectation for level of risk taking; rather, each person needs to move at the speed appropriate for that person. For example, people who are group veterans and know what to expect might take risks and reveal personal matters much quicker than someone who has never been in a group before and is still learning how group works.

Casualties occur in groups when people are pressured to do or say things they are not ready to do or say. They are forced to take risks and then regret it later. They are shamed into revealing secrets and then feel such embarrassment that they do not return. They are emotionally blackmailed into saying things that, afterward, they can disown because there was no freedom of choice. Worst of all, they can be pressured into letting down defenses to the point where real harm can be inflicted. Group members need support and assistance to be able to have more efficacy and control over when to share. Rather than pressuring someone to talk about risky content or experiences, a more useful intervention is to ask a person to talk about what makes it hard to share in this group.

In the group that began this section, it is the leader's responsibility to intervene on Tommy's behalf and to stop the others from applying so much pressure. This might take the form of the following:

Leader: I think it's really great that many of you feel such strong attachment and loyalty to our group that you want everyone to belong. Tommy, I guess what Alice, Jean, and Mickey are saying to you is that they have taken risks in here and they perceive that you have not taken the same degree of risks. I am not sure that all risks taken are evidence or equal. I think you have put yourself out there, but just in a different way. Right now, you seem reluctant to go further with this.

Tommy: Umm, yeah, I really don't want to talk about my sex life in group at this time. You know, it's pretty personal.

Leader: That's totally up to you, Tommy. In spite of the pressure you might feel right now, it's important that you go at your own pace. I think what you are hearing from others is how much they'd like to know you better. Maybe there's a way that you can share more about yourself and still feel safe. What would that be like for you?

The leader intervened to stop Tommy from being coerced (which can lead to casualties). She shifted the focus from risky content (Tommy's sex life) to the more useful process level of looking to engage Tommy with the group. It is very important that group members accept responsibility for their own behavior and not have an excuse if things do not proceed as expected. Whenever anyone is offered feedback, it is important to ask permission to see if it is welcomed and if that person wants to hear it at this time. You are not only protecting the rights of each member, but you are demonstrating to the more reluctant participants that you are present and available to provide a safety net for them if and when they are ready to jump in.

CLOSURE

One final instance when intervention is required is when time is running out in a group meeting. Somewhere before the end of session—usually anywhere from 5 to 20 minutes, depending on the size of group, the length of the session, and what happened that day—you will announce that it is time to bring things to an end. This can be done simply by saying, "We have about 15 minutes left in the group." Ideally, this would signal to everyone that they should move toward closure. Often, however, this may involve more direct intervention in which you have to interrupt someone to help this process along. Although you will find this uncomfortable, it is absolutely necessary to manage time and end promptly.

Another common situation at the end of a group is when a group member takes this moment to introduce a heavy topic or reveal something risky or distressing. We call this "dropping the bomb," as it alludes to creating a significant change in the group. But waiting to do this at the end of the session allows the "bomber" to walk away, leaving the group in chaos and worried about what has happened. Examples might include statements such as the following:

- "Oh, one more thing I forgot to tell you guys: I've been thinking about not coming back after today."
- "I know we're almost out of time, but I just wanted you to know that I've been thinking more about suicide lately."
- "I can't remember if I told you or not, but that problem I've been having with my husband? It's been getting a lot worse. I'm thinking of moving out."
- "I guess I should say something before we leave. I saw a doctor this week, and she thinks I might have something seriously wrong."
- "I've been trying to decide whether to say something or not, but I guess I'll just get it out. Loren, I have a really hard time listening to you."
- "I'm not real pleased with the way this group has been going. I know we're almost out of time today, but I wondered how the rest of you were feeling."

It may sound easy to blame the "bomber" here for poor timing, yet it is often more complicated than that. We believe that members often come into a group with a hidden goal or plan about what they hope to do. Sometimes it is a very significant hope that carries a big risk. As the group meeting goes on and the member has not taken the risk or revealed the goal, anxiety often builds until the end of the group. When the group is ending, the adage of "now or never" seems to apply, and the member finally acts and does what he or she was planning to do. The problem with taking this step at the end is that time does not allow the group to adequately process or support the group member, and so the group concludes with an often shocking or disturbing ending. Of course, sometimes members consciously or unconsciously "drop bombs" at the end of group for precisely that reason: They do not want to deal with the consequences of their actions or statements, and so it is easier just to leave. Here is a way to address this in the group:

Leader: Okay, we have about 10 minutes left, and so I am wondering if we need to follow up with anyone before we end.

Thom: Um . . . I have been meaning to talk about something really important for the past few weeks, so I guess now might be a good time. This thing has been eating me up for weeks.

Leader: Thom, this sounds really important to you, and clearly it is something that you have been thinking about.

Thom: Yeah, it is a really big deal.

Leader: It's encouraging to see you ready to take this step, but I have to say that I have some concerns about the time we have left. It is one thing just to bring something up, but it sounds like you are wanting to have some time to talk about what you plan to bring up. We would only have a few minutes to do that, and so I worry you might not get what you hoped in that amount of time.

Thom: Um . . . well, I can see that, and it is a big deal to me. I really want to tell people something about me and my past.

Leader: It does not sound like you need immediate help for this but, rather, like you would really like some time to explore it with the group. Now the group knows you are ready to talk about this, so how about it we start with you next week when we will have adequate time to honor what you want to share?

The example above illustrates the directive nature of protecting the group by bringing closure to the meeting. In that situation, the leader felt that it would be more important for Thom to have the needed time to really get what he wanted, rather than a time-limited opportunity that might shortchange him and the risk he took.

Some groups end with a final go-around, or checkout, in which members mention how they are reacting to what just happened, what they will take home with them, and possibly what they intend to work on before the next session. The checkout is not for giving feedback or any last-minute barbs to others but, rather, to comment on the process of the group and gain an eye toward the next group meeting.

For a Class Activity

Much of what we are discussing about therapeutic groups can be applied to any setting, including your classroom. Take turns bringing the class closure by using the last 5 to 10 minutes to process what happened and helping classmates leave with something constructive to work on.

The Power of Language and What to Say: Group Leaders as Language Coaches

In describing the principal instances when some form of intervention is required in groups, it is obvious that language plays a major role in the process. We have said before that what you do is less important than how you do it. You must choose your words and gestures carefully to communicate clearly and also sensitively. Furthermore, the precise selection of language is key to the effectiveness of most interventions.

SELF-DEFEATING AND DISTANCING LANGUAGE

Leader interventions often involve responding to the specific things members say or the ways they choose to express themselves. Depending on theoretical orientation and style, there might be more attention paid to thoughts over feelings or vice versa, or to shoulds, musts, can'ts, or other forms of syntax, vocabulary, or communication style that reinforce dysfunctional and self-defeating ideas. Remember that language is one of the best ways to know what is going on inside someone's head.

Below are some examples of language use that might lead to an intervention:

- The use of *we*, as in "We think it would be best . . ." or "We all know the pain of feeling like we don't matter to others . . . ." This plural pronoun is a way group members avoid responsibility for their own beliefs by spreading around the blame. Furthermore, it is a way people defend against taking ownership for a statement or reaction. It can be therapeutically beneficial for leaders to help clients see themselves as unique individuals within the group and their larger family systems. Speaking about what "we believe" or what "our family feels" can be corrected by determining whether the speaker is expressing the true beliefs of *all* persons present and is doing so with their consent. Generally, when this happens, you can easily ask whom else the person is speaking for, or ask the person to say it again in the first person: "I know the pain of feeling like I don't matter." Can you feel the power of using *I* compared with *we*? Using *I* means owning one's own feelings and experiences.

- "He *makes me* upset." Verbalizations such as this imply that someone is controlling the group member's internal emotional states. "He *makes* you upset? How does he do that?" You might ask, "Don't you mean that you *make yourself* upset over what he's doing?" Remember also that you are not only talking to the person who used the illogical language but also to everyone else in the group who is learning this principle vicariously.

- "*It* is just so difficult." *It* is an ambiguous pronoun that allows the group member to speak in a general rather than specific way. "What is the 'it' you are referring to?" might be a way the group leader would help the person be more detailed about the assumed source of the difficulty.

There are dozens of other instances when you might also focus on the language employed, depending on the type of group and approach you prefer. When a group member says, "It's not fair!" a leader might reply with, "Who says the world is fair?" When someone says, "I really need that job," the intervention might be, "You mean you *want* that job." When people use the words *never* or *always*, they might be challenged to substitute *sometimes*, which is probably a more accurate description of frequency.

Student Voice

The Pronoun King Speaks

I had some pretty big goals for group, but oddly enough, what I learned most was a rather little thing. In fact, writing the word I is pretty much what I got from group. Most of my life, I have been pretty private, and I learned that from my family. So sharing myself is not something that comes naturally to me. So most of my life, I did not share, but rather just talked in generalizations as a way to mask my own thoughts and feelings. Well, the fifth night in group, the leader pointed out that I often used we and people when talking, like, "It is normal to be upset about a low grade, people get upset all the time." I discounted it, but then later that night another group member said the same thing to me. And what do you

> *know, I tracked myself all week, and I did it all the time. I made a pact that week to use I when talking about myself, and I have not looked back. It also makes a difference, since it reminds me to put myself out there for others to experience rather than hiding. Also, I talked about it with my wife, and she welcomed the change, and it has made communicating much better. That was a simple lesson with a big reward.*

Just because you are aware of illogical, irrational, or self-defeating language patterns does not mean that you will necessarily intervene each time. Most people do not appreciate being interrupted, especially when they are in the middle of a heartfelt personal disclosure. Timing is therefore important when you choose to point out that someone is talking in a way that reinforces negative thinking or dysfunctional behavior. More than half the time, you might want to file the observation away and return to it at a more opportune moment.

For a Field Study

Keep a journal for a single day in which you jot down how often you hear people say things such as "I can't" (instead of "I won't"), "I should," "I must," "never," "always," and other evidence of illogical thinking, overgeneralizations, and distortions.

Imagine the ways you might effectively point out what people are saying, and what this means, without offending them. How would you phrase the observation?

Words to Avoid in Therapeutic Groups

Words, in and of themselves, are neither good nor bad. Nevertheless, some words that group members commonly use act as symptoms of underlying illogical, distorted, or irrational thinking patterns. Most experienced group leaders have trained themselves to monitor group member speech patterns and language use, both to collect meaningful data about how group members characteristically speak and also to attend more closely to the subtleties of communications. Sometimes a little bell rings in our head, an alert that some principle of reality has been violated.

Certain words, usually indicative of cognitive distortions, make it much more difficult for group members to experience change. These words, such as *fate, luck, it,* or *them,* thrive on the force of externally controlled factors. An attitude of resignation, despair, and hopelessness sets in when one verbalizes statements that imply, "I can't help it; it's not my fault." Below is a sampling of the kinds of destructive language that signal reality distortions and obstacles to change. These are often vocal symptoms of underlying cognitive and affective processes.

FAIR

The question, "Who says the world is fair?" echoes through the offices of counselors throughout the world. Obviously, if the world were a fair place, people would always treat one another with respect. There would be no crime, poverty, or sickness. All people would get what they want; they would also get what they deserve.

Sometimes group members need to be challenged: "I guess this is one of those times when you didn't get what you want. Has that ever happened before? Is it likely to happen again?"

PLATITUDES

By borrowing someone else's tired and trite formulation of language, therapists can conceivably conduct an entire group session without uttering a single original statement. Classics for the "platitudinal" group leader include, "It takes two to tango"; "Don't take life too seriously; after all, you'll never get out of it alive"; "Don't worry, it will be a better day tomorrow." Platitudinal comments spare us from having to *think* about what we are really saying. They also help group members feel as though they are insignificant repositories for other people's trash.

NEED

To *need* something is to require it for continued physical survival. The only things we ever truly need are oxygen, nourishment, and shelter from the elements, although a case could also be made for sex and human touch. No one ever *needs* anyone or anything else. A great many things in life are desirable, preferable, or terrific but not actually needed. People whose *needs* go unfulfilled experience panic and fear; unsatisfied *wants* produce only discomfort or inconvenience.

Whenever group members use the word *need*—as in, "I need this job" or "I need feedback from the rest of you"—they should be helped to substitute the words *want, prefer,* or *desire.* It is no great catastrophe to do without a thing we might *prefer* to have in life; after all, we've been disappointed many times before. But the deprivation of a *need* implies torture or death.

CAN'T

Group member:	I can't come to the group today.
Leader:	You *can't* come today? I see. You mean you're either chained to your bed or in an advanced state of coma?

This little helping verb, so anonymous when buried in a sentence, is among the most abused of all words. *Can't* relinquishes your power and control. It means that you are unable to do something. Saying, "I can't get a job," is very different from saying, "I don't know how to get a job" or "So far, I've been unable to find a job." Similarly, "I can't confront him in this group" is different from "I *won't* confront him," "I *choose* not to confront him," or "I don't *want* to confront him." In reality, there is very little you can't do in this world as long as you are willing to suffer the consequences.

NEVER

First cousin to *always* and *forever, never* is an overgeneralization that exaggerates reality. The use of these words leads to a false sense of hopelessness. Who can say what might happen in the future? "Perhaps you may not feel happy very often in the future, but you would have a bitter task ahead if you were never to feel happy again, not even for an accidental instant, and were *always* to feel depressed."

Because these words reinforce a sense of helpless resignation (why try since you will *always* be this way?), the group member's motive to change becomes handicapped. By altering *never* or *always* to the more flexible *sometimes* or *occasionally,* people admit that they can function effectively in some situations: "Much of the time I feel slightly depressed, but sometimes I feel quite good."

EXPECT

Expect goes hand in hand with disappointment, for the latter is not possible without the former. The amount of time spent anticipating an event is directly related to subsequent disappointment if the event does not turn out as expected. To minimize expectations is to reduce or prevent future disappointment.

It is one thing to attempt to predict future occurrences but quite another to indulge in fantasies that only preempt what one hopes will occur. How bored one feels, how much one lives in the future and in fantasy, how much one tries to control and anticipate will all contribute to the frequency of *expect* in one's vocabulary. The oracle on the mountain advises, "Expect nothing, and you will never be disappointed."

MUST

The use of *must* implies a demand that things be a certain way; it is a command to the universe to pay attention and cooperate extra hard with one's wishes. As children pout when they don't get their way, grown-ups sometimes unrealistically order the world to deliver on demand. Group members play variations on this linguistic theme: "I *must* do well"; "Other people *must* treat me fairly"; "I *must* get my way." The obvious retort is that time-tested strategy perfected in childhood: "Who says?"

PROBLEM

Problems usually have solutions, and people who have problems spend their time trying to find solutions for them. They mount a mission in search of the Holy Grail, Truth, or some such answer that will disperse this storm cloud forever. Only in mathematics do problems have single solutions. Geometric theorems can be proved; algebraic equations may be factored; sums, dividends, and products can be calculated to find solutions to problems. In group work, the words *concern* or *trouble* can be substituted for *problem*. Concerns don't necessarily imply that something must be rectified or that there is a single answer that will fix everything.

I'M

These two letters separated by an apostrophe have kept more people from changing than all the excuses in the world. Short for "I am," *I'm* is a self-defining descriptor that irrevocably reduces the totality of a human being to a convenient label. *I'm*s are overgeneralizations, oversimplifications, and more: They offer a flawless excuse for running in place. When "I'm shy," I am blessed with a condition as certain as "I'm North American" or "I'm 30." "I'm shy" also brings with it "I'm always shy, I was born this way, I will always be shy, and I can't help it." Statements can be rephrased in a way that implies control, temporary states, and situation-specific behavior: "I *act* shyly"; "I *behave* shyly."

MAYBE

Maybe, perhaps, I think so, I guess, possibly, I don't know—these are all safe ways of avoiding a commitment. They are evasive words that group members use to back out of tight situations. When these ambiguous responses are used, the group leader has to work extra hard to get some clear declaration of opinion or intent. Shown here is a typical evasive dialogue that can sometimes be stopped through persistence.

Leader:	How do you feel right now?
Nikita:	Kinda strange.
Leader:	Strange, meaning nervous?
Nikita:	I guess so.
Leader:	What is going through your head that is making you feel strange?
Nikita:	Um—ah—
Leader:	That you aren't in control of this situation?
Nikita:	Yeah, maybe.
Leader:	And that you don't like being in this vulnerable situation?
Nikita:	You could say that, I guess.
Leader:	Well, what do you believe will happen next?
Nikita:	I don't know.
Leader:	What do you imagine is in store for the future?
Nikita:	I just can't say. How should I know?
Leader:	Take a wild guess. What do you think is going to happen next?

MADE

The misuse of verbs creates an unhealthy distortion of reality in which cause-and-effect relationships become confused. Since one's own neurons and synapses, the stuff from which feelings are constructed, are inaccessible to others in the world, it is difficult to believe that anyone can *make* another feel anything. Short of physical contact, feelings are self-manufactured states. When language signals that cognitive distortions are occurring inside a group member's head, the group leader vigorously challenges the rational base for the distorted beliefs: "He *made* you cry. How exactly did he do that? Do you have a 'cry button' on your forehead that he can push at will? Did he reach inside your brain, perhaps through your mouth or ears, twist a few neurological connections, and thereby make you cry? In fact, you did it to yourself *after* you heard what he said."

WRONG

Right, wrong, good, bad, and other value judgments imply that there is some absolute standard of measurement by which all behavior in every culture can be assessed. There really is no touchstone for determining whether anyone else's behavior is absolutely right or wrong; the context is usually needed to better understand what happened.

One behavior might be better than another, more productive or effective relative to some other choice, but it would be inaccurate to label someone or something good, bad, right, or wrong. Only when the language of value judgments has been eliminated from group members' vocabularies can they hope to be accepting of one another:

- Who says it is wrong?
- How do you know it is bad for him just because it is bad for you?
- It sounds as though that is something you object to personally, but can you judge everyone in the group against your standard?

SOME CLOSING WORDS ON WORDS THEMSELVES

The purpose of reviewing the words above is not to make you a word-sleuth group leader who constantly stops group members from saying these words. Rather, our intention is more to help you become aware of some of the common sentiments and psychological meanings behind these words so you can intervene with group members to help them speak about their true feelings and reactions, rather than hiding behind carefully constructed words and phrases that distance people from responsibility and experience. Once you begin to make small interventions around word choice, chances are you will set in motion a process in which group members begin to catch themselves when they use words that distance them from others and their true emotions and feelings.

Review of What You Learned

- Being a group leader is often a directive role. There are specific instances in group when you must intervene to protect member safety and facilitate cohesion and progress.
- There is rarely only one intervention that works best in any given situation. Rather, there are multiple ways to help group members communicate and be with one another in more effective ways. Prepare yourself with three or four options, since the first try may not be successful.
- How group members interact and communicate is often more noteworthy than what is being said. Many of the interventions above target rambling, withdrawal, passivity, manipulation, and attention seeking.
- Feedback is often the core of group interaction and an opportunity for interpersonal learning. Feedback is a process for both the one who provides and the one who receives the feedback. Group leaders must actively facilitate this process.
- Group leaders often serve as language teachers to improve group communication. Leaders employ specific interventions to highlight how language is being used.

Group Techniques and Structures 10

Group leadership is not about techniques, although it is always handy to have options available to pull out just what the situation calls for. Over time, you will collect various interventions from ideas you have read or witnessed, those suggested by supervisors and coleaders, as well as techniques you adapt or invent yourself. We will warn you, however, that the challenge of running groups involves not a scarcity of options about what to do but, rather, having too many choices and not knowing which seems most appropriate.

The goal of this chapter is not to equip you with all the techniques you might need in any situation. Instead, we will review some of the common structures in a group and outline a few representative techniques that might be used at various intervals during these periods. This will give you the background you need to understand the ways techniques are constructed, the means by which they are employed, and the timing for when to use them.

For a Class Activity and Field Study

In small groups, share your favorite method to enliven a party or social gathering that has run out of steam. Build on one another's ideas by discussing ways this method could be further refined or developed.

Have one person act as a scribe and take notes on each person's contribution. Agree to make copies for everyone in the group.

Identify what you consider to be your one or two most creative or brilliant ideas, and share them with the rest of the class. Have the scribe of your group add to the list by including ideas offered by other groups. This is exactly how you might collect the "greatest hits" of each veteran group leader you meet. Make it a habit to find out what his or her favorite, most foolproof technique is.

As a corollary to the group activity, initiate a field study to interview experienced group leaders about their most effective, powerful techniques. Report back to the group (or class) what you learned.

Ways to Prepare a Group

The group begins before anyone walks through the door for the first time. This is true for all learning/therapeutic experiences. Once the person first contemplates getting help, the process starts. It could take months, or even years, before the person is ready to seek help; nevertheless, the change process has already begun with the first awareness that help might be needed. Even though the change process has begun, keeping it going can be difficult (Kottler, 2014). For many people, the idea of being in a group setting creates feelings of anxiety and fear. Dropouts from group are not uncommon, yet group dropouts often significantly influence the effectiveness of the entire group. Thus, group leaders need to work actively at the beginning of every group and adequately prepare members for the group to alleviate some of the stress and anxiety of beginning.

Remember that many groups can be a challenge to organize and maintain. As opposed to working with individuals, the group leader must be able to coordinate and assemble the group members to begin at the same time. Many people have some sort of resistance to group work, since they anticipate and experience less control in group settings. Many people, not just a few, influence the flow of events, and many people experience a loss of individuality (Piper, 2008). Thus, any prospective group leader must work with the concerns of all potential group members to help the group start with everyone informed about the group process and ready to begin.

Without a doubt, a group with a successful outcome is predicated on the group leader's doing the work up front to prepare and assemble the people to form a good working group (Burlingame, Whitcomb, & Woodland, 2014). Selecting group members who have a high probability of remaining and working in the group helps enhance the likelihood of a good outcome (Barlow, 2013). Often, the best predictor of a group member's success in a group is that person's prior success in other group settings (Piper, 2008). People with prior group experience tend to report higher expectations for group work (MacNair-Semands, 2002). Even though that is a great way to select group members, it is important to note that people who may appear to be poor candidates for group can be successful if they are supported and encouraged within the group structure.

Before beginning any group, several practical factors should be considered:

- Clarify what kind of group you wish to run. Homogeneous groups are easier to market and get going; heterogeneous groups offer more resources and balance. Decide, as well, whether you will have a "closed" group or "open" group, to which new members can be added, and whether it will be time limited. You will also need to identify the theoretical orientation and leadership style you will adopt.
- Undertake far more promotion than you think you need to fill the group. In our experience, only about half the people who say they will come actually show up. Some of those who attend the first meetings will not continue. That means that if you want 8 active, committed members, you may need to screen and interview 20 viable prospects.
- Provide guidelines explaining confidentiality, informed consent, established ground rules, and appropriate member conduct.
- Keep the number of participants manageable—6 to 8 if you are leading alone, 8 to 12 if working with a partner. Groups containing 3 to 8 members are often more productive and more developmentally advanced than groups with 9 or more members (Wheelan, 2009).
- If possible, work with a coleader who is more experienced. If this is not feasible, make sure you have weekly supervision available to help you debrief each session.
- Remain clear about what you want to accomplish during the first induction stage. Think through the most appropriate structure for building trust and cohesion.
- Screen the participants to make sure they are good candidates for the group (Burlingame et al., 2014).

If you don't already know the people who will be participating in your group, it would be useful to collect some preliminary information from them, either by phone, personal interview, or questionnaire. Almost all clinical settings employ some type of intake process that can be easily adapted for group formats, and pregroup selection, screening, and preparation of group members are widely considered best practices in the field (Jensen et al., 2012). When group leaders prepare potential group members for entering group, these members will better understand what they are about to experience and how it can help them. Further, these new group members will enter the group with higher levels of confidence, hope, and expectancy.

No matter how you choose to collect basic information about the group participants, your interview or questionnaire should help you screen out those who might not be suitable. Ideally, such an exercise should not only help you find out things you need to know but also help the group members begin thinking about how they want to make the best use of their time.

The screening interview tends to focus on outlining the objectives and norms of the group, clarifies typical behavior of group members, outlines basic group processes so members know what to expect, and helps members begin planning issues they want to work on in the group (Corey, Corey, Callanan, & Russell, 2015). Part of the interview is focused on clarifying misconceptions about group, exploring some of the fears and unrealistic expectations associated with group work. Clearly, part of this interview is logistic and informational, but it is also strategic and therapeutic. During the interview, the group leader can help plant favorable expectations about the group to begin to develop hope and expectancy about the benefits of the experience. Caplan (2005) noted that many potential group members want confirmation that they are not "sick" and validation of their decision to seek help at this time. The group leader can also provide new group members with a cognitive structure of the group that explains the method of group and how it will be run. That helps with group participation and creates informed group members who share the same notions of what is to happen. Also, the group leader can clarify some of the anticipated pitfalls and concerns of the potential group members (e.g., trust, safety, confidentiality, privacy) to decrease the likelihood of premature termination (Piper, 2008).

Whether you schedule pregroup screening interviews; talk to prospective participants on the phone, via e-mail, or as part of large group; or distribute informational literature, you will want to prepare members on what to expect, get them thinking about ways they could use the group, and even get them started in the change process.

QUESTIONS TO CONSIDER DURING SCREENING

One of the goals in the screening process is to help frame how each group member's concerns can be understood. Since most groups operate with the notion that change occurs as a result of giving and receiving feedback, the group leaders can explore how the group member will benefit from being in the group. One way to do this is to frame the presenting concern from an interpersonal perspective, considering how that concern will appear in the room and how it might affect the relationships in the group. For example, someone presenting an initial complaint of acute panic disorder, often leading to dramatic displays of anxiety and agitation, may not be the best candidate for a group in which such behavior could provoke contagious reactions. However, if the panic is less acute and the potential group member can talk about how panic often impacts her relationships with others, since she thinks people are afraid of her and so withdraws, then that could be explored effectively in a group setting.

Here are some examples of the questions you might ask during a screening session:

- What are you hoping to gain from the group experience?
- What would you work on in this group?
- Why did you choose to join this group?
- What other group/counseling/therapeutic experiences have you participated in?
- What was helpful in previous groups, and what was most difficult for you?
- How is it for you to speak in front of others?
- How do you respond to conflict?
- What are some of the characteristic roles you usually play in groups? How might you like to change these patterns?
- Describe any emotional problems or mental disorders you have experienced or are currently struggling with.
- Describe any medical history or physical problems that concern you at this time. List medications you are taking.
- What else about you that would be relevant to this group experience might be helpful for me to know?

EXPLAINING THE PROCESS AND DETERMINING FIT

If you perceive a good match between the group member and the group you are conducting, then the screening moves to specific preparation for logistics of the group so the expectations and rules of the group are clearly understood. The goal here is to confirm that the group member can meet the expectations and commit to becoming a member of the group.

You would want to discuss what is expected from a member of the group in terms of responsibilities. Explain the importance of punctuality, the starting and ending times, and the consequences of coming late or missing sessions. There would likely be some rules that are part of the group, such as giving notice prior to leaving the group, how payment is handled, and what is considered appropriate behavior. Confidentiality and informed consent would be discussed, as well as their limits in a group setting. Finally, any of the person's concerns and questions would be addressed.

In addition to the in-person interview, some formal measures are available that have the potential to provide useful data that enrich the process and supplement decision making about selecting group members. For example, the Group Therapy Questionnaire (MacNair-Semands, 2002) examines client variables pertinent to group participation, such as previous therapy experience; expectations, goals, barriers, and fears about group; substance abuse symptoms; and suicidality. The Group Readiness Questionnaire (Cox, Burlingame, Davies, Gleave, & Barlow, 2004) is a quick way to identify prospective group members who have higher levels of expectancy for the usefulness of group work and are likely to participate in ways that benefit the group process. The Group Selection Questionnaire (Burlingame, Cox, Davies, Layne, & Gleave, 2011) assesses the degree to which a potential group client believes that group therapy will be beneficial, attitudes and skills associated with interpersonal exchanges in small groups, and behaviors that might be problematic in small-group settings.

Basically, during this assessment, you are asking yourself whether this person is a good match for the group you are running, given life circumstances, personality, presenting complaints, and readiness level of the potential group member. If it seems like a good fit, your next step is to confirm that the person wants to and can attend the group. If you think this person might not be a good candidate, you will wish to make a more appropriate referral.

Voice of a Group Leader

I know all the books say you're supposed to screen members, but I've never had that luxury. There is just not enough time in the day, and so in my organization it's the luck of the draw—you get people based on their expressed need. If they want to come to the group, then they show up. Often, there's only a minimal intake so I get stuck with all kinds of people, some of whom are definitely obstructive and belligerent, or who are so withdrawn they will never speak. So I spend the first few times trying to figure out how we are all going to work together and basically who is going to be committed to the group. Usually, I have to schedule a private session with a few people after the first few sessions—after I figure out what's going on—to refer them elsewhere if it seems like a poor fit. Some people just aren't ready for a group—so they need other types of care first before they are able to benefit. So it seems like I spend our first two to three sessions together doing a screening of everyone in the group. Maybe that is not ideal, but it is reality for me.

Ways to Begin a Group

The first group session is critical for establishing the tone and norms of the group experience. As you think about the goals or objectives of that first meeting, take a moment to consider the context and perspective of the new group members. Most people are rather nervous, if not downright terrified, of coming to the first group meeting (think about your own apprehensions when anticipating this class). Up until this point, each member's contact has been limited to you as the professional; but as the group begins, they now face a bunch of strangers. Even though you may have prepared each person in advance about the group and the process, all that has usually been forgotten. Group members are wondering what the heck they are to do and how the time will be filled.

For Reflection

Before we even begin talking to you about what you want to do to launch a group, think on your own about what objectives would need to be addressed in that first group meeting. What are all the things you would wish to accomplish in any introductory structure to get a group going? What would you need to accomplish?

Make a mental list of the most crucial factors. Just to get you started, consider that the most important thing to do in *any* first session, whether individual, family, or group therapy, is to get the clients to come back; if you can't get people to return, you can't help them. In a voluntary group, what does it take to capture sufficient interest so that members are willing to return? You had better figure out a way to build trust quickly, to get each member to "buy in" to make a commitment, and to create enough safety that it seems worthwhile to come back.

With that as the backdrop, it is time for the leader to get to work. It is hoped that, if you took the time to think through the possible objectives for launching a group, you came up with several goals for the opening meeting that struck you as most important. Obviously, for instance, you want to devise a way to reduce the anxiety and eliminate the feeling that everyone in the group is a stranger. You want everyone (including yourself) to quickly learn one another's names and get to know who you are as a leader as a way to build initial trust. Already you can see that safety, trust, cohesion, and universality are coming to the fore as important variables to establish in the group. There are several ways to start a group, but any technique you use should accomplish the following:

- *Plant favorable expectations.* Get the members excited about their journey and give them the hope and expectancy that it will be worth their while in meeting their goals.

- *Create efficient intimacy and cohesion.* Help them get to know one another immediately, with minimal fuss.
- *Begin to develop a sense of universality* by acknowledging some of the similarities in the group. You can even do this by connecting/linking people around the shared anxiety of being together for the first time.
- *Establish a productive atmosphere that clarifies ground rules* so that all the group members have a shared idea of what is expected from the leader, the other group members, and especially themselves.
- *Capture and maintain the members' attention* so they are focused on the tasks at hand.
- *Identify goals and problem material to be worked on.*
- *Get the members to come back.*

If you start on the path toward accomplishing the goals above, then you have gone a long way toward reducing the fear and anxiety of starting a group and have moved the members into planning how the group will be of greatest assistance to them. This may sound like a lot to do in a single session, much less one introductory structure, but most of these objectives are linked together. The last one, getting the members to come back to group, is the most important of all: If you can't do that, you can't help anyone.

Obviously, the choice of what you do to launch your group is very important. You want to "hook" the participants in such a way that they feel they have made a good decision in coming. You want to make sure that everyone gets involved and nobody is left out. And you want to make sure you provide the kind of meaningful experience that meets their needs but doesn't scare the timid ones away.

For a Class Activity

Get together in groups of six to eight. Pretend you are all meeting in a first group session. Take on the role of someone else you know—someone whom you can play realistically and fluently, preferably someone with a problem or two.

Introduce yourself to the others in your group by talking about how you feel about being in the group, what you want from the experience, and what concerns you have.

After you are done with the exercise, abandon your adopted roles and talk to one another about what the experience was like and what you learned from it.

This is indeed a tall order. Fortunately, there are loads of introductory techniques that work well to accomplish these goals. Icebreakers are designed to build a working level of familiarity to get a group going; there are hundreds of such exercises. Generally, we like to start a group by having members talk about who they are and what they are looking for in the group. Since you want to minimize small talk, rambling, digressions, and self-indulgence, the key is to get people to say something new and unrehearsed about themselves that begins the process of revealing to the group who each person is. We will actually say this out loud and then model the kind of introduction we would like them to try. During the beginning stages of group, members will often model the leader and do what is asked of them; by taking the first step to model how to check in, the leader is trying to establish the norm of being honest and open. When we lead, we try to present ourselves as authentically, genuinely, and spontaneously as we can, showing group members how it is possible to be vulnerable and appropriately disclosing. We want the group members to gain some confidence in us as the leader of the group while realizing that the group can be a unique place to be honest and real with one another.

Since group members are often unskilled at this task, anxious about being in the group and nervous about making a particular impression with the other group members, this is a good place to work on reducing the tension in the room and providing guidance. That is why modeling the introduction to show the group members how it can be done is so important—something along the following lines:

Why don't I begin the introductions? My name is Matt, and I am fine with my first name, Dr. Englar-Carlson, or Dr. Matt since my whole name is pretty long to get out. I am really excited to be here today, and I can feel my heart pumping with anticipation. I love to lead groups; in fact, it is the most exciting professional thing that I do. I have led groups for all kinds of people, concerns, and problems, and I have grown as a person from my own experiences of being a group member. I guess you could call me a group-junkie.

What do I want you to know about me at this time? As a leader, I need to let you know that I get pretty engaged and animated with the group, and sometimes it's hard for me to sit still. I like to be playful and goofy, but I also really value the power of being in a room together like this and the opportunity to take risks and try new behaviors with each other. Above all, I value the relationships you will develop with each other and with me. I think a real strength of mine is as a supportive and encouraging person. I can tell you up front as a leader that I will not push you to reveal or do things that you are not ready for, and in that sense I will support you. But, at the same time, I will lean into you to help you expand your limits to how deep you think you can go and what makes it hard to reveal yourself.

As far as what I could work on in a group such as this—if I were a member rather than the leader—I would most likely work on reducing my wall of vulnerability with others and exploring some of my own fears about myself and the

direction my life is taking as I navigate my early 40s. I struggle at times with being
torn between work and my family, and my level of accomplishment. I know that I
hold my cards pretty close to my chest, and people have given me feedback that I
support others well but that sometimes the "me" in that support is hard to delin-
eate, and thus I am hard to read and really know. And so I would most likely work
on being more spontaneous with my emotions with others as a way to build more
real and honest relationships.

Who would like to go next?

This introduction took less than 2 minutes to deliver. Matt tried to be precise
and efficient, since there is so much to do in this first session and so little time
to do it. If you could have watched him, you would have noticed he used a calm
and deliberate tone and maintained eye contact with the group the whole time,
making sure to look at each group member. Notice what he did not include in
the introduction. He didn't talk about his job, family, or the usual roles he plays
in life. It's not that these things are unimportant; they will certainly emerge later
as people get to know him. For now, however, it is more important to reveal as
much about Matt's "essential" self as he can in the briefest period of time. He also
demonstrated a degree of vulnerability by sharing a number of concerns he
might use the group to work on. The other thing Matt did was take responsibility
for what he would have to do to create change. It is important at this point in the
group to establish that group members can direct the group treatment toward
their own individual needs rather than expecting the group leader to do that.

For Reflection

In your journal, write out one way you could introduce yourself to a group for the first
time that reveals as much as possible in less than 2 minutes. Include not only the most
essential parts of who you are but also the particular personal issues you could work
on in group at this time in your life.

In this introduction, present yourself in the most authentic, honest, genuine way
possible, highlighting the major unresolved issues you'd like to work on, as well as
what you bring to the group in terms of your strengths and resources.

This is the basic structure for beginning a group, in all its various forms. Limitless variations are also possible. Some examples are given below:

- You can have members work in dyads, triads, or subgroups, interviewing
  one another for the purposes of introducing one another (as we did in the
  introductory chapter).

- You could have people share their first impressions of one another after each introduction.
- You could have them reveal something about themselves that nobody else knows or has heard before.
- You could have them talk about how they are feeling in the present moment, what it's like to be there now.
- You could structure the introductions in such a way that attention is directed toward one facet that is relevant to the group. In a grief support group, members could talk not only about the present losses they are currently suffering but also about the most devastating loss they have recovered from in the past (notice the emphasis on recovery).
- You can do a goal-setting introduction, in which people imagine what it would be like to end the group having met all their goals. It can be phrased like this: "Imagine that it is the last day of our group and we are saying our goodbyes to each other. If you were to say to the group, 'I got exactly what I needed out of this group,' what would that be, and what would you have had to do during the group to meet this goal?"
- You can have them pretend the group is now over and speak in the past tense about what they learned and how they grew from the experience, starting the group by saying, "This is the last session, so I'd like to have each person report on what they are taking with them."

In any structure you use, remember that you must watch the time so you have the opportunity to start identifying and working on concerns in the very first session. Don't be surprised if some powerful experiences occur during the first hour together. After all, often many group members have been waiting weeks for the group to begin and are eager to share themselves and their concerns. It is also important not to push people too far, too fast, or to explore topics that the group may not be ready to process. Challenging a group member prematurely and not validating someone can also frighten some members into withdrawal or caution (Caplan, 2006).

You want to create a meaningful and therapeutic opening encounter that leaves the members wanting to come back, not a shocking or terrifying interaction that leaves them frightened or more anxious than when the group began. In groups with voluntary participants, each person is making a decision as to whether it is worthwhile to come back another time. Therefore, one good way to end that first session is to ask members to talk about how they are feeling about things so far. You might also ask them to mention what they are taking with them as the session ends, or what they already learned from the experience. For those mandated or required to attend, the goal of the opening session is to reduce resistance or defensiveness, and potentially move group members to a point of considering how the group could be helpful (Schimmel & Jacobs, 2011).

> ### Student Voice
>
> #### First Impressions
>
> *When the group started, I had little hope that things would get better for me. I hated being in group, hated it! I was scared, anxious, teary-eyed; basically, totally freaked out. But that first day changed my mind. I sat in a circle looking around to see no friends, nobody looked like me, and everyone was a stranger. I was the only Asian female. I realized I was going to be expected to open up to these people, to trust them. I was so afraid of being judged by the other members for some of the things I might say or share in the group. I was unsure if I was going to be able to handle some of the raw, uncensored stories and experiences of other group members. I was afraid that I would not know how to respond correctly to other members' emotions. I also told myself, "I am not going to cry." I had heard stories about how emotional people got during group therapy and I just told myself that it would not be me. I would not cry in front of a group of strangers. As it happened I was the second person to spill my guts and the second person to cry, so basically I faced my biggest fear right from the start. And in that moment of being so vulnerable, the leader was great. He was so attentive to me and supportive. And then the group started to be supportive, and right then, I felt that maybe this might be okay.*

Up until this point, we have focused primarily on starting the first group meeting, but it is worth noting that norms and routines for how every meeting will begin are quickly established. There is no set formula for starting the meeting, but the beginning of the meeting is a critical signal for members to shift from their day-to-day lives and experiences into the context of that particular group meeting. For example, in many 12-step groups such as Alcoholics Anonymous, members may mill around and make small talk, but there comes a point when the meeting is called to order and someone begins the familiar induction: "My name is Bob, and I am an alcoholic." At that point, the familiar ritual has begun and a process shift occurs.

Some leaders may decide to start groups with a 1-minute moment of silence or a meditation to shift the process. We often begin our groups with a "check-in," which is a brief go-around in which members take turns talking about what they are bringing to the group that session. During the beginning stage of group, we have the members say their names so the group gets names down. Usually, we ask every group member to take less than a minute to update the group on progress, reveal what they are working on, and then ask for time during group to explore a concern. One immediate benefit of a check-in is that each person gets to speak, so there will never be a group where someone goes home without saying a word. The other benefit is that the check-in can set the agenda for the group in terms of who is asking for time.

Ways to Build Cohesion and Intimacy

Whenever you deduce that trust in the group is not sufficient for deeper work, it is time to initiate some intervention to correct this matter. How will you know when you have reached this point? Several signs and symptoms will be present (Corey, Corey, Callanan, & Russell, 2015; Hornsey, Dwyer, & Oei, 2007; Joyce, Piper, & Ogrodniczuk, 2007; MacNair-Semands, 2002):

- Members make overt statements that the group does not feel safe.
- There is little identification with the group.
- There is a lack of homogeneity among group members.
- There seems to be a marked reluctance for people to volunteer or reveal themselves.
- Members engage in rambling, distractions, intellectualizations, and other means by which to hide.
- Personal disclosures are vague and lack personal meaning.
- Repeated silences last long periods of time.
- Participants confide to you privately that they do not feel comfortable.
- Members deny that they have any problems to work on.
- Conflicts and disagreements are side-stepped.
- Attendance, with members either not showing up or being consistently tardy, is becoming a concern.
- There is a lack of frequent and intense feedback.

These are, of course, quite natural reactions to a strange, threatening situation. To move things along to the next level, and as a prerequisite for risk taking, you must do what you can to build a greater sense of community and connection. To build cohesion, group leaders must emphasize group member interaction (Burlingame, McClendon, & Alonso, 2011a).

Rather than employing a "technique" to create deeper intimacy and cohesion, the most direct route is simply to label what you observe: "I notice that some people seem unwilling to move beyond the superficial. I wonder if we could talk about what is going on." This direct naming of the process can allow the group members to focus on the barriers within and among them—and it gets the group interacting with one another. The group leader must also directly address concerns about safety and confidentiality that are voiced in the group.

There are some specific interventions group leaders can use to build cohesion and intimacy (see Burlingame et al., 2011a, for an extensive list). These include, among many others, modeling appropriate self-disclosure, encouraging "here-and-now" rather than storytelling disclosures, highlighting corrective feedback while reframing injurious feedback, encouraging active emotional engagement among members, and eliciting verbal expressions of support.

Depending on the type of group you are leading and the setting, there are dozens of manuals that supply thousands of trust- and community-building exercises. As just one example, adventure-based group activities involve people in a series of games and physical activities designed to break down barriers, improve communication, and build a sense of community (Gillis, Gass, & Russell, 2014; Midura & Glover, 2005). You probably played a lot of these games as a kid, such as the "trust walk," in which you walk around blindfolded, led by partners, or the "trust fall," in which you fall back and let others catch you. Some programs, such as Outward Bound and Project Adventure, have incorporated these structures into their warm-ups as a way to facilitate team work before participants venture into the wilderness together.

Photo 10.1 The leader is taking a "time-out," stopping the action to process whether the level of trust and cohesion established is sufficient for some members to take constructive risks with one another. Prior to this intervention, there was a lot of hesitation, avoidance, stalling, and superficial responses. The leader asks members to reflect on what they observe, as well as on what they are experiencing. Such time-outs can be used in a variety of ways to focus on process, as well as to talk about what is going on at any moment.

Ways to Promote Risk Taking

Once you are well into the working stage of a group, you will want to introduce structures that take interactions to a deeper level. This is a tricky part of your job because the members' readiness levels to take risks are so variable. Some participants may feel free to say whatever they want, to say out loud anything that comes to their hearts or minds, while others find it utterly terrifying just to make direct eye contact with someone else in the room. Leaders have to support all the levels of readiness within a group.

Risk taking is central to all that change involves. Unless one is prepared to take chances, to experiment, to try out new strategies, to look into the unknown and pursue what lies ahead despite hesitation and fear, then all the talk in group is rather meaningless. Since risking necessarily involves the possibility of a loss or an emotional or psychological injury, there is often justifiable effort on the part of the group members to minimize adverse consequences such as heightened vulnerability, rejection, reputation damage, or loss of self-esteem.

As part of informed consent, leaders should educate clients on the risks they may encounter as a result of participation in a group. Informed consent is addressed not only during the first session but also during the course of a group, when process events present situations containing possibilities of confrontation, emotional outbursts, coercion, and judgmental comments (Rapin, 2014).

Much of what group work accomplishes is to provide a safe structure for participants to practice taking risks. Whether a decision needs to be made, a confrontation must take place, or a new skill is to be learned—basically, whenever change occurs—an element of risk is involved. Any risk-taking exercise should be undertaken to deepen the levels of intimacy, sharing, and cohesion in the group. Yet safeguards should be in place to give people choices about how much (or little) they reveal. Efforts must be made to ensure that people are not coerced to say or do more than they feel ready for so that group members decide for themselves when to take risks. On the other hand (and this is often delicate and confusing), your job is also to encourage people to go beyond what is comfortable and to risk new ways of being.

Before getting too far into the group, we see the first step in this process as talking openly about the fears of risking with the group. We like to ask participants to imagine that, in this group, they will say out loud their deepest, darkest secrets, or blurt out all the things they have been thinking and feeling but can't imagine ever having the courage to reveal publicly. As they think about what it would be like to reveal these things, we ask them to look around the room, making eye contact, and imagine how each person might respond to their revelations. This usually provokes a rather spirited discussion about fears of risking and being judged by others. The very act of talking about risk taking in the group often creates a feeling of universality about fears and normalizes many of the concerns shared by group members.

FEAR OF CONSEQUENCES

The most readily apparent inhibitor to taking risks is the perceived consequences each person imagines. Before taking any action, especially one that involves unknown factors (such as how others might react), people spend considerable time estimating probable and possible outcomes. Group members tend to exaggerate what could conceivably occur and to magnify the potential dangers. They often inflate their sense of self-importance, believing that everyone else has nothing better to do than constantly scrutinize their behavior. In actuality, however, the worst possible reaction to any risky disclosure would be that members don't do or say *anything* at the time, leaving the risk taker to wonder how the group members experienced the revelation.

Though most group members ponder consequences, there is usually at least one group member who is relatively fearless or highly motivated to take risks. That person usually takes the first plunge. You can often use this person's courage as an entry point for others to explore risk taking. Remember, however, that such structures must always include volunteers rather than those who appear pressured to reveal.

An individual's willingness to take risks is also stifled by distorted views about what risk taking involves. The human propensity to think in dichotomies has no basis in reality—except perhaps in physical laws, such as the absolute minimal threshold necessary for a nerve impulse to be conducted. When a group member reasons that the only two options available are either to clam up or self-disclose unreservedly, the likely course of action is clear. For this reason, group members must be helped to dispel their absolute notions in favor of seeing behavior along a gradual continuum. In an effective group, risk taking deepens over time as members reveal layers of disclosure rather than everything at once. This can enable members to gradually expose their vulnerability at a rate that allows provision of support and validation by the group.

One way to understand this is by using a developmental scheme, beginning with self-disclosure, the least threatening variety; then moving to interpersonal feedback, which requires considerably more skill, yet involves less predictability of outcome; and finally coming to group confrontation, the highest possible level of risking. Group confrontation, in which a member shares dissatisfaction with a current activity, can virtually explode with negative consequences.

Everyone could unanimously boycott the outspoken member, ridicule the member's opinions, and use the outburst as an excuse for devious psychological torture. Worse, the person could be totally ignored. That would be a very difficult risk to take with the group. Further, effective confrontation usually requires some shared history with the group to develop support and trust. Clearly, confrontation takes time to develop and is not the best risk to take at the onset of a group.

These different levels of risking can be ordered on a gradient so that the leader may progressively encourage low-level toward high-level risking, slowly inoculating participants' exposure to perceived danger. In this way, absolutism is replaced by relativism, allowing more possible choices for client action.

FEAR OF FAILURE

Individuals naturally differ in their propensities to take risks; also, great variation exists in the degree to which people will make rational choices. People who are preoccupied with winning approval and who have a high fear of failure are often less able to adjust their risk-taking strategies to fit situational requirements; they will consistently act inappropriately conservative or reckless. Those who are less concerned with group members' opinions will make more intelligent decisions about when and how to take a risk.

The alternative to a failure-avoidance orientation is to behave without accompanying self-judgments. The group leader must work with members to wipe out anticipatory regrets that inhibit experimentation. A group atmosphere conducive to risk taking is one in which the possibility of failure does not exist. People either do or they don't do, period. In one example of a risk-taking exercise, adolescents were given practice at handling rejection and eradicating the word *failure* from their vocabularies. They were instructed to ask one another for things they knew they would never get and then to remain calm in the face of disappointment. If, when they took interpersonal risks, the worst thing that could occur was not that they might fail but that the other person might not respond, then they felt freer to take risks.

It is well-known that, whereas a little anxiety improves performance of a well-rehearsed task, too much anxiety can result in stage fright. Unfortunately, the situational factors prevalent in groups may produce toxic levels of stress that curtail risk-taking actions. The pressures to conform, performance anxiety, comparisons with peers, approval seeking, and other group norms are all anxiety-provoking stimuli. Hypervigilance is also evident in group situations in which a person enters a state of helpless panic in the face of an oncoming threat for which there is insufficient time to prepare evasive action. For the same reason that people may freeze during a fire escape or other group crisis, group members may allow the prospect of an impending risk to cripple thought processes and constrict effective strategies for countering the threat.

Novice group leaders often make the same mistake in their efforts to expose clients to taking risks. When an introductory exercise requires people to tell something about themselves, each in turn around a circle, group members usually spend the time rehearsing their introductions instead of attending to others'. After their turn is taken, they will spend the rest of the hour patting themselves on the back in relief. Basically, no one is paying attention to the group members or focusing on them except for the group leader.

Photo 10.2 The leader encourages a group member to take the risk of confronting an authority figure in her life, someone who has been a source of great frustration for her. He is using the "empty chair" technique to ask her to imagine her boss sitting there and then helping her practice different assertive responses. Other group members join in, offering feedback, suggestions, and their own similar experiences. Such experiential work in groups begins at the point when members feel safe enough to take risks and experiment with new behaviors.

The inhibiting stress can be intensified or diminished through the use of structure, depending on when and how it is introduced. Early group structure in which expectations, goals, and roles are clarified helps make risk taking easier. When members understand what appropriate behavior is, how the group process will emerge, and what is likely to happen, they are a lot more willing to take risks.

We can soften the impact of anxiety-provoking stress by preparing participants for the experience. Here are a few examples.

- Giving guided constructive feedback to one another reduces stress by providing certain guidelines for diminishing the ambiguity of the situation.
- Risks can be structured according to spontaneous circumstances where rehearsal anxiety won't get in the way: "Just now, you gave me that look where you stare down at me as if I were a bug you want to squash."
- Structure can involve specific declarations of risk and planned rehearsal: "When I get home tonight, my husband will be dozing in front of the television. I'll explain to him that I'm uncomfortable and dissatisfied with the amount of work he does around the house and then negotiate a more equitable arrangement."
- Providing minimum structure works to reduce inhibiting stress; so does encouraging familiarity and intimacy. If people can be helped to feel more comfortable, they will be much more willing to try out new behaviors.

DEGREE OF COMFORT

At the other extreme, feeling too comfortable with oneself may also diminish a person's motivation to take risks. As noted earlier, people don't change as long as they are minimally comfortable with the way they are. Often group leaders must intensify the dissonance in people so that they will work to reconcile their inner conflict between the status quo and the desired future. Group members are not likely to take risks until they feel externally—or, preferably, internally—pressed to do so.

Many group techniques are designed to make group members feel uncomfortable with their ineffective selves. Once the ball is rolling and a few courageous people jump in with both head and heart, the others begin to notice how attractive the risk takers are. They may at first be resentful and later jealous, but eventually they will be respectful of their more venturesome colleagues. "If they can do it, so can I" is the hoped-for conclusion they will reach.

In one group, a middle-aged man listened restlessly to the tearful complaints of a college student who had just broken up with her boyfriend. Apparently, they had been dating since high school and had settled into a fairly comfortable routine. Eventually, bored with the relationship, the young woman decided to break it off even though she was giving up some great times. "What has this to do with me?" wondered the older gentleman, suddenly aware that he was feeling hot and sweaty. He thought to himself, "After all, my marriage has been good for the past 24 years. We've raised two pretty nice kids. We have a nice house, kind friends, and we're very considerate of each other's needs. But this woman gets rid of her boyfriend just because she doesn't love him intensely. What the hell is love, anyway? That's the stuff you see in movies!"

Another group member supported the woman by disclosing that she had wanted to do the same thing with her partner. She had lived with her first and only boyfriend for some years until she, too, had settled into a comfortable but dependent routine. It had taken her almost 6 months to work up the courage to leave. "I really admire your spirit for not letting things drag on," she said. "There was a great temptation for me to wait until I could find another guy before I left my old relationship. What you're doing takes a lot of strength, especially when what you're leaving is so convenient." With this support, the college student acknowledged that she was feeling so much better for talking about her relationship.

Student Voice

Taking the Plunge

When the group started, I had an immense preoccupation with how I was seen by others. I wondered how other group members viewed me as a person and member, yet I was too afraid to ask, so I just kept quiet. Over time, I began to notice my own connection to members who were making themselves vulnerable by opening up. At first, I expressed these feelings by expressing my respect and admiration for others. In a sense, I was learning vicariously through the risk takers and did not feel safe enough to be such a participant. My role was mostly to go to people's rescue or offer words of encouragement without taking big risks myself. There came a point when I had an "aha" moment of realizing that sharing ourselves only brings others closer. Along with that, I came to the realization that negative reactions are not as bad as a lack of closeness. This recognition was not without anxiety; however, it gave me enough strength to let some of my guards down and to welcome any opportunities to reveal myself. When I did get the chance, I did not hesitate, and that led to an immensely positive developmental growth in me. For the first time, I became truly aware of the impact of my own beliefs and how far from reality they can be. I felt a great deal of acceptance as a result of this experience. I was able to experience firsthand what an impact I can have on others when I allow myself to be seen. Once I opened up, I began to take a much more active role in the group. I came to the realization that once I get past my own insecurities, I become very expressive.

Then the older man began to sweat profusely. His heart was pounding. Finally, he blurted out:

Is it really so terrible to have a comfortable relationship? I mean, sure, some things are boring and predictable. We have sex every Wednesday and go out for dinner every other Friday. We go to sleep every night after the late news, though on Mondays we sometimes watch a talk show. Sure, it's gotten to be a drag. I don't believe I've really loved my wife for over 10 years. But is it really worth giving up a 26-year investment just because it isn't all that exciting? Well, maybe it is. What should I do?

This man's discomfort was multiplied in direct proportion to the risk taking going on in the rest of the group. As others shared their apprehensions, it became more acceptable to admit his own fears, since he could sense support in the group. Finally, he was motivated to risk opening up because his discomfort had become intolerable. Keeping his secret safe did not seem all that attractive compared with the great relief he could feel in unburdening his soul.

SELLING RISK TAKING

Perhaps the most difficult task for group leaders is to "sell" productive risk taking to the group. Group members are naturally skeptical of a leader's urging and admonishment about risk taking, since the leader is supposed to say that and is not the one who will be taking the risks! We find that a dramatic risk-taking pitch is usually necessary in almost every group. Usually, the group has reached some impasse and people have begun more skillful dodging. Conversation has become safe and predictable, involving low-risk topics or those that have been previously brought up. Sometimes, members will revert to their old standard defenses: "I just don't have anything to work on right now. My life is going pretty well."

Particularly in the early sessions, members will exhibit much reluctance as they cautiously test the water. Stubbornly, they cross their arms and seemingly demand: "Prove to me that any of this will make a difference. Why should I go out on a limb when it can so easily break off?" At this point, the ball is in the leader's court. It is up to the leader to recruit potential risk takers to take the plunge.

Sometimes, leaders need to give a hard-sell speech to promote risk taking, which is one of the few times leaders resort to lecture tactics as a matter of choice. If pep talks work well as a motivating force when coaches give them to athletes, why shouldn't they also work for us? Occasionally, we check whether the time is right and the players are ripe for such a pitch. We take a deep breath, bore holes in their heads with the intensity of our gaze, and then deliver one of our favorite therapeutic speeches, usually intended to shake group members out of their inertia. This speech always contains certain elements, although its form may change:

1. It must be entertaining.

2. If long-winded, it is for the purpose of repeating important themes.

3. It makes things seem easy.

4. It is educational and informative.

5. It is self-disclosing. We admit that we had the same concerns but did something about it.

6. It is not too scolding in its tone.

7. It gets clients enthusiastic about starting on their productive risks.

8. It is aspirational, tapping into the potential of a something better out there—if they are willing to reach for it.

9. It brings people back to the here and now within the group and the opportunities available in that space.

You might begin by saying something like the following:

Right now, think about the risky things you've wanted to do for a long time but continuously put off because of fear. Is it making a career switch? Telling someone what you really think? Speaking up more honestly in this group? Sharing something personal for which you are afraid others will condemn you? Whatever it is, you are probably giving yourself a lot of excuses for not taking action.

You have named that which is most fearful to group members. It is natural and normal for them to play it safe and avoid putting themselves on the line, but your job is to push them to go further—and deeper—within safe, constructive limits:

Think again about the things you don't like about yourself, the things that if others knew, you are certain they would also dislike. Consider the behaviors you would like to change, anything from being overweight to feeling excessively guilty. Whatever the undesired behavior, you've learned to live with it. It brings comfort because it resembles a stable character trait. After all, you've always smoked, worried, been dependent, overweight, unhappy, or nervous. Why change now?

Finally, you throw out the challenge that they always have opportunities—and options—to go beyond their self-defined limits, to reinvent themselves in new ways:

> It is totally up to you. For me, in the past, here is where I really began to get serious about making a change. The next time you catch yourself censoring risky thoughts or hesitating to speak up in the group, ask yourself what you really have to lose. I mean, you could just continue to be unhappy and beat yourself up, right? But why not question your motives for playing it safe. Take a deep breath and then plunge into this group, with these people around you. Isn't that why you're really here?
>
> It is only by taking risks that you can ever expect to make changes in your life. If you don't venture forth in this group, exploring new territory, encountering people more intimately, you will be condemned to a life of stale mediocrity. The choice is yours. Now, does anyone have anything to say?

If the mini-lecture has had its effect, group members will start to get fired up (or at least one will). They will also feel a little guilty for hanging back, but the momentum will have begun. Since risk taking involves a response inhibition behavioral model rather than a response deficit model, a great part of the group leader's work involves coaching clients to do what they have already learned to do selectively since birth. Promoting risk taking is among the most difficult challenges for group leaders. And the irony, of course, is that people are usually in the group because they want to change and take risks, yet many clients fight against risk taking every inch of the way, occasionally forcing leaders to wonder why they must constantly sell an idea that is so obviously beneficial and often the main reason people have come to the group in the first place.

RISK-TAKING INTERVENTIONS

There are quite a number of interventions that leaders can use to actively encourage risk taking. The "hot seat" is always a good icebreaker for risk taking. In this exercise, members take turns agreeing to answer any personal question directed their way. In another variation, members are randomly divided into subgroups, or allowed to choose those they trust the most, and then they share with one another aspects of themselves that have yet to be revealed. Afterward, participants can talk about what it felt like to take such risks and then be encouraged to do so in the larger group.

Here are some other risk-taking structures:

- All members write down something so personal about themselves that they would be unwilling to reveal it except anonymously. Make sure that all the members use the same kind of paper and pen so their disclosures will not be revealed unless they choose to do so at a later time. Collect the papers, shuffle them up, and pass them out so everyone gets one to read out loud. Afterward, see if anyone is willing to own their disclosure.
- Ask members to choose someone in the group with whom they have some unfinished business. Have a volunteer sit right in front of someone else (who also agrees to participate), and then have them take turns telling each other things that have not yet been said.
- All members share a time in their lives when they took a major psychological and emotional risk that ultimately had a positive outcome, even though it was initially very difficult.
- Ask members to identify roles in the group, such as who is the most/least active, most/least likely to take a risk, most/least likely to give honest feedback, most/least defensive. You can also name the caretakers, most honest and truthful, most direct and risky, most frightening and/or combative. This process calls out people for playing certain roles and does provide feedback on how people are being perceived in the group.
- Ask for and receive honest feedback from others in the group.
- The most risky thing of all is to speak in the present about something you are feeling toward someone else in the group. Imagine, for instance, what it would be like to tell a classmate how attracted you are to her or him, or how difficult you find it to be around her or him.

For a Class Activity

Sit in a small group so you can easily make eye contact with everyone else. Sit as close as possible to one another to create an intimate atmosphere.

Each of you will take a risk by sharing something about yourself that nobody else knows. You have wide latitude about what sort of thing you reveal, depending on the trust level you feel in your group, as well as your own inclination at this time. Select from the choices above, or others that might occur to you.

Before you decide to say your risk out loud, rate on a 1-to-10 scale how risky it feels to reveal this. A 1 means it isn't risky at all, while a 10 means your heart is thumping so hard inside your chest that you can barely breathe. A 5 is medium risk, whatever that means to you.

First, tell your group members what your risk is, and then tell them how relatively difficult it was for you to share it.

If time allows, do a second or third round in which you go a little deeper.

Afterward, talk about what happened for you in this experience—what you learned about yourself, about others, and about the role of risk taking in groups.

Ways to Solve Problems

Problem-solving and other skill development models have been developed for use in group settings (D'Zurilla & Nezu, 2007). The intent is to teach participants the systematic steps involved in making good decisions in their lives, a process that can be applied to a variety of situations. Quite spontaneously, a member may signal that he or she needs help making a decision about whether to end a relationship, quit a job, relocate to another state, or take a dramatic step in another direction. The leader may then announce to the group as a whole that it would be profitable for them all to learn a process for making sound decisions.

Several problem-solving models, such as those developed by Johnson and Johnson (2012) and Ray and Raiche (2006), follow a process that invites members to do the following:

1. *Identify the problem and define the issue.* It is preferable to select one part of an issue that can be specifically addressed and that lends itself to resolution within the time and using the resources available.

2. *Gather information that is relevant to the situation.* Explore the nature of the difficulty and its context. It is helpful to know, for instance, what has been tried before, under which circumstances the problem is not present, and who else is involved in this situation.

3. *Consider alternative courses of action.* Initially, as many different options as possible should be considered. Afterward, these can be narrowed down to those that seem most feasible.

4. *Examine barriers to making a decision.* This is where you anticipate where things might go wrong and prepare ways to overcome the obstacles.

5. *Decide on a solution.* Based on the exploration, analysis, and discussion that have taken place thus far, what is the person willing to do at this time? Preferably, this goal, or at least a small part of it, can be completed before the next session.

6. *Take action.* In groups, action takes two different forms: Rehearsal or practice in the group (e.g., role-playing, confrontation) and homework outside the group. In either case, the group members act on what they understand.

7. *Evaluate the outcome.* Any problem-solving attempt should be assessed in terms of its relative effectiveness in reaching desired goals. Most of the time, adjustments need to be made for continued efforts in the future.

For Personal Application

As with any technique or structure you use in groups, you must develop sufficient familiarity that you can make needed adaptations. One way to do this is to try out every one of them first.

Working with a partner or on your own, proceed through the problem-solving stages listed above to address some unresolved issue or decision in your life. As you go through the process, notice the places where you feel stuck or resistant. Consider how group support, input, and feedback might make this procedure go more smoothly.

As a technique in action, whenever a group member seems stymied by potential courses to follow, unable to decide on the best solution, you can invite the whole group to become involved in the process of learning about problem solving and, subsequently, working to solve the problem. This kind of skill-development approach can be used with a whole variety of content areas, depending on what emerges in a group and what needs are identified.

Ways to Facilitate Task Completion

One of the challenges you will face is finding ways to help group members apply what they are learning to their lives in the outside world. You will recall that the insights generated, or the changes people make, do not endure unless people have the opportunity to generalize concepts and practice new behaviors. In fact, most of the changes that people initiate don't last over time because of a number of factors, including inertia, procrastination, self-sabotage, lack of ongoing support, and unrealistic expectations (Kottler, 2001a, 2014).

A number of standard operating procedures can be used to facilitate this task completion. The "go-around" or "checkout" is often used to end each group session. In this exercise, members take a minute or two to declare one thing they learned that day and one thing they intend to do before the next session. Depending on the type of group and your leadership style, these "homework assignments" can be rather specific, such as confronting a specific person or taking a particular action. The next session would then begin with each person reporting on what was thought about and what was done. This lends consistency and continuity to the structure of the group so members understand they are held accountable.

For a Class Activity

In small groups, or in the class as a whole, do a "go-around" in which each person says something he or she intends to do before the next class. This self-declared goal should be as specific as possible but also reasonably modest and attainable. Ideally, it should be a goal that brings you closer to your ultimate objective of becoming more fully functioning in an area of your life. While you could certainly declare something related to your body (e.g., exercising, dieting) or an unhealthy habit (e.g., smoking, poor eating), it would be desirable if you could select an interpersonal goal that involves working through a conflict, initiating a new relationship, creating more or deeper intimacy, facing an unresolved issue, asserting yourself, or finding/creating more love in your life.

Journaling is another adjunct structure commonly introduced as a way to promote work between sessions and process insights along the way (Charles, 2010; Cummings, 2001; Haberstroh, Parr, Gee, & Trepal, 2006; Lent, 2009; Parr, Haberstroh, & Kottler, 2000). A benefit of journaling is that it is culturally sensitive, meaning that it is not allied to specific cultural norms, and it can be implemented at age-appropriate levels across a wide range of group populations (Gullette, 2003; Tyson & Baffour, 2004; White & Murray, 2002). This can be a relatively unstructured assignment in which members are encouraged (or required) to write in journals several times each week and then to share them periodically with the leaders, or more structured logs can be introduced in which members must complete self-assessment forms. In some cases, journals can be shared systematically not only with the leader but also with one another. Journaling can integrate new technology as well through the use of therapeutic blogging (Lent, 2009) or video journaling (Parikh, Janson, & Singleton, 2012).

The intent of such journaling is to help members accomplish several tasks (Kerner & Fitzpatrick, 2007), many of which you could review during the first session:

- Reflect systematically on what transpired in group and personalize the content
- List important points or ideas to be remembered and retrieved at some later date

- Talk to the leader(s) in a private forum
- Explore more deeply personal issues that were triggered by work in session
- Describe vividly what is seen, heard, observed, perceived, and felt during the session
- Create memorable portraits of each participant
- Release pent-up feelings and unexpressed emotions
- Declare personal goals that can be worked on
- Construct letters (never intended to be sent) that express heartfelt reactions that have yet to be expressed
- Express creativity through poetry, artwork, or freeform writing
- Practice new ways of thinking or acting, rehearsing planned strategies
- Monitor progress and growth over time
- Carry on self-dialogue about some conflict or issue
- Capture the moment by writing vividly about something that has been observed, felt, or experienced

Believe it or not, this is only a *partial* list of possibilities. Generally, when we first begin a group, we spend considerable time talking about the ways a journal can be used throughout the experience. At various intervals, we will ask members to talk about what they are reflecting on and doing in their journals. Sometimes, they even bring them in to use as resources or share especially poignant entries. Do not be surprised to hear group members say, "Oh, I journaled about you last week." This can lead to a deeper discussion in the group about what the member was writing about in the journal and why.

One of the most meaningful comments you will ever hear from a former group member is, "Guess what? You know that journal you had us keep in group? Well, after all these years, I'm still writing in it almost every day!"

Ways to Rehearse New Behaviors

You have heard before that groups have the distinct advantage of providing opportunities for members to practice new behaviors in a safe environment. Role-playing and psychodramatic enactments make it possible for people to confront antagonists or experiment with alternative styles, all the while receiving continual feedback on what works best.

As originally conceived by Jacob Moreno, psychodramatic techniques were synonymous with therapeutic groups. In fact, he is the one who first coined the term *group therapy* to describe what happens when people get together to help one another work through unresolved issues. The object of these methods was to help someone work through a struggle by acting out feelings toward a "double" or "empty chair." Since that time, a number of refinements have developed role-playing techniques into standard procedures for groups (Baim, Burmeister, & Maciel, 2007).

The essential notion behind these methods is that rehearsal is provided for the real world, with appropriate support and critical feedback. Basically, the following structure is followed:

1. *Exploring and understanding the situation.* The member talks about what is most troubling. Others ask questions and draw the person out, exploring fully what is going on. The issues are clarified, defined, and narrowed to one situation that can be worked on profitably.

Leader:	So let me review what you've said so far. You resent the way your husband tries to control you. When you tell him how you feel, he either ignores you or says that you are imagining things. Then you withdraw and pout.
Felicia:	Well, I hate the way that sounds, but that about covers it.

2. *Selecting the cast.* The member chooses people in the group who she believes are most capable of playing the various parts. In addition to the main antagonist, the husband in the previous example, there are other characters involved in this conflict, such as her two children and her mother-in-law. In addition to the active characters, the leader may designate others in the group to act as "auxiliary egos." These members serve a supporting role as needed, reflecting unexpressed feelings, offering encouragement or advice, serving as a consultant when action is stopped, or saying out loud things that are sensed but not articulated.

Leader:	Felicia, let's reenact the typical way you might attempt to confront your husband, and then we can try some alternative strategies that might work better.
Felicia:	[Hesitantly] Ah, okay.
Leader:	You seem a little reluctant.
Felicia:	Well, maybe a little. I'm just a little scared doing this.
Leader:	That makes sense. Maybe a first place to start would be to pick someone in the group who you trust completely, someone who can sit at your side and be there for you during the whole episode. This consultant's job will be to whisper in your ear when you get stuck. So, who could that be?

> *Felicia:* Um, how about Michele? I mean, if that's okay with you?
>
> *Michele:* Sure, I'd love to! It pisses me off to hear you cowering like you describe. You just seem so much stronger than that to me.
>
> *Leader:* Okay, Felicia, next let's pick the others in the cast. Choose those who you think would be especially good at playing your husband, your mother-in-law, and your kids.

3. *Switching roles.* Since the group members do not know what the family members look, sound, and act like, they need some coaching from the client. Even better than having the group member describe the people is asking her to become them to show how they behave. This has the added advantage of forcing her to experience what it is like to be the antagonist and to get inside his head. Many clients report that this experience alone helped them develop greater understanding and empathy for others.

> *Leader:* Felicia, we don't know what Antonio is like, except as you've described him. Why don't you show us what he's like? Sit in the chair just like he would. . . . That's right. . . . Now, talk like him. Use his tone of voice and vocabulary. Gesture just like he would. . . . Come on. . . . Really get into it.
>
> *Felicia:* Well, he'd probably . . .
>
> *Leader:* Don't tell us. Show us what he's like.

Clients are often a little resistant to doing this part. Not only might they feel a little inhibited acting in front of peers, but on another level, it is very threatening to become the person you fear the most. Nevertheless, clients should be gently encouraged and guided to proceed with role switching, because it is critical to see and hear, as realistically as possible, how the antagonist behaves. The group leader can act like a supportive coach, encouraging and supporting the performance.

4. *Setting the scene.* Arrange the situation exactly as it would take place in the real world. Set up the room just as you would a stage. Ask the person to explain the exact circumstances under which the confrontation will take place. By the way, notice the use of the future verb *will* in the previous sentence, reinforcing the idea that what is being rehearsed will actually take place.

> *Leader:* Felicia, please describe for us exactly when this conversation would take place between you and Antonio. Place everyone in the room just as they would be at home. Arrange the furniture any way you like. Then tell us how this interaction will begin.

5. *Acting out the confrontation.* In this first round, the performance will be dismal. After all, the client is not really doing anything differently. And the

group members playing their parts will probably really enjoy their antagonistic roles, giving the person a harder time than usual.

Felicia:	Um, honey, I was wondering . . .
Antonio (played by group member):	Hey, will you get me another beer?
Felicia:	Yeah, sure, but first I wanted to . . .
Antonio:	Not now! Can't you see I'm watching the game?

Even with the support available, Felicia lapses into the same old patterns of being deferential. That is actually quite a good thing, since it means this simulation will be as realistic as possible.

6. *Providing feedback and analysis.* At various intervals, the leader will stop the action and elicit feedback from the group and the assigned consultant to create alternative strategies. At this first juncture, Felicia hears that choosing to confront her husband in this situation is probably not wise, especially with all the distractions of the television and her kids.

Photo 10.3 The leader is guiding a role play in which she acts as director of the process, helping a member work through unresolved issues with his partner (played by another member). At various points in the enactment, the process is paused to solicit feedback and suggestions from other group members, even to add additional characters and helpers to the role play.

During the course of the scenario, the action can be stopped frequently to give suggestions, offer alternative strategies, and provide support. In some cases, other group members, or even the leader, can take Felicia's chair to demonstrate different styles that could be introduced. The group leader may even jump in if the client is getting discouraged or beaten down by the experience, to show how different outcomes are possible with alternative strategies. The key here is not to lose the group member in the process of acting out the scene. Be sure to keep the subject of the role play engaged.

The example above, of course, is just one role-playing format. You can use this method in many other ways:

- Dictate a letter to someone in your life (dead or alive) who needs to be confronted. A designated scribe can take notes and give the draft to you afterward.
- Talk to an empty chair, imagining that the antagonist is seated there, tied up and gagged, so you can say anything you like without being interrupted.
- Imagine that the empty chair contains another part of yourself. Talk to that alternative part of you, then switch chairs and respond back.
- Reenact an incident from childhood, but add a different ending.
- Act out a fantasy.

For a Class Activity

Get together in groups of five or six. One member volunteers to work on the need to confront someone in his or her life. Preferably, this would be a relatively minor situation, since you are working without a professional leader present at all times.

Go through the various steps described earlier, but do so in an abbreviated manner: (1) Say something about the situation, giving basic background information; (2) choose and coach the cast in how to play their roles effectively; (3) act out the confrontation; and (4) solicit feedback to incorporate into the continued enactment.

Talk about what you found most frustrating and most instructive about this exercise.

Ways to Work Briefly

If you intend to run groups in schools or community settings where brevity and efficiency are necessary, you must adapt structures to the requirements of the time available. Several sources have been designed for this purpose (see Falco & Bauman, 2014; Hunter, 2006; Jennings, 2007; Joyce et al., 2007; Keats & Sabharwal, 2008; Piper, 2008; Piper & Ogrodniczuk, 2004), responding to the demands of managed care as well as the need for more brief interventions. Time-limited methods and interventions are considered more cost-effective and make it possible to reach more people in a shorter period of time. Of course, there are limits and disadvantages to such methods as well, since they are certainly not designed for everyone.

If you find yourself in a work situation in which you must lead a group in an abbreviated format (say, fewer than a dozen or even half a dozen sessions), then you must make certain changes to the structures you introduce:

1. Work with homogeneous groups so it is easier to build cohesion, trust, and intimacy quicker.

2. Start the group way before the first session. Use advance preparation to get members working on goals and issues before they meet for the first time.

3. Remind participants that the "meter is running," that time is limited, so they don't have the luxury of waiting until the perfect opportunity to do something.

4. Help participants set limited, realistic goals that can be reasonably completed in the time available.

5. Employ the use of adjuncts (such as homework, journaling, field studies, readings) to supplement what is done in sessions.

6. Spread out the frequency of sessions over a longer period of time to allow for follow-up.

7. Use action rather than insight methods more often, since observable progress must be attained rather quickly.

8. Teach problem solving and other skills that can be applied immediately.

9. Use group time for rehearsal, practice, and application of new behaviors and skills.

For a Field Study

Find a setting in which leaders work within abbreviated time parameters. You might try talking to school counselors, community mental health or hospital-based social workers or nurses, or crisis intervention specialists. Discover what adjustments have been made to the group format to accommodate for the limited time. Ask about favorite strategies and methods that seem to work especially well in these settings. Explore the types of goals and changes that the leaders observe in the time-limited setting.

Ways to End a Group

We can't emphasize how important it is to close a group with momentum at its peak. For the group members, the last session will form one of the lasting impressions of the whole group experience; thus, leaders have an imperative to create an effective ending that is therapeutic but also honors the work accomplished over the lifetime of the group. Group endings are not easy, as they are often emotionally charged events with many challenges. The goal of the group leader is to keep the group focused all the way until the end, with an emphasis on creating endings that allow members to say goodbye to the group while finishing their own individual goals (Corey, Corey, Callanan, & Russell, 2015).

One of the disadvantages of group work that we have discussed previously is that sometimes people do not follow through with their intentions. Though people appear committed to their goals and to staying engaged with the group until the end, other factors can intervene to derail these intentions. Group leaders must be aware that this is natural and to be expected. Endings are difficult for most people, and a popular strategy to avoid ending is simply not to do it. Our experience has shown that group members tend to end groups in a similar fashion to how they end relationships in their lives. Again, for many people, that equals avoidance. Therefore, the leader must be active in the final session to make sure that the ending of the group is both planned and intentional. The leader will have to be the one who draws attention to the ending of the group (reminding the group of its approach weeks in advance) and who is purposeful about facilitating direct contact until the very end. In many ways, the final group meeting is akin to the first meeting, as the leader does have an agenda to accomplish in the group that day. You must devise ways to end your groups so that several objectives are reached:

1. Main themes are reviewed and processed, with an emphasis on summarizing what has been learned.

2. People are able to reach closure with the experience, expressing their grief and loss for the end of the group but also their excitement for the future.

3. Unfinished business is named, even if there is no time (there never is) to resolve everything.

4. Potential setbacks and relapses are discussed, including ways they may be overcome in the next weeks.

5. Members are helped to say goodbye to one another in a way that honors their mutual caring but does not reinforce dependence.

6. Opportunities are provided for giving one another final feedback. That feedback should often have a positive or encouraging tone, since there is no time available to process constructive or negative feedback that has an edge to it.

7. Plans are set in motion for continuing the work that each member has begun.

8. Follow-up plans are proposed and implemented.

You don't have to use any particular gimmicks, exercises, or techniques to end a group effectively. You can readily see from the objectives just listed that the structure runs itself. Essentially, you ask participants to talk about how they are feeling now that the group is drawing to a close. You provide a framework and sufficient time for people to talk about what they had hoped for initially, what they actually experienced, and what they want for the future. Rather than springing this on the group during the last session, tell them during the second-to-last meeting what the final group will look like. Ask group members to think in advance what they want to say about their experience, and what they want to say to the other members of the group. A powerful goal of ending the group is to walk away with no regrets—with nothing left unsaid about progress or things that are appreciated about others in group. Suggesting goals can often propel group members to think purposefully of what they want to say publicly to the group during that last meeting.

One technique that often works well at this time is a final go-around, in which members can share what they learned that was most meaningful and what they are taking from the experience. Afterward, other members can give some feedback to each person as "last words" or "final impressions" to remember. Because it is so difficult to remember things that were said, it might be useful to have each person choose someone to write down everything that is offered. Alternatively, you can even record the closing "speech" that each person makes, including the feedback received, and then give the tape as a final gift. During this process, ask the receiving group member just to listen and take it all in without responding to each person. A more structured variation of this uses an empty chair (in the middle of the group), with members taking turns talking to themselves in front of the group about what they have learned in the group. The empty chair represents the self that arrived at the group on the first day, now being addressed by the group member who is finishing the group. After the group member has spoken to the past self, the other group members provide feedback on what they observed and give support for the changes made.

For a Class Activity

This exercise is called "The Reunion" and is designed to help participants set goals for the future in a dynamic, fun, and subtle way. For this activity to work well, you must take it seriously and pretend that the scenario is real. There are aspects of this experience that participants may find a little threatening, so you may feel the temptation to treat it as "only" a game. For this to work well, you must act as if it is real.

Everyone leaves the room and stands in the hallway, but resists the urge to look at or talk to anyone else. Go inside yourself until you can imagine you have journeyed 1 year into the future. Pretend that a whole year has elapsed since the last time you attended this class. During that interval, you have not seen anyone else in the room. You are now meeting for a class reunion.

From the moment you reenter the room, act as if it has been a year since you have greeted one another. After you say hello, sit down in your "old" seat that you last occupied a year ago. Each of you take turns telling everyone about what has transpired in your life during the previous year. You must speak in the present tense. Talk about what you have done, how you are different since your classmates last saw you, and what significant events have transpired in your life. How has your living situation changed? How have your relationships evolved? Anyone new in your life? What about those issues you were struggling with a year ago? How are you doing now?

After each of you has had a chance to make a brief report, talk about the ways this exercise has helped you clarify goals for the future.

How you handle this closing phase is really up to you, but what is most important is what you do to help members feel good about the group and what they have accomplished. You must reflect the underlying fears and apprehensions the group will likely feel at this juncture, just as in any transition. Endings are tough for most people, and so they tend to end poorly. An underlying goal for you as a group leader is to change that trend and to impress on the group how they should aspire to a unique and complete ending. In the last session, you must also plant the most favorable, but realistic, expectations possible for what will happen in the future.

We like to tell members something like this:

Of course, you are going to have setbacks. At times, you will forget everything you learned and make the same mistakes you have made before.

Here, we like to wait a long beat and watch them take that in. After all, we are saying their worst fears out loud.

But this is no big deal; so don't let it get you stuck. These setbacks are only temporary, if that is the way you want it to be. Just as you were able to apply in this group the new skills you learned, you can do so in your life whenever you want. While it is true that you won't have this group to report to, we will all remain alive inside you, as long as you keep us there. The support you offered to one another here endures far beyond the tenure of this group.

There is one final point to make, related to the dependency that sometimes can develop in experiences such as this. As you are well aware, "groupies" become addicted to one support group after another, unable to function on their own.

The key question is what you are going to do to re-create a group like this in your own life. What you are willing to do with your family and friends and coworkers and neighbors to include the same spirit of trust and caring that you found here?

This is another tall order, of course. The truth is that you can't really re-create a spirit that has all the same elements as a helping group. Nevertheless, your job in this final stage is to encourage members to take what they have learned and apply all they can to the other facets of their lives. Changes truly last when people find as many ways as possible to internalize the lesson learned, practicing every day what has now become second nature.

Review of What You Learned

- The main problem you will face is having too many, rather than too few, techniques at your disposal.
- Any group technique must be adapted to the particular context, situation, leader style, and member needs. The best techniques and structures are not even recognized as such, because they are introduced so smoothly.
- Techniques are best collected by asking experienced leaders about their favorite methods. The hardest part is cataloging the options so they may be retrieved on demand.
- When introducing group structures, you may often wish to model the sort of spontaneity, openness, honesty, and authenticity you want from others.
- Good group preparation often leads to better group outcomes. Clinical research demonstrates that preparation leads to decreased dropout rate, improved attendance, and a greater incidence of the types of behaviors that move members toward their goals.
- Just as group leaders must give special attention to the beginning of group, the ending of a group is equally important. The ending of the group is a chance to reflect on progress, celebrate the work completed, and plan on how to maintain change in the future.

Part III

Applications and Significant Issues

Coleadership 11

The best way to learn group leadership is not from a text, a class, watching groups in action, or even participating in a group. All these are important components of the training process, but in an experientially based educational model, the best way to learn anything is by *doing* it. Of course, practice by itself might not be all that useful if you end up making lots of mistakes and do not know enough to learn from those lapses. You need a way to test what you know, practice your skills and interventions, try out your theories, and then receive immediate feedback on their relative effectiveness.

If you know what to look for, and watch carefully, you will receive lots of valuable information from group members; ultimately, they are your best teachers. It is stunning sometimes to watch videos of your groups in action, noticing all the cues you missed and the signs you ignored. But that is not enough. You need a more experienced colleague to monitor carefully what you are doing and then provide you with supportive and constructive feedback about what you can do to improve. Of course, one of the difficult aspects of coleadership is that, as in any other successful relationship (e.g., friendship, marriage, partnership), the coleaders must work well together to develop a balanced and healthy dynamic. Thus, working in tandem with a partner not only helps you understand group leader interventions; working on the coleader relationship helps you develop awareness of your own interpersonal style and its influence on groups.

The coleadership training model has been widely employed across training and treatment settings (Fall & Menendez, 2002; Luke & Hackney, 2007), and it has been viewed as the cornerstone of therapeutic work by a number of prominent practitioners (Goulding & Goulding, 1991; Napier & Whitaker, 1988; Yalom & Leszcz, 2005). Furthermore, the coleadership model has been accepted across most theoretical orientations and mental health domains (Markus & King, 2003). As traditionally practiced in the field, novice group leaders will often pair with an experienced or senior group leader to begin their group training. This model allows the experienced leader to provide direct supervision and support both during group sessions and afterward during debriefing or group supervision. Other models of group coleadership include pairings of novice members and pairings of experienced leaders.

There is some question regarding the efficacy of the coleadership model for the coleaders, the group itself, or both. In an extensive review of the literature on group coleadership efficacy, Luke and Hackney (2007) noted the relative lack of documented support for this training model in relation to the widespread acceptance of the coleadership model. Despite the lack of empirical evidence, they found strong anecdotal support in the scholarly literature for the use of coleadership as the treatment of choice. They concluded that the coleader model offers different and potentially better leadership dynamics than those with a single leader. In a comparison of individual and co-led groups, Kivlighan, London, and Miles (2012) found that group members in co-led groups reported greater benefits than did those in individually led groups. They also found that coleaders became more important as group size increased. Clearly, an individual group leader, regardless of skill and experience, cannot keep up with the increased wealth of the group experience (Breeskin, 2010). Many of the distinct strengths and advantages of coleadership will be reviewed in this chapter.

Power of the Coleadership Model

Even experienced leaders will continue to work in tandem because they recognize certain therapeutic advantages that are not possible with solo leadership. In addition to the advantages of an apprenticeship model for beginning group leaders who are teamed with more experienced colleagues, this structure offers a number of unique advantages for the participants as well (Fall & Menendez, 2002; Hendrix, Fournier, & Briggs, 2001; Kivlighan et al., 2012; Kline, 2003; Kottler, 1992; Luke & Hackney, 2007; Roller & Nelson, 1991). In fact, close to 9 out of 10 leaders prefer to work with a partner if given the opportunity (Yalom & Leszcz, 2005). This isn't very surprising when you remember how much there is to do in a group and how little of you there is to go around.

There are many strengths of coleadership, but for teamwork to function effectively, you must communicate with your partner throughout the experience so you are working together in a synchronized way. Like a pair of graceful dancers or ice skaters, there is something elegant and amazing about two coleaders working well together. However, we imagine you have seen just as many disastrous performances when the pair is just not getting along or in sync. The same occurs in group. There is nothing more frustrating than pushing in one direction when your coleader is pulling in another. In these situations, the group members suffer. Coleader relationships become dysfunctional when one or both partners are oblivious to the issues highlighted previously, or are unwilling or unable to work through them. In these cases, the facade of cordial respect is dropped and leaders begin acting toward each other as bickering spouses or siblings would, a situation that group members from dysfunctional families will recognize.

Many experienced leaders attribute their high morale, continuing growth and confidence, and avoidance of burnout to their willingness to work in tandem with compatible colleagues (Cohen & DeLois, 2001; Corey, Corey, & Corey, 2014; Kline, 2003). Coleaders are able to complement each other by picking up on things the other might have missed (Breeskin, 2010). Coleaders can scan different sections of the group, monitor more effectively each person's reactions, and attend to simultaneous issues that crop up. Just as important, they can watch each other to synchronize leadership. Simply stated, two heads are better than one.

With mutually vigilant partners, the biases, prejudices, weaknesses, and shortcomings of each leader can be minimized. Coleaders become responsible to each other for their actions, in addition to their societal, institutional, group member, and self-responsibilities. This added safety feature may even further reduce the frequency of casualties.

GREATER COVERAGE

Group work has been criticized for affording individual members less opportunity for therapeutic time. When a 1:1 ratio between client and therapist is increased to a 12:1 ratio, there are bound to be people lost in the shuffle. Whereas a client in individual counseling has the luxury of being an "only child," commanding the therapist's total attention, the client in a group setting is only one of maybe a dozen competing siblings. In a 2-hour group of 12 participants, each member is entitled to an equitable share of only 10 minutes. Two group leaders, however, can ensure better coverage and more efficient use of therapeutic time. One leader can take the primary responsibility of ensuring that each person has an opportunity to speak.

The strength of coleaders becomes more important as the size of the group increases (Kivlighan et al., 2012). More people means more interactional complexity. An extra set of eyes and ears can make a huge difference when group leaders are trying to keep track of multiple interactions. Further, larger groups often lead to greater disengagement by group members; thus, an extra leader can work to keep group members connected. Further, two leaders maximize the group's chance of utilizing the additional resources that increased memberships brings.

We have mentioned before that when coleaders sit on opposite sides of the group, not only can they easily communicate with each other, but they can also more effectively monitor how everyone is doing. Generally, it is hard to see the people sitting right next to you, but a coleader can be responsible for scanning your side of the circle while you take the other half. The group gets divided between coleaders in ways that can lead to more attention for the group members.

If dual scanning provides for better coverage of member reactions, the division of labor operates in other ways as well. Coleaders can specialize in attending to some facets of group behavior over others, or even take turns doing so. For instance, if one leader is listening for content, then the other can focus on process variables. Or while one is facilitating an interaction among a few members, the other can take care of the rest of the group. This is especially useful when there is a conflict among members or between one of the leaders and a group member. While one leader is engaged in the conflict, the other leader can monitor the group and facilitate the conflict. We have both led groups alone and found ourselves at odds with a group member or vice versa. As you well know, it is hard to evenly facilitate a conflict in which you are engaged. Those are the times when we wish we had another leader in the room to process the interaction and help mediate or facilitate the conflict.

For a Class Activity

Take turns working with a partner to lead a particular part of class, whether that involves discussing an issue, demonstrating an exercise, or even talking about a part of this chapter. Before you begin, talk to each other about the following:

1. One of you will begin the group, while the other (the one with a watch) will end it.

2. Sit on opposite sides of the group so you can see each other at all times and also observe different members.

3. Make an effort to scan the room continuously, watching carefully to see how each person is responding to what is going on.

4. Occasionally make eye contact with each other to ensure that you are operating together.

5. Take at least one "time-out" to speak to each other in front of the group.

After your leadership is over, elicit feedback from the group regarding how you did. Structure the feedback so you hear constructive things you can work on in the future. Make plans with your partner after class to debrief each other and process the experience.

MORE CONTROL

This can be a mixed blessing, as we will see in the section on limitations later in this chapter. Nevertheless, safety is often a big concern in group work because members receive less attention; it is more difficult to protect people's rights. With two leaders present, the odds that someone will slip through the cracks, remain ignored, or end up as a casualty decrease. Members often feel comforted knowing that there are two leaders in the room. Furthermore, it is simple fact that individuals are drawn to different people.

Double coverage is especially important when working with rowdier populations—hormonally charged adolescents, rambunctious first-graders, prison inmates, outraged or angry folks—as it is important to maintain sufficient control so nobody ends up hurt. Yet the extra coverage is also helpful when working with populations that need emotional connection, such as those experiencing grief and loss. Furthermore, coleadership is probably the only way to provide sufficient support and supervision to low-functioning clients, such as those manifesting psychotic or borderline symptoms; this structure allows the leaders to maintain their own emotional stability in the face of intense conflicts (Breeskin, 2010).

Functionally, coleaders can divide up responsibility for watching certain group members and observing different parts of the room. As shown in the example below, you can also remind each other, as needed, when follow-up is required:

Coleader A: Okay, then, I think it's time to move on. I'd like to check in with you, Scott, to see how you're doing this week.

Coleader B: Excuse me, but before we change the focus, I'm not sure that Rita is done yet. I know she said she doesn't want to say anything more, but I sense that she . . . [looking at Rita to address her directly] . . . that you, Rita, have some things you would still like to say.

Coleader A: Thanks for noting that. I didn't notice. But while you were pointing that out, I saw that others were nodding their heads in agreement. So let's stay with Rita for a little while longer before we go to Scott.

Perhaps you can breathe a sigh of relief, vicariously, as you think about the security of knowing that someone else is watching your back. You don't have to remember everything, or check everything yourself, because you have a partner who is helping you and sharing the load. For novice group leaders, the simple realization that you are not alone in leading a group can provide the confidence to take some risks, knowing that support is available.

MODEL OF A GOOD "MARRIAGE"

In more ways than one, a coleader is like a marital partner. You must read each other's moods, be sensitive to nuances in behavior, and take care of each other's welfare. You share "children" who occasionally need discipline and always need nurturance. Your effectiveness is based on the quality of your communication with each other (Bridbord & DeLucia-Waack, 2011). And of course, like children in a family, group members take their cues from their parents. If the coleaders model good communication, group members often follow suit. Yet if coleaders argue, or indicate a level of disagreement that members can pick up on, it often provides permission and encourages group members to act out.

Remember that many clients have never experienced being part of a "family" with healthy parents. Many come from difficult families and potentially abusive homes. Even the ones who lived in reasonably "normal" families may still not have observed parents negotiating with each other in constructive, sensitive ways. For the first time in their lives, they will see two adults disagreeing in a respectful, sensitive manner, and that can represent the replication of the family in coparenting roles. They will observe the ways two parent figures make decisions, give and take, and negotiate the challenges of a family in turmoil (as most groups tend to be). Furthermore, remember that most people come to groups because their interpersonal lives and relationships are not going well—this is a population that needs modeling of complementary and cooperative relationships.

In the following dialogue, for example, notice how the two leaders disagree with each other respectfully, demonstrating how it's possible to take an alternative position without jeopardizing the relationship:

Coleader A: Debbie, I want to try something with you. I'd like to ask you to pick someone out of the group who you think could do a good job role-playing your father. And . . .

Coleader B: One second. I have an idea of what you want to do, but before we proceed with a role play, I'm sensing that Debbie might not yet be ready for this. Perhaps we should give her some time to think about this before we push her into action.

Coleader A: I am not sure about that. I think she is ready, but I do appreciate your sensitivity for her pace. Let's ask Debbie what she wants to do.

Coleader B: Sounds good.

The members, of course, are watching this interaction *very* carefully, as it reminds most of them of those times when parents or other authority figures argued about their preferences. In this case, however, the participants are watching two partners talk things out and negotiate where they want to go next. Of course, mutually respectful relationships do not happen automatically. For this to work well, the two leaders must invest considerable time and energy in their relationship, as with any partnership.

For a Field Study

Arrange to interview two leaders who have worked together for a period of time. Like most of the assignments in this book, it will take some persistence and persuasion on your part to make this happen. People will tell you they are too busy, that their schedules don't permit such an interview. In one sense, they are right: After all, you aren't paying them for their time.

We have heard many students complain that they were not successful in finding one group leader, much less two, who would agree to talk to them about their professional activities. When we hear such reports, our first temptation is to offer sympathy—that is, until we hear a chorus of others who report quite a different experience: They had no trouble at all getting group leaders to meet with them. All we conclude from this discrepant feedback on assignments such as this is that you shouldn't give up if your initial attempts prove futile.

Assuming that you can find two coleaders who will meet with you, or even visit your class, talk to them about the ways they work together. Ask them these questions:

- How would you describe your relationship?
- Over time, how has your relationship evolved?
- What are the strengths that each of you brings to the room, and how do you complement each other?
- How do you resolve disputes between yourselves?
- How do you communicate with each other before, during, and after the group?
- What do you like best and least about working with each other?

DOUBLE THE EXPERTISE, RESOURCES, AND PERSONALITY

Practically speaking, having two leaders is more convenient for clients, giving them better value for their money. If one leader is sick, on vacation, late, or tied up, the other can take over. Or if one leader is having a tough day, is run-down, or feels temporarily lethargic, the partner can keep the level of enthusiasm up. Far from encouraging a leader to "slide" and lazily defer decisions and actions to a peer, coleadership involves shared responsibility for more territory. There are fewer excuses for making mistakes or overlooking valuable content when double the resources are available.

The likelihood of group member identification and compatibility with the leader is increased if two options are available. Two coleaders may come from different cultural backgrounds, represent different cultural identities, embody different gender and sex roles, and have different perspectives on life. They most likely follow slightly different theoretical orientations, and they certainly behave with unique interpersonal styles. Each personality is different as well. This means that a group has double the potential resources and strengths. In addition, group members can gravitate toward the person they perceive as being most like themselves.

One leader may be better at confrontation, the other at dealing with feelings. One leader is an expert at role-playing; the other is a specialist in thought disorders or career indecision. One is low-key in his approach; the other is passionate and dramatic in her style. One leader likes to use metaphors in her speech, while the other is a concrete talker. One is warm and the other firm. One becomes the "mommy" of the group (not by any means determined by gender), the nurturing figure; the other is the firm and forceful "daddy." All these variations in style create more opportunities for members to respond to different aspects of leadership. I (Matt) remember one of my early coleaders. He was nicknamed "the sledgehammer" because he was skilled at confrontation and being concise and direct. At that time in my career, I was a little quieter and more adept at supporting and exploring emotions. As for my group role, I quickly became the broom and dustpan to pick up the pieces after "the sledgehammer" hit the group. As a team, we actually worked well together and complemented each other's strengths and areas of growth.

With two skilled leaders on the task, when one leader gets out of line, loses objectivity, or gets embroiled in a conflict (yes, this does happen), the other leader can intervene to get things back on track. There is always someone else available whom you can count on to help you out of a jam, or at least to share the chaos.

With coleaders, clients can experience support and confrontation simultaneously. There is a greater willingness to accept constructive feedback when it is offered nonthreateningly. It is therefore possible for one leader to circumvent a client's defenses and resistances by playing a nurturing, soft role at the same time as the partner is pointing out inconsistencies in that client's behavior.

Coleader A: I can really feel for you. I know it hurts. I can see by your tears how much pain you are in. It is so overwhelming to be in the single world again, forced to fend for yourself. You wonder if you'll ever find a lover again.

Coleader B: Yet feeling sorry for yourself won't make things any better. Wishing and hoping for deliverance won't make it happen. You keep blaming yourself for everything you might have done differently if you had another chance. But there is not another chance for your wife to come back. That's over forever. And I am sitting here wondering why, week after week, you play these same games. The tears; the dejected, pitiful looks; the same old stories. We've heard them over and over again. What does it take to get you to work and create a new and better life for yourself?

Coleader A: I know that was difficult for you to hear, but perhaps she is right. You know that we care for you, that we hate to see you suffer like this. How do you feel now? What are you thinking?

SUPPORT FOR EACH OTHER

Many novel ideas expressed in a group are initially rejected because they seem so foreign. Two leaders can endorse each other's verbalizations, reinforcing and supporting the attempts of each to motivate client change. After one leader introduces a concept, confronts a client, or initiates a process intervention, the second leader may choose to offer supportive examples and substantiating data. Each intervention becomes more powerful when implemented with forceful consensus. Look at the following example:

Coleader B: I noticed that you had a smirk on your face while my partner was explaining the ways you deliberately seek attention in the group. I, too, have observed you in action. Earlier today, for instance, whenever you spoke, you would only make eye contact with me and ignore everyone else. Even when I averted my gaze, you would stare at my forehead rather than talk to anyone else. It is as if my opinion is the only one that counts.

Many counselors and therapists shy away from running groups because of the strain on their attention span. It is virtually impossible for a solo leader to attend fully to every subtlety requiring individual focus. In addition to possessing the skills and knowledge necessary to counsel an individual in the group, the leader must also continuously take the pulse of every other member. The single leader's brain easily becomes overloaded with busy signals. Having a coleader helps share the load and keep each person actively engaged. It would not be uncommon for a leader to have the following reactions during a group:

> *I've got to press Sandra harder. She's slipping away with her typical game-playing manners. Perhaps I could . . . oops. Why is Rob squirming over in the corner? Did I hit one of his nerves? There go those giggling guys again. I better interrupt them before they begin their distracting jokes. Where was I? Oh, yeah, I was formulating a plan to motivate Sandra. But she keeps looking to Jody and Melanie for approval. I must break that destructive bond between them. They keep protecting one another from any growth. And there's Cary acting bored again, dying for attention. I've got to ignore him and get back to the problem at hand. But what is the problem at hand?*

With all that mental activity, it can be crucial to have another person helping steer the ship. Two leaders working in tandem can systematically divide the duties that require a leader's attention. While one leader is leading an exercise, the other can help moderate. While one is talking, the other can be scanning member faces for reactions. While one is preoccupied with counseling a client, the other can divide his or her energy among cuing other members to respond, making sure they stay involved, and objectively assessing the progress of interventions.

OPPORTUNITIES FOR IDENTIFICATION

The transference possibilities increase with two different authority figures on which to project their feelings. For group members, that means double the fantasies and reactions to different authority figures. Transference is inescapable in group, and it provides great opportunities for insight (Hopper, 2006, 2007). The beauty of having a coleader, of course, is that when you are the object of such intense transference feelings or reactions, it is very difficult to remain neutral, detached, and uninvolved to the point where you can help the person work through the unresolved issues. With a partner, however, it is relatively easy to observe this occurring in the room: "I notice that you are having some rather strong reactions to my coleader. Let's explore what's going on." In these situations, much as in mediating or facilitating a conflict, coleaders can work in a manner that allows one leader to facilitate the interaction between the involved parties (i.e., the other coleader and a group member). That format frees the involved coleader from a strictly leadership role for the whole group and allows him or her to engage specifically with the individual group member.

It can be useful for coleaders to represent various forms of cultural identities. Visible diversity in the coleadership team may maximize the opportunities for member identification. For instance, having a male and a female coleader can present certain advantages to the group, and mixed pairs of coleaders do not report less leadership satisfaction (Bridbord & DeLucia-Waack, 2011). In these groups, the image of the group as a primary family may be more strongly evoked. Furthermore, member fantasies and misconceptions about the type of relationship between the coleaders may arise and be explored. Members benefit from seeing a model of an egalitarian male–female relationship that works together with mutual respect and is absent of competition, exploitation, degradation, or an element of pervasive sexuality.

Although sometimes it is not possible to work in a culturally diverse coleadership team, given the staff available, every opportunity should be made to team up with someone who can offer group members a different perspective from your own. Not only does it add a needed dimension for group members, but we both agree that working with someone vastly different from you allows the leaders to develop in new ways. Coleaders can provide fantastic modeling of how to address power issues, gender issues, cultural differences, and relational issues (Luke & Hackney, 2007).

Although one criterion for choosing a coleader to work with should include variables such as a different culture, gender, age, and personality, those are certainly not the only factors to consider. Here are some recommendations:

- Choose someone who complements your style, someone who can supplement what you know and can do it in a way that is compatible with your preferences.
- Pick someone you can trust. This is such an intimate relationship that you will want to work with someone with whom you can be vulnerable, admit your mistakes and failures, and ask for help when you need it. Your coleader is going to see you at your absolute worst and best.
- Make sure that your approaches to leadership are relatively compatible. You are in for trouble if you like to work primarily in the past and your partner values only the present (or vice versa). Certain theoretical orientations blend well together, and others do not. Keep in mind, though, that flexibility is probably a more important consideration than espoused beliefs.
- If you have a choice in the matter, find someone who has more experience than you do but who respects you as an equal. You are likely to learn more

from a partner who is an expert in areas where you are not; however, it is better if this person is also comfortable sharing responsibility in an equitable manner, rather than treating you as a lackey.

- Start dating before you get married (much less have children). In other words, spend some time with your potential coleader before you commit yourself to a working relationship (more about this later in the chapter).

For a Class Activity

In line with the recommendation about spending time with a coleader, pair up with someone in the class and imagine that you will be a coleadership team for a new group. Take 20 minutes to talk about yourself as a leader and how you work. Consider the following questions:

1. How would you describe your personality or interpersonal style?

2. What do you see as your strengths as a leader?

3. What do you see as your areas of growth as a leader?

4. What types of interpersonal interactions do you tend to notice? Tend to miss?

5. What do you find annoying in groups?

6. How are you with setting and enforcing limits?

7. How do you feel about working with emotionality?

8. How do you cope with conflict?

9. What are your thoughts on self-reflecting and self-disclosure as a leader?

MENTORING OF BEGINNERS

Since its inception by Hadden (1947) a half century ago, coleadership has been the preferred model used by advanced practitioners to train less experienced ones. It should be of special interest to you, as a beginner, that the coleader format is ideal for increasing your confidence and skills. There is perhaps no better way for you to get your feet wet, gain experience, and yet work with a safety net. Besides the new skills and techniques you can learn, you will also find a high degree of mutual support, someone to debrief with after each session.

When advanced practitioners function in the role of supervisors as part of a team, it is important to consider the following:

1. *Address the beginner's fears of failure.* "What if I don't have what it takes? What if I make a mistake? What if I hurt someone? What if I am not doing enough?" This is but a sampling of some of the internal doubts that run through the beginner's (and many an advanced practitioner's) mind.

2. *Make it safe for the beginner to make mistakes.* Learning comes from experimentation and constructive risk taking. It is important to provide sufficient support for the less experienced coleader to practice what he or she has learned.

3. *Help the beginner process what was learned from miscalculations and misjudgments.* Review each session with an eye toward constructive suggestions that are framed in nonthreatening ways.

4. *Model an honest confrontation with your own imperfections.* Demonstrate a willingness to solicit feedback from your partner and openly disclose those aspects of your leadership that you are working to improve.

5. *Monitor the usual errors of beginners.* These may include being too passive, taking too much responsibility for outcomes, showing difficulty following or tracking proceedings, tolerating silences poorly, or exhibiting a lack of confidence.

6. *Confront approval seeking as well as competition.* Since coleaders should be modeling effective cooperation between partners, attempts should be made to address dynamic issues between them.

Coleading with a more experienced colleague is the best source of on-the-job training. It is one thing to tell a supervisor or coworker about your group and ask for feedback; it is quite another when that person is actually present as a participant. As you have probably realized, this sort of work can be very lonely. Confidentiality requires that we keep most things to ourselves. Yet with a partner involved in the process, the journey becomes a shared enterprise.

Even when you log sufficient experience to fly solo, you will often find it frustrating that there is nobody to talk to about what happened in your groups. Certainly, you will review things with supervisors or talk to trusted colleagues about what happened, but this is no substitute for the kind of camaraderie that occurs when you have worked together with a coleader.

For Reflection

Remember a time when you worked closely with a partner on a project. What were some of the things you enjoyed most and least about this collaboration? What are some aspects of such teamwork that you struggle with the most? Jot down a few notes to yourself that you can eventually share with a coleader you might work with.

For instance, when we begin with a new partner, we like to spend time telling each other about trouble areas we most consistently encounter. We might review areas where we are working to improve, as well as what we like to bring to each group session. Based on your own previous experiences in collaboration or partnership with others, create your own list of trouble spots you can share.

Some Dangers and Limitations

Despite all the positives that come from coleaderships, numerous pitfalls and difficulties exist. Critics warn that the partnership is more for the benefit of leaders than of clients and that it can set up destructive and toxic relationships. In fact, Luke and Hackney (2007) noted that the majority of scholarly articles on coleadership attest to the potential difficulties between coleaders or between coleaders and group members. Therefore, we want to make the next point loud and clear: Coleadership presents some special challenges that must be closely addressed. Almost all the problems result from some aspect of the relationship between the coleaders that gets in the way. When jealousies or resentments arise, when one member feels misunderstood or unappreciated by the other, even undermined, then serious problems will leak into the group. That is why it is so critical for coleaders to continue to monitor and work on their relationship, just as partners in any business enterprise or marriage would.

One of the significant difficulties that occur between coleaders is associated with competency concerns. When coleaders view themselves as less competent than their coleader, they become anxious about their partner's perception of them and the coleading relationship suffers (Cohen & DeLois, 2001; Okech & Kline, 2006). Okech and Kline (2005) found that group leaders' concerns about their competence were among the most significant factors influencing the development and enactment of the coleader relationship.

REALITIES TO CONSIDER

Even if it is true that coleadership does result in better groups, the reality is that most leaders have to work alone. It is often too expensive and impractical to assign two leaders to a group, especially in schools and organizations that already have a shortage of personnel.

A second important reality is that in many work situations you do not have the luxury of choosing your partner; that decision might be made by a supervisor or no decision at all because only one other person is available. Just imagine how frustrating work can be when you are forced to work with someone you do not trust or respect. And if you think that group members will not sense this animosity or tension, you are very wrong. Many people in groups live by feeling and exploiting conflict in others; it is their favorite survival mechanism.

Third, if you are so fortunate as to work with a coleader who does have skills and expertise you admire, that does not mean that person is favorably disposed to mentoring you. If you feel continually evaluated and judged by your partner, you are not likely to be very comfortable in this situation. Therefore, probably most of the problems and dangers associated with the coleader model are the result of partner incompatibility or mismatch. Here are some of the situations that can arise as a result of coleader mismatches.

Tug-of-War

Posthuma (2001) warns of the competitive temptations inherent in any professional partnership. These can stem from interpersonal dynamics between two individuals struggling for recognition or even fighting for member approval: "Which one of us do you like better?" The competition can be further exacerbated by the inevitable conceptual and value differences between two leaders who have their own strong ideas about the best ways to do things.

If coleaders do feel competitive toward each other (and it is difficult not to), there will come times when each of you is fighting to go in your preferred direction. Let's say that you think you are onto something important with one person who is exploring issues related to mortality. Right in the middle of your exploration, your coleader interrupts:

Coleader: Excuse me for a moment. I think there is something else going on that needs our attention right now. Besides, I don't think this person is ready to go much deeper right now.

You: I'm not sure I know what you mean. I don't know who else you think needs time right now, but I'd like to finish up here first, and then we can move on.

Coleader: Well, if you want to. But I still think . . .

You: Yes, I heard what you think. You always interrupt me. Why don't you back off, you sanctimonious jerk!

Okay, we got a little carried away there at the end. But we couldn't help it. Whether you say the things you are thinking out loud or not (maybe you would not), you can't help but feel a degree of annoyance when your partner does not agree with what you are doing. And if you think that it's best just to let your coleader finish before you change directions, remember that lots of times the roles will be reversed: You will be the one who believes your partner is wasting time or heading down a blind alley.

Shortly, we will discuss some methods for coordinating your different agendas and resolving differences of opinion. That does not mean, however, that coleaders will always take the time to say what they are really thinking about each other's work. The differences, per se, are not disastrous. The problem arises when these issues play themselves out in your public interactions.

What My Partner Means to Say . . .

When one coleader is more experienced than the other, or has more seniority (and this is often the case), there may be inequitable status and power in the group. When members know this, they may react either by marginalizing the leader without real power or by siding with him or her against the perceived oppressor.

Another variation on this theme occurs when one leader is significantly more dominant than the other as a result of differences in style. Some people are naturally loquacious—they talk a lot (too much). Others have a more low-key, quiet style. If one leader is allowed to take over, to fill in the space, then the other is going to be left behind. This happens a lot in couples counseling when one partner speaks for the other, who then takes a deferential position. With a mediator present, adjustments can be made to force the dominant partner to back off so the quieter one can become more involved. In your coleader relationship, however, it is up to *both* of you to monitor and adjust your relative contributions and involvement.

Value Conflicts

We have mentioned already the dangers that arise when two leaders subscribe to radically different theoretical orientations. It can be equally problematic when you share the same approach to group work but not to life. You can be separated by religious or lifestyle differences. One of you may be very conservative, the other liberal. We happen to think that differences between coleaders can actually be a great strength, but only if you exhibit essential tolerance and respect for each other. If I think you are wrong because of your beliefs or think your ideas are not sound, then we are probably in for some trouble.

During your "courtship" period, you should spend some time with your coleader finding out potential sources of conflict between you. How will you deal with abortion, extramarital or premarital sex, recreational drug use, and other controversial issues? If you cannot work out these differences during your initial contacts, you may see them play out in your group.

Leader Dominance

Having two leaders can also increase the likelihood that the group will become overstructured. Members can get lost in the process of two leaders working hard (harder than they need to) to control every facet of the experience. One principle to remember is that the more you do in a group, the less there is for the members to do. That is not to say that you should do as little as possible but, rather, that with two leaders you must take more than usual care not to overstructure or dominate the sessions.

Basics to Keep in Mind

Even with the limitations and dangers previously reviewed, the coleader model is still the preferred way for you to develop your skills and expertise (Breeskin, 2010). Taking a beginning course is just not enough to prepare you for all the difficult challenges you will face. While supervision and further training will definitely help, there is no substitute for receiving the kind of immediate feedback that is possible with a partner in the process. For group leaders, the coleader model is the closest thing to an apprenticeship.

For novice group members, understanding how coleaders develop can be useful knowledge, since it can normalize the process of working with a new partner. Furthermore, this model provides an additional perspective on the difficulties and successes of the coleader relationship. As with a group, the development of coleaders progresses through stages. Fall and Wejnert (2005) proposed that this development parallels the classic stages of group (i.e., forming, storming, norming, performing, adjourning) as outlined by Tuckman and Jensen (1977). What this means is that you first develop a relationship with each other, identify respective strengths and resources, and then negotiate a way to function effectively together. It is critical that coleaders are on the same page in working toward the common goal of positive group member outcomes. When coleaders conceptualize their group in a similar way, they help develop a more cohesive group and facilitative group climate (Miles & Kivlighan, 2008, 2010).

COLEADER MATCHING

From Lennon and McCartney to Batman and Robin to Abbott and Costello, all successful teams feature similar qualities. World-class doubles tennis partners can anticipate each other's moves with uncanny accuracy; they know exactly where their partner will be positioned on the court at any moment. Tag-team wrestling partners well understand their limitations and physical endurance; they know when to rest and let the other partner take over. Master bridge players can read the subtlest signals in their partner's face so that they can expertly play into each other's hands. Coauthors tend to choose their partners on the basis of complementary experience, style, temperament, and skills. Selecting a compatible coleader for group work should not be a random process any more than choosing a partner for any other important endeavor.

As for specific requirements in coleader matching, the decision should be based on a lot more than just personal attraction. Trust is an essential element. The partnership should be an open relationship, a model of constructive compromise. There should be a great willingness to learn from each other. Coleaders should be extremely flexible in their style and orientation to maximize the advantages of having complementary personal styles, as in pairing a spontaneous person with one who is more reflective and deliberate. Some are drawn to coleaders who are theoretically compatible, as evidence suggests this can lead to greater coleadership satisfaction. There is also greater relationship satisfaction between coleaders who practice self-disclosure and directness (Bridbord & DeLucia-Waack, 2011). It can be best to have a coleader with similarities in terms of viewpoint who also brings a different skill set, as that can provide more tools to fully address the needs of group members (Miles & Kivlighan, 2010). The bottom line is to find a coleader with whom you can work effectively.

Mutual respect is important so that coleaders feel safe in disclosing their fears, limitations, and weaknesses to each other. Only by being aware of mutual strengths and limitations can coleaders know how to best use them. Once relevant variables are matched according to these established criteria, coleaders can form a meaningful division of labor.

The coleadership model is not merely a technique used for particular purposes in a group; rather, it is a *relationship* between two professionals that demonstrates high levels of cooperation, congruence, balance, and crystal-clear communication (Huffman & Fernando, 2012). Goulding and Goulding (1991) elaborate on the intangible aspects of therapeutic partnerships: "If you define *technique* as a trick or artificial maneuver, then good and effective cotherapy can never be a technique" (p. 197). It is first and foremost a *public* relationship.

CHOOSE A PARTNER WISELY—IF YOU HAVE A CHOICE

Choosing a coleader, a process much like selecting a spouse, is too often random. Therapists and counselors are more often matched according to convenient considerations, such as friendship or the proximity of their offices, than by any systematic rationale. Evidence suggests, however, that coleaders who choose to work together are more satisfied with the coleader relationship compared with those who are randomly paired (Bridbord & DeLucia-Waack, 2011). If you are scheduled to lead a group and do not yet have a coleader, recruit one. Throughout our careers, we have been systematic in picking out prospective mentors from whom we could learn and then arranging to colead a group with them. In some cases, we worked just for the experience. In other cases, we volunteered to be process observers (trainees who are silent members in the room, often sitting outside of the circle, whose task is to record the group process as a way of learning about group dynamics) in groups our mentors ran just to get a glimpse of what the groups and group leaders were like. When our prospective mentors were less than enthusiastic, we did not give up until we found a way to work together.

If a more experienced colleague is not available to mentor you, then pick a peer who has experience and qualities you admire. If you can both arrange to participate in supervision together, that is all the better as a means to structure your continued learning.

For Reflection

Look around the room at your classmates and consider the relative merits of working with each of them as a coleader.

- Whom would you want to work with most and why?
- Whom would you be least inclined to work with?
- Now imagine that you are paired with the person you would least like to work with. How could you address your apprehensions in such a way that you both would be able to function effectively?

PREPLANNING WITH YOUR COLEADER

Though coleadership teams may be hurriedly thrown together, time must be set aside to develop the coleading relationship and to plan for the group. Co-led groups can be potentially frustrating experiences for all parties concerned, even when the leaders genuinely like and respect each other. While one leader is heading in one direction, attempting to facilitate a group member's insight, the other leader may be pursuing a different goal, thereby short-circuiting both helping efforts. Clients can be caught in the middle of a psychological tug-of-war to determine who will win a senseless power struggle.

Coleader A: And so it is very important that you practice being more assertive when . . .

Coleader B: Even more important than the practice, you absolutely must stay in touch with your feelings. Do you know what I mean?

Client: Yes, but . . .

Coleader A: Let's give you an opportunity to practice being assertive right here in group. Pick out someone . . .

Coleader B: . . . for whom you have strong feelings, and share them with that person.

Coleader A: Actually, I was about to ask her to confront her boss in a role-play situation.

Client: I'm confused.

Coleader B: Yes, that's apparent. That's why I want you to work through the confusion before you confront anyone.

Coleader A: But first shouldn't we help her . . .

In addition to competition between leaders, most conflicts and instances of inefficient functioning are the result of inadequate preparation on the coleaders' part. Just as a vocal duet must rehearse endlessly or tennis partners must devote hours of practice to learning each other's moves, so must coleaders negotiate their roles ahead of time.

During preliminary planning sessions, coleaders can decide who will open the group and who will close it, who will take responsibility for timekeeping, and other practical functions. At this time, coleaders should negotiate their roles, deciding who will specialize in particular strategies or conflicts. Specific procedures should be standardized and instructions for implementing psychodramatic structures talked through.

There can also be considerable discussion of a philosophically compatible format that is flexible enough to allow for individual differences in leader style and background. Although working only with identical theoretical affiliates is unnecessary, it is probably counterproductive to pair an orthodox psychoanalyst with a radical behaviorist. Mixed marriages work quite well if both coleaders are open, flexible, and motivated enough to learn from each other. Actually, the greatest benefit for leaders in the coleader structure is that it not only allows for but also maximally facilitates an open exchange of ideas. Leaders cannot help but increase their repertoire of group skills as a result of observing and working with a respected colleague.

A part of initial planning sessions can be devoted to learning how each other's minds characteristically function: "What do you do when a group member refuses to participate? How do you handle silence? What goes on inside your head when you are waiting for responses? How do you anticipate dealing with conflicts that arise between us in the group?"

At this time, one leader may cue the other to observe leadership behaviors, paying particular attention to a skill that is being refined: "After the group, I'd appreciate your assessment of my ability to stay neutral and not inadvertently let my biases show. Please watch me carefully in this regard, since I have been told that I tend to shape clients to answer questions according to what I have in mind."

Photo 11.1   These two coleaders are consulting with each other prior to leading a group. Since they have not worked together previously, they are negotiating their respective roles, sharing resources they bring to the partnership, developing a signal system, and planning how they might proceed. They are also working through some of the differences reflected in their backgrounds, training, and experiences that could sabotage their efforts to function collaboratively and respectfully.

SIT OPPOSITE FROM EACH OTHER

For reasons already been mentioned, it is preferable for coleaders to sit on opposite sides of the group so they can observe different perspectives. This seating arrangement also facilitates easier communication between the two of you. In some cases, you can plan more intentionally to seat yourselves next to members who you think might need extra support or supervision.

For a Field Activity

During a class session or meeting, practice scanning the room rather than just attending to the instructor or person who is speaking. Try to be as unobtrusive in your efforts as possible so you don't draw attention to yourself. Just casually look around the room at intervals, taking in everything you can about how others are responding internally. Form some hypotheses about the ways you think people might be feeling or reacting.

- Who looks bored?
- Who seems distracted or anxious?
- Who is completely engaged?
- Who seems to be only pretending to listen while really lost in a fantasy?
- Who is making eye contact with whom?

Take notes about all the things you learned as a result of scanning systematically that would ordinarily have escaped your notice.

DEVELOP A SIGNAL SYSTEM

In pregroup briefings, coleaders may create a set of signals to use as an abbreviated private language system. Standard cues can be developed for pacing time, switching counseling focus, or indicating future direction; specific signals can be selected for temporary communication channels. If one leader, for instance, wants to be monitored on a tendency toward rambling, the coleader can, in appropriate instances, unobtrusively signal to bring this behavior to the partner's attention. Another prearranged hand movement might indicate the beginning of a planned sequence to focus on a particular group member or exercise. The longer you work together, the more hand signals you can develop to communicate with each other unobtrusively. Now, we are not asking you to mimic a third-base coach telling a base runner to steal a base or suggesting that you create a new version of the hand jive; rather, we are suggesting that you develop natural and nonintrusive ways to communicate with each other silently about important process events in the room. At the very least, you will want to signal messages such as the following:

- "Time to end the group." (Pointing at watch)
- "Let's move on to someone else." (Moving hand in circular motion)
- "I'm confused and don't know where you are going." (Placing hands palms up)
- "Help! I'm stuck." (Sending pleading look)
- "Keep it up; you're doing fine." (Nodding head)

- "Start to wrap things up." (Rolling hands)
- "We're messing up, big time." (Grabbing own neck in chokehold)

As you work together over a longer period of time, you can customize your signals to the situation and to particular members. For example, if you have a difficult group member who has been rambling too much, you can signal each other when it is time to move in and redirect. The same might be true for a passive member who rarely says much. Our experience has been that over time, veteran coleaders no longer need to send each other signals, since time together has taught them intuitive skills about what the other is thinking.

TALK ACROSS THE GROUP TO YOUR COLEADER

There often comes a time in group when one partner doesn't understand where the other is going, becomes confused by events that have developed, or experiences frustration over intense resistance. One of the more interesting options available to you with a coleader is the technique of calling a "time-out," in which you talk across the group as if the two of you were alone. We mentioned this in the previous chapter when we talked about ways a leader can temporarily suspend the conversation to talk about a process as it is unfolding.

The dialogue may be initiated for a number of reasons, most notably to share thinking aloud. An example is given below:

Coleader A: Miriam, we've been working with Gail for the better part of an hour, and I've yet to see much progress. Every time we get close to the root of things, she backs down. I can't decide whether we should move on to someone else while she rests, or whether she is actually inviting us to push harder.

Coleader B: I agree, Ronnie. This is getting us nowhere. Personally, I think Gail is having a great time playing games with us, though she's probably unaware that they are games. Let's confront her directly and force her to make a decision.

Gail, of course, attends carefully to this interaction, gleaning insight into her behavior, and then has sufficient time to prepare herself for the next phase. The other group members also listen to the interchange carefully. They learn a lot about how the leader's mind functions, how it analyzes problems and comes to a resolution. As they become more fascinated with the process of group work, with the skills of promoting insight and action, they also grow more proficient at applying the concepts to themselves.

Communicating across the group also allows leaders to synchronize their actions. It often happens that one leader will begin a series of interventions on the basis of a hunch. When the direction is not readily apparent, the other leader is left behind. This problem can be overcome by sharing the agenda aloud. Another time to use this technique is when there is some confusion about which direction the group needs to go. An example of this follows:

Coleader A: I wonder if we can stop for just a minute. It seems like there is a lot of energy in the room right now, but I cannot really get a sense of what would be a good starting place. [To the other leader] I am wondering what you are aware of right now.

Coleader B: I am also noticing the energy in the room. Part of me is really drawn toward Michael and what is happening with him, but at the same time this is one of the first times Mahsa has asked for time in the group. It seems like we have a choice as a group about where to go.

Coleader A: Good point. Maybe we can start with Mahsa and then explore what is happening with Michael.

Here are other examples of this technique and its purposes:

- When you and your coleader are not together: "Stop for a second. I'm not sure where you are going with this."
- When you want to confront someone indirectly: "Time-out. I don't think we should proceed any further with Franklin. I sense he's very resistant."
- When you want to discuss strategy and allow the members to listen in: "We keep pushing for greater intimacy but only get to the brink before people back off. What if we try something different . . ."
- When you want to make a decision and demonstrate your cooperation: "I'm not sure whether we should continue with this or move on to something else. What do you think?"
- When you want to explain some dynamic that is happening: "Let's stop for a second and look at what's been going on."

Of course, the coleader dialogue is as much for the audience as it is for the coleaders to synchronize their efforts. It is a subtle, indirect way of informing members about things beyond their awareness. It demonstrates the way cooperative partners can work to negotiate options. And it can become an impetus for getting members more involved.

Whenever we are stuck in a group, or don't know where to go next, we will talk to our coleader about the dilemma. If we don't have a coleader, then it is always possible to deputize one on the spot:

Leader: Manny, I wonder if you'd mind helping me for a minute. I'm not sure what this silence means that's been going on for so long. I'm tempted to just let people stew for a while, but maybe it's better to rescue them. What do you think?

Regardless of what Manny says, you have brought the issue into the open. Generally, the conclusion reached is that we should ask the group members what they think is happening and then move on from there.

For whatever reasons across-the-group talking is used, the result is usually desirable as long as leaders have a specific, defensible rationale for doing so. Certainly, coleaders can operate more efficiently as a team when they keep each other informed. And clients definitely appreciate the opportunity to watch their leaders demonstrating their most open, genuine, and honest style.

For a Class Activity or Field Study

Team up with a partner to colead a group for 5 minutes. During that interval, find one excuse to take a "time-out" and talk to each other in front of the group. This could involve something such as not understanding where your partner is going, or it could take the form of talking together about what you observe. A third possibility is to stop the action to make a decision in front of the group about where to go next. After you are done, talk about what it felt like to use the "time-out" strategy. What are some concerns you have for applying this in the future?

BALANCE YOUR CONTRIBUTIONS

Successful coleaders feel responsible for making certain that both leaders are included in the process and are "on the same page." Remember that you are modeling this behavior for group members as well, showing them how a high-functioning team operates. It is a good idea to check in with each other to make sure you are synchronized (as you've just seen, you can even do this during the group). It is also a good idea after the session to talk about the extent to which you felt included and whether the workload was shared equitably. Beginning coleaders often find it useful to divide some of the known tasks of the group before each session to structure equity in contributing. For example, one leader will agree to open the group and summarize the check-in, while the other leader agrees to facilitate the checkout and ending process.

CUE EACH OTHER

Feel free to cue each other if an appropriate situation arises. If you happen to know, for instance, that your coleader has resolved a particular issue in her life, you can elicit this contribution at the opportune time. If you need some help during an interaction, ask for what you need. You might say to your coleader something like this: "I'm not sure where to go with this next, so feel free to jump in anytime."

Surprisingly, group members often like it a lot when you reveal your uncertainties and doubts, showing them that you are human, too. They are also able to see more clearly how you manage to do what you do. One of the benefits of group work that we've both observed is that participants learn the skills of helping at the same time as they work on their personal issues.

Everything you do takes place on multiple levels. In groups, you are not only speaking to one person but to an audience that is also personalizing what is going on. That is certainly the case whenever you and your coleader communicate with each other. Members are watching carefully how you react, negotiate, and resolve differences. Whether you encourage it or not, most group members put their leaders on a pedestal and look to you as a teacher. They are learning as much from you through these interactions as they are from any other therapeutic intervention you might initiate.

INVITE GUEST COLEADERS

For a group with the right sort of composition, the possibility exists of introducing an occasional guest coleader who has expertise in some needed area. Presumably, this guest would neither be resented nor destroy cohesion if a fairly well-developed, secure atmosphere already existed and if all persons involved were adequately prepared.

A coleader might be recruited who has specialized knowledge of human sexuality or career decision making or the like, depending on stated needs. Theme sessions could be structured around topics such as logical thinking processes or the spirit of Zen. In every case, the regular group leader(s) provide continuity, while the guest coleader(s) add diversity and excitement. Because of his interest in helping clients confront fear of death (and fear of living) issues, Yalom (2008) has been known to bring into the group a guest who has a terminal illness. Similar strategies could be introduced in any area in which someone has special expertise—as long as inviting a stranger doesn't significantly compromise trust and cohesion in the group.

Guest coleaders add a unique dimension to the group process. It is always crucial to discuss with the entire group the possibility of bringing in a guest coleader and to ensure that the entire group would like the guest. Group members often find that it is worth sacrificing a little intimacy by bringing in an outsider if the person is sensitive to their needs, has a low-key approach, and can be a compatibly functioning partner with the principal leader(s).

How to Debrief a Coleader and Get the Most From These Sessions

In addition to the sizable advantages to clients, the cotherapy model offers many educational benefits for group leaders. Indeed, the most prevalent use of co-led groups is in counselor/therapist training programs in which trainees can receive hands-on experience while under close supervision. Even for group leaders with roughly equal status and experience, there are ample opportunities for mutual growth.

At various stages in the group's development, certain inevitable issues must be carefully examined by coleaders, not only to keep the group on track but also to support their working relationship. These types of interactions often occur after the group in a debriefing or group supervision session.

Regular debriefings should therefore be scheduled to process the events of the previous session. This is most often done on an informal basis. As the last client leaves, the coleaders inevitably pivot on their heels and ask each other, "So what did you think?" In the debriefings, coleaders will first want to critique each other's performances as honestly as possible, giving specific, constructive feedback about interventions that appeared helpful, wasteful, or harmful. They will next check in with each other regarding any behaviors they did not understand. Certain "lessons for beginners" will predictably crop up if one of the leaders is a student, intern, or less-experienced clinician. The supervising leader might point out the following common mistakes:

- Not sufficiently scanning client nonverbal behaviors to interpret reactions
- Being too passive, safe, and timid about getting involved
- Acting self-indulgent by rambling excessively or using self-disclosure inappropriately
- Following one's own agenda so closely that actions were in conflict with the coleader or needs of the group
- Staying on a superficial level by not sufficiently exploring the individual or group dynamics
- Speaking in a monotone, showing little enthusiasm or excitement

- Wasting valuable group time by letting clients engage in intellectual small talk
- Not using the coleader enough in supportive ways
- Using too limited a variety of interventions, mostly restricted to reflections of feeling and summarizing responses
- Trying to solve problems too quickly because of one's own discomfort with ambiguity or conflict
- Becoming too interrogative, bombarding clients with inappropriate questions
- Allowing clients to use general pronouns such as *we* and permitting some clients to talk for others without their consent
- Permitting clients to use the group for griping about people and things that can't possibly be controlled
- Rarely helping clients focus on concrete goals that they could commit themselves to work toward
- Becoming too intolerant of silent periods, forcing people to talk before they feel ready
- Not attempting to generalize the stated concern by drawing in other participants and looking at common themes
- Asking clients "why" when they don't yet understand what the problem is, much less why it happens
- Not managing time properly, allowing a few people to dominate and then focusing disproportionately on one idea
- Reinforcing precisely the behavior that needs to be eliminated

For experienced group leaders, who make fewer mistakes of this sort, debriefing sessions might be devoted to analyzing group dynamics and identifying possible therapeutic goals for each client. As the pathologist conducts an autopsy to figure out what caused someone's death, coleaders can similarly use their debriefing sessions to identify cause-and-effect occurrences or circular casualty dynamics. With each hour they work together, coleaders can become even more committed to growth, questioning their actions, noting their effects, and filing for later use those techniques and skills most likely to produce positive results and allow for calculated therapeutic risks.

Debriefing a coleader is one kind of peer supervision that has the advantage of avoiding dual-relationship issues of evaluation. It is not intended to replace traditional, hierarchical supervision in which you are held accountable to a supervisor, but it provides a different kind of support, feedback, and stimulation (Riva, 2014). We have found that consistent use of debriefing sessions is one of the ways to strengthen the coleader relationship. Though it takes additional time each week, your groups will most likely energize you and you will

> ### Student Voice
> ### Learning From My Coleader
>
> *I was way too nervous when the group started. Maybe I put too much pressure on myself to achieve success. I lost my grasp on language and couldn't find the proper words to give feedback and communicate effectively. My coleader seemed to constantly bail me out. It felt like I was the rookie and she was the veteran. After the group I blamed myself for not knowing enough, not having the necessary skills, not being sensitive enough, and not being able to express my thoughts more. My coleader actually agreed with my assessment, but she did so in a caring and supportive way. Looking back, I learned the most from my mistakes, which is exactly how my coleader reframed the whole experience. I realized that I was creating my own frustrations and actually fighting the group and my coleader. I was angry that the group was not where I wanted it to be. So what? As a counselor, I have learned how important it is to trust in people and process. Did they get there eventually? Yes. I have learned what I consider to be three significant lessons: (1) Trust in the group, (2) forgo your own agenda, and (3) work as a team.*

want to talk about the experience with someone who understands. Who better to debrief with than someone who was there? Whether you work with a coleader who is a peer or one who is a supervisor, here are a few suggestions to follow during your debriefing process, which should take place before and after each session.

TELL YOUR PARTNER
WHAT YOU ARE WORKING ON

Let your coleader know with which areas of your professional functioning you have historically had the most difficulties. Review the work you have done previously in supervision (and personal therapy or counseling). Inform your partner in which areas you are especially interested in having your behavior monitored. Basically, tell your partner what you need most and what you are most looking to learn from the experience.

If we were working together as coleaders, Jeffery would tell Matt something like this:

- "I tend to be impatient. I work too fast and push people too quickly. Please stop me if you sense I'm rushing things."
- "I've been told before that I sometimes have a blank look on my face. Group members have told me that this bothers them, that they don't

know where they stand with me and how I'm reacting to what they're saying. There are a few other things to help me with as well. I tend to overpersonalize things too often. If you catch me becoming defensive, please stop me."

- "One other thing: Sometimes I get a little too goofy and irreverent. I get bored easily so I make jokes a lot, sometimes at inopportune times."

In turn, Matt would tell Jeffrey something similar to this:

- "I am also pretty impatient, and I tend to get bored easily. So at times I might try to move things along too quickly."
- "At times my mind can get ahead of me. Sometimes I have ideas about what is happening in the room and I push that agenda too much. If that happens, try to slow me down and have me explain what I am seeing or trying to do."
- "My clinical specialty is working with male clients, and I am aware that we are both men, so I might have a tendency to overidentify with the male members of the group. We will need to watch that in this group."

ASK FOR WHAT YOU NEED

As should be apparent from the previous example, it is your job to let your partner know what you need. If you are not happy with the way things are going, say something. If you are struggling in some particular area, ask for help. While your coleader is not your therapist, and may not be a supervisor, you share a mutual responsibility to support each other as best you can.

- If you are about to try something new, tell your coleader to provide a safety net.
- If you are feeling stuck in some aspect of your development, ask for help to break through the impasse.
- If you are confused about what has been happening in the group, stay with the process analysis until you are reasonably satisfied.
- If some countertransference or other personal issues arise, discuss these with your partner.
- If you are feeling resentful, frustrated, or dissatisfied with some aspect of the leadership experience, work through this with your partner.
- If you are having trouble with something your partner is doing, or not doing, then let that person know.

REMEMBER POINTS OF CONFUSION

There will be at least a dozen times in every group session when you don't have a clue about what is going on. The process is really so complex and multi-faceted that a team of scientists could spend their lifetimes analyzing a single group session and still not hit everything. So confusion is not only normal but desirable: If you don't feel confused, then you should if you want to know what's going on.

Consider making notes to yourself about things that happen in the group that you do not understand. This could involve some interaction between members or between yourself and someone else. It could also be about something your coleader is seeing and trying to address in the group that you are just not seeing. This could be a clinical issue or a cultural consideration. Your intuition could tell you that something funny is going on, but you cannot get a handle on what it is. Certainly, there will be numerous times when you try one intervention but could have chosen many others. Take notes that you can return to after the session, during the debriefing process.

After one group session, the leader jotted down the following areas to explore with his coleader:

1. What's with David? Why was he being so evasive? Normally, he's the first to jump in.

2. When I jumped in after Flynn spoke, I wondered if I was rescuing him. What else could I have done?

3. I had no idea where you were going with that about "life decisions."

4. I noticed that several times in the session there were those long silences. At first I thought that people were just thinking about stuff, but now I'm wondering if something else might have been going on.

5. Did you catch that look that Megan gave Stella every time you spoke? Is there some resentment there?

6. I thought we were more than ready to move into the working stage, but now I'm not sure. There was a lot of reluctance today to go much deeper.

This happens to be a very abbreviated list. We can come up with a hundred questions about things we don't understand after any given session. The true joy of coleadership, though, is that you have a partner with whom to talk these things through. You get the benefit of another perspective on matters. Even if you must remain confused, you will not feel so alone in your bewilderment.

For Reflection

In your journal or on a separate sheet of paper, jot down notes about all the things that happened in your class that confused you. We are not referring to the content but to the dynamics and process of what occurred. Make a list of at least a dozen distinctly different things that puzzled you. These could include the following:

- *The instructor's behavior.* What are some things the instructor did or said for which you were not sure the intended outcome?
- *Hidden motives.* What are some interactions that took place in class that seemed to involve hidden agendas?
- *Peer interactions.* What are some communications between individuals that appeared far more complex than you would first have guessed?
- *Dynamics and process.* What is it about the group dynamics of the class that puzzles you?

COMPARE NOTES ON CRITICAL INCIDENTS

One of the ways you will get better as a practitioner is in discovering other ways various situations could have been handled. During a critical incident, your brain can process only so much information in the allotted time. You see what you think is going on and then react. It is fascinating, however, to hear your partner offer an alternative view of what was happening (often completely different from your own perspective) and then suggest ways the situation could have been handled differently.

Even when the choice of intervention is exactly the same, it is still informative and stimulating to hear the different ways an incident or interaction may be interpreted. This is what will increase your flexibility and resilience in dealing with new challenges that arise in the future.

For a Class Activity

Working in pairs, compare your perceptions of an event or situation that came up in class. Reconcile your differences of opinion to the point where you can reach a consensus about what probably occurred.

After you are done with this task, talk to each other about the process of how you worked together. Talk about strengths and weaknesses of your communication, as well as what it would take for you to work better together in the future.

WORK ON YOUR RELATIONSHIP

If working with a coleader is a kind of partnership, if not a marriage, there will be times when you will encounter difficulties. Occasionally, you will get on each other's nerves. You will feel slighted. You may feel competitive toward your coleader, who can probably do some things better than you can. There will be times when you just don't like how things are happening in the group. Even if you get along almost perfectly, you will still need to communicate a lot about your respective positions. This may sound rather obvious, that the quality of your work together depends on the amount of time and energy invested in the relationship, but the reality is that coleaders often take each other for granted.

You may think it's a great idea to debrief each other before and after group, but a lot of obstacles will get in the way. The legitimate excuses are endless: You were catching up on paperwork, you got stuck in a meeting, or you have another appointment scheduled right before or after. Another possibility is that you are tired and just plain don't feel like it. Our experience has been that one of the most powerful, yet hidden reasons why group leaders do not debrief is because people want to avoid confronting others or giving constructive feedback.

Just as in a marriage or friendship, it takes a degree of commitment to make the coleader relationship work. You must build time into your schedules, just as you do for running the group or any other professional appointment, so you can meet on a regular basis. And, as in any relationship of any significance, there must be honesty between the parties.

An example of honesty between coleaders is provided by Ouyporn Khuankaew from Thailand and Kathryn Norsworthy from the United States. They have worked for many years coleading support groups with the refugee women's communities of Burma. They recalled a difficult dialog associated with a 4-day group they were leading as they debriefed during an early break (Norsworthy & Khuankaew, 2013, p. 231):

OUYPORN:	"Have you noticed what is happening?"
KATHRYN:	"It seems to be going pretty well, don't you think? The participants are really speaking up and seem to be into it."
OUYPORN	(serious facial expression and voice): "The group members are mostly speaking to you, looking at you when they respond to our questions or report on their small group work. I feel invisible."

KATHRYN (surprised):   "I didn't realize this! And I think I am reinforcing their behavior because when they do it I respond back."

OUYPORN: "Yes, you are. How do we deal with this to change the dynamic?"

KATHRYN (embarrassed):   "I am so glad you told me and I am very sorry. Let's figure this out before we start again."

Their concern was focused on Kathryn being given more respect due to assumed privilege and power as the "Western expert." Participants were ignoring the Thai facilitator, Ouyporn, who was quite experienced, skilled, and knowledgeable, instead focusing their attention on the White, Western facilitator, Kathryn, who had fallen into the "expert" trap and was engaging with them, to the exclusion of her Thai cofacilitator. In their ensuing discussion, they decided that Ouyporn would take the lead and Kathryn would step back, in terms of facilitating and also by sitting down rather than standing. They talked honestly, developed a strategy, and shifted consciously into a "power-sharing" approach where they worked to share the space so that neither of them were dominating the facilitation or subordinating each other's contributions. As they noted, "the group members saw and experienced a Thai–U.S. collaboration, in which a woman of color and a White woman were enacting values of mutuality, respect, and egalitarianism" (p. 231).

Though we are presenting these debriefing sessions as a sort of obligation, we are trying to imply that they are the absolute best part of the job. Most group leaders are hungry for camaraderie in this type of work and needy for feedback on how they are doing. You will get some of this from informal contacts with colleagues and supervision, but that isn't nearly as fun as being able to compare notes with a "coparent" who shares the same experiences. It is like the bond shared by teammates who have played many games together. You have pulled each other out of trouble and have seen each other do amazing things. You have taken your share of losses but also enjoyed the glory of many victories.

For Field Studies

1. Volunteer to colead a group in another setting. Approach someone you respect greatly who you know is leading groups on a regular basis. Ask if you can serve as an apprentice, just for the learning opportunity. Surely there is someone in your community who would serve in the role of mentor.

2. Ask a faculty member to colead a group with you. Instructors tend to be way overscheduled and overbooked in their lives, but sometimes they might be willing

to colead a group with you where you work. If time does not permit an extensive commitment, sometimes brief observation visits can be scheduled.

3. Partner up with a classmate to colead a group. This should be a last resort, because it may be like the blind leading the blind. If, however, a more experienced candidate is not available, then the next best choice is to work with a compatible peer so you can mentor each other. Remember, as a beginner, you will be receiving some supervision anyway.

Review of What You Learned

- Working with a coleader is both much easier and much harder than working alone. On the one hand, you have support and added resources available. On the other hand, you have another potential source of conflict. Working with a coleader requires diligence toward fostering a supportive relationship that is healthy for the coleaders and the group members.
- When it comes to coleading, attempt to select a partner who is more experienced, yet will treat you as an equal and devote the necessary time for debriefings. In that sense, look for a partner who can complement your own style of group work.
- Before the first meeting, spend time planning with your partner how you will divide up tasks, communicate during the sessions, and resolve disputes. As the group progresses, continue to engage in group supervision in which you offer feedback to each other to develop individual areas of growth and the effectiveness of the coleadership team. During debriefings, talk openly with your partner about your needs, frustrations, and weaknesses. If you don't feel comfortable doing so, talk about that as well.
- There are multiple techniques unique to coleaders. At times, you can talk across the group to your coleader when you are stuck, confused, wish to confront someone indirectly, or want to cue your partner to do something. Your coleader can also be used to effectively facilitate interactions you may be engaged in with specific group members.

Critical Incidents 12

Challenges and Obstacles

Throughout its duration, a group goes through a series of predictable stages. In groups, as in human evolution, progressive development can lead to potential problems. Every experienced group leader comes to recognize these critical incidents that can so easily sabotage therapeutic effectiveness. In a single instant, all our training and preparation must come into play, a split-second decision must be made as to the best way to handle the situation, and the group must live with the consequences. Critical incidents, crisis stages, and pivotal moments are often the crux of any group—they can short-circuit progress or ultimately lead to positive experiences for members.

Just as airline pilots sometimes have less than a second to make a critical decision that will affect everyone's immediate well-being, group leaders are regularly faced with conflicts in which their chosen course of action, selected within an instant, will ultimately affect the safety of a dozen persons in their charge. If a belligerent and abusive group member comes barreling down the runway, so to speak, determined to wreak havoc on unsuspecting peers, the leader must make one of three choices: (1) confront the client with the inappropriate behavior (and risk alienating, embarrassing, ridiculing, or damaging that person); (2) ignore the behavior and attempt to extinguish the actions (and allow potential abuse to ripple throughout the group, destroying intimacy, cohesion, and perhaps the defenses of a vulnerable member); or (3) try to use the outburst as a stimulus for openly working through the issue (allowing the client to manipulate group time and monopolize the focus, inadvertently rewarding his deviance). All this happens fast, requiring swift, strategic action (Motherwell & Shay, 2014). There are perhaps a dozen legitimate courses of action but none that leads to a single, "correct" solution to the problem. That is one of the important points we hope to impress in this chapter—that there are many different ways to navigate through solutions if you can thoughtfully assess and think through the situation.

Common Critical Incidents

A group problem may be defined as any interactive event, or result from such an event, that interferes with the completion of therapeutic tasks or the attainment of client goals. A number of critical incidents and predictable problems come up in groups, mostly signs of resistance or confusion (Donigian & Malnati, 2005). Below are some of the most common problem behaviors that group leaders might face on a regular basis:

- Physical flight (absences, lateness)
- Nonparticipation (silence, withdrawal)
- External focus (blaming, gossip)
- Ventilation (grievances, anger)
- Monopolizing (attention seeking, rambling)
- Intimidation (emotional blackmail, verbal abuse)
- Seduction (helplessness, eroticism)
- "Red Crossing" (rescuing, avoiding conflict)
- Intolerance (peer pressure, prejudices)

Most noteworthy among the critical incidents are several significant nominations that must be handled with particular skill, sensitivity, and diplomacy. For instance, in every group a number of "firsts" command the attention of every participant until they can be integrated into the existing scheme of things. When a first occurs, the group will often look to the leader for guidance and direction, as this is where many expectations and norms will be modeled for the group. The first time the group leader says, "I don't know," shock waves ripple through the group members until they figure out the implications of having a leader who is less than perfect. Other firsts can be just as challenging.

Student Voice

The First One to Cry

I have never had a hard time crying in front of a friend, but I had never experienced crying in front of a group of people, and the experience was quite different. I did not plan this, but on the first day it just came out. When I cried in front of the group, it was a humiliating experience for me, and at the time I wasn't sure why. I just wanted to stop since it seemed too intense for our first meeting. In my family, I was always put down for being too sensitive or overly emotional. I think I assumed that members of the group would become annoyed with me for being emotional because that was my past experience. When the group did the opposite and instead supported me in my emotional state and encouraged it, I felt validated, and it was the beginning of changing my own self-perception. Even though I felt out of control at the time, the leader seemed calm, confident, and constantly assured me and the group that this was okay. He was not worried about my tears and emotional outburst, so I guess that was what we were going to do in the group.

Alternatively, the transition points between group stages are often precipitated by particular incidents that occur with a sense of drama. Imagine as examples that the following situations arise in a group you are leading:

- When everyone in the group is asked to report on what happened during the preceding week, one member responds, "Nothing," and indicates that he should be skipped.
- It is revealed in the group that one member broke confidentiality by telling others what happened the previous week, identifying specific people by name.
- A group member attacks you as being incompetent because you confronted someone before she was ready.
- A member walks into group 15 minutes late. This is the third time in 5 weeks that this has occurred.
- A group member is very emotional, and after a long sigh she says that she has to leave the room and starts to gather her things to go.
- A group member is about to disclose something rather powerful, when another attempts to make a joke.
- Someone discloses that he might not be returning next week because he's been "doing some thinking and maybe there's no point in all this, no point in even living."

Of course, one of the most disruptive problem behaviors is not showing up to group or having poor attendance. Whereas this may be a personality trait associated with an individual or indicative of an inability to commit, there may be other reasons associated with what is happening in the group. Kivlighan, Paquin, and Miles (2011) found that being the group member exhibiting the highest or lowest number of intimate behaviors was associated with not attending the next session. This may be connected to feeling like an outlier in the group, or the "black sheep." Group leaders are in a good position to assess which group members might be feeling like outliers, and then to intervene to encourage those group members to attend the next session. Further, experiencing a low level of intimate behaviors by other group members also contributed to members' not showing up. Group members may be wondering if coming to the group is worth their time, and they may weigh the costs and benefits of attending the group. To address this, group members can work to develop cohesion and intimacy within the group.

For Reflection

If faced with the situations just described, how would you handle them? What issues are at stake in each of these examples? As you think through these scenarios, we are sure you can imagine how each of these situations has the potential either to shift the group toward a deeper connection or commitment or to create uncertainty among group members.

FIRST IMPRESSIONS

As group members first enter the room and begin to make themselves comfortable (or uncomfortable), they check out the other members. On the basis of their perceptions and biases, they will form limited, narrow first impressions of one another:

That girl looks like she's mad at the world. I like that guy she's sitting next to, although he seems even more nervous than I do. I *know* I'm not going to like these older guys with their snotty attitudes. I wonder what these people think of *me*?

Though group members will often deny it, everyone forms these initial impressions that are often grounded on judgmental first impressions.

In the initial encounter, group members will tend to write off those whom they perceive as different or strange and will attach themselves to a few persons who may hold values similar to their own. Coalitions are established that must eventually be expanded to reflect more open acceptance of all persons, regardless of their lifestyle preferences and personal traits. Members will need to be helped to move quickly beyond superficial encounters and predictable small talk to deeper levels of honest communication.

Opening exercises designed to start the group with structured introductions often help dispel negative reactions, because people usually become more attractive after they have made disclosures. Residual limiting impressions, those that were reinforced during the introductions, will dissipate further if participants are given an opportunity to express them aloud. In one such exercise, group members are instructed (on the pretext of remembering one another's names) to select the animal that a given person most reminds them of. After clients creatively introduce themselves, they are offered the chance to hear how they initially come across to others in the group.

Violet: Arthur, you actually remind me of a turtle. You seem quiet, lazy, and unassuming. You are content to bask in the sun. Yet you love to swim and explore beneath the water where no one can see.

Conrad: Nicole, my first impression of you is of a basset hound. You appear loyal, protective, and cuddly. You're a good tracker, with your nose to the ground. But you seem a bit awkward, ungainly, and powerless—or at least you sit in your seat that way.

This exercise, or one like it, will bring first impressions out in the open. It provides feedback to people in a relatively structured, nonthreatening manner. It helps clients (1) hear nondefensively how they come across to others, (2) become more accurate in interpreting others' behaviors, (3) get practice in giving constructive feedback, (4) become more congruent between the images they believe they project and the ones people actually see, (5) collect significant data about one another, and (6) be more accepting and flexible in their perceptions of others, more willing to appreciate individual differences.

UNEQUAL PARTICIPATION

Within minutes of the first group session, it becomes evident that the willingness of group members to participate is often uneven. You will be able to observe these behaviors in the first session, but many group members will flatly reveal that they are shy, reserved, outspoken, or talkative. Some persons enthusiastically contribute all that is available to their consciousness, while others pout, sulk, or cautiously observe to see what befalls those who leap before they look. Rather than viewing participation simply as personality traits, it is important for group leaders to take a broad view of participation to assess some of the underlying factors that guide it. Consideration must be given to cultural influences (gender, ethnicity, race, age, etc.) and how they contribute to perceived permission and opportunity to speak. Consider the cultural identities of each group member, and also observe how these identities interact in the group to create power hierarchies (Burnes & Ross, 2010; Chen, Kakkad, & Balzano, 2008; Singh, Merchant, Skudrzyk, & Ingene, 2012).

Over time, resentment often builds in those who have given much but don't see their partners reciprocating. Yet cautious and reserved members may resent those who "hogged" most of the group time, feeling as though they would have spoken up if they had been given more time. Frustration levels increase as feelings of inadequacy become evident during introductions.

Student Voice

Learning to Listen

I have no problem speaking my mind, and I am always the one in classes who answers questions and is active. In my group, I did the same thing. During the first session, I expressed how excited I was to work on myself, and I admitted to being a talkative guy. Over the next month, I was one of the more active group members, I checked in early, had things to talk about, gave feedback, and found myself getting a little frustrated at the contributions of more shy and quiet members. They seemed to be along for the ride and did not really add too much to the group. So after about 6 weeks, I made a comment about feeling a little frustrated at the pace and the sharing level; after all, I was all in the group from the beginning. I thought that this was not a big deal, but we spent the whole time talking about this, and I have to say that at first I did not get it. It seemed like we were wasting time talking about talking. But then something happened—maybe I was being too pushy or something—finally a woman in the group said, "I would talk more, if you would shut up and give me a chance." A few other people nodded in agreement at this statement, so I said, "Help me understand this more." And so I learned something that maybe should have been obvious, but it was not. I did need to listen more, and clearly there is a connection between active talkers and shy people. We both needed to change: I needed to take the risk to listen and be quiet; if I did that, then more space would be there for a quiet person to take the risk to speak up. I used to think that being quiet was someone else's issue, but I can see how my being overtalkative plays into it.

Often the leader will deliberately use a well-tested, structured exercise that is designed specifically to ensure equal input among members. A leveling effect can be programmed into the introductory activity by providing specific instruction on appropriate behavior and by allowing all members the same amount of time. A 3-minute timer can be used to encourage conciseness and meaningful introductions that include such basics as expectations of the experience, present feelings, stated goals, characteristic functioning patterns, troublesome behaviors, apprehensions, and predictions of what will occur.

In later stages of the group, unequal participation is confronted more directly by drawing out the passive members (while also protecting their rights to privacy) and encouraging overactive members to be more discriminating in their decisions to speak up. Generally, additional feedback is invaluable in this situation, because passive members will receive support that their opinions are valued, while overactive members will learn of specific instances when they ramble and focus too much on themselves. Only when participation becomes equally distributed will feelings of belonging, identification, cohesion, and intimacy develop.

STATEMENT OF SUPERFICIAL CONCERNS

It can be difficult for group members to speak honestly about themselves, even to the point that they are not sure where to begin. The inherent ambiguity of the group situation, together with diversified member expectations, can easily lead to confusion and uncertainty. Members may argue about the "real" purpose of the group, stalling progress until some unifying themes and common goals come into focus. Early attempts to resolve differences in interests, backgrounds, styles, needs, and goals will be unsuccessful until a common language has been developed. The group leader works to restate and clarify group member messages in a way that creates greater cohesion and mutual identification. Through all this, the leader is working to get members to talk about what is truly important and real during the time in group.

After group members initially state their reasons for joining the group, their goals, and how they intend to use their time, it will become evident that there are varied interpretations of what is expected. After the first go-around, some group members will have bravely volunteered deeply serious concerns—about their marriage, sanity, or sexuality, for example. Others will decide to play it safe (or perhaps they just aren't skilled at self-diagnosis), declaring such goals as, "I want to get my parents off my back," "I'd like to get a promotion in my work," or

"I want to understand myself better." Over time, this will be repeated in the check-in that opens each group session. Some group members will take risks in the check-in, whereas others will talk about daily stressors or what they did last weekend—or they will say, "I am fine, and I just want to listen to others today."

It is the job of the group leader to universalize these concerns and encourage people to go deeper, translating each from a superficial, narrow orientation into one everyone can relate to: "When you say you are stressed, it sounds like others can relate to being overwhelmed, but I am wondering if that is what you want to explore today. Your stress over your papers and exams must have a different flavor than the stress that other graduate students experience. So what is beneath your stress?"

SMALL TALK

Until group members learn the rules about appropriate topics for discussion, there is much rambling, small talk, and digression that is unrelated to therapeutic growth. Most people attempt to generalize their behavior in other group encounters, such as parties and meetings, to their actions in therapeutic groups. They have learned to wear plastic smiles, engage in trivial conversation, hide their true feelings, and play games of deception that are patently unacceptable in a counseling setting. If the group leader allows such chitchat to continue, members will assume that they are acting as they are expected to act. But if the chatter is cut off and their usual defenses stripped away, they will begin to feel even more vulnerable. The group leader's task is to model appropriate socializing behavior that is sensitive, direct, and concise, while encouraging group members to avoid small talk. Silence is preferred over an incessant outflow of trivia.

Some members will persistently bring discussion back to small talk about politics, baseball, reality television, or the weather. Only by modeling how therapeutic groups are different from social groups will members begin to realize how and why they waste valuable group time. After a while, group members will begin to monitor themselves with regard to trivial, distracting discussions, to the point where they long to avoid those conversations in group because an expectation for deeper connection is the norm.

COLLECTIVE SILENCE

Beginning group leaders often list prolonged silence as the situation in group they fear the most. Just imagine: There you are—you just gave what you believe are very clear directions and asked people to respond. The group members sit there, staring at the floor. Or at the ceiling. Or at you. But nobody says a word. The silence seems to last forever, although you glance at your watch and see it has been only 40 seconds. Should you say something? Maybe you should wait just a little longer.

What you do in a situation such as this depends on what the silence means. We could say this about *any* critical incident that arises in a group: The first thing you have to do before deciding on a course of action is decode what the behavior means.

If we take silence as one example, silence can mean a whole bunch of different things, and of course it can mean different things for different group members at the same time (Brown, 2008; Rutan, Stone, & Shay, 2007; Urlić, 2010):

- Some group members wait patiently, knowing that they are not yet ready to contribute anything meaningful.
- Others are silent because they don't understand what is expected of them. Your instruction or question wasn't clear, and members are confused.
- A few will be using the silent time productively to gather their thoughts, integrate new ideas, or formulate a plan. In this sense, the silence is very helpful to them.
- At least one group member will deliberately keep quiet just to see what the leader will do. Such people are being manipulative and playing power games to test you, and so they stubbornly stay quiet.
- Some members may be quiet because that is their usual style.
- Another might be working on a self-defeating behavior of talking too much and so refrains from giving any input.
- Trust may be an issue, and group members may not be saying anything because they don't feel safe.
- Someone else may be relaxing, resting, or regrouping energy after a period of intense interaction.

The point is that people choose silence for their own personal reasons. So how do you determine what is happening? And how do you cope with your own anxiety and reactions to silence? A beginner usually makes the mistake of assuming that all group members are part of an uncooperative conspiracy to resist treatment. Their lack of dramatic, *observable* behavior is interpreted as a sign of reluctance to participate. But since only one member at a time can speak, there is *always* group silence except for the voice of a single person.

The group leader who approaches this critical incident with the goal of reducing personal discomfort is likely to find trouble along the way. Such an attitude might be interpreted by the group as, "I don't know what's wrong with everyone today. I thought we were making some headway; I guess I was wrong. That's okay if you just want to sit there, but it's such a waste of time." Group members usually do not respond well to this type of intervention, as it often builds resentment or resistance due to being shamed.

A more helpful approach is to start from a place of curiosity. Depending on what you interpret the silent behavior to mean, you might address this problem in a number of ways. It is almost always helpful to select one person (usually the group member who seems most responsive at that moment) and address an inquiry in a more personal fashion.

Leader: Manny, I notice that you have been very quiet for the past few minutes. What do you imagine Chan and Louise are thinking about over there in the corner?

Manny: Uh—ummmm, I don't know. I was just thinking about whether I wanted to use group time tonight. I think Louise looks kind of bored, because she keeps yawning and looking at you to do something. Chan just looks like he's daydreaming.

Leader: Well, Manny, what do you think we should do now? It seems like you are pondering something.

When working with a coleader, it is tempting to drop the problem in the coleader's lap: "What do you make of this silence? I'm a little confused because a number of people look like they want to speak but seem to be holding themselves back." When group silence does not feel productive or seems hostile, the leader can also make a process comment back to the group acknowledging the silence as something that has been overlooked, ignored, or minimized (Brown, 2003, 2008).

Sometimes, the simplest response is the best, as the group leader can comment on the group process, "I notice that we are silent" or "It seems like we are silent now, and that is uncharacteristic for this group." Once observations are noted, group members often respond. Regardless of how the problem is managed, the style of execution is most important. The group leader wants not only to state that silent periods are acceptable, even desirable and necessary, but also to encourage risk taking by group members who are too intimidated to speak their minds. By keeping their fingers on the pulse of each group member, leaders can readily interpret the meanings behind "silent action" and so gear their strategies to meet the requirement of each situation.

FIRST ANGRY OUTBURST

Even though we can predict that at some point during the early group sessions someone will have an angry outburst, the foreknowledge doesn't often reduce the startled response when the event occurs. We tell group members that spontaneous emotional expression is good, that it is an example of what we are here for—to work through negative feelings. Still, the first uncontrolled tantrum is almost always jarring to everyone, including the group leader.

In whatever form and manner the first angry outburst arises, the group leader must deftly intervene to prevent casualties among other group members who are not prepared to handle the confrontation constructively. An explanation may be needed in which the group leader simultaneously acknowledges the validity of the anger, gives permission for it to continue (unless it is grossly abusive), and reassures group members that the steaming party is indeed playing by the rules and this can be useful for everyone in the group.

Once the anger has been labeled, the catharsis is redirected toward focusing on some resolution of the problem (Yalom & Leszcz, 2005). The most important point is for the group leader to treat this spontaneous conflict in the same calm, accepting, controlled manner used to resolve any other conflict. After analyzing the reasons and motives behind the anger and working through destructive attitudes that were responsible for the outburst, as well as through any interaction variables with other members who were involved, the group leader can lead the group member to express the anger more effectively. One of the therapeutic goals in dealing with anger is learning to resolve and express it in more productive ways. There are many therapeutic ways to work through anger (see Cavell & Malcolm, 2007), and groups are routinely viewed as one of the modalities for best addressing anger (Fleckenstein & Horne, 2004). Four ways of guiding therapeutic anger are as follows:

1. Encouraging directness, honesty, and precision of expression

2. Making certain that complaints are specific and complete

3. Following through the topic of anger with involvement in the conflict or with the target person(s)

4. Teaching more socially acceptable alternatives for working through hostility

The group leader may choose to cap the erupting volcano with instruction on controlled anger—how group members can dissipate anger when they feel it rising, how they can express anger nondefensively, and how they can use angry experiences for future growth. For the other members of the group, this is an opportunity to work through their own issues related to being victims of explosive or abusive outbursts.

Photo 12.1 The leader (with back showing and hand outstretched) intervenes during an episode of explosive anger. The first priority is to protect the safety of any member, especially the target(s) of the outburst. Second, the leader will help the angry person express himself in ways that are more appropriate. Finally, the whole group will be invited to respond by providing feedback and reactions, as well as talking about their experiences during this critical incident.

GIVING ADVICE

From movies and television, group members often acquire distorted expectations of what will happen in therapeutic groups. Since most people operate from a problem–solution orientation anyway and are used to telling people what to do, there is a strong drive to solicit and give advice as soon as the presenting concern is expressed. Group members feel pity and empathy for their friend in trouble. They want to help the person solve his or her difficulties in the quickest way possible—by dispensing advice.

Even before the concerns have been sufficiently explored, group members may jump in with, "Have you tried . . . ," "If I were you . . . ," or "My advice to you is . . . ." The advice givers feel great because they believe that they are *doing* something to resolve the ambiguity of the situation and make the pain go away. They breathe a sigh of relief: "Well, we fixed that problem. Who's next?" The group member in focus, of course, loves the advice and soaks up as much of it as possible, at least for a short time. The group member doesn't have to take responsibility for the advice's outcome when someone else offers it. Yet is it really that easy to help people? As you know, advice is easily given and forgotten; rarely have we found that the solution to most people's concerns is just the right information for a specific situation. Further, giving advice sidesteps providing empathy, which is what most people need when they are experiencing pain.

The group leader must step in during these early "home-remedy" swap sessions, explain how and why they are going on, and describe the reasons why they can be destructive in the long run, even though they provide everyone temporary relief:

> Micah, is it helpful for you to hear these suggestions before you are done sharing what is really going wrong? And even if this advice is followed to the letter—you go home and say what they told you to—what will you have learned to do next time? You will have learned that when you have problems in the future, you must find someone else who will tell you what to do.

In a relatively high-functioning group, you might also say something like the following:

> Nathalie, you seem like a pretty smart woman, and it seems like you would have tried all different angles to solve this problem. So even though these ideas you are getting seem useful, I get the sense that you are looking for more than advice right now.

Another intervention is to work with those giving the advice. Many group members give advice because they don't know what to do but do want to help and convey their concern. The group leader can stop advice giving by probing the meta-message behind the advice:

Jorge: Nathalie, I think you should call your doctor right away and get an appointment. Talking with the doctor is the only way to know what is happening . . .

Leader: Jorge, let me stop you for a moment. It sounds like you are really concerned about Nathalie.

Jorge: Well, yes, I am.

Leader: So I am wondering if you can tell her that directly.

Jorge: Okay. [Turning to Nathalie] I am really worried about you.

POWER STRUGGLES

It is normal and natural, if not healthy, for the leader to cede power to the group members. Power struggles begin in earnest once group norms become reasonably stabilized. Those who have initiated discussions fight for control, believing that they have contributed the most and so deserve recognition and time. Actually, the early initiators are smooth talkers, usually with experience in other groups. They are overly prone to giving advice to others based on the delusion that problems are easily solvable if only they can find the "right" solution.

Other members try to ace the leader out of the authority role, challenging actions and blaming mistakes, whereas others align themselves in a protective posture to defend the leader against all criticism. Group members try all their tricks to win leader approval, some by demonstrating compliance and flexibility, others by being rebellious and independent. And when they speak, all group members' eyes will be intently focused on the leader, looking for the slightest sign of displeasure. Rather than displeasure, however, as the group progresses, a leader is better positioned to offer no response except nonverbal encouragement for the group members to naturally become more active in the group.

When this occurs, dependency issues come to the forefront, producing simultaneous resentment and relief. Group members expect the leader to take full responsibility for providing entertainment and so tend to hang back. The leader tries to extinguish such dependence by slightly withdrawing, allowing leadership spaces to be filled by those who want the responsibility. By voluntarily yielding power, the leader is automatically seen as less threatening. The power struggle takes a backseat once the godlike aura is stripped from a leader who is perceived as perfect in all ways. When limitations and weaknesses are willingly displayed, the leader is a less attractive target for hostile acts, and the group members can then move their gaze to one another.

Power struggles are also common in groups with involuntary members (Morgan, Romani, & Gross, 2014). These groups can be difficult since the members did not choose to be there, and many are content to let the leader and other members of the group know this. Since these members are powerless over attending, they often look to obtain some sense of power in other ways, including being an impediment to group cohesiveness. Schimmel and Jacobs (2011) suggest that leaders meet this power struggle in creative ways, such as using adjunct structures (e.g., movement, writing, props; see Chapter 15) and doing the unexpected. The key is not letting the power struggle become negative and impact the entire group. Effective leaders look for ways to help involuntary members find their own purpose and ways the group can be helpful for them. If the most beneficial outcome an involuntary member can think of is finishing the group so he never has to go to group again, reframe finishing the group as his goal.

ACUTE ANXIETY

When a person is matched to a challenge that is perceived as too difficult or that requires the use of unavailable skills, anxiety results. The overwhelming, panicky realization that you might be over your head, that things might get out of control and ultimately destroy your existence, is the subjectively experienced state of anxiety. The anxious person might break into a cold sweat and start shivering. Breathing rate will increase, as will hand tremors, body shakes, and feelings of unsteadiness. A spectacle unfolds before the group. The anxious person, attempting to control the symptoms, finds that panic becomes even more pronounced as a breaking point is approached. It is frightening enough to brave anxiety in the privacy of one's own home or in a therapist's office, but to do so before a group of persons whose approval has become important is excruciatingly painful.

Freud (1926) was among the first to suggest that anxiety serves a useful function as a danger signal that prepares the organism for combating threat. Spontaneous anxiety, such as might occur in a group, can be triggered by a number of factors, the most common of which involves helping efforts' getting too close to the mark before the group member feels fully prepared to change. When a group member with a low tolerance for frustration and impoverished interpersonal skills attempts to express ambiguous feelings or integrate confronting feedback from other participants, anxiety can arise. One group member's anxiety can become contagious and spread throughout the group unless the leader swiftly and confidently intervenes to offer relief.

A display of severe anxiety quickly becomes a critical incident, and the leader needs to respond. The use of meditation, relaxation, or hypnosis to dispel acute anxiety in groups is often helpful. Before any further action can take place, the anxious group member's fears must be pacified, and the observers must be convinced that the situation is under control. Using a firm, commanding voice, the leader can distract the anxious group member from panic feelings by directing the group member's attention to rhythmic breathing, a focal point to stare at, and/or the systematic relaxation of muscle groups. The leader might say the following:

> Audrey, let's take a break for a moment. I want you to just focus on your breathing and let the tears do what they will. That's right, a few deep breaths, and the rest of the group can breathe with us. Good, keep taking slow, deliberate breaths.

The goal here is to calm the group member down and show the whole group that you are taking action; after things have quieted down, you can determine where to go next. One place not to start is back in the anxiety-provoking incident. More appropriately, start by dealing with the feeling of anxiety in the room. Processing this as a group is often a good way for the group to learn about many of the fears that were activated.

PREJUDICIAL INCIDENTS

Once the ice has been broken and an atmosphere of honesty prevails, people are more willing to reveal their prejudices and biases toward those different from them. Sometimes group members are just trying to speak honestly and may not be aware that they are the source of microaggressions in group (Sue, Lin, Torino, Capodilupo, & Rivera, 2009). Group members will start to denigrate people based on race, class, sex and gender, sexual orientation, geography, immigration status, and so on. Since participants feel that permission has been granted to say whatever is on their minds, they open an attic of stored judgments about every conceivable ethnic, socioeconomic, racial, or religious lifestyle represented in the group. The magic label "you people" or "those people" will then preface any number of creative combinations of abuse. These statements and actions often have stinging emotional consequences for the targets (Wang, Leu, & Shoda, 2011).

Sexist stereotyping, racial tensions, and other critical incidents that result from overgeneralized thinking are best handled by addressing the confrontations on a personal basis rather than on a cognitive plane. All the ignorance and rigidity that stems from a lack of personal involvement with the scorned population can be dissipated after people are given the opportunity to confront one another on a personal level. Contact in group can be a way for members to experience one another and the pain of prejudicial actions and attitudes, and also to work through these experiences in a supportive environment (Burnes & Ross, 2010; Ibrahim, 2010).

In one group, a member was late for a session; when asked why, he proceeded to talk about his difficulty driving to the group and how he had once been rear-ended on the freeway by an elderly Japanese man. It was clear that the incident was still fresh, as he went on to talk angrily about how bad drivers tended to be either Asian or old people and he had hit the jackpot with both. The group had been meeting for more than 3 months at this point, and there was a pause as the leader noticed multiple strong reactions. At that point, two group members, an elderly woman and a Chinese American man, both delicately validated their fellow group member's anger but commented on how his stereotypes were hurtful to them. The angry member was able to hear them; he apologized and said that he needed to work on his prejudice, and then he thanked the two members for being honest with him. The two hurt group members were able to talk in more detail about how prejudice, stereotypes, and microaggressions impacted other aspects of their lives.

SETBACKS

After significant progress has been made, group members often regress to previous self-defeating behaviors when they are under duress. Group members' worst fears are confirmed—that any changes made are only temporary reprieves. Once a group member backslides, all the other group members vicariously experience the setback, as the discouraging sight makes everyone wonder when it will happen to them. In these situations, hope and expectancy are both on the line.

One of the best ways to address this is to sufficiently prepare the group for the realities of change—two steps forward, one step back—as a way to minimize panic reactions and normalize the situation. The leader might say the following:

> Piper, you have made great strides these past 3 weeks with your negative self-talk, and the flood of negative self-talk you are experiencing today might just be the negative self-talk trying to fight back. That is normal, as any entrenched behavior or problem will not go away without a fight. So the important thing here is to stand firm through this and continue to chip away. You will make more progress.

Confidence grows with the knowledge that even if a return to previously ineffective functioning should occur, the group member can readily fight back to the new line of scrimmage, just as before.

Somewhere during the middle of a group's life, once members have had a taste of personal mastery, the leader can deliberately provoke situations that require the use of newly learned skills. The group members can then practice recovery strategies within the safety and support of the group. Certain themes—for instance, the subject of death—become critical incidents because of their emotionally charged nature.

For example, Yalom (2008) sometimes introduces a dying cancer patient to a group of reasonably healthy individuals, hoping to provoke a confrontation with the inevitability of death. Instead of eliciting an atmosphere of morbid fatalism, however, the content spans the usual assortment of presenting concerns. In addition, at one time or another, each group member is given a bonus of facing one's own death anxiety as both a participant in the struggle and a spectator in the dying process of a peer. The concept of setback is reframed within a positive context, providing opportunities for flexing one's newfound strength rather than highlighting the weaknesses.

BOREDOM

After working patterns have been established and group members can reasonably predict the outcome of each session, the following will typically occur: The leader will get reports from members, all saying how much they enjoy the group. People will fight over who gets group time. They will all do a little exercise to get their heads primed. Someone will cry; someone will laugh. A few people will get most of the attention. They will summarize what they learned, get feedback from others about how wonderful they are, and you will think that you have a nice little group on your hands. And then the excitement will stop, and an atmosphere of boredom may take over.

Unless there is a liberal supply of spontaneity, humor, varied formats, unpredictable agendas, intensity, emotionality, and free-flowing flexible structure, group members will grow restless and lethargic. And because the early stages of group tend to be so charged with anxiety and uncertainty, it is hard to get the later stages to match the constant emotional activation. Boredom is the supreme enemy, the state of existence in which time moves intolerably slowly. When group members become bored, their perceptions of time in the group alter dramatically. Most group members require a constant bombardment of stimulation to keep them occupied. They cannot stand being alone in a room unless the television is on, their cell phone is on their lap, their iPod is blaring, or all those things are happening at the same time. These people can't eat without reading the paper or looking at their laptop. They can't sit still for more than a few minutes. Their counterparts, who are relatively immune to boredom, enjoy a never-ending fascination with involving themselves in any activity. In the dentist's chair, they will count the hygienist's nose hairs. In a faltering group, they will have a list of favorite activities to keep themselves occupied until things pick up; they might place odds on who will speak first or reflect on what is holding people back. However they choose to handle the situation, they obviously have skills that bored group members lack.

The beauty of group work is that the heterogeneity of participants encourages people to teach from strengths:

> Kathryn, while you sit there restless, sulking, and yawning, staring out the window, wishing you were somewhere else, hoping that I'll do something to rescue you from this fate worse than death, Becky sits over there as happy as a clam. I wonder how she is so content with her thoughts, how she gets herself involved when she is restless, while you are powerless to do anything but feel bored.

There is something remarkably unsettling about being bored in group, especially in a group setting that is focused on building connections. If you sense that people need more challenge, you can have members publicly assess and reset their goals for the group, which can motivate some. Another rather rough but straightforward intervention is simply to ask the group the following:

> How can you possibly be bored in here when you have so many amazing opportunities available to you? If you are bored, then I have to ask you, what are we not talking about or deciding to ignore? So think about that for a moment—what are you choosing not to talk about in here that if you shared instead, it would be impossible for us not to be engaged?

In the above sections, we sampled some of the common critical incidents you will face on a regular basis. Their order is not predictable, but you can be assured that they will occur. In each case, there are any number of ways to proceed. The first step, before you can intervene effectively, is to assess the situation to determine what the behavior is all about and what you can do to prevent collateral damage to others. Once you have an idea of the group and individual dynamics at work, you can move toward an intervention.

Interpersonal Conflict

One of the more critical incidents in any group is conflict. If you do not have a group in which people are disagreeing and arguing with one another, then you do not have an atmosphere where it is safe for people to speak their minds. Conflict presents groups with both an obstacle and an opportunity; it can be dysfunctional—harming performance, breaking down cohesion, deteriorating trust and cooperation—or it can be beneficial—advancing the group by circumventing the natural tendency toward stability and status-quo thinking (Brown, 2011;

DeChurch, Hamilton, & Haas, 2007). Group conflict can be viewed as a process, rather than an event, that begins when at least one group member perceives a difference of opinion regarding something important (Brown, 2011; De Dreu & Weingart, 2003). Many group members' greatest fear is conflict, because they worry that somehow the disagreement will get out of control and the individual and the group as a whole will be irrevocably hurt. Of course, one reason why most group members fear conflict is that, as a whole, most people process conflicts poorly, so that the inevitable result is a winner and a loser. Conflicts become a way to flex physical, emotional, or psychological force, and listening and compromise get shortchanged. In a group setting, the leader must help create a different outcome.

Conflicts are not only inevitable in groups but, as we mentioned before, also highly useful (we will keep mentioning this point to encourage you to delve into conflicts as a group leader). Conflicts actually serve a number of constructive purposes (Kottler, 1994):

1. They bring attention to important issues that may have been previously ignored.

2. They underscore underlying issues of power and control.

3. They prevent stagnation.

4. They regulate distance between people.

5. They ease tension.

6. They promote reflection and growth.

7. They can lead to greater intimacy.

8. They provide a learning experience in which a conflict can emerge and yet be addressed in a nonconflictual manner.

For Reflection

Think of a recent time in your life when you were involved in some sort of conflict. This could have been with a family member, friend, coworker, or acquaintance. Although this situation may have been tense and uncomfortable, and may even have ended on a negative note, consider what good might have emerged from the disagreement. What did you learn from the experience? How did you handle the incident? Use this example to analyze your normal reactions to conflict, as this will be a good indicator of how you will respond as a group leader.

Since conflict is the inevitable result of any group activity, it is your job to facilitate the interaction in such a way that the participants (and the audience) leave the encounter feeling good about the experience. In fact, one of the things that distinguish experienced group leaders from their less experienced peers is greater comfort with and confidence in dealing with periodic upheavals. This "calmness under fire" models for group members the salient attitude that what is happening right now, although heated and passionate, is a constructive exchange that will lead to positive outcomes. This can occur only under the stewardship of an able leader who works to protect people against becoming casualties.

There are several basic courses of action you can take when faced with a conflict in the group (Brazaitis, 2014; Sole, 2006):

1. *Beating a hasty retreat:* If, in your judgment, the conflict is not a constructive engagement at that moment in time, then you can work to divert the negative energy in other directions. Perhaps the timing is not good because someone is in the middle of something else that is important. Another possibility is that this has been a recurrent source of struggle between combatants that has not led to anything useful. Or maybe you just want to wait awhile, observe the situation more closely, and collect more information before you attempt to work things through. Since most group members can clearly sense a conflict or one in the making, if you choose to move away from it, it can be useful to note verbally to the group that you are making this choice deliberately. If you do not acknowledge this, then an incorrect message may be sent to the group that you do not like conflict or that avoiding conflict is okay in this group.

Of course, in this case, you are not necessarily avoiding the conflict altogether; you are merely postponing its resolution until a more opportune time. When the issues are relatively minor, such as a skirmish over who sits where, you may elect to ignore it altogether. It all depends on what the conflict means in the context of the interaction. If you do not know (which often you will not), you can always ask the group to help you sort it out:

> I'm puzzled by something I'd like to understand better. I notice that every time you, Nate, and Michelle talk to one another, you usually resort to teasing and ridiculing. I can't tell if this is good-natured fun on your part, or whether there is something else going on between the three of you. What's happening?

2. *Finding a consensus:* In this case, you have decided to mediate the disagreement by helping the participants develop a solution that meets all their needs. This means that each person is going to have to compromise to attain peace. Mediation efforts

usually involve helping all parties express their points of view and acknowledge to one another that they have heard what was said. They are then encouraged to find some common ground that each can live with. Of course, any mediation in this setting happens with the other group members as active observers. You can use group members to help mediate conflicts when they get stuck:

Leader: Let's stop for moment. Addie, you have been watching Vong and Adam go back and forth for the past 10 minutes with no resolution. What do you see that each of them is missing from the other?

Addie: Okay, well this is just my observation. You stopped listening to each other about 5 minutes ago, and now it seems like you just keep saying the same thing. Adam, you seem really defensive, since you keep trying to explain how you didn't mean what you said in that way. And Vong, it seems like you are really stubborn right now, as if you are unwilling to alter your perspective.

3. *Using a power position:* From your position of authority, you can intervene decisively to stop an altercation if someone is getting hurt. This has the advantage of ending the conflict quickly. The disadvantages, however, are that you may not address the source of the problem and you may have taken over the group instead of allowing the members to resolve their own issues. This course of action is usually used only in rather extreme circumstances or when there seems to be no resolution in sight.

Because of the inevitability of multiple perspectives in any group, group leaders play an important role by synchronizing members in such a way that all participants can understand one another, even if they do not agree. When it comes to mediating or facilitating conflicts, there is not one way of doing it; rather, a combination of skills and interventions is used. You might try any mixture of the strategies given below:

1. Directing the people in conflict to speak *to* one another rather than *about* one another to someone else

2. Blocking insensitive or inappropriate attacks

3. Reflecting the feelings of what is expressed

4. Clarifying the content of the communications

5. Linking common points of agreement

6. Cuing others to get involved

It is hard to spell out what the desired outcome of any conflict should be. Usually, the leader can get a sensation about the process and dynamics in the room that indicates how well the conflict was resolved. Since conflicts are an important event in any group, we do suggest taking the time during and after the conflict to assess the reactions of group members to learn how they are feeling about the group and the process that has just occurred. If the resolution is successful, group members often learn the following from such conflicts:

- Confrontation, when communicated appropriately, can lead to tremendous growth.
- Resolution occurs only through collaboration and compromise.
- Avoidance or diminishment of conflict is often unhelpful in the long run.
- There are as many different perspectives on what is happening as there are participants.

Student Voice

Dealing With
My Conflict Over Conflict

It took months for me to really talk about stuff, and in the process of sharing, I let out a bad experience that I previously had with a current group member. It was just part of my story, and I did not name him, but I could feel the tension between us that night. I felt that it was appropriate for me to have said what I did, but he didn't feel that way. Next week, he started by telling the group about how hurtful last week was because I had alluded to him. We could not avoid talking about this, and it was really tense between us and the group since all this was news to them. We were both pretty defensive and angry and began to play out our old conflict, but the leader stopped us and had us keep it in the present. The other group members got frustrated with both of us, since we both were on the attack and not listening to each other. So they gave us some feedback and helped me hear things that I had been closed off to. There were many times when it seemed like we would agree to disagree or just not deal with it, but the leader kept bringing it back to us, using the group to help us, and eventually we began to thaw. Working out that conflict in front of the class helped me see how defensive and closed off I am. I wasn't able to fully process what was going on at first, because I was too concerned with keeping myself safe. But working that out was the pivotal moment for me, and it was a real turning point for the group. We had hung tough and resolved a difficult situation—after that it seemed like we took big steps and began to be much more real with each other.

For example, after speaking at length about her lifelong struggle with trusting men, Samantha viewed her own disclosure as clear, cogent, and incisive. Li, however, thought Samantha sounded whiny and embittered, stirring up trouble by forcing the men and women in the room to choose sides. Colin, who had been speaking earlier, thought Samantha was attempting to control the session and draw attention away from him. And he also sensed somehow that Samantha was talking about him as one who could not be trusted. Felipe, on the other hand, felt profoundly moved by Samantha's story; he began examining his own trust issues toward members of the opposite sex.

After the session ended, other group members processed Samantha's comments as they walked out to their cars. They also reflected little consensus in their points of view about the relative meaning of this incident. It seemed that Samantha was alternately perceived as bitchy, courageous, manipulative, and vulnerable. Even the two coleaders didn't agree on how they viewed Samantha's behavior. One leader thought Samantha's disclosure was a significant catalyst for future action in the areas of love and trust; the other leader felt that Samantha had diverted the discussion to avoid the more potentially frightening issues of self-destruction that Nigel had been on the verge of bringing up.

Leaders must plan for and expect group conflict, before it ever begins. One of the ways to do this is by negotiating and clearly defining the contractual goals for the group so that there is shared ownership of the rules. Those rules serve as guidelines for all communication, including conflict. They might include a number of items, depending on the type of group. Some examples are given below:

- That physical or emotional abuse will not be tolerated
- That each member will not speak for others without their consent, and that each participant will take responsibility for getting one's own needs met
- That there will be an equitable distribution of group time, with each member getting a fair share
- That members will not be permitted to complain and gripe about things and people over which they have no control
- That members will be respectful of and sensitive to others' rights
- That nobody will be pressured to do or say anything for which they do not feel ready
- That participants agree to reveal themselves in honest and authentic ways

Strategies for Handling Critical Incidents

The ways to address critical incidents are as varied as the groups themselves. With any intervention, you want to assess the group's needs, both overt and covert, and then tailor the intervention to those needs at that time. Other critical incidents and predictable problems frequently occur: termination and reentry problems, conflicting goals between the leader and participants, degeneration of the group into a gripe session, or difficulties with oversolidarity, in which the pervasive closeness that has developed within the group only confirms the suspicion that people outside the group cannot be trusted. All these incidents may be dealt with in a systematic fashion that involves several sequential steps.

First, the group leader must be able to recognize critical incidents when they are occurring. This process involves some fairly clear notions of what exactly constitutes a critical incident. The operational definition will probably be consistent with one's theoretical framework.

Second, the group leader must be able to identify the specific variety of critical incident that is occurring by noting its effect on individual members and their reactions. This involves examining the context in which the event takes place, including precipitating factors that led up to the incident, relevant background, group climate, timing, and the intensity of member responses. The specific diagnostic decision may then include figuring out what happened, why and how it occurred, and whether a leader intervention is called for to resolve the therapeutic issue. It is important to note that sometimes Steps 1 and 2 do not occur during the actual group but may come to light during a group supervision session or a debriefing with your coleader. One benefit of this is that you will have time to thoughtfully conceptualize what is occurring in your group.

Once the critical incident has been clearly dissected, the leader formulates an optimal plan for creating therapeutic insight from the wayward ingredients that are most prevalent. Consider a group in which one member is chronically late for sessions. Other members become impatient and resentful. Soon, voices and blood pressures rise and acceptance, tolerance, and politeness decline. The leader takes a deep breath, offers reassuring words to the effect that the group may have gotten carried away, and then attempts to use the outburst as a constructive lesson for understanding effective confrontation. In this example, the lateness of the group member may seem like the problem at hand—and, without a doubt, it is a concern—but for the leader, the more pressing concern is coming up with a framework to express conflict and displeasure about the lateness. Thus, the process in this situation is the intervention of expressing conflict rather than the content of the problem of lateness. Members will be much more concerned with sharing their opinions about the situation, but the leader is focused on how members are communicating.

In resolving interpersonal conflicts such as these, the leader will want to clarify communication and structure-specific goals satisfactory to all parties, filter out distracting variables, and use compromise and consensus strategies to avoid win/lose situations. Critical incidents are critical because they can be used for better or for worse. Rather than dreading and avoiding them, the group leader should calmly face such predictable problems and sometimes even encourage their development, secure in the knowledge that they can be transformed into stimuli for accelerated growth. It is important to remember that the leader will most likely have to be the one to draw the attention of the group to the underlying critical incident.

As you no doubt realize, there is no single best way to respond to a critical incident that occurs in a group. There are, however, some sound strategies that can be employed. If we take, as an example, the rather structured type of group found in a school classroom, you can see the way a number of common challenges might be addressed (Kottler & Kottler, 2006). This will give you a flavor of how you might deal with similar situations in any group you lead.

The situation:	A member asks you a question to which you don't know the answer.
The response:	"Good question. What do you think?"

Group leadership (and all helping) is often like tennis; the object is to keep the ball in the other person's court.

The situation:	A member shows resistance, makes excuses, or argues about why something wouldn't work.
The response:	"Don't argue with me. Argue with yourself."

Don't try to talk people into something they are not yet ready to hear. Extricate yourself from arguments by reminding yourself that sometimes people don't want what you are selling.

The situation:	You ask people a question, and they say they don't know.
The response:	"Take a wild guess."

Many times, people are just unwilling to risk being wrong. Once you give them permission, they will often surprise you (and themselves) with how much they really know and understand.

The situation:	A member is wandering, digressing, or distracting.
The response:	"I wonder if you would mind summarizing what you really want us to know."

This is much more polite and less threatening than saying, "I'm lost," "You aren't making much sense," or "I wasn't paying attention."

The situation: A member is passive, withdrawn, or quiet.

The response: "You seem awfully reflective."

This is, of course, an invitation to join in. On the one hand, you can't ignore members who are withdrawn; on the other hand, you don't want to pressure them to do more than they feel ready to do.

The situation: What you're doing is not working.

The response: "I'm aware that what I'm doing isn't working. So I need some help from the group today."

Members often like it when you own up to your confusion, making it easier for them to do so as well. This also allows members an opportunity to take more responsibility for what is occurring.

For a Class Activity

In groups of two or three, discuss ways you might handle some of the critical situations described above. For each of them, list the motives, goals, and hidden agendas that might be operating for the individual who initiates the incident. In this situation, what would be hard for you to do? Next, figure out what you might do to limit the destructive aspects of the behavior, as well as to use it as a learning experience in the group. Share your strategies with other groups, coming to a consensus on the preferred methods.

For a Field Study

Talk to several experienced group leaders about the critical incidents and challenges they struggle with the most. Find out what they have discovered works least and most effectively when faced with such situations. What would they recommend you do to prepare yourself for similar struggles?

Review of What You Learned

- Critical incidents represent situations in group work that become pivotal because of what is at stake. These incidents require group leaders to act with confidence to reassure group members to proceed.
- A dozen or so critical incidents are common and predictable, meaning that you can prepare yourself for handling them ahead of time.

- There are many "firsts" in the life of a group, and each first represents a new hurdle for the group to overcome. Group members look to leaders for guidance and for assurance that what is happening is okay.
- Conflict in a group is a certainty. Conflicts present unique learning opportunities for the group to grow, and they can teach individuals ways to approach conflict more effectively in life outside the group.
- Each incident is unique and is based on the group dynamics at any given time. Assess the situation and then determine what issues are present for individuals and the entire group. There is no one right way; rather, good assessment of your group, group members, and group process often provides the compass for where and how to intervene.

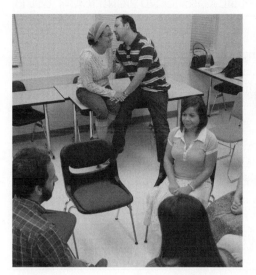

Ethical Issues Unique to Group Work 13

I n every class you will take, there will likely be some treatment of ethical, legal, and moral issues that must be considered in professional practice. Group work is no exception; in fact, it has some unique challenges that place it among the most complex helping endeavors. The very fact that multiple people are in treatment together means that, by definition, the best outcome for everyone will vary. Concerns about confidentiality, informed consent, diversity, group pressure, and managing multiple relationships all require special attention. Interestingly, although all the major professional organizations to which group leaders belong—American Psychological Association, National Association of Social Workers, American Counseling Association, American Association of Marital and Family Therapy, and others— have their own ethical codes that cover basically the same areas, there has still been a need for group specialists to develop their own ethical, practice, and training guidelines (American Group Psychotherapy Association, 2002, 2007; Association for Specialists in Group Work, 1998, 2000, 2012).

Special Challenges

Throughout this text, we have examined how group work has the potential to be far more potent, and also more dangerous, than other helping modalities. This situation exists for a number of reasons that are associated with having so many different people involved in the setting, with multiple interconnections among problem areas (Barlow, 2013; Brabender, 2007). Ethical decision making for the group leader presents a formidable challenge for many reasons unique to this setting, including the following:

1. Verbal abuse and subsequent casualties are more likely to occur in groups than in individual treatment.

2. The leader has less control over proceedings and group member behavior; so more things can potentially go wrong before the leader is able to intervene.

3. The leader has more control in influencing capabilities, a power that can be used for better or for worse.

4. Peer pressure and coercion create undue influence.

5. Group members receive less attention than they might in a one-on-one setting.

6. Confidentiality can be neither guaranteed nor enforced, because other group members don't necessarily live by the same ethical codes that leaders do.

7. Many group leaders practice without benefit of training, education, or supervision. There are no standardized criteria for acceptable qualifications. In the same city, a psychiatrist, psychologist, astrologer, palmist, and fortune-teller can all label their professional activities as "group therapy."

8. Because groups are such intense environments in which interactions occur at a rapid pace, the risks for each member are greater. Change and damage are accelerated.

9. The screening of group members is frequently haphazard. Many group members are often required to participate in the experience involuntarily (i.e., for court-mandated treatment).

10. Group work presents special reentry problems for participants when the sessions have ended.

11. Dependency effects are more pronounced in groups.

12. There is no licensure, certification, or regulation that can effectively enforce the practice of responsible group leadership.

Like so many of the subjects we have covered in this text, there are whole books devoted to the topic of ethical issues in helping professions (see Corey, Corey, Corey, & Callanan, 2015; Cottone & Tarvydas, 2006;

Pope & Vasquez, 2011; Welfel, 2013; Wheeler & Bertram, 2012). While there is a risk of redundancy in reviewing ethical issues you may have considered before in a broader context, it is always useful to examine the ways these dilemmas manifest themselves uniquely in special circumstances such as group work.

Major Ethical Issues in Group Leadership

In this chapter, we will review those ethical challenges that are part of group leadership practice. We will assume that the more general ethical principles that apply to all helping professionals will have been covered in other classes. If not, you will want to familiarize yourself thoroughly with ethical conduct related to concepts such as informed consent, privileged communication, dual relationships, and scope of practice.

For Reflection and a Class Activity

Among all the issues raised in this text and in your class, there are most likely a few that strike terror in your heart. Write down several ethical or moral dilemmas that you can imagine facing in your work as a group leader.

To get you thinking about possibilities you might overlook, or conveniently push out of your mind, consider these realistic scenarios:

- A group member confides to you that she knows something awful about another member, but she warns you not to say anything.
- It comes out in the group that someone may be suicidal, but you aren't sure if the person is serious or not.
- A group member tells you that he or she is very attracted to you and wants to have a relationship after the group ends.
- Someone in the group appears toxic to others and is constantly disruptive but refuses to leave; this person threatens to sue you for negligence or abandonment if you force him or her out of the group.
- A number of group members conspire to impose values on others in the group that you find distasteful, if not immoral.
- You find out from a secret source that confidentiality has been breached in group, yet no one in the group will admit to it.
- A member of the group says that a friend outside of the group pointed out that one of the group members is posting personal information about the group and ridiculing it on Facebook.

In small groups, talk to one another about the ethical dilemmas you fear the most. After each person has had a chance to talk, look for common themes in your disclosures.

CONFIDENTIALITY CANNOT BE GUARANTEED

Just imagine the dilemmas associated with a situation in which you are the only one who is ethically bound to maintain the privacy and sanctity of disclosures. As much as you can urge group members to respect the right to privacy, as much as you can stress that this safeguard is the key to any trust that develops in the group experience, you can't guarantee that this promise will be honored (Barlow, 2012). It might be unfair, even immoral, for people to betray confidences, but you are the one who is ultimately responsible for the outcome. All you can do is strongly encourage group members to keep one another's confidences, as you are the only one who must keep confidentiality (Weinberg & Schneider, 2007).

Imagine that someone in your group discloses that she has been sexually abused, or someone else reveals that he is gay, or another person is contemplating suicide. Now, imagine that these secrets slip out so that others know them. Although there is little you can actually do to prevent, with complete certainty, such circumstances from happening, you need to take steps to protect members as best you can.

The first step is to stress how important confidentiality is in the group. The confidential relationship in a group is critical so that change can take place that benefits those in the protection of the group by helping them relate to the outside world. The rationale for confidentiality is that it provides the optimal condition for personal growth (Behr, 2006). Group members will need to be educated and reminded from time to time about the subtle ways confidences can be revealed. Discuss the problem frankly at the beginning of the group and then any other time concerns come up. Part of the difficulty with confidentiality may arise from confusion between the terms *confidentiality* and *secrecy* (Cohen, Ettin, & Fidler, 2002). Confidentiality requires that the identity of the group member be protected, but in many circumstances, what was said may be revealed. The key distinction is whether a group member's identity can still be protected if the information leaks. Therefore, group members have to learn how to talk about their group experience in a way that disguises other group members' identities (Weinberg & Schneider, 2007).

Role-play how to handle tempting situations that will inevitably arise, such as when a spouse or best friend directly asks a group member what was talked about. Explain how to handle the situation by saying something like the following:

> While you are permitted, even encouraged, to talk about what happens in this group with respect to your own behavior and issues—in fact, I hope that you will be proud of the work you are doing and that you will talk about what is important

to you—you are not allowed to mention anyone else, either by name or by identifying features. So, for example, let's say the issue of fathers came up in the group, and when you went home, your partner or roommate asked about the group. You could not say, "Well, Rachel talked about her father, Frank, who works down at the library." But you could say, "The issue of fathers came up tonight, and I found myself thinking about my relationship with my father and the things I appreciate about him."

The key here is to give group members the impression that they can always talk about *their* experiences (and most likely should share their growth and insight with those they trust) but that they cannot talk about the details and identifying information of other group members.

Group members must be informed accurately and realistically about the risks they are facing as members of the group (Fallon, 2006; Rapin, 2014). These risks include the possibility that someone else present might not honor their commitments and their promise to keep group proceedings confidential. Many group leaders follow the guidelines of professional organizations devoted to group work (i.e., Association for Specialists in Group Work and American Group Psychotherapy Association), which advocate providing participants with written disclosure statements that include information such as the following:

- Purpose and goals of the group
- Scope and parameters of the sessions
- Expectations for members' participation
- Roles and responsibilities of the leader
- Policies regarding attendance, fees, and scheduling
- Discussion of norms and ground rules
- Risks associated with the experience
- Limits of confidentiality
- Respect for cultural and individual differences of members
- Protection against coercion
- Notification of any recording of sessions that might take place and what will happen to those tapes

The key is to do your best as a leader to clarify and explain the expectations and responsibilities so that group members all share the same understanding and expectations about member behavior. Yet, despite these efforts, confidentiality is often broken in group work. When this happens, it will have to be addressed immediately to rebuild trust and cohesion.

For a Class Activity

Either in a "fishbowl" in front of the class or in a private area, role-play a group of some very concerned, fearful members who feel reluctant to reveal very much about themselves. With this as a setting, take turns as coleaders explaining confidentiality and then helping members talk about their concerns.

Give feedback to each set of leaders on things they might do differently to operate more effectively in the future when they talk about confidentiality in groups.

Process what it felt like to be part of a group in which safety is such a deep concern. What are some steps that could be taken to alleviate these fears?

COERCION AND PEER PRESSURE ARE COMMON

One ethical issue has great relevance for contemporary group leaders: the innate conflict between the coercive force of groups and the individual autonomy of each member. Once people decide to pool their resources and work toward a common purpose, individual needs are necessarily shelved in favor of what is good for the majority.

You have heard this one several times before, but in group settings it bears repeating, because it is so critical. When group members take the risk of jumping into the cold water and becoming vulnerable, they want others to join them. If someone balks, intense pressure will be leveraged to force this person to join the crowd. There is a feeling something like this:

> I paid my dues. I spilled my guts and told you my secrets. You sat there and took it all in. You have me in a vulnerable position because you could use what you now know against me in some way. Now it's your turn. Now you have to pay your dues by working on your stuff, or at least telling us something really juicy. That way, we will both have something on each other.

Ultimately, peer pressure can have its positive functions in that it does create risk-taking norms. The problem, however, is a matter of timing, since individuals have different readiness levels for taking such risks. Most group members want to take risks, but they don't want to feel coerced to do so. It feels better to know that one made the choice to be vulnerable, rather than sensing that one has to share to be accepted by others. It is your job to protect the safety and rights of each group member, to make certain that nobody is coerced or forced to comply with norms that are not consistent with that person's best interests.

In society at large, there is also tremendous pressure for members of minority groups to conform to majority norms. Individual and cultural differences are often seen as a threat to stability. Knowing this, you can expect that a similar phenomenon, in which minority members are coerced into abandoning their core values and beliefs in favor of the group's dominant culture, will develop in your groups (D'Andrea, 2014; Debiak, 2007; DeLucia-Waack & Donigian, 2004; Pack-Brown, Whittington-Clark, & Parker, 1998). On the surface, everything may appear okay in the group, but these shifts can create incredible internal conflict for some group members, who may experience feelings of shame, fears of betraying their family or cultural group, and, most notably, anger at being forced into a role that does not recognize their cultural identity as important or noticeable.

Imagine the pressure a Mormon would feel in a group of atheists; an African American woman in a group of White males; or a rebellious, creative teenager in a group of overly compliant peers. Unless you intervene decisively in such situations to validate and protect each person's ability to exercise autonomy in personal expression, individuals can be scapegoated, marginalized, or coerced, causing great harm.

For a Class Activity

Conyne (1998) recommends the following activity for sensitizing students to multicultural issues in group settings that might lead to coercion or peer pressure. Organize yourselves in groups of eight. Choose two members to sit outside the group and act as observers of the process. Their job will be to take notes on the process that develops. Group members are to take half an hour to talk to one another about the following questions:

1. What are the cultural similarities and differences in your group that are most influential?

2. What norms have developed (or could develop) that lead to oppression or empowerment of some cultures over others?

3. How could you better sensitize yourselves to the various multicultural influences in groups, responding more effectively to members of minority cultures?

After the discussion, observers will report on what they noticed, paying special attention to the various processes being discussed in the group. What are the cultures represented in this group? What cultural norms evolved? In what ways were members of minority cultures forced to comply with the dominant culture?

The ethical issue for group leaders, then, is to capitalize on the therapeutic advantages of group settings while simultaneously protecting individual rights and values, a difficult proposition for even the most clearheaded and advanced group leader.

MULTIPLE RELATIONSHIPS BECOME MORE COMPLEX

It is highly likely that there are multiple-relationship issues in your participation in this experientially oriented course. Here you are, sitting in a class to learn about group work, being evaluated and graded based on your performance, and yet you are also asked to reveal very personal aspects of yourself to an audience of your peers and fellow students. You might be worried about how information will be used if you choose to reveal yourself. You may be confused about how to react to your instructor and uncertain about how much personal material you are able and expected to reveal at this time. Some of your friends might be in this room, or people you come into contact with through social media. Most of these concerns can be addressed through certain safeguards, but you can nevertheless feel the confusion of relating to your instructor and peers in a multitude of roles across different settings.

The issue of drawing specific boundaries for group members in regard to social media such as Facebook is gaining more importance (Brew, Cervantes, & Shepard, 2013). Young people and others are using social media in ever-increasing ways, and it is a normal form of communication for many. Social media are unique in that the number of outsiders observing the communication is often unknown, and it can be easy to develop new lines of communication through comments and other subscribers. Material from group can seep into social media if group members maintain poor boundaries, and confidentiality can be easily compromised. Over the past few years, we have seen emerge within our groups more and more concerns and disputes regarding group member use of social media. Group members become "friends" with one another and then inadvertently refer to or directly talk about group interactions or other group members. That is a breach of confidentiality. When discussed in group, some group members feel left out if they are not connected with those who are, and it can easily spiral into a quagmire of trust concerns, hurt feelings, and uncertainty about where group information is going. Group leaders need to be specific about social media expectations for group members. Spell out clearly what is okay and not okay, and speak frankly about the cost of violating group boundaries with social media.

Though this may seem like a concern specific to the academic setting, we can assure you that it is not. Group work often becomes caught up in a web of other relationships. It is possible that you or someone else in group once had individual counseling with the group leader or shared some other prior professional or personal relationship. Furthermore, group work is often supplemented by conjoint sessions in which a participant might see the therapist or counselor for individual consultations. This has some distinct advantages in that participants have the opportunity to process what happened in group during their individual sessions, personalizing the material. Likewise, during these consultations, they can plan new behaviors that may be practiced in group. For members who are unusually timid, anxious, or in crisis, this structure can be invaluable.

Unfortunately, this also means that some people will have a "special" relationship with the leader that others do not. Again, due to the complexity of relationships, this often cannot be avoided. The important aspect of this for group leaders is to openly acknowledge it in the group but also consider the ramifications for the group members. There is a common fantasy, imagined or real, that members will gossip or talk about others from the group, thereby exacerbating potential resentment. Other problems mentioned include greater risks of compromising confidentiality, overdependence on the leader, and possible financial gain for the leader (Welfel, 2013).

Student Voice

I Did Not Realize Having Coffee Could Be So Complex

In my group class, I had a few acquaintances from previous classes, and it seemed like it would be easy to keep our group class experience separate from our social relationship. At first, I thought no big deal, but then the class started getting pretty intense and there were things I wanted to talk about. I remembered having coffee with one of my friends in group, and even though we tried to steer clear of talking about the previous session, we did process a few things. I felt bad at the time, but I felt even worse the next week when during check-in another group member commented that he saw us having coffee and he wondered if we talked about group. We were so busted and I felt so low about this. I got a little defensive at first, but the leader seemed to open this up to a larger discussion of how to navigate our relationships outside the group. So I came clean and talked about the conflict I had experienced and that I needed some help with keeping group separate from my social life. I expected people would hate me, but instead most people sympathized and admitted to some of the same questions. It became kind of a joke in the group, as we developed guidelines and expectations for "How to Have Coffee."

Finally, group members may have other relationships with one another outside the sessions that are preexisting or form after the group has begun. It is easy to imagine how this occurs. In the group setting, members learn intimate details about one another and share powerful experiences. For the first time, group members might feel connected and supported by others, and it is natural to want to further that kind of relationship. Coalitions and alliances are formed in the group that can easily be extended and solidified in the parking lot before and after group meetings. The exchanging of phone numbers and e-mails among group members is common, and it is easy to connect through social media if you just know someone's name (Brew et al., 2013; Wheeler & Bertram, 2012). Cliques can develop when some members are included in coffees or meals and others are deliberately left out (often because they are the subject of discussion). In many ways, groups are like any social setting where people get thrown together and form close relationships. Again, it is not surprising that in a setting that is emotionally charged, romantic attractions develop and lead to liaisons. When this occurs, group members may attempt to hide what has occurred. Phone calls, e-mails, and text messages race back and forth among members, potentially undermining the group. Plots are hatched. Plans are made. As you can easily imagine, these extracurricular relationships can turn out to be a real mess, since they create relationship dynamics developing covertly in a setting that values overt interaction among all members.

For all these reasons, you must closely monitor what goes on outside the group. Some leaders attempt to forbid such contacts, but that is usually unsuccessful and in many ways only functions as further motivation to keep outside-of-group relationships hidden. Yet, without a doubt, extracurricular relationships will undermine the group's cohesion and connectedness. Group leaders must therefore be proactive from the beginning in bluntly revealing how toxic these relationships can be to the group. Here are a few rules that might help:

1. Anything said to anyone outside the group (by the leader or other members) is fair game to be brought up to everyone else.

2. If you find yourself saying to a group member something like, "I wanted to say this during group . . . ," then stop yourself from saying it and wait until the next group.

3. If you do slip and have a conversation that is about the group or any of the group members, or that has even the slightest twinge of being of interest to what is happening in the group, then you need to bring that back to the group and reveal at the beginning of the next session what was discussed.

4. Members should agree not to post pictures, comments, or any other type of confidential information about members online (Wheeler & Bertram, 2012).

5. Even with all these rules and precautions, it is possible that deeper connections and relationships will form that extend beyond the group setting. Be honest and forthcoming about these relationships in the group so all the group members are privy to the extent of the relationships within the group.

If you do not have such clear expectations, you will find that group members even begin to pull you into outside relationships, and you may find yourself in a situation where people confide things to you or others, resulting in secrets and hidden agendas that compromise the group trust. Therefore, as leader, you have to model the expected behavior before, during, and after the group.

TRAINING IS OFTEN INSUFFICIENT

You should by now be convinced that leading groups is quite unlike other forms of helping. It requires additional skills and expertise, greater flexibility, the ability to juggle multiple tasks, and a different sort of mind-set. This includes assessment of group members, familiarization with the unique ethical issues, planning and implementing effective group interventions, and outcome evaluation. While many of these areas are suitable for all kinds of helping, many others must be adapted to the specific requirements of a group situation.

Ask yourself whether a single course in group leadership is nearly enough to prepare you for what you are likely to face. Would even a second course be enough? What would it take for you to be sufficiently trained? We expect your answer will be something along the lines that there is never enough preparation.

With confidence, we can say that more than a few professionals out in the field leading groups do not know what they are doing. Either they were poorly trained, they did not receive adequate supervision, or they are not well suited to this type of work. In some cases, group leaders are affecting hundreds of people without any systematic training at all. You can imagine what we think about that. But how do *you* feel about that? Would you like to attend a group in which the group leader is flying solo and has little previous training?

Among the professionals who have taken a group course or two, many still do not feel comfortable leading groups because of the added burdens and unique challenges that make group work more complex. Rather than taking our word for this, do your own sampling in your community. Visit your local high school and check out how many counselors are actually leading groups. Look at the websites of local counseling agencies or your university counseling center to see the scope of their group program. Survey therapists and counselors in any setting and you are likely to find that the majority are not doing groups because they do not feel adequately prepared.

We are saying this to be honest with you about the reality in the field. Groups *are* everywhere, but a well-led group is a bit harder to find. If you are serious about doing this type of work and you want to get very good at it, then you are going to have to make a major commitment to your training beyond this course. Continue to be a group member beyond this course, observe groups in multiple settings, and continually look for chances to colead groups. This is not optional but mandatory if you wish to practice in an ethical manner that is consistent with the highest standards.

Photo 13.1	Because leading groups is so much more complex and challenging than doing individual sessions, regular supervision and consultation are even more critical, especially as they relate to managing ethical issues that inevitably arise. Two coleaders are pictured here meeting with their supervisor to talk about problems from the previous group session, in which two members confessed that they had been overheard talking about the group in a way that may have breached confidentiality.

How can you get the additional training you will need? Continuing education and workshops make up one viable alternative, an option that is actually required by most licensing boards. We have mentioned previously the kind of peer supervision that is possible with an experienced coleader. You can also take additional courses, participate in training groups, and recruit mentors who have skills you admire. You can join and become active in specialized professional organizations such as the American Group Psychotherapy Association (www.agpa.org) and the Association for Specialists in Group Work (www.asgw.org).

Slightly Unethical Behaviors That Create Deception and Moral Conundrums

In addition to the issues that clearly present ethical problems in group, you must also wrestle with several subtle complexities around group work. After all, certain assurances that are not quite true are often offered in groups. We present these to you to raise your awareness of how subtle group pressures and dynamics can easily undermine your attempts to be ethical and supportive in your leadership role.

It is one of the secrets of our profession that practitioners rarely acknowledge or speak about their mistakes, misjudgments, and incompetence for fear of the consequences. Yet when notable theorists do admit their most common imperfections and failures, certain consistent behaviors emerge, such as being excessively self-disclosing, not listening to the clients, being self-indulgent, losing compassion, misdiagnosing, and being overly rigid (Kottler & Blau, 1989; Kottler & Carlson, 2003). Several "slightly" unethical behaviors associated with group are reviewed below.

LITTLE WHITE LIES

You Don't Have to Say or Do Anything in Here Unless You Want To

This, of course, is bunk. Lots of pressure will come to bear on those who try to hide or pass in group. Like "The check is in the mail" and "My dog ate my homework," this is one of the great lies of our time. Although we never begin a group without making this claim, we have to admit honestly that no matter how earnestly the leader attempts to protect each member's rights, incredible pressure—subtle, unconscious, sneaky, and overt—will be imposed on those reluctant to get involved. Furthermore, even though a group member can keep quiet, that will not prevent the other group members from talking about the effect of that silence on the group. Occasionally, we will jump on the bandwagon, temporarily ignoring our previous promise, and use all our skills to manipulate reluctant clients to join in, even against their will. Are we excused from such transgressions? Certainly; after all, we're only human. But copping a plea doesn't diminish the nature of an essentially unethical act.

It is important to remember that there are constant tugs on every group member to conform, to contribute, to be a "regular group member," and we underplay these forces for good reason, attempting to reassure clients that their privacy will be respected. Realistically, we couldn't even begin a group without convincing participants that their freedom of choice will be encouraged. Nevertheless, this is one of those promises that is pretty hard to keep or even control.

This Is a Safe Place to Work on Yourself

We discussed earlier all the reasons why groups are much less safe than individual sessions: Confidentiality can't be guaranteed, toxic members can be abusive or hurtful, and interactions can get out of control with little warning (Barlow, 2014). Group work is a unique professional activity in which clients who have not received training and are not bound by confidentiality or any formal ethical codes essentially function as coleaders. They probe, confront, participate in role plays, and do many of the same things that therapists and counselors do. That is one of the principal benefits of group work—participants learn to be skilled helpers at the same time as they work on their own issues. This situation, however, presents quite an ethical dilemma.

When we promise participants that their group is a safe place to disclose personal secrets, explore sensitive areas, and take risks, can we really guarantee that other members will not (1) act insensitively, manipulatively, or even abusively; (2) violate confidentiality by telling others what was revealed in group; or (3) pollute the therapeutic experience by being obnoxious, obstructive, or excessively self-centered?

The reality of group practice is that confidentiality cannot be enforced, individual privacy is diluted, participants feel coercion and pressure to conform, and verbal abuse is likely. Also, the leader has less control over proceedings, and clients receive less attention and close monitoring than they would in individual treatment (Barlow, 2013; Brabender, 2006; Rapin, 2014).

I Neither Like nor Dislike You; You're a Client

Inevitably, some group members will ask directly how you feel about them. And if they do not ask you, we can promise you they are thinking about it. Recognizing the dangers of saying what we really think (whether positive or negative) because of the weight of the group leader's word, it is easy to pretend that we don't have feelings at all toward the group. And most of the time, during group meetings, we do guard against allowing our personal feelings to get in the way of therapeutic actions. Again, however, the therapeutic options are limited:

1. If we respond honestly, we risk being seen either as seductive (or playing favorites) if the feelings are positive or as hostile if the feelings are negative.

2. We could employ therapeutic maneuvers such as, "How would that be helpful for me to tell you?" or "What difference would it make to you?" or "I'm sorry. I didn't hear you. Does anyone else have something to say?" Yet the problem here is that we look evasive and as though we will not answer the question, creating the impression that the group member should not have asked it. This raises the likelihood that the group member will feel shamed for asking such a question.

3. We could share our problem: "I feel uncomfortable telling you my feelings because then I compromise my neutrality." But members might wonder why they should be honest when their leader is so evasive.

Each of these responses creates potential problems that we would prefer to leave alone. So, instead, we resort to little white lies, with the excuse "but it's for their own good" in mind, though not altogether certain that excuse is valid. One way to navigate this dilemma is to focus your response on what you have observed in group (e.g., "I have seen you show plenty of courage in group over the past 3 months as you decided to face your fears") and how that impacts your connection with the group member (e.g., "When you were more evasive with your feelings, I found it hard to connect with you, but lately as you have changed course, I feel like I know you a bit better—and I like getting to know you in here").

I Remember a Time When . . .

Inappropriate self-disclosure is a way group leaders focus on themselves at the cost of valuable time and at the expense of the whole group. Unless a therapist has a specific, defensible rationale, sharing personal stories is likely to be digressive. Each time a group leader engages in a long-winded anecdote that is not specifically intended to deliver an important message or to help a group member work through the presenting concern, the action is unethical in that it negates the clients' importance and wastes time.

Facilitative self-disclosure that is well timed and appropriately implemented satisfies certain criteria mentioned by Corey, Corey, Corey, and Callanan (2015):

- How crucial is it that group members perceive you as being human?
- What specific intentions do you have for revealing your personal life?
- How might clients' progress be hindered as a result of your self-disclosure?

Only after these questions are addressed may the group leader be reasonably certain that self-disclosing interventions are indicated. The key is being fairly clear that your self-disclosure will benefit the group or give voice to a therapeutic perspective or direction that other group members are not expected to reveal. If you sense that another group member will say something similar to your story or disclosure, then let the group member speak and allow the attention to stay on the group members.

I Know We Can Help You

It follows sound therapeutic principles to promote positive expectations (the placebo effect), but sometimes we exaggerate to give the person hope. Although uncertain that we can keep our promises, we believe that such claims are necessary to keep up group morale. Group members enjoy hearing this little lie, since they desperately want optimistic assessments. In the same way a physician prescribes a placebo, saying, "I believe this will make you feel better," we justify our own little deceits.

What I Think Does Not Matter

We pretend that we are value neutral, that we will not take sides or impose our beliefs on others. More truthfully, we often have strong convictions about what is best for others. To reveal or not to reveal our values, that is the question—if indeed it is a question at all. Even if we decide that withholding our beliefs regarding what is good or bad, right or wrong is desirable (and this is by no means a universal value in itself), is this physically possible? In spite of our best efforts to remain perfectly neutral, to restrain or disguise all personal preferences, it is utterly impossible to do so completely.

Suppose a group member discloses that he is about to leave his wife for his 19-year-old secretary; although we may show our mask of neutral, accepting, unconditional regard, we may find our lips curling against our will. Indeed, we have strong opinions about almost everything clients do or decide. We are able to restrain most of these value judgments (on the outside anyway); a few slip through our guard; others, we deliberately reveal.

We thus make no apology for espousing a number of values that we believe all members should adopt. A sampling of these universal truths that we not-so-subtly impose includes the following:

- Being open, revealing, disclosing, and taking constructive risks in group is a good thing.
- Sharing and feeling emotions in the present is preferable to simply talking about one's feelings.

- It is better to have more choices in life than fewer (except when you already have too many, in which case the opposite is true).
- It is not all right to settle for mediocrity; one should strive for excellence to be happy and satisfied.

Everybody in This Group Will Be Treated Equally

Obviously, group leaders have their favorite group members, as well as those who push their buttons, cause them grief, or just come across as annoying. After all, being the leader does not excuse you from the social microcosm in groups. Who you are in real life will also come forward in the group setting. The Constitution of the United States guarantees that all people, regardless of age, sex, race, and religion, will have equal status under the eyes of the law, but we know that marginalization and inequality are rampant. Just as in society, not everyone in group is equal, as people have definite preferences for the sorts of people they would like to be around, and group leaders are no different. We often like group members who are attractive, enthusiastic about what we do, and share familiar backgrounds and interests. In spite of our restraint, we may give more attention to those who smile and laugh more often at our jokes. Although we attempt to hide our biases, there are some in the group to whom we give less of our time and patience. In short, it is no more possible to treat all clients alike than it is for parents to love all their children equally. It is important for leaders to recognize our biases through consistent self-supervision or by talking with a coleader about our reactions to group members.

WHAT CAN YOU DO ABOUT ALL THESE ISSUES?

We don't wish to alarm you unnecessarily about these concerns, but we do want your eyes wide open to the dilemmas and pitfalls that await. We would rather you were an aware traveler on the road rather than one who constantly encounters pitfalls and is not sure why. Being a group leader carries with it an awesome responsibility, but you will never be able to resolve fully the ethical challenges you must face. The best you can hope for is to remain vigilant and cautious, to follow the ethical guidelines as closely as possible, to work hard in supervision, and to be honest with yourself about the impact of your behavior. Inevitably, we all act unethically because we are all imperfect beings, inconsistent and hypocritical. We muddle in the dark doing our best to be genuinely helpful, but we know we can't possibly please everyone all the time.

For Personal Application

Make a list of all the values and beliefs you hold most dear that you think are also best for everyone else. For instance, you might think that everyone would be better off with more education, more choices, and more freedom. As a group leader, which of your cherished values and beliefs are most likely to become evident in your work?

What are the ethical consequences of this phenomenon? How will you be aware of the times when you are pressing these values on the group?

Making Sound Ethical Decisions

You will be relieved to know that models for making sound ethical decisions (see Barlow, 2013; Brabender, 2006, 2007; Corey, Corey, Corey, & Callanan, 2015; Rapin, 2014; Welfel, 2013) have been developed to help you take the following steps:

1. Identify the problem and context

2. Reason through the problem to see which ethical standards might be involved

3. Consult and apply the relevant ethical standard

4. Formulate a preliminary response

5. Predict the likely consequences of this choice

6. Decide how you might follow through on the best plan of action

7. Process feedback with peers and supervisors along the way

At least one advantage of ethical challenges in groups is that you are not alone in your struggle. Even if you do not have a coleader with whom to share the dilemma, you do have the group to consult with. If you have empowered the group to be mutually responsible for all its proceedings, then group members are also involved in the process. You may be the one who is held legally liable and ethically responsible, but the group members are also part of the community that makes decisions.

Ethics involve not only professional conduct but also the behavior of all participants in the experience, especially one that involves such mutual trust. One way to develop a cohesive group in which members deepen this commitment to the group is making ethical standards part of the established group climate. Such an ethical atmosphere would include the following values:

- Privilege—belief that it is an honor to share in the experience
- Caring—essential compassion and respect for others
- Responsibility—commitment to protect the safety of others
- Confidentiality—holding what is said sacred and private
- Honesty—being truthful with oneself and others
- Dependability—honoring commitments
- Cooperation—honoring established norms
- Integrity—being true to convictions
- Proactive—opposing injustice or abuse

If such a group climate can be established, then ethical issues that arise can be handled as a group responsibility. These values will not magically appear in your group; you will have to talk about them during your first meeting and purposely revisit them along the way. When we have been faced with dilemmas similar to the ones examined in this chapter, we have been inclined to bring them to the group for discussion. We might say,

> Look, I've got a problem. I am aware of something that has occurred that must be dealt with. I have certain professional and ethical obligations that must be considered. But you are also involved in this process. Let's talk about what we need to do and how it will affect the group.

The operative word in the preceding invitation is the plural pronoun *we*, meaning that this is a shared problem. Sometimes you don't agree with what many group members decide to do. Occasionally, as a leader, you cannot live with the consensus that has been reached. When it comes to ethical issues and group member safety, groups are not democracies. Yet even if the outcome is not ultimately decided by member contributions, they have at least been a part of the process and had some time to think it through together. This is what happens in good organizations, businesses, and families, in which the person in charge says,

1. What do you all think about this?

2. Thank you for your input.

3. This is what I heard you say.

4. This is what I've decided to do.

In high-functioning groups, members will often come to the same conclusion you would, but that is not always the case. Depending on the particular problem and what it means for others, they may decide to take a very different course of action. Since during your announcement of informed consent at the beginning of group, you explained your role and responsibility and your professional obligations, you must then do what your ethical codes, laws, and conscience dictate. The hard part is living with your decisions.

For a Field Study

Talk to practicing group leaders about the most difficult ethical challenges they have faced as part of their jobs. Explore the specific issues involved and what they did to resolve the dilemma. Also find out how they handled things internally. What advice do they offer you as to how you can best prepare yourself for the inevitable problems you will face?

Becoming an Ethical Group Leader

This chapter has summarized and reviewed many of the common ethical difficulties that arise when working in group settings. Becoming aware of many of the ethical issues unique to group work is a beginning step to gaining more awareness of effective group practice. Brabender (2007) highlighted five areas that cut across most ethical concerns in group work and help form a solid foundation for successfully navigating many of the concerns noted in this chapter.

- *Acquire an ethical foundation.* The only way to work through ethical concerns in group is to develop a solid knowledge base about ethics and a set of skills that allows one to proceed effectively. For the new group leader, this requires extended reading and honest supervision about the concerns that present in group. For the more advanced group leader, this necessitates a commitment to continuing education on ethical issues specifically relevant to group work.
- *Develop the person of the group leader.* Navigating ethical concerns requires personal qualities that support thoughtfulness, reflective thinking, and the ability to act. These personal qualities can include courage (Mangione, Forti, & Iacuzzi, 2007), as in being able to decide whether to confront a disruptive group member, or humility (Debiak, 2007), as in recognizing one's limitations or biases in relation to difficulties associated with cultural or identity differences, or in knowing when to consult for supervision and assistance.

- *Focus on your own self-awareness.* A key aspect of self-awareness is knowing the social and emotional forces that act on you in any ethical decision. This reflective knowledge can lead to reflexive thinking in evaluating the choices you are inclined to make. For example, recognizing your desire to be liked by the group can help you reevaluate an ethical decision if the correct course of action might not be a popular one within the group setting.
- *Examine the information within the larger context.* Though many ethical dilemmas and decisions are made within the smaller confines of the group, the ramifications and extenuating circumstances can easily reach far beyond the group. Take care to appreciate the complete context in which the problem has arisen and where the impact of the decision will be felt.
- *Take a continuous rather than an episodic focus.* Few ethical decisions are easily made and presented with a black or white answer. Ethical decision making, by its very nature, is complex and confusing, especially in a group setting. One course of action may aspire to one set of ethical guidelines and principles but be at odds with other ones. It would be much easier if there were a guidebook that listed what to do and what not to do, but it is seldom that clear-cut. Rather, decisions need to be made with an eye to the current situation and the long-term evaluation of how that decision will evolve within the group. One can hope to honor as many ethical principles as possible in making the appropriate decision for the group at the time.

The final caveat, and one that is repeated in every ethics course and book, is to consult, consult, consult. Oftentimes, you do not have to make an immediate decision, and it is imperative to consult with other professionals or professional organizations, or even to obtain legal advice. Talking through your ethical dilemmas and decisions with others who share the same ethical obligations leads to more thoughtful decision making. We often consult with each other about events that happen in our groups. These conversations help us consider alternative options to discuss with our groups.

Review of What You Learned

- Group leaders face unique ethical challenges in balancing the need to protect members' welfare with the need to promote risk-taking behaviors.
- The risk of casualties in groups is far higher than in individual sessions, because the leader has less control over the proceedings due to the increased number of participants in group settings.

- Special ethical challenges you will face involve enforcing confidentiality, negotiating multiple relationships, protecting members against coercion, and ensuring that you have the appropriate amount of training and/or supervision for the group you are leading.
- Group settings also involve several subtle complexities related to appropriate self-disclosure, the scope of the leader's influence on a group, and the ability of the leader to control the group and group members.
- One of your jobs is to help everyone in the group feel ethically and morally responsible for everyone else's welfare.

Part IV

Advanced Group Structures

Advanced Group Leadership 14

Creative Interventions and Difficult Members

Most group leaders can reliably demonstrate a core of basic interventions. These interventions include such skills as assessing individual and group behavior, identifying themes as they emerge, keeping members on task, soliciting feedback, seeking consensus on courses of action, blocking inappropriate behavior, and others mentioned in earlier chapters. Although these are necessary and basic skills, as you gain experience you will wish to expand your repertoire to include more advanced interventions, especially those that foster greater creativity and flexibility.

Expanding your base of fundamental group helping skills is necessary for survival in the field. The unique demands of group work require that leaders continually augment their options in a given situation. When you confront someone who is being obstructive, resistant, manipulative, domineering, withdrawn, or highly anxious, it is far better to have multiple alternatives to deal with the situation effectively. To hold group members' attention over the long haul; encourage creative solution seeking; facilitate spontaneous, productive interaction; and help group members take risks, the group leader must have the widest range of tools available.

The Role of Techniques for More Experienced Leaders

Some students have never led a therapeutic-type group in their lives, or perhaps even seen one except in movies; other students are quite experienced in leading groups, having worked in the field for many years. Regardless of your level of expertise and experience, there are many ways you can gradually add new strategies to your range of options.

To summarize much of what you have learned so far, leaders essentially serve four functions in groups:

1. Provide a supportive climate in the group that is conducive to safety, trust, cohesion, and growth

2. Process events, experiences, and interactions as they take place

3. Stimulate interactions among and between members that provide feedback, encouragement, and insight, and promote constructive action

4. Facilitate healthy norms in the group, as well as promote goal attainment

Of these leader behaviors, the first two—providing a supportive climate and processing experiences—have a direct, *linear* relationship to positive outcomes; the more support and constructive processing that is built into the group experience, the more likely that members will have a good outcome. The second two functions, stimulating interactions and facilitating norms, have a *curvilinear* relationship to outcomes; if too little or too much of these ingredients is present, the group will either become lethargic and predictable or chaotic and emotionally charged (Burlingame, Whitcomb, & Woodland, 2014; Kivlighan & Kivlighan, 2014; Meier & Comer, 2011).

Each of these four functions is carried out by the group leader through the use of techniques—that is, leader behaviors, strategies, and interventions that are designed to provide structure, initiate action, stimulate insight, facilitate goal completion, or otherwise accomplish therapeutic tasks. What this means is that during any moment in a group you are leading, you are asking yourself, (1) "Do I need to do something?" and (2) "What is it that I need to do?"

How you answer these questions depends on a number of factors, including your theoretical framework and personal style, as well as the context of the group and needs of the members (Barlow, 2013; Corey, Corey, Callanan, & Russell, 2015; Kane, Zaccaro, Tremble, & Masuda, 2002). You review what has worked previously and what has not. You consider this group in light of other groups you have observed or led. You review options that you know, and can recall at the time. Finally, based on your intuition, logical reasoning, and perceptions, you make a choice about what you think is going on. You observe carefully the outcome and make adjustments as needed.

Note, for example, how this process works in the mind of a group leader selecting particular interventions and techniques:

> Things seem to be bogging down. The group needs some direction to get refocused *[needs of the group as a whole]*. This lethargy is probably the result of the members' apprehensions regarding their own fears of death *[leader's theoretical framework]*. As Tim talks about his impending surgery, he seems to be asking for guarantees that his cancer will stay in remission *[needs of an individual group member]*. Yet others seem so introspective; they have retreated deep inside themselves and don't appear to be listening to Tim anymore *[the group atmosphere]*. I recall a marked reluctance on the part of these folks to share honestly reactions and feelings that are unpleasant *[history of the group]*. But I think that this is fairly typical of people when issues of death come up *[history of previous groups]*. Besides, Tim does not seem ready yet to be confronted with how frightening his plight is to others *[history of individual group member]*. I think it is time *[logical reasoning]* to draw people out of their cocoons and help them reconnect with one another. I sense *[intuition]* an undercurrent of interest, even fascination, with exploring this issue further. Then again, maybe it is my interest in this subject, since I tend to explore issues of death *[leader's mood]*. What I need to do, then, is bring them back to the present, but in a way that is neither going to frighten them too much nor going to ignore Tim's craving for honest feedback *[needs of the group as a whole]*. I think I will try . . .

And so goes the internal dialogue of selecting a technique, a process that is always changing—whether the decision is to use an individual intervention to reflect a group member's feelings, an interactive technique to bridge connections among members, or a structured exercise to help assess progress toward goals.

Over time, you will develop a reservoir of structured techniques you can use when you sense that they might be helpful. There are a number of reasons to initiate a structured technique in a group:

- *To help focus discussion on a particular issue:* "Since a number of you seem to be struggling with a fear of death, let's try an imagery exercise."
- *To invigorate the lethargic, passive mood:* "Okay, everyone stand up for a minute and face out from the group."
- *To increase comfort levels with an ambiguous situation:* "Perhaps it would be helpful if each of you wrote down on a sheet of paper what your impressions are."

- *To create some fun:* "Pick somebody in the group to imitate for a few minutes."
- *To deepen the level of interaction:* "It would be helpful if you formed three different subgroups so each of you has more time to explore your reactions to what took place."
- *To move the focus from one mode of experience to another:* "Rather than talking about this issue with your families, let's sculpt a typical interaction."
- *To lessen tension or anxiety associated with intense affect:* "Perhaps each of you could take a step back and describe what you observed."
- *To ensure greater participation among all members:* "Before we move on to something else, I would like everyone to have a chance to respond to what was said."
- *To make group decisions or reach consensus:* "You have 10 minutes to reach a unanimous agreement on what to do next."
- *To encourage more creativity:* "I would like everyone to draw a picture representing how you feel about this group."
- *To motivate a group:* "Let's go around and review your progress toward your goals. Talk about what you have done or what you have not. State what you will do between now and the end of group to meet your goals."

Just as important as selecting and implementing the most appropriate technique is how the group and the group leader process it afterward, either individually or in group supervision. For the group, the leader usually explores the process of the technique and what members are taking from the experience. For the leader, the evaluation is more of an assessment of how well the leader is operating with the group. This usually takes the form of a series of questions: "What did I observe? Why did I do what I did? What are some other ways I could have done something more effective? What might I do next time in a similar situation?"

Personal and Physical Considerations

In this section, we want to get more specific about areas of intervention. In examining what differentiates an "advanced" group leader from a neophyte, several areas are most prominent.

PERSONAL CONTROL

First and foremost, advanced group leaders are maximally in charge of their own bodies and minds. Just as an athlete rigorously exercises to improve muscle tone, strength, agility, and endurance, the group leader, too, must be in good physical condition. The mind is similarly fine-tuned and trained; vocal tonality is extremely well developed, providing a range rivaling that of an operatic soprano. Facial expressions are constantly monitored. Sometimes a poker face is shown to hide inadvertent value judgments; at other times, the face is openly expressive for the purpose of providing clear feedback or reinforcement. To demonstrate support or authority, the body, too, conveys subtle nonverbal messages on demand. Effective group leaders learn that many interventions are not verbal but, rather, nonverbal behaviors that convey acceptance, calm under distress, control, and a wide range of other intentions and emotional states.

In short, group leaders are meticulously in charge of their personal space so they may send the fullest range of clear messages at will. Hence, the more therapeutic skills and choices leaders add to their repertoires, the more effectively they can accurately read and convey verbal messages.

MASTERY OF SPACE

The next consideration, after personal control, is that of understanding and readily employing therapeutic variables in the physical environment. In a sense, the group leader becomes a spatial engineer who can manipulate physical space with the assurance of a chiropractor rearranging spinal alignments. You will quickly observe in your groups that group members are often reluctant to give up their seats once they have claimed them; ownership is determined by squatters' rights. Invisible boundaries pervade group behavior. Characteristic interaction distances are established depending on factors such as age, gender, race, social status, and cultural differences. In addition, many other physical factors may affect group behavior, including lighting intensity, noise, and physical proximity—all variables that the group leader can manipulate through intervention strategies.

Most group leaders are addicted to the use of circles, based on the notion that circles provide clear line of sight for all group members. Yet many group members come into a group and move their chairs as a means to hide or, alternatively, stand out. It is good practice to begin each group by scanning to make sure everyone can clearly see the others; if you detect that someone cannot be seen, ask that member to move. Yet leaders can also work within the circle to deliberately intervene where a need has been identified. For example, the leader may sit next to antagonistic group members to keep them in check or across from passive ones to draw them out. Leaders can break up destructive coalitions by rearranging the seating order when the group begins.

A leader can, of course, carry this a step further by creatively enlarging on the physical dynamics of groups. For example, we may attempt to centralize communication patterns by spreading the more talkative group members around the group or may try to stifle approval seeking by deliberately seating ourselves outside the group for a time. This typifies the attention the leader pays to physical interventions.

SUBGROUPING

There is no rule saying that the group has to remain together and complete for the duration. Though we are fond of dyads and triads, many other combinations are possible, depending on desired outcomes. For instance, after two group members have used group time to confront each other about longstanding conflicts, they may each be asked to take half the group to receive structured, private feedback in a small group before they reencounter each other. In one subgroup, all five colleagues may agree that a group member has overstepped her bounds by ignoring the other person's rights or that she should stop responding so defensively to every attempt at being helpful. In the other subgroup, the group member may be cautioned that he is playing it too safe, being dishonest with himself, and trying to placate everyone's wishes. After the feedback, the group may be reunited to help the group members reach some resolution.

Group members may also be paired in fishbowl structures. Two members who rarely listen to each other may be asked to move their chairs to the middle of the group, tune out the audience, and practice listening and responding skills. The others will remember the same principles in their future encounters. As witnesses to the exercise, they can also help process what happened and offer valuable suggestions for improving communication.

USING TIME

Time is not only an absolute that is measured by a clock. Time seems to expand during boredom and contract during involvement. The subjective experience of time is affected by a number of factors that radically influence the behavior of different people.

In therapeutic groups, the concept of time becomes most significant in the *relative* value it has for group members. People escape from the present by living in the past through nostalgia, guilt, or reminiscence; people live in the future through fantasy, anticipation, or worry, often talking about all they are *going* to do. Some members will constantly tell stories about the past, and this often leads to boredom within the group, since it makes it harder for interpersonal interactions to occur in the present. Group leaders must think in terms of cost-effectiveness and be guardians of time to make certain that it is neither wasted nor abused. In many ways, group leaders will keep the group engaged to the degree that the group can interact with one another in the here and now.

Perhaps a primary technique of group leaders is to use the concept of time as an overriding factor to motivate the group:

- "Do we want to be using our time in this way?"
- "We have 20 minutes left today, and Rachel, your opportunity to talk about your concern is fading."
- "How have you maximized your time in the last 3 minutes of silence?"
- "In what ways are you not appreciating your time as much as you could?"

Time is also important in the pacing of certain interventions. The group leader must time comments to coincide with the readiness of group members to hear them, or limit interactions from becoming too intense at the end of the group. As mentioned previously, it is not uncommon for the end of a group to bring a rush of group members' trying to share. The leader must directly note the amount of time left in the group to help members regulate their emotions and depth of sharing. Advanced group leaders have a knack for controlling the process in a group to match the time allotted. This often means moving a group rapidly back to an emotional spot from the previous week, or managing an emotional or conflictual situation at the end of a group so there is some time for cooling off, finding a take-home message, or regaining composure before leaving.

BRIDGING

Group leaders who are used to staying on top of things may be doing the group members a disservice by intervening too quickly when one group member acts out. Although leaders certainly have a responsibility to curtail members who act inappropriately or disrupt others' work, the more leaders do, the fewer opportunities other members have to learn to be more assertive. Also, leaders who are too directive and controlling create constrained groups that are somehow contrived in the image of the leader, rather than groups that accurately reflect the best and worst of the group members. Advanced group leaders learn to assess when to intervene and when to hold back to see how the group responds and adapts.

It takes tremendous restraint on the leader's part to exert the patience to wait far longer than preferred until other group members reach their frustration tolerance and gather the courage to do something decisive to cut off the distracting member. Group leaders, of course, can move this process along by cuing members who we sense are on the verge of enforcing group norms; at the same time, we forge closer connections among members. One way of doing this is by looking for behavioral cues in group members that reveal their impressions and reactions to other group members.

Leader: Jude, I notice that every time Eamon speaks, you roll your eyes toward the ceiling and seem to withdraw. Why don't you tell him what you are experiencing?

This craft of *bridging* involves making more and more connections among group members in an effort to build open communication and greater cohesion. Group leaders can expand their repertoire of bridging techniques by adapting the following time-honored interventions:

- *Open-ended questioning:* "What do you sense she is feeling when she folds her arms like that?"
- *Directed questioning:* "Are you aware that he started to withdraw right after you pointed at him?"
- *Questioning about interactions:* "What are they doing right now?"
- *Behavioral observations:* "Muna, I notice that you were leaning toward Shelly as she was talking about her mother."

In each case, the group leader is indirectly guiding the group's movement while bridging connections among members in such a way that they become more active. That is the hallmark of the advanced group leader—ability to lead by encouraging others to do the work.

CREATING HOMOGENEOUS GROUPS

One of the trends in contemporary group work is specialization with very specific populations (Barlow, 2013). Without looking very hard, we are sure that in your community you could find specific groups for the elderly, men, women, widowers, Alzheimer's patients, high school students, adult offenders, divorcees, college-age children of alcoholics, and so on. There are a number of distinct advantages to organizing homogeneous groups, the most important of which is that it allows leaders to tailor group structures and interventions to the specific needs of the population. Certainly, adults experiencing social anxiety have different needs and are likely to respond better to certain kinds of group structures than would college students who have study-skill deficits, adults who are undergoing divorce, or individuals who have psychotic conditions. Furthermore, the fact that each person must meet a specific requirement (e.g., being an elderly woman, experiencing depression) to be in the group can create immediate feelings of universality for group members, knowing that they will encounter people like themselves.

Let's use men's groups as an example. The leader must be experienced and knowledgeable enough to design the group in a way that is consistent with the research on the subject and responsive to the needs of the group members (Kiselica & Kiselica, 2014). Male group members can present a unique challenge to group leaders who operate in a traditional manner. Many men are socialized to fear core components of the group therapeutic process—the language of feelings, the disclosure of vulnerability, and the admission of dependency needs (Englar-Carlson & Stevens, 2006; Rabinowitz, 2014). Male clients' discomfort with the developing intimacy of close relationships, especially with other men, can manifest as early termination, anger at the counselor, unproductive intellectualizing, and other forms of resistance (Englar-Carlson, 2014). Men's groups can address these challenges in a manner that feels more in line with how men interact with one another. Of course, there are multiple differences among men of different ethnic and racial backgrounds, creating unique ways of interacting (Appiah-Boateng, Evans, Zambrano, & Brooks, 2014). To address these concerns initially, there is often a greater emphasis on action rather than emotional processing, with more attention on making things active and engaging. Furthermore, leaders may self-disclose and model vulnerability as a way to join with the group and demonstrate that the leader is willing to do what is being asked of the group members.

It is clear that the advanced group leader must attend to myriad variables unique to this or any specific population. Homogeneous groups require more specialized expertise, thoughtful research, and experience working with the targeted population. Leaders must have knowledge not only about the intricacies of the specific disorders of group member populations but also about the greater burden placed on leaders of having to deal with problems that will inevitably arise (members' protecting and enabling one another, ganging up against the leader, presenting deficits similar to one another, etc.). These greater demands placed on the professional require leaders to be fluid enough in their craft that they can adapt their methods to the specific needs of each unique population.

USING PSYCHODRAMATIC STRUCTURES

No other group technique has been adopted by so many divergent leadership approaches as has psychodrama. Behavioral group leaders may call it a form of social modeling or behavioral rehearsal. Gestalt practitioners routinely employ "double chairing." Cognitive therapists act out elaborate role-played scenarios in which group members confront their irrational beliefs. Existential, psychodynamic, and Adlerian groups make liberal use of psychodramatic structures to facilitate insight and work through conflicts.

What makes psychodrama such a spontaneous, powerful, and creative enterprise is that it simultaneously makes use of behavioral principles (modeling, giving feedback, reinforcing healthy behavior), phenomenological ideas (dramatic experiences), psychoanalytic concepts (catharsis, transference, unconscious motives), existential premises (authenticity), group member–centered values (empathy, encounter), object relations theory (role reversal), and even spiritual components (Baim, Burmeister, & Maciel, 2007).

Advanced group leaders have already mastered (or at least are familiar with) the basic psychodramatic process in which a protagonist (the group member in focus) first describes the presenting concern and is then directed to act out a scenario as if it were really taking place. The action is stopped at various points so that other group members can offer feedback; auxiliary roles can be included; certain behaviors can be redirected, exaggerated, or expanded; or the leader can help process what has occurred.

A number of psychodramatic therapeutic structures seem particularly well suited for advanced group leaders. A few representative samples are described here.

Childhood Regression

Because of the potential for decompensation and extreme affective expression, only the most experienced group leaders should attempt to take a group member back into childhood to relive traumatic experiences. This is especially the case with those who we may suspect were victims of sexual or physical abuse but are repressing the episodes.

Even with the potential dangers of a group member losing control, childhood re-creations can be among the most potent of therapeutic structures. One illustration that stands out is a case in which a member of a counseling group for therapists felt blocked in her work with her own group members. She was feeling less and less satisfaction doing therapeutic work and sensed that the origins of her struggle lay in the past. Because of the high degree of trust she felt in the group and the respect she had for her peers and the leader, she consented to re-create a scene from childhood that seemed particularly significant.

The psychodramatic enactment that followed was indeed powerful. The woman did not *play* being a little girl; she *became* herself as a little girl. With the help of several group members who took on the roles of her parents, siblings, and auxiliary egos (including the persona of her present-day denial), she was able to identify the original introjections from her parents that were still blocking her from experiencing life and work more fully.

As is so often the case with creative group structures, what eventually evolved over time bore little resemblance to the originally constructed role play. By making continual adjustments according to this group member's reactions and the other group members' individual and collective responses, the group leader helped a spontaneous process develop, rather than staying with a prescribed sequence of stages.

Sculpting

As much a part of family counseling lore as group work, sculpting is the act of allowing or guiding participants to shape themselves into a symbolic representation of the ways they interact with one another (Bitter, 2013; Satir & Baldwin, 1983). What makes this creative structure so challenging is the demands it places on the group leader to help members process their experiences and identify their scapegoating, placating, and other defensive roles (Satir, 1972).

There are basically two versions of this methodology used in groups. In one, an individual group member sculpts his or her own family using other group members as "fodder," such as in a family reconstruction process. The second, and somewhat more interesting, version for groups that have worked together for a while is to create a collective sculpture depicting everyone's role in the group. In its most ingenious form, coalitions become clearly evident, as do codependent and conflicted relationships.

Student Voice

The Group Sculpture

I had read about sculpting in our group book, and so I asked our leader if we could try it during our training group. It was good timing, as the group was feeling kinda boring and we were seemingly at an impasse due to a couple of entrenched conflicts that had never

(Continued)

(Continued)

really been resolved. The leader suggested I be the sculptor, and the group agreed to try this out. It was hard at first, since I knew that by sculpting the effect of these two conflicts on the group I would be giving clear feedback that the four group members involved were holding us back. I ended up putting four members together as if they were ready to start a race, and then I put the four people in the unresolved conflict in front of them, blocking their progress and blocking each other. I really accentuated their facial expressions of not listening to each other and being clueless as to how they were influencing other group members. It was a cool process, and when we began to talk about it, we began to make some progress as a group.

Fishbowl

One other example of a psychodramatic structure that offers multiple creative opportunities for the experienced group leader is one in which two subgroups are formed to monitor each other's behavior.

In its generic form, the group is divided in two, with about half a dozen members huddled in the center. Each participant is assigned a partner on the outside circle who may be asked to do a number of things: to observe that individual during the process and provide feedback later, to engage that person in a personal exchange, to serve as an auxiliary or silent ego to the partner during the exercise, and so on—the possibilities are endless.

The intent of fishbowls is to heighten participants' awareness of group processes. With members subdivided into cohesive units, it is also likely that overly strong coalitions can be diluted in favor of other interpersonal connections. The most difficult part of running these activities is controlling the "chaos" to the extent that people remain task oriented during their spontaneous experiences.

Many of the advanced techniques just described seem inviting and stimulating—at least when read in the pages of a book. A few words of warning, however: These ideas are presented more to stimulate your creativity and imagination than they are to give you intact strategies to incorporate immediately into group settings. The hallmark of advanced versus beginning group leaders is their ability to be flexible and adaptable in their implementation of group interventions. We mention this point primarily because of the potential for any innovative strategy to do as much harm as good.

Using Metaphors in Group Settings

Metaphors are common in our everyday conversation, but when they are used in a group context, they can provide a powerful tool to create insight and awareness. Simply stated, metaphors are a comparison of two similar things. From a clinical perspective, therapeutic metaphors help people make sense of their own experiences and restructure meaning (Davies, 2013; Nadeau, 2006). Good metaphors are both appropriate for the situation and tailored to the audience. They are designed to heighten certain aspects of a message in a manner that will be best received by the listeners. Metaphoric language can be used by group leaders to depict group member experiences more graphically without triggering defensive reactions. Metaphors also create lasting images that can be referred to again and again as memory anchors, especially when they have been designed specifically for a member. Burns (2001, 2006) notes many advantages of using metaphors in helping settings:

- Metaphors tap into a long historical means of communicating that transcends all cultural groups and backgrounds. As such, the process is familiar to group members.
- Metaphors are atheoretical; thus, they can be used regardless of the particular orientation or model one is implementing.
- Metaphors tap into a different way of teaching that is less about facts and more about the experience of taking in the metaphor and applying it to one's life.
- Metaphors bypass resistance that may usually accompany advice or psychoeducation in a group. Metaphors can do this since they are often linguistically packaged not as advice but, rather, as a story or anecdote. If the metaphor comes from the group or a group member, then there is often nothing to resist.
- Metaphors nurture imagination and creativity. This new way of thinking can transcend a communication rut a group has fallen into.
- Metaphors engage members in a search process—the search for their own meaning in regard to the metaphor. Most metaphors offer a somewhat ambiguous stimulus, even though the leader has offered it for a reason. The leader knows the reason for using the metaphor of the beach, mountain, volcano, or castle, but the group member often asks himself or herself, "Why am I being told this?" "How does this fit for me?" "What purpose does the group leader have in relaying this metaphor?"

TYPES OF METAPHORS

When a metaphor is adopted by a group, group members create their own language system, complete with an invented jargon that helps define their unique identity. Metaphors become a significant part of this group vocabulary; they symbolize the past that has been shared and represent a shortcut to bringing specific themes to collective attention. Group leaders can use different types of metaphors. Burns (2006) identified three categories that are appropriate for groups:

1. The first type is a member-generated metaphor that comes straight from group members. A group leader uses images, ideas, or words from the client to explore different ways to create change or insight. Examples of these would be a client stating any of the following ideas:

   "I feel like I am stuck in a box."

   "Talking with my spouse is like yelling at a brick wall."

   "I am like a turtle when there is a conflict."

2. The second type of metaphor is a group leader–generated metaphor, which is created by the leader to match the group or group member's concerns. This might be told as a story or given to the group as an image. It is often used when the group is at an impasse or stuck. Examples include the following:

   Leader: I have watched Trevor and Rubin go back and forth for weeks like two boxers who will not back down, and the rest of the group seems like a stunned audience.

   Leader: I can see this as compelling, but at some point the audience or the boxers need to stop the fight, call it a draw, or look for a different way to address these concerns. Because everyone in the group is just getting bloodied and nobody is healing in here.

3. The third type of metaphor is a collaborative metaphor that comes from the combined efforts of the leader and the group. These are common in group settings where the group begins to take on an alter ego and the leader builds on the story. An example of this would be a group of maligned individuals who started out being pretty discouraged. Over time, things got a little better with some success, and the group adopted the nickname "The Underdogs." As the group progressed, the "underdog" theme strengthened to the point where the check-in became a roll call of

how the "underdogs" were improving each week. The leader could feel the energy and acceptance of this image, and worked to strengthen it by validating success and saying, "You did it just like an underdog would." It is not uncommon for groups to find metaphors emanating from their work together that serve almost as mascots for the group. These metaphors become symbolic of the group's identity and how they envision their work.

A Favorite Group Metaphor: The Group as a Swimming Pool

One of our favorite metaphors that we have used in many groups is comparing being in a group with being at a pool party and wondering if one should go for a swim. The metaphor is a helpful way to talk about group stages and cohesion without using jargon or intellectualizing. We might begin by saying, "Starting a group is much like standing with a group of people around a swimming pool. Everyone is looking at one another, hiding behind their towels, wondering who will jump in first and get wet. You might be wondering, 'Are people going to like my suit? How cold is the water? Will everyone go swimming?' You fear that someone might push you in the pool before you are ready. It may seem as though the best thing is just to do a cannonball and jump in, but usually we observe that people like to slowly move toward the water and dip in a finger or toe to see what the pool is like. Is the water warm or too cold? Then the toe becomes the leg, and eventually the whole body goes underwater. You might notice that everyone has their own path and pattern of getting into the pool, and at some point you might notice that everyone is in the pool together. As leaders of the group, we want you to know that we will be like trusted lifeguards at the pool. We won't push you in the water, and we will enforce the rules of the pool. So it is really up to you to determine how you want to get in the water."

THE STRUCTURE AND CHARACTERISTICS OF METAPHORS

Group leaders have choices regarding how to facilitate members' awareness that metaphoric communication is occurring. Leaders can (1) label what is taking place, interpreting possible meanings ("This could mean . . ."); (2) involve members in the process of illuminating ("I wonder what this means"); or (3) match the figurative language that is being used ("So this *thunderstorm* that stopped you from venturing outside . . ."). One of the benefits of employing this third option whenever possible is that resistance is more often circumvented and the complexity of the full communication preserved if leaders stay with the members' own metaphoric language.

Metaphors convey abstract ideas as visual images; usually, they provide new ways of seeing something or cast it in a different light. For this transformation to take place, for affective insight to occur, the images must be vivid in their descriptions. But more than having the poetic and powerful primacy of the description, a metaphor must carry a compelling therapeutic message.

Metaphors are most likely to be influential if they are deliberately vague in their use of nominalizations, unspecified verbs, and referential indexes. Group members can personalize the themes to fit their unique situations if they are allowed to fill in the details.

Effective metaphors are concise and efficient, using the fewest possible words to convey the most powerful images. They are an economical form of communication insofar as they say more than ordinary language but in a more memorable way.

Difficult Group Members

You will end up with people in your groups who don't really want to be there (Schimmel & Jacobs, 2011). The honest ones will say directly, "I don't want to be here." The *really* honest ones will add how they feel about that: "Not only do I not want to be here, but I think it stinks that I have to come." Almost nobody will state what they intend to do about the situation: "Since I don't want to be here, and I am being forced to come, I intend to make everyone else's life as miserable as I can." There is little sense in complaining about involuntary participants, because they account for so many of the people with whom you will work (Morgan, Romani, & Gross, 2014). Children are referred by teachers or parents against their will. Adults are forced by their partners via ultimatums and blackmail. The criminal justice system mandates group work for substance abuse, driving under the influence, anger management, and parenting skills. Hospital or prison inmates are required to attend as part of their treatment. And a whole lot of members who may look like pretty cooperative people are secretly resentful about the idea of having to be in the group. Thus, the question is not *whether* you have resistant, noncompliant, difficult, uncooperative group members but *how many* there are in any given group and how determined they are to take others down with them.

This section is devoted to individual group members who tend to make the process difficult. Although this may seem surprising, what makes someone difficult to work with is often in the eye of the beholder (Brown, 2006; Kottler, 1992, 1994; Schimmel & Jacobs, 2011). The people you may experience as tough to deal with may not necessarily be those with whom we have the most trouble. We know some group leaders who prefer their participants to be well behaved and relatively compliant, whereas we consider this a form of resistance, much preferring people to "act out" if that is the way they are feeling.

For Reflection

Think about the people you have had the most trouble with in your life. This has likely been a consistent pattern in which the same sorts of individuals consistently get under your skin and irritate you. What are the typical characteristics of these people? How do you usually respond to those individuals who push your buttons or otherwise provoke strong reactions in you?

In spite of the differences in the ways some group leaders react to particular kinds of group members and provocative behavior, there is a consensus on which ones are the most challenging to work with (Brown, 2006; Gans & Alonso, 1998; Gladding, 2012; Kottler, 1994; Leddick, 2011; Roth, Stone, & Kibel, 1990; Yalom & Leszcz, 2005). This agreement indicates that leaders share certain expectations for how group members ought to act: They should be respectful of others, cooperative, responsive, and grateful for help, and they should do what they say they will do. The more a given group member deviates from our prescribed roles and expectations, the more likely we will perceive that person as difficult. Of course, it is important to remember that the irritation you feel is quite likely the same reaction the group member provokes in his or her life outside the group. So, often, the exact issue that is creating difficulty is the one that can be worked on in the group setting. And make no mistake, the group leader and other group members need to address problematic roles developing within the group, regardless of their form, to ensure the safety and optimal development of the group (Goodrich & Luke, 2012). If left unaddressed, any of the previously discussed negative roles have the potential to impede the group process (Leddick, 2011), reduce trust, and retard the group's development. In the sections below, we discuss some of the difficulties that stand out in group work.

MANIPULATION AND HIDDEN AGENDAS

Whether as a situational or characterological pattern, you will face group members who have in mind little else except undermining the group. They may feel that some injustice has been committed against them and want to have their revenge. They may enjoy the sense of power and control that accompanies destructive acts. More than likely, they are just trying to keep you and the group off balance so you don't get too close to them.

This is one of the most difficult challenges you will face, because people who are really good at being manipulative are also highly skilled at disguising their efforts—until it is too late. Assume that they are smarter than you are, at least in the domain of clandestine sabotage. Needless to say, you will have your hands full.

When encountering members who are being manipulative, the first order of business is to bring the issues out in the open. Since they are unlikely to respond to direct confrontation, except with another manipulative act to pretend compliance, you may have to resort to enforcing the strictest possible boundaries. In extreme cases, you will have to get the manipulative person out of your group, but that will come with its own price, since the member is unlikely to leave without a fight. Be clear and firm, and try not to fight.

We don't wish to frighten you with the possibility that there is a monster lurking in every group, just waiting to tear things apart. But you will wish to be vigilant and monitor carefully the extent to which group members are acting in ways that are not constructive. And when you sense that something is amiss, be sure to name it and bring it out.

SELF-CENTERED AND ENTITLED BEHAVIOR

The entitled or monopolizing group member has a number of ingenious ways of keeping the entire group's focus. This person's behavior might manifest through presenting as the recognition seeker/attention getter, constantly working to hold the group's focus, to the detriment of other members (Leddick, 2011). Persistence and sheer single-minded devotion to self-centeredness can often compensate for a lack of variety in monopolizing methodologies. For example, a group member may respond to input from someone else by beginning with, "That reminds me of the time . . . ." Filibustering is another common variety of group domination, in which the group member drones and rambles endlessly, ignoring others' frustration and boredom, even failing to respond to repeated intervention. At first, this may be subtle and even charming, since this member appears willing to fill in silences and takes an active role in the group. Yet, over time, you begin to sense something disconnected about the way the person interacts in the group.

There are many other reasons certain people attempt to monopolize group time. They may feel a sense of entitlement, believing that they are special, deserving of extra time. Some members lack interpersonal sensitivity and skills; they miss cues and remain unaware of their impact on others. Still others keep attention on themselves as an expression of power or control. Regardless of the reason, you must do something to intervene in such a way that this behavior is challenged.

Photo 14.1   The use of humor in groups is one way to defuse tension and conflict, especially with members who attempt to be controlling or manipulative. Humor can be used safely and supportively to provide a bridge between client reluctance and client motivation to change. Initial attempts to explore sensitive issues often take a jesting form to test the water before taking the plunge. Humor can also build group cohesion through in-jokes and shared laughter; yet it can also be used to express hostility, ridicule, or aggression.

Your job is to make certain that no one person dominates the group, captures an inequitable share of time, or holds center stage. This will be far more difficult than it sounds. Ideally, you can train everyone in the group to be responsible for intervening when necessary. In the early stages, however, the job will fall on you to do something to limit overindulgence by some members. You will be able to read the process in the group and know that an intervention is needed; yet unless you do it, most group members will placate the dominating person even though they wish the member would stop talking. The challenge is to give such people feedback that they need to stop talking but to do so in a way that doesn't cause them to feel censured or threatened.

The most challenging part of any intervention with monopolizing group members (or with any difficult group member, for that matter) is to retain one's composure and sensitivity. Beginning group leaders will naturally be cautious—even hesitant—to intervene, and thus the behavior can get out of control quickly. Experienced leaders may recognize more immediately exactly what is taking place: "Uh-oh, a monopolizer. The others are getting restless. Better stop this before it gets out of hand." Experienced leaders, therefore, are inclined to jump in more decisively—sometimes prematurely.

With any difficult group member, leaders have to assess both the consequences of the behavior on the member's own life and the effects on others in the group. If you respond harshly, you may shame the monopolizing group member and scare the other group members. Thus, leaders have a responsibility to give the monopolizer feedback on inappropriate or self-defeating behavior but to do so in ways that are therapeutic for others. At first, you might try waiting things out, hoping that either the person will run out of steam or someone else will jump in and tell him or her to shut up. This almost never happens in the beginning of a group; thus, you have to act.

One way to intervene is to wait for an opening (or create an opening with nonverbal body language) and then politely thank the person for the contributions, moving things along to the next contributor. Those who are skilled filibusterers usually ignore these subtle cues, requiring more direct intervention. Here are some options that might be used with Dirk, a member who has been talking way too much.

- *Try to use the group:* "I noticed that when Dirk was talking, some of you were having some strong reactions. Grant, you seemed a little bored; Mavis, I noticed you sighing a few times; and Esther, you kept looking intently at me. So what was going on?"
- *Summarize the point:* "Dirk, you have been talking for some time about what has been happening. What do you really want us to know?"
- *Comment directly on the process:* "Dirk, as you have been talking, I have lost my focus on you. I notice that happens often when you share. I find myself disconnected from you even though I realize that what you are sharing is very important. Have others had that experience today?"
- *Be directive and shift to someone else:* "Excuse me, Dirk, I'm sorry to interrupt, but we seem to be running out of time, and we have others who want to say something. I wonder if we might get back to you a bit later, after others have had a chance."

For Reflection

Think of a time when you were speaking in a group and got a clear message from the leader or teacher that what you were saying was not what he or she wanted to hear. How did you feel inside? How did you feel toward the leader, even if you knew that what he or she was doing was for the good of the group? Ideally, how would you have liked the interaction to go?

All these interventions speak to the point that eventually the leader must intervene with the monopolizing group member. If subtle or soft directives are ignored, then more direct methods will need to be used. As your efforts increase, you can also be assured that this action will come back to haunt you later. Even though some group members are impatient, frustrated, and bored, there will be some repercussions from others who resent the authority figure's cutting off one of their brethren.

For a Field Study

Ask a number of experienced group leaders, faculty, or teachers how they handle a situation when someone is talking too much or taking up more than one person's fair share of time. When the situation can't wait until the session is over, how do they intervene in a way that gets the point across without being offensive?

Obviously, this is a tough situation. One option is to confront the person privately before or after the group to help that group member interact in a more appropriate manner. The goal of this is more of a teaching and guiding opportunity rather than a shaming one. This is especially the case when working with members of cultures in which a public censure, no matter how well intended, is experienced as deeply humiliating. The problem, however, is that you can't often wait until the group is over to say something. You must intervene to stop behavior that is patently inappropriate and selfish. The challenge you will face is in doing this in a way that does not stir up more trouble.

THE SILENT GROUP MEMBER

In every group, there is a member (or two) who stays out of the main flow, not apparently connected to the others. Members who choose to isolate themselves often leave the group feeling dissatisfied (Corey, Corey, Callanan, & Russell, 2015; Ormont, 2004). Of course, this silent group member can "speak" even louder than do those who monopolize in terms of drawing attention and disrupting group movement.

Leaders need to model respect for and show interest in group members who remain silent. The group leader must continue to create a safe group where the invitation to speak remains. Members can remain silent for a number of reasons, some related to hidden agendas or seeking attention; others are just fearful and mistrustful of the climate—they are simply protecting themselves. Regardless of the reason, silent behavior has a profound effect on others in the group, as it brings out sympathy and concern, as well as anger and feelings of inadequacy: "We are a failure as a group as long as one among us is so disengaged."

Before you can intervene in such a situation, you must first assess what is going on and what the silence means (Brown, 2006). Does the person wish to join in but not know how? Is the behavior within voluntary control? What is the silence or withdrawal communicating? Is there an endogenous or organic process operating in the group member? What are the motivational and secondary gains underlying the behavior? When has the member demonstrated minimal responsiveness, and to what, when, and to whom, specifically? What is this person being asked to do that is beyond his or her present capability?

The key to these and any other questions that come to mind is to find some leverage or a bridge for engagement, even if it is just a token gesture. Once the meaning of the behavior is identified, whether as a form of defiance or protection, efforts can be made to address these issues more directly. For example, when members are involuntary participants in the group, forced to come against their will, withdrawal or silence is one of the few ways they can assert themselves. Being able to convey that understanding may help the leader connect with a silent member, since it validates this behavior and acknowledges the utility of being silent; yet, at the same time, it brings the issue front and center to the group so it can be discussed.

You have quite a number of options when confronted with silent group members. First of all, look at it in context of the group as well as of the individual member. Cultural, age, and gender factors will have an influence on how members interpret their permission to speak and when they are permitted to do so. Note the effects of the silence in terms of how members are processing what is happening: Are they sitting patiently, or do they appear anxious? Consider changing the structure of what you are doing to encourage more active participation and more equitable contributions. Sometimes this means more explicitly drawing out quiet members, inviting them to speak. Better yet, cue other members to draw people out:

Leader: Mack, I notice you looking over at Tanya repeatedly. What's going on?

Mack: Nothing, really. [Pause] Well, I was just wondering why she never talks. All the rest of us have said something.

Leader: [Pointing to Tanya] It sounds like you are curious about her and why she does not speak as much. Why don't you ask her?

Mack: [Shrugs] Okay. Tanya, why don't you ever talk? It worries me that you are watching us all the time but never saying anything.

In other situations, when a group member may feel terrified, intimidated, or extremely inhibited, you could also schedule a private conference to explore what it would take for the person to feel more comfortable speaking. Most of the time that will be enough. In other circumstances, it may be decided that the group is not an appropriate place for the person to do the work, and that group member can be referred for individual counseling. Finally, it should be understood that people learn in different ways. There is probably no relationship between how much people talk in a group and how much they are really learning and changing; sometimes people who talk the least are actually experiencing the most growth. You can test this idea yourself by reading journals of group members and noting what is going on behind the scenes, outside the group, and within each person's head and heart.

THE DISTRACTING AND DIVERTING MEMBER

There are so many varieties of this behavior that it is hard to catalogue them all. What they have in common is a desire to sidetrack what is going on to keep the interactions in safe territory. Members will do this through a filibuster—a long-winded story that can easily fill up a whole session. They will ramble a lot, create crises on cue, change the subject, ask nonrelated questions that go in a different direction, or do anything in their power to divert discussion away from what they feel is most threatening (and what you may believe is most useful).

The preferred intervention is to label what you observe going on; better yet, cue others in the group to do so, as illustrated in this interaction:

Frank: It was a tough time . . . maybe the toughest thing I've ever faced. . . . I don't know . . .

Candy: Well, let me tell you about something tough. A couple of years ago, my sister had to . . .

Leader: Wait a second, Candy. I noticed that Flynn flinched a second ago, and I wonder what he's thinking.

The leader obviously knows why Flynn is startled—for the same reason everyone else is appalled at Candy's interruption when Frank is trying to talk about something very difficult to share. Rather than confronting the distracting behavior directly, the leader cues Flynn to do so. You are essentially training everyone in the group to think like a leader, to monitor progress, to protect everyone else's rights, and to make sure that everyone gets their fair share of attention.

THE ARGUMENTATIVE AND ABUSIVE GROUP MEMBER

Some people enjoy verbal combat. They like intimidating others and would love to take on the leader or create as much havoc as possible in a group. If you think about it, this could make someone feel very powerful. That is why acting out, especially by those who feel powerless, is such a common occurrence in groups, as in life. In its most overt form, acting out involves some sort of dramatic attention-seeking scene, such as initiating an argument. This behavior can play itself out in other ways as well—the member who comes late or misses sessions, the person who refuses to talk or otherwise refuses to be pinned down, the person who consistently seems prickly during interactions in the group.

It is unlikely that you would be able to screen out such a person in your interviews. In some cases, you could have seen this person for years in individual counseling and never realized that the client had such potential to act out in group settings. More likely, you viewed the group member as feisty and spirited but had no idea that this person could wreak such havoc. The adage about how one sour apple can ruin the bunch applies to this person. The argumentative and abusive quality of the interactions is what creates such toxins. Under any and all circumstances, you must stop the abusive behavior. If the person does not respond to confrontations in the group or to feedback during a private conference on the need to be respectful and attempt to change, then you will most likely need to recommend an alternative treatment setting.

Student Voice

Am I the Difficult Group Member?

I was in a training group that paralleled my group counseling class for about 12 weeks. I had shared a bit here and there, but I was definitely more on the quiet end of the continuum. The leader and other group members had encouraged me to share and even invited me multiple times to talk, but I was able to deflect and use other methods to keep myself protected. I didn't think too much about this, and I wasn't really conscious of my efforts. I was reading a book chapter on difficult group members when it became clear to me, and I had to ask, "Was I being the difficult group member who stayed silent and resistant while the group tried to move on?" I brought that to the next group and asked the question. Confirming my suspicions, most of the group members said yes, I was being that type of member. I got feedback that I sent nonverbal messages to stay away, with members commenting that I drew a line where people weren't supposed to cross. People seemed to like me, but could not get close to me. Wow! That was news to me, and not the message I wanted to send. As I thought about that more, it seemed to be true in so many other areas of my life. So that day I really began to the join group and made a big effort to engage with the group and others.

THE RESISTANT GROUP MEMBER

Whereas conflict is often an overt event, it is easy to understand resistance as covert static that is constantly making noise in the group setting. Like conflict, resistance is normal and understandable given the expectations that group members face in a group setting. It is not a surprise that part of a person might want to flee the scene of a group rather than take a big risk and be vulnerable. Yet constant resistance to engagement with the group that undermines cohesion and trust is a concern (Brown, 2011). Furthermore, the resistant group member becomes problematic because this person can act as a road block within a group that wants to advance and deepen the process.

Resistance to the group process is often shown through unwillingness to share, acting withdrawn, or intimidation of fellow group members (Gladding, 2012). Resistance in the group can be addressed by providing sufficient structure and comfort in early sessions, gently encouraging and validating risks as they occur; leader modeling of cooperative group behavior; and realistic expectations on the leader's part for predicting when, how, and why such behavior occurs. A great many explanations are viable for a variety of motives behind resistant activities, which is why this behavior is so difficult to handle. A group member may exhibit resistant behavior for any of the following reasons:

1. The group member doesn't want to be in the group in the first place but is attending to satisfy the demands of someone else, such as a spouse, teacher, friend, or supervisor. Or they are mandated to attend by an outside force (Morgan et al., 2014). Surprisingly, this is one of the easiest types of resistance to handle, because the group member is usually outspoken and honest about resentments.

2. Resistance is frequently an adjustment reaction to a novel situation. Groups are strange places to the uninitiated, and in many ways it is normative to be cautious in such a setting. Only a fool would take the apparent concern, empathy, and safety at face value before doubts are addressed and trust is earned.

3. Under pressures to conform to group norms, all but the very meek feel the need to flex their individuality. Resistance can thus be an expression of rebelliousness, an unwillingness to be grouped as a part of the whole.

4. A fear of being judged by others and of interacting in groups sparks a lot of resistance in those who want to speak up but worry that they can't perform adequately in front of their peers.

5. A corollary of the social-fear motive is resistance due to a fear of failure. Persons who are used to feeling totally successful in their chosen profession and their peer groups may feel out of their element in this kind of group. They expend energy trying to maintain good impressions and spurn opportunities that involve being spontaneous or unpredictable, where perfect competence isn't guaranteed on the first try.

6. Resistance can be a sign of someone who enjoys manipulating others. It is, after all, an attention-getting ploy that evokes emotional responses in other members and even in the leader. The resistant group member can stop leader actions dead in their tracks, collect laurels of pity from others, and at the same time feel like a poor victim who can't help the situation.

7. Resistance can also be an act of jealousy to sabotage forward motion. Every time a group member makes significant life changes, it helps other

group members feel more dissatisfied with their inertia. A group member can then refuse to cooperate with group proceedings, knowing that by resisting, she or he no longer has to feel threatened by the rules the productive members are following.

8. Resistance is also a pacing mechanism to stall for time. In the language of physics, resistance is the drag that slows down the force of movement. When change accelerates too quickly, the human mind will attempt to decelerate progress to more comfortable levels that allow breathing space.

For Personal Reflection

We have framed resistance as being the result of myriad possible intentions, but we noted that it can also be understood as a normal reaction to the group situation. Think back to situations in your life where you were reluctant in a group. This could be within your family, with friends, at work, or even in a therapeutic group setting. What do you think was the cause of your resistance? How did you deal with it? What did you learn from that experience that might help you when you encounter such behavior from members in groups you lead?

Why Group Members May Create Difficulties

It is important to understand that in almost all the cases mentioned above, people are not acting uncooperatively to make your life miserable. They are doing the best they can to protect themselves from a situation that feels very threatening. Perhaps they don't want to be in the group in the first place but are being forced/coerced/blackmailed into participating; this would put anyone in a bad mood and predispose anyone toward belligerence. It is also likely that the environment does not feel very safe, and entirely possible that your expectations for group members' behavior may be beyond what these members are willing or able to satisfy. In such circumstances, acting out in some way is actually the "sensible" solution to protect themselves against perceived threats. If you can see resistance from this perspective, then you ought to be able to muster empathy for resistant or "difficult" group members—so much so that you do not view them in those terms. Rather, you can join with their fear or anxiety, show understanding and compassion, model that sensitivity for other group members, and, in so doing, likely reduce the perception of fear and anxiety in the group. Some specific tools for doing this are listed below.

For a Class Activity

In small groups, talk to one another about a time when you were forced to participate in a group situation that did not feel comfortable or safe. How did that feel to you? What were your reactions to coming to the group? Share examples of what you did to protect yourself and ways you acted out in the group.

The first step in working with challenging group members is not to take things personally. A group member's behavior represents an attempt to help himself or herself in some way, even if this strategy has some annoying side effects. In that sense, we encourage you to find the functionality behind the behavior that appears uncooperative to the group. That very process might help you build a connection with the offending group member. Look for ways the behavior is somehow adaptive. What benefits and payoffs is it serving in the group but also in the person's life outside of group? Generally, people tend to act out because it serves one of the following purposes:

1. It allows the group member to procrastinate, put off action, or avoid taking risks.

   I distract you from my issues.

   I prevent others from getting close.

2. It maintains the status quo.

   I may be miserable, but at least there are no surprises.

   I don't have to grow up or make any decisions.

3. It aids the person in avoiding responsibility.

   It's not my fault.

   I can't help it.

4. It gives the person an opportunity to revel in his or her power.

   I am destroying things on my own terms.

   I get lots of sympathy.

Whether or not the time is right to confront the difficult behavior and help the group member look at payoffs and secondary gains from acting out, it is important that you realize what is going on so you don't take things personally. In summary, people act in ornery, difficult, obnoxious ways not because they are cruel, heartless folks who want to ruin your group (although it may feel that way) but because they are just trying to protect themselves against something they perceive as terrifying. They are also engaging in behavior inside your group that has consistently gotten them in trouble (or gotten them attention) outside the group. But then, that's why they are getting help in the first place: It is their job to act in the same annoying ways that have created problems for them in their lives. When you see someone acting that way in the group, you get an in vivo experience of that person, and the group can give feedback on real behavior. But then, it is your job to help them learn alternative ways of getting their needs met, without disrupting your group.

For a Class Activity

In groups of six, decide on some common point of discussion that involves making a decision. Pretend that you have been given the choice of inventing an alternative way to be graded in the class or that you have been asked to devise other assignments you could complete.

During this conversation, each of you is to role-play your anticipated most difficult group member, whether that person is a whiner and complainer, a screamer, a controller, a manipulator, a distracter, a compulsive talker, or whoever. Really get into the role of being that person, talking and acting just as you imagine he or she would.

After the chaos is over and the laughter has died down, talk about what it felt like to be that person.

SET BOUNDARIES AND LIMITS

Under no circumstances can you risk losing control of your group. People will get hurt. Chaos will result. Manipulative and controlling members will be reinforced for their behavior. You must, therefore, intervene decisively whenever someone acts out in ways that are dysfunctional or destructive. This doesn't mean you have to be the one to say something, but you must cue others to take responsibility for reining in someone who is out of line.

In previous chapters, we discussed the sorts of circumstances that require intervention, such as when someone is being distracting, disoriented, provocative, abusive, disrespectful, and so on. You must be the one to jump in when things show signs of getting out of hand, keeping challenging members in line. This might look something like the following:

Connie: I've tried so hard to do something about this, but . . .

Ruth: God, this is just so boring I could scream. I've heard this shit so many times before.

Connie: Excuse me?

Ruth: Blah, blah, blah. . . . Do you have a hearing problem as well? I said this is boring and I hear this type of whining all the time from my friends, and also from you, so let's move on to something interesting.

Connie: I can't believe you just . . .

Leader: Connie and Ruth, let's stop for a minute. Steve, I can see by the look on your face that you're pretty stunned by what just happened. Perhaps you'd be willing to tell Ruth what you are experiencing right now.

The leader could have confronted Ruth directly or gone to Connie and invited her to confront Ruth on her inappropriate behavior. It may very well be that Connie is being just as difficult as Ruth is. Maybe Connie does ramble and repeat herself a lot. Perhaps Ruth is just expressing the exasperation that many others feel but chose a particularly harsh way of getting her point across. Multiple factors are likely operating. Going to another group member is an attempt to establish the norm that members can confront and react directly to one another rather than depending solely on the leader to intervene. If Steve, however, does not respond, then the leader will need to intervene directly.

What you will do in your groups is establish clear norms about what is considered appropriate behavior. You will also set boundaries for each group member who has trouble complying with consensual rules. You have already decided, for example, that Ruth is impulsive and must be restrained at times. You also have limits in mind for Connie and her repetitious storytelling but didn't get a chance to cut her off before Ruth jumped in. Another member in the group hardly ever talks, so at some point you intend to intervene and draw her out. In each case, you do what you can to help members learn appropriate ways of expressing themselves. In the best case, they will generalize what they are learning within the group to their lives outside the group, which may be the greatest therapeutic benefit of all.

LOOK AT YOUR OWN CONTRIBUTIONS TO THE PROBLEM

Although we have focused on the special problems in working with manipulative, entitled, or resistant group members, many of the same principles apply to any difficult group members. These clinical situations invite group leaders to invent creative means by which to work with or around group member deficits and design potent, individualized therapeutic experiences.

We have an obligation to protect the rights of other group members, a responsibility that can be applied only through consistent limit setting and compassionate, yet firm intervention (Barlow, 2013). Most of all, group members perceived as difficult require honest and caring feedback from others to help them act in ways that are both in their own best interests and consistent with healthy group norms. This requires that group leaders demonstrate tremendous flexibility, patience, and a willingness to look at their own contributions to conflicted group interactions. That's right; you must acknowledge when the difficult person in the room is actually you.

Most group leaders prefer to blame difficult members as being the problem. We call them "resistant," or other names that are less than flattering. Indeed, there are individuals who are a gigantic pain to deal with; after all, that's why they are in our groups in the first place.

Yet some members become difficult because we have made them that way or boxed them into a corner. Leaders can be as much of a problem as members because of things we do that are insensitive, inflexible, overly controlling, misguided, inappropriate, or provocative. It would be downright negligent, therefore, not to examine your own contributions to the difficulty.

Earlier, we wrote that you should not take things personally, but you would not wish to take this to the extreme where you refuse to examine what you might be doing to make group members more difficult than they need to be. It might be useful to ask yourself a series of questions such as these:

- What am I doing to create or exacerbate the problems?
- How am I being unusually inflexible in my style or manner?
- What personal issues of mine are being triggered by this incident?
- Whom that I have encountered previously does this group member remind me of?
- How am I acting out my impatience with the member's (or group's) progress?
- What expectations am I setting for this individual that he or she is unwilling or unable to meet?
- What needs of mine are not being met?

CHALLENGES OF GROUP LEADERSHIP

In one sense, difficult members are taking risks, making themselves vulnerable, putting themselves on the line, and volunteering themselves as targets of opportunity. In that sense, they may be doing more work than anyone else, especially those who are being polite and compliant.

That is not to say that you want to do everything you can to bring up problems or provoke difficult behavior. Obviously, you've got enough to do in the group without creating more work for yourself. This is just a reminder not to complain incessantly about difficult members or challenging situations but, rather, to view them as opportunities for learning and growth. We can guarantee that you will hear such complaints a lot: Leaders spend an inordinate amount of time whining about how ornery and uncooperative and resistant their group members are. Resist the impulse to join in on these sessions, which only encourage feelings of victimization and powerlessness and further reinforce the idea that members are the problem, not the leader. If you really feel stuck, work with a coleader or supervisor to work through the struggle. Examine not only what is happening in this particular struggle but also what it means in the larger context of your work and life. That is one of the benefits of this type of work, at no extra charge. After each challenge you face, you have the opportunity to learn from the struggle in such a way that you become more effective in facing similar situations in the future.

CONFRONT FAILURES, REFRAME THEM, AND APPLY WHAT YOU LEARNED

Inevitably, you are going to encounter a number of people you can't help, no matter what you try. Similarly, no matter how much experience you accumulate, how many workshops you attend, how much training you receive, how many books you read, and how much supervision you get, you are still going to lead groups that just don't work well. This could be because of a variety of reasons, some of them related to the members, some to the environment and context, and some to you as well.

Failures represent an opportunity to learn and grow from mistakes—but we also know that when you are the one who feels as though you messed up or made a mistake, this advice is hard to take in. What we can tell you is that you are going to make plenty of mistakes, many group members are not going to like you, and you will have many restless nights where you replay a group over and over again, trying to figure out what you could have done differently. Such are the depressing ruminations of a group leader who encounters failure. We implore you now, in the early part of your career, to acknowledge imperfection in practice while striving to do better when you can. And remember that mistakes and imperfections are not always flaws. Since failure is a certainty, you can decide now how you are going to reframe and make sense of it.

For Reflection

Think of a time recently when you attempted to serve in some leadership role. It is likely that you did some things that were quite effective and others that were less than inspired, if not obvious failures. In a balanced way, review what you did best and worst. Ask yourself what you learned from the mistakes and what you intend to do differently in the future.

Failures can indeed provide excellent opportunities to reflect on your leadership skills, consider ways you could handle things differently in the future, help yourself grow to new levels of flexibility, and open new opportunities that were not there before (Kottler & Carlson, 2003, 2014). For this to happen, however, you must be brutally honest with yourself about mistakes and misjudgments you have made, and allow yourself to learn from group members. This means that rather than blaming certain group members for being uncooperative or certain groups for being resistant, you must own your share of the responsibility for things you could do differently. This means that one of the most useful personality traits of an advanced group leader is humility. Owning up to a mistake or acknowledging that you did not do something well in group can be a tremendous growth experience for the group.

Matt remembers a group he led that had become stagnant in growth:

A group member confronted me in session about not being validating enough about a risk she took a few weeks earlier. I was surprised, since she was one of my favorite people in the group. Yet I took in what she said, acknowledged the risk to confront me, and then apologized for not being there for her. I tried to validate her at that moment—and something then sparked in the group. She accepted the apology and said she felt energized, and then other group members seemed to get more engaged. Later, as I reflected on that moment, up until that moment it seemed that I had been the omnipotent leader and too directive and controlling. Acknowledging the misstep helped model that I was not always right and that group members had the freedom to act without my permission. That was the crux of the group, since it empowered group members to act on their own.

A SUMMARY OF MANAGEMENT PRINCIPLES

Our experience leading groups has taught us that it is often one or two difficult group members who consume the majority of our group supervision and

planning time. With that in mind, we close this chapter with some general principles to keep in mind when addressing problematic behavior in groups:

1. Keep yourself calm. Address your own countertransference or exaggerated
   personal reactions to what is going on.

   Who does this person remind me of?

   How am I overreacting to what is going on?

   How is my sense of control being threatened?

2. Label what you see—or, better yet, help others do so.

   "I notice that as Fred is talking, a number of you are looking frustrated.
   Perhaps you could tell him what you see happening."

3. Ask yourself, or the group, what is really going on.

   What is the meaning of this behavior?

   What is this person really saying at this moment in time?

4. Model the kinds of behaviors you would like others to employ. Encourage
   others when they follow your lead.

   "I'm having trouble hearing you right now when you appear so angry and
   out of control. I agree with Sandy when she was telling you to calm down."

5. Give immediate feedback to members who are out of line.

   "Stop for a second. Before you continue, I think it might be helpful for you
   to hear how others are reacting to what you said and how you said it."

6. Schedule individual, private conferences in cases when direct, public
   confrontation may not be indicated.

   "I know you get embarrassed easily, so I didn't want to say this in the group,
   but I'd like to talk with you about ways I can help you get more involved and
   hopefully help you meet your own goals."

7. Uncover and confront hidden agendas that are at work.

   "I'm confused by what is happening right now. It appears as though several
   of you have talked about this outside of group. One of our agreed-on rules
   is that such discussions will be disclosed openly in front of everyone."

8. Reframe challenging or provocative behavior as an opportunity for learning and growth, rather than merely an obstacle to be overcome. Some of
   the best stuff that happens in groups occurs as a result of some critical or
   disruptive incident.

"I can see that many of you are upset by what just took place. It is uncomfortable to resolve conflicts like this, and I certainly wish we could have prevented it. Yet at the same time, I think this presents a wonderful opportunity for this group to grow. Clearly, this conflict has sparked thought and growth, so let's talk about what you learned from this."

9. Get some help, either in the form of supervision, from a coleader, or from a recruited assistant in the group.

    "I'm not sure what this is about. I'd like to ask for some help from those of you who might have something to add."

Review of What You Learned

- As leaders gain more experience, they learn how to intervene in ways that are more complex and responsive to the needs of the group.
- Advanced group leaders become attuned to changes in the physical environment where the group is being held and then intervene to modify or clarify the group dynamics.
- Metaphors are useful tools to break an impasse in a group or help group members see concepts or solutions in a new manner. Metaphors can help build group cohesion by developing a shared language and understanding among group members.
- The most honest resistant group members will display their dissatisfaction overtly; the really tough ones will pretend they are enjoying themselves while they play games and attempt to sabotage the group's work.
- Group members don't necessarily start out difficult and resistant. They may become that way in response to things you are doing that appear confusing or threatening to them. Further, they may be scared and anxious for good reason; so explore that with group members before confronting them.
- Whenever possible, cue group members to do the work when a distracting person needs to be confronted or limits must be set.
- Group leaders have to be active when working with difficult members. This means drawing limits and boundaries, protecting other group members, and potentially confronting the group members during or outside of group about their ability to be proactive in the group setting.
- Not all difficult situations in groups are about the members; sometimes the leader is the one being difficult or causing an obstruction. Get in the habit of reviewing what your contribution to the problem in groups is, and then develop a support system of peers or supervisors with whom to consult about ways to modify your interactions.

Adjunct Structures to Group Work

15

The goal of therapeutic adjuncts is to intensify any work done within the more traditional latitudes of group practice. Since the average group member spends more than 100 waking hours each week *outside* the therapeutic encounter, the time logged in the group represents less than 2% of the thoughts and feelings that group members experience. A group member may enter the hallowed chamber each session, itching to get started on two intensive hours of hard work—introspection, confrontation, and integration. But then the group disbands until next week, and the group member reenters the real world, perhaps acting just as ineffectively as before.

In the safety of the group, the group member may be a superstar at risk taking, because the atmosphere is conducive to trust, respect, acceptance, and human kindness. The group member's comrades praise every intelligent comment; confronting a conflict head-on wins enthusiastic support. The group member is continually reinforced for growing, at least until the following week. Once outside, however, smiles fade, support is hard to find, and the group member may regress to prior behavior for a week. Tempers are lost. Self-pity returns. All is forgotten, or temporarily suspended, until the next group meeting.

This doesn't happen all the time, perhaps not even frequently, but group members report often enough that the glowing effects of the group experience don't even outlast the weekend. Unless members are given opportunities to think about their insights every hour—while they eat or drift off to sleep, when they are anxious and depressed, during television commercials or rides in the car—the memories quickly fade. If people do not practice new skills regularly, the skills will never become part of natural functioning.

To maximize gains and progress from the group session, many group leaders incorporate adjunct structures for maintaining therapeutic changes outside of the group. Unlike our colleagues in medicine who have the use of high-technology tools for assistance, we create tools to remind our group members to continue working on themselves between sessions. We use all the help we can get to ensure that each group member individually personalizes changes and that these desired changes are perpetuated long after the last group session.

In this chapter, we review some of the most functional adjuncts currently in use by group leaders who seek innovative ways to supplement their "talking cures." By combining the technology from the creative arts, pharmacology, electronic media, cultural geography, and the biological and social sciences, we can more powerfully promote long-term group member changes. Furthermore, the burgeoning self-help field can be used to provide group members with consistent resources to work on their goals and create change (Bruneau, Bubenzer, & McGlothlin, 2010; Norcross, 2006). Self-help resources are now more available than ever before, particularly online (Chang, 2005). Further, there is evidence that self-help reading encourages active coping and promotes insight (Bergsma, 2008). Therapeutic changes can happen at any time, whether or not people actually pay attention to them (Kottler, 2014). Group leaders can help group members focus on everyday events and situations, such as reading a book, watching a movie, or writing in a journal to capture insights, emotional reactions, and new ways to solve problems, as a parallel change process to being in a group (Lampropoulos & Spengler, 2005).

We now have access to endless forms of advanced communication technologies, such as handheld devices and cell phones that contain audio- and video-recording equipment, computer systems, and absentee-cuing systems. Yet main adjunct structures rely on some of the simplest forms of communication—a pen and paper. From writers such as Anaïs Nin and Albert Camus, we have inherited the literary legacy of journal keeping. Many novelists, as well, have provided psychologically sophisticated literature for self-reflective study, spawning the field of bibliotherapy. We can use behavioral technology such as environmental programming, contingency reinforcements, psychological homework, and people monitoring. We can access the Internet and online discussion sessions to supplement what happens in group or to give members opportunities to report on daily progress. Field excursions are ways of creatively augmenting group experiences by taking members outside the usual environmental parameters. In each case, other disciplines have contributed valuable tools that innovative group leaders may incorporate into their repertoires.

Therapeutic Writing

The use of writing in a therapeutic manner can be traced back to psychotherapeutic traditions that encourage the expression of emotions and self-reflection. Almost all psychotherapeutic paradigms, regardless of theoretical orientation, consist of some form of disclosure that includes identifying, labeling, and disclosing emotional experiences (Smyth & Helm, 2003; Smyth, Nazarian, & Arigo, 2008; Thompson, 2011). *Expressive writing* and *therapeutic writing* are terms used, often interchangeably, to describe writing as a psychotherapeutic intervention. *Expressive writing* is the term most often cited by researchers who investigate the physical and psychological benefits of emotional disclosure. *Therapeutic writing* is a more global term used to describe any writing exercise undertaken to support therapeutic work (Thompson, 2011). It is "a means of dealing with stressful or traumatic events . . . that involves writing (without feedback) about the thoughts and feelings surrounding a stressful event" (Wiitala & Dansereau, 2004, p. 187).

Expressive writing has increasingly been applied as a psychosocial intervention across multiple settings (Jolly, 2011) and represents an effective supplemental intervention that group leaders can add to their array of therapeutic tools for group members—both inside and outside the group session. Writing is a strength-based technique that can be used to engage group members in the process of therapy to promote positive life changes (White & Murray, 2002). The technique is culturally sensitive; it is not allied to specific cultural norms and can be implemented at age-appropriate levels across a range of group populations (Gullette, 2003; Tyson & Baffour, 2004). Journals can also be created through reflective video journaling, which may be more appealing to some people (Parikh, Janson, & Singleton, 2012).

In a group setting, even though members may have a desire to disclose their thoughts and emotions about a distressing experience, social constraints in the group may limit such interpersonal disclosure (Lepore & Smyth, 2002). As you know, group members always leave with a variety of content or emotional material that was not revealed. Some group members may refrain from discussing negative events due to the social stigma associated with the experience. Others may lack a social support system and/or receive insensitive or inappropriate support. In contrast, written emotional expression outside of the group offers the opportunity to express one's thoughts and feelings without regard to social constraints or barriers that might accompany interpersonal disclosure, and reduces the likelihood of negative interpersonal responses. Writing has long been a common strategy for expressing strong emotion and has informally been used both personally and in therapeutic settings for a variety of purposes and goals (Jolly, 2011).

Disclosing information, thoughts, and feelings about personal and meaning-ful topics (experimental disclosure) has positive psychological consequences (Frattaroli, 2006; Graybeal, Sexton, & Pennebaker, 2002; Klein & Boals, 2010). Therapeutic writing is viewed as having a wide range of benefits for health, psychological well-being, physiological functioning, and general functioning (Pennebaker & Chung, 2011; Troop, Chilcot, Hutchings, & Varnaite, 2013). Studies have demonstrated that writing about difficult experiences or events can promote effective coping (Lumley & Provenzano, 2003), promote forgiveness (Romero, 2008), decrease depressive symptoms by attenuating the negative emotional effects of intrusive thoughts (Lepore, 1997), decrease the occurrence of physical illness due to stress (Greenberg, Wortman, & Stone, 1996), and promote positive growth (e.g., improved interpersonal relationships, greater appreciation for life) following a difficult experience (Ullrich & Lutgendorf, 2002). When compared with other creative forms of therapy, such as drawing, writing was found to encourage a greater decrease in psychological symptoms, especially for individuals who had higher baseline levels of psychological distress (Chan & Horneffer, 2006). All in all, writing can serve as a strong accompaniment to working in a group setting.

Group leaders can be directive in prescribing writing assignments for group members. Programmed writing is a therapeutic technique with a high degree of structure. It is usually more on the cognitive end of the continuum. Programmed writing uses structured writing assignments or lessons completed between group sessions (Jordan, 2000). This can mean assigning specific prompts or themes for the whole group or tailored assignments for individual group members. Writing about positive experiences has been linked to improving one's mood (Burton & King, 2004). Those who use more positive emotion words in their writing achieve the greatest benefit physically and psychologically from the writing interventions (Pennebaker & Francis, 1996); the use of more negative and fewer positive emotion words has been related to an increase in depressive mood (Pennebaker, Mayne, & Francis, 1997). Thus, using writing to infuse positive emotion words into one's writing can act as a regulatory measure that buffers the impact of negative emotions that either came up in group or come out in one's writing. Therefore, a group leader can instruct members to write about the positive experiences from the previous group.

Some prompts from a group leader could go as follows:

- Write about your positive insights since the last group, and identify how you can apply them in your life.
- Identify the ways you have progressed toward meeting your group goals over the past week.

- What personal strengths are you discovering about yourself in group?
- Identify three moments in the last group when you were proud of yourself or another group member. What happened in the group to allow these moments to occur?

Although we have been speaking about prescribed writing in the context of pen and paper, it is also possible to use the online technology that has become so common in classrooms. Of course, there are additional problems and challenges for the leader in managing such outside communications, since it becomes quite easy for things to slip out of control, for members to abuse the privilege, or for people to inadvertently or deliberately wound one another. There has yet to be significant research in this area, because the technology is still being tested in therapeutic settings.

JOURNAL WRITING

There is an established history of using journaling as an adjunct structure in group work (Falco & Bauman, 2004; Hall & Hawley, 2004; Parr, Haberstroh, & Kottler, 2000; Thompson, 2011). Some people also keep daily or weekly records of their lives in the form of journals or diaries. Journals in a therapeutic setting are used to provoke reflections on the self and the environment (Stone, 1998). Journals are often less structured than programmed assignments or thought diaries. The main structure involved is often around time—for example, writing each day or three times a week. The daily rhythm of writing can help develop the habit of regular reflection. When journaling is used as an assignment, the group leader may collaborate with the group to structure the topics that will be considered.

Journals are often organized around the emotionally relevant aspects of one's group experience and can help address the difficulties associated with those experiences. Because journaling is less interpersonally intimate than actually being in the group, group members who find face-to-face disclosure and exploration challenging may be encouraged to venture into emotionally difficult areas. The journal can help one organize one's reactions and be better prepared for the next group. Writing about personally painful experiences in unstructured, yet reflective ways may also help group members better articulate difficult topics in the group.

One of the benefits of using a journal as an adjunct to being in a group is that it capitalizes on techniques active within an individual that are not available during group meetings. It counterbalances the *we*-ness of groups or the helper's role in individual counseling by encouraging the creative and spiritual enrichment of one's inner life. Furthermore, the journal teaches self-reliance; it provides an inner sanctum where a group member can practically and safely experience greater personal mastery. A daily, intensive journal is perhaps the single most useful therapeutic adjunct available to group members for deepening work accomplished during sessions. Journal keeping has become a standard operating procedure among many group leaders of various theoretical persuasions for many sound reasons.

Journaling does not necessarily need to be a private affair. Haberstroh, Parr, Gee, and Trepal (2006) outlined a form of interactive e-journaling among group members. This format included group members' sending a journal that summarized their thoughts, reflections, and experiences after each group to all the group members before the next session. Members did not respond to one another or interact online about these journals but, rather, were able to use the face-to-face group time to process any reactions. Group members found that the e-journal paralleled the group process and helped facilitate the progression through the group stages. Furthermore, the journals provided opportunities for members to reflect further and gain perspective on happenings in the group.

CATHARSIS

Writing and journaling has a purported cathartic effect. First and foremost, a journal is a convenient repository for all thoughts and feelings swelling inside and bursting to express themselves. Freud had originally intended therapy to be a vehicle for releasing stored psychic energy, and the journal is a more appropriate place for self-expression than the group sessions themselves. All too often, group members waste valuable group time complaining about their lives beyond the point where complaint is helpful, but the journal offers an eternally vigilant ear, always ready to accept unconditionally any and all cathartic entries.

Sample Journal Entry

I really hate my job, and I despise this two-faced place. I'm so damn tired of all these idiots telling me what to do with my life, how I should think, what I should wear, how I should speak, and so on. It would be different (maybe) if they could get their own acts together first before they try to direct my life. I hate nothing worse than a bunch of loud-mouthed hypocrites who get off on the power of making other people feel miserable. I would so much like to stand up to these assholes and tell them what I really think, that they are self-centered, rigid-thinking, insensitive, irresponsible peasants who delude themselves into believing that they are royalty.

INTROSPECTION

We all have human needs for completing unfinished business and finding meaning in our actions. The principal shortcoming of group experiences, where there is so much to do and so little time, is the lack of opportunity to draw closure on each participant's processing of whatever is occurring in group. Writing in a journal, Pennebaker (2004) enthusiastically explains, provides the group participant with a structure for completing the "teasers" that may have begun in the group. We can also reduce rumination around replaying specific incidents or thoughts. Closure on accomplished personal goals can also be gained, and the journal can provide a chance to develop new goals. King (2001) noted that the journal could be used as a place to write about one's best possible future self, and then begin to envision how to become that person.

The journal is a place to talk to ourselves, to reflect on significant events both in the group and in the real world (Thompson, 2011). Systematic writing trains us to think more analytically and introspectively about our actions, to ponder inconsistencies and underlying motives, and to reconcile others' perceptions with our self-image.

Sample Journal Entry

The feedback from the other group members as to their first impressions of me is incongruent with how I think I come across. I appeared shy and studious, which is certainly a new image for someone like me, who pretends so much to be a "man of action." So who do I want to be? The shy guy or the man of action? Maybe I can really ask myself, Who am I really? I pretend to be the life of the party, but maybe that is a façade to hide the quiet and introspective me. I guess for so long I believed that that person was not okay and that others would not like that guy. So maybe I can try to experiment in this group and be who I am, and then see how people like me. Funny to imagine that the experiment is just trying to help me be "me" for the first time.

SELF-INTIMACY

Whereas group sessions usually focus on people as social beings, journal writing complementarily concentrates on the private self. By exploring their own intimate thoughts in conjunction with the interactive group work, group members are better ensured of making independent decisions, as well as preserving personal identity (Jolly, 2011). A particular group meeting can often act as an impetus for group members to turn inward, explore the implications of an issue for themselves, and then further explore the most relevant dimensions in their journals. The journal can provide a place of solitary disclosure for group members to figure out what they need to do next and how much to put forth in the next group (Pennebaker, 2002).

Sample Journal Entry

I left the group with a bored, wasted feeling in the pit of my stomach, like I hadn't grown any. And I wasted my time watching one of my cohorts getting thoroughly grilled. It wasn't until now, after becoming more aware of my own dependencies on people I love, that I realized that I had, in fact, been pounded on the head. I, too, feel guilt—obligation toward my grandparents who love me so devotedly and live their lives through mine. And I felt that guilt in group, too, like I must repay or be obligated to people in the group. Yet I now wonder, must I really repay this perceived debt to others? How would I be different if I did not feel that guilt in group? How would my life be different if I did not feel guilt toward my grandparents? Would I still be living here or would I have moved to New York last year when I had the chance?

PROCESSING INSIGHTS

Even an exceptional human mind cannot keep pace with the kaleidoscope of new ideas presented in a typical group meeting. Concepts are often introduced on an abstract or general plane, requiring systematic personalization of the material. Each participant must continually ask questions: *What are they really saying? What does this mean? What has this to do with me? How might I apply this to my life?* One of the benefits of journaling about one's group experience is the opportunity to process insights in a timely manner, thus regulating how much information and awareness one can process (King, 2001).

Each novel concept, every lesson worthy of recall, must be fully understood, interpreted, generalized, applied, coded, and stored in memory for retrieval on demand. To accomplish these tasks, it is not only desirable but necessary for group members to process insights gleaned from group sessions into bite-size pieces that can be swallowed without indigestion. And writing, rather than just thinking about insights, is associated with greater benefits, since it allows people to organize their experiences (Lyubomirsky, Sousa, & Dickerhoof, 2006).

Sample Journal Entry

One of the main points of the last session was that a person is ultimately responsible only to himself. Problems that arise as the result of another person's actions must be seen only within the context of how I allow it to affect me. The implications of this are awesome: I need never feel helpless again.

DIALOGUE WITH GROUP LEADER

One of the principal disadvantages of groups is the premium placed on leader accessibility. The group leader is simply not readily available to group members in this time-shared structure, in which each participant may command only a one-sixth or even one-fifteenth share. When many people vie simultaneously for leader attention, some will inevitably be shortchanged. Moreover, even a socially skilled and assertive group member who is able to maximize leader expertise during sessions will be left out in the cold between meetings. Questions and comments that come to mind during the week must often be shrugged off.

A possible solution to this problem lies in using the journal as a place where group members can create dialogues with the leader. The leader's ear is thus always on call, at any time of the week, whenever the group member has need for a confidential conference. If group members later decide to share their journals with the leader, any responses, reactions, and feedback can be inserted throughout the pages.

Sample Journal Entry

I don't much like the idea of not being in control of what goes on in this group. And yet you seem perfectly fine with not knowing what is going to happen each week? I have encountered some leaders who act like they know it all, and I never really trusted them. It seemed like their certainty was just another form of control, which is the same thing I struggle to maintain. But with you, it seems different. I know you are going to read this journal, so I am going to take the risk of being a little out of control and ask for some help in living with uncertainty. I want to come into group and not freak out beforehand worrying about what is going to happen and what I am going to do. I just want to be in the group, and I just want to be in my life. Maybe I am reading you all wrong, and you are a control freak just like me, but it seems like you wear it pretty darn well.

Of course, with the arrival of web-based discussion groups, listservs, and secure e-mail technology, using a journal as a way to dialogue with a leader and other group members is an easy option (Atkinson, Hare, Merriman, & Vogel, 2009; Haberstroh et al., 2006; Page, 2003; Page et al., 2003). Furthermore, it can be a convenient and effective option. Journals written under interactive e-mail conditions are more likely to contain evidence of reflections than are traditional journals (Kaplan, Rupley, Sparks, & Holcomb, 2007). Leaders need to be clear about the expectations for group members in terms of how to use the journal, and they also need to convey how members should respond and use the journal as an adjunct to the group.

SELF-DISCIPLINE

People experimenting with journal writing often complain that it is hard work. It takes time, dedication, and focus. Sometimes you're too busy or feel as though you have nothing to say; other times it's too painful to get into personal matters. In either case, it takes resolve and effort on a member's part to carry through with the task. Like the change efforts attempted in therapy, journal keeping requires considerable self-discipline.

Sample Journal Entry

I find myself, day by day, growing stronger. The reinforcement mechanisms for change are operating at an extremely effective level. I can't even put my finger on how I've changed; I just think differently. I'm much more positively critical, demanding of myself. Just by nature of the fact that it is 8:00 a.m. on a Saturday and I'm sitting here writing instead of sleeping is indicative of my new self. I am more disciplined—heck, I have already filled two notebooks of journals. When this started, I thought I would only write once a week, and that was just to get it done. Now I look forward to writing each day. It is funny, but I feel kind of cool to be drinking coffee and writing intensely at the café—it makes me appear serious and studious in an okay way.

CREATIVE EXPRESSION

The unique communication style of group work lends itself to an emphasis on scientific inquiry, inquisitive exploration, and a playful experimentation with novel ideas. It is hoped that these qualities will become part of the content of the journal, making it a forum for creative expression.

Sample Journal Entry

Organization is the hardest part of writing, deciding what to put where. With the greatest fluidity, I can sit down almost anywhere and write acceptable, if not interesting, prose. But my writing style does not include a sequential flow of pages from beginning to end. Like the free association of a slot machine, a spark clicks, triggered by a memory, a sight, and a sound. From there, the idea writes itself from the nucleus outward. A string of jumbled beads is thus left around my neck, in need of sorting. And that is the most confusing, challenging task of all. I get frightened by the power of a writer to alter pieces—first to create them from nothing, then to put them anywhere.

In addition to journal writing, members can use other forms of self-expression, such as poetry. Poetry helps group members access emotional material in an unstructured way. It can help group members articulate thoughts that are difficult to express, tapping into certain aspects of their lives from a perspective that may be inaccessible in a normal group setting (Heimes, 2011; McArdle & Byrt, 2001). For many, the point of entry is expression and disclosure of emotions. Poetry writing often begins with emotional disclosure and, in the process of writing, moves toward creating empowering or helpful narratives that bring one closer to a personal voice that can be expressed in the group (Heimes, 2011; Kempler, 2003). Below are some examples of written self-expression:

- *Goal setting:* "I notice that I keep trying to win my father's approval for the things I do. Alternative: to keep my own counsel and quit running to him each time I accomplish some task. Goal: to stifle the urge for others' approval. In the group I must restrain myself from saying things I don't necessarily believe in—just to win approval and strokes."

- *Structured self-counseling:* "I have a desperate, neurotic need for recognition by an impartial audience. I am not at all concerned about the approval of my parents or friends or anyone else close to me. That is the confusing part: I don't feel I have to prove my wonderfulness to anyone I know; it is the people I don't know whom I make so important. I must make extraordinary efforts to remind myself that (1) I don't become a more worthy human being just because I convince strangers that I am important, (2) it is a losing proposition anyway since I cannot convince everyone, and (3) I am important to myself and those who love me—what difference do other opinions make?"

- *Systematic practice of new thinking:* "What an interesting idea we learned today—that other people can't reject me unless I permit them. So often,

I let myself be put in vulnerable positions where other people can control my life. This evening I tried something new. I walked up to a girl, as usual, but this time when she didn't respond to me, instead of feeling dejected, I told myself, 'Big deal. So she didn't like you. That doesn't mean you are ugly or stupid. Maybe next time things will work out differently. And if they don't . . . I can live with that, too.'"

- *Dream analysis:* "Only since my baby was born have I had these incredibly vivid dreams. I am being pursued by some suitably grotesque creature, and it goes after the baby instead of me. I struggle. I fight. Just as the baby is devoured I wake up screaming, in tears. Never have I felt so damn vulnerable. It is bad enough to have to protect myself, worse still this little one who cannot fend for himself."

- *Remembrances, memory:* "In this book I've been reading, a little boy asks his mother if raindrops are alive. His mother nonchalantly replies: 'I think so. Isn't everything alive and infused with the spirit of God?' The boy, not to be put off, asks: 'Then does the rain have dreams, too, like us?' While his mother stammers, searching her memory for the correct response, the boy inwardly smiles, points toward the sunlit mountains in the distance, and answers his own question: 'Rainbows are the rain's dreams. If rain dreams, can it also cry?'"

- *Progress and growth:* "Last night I stumbled onto an opportunity to use the confrontation skills that I have unknowingly acquired from this group experience in the past few weeks. I found myself using phrases I had heard in the group. To be quite honest, I thought that last week wasn't that useful. Apparently, I learned more than I thought."

- *A celebration of life:* "Today I have fulfilled my greatest dreams. Perched atop an overhanging cliff at 10,000 feet (higher than eagles dare fly), overlooking the valley below, my skis swinging in a rhythmic pattern to the wind and snow, I lived. It was then that I realized that I had been thinking about absolutely nothing—my mind was a complete blank. How precious are these moments, devoid of thought and feeling? I never once thought to myself, 'This is beautiful.' My unconscious self had already accepted this fact; it felt no inclination to bother the rest of me with a lapse in concentration."

For Reflection

What have been your experiences while journaling or keeping a diary? How has this been a helpful experience for you? What did you gain? One of the tasks leaders face with using journals in groups is ensuring that group members are able to keep writing consistently. Leaders often have to troubleshoot some of the barriers (e.g., not having enough time, not knowing what to write about, forgetting to do it). How would you introduce a journal assignment to a group? How would you outline the benefits? How would you create compliance in keeping the journal?

SOME LIMITATIONS OF JOURNAL WRITING

Journals are sometimes structured as group logs, in which participants are expected to document after each session what was accomplished, which personal goals were attained, observations of what transpired, what in particular was learned, and their personal reaction, including what the session felt like. The logs are then collected regularly so the leader may read and react to each member's comments, giving individual attention to issues that are not possible in group formats.

An assignment like this, however, is not without hazards that can be typical when using writing as an adjunct structure. Members may resent that even their most private written reflections are open to scrutiny. In addition, knowing that the leader will read what has been written can foster greater approval seeking or even lead to manipulative games: "There is something I have wanted to say to you that I have been unwilling to say in the group . . . ." Because opportunities are available for members to disclose things in the log or journal, some may avoid doing so in the group. For the same reason, many group leaders are reluctant to communicate privately with any group participant for fear that they will be triangulated into a group conflict.

Although there are many uses or benefits of journal writing as an adjunct to group work, Pennebaker (2004) warns that overreliance on this structure can also create some problems, many of which are quite evident to those of us who have been reading member journals for many years. Some of them are as follows:

- Journal writing can be a substitute for action. In the same way that talking about a subject can prevent someone from taking care of business, writing about one's plight can take the edge off the need to act.
- A journal can become a vehicle for complaining. Depending on how it is used, some group members have a tendency to write mostly about what upsets them. They focus on what is going wrong rather than on what is right and become almost obsessively critical of themselves and others. Rather than serving as a means to apply the best lessons of what was learned in group, the journal becomes an endless stream of complaints.
- Self-dialogue can become intellectual game playing rather than truly self-reflective. In a similar vein to the complaints just described, group members may act out their worst behaviors in their writing. Left unchecked and unsupervised, the journal deteriorates into an exercise of pompous self-absorption.

The key is to remember that any group activity or therapeutic adjunct can be useful, benign, or harmful depending on how it is introduced and applied. It is not enough simply to suggest that writing might be helpful and then leave it at that; these entries must be treated as an extension of the group process itself.

Homework

We could make a case that all effective counseling and therapeutic groups involve some form of "homework," or adjunct tasks that involve completing work that was started in the group sessions. No matter how engaging, interesting, dynamic, and powerful any group session might be, unless members are helped to apply the concepts and skills in their lives during the week, nothing much is likely to change. As such, between-session assignments are not so much optional as they are necessary to solidify any gains that have been made.

Homework has generally been related to beneficial therapeutic outcomes (Kazantsis, Deane, & Ronan, 2000), and many homework activities involve some kind of writing (Rosenthal, 2011). Homework assignments in behavior therapy often merely record or briefly describe some aspect of daily or weekly functioning. Many consider working on outside-group homework assignments to be the most important therapeutic process (Viers, 2007). Homework assignments give group members opportunities to practice new behaviors in real-life situations and to make any necessary modifications before continuing to experiment in the group. They help group members generalize what they learned in group to other aspects of life. Finally, such structures provide ways for group members to function autonomously so they do not remain dependent on the group setting for approval.

For Your Own Homework

Get together with a few partners, and each of you share some issue you are working on in your life right now. Collaborate with one another to declare some homework assignment that you can accomplish in the next week that helps you get closer to your ultimate goal. Make sure that what you agree to do is actually meaningful and important to you, not just concrete and specific (see Chapter 16). Common examples of what students might work on include confronting someone who has been giving them a hard time, initiating new relationships, following through on tasks that have been avoided, increasing intimacy in relationships, or initiating and following through on more healthful habits related to diet and exercise.

One mistake beginners often make is being too ambitious or unrealistic; so make sure you settle on an assignment that is realistic and attainable within 1 week.

Make a commitment to hold one another responsible for following through on your declarations.

If you want to increase the probability that you will accomplish what you say you want to do, make a *public* commitment to the whole group, saying what you will do, when and where you will do it, and what the consequences will be if you wimp out.

Below are some of the more common examples of homework as an adjunct structure to group work:

- *Interactive tasks* are those in which the group member agrees to do or say something to someone else: "Okay, so what I will try to do—I mean, what I *will* do—is approach Kevin and introduce myself. I will talk to him for at least 2 minutes."
- *A behavioral experiment* is a task in which a group member tries something new and then collects data from the result: [Group leader] "Elias, I know you are nervous about dating and believe that you don't know even where to begin, so I have an experiment for you. Go to a local café on this Friday or Saturday night, and scan the room for a couple that looks like they are on a date. Find a table close to them, and then eavesdrop on their conversation for about 1 hour. Remain inconspicuous and write down the basic things they talk about, and bring that into group next week. We will then see if these are topics that you can talk about."
- *Simulated tasks* are role-played interactive opportunities that take place outside of group: [Group leader] "Since you and Tim are both in the same health class, perhaps you could find the time to practice cuing each other."
- *Cognitive tasks* help the group member rehearse new ways of thinking in response to an event that may take place: "When my spouse yells at me for not cleaning the garage the way she believes that I should, I will tell myself, 'She's not being mean but only doing what she thinks is best.'"
- *Individual tasks* involve any assignment that helps a group member meet personally stated goals. These could include anything from performing meditative exercises and writing in a journal to completing a budget.
- *Metaphorical tasks* are designed to get clients outside their comfort zones. They don't necessarily logically flow from what was discussed but often are deliberately ambiguous and only slightly relevant to the presenting problem. In the tradition of Ericksonian interventions, members may be asked to do things that appear ridiculous or wacky; they don't have to make sense, since the client is asked to create the meaning. One example might be introduced as follows: "When you get home tonight, I want you to think

about everything we did in group today and everything you learned, and distill the essence into a single word. Write that word down on a small sheet of paper, and put it inside your pillow case. Whether you have a dream or not that you remember tonight, this word, this essence, will stay with you throughout the week. Take the paper and bury it somewhere that is special to you. Leave it there until the next full moon, when you will return to that exact spot and reflect on how you have changed since the last time you visited there."

There are limitless possibilities for what can be assigned or, better yet, what the group members can *choose* to do that helps them apply the new learning and skills. Nothing they learn in sessions will become part of them unless they find ways to use the skills in their lives. Some prominent therapists describe the things they ask clients to do (see Rosenthal, 2011), often designed to break them out of their normal routines and shake things up. These include asking a client to go on a quest in the desert to look for a particular tree, stand on the beach and watch the sunset between two spoons, plan a family party to celebrate the naming of a stuffed deer head, convene all the client's friends for support during trying times, build a box as a retreat from stress, and other pretty outlandish tasks that are all intended to encourage alternative coping strategies (Kottler & Carlson, 2009). The key with any homework assignment is that it must help members actually practice what they are talking about in groups, as well as hold them accountable for what they say they want most.

Questionnaires and Logs

There are ways more structured than journaling to systematically record reactions to group proceedings. One such method is questionnaires and logs that members complete at set times during the week. Calley (2007) outlined a solution-focused self-assessment designed to increase self-management skills after each group and expedite the group process. The outcome of this assignment was the promotion of group member empowerment by increasing focus on self-management.

One way to access unexpressed affect and dissatisfaction of group members is to have them complete brief questionnaires at the end of each group in which they describe their degree of satisfaction with the proceedings, as well as things they would have liked to have said or done. These questionnaires are then shared with the group leaders, providing immediate feedback on the group. They can help assess potential dropouts as well as encourage inhibited group members to express themselves more fully. Some researchers, such as Miller, Hubble, and Duncan (2008), have found that the best predictor of successful outcomes, in *any* form of therapy, is continually assessing how the client feels about the sessions. They advocate distributing brief questionnaires at the end of every session basically asking what worked and what didn't, and what the clients would like to do more or less of in the future.

Edelwich and Brodsky (1992) also describe a postgroup log as a means to help participants focus their attention on specific areas after each session. They suggest that, between meetings, participants address some of the following questions:

- What was the best part of the group for you?
- What changes have you made during this week?
- What things could you do differently?
- What unfinished business might you bring to the next session?

This type of writing assignment gives more structure and direction to the group process than does the more traditional open-ended journal.

Using Videos and Films

One unique adjunct structure is the use of audio or video recordings to help group members examine the impact of their own behavior. The camera does not lie, and videos of group behavior can provide immediate evidence of how one behaves in the group. Group members may be more likely to accept feedback, remain open to altering views about how they appear to others, and be more responsive to confrontation when they see themselves on video. Observing oneself on video provides a kind of information about one's behavior and interaction patterns that is not available through any other process. It allows group members to observe both verbal and nonverbal aspects of the way they present themselves. They are able to relive poignant or significant moments and yet reflect constructively (rather than critically) on what took place and what they might do differently in the future. Setting up this type of structure requires advance planning by the group leader. Some leaders routinely videotape their groups as a way to provide a review of the group for those who are absent. If this structure is already in place, the video of the group could be used by group members to review how they interact in a group setting.

Smokowski (2003) outlined a variety of ways advanced technology such as videotape and computer simulation can be used to enhance group work.

Video modeling is the practice of taping expert models demonstrating desired skills. These can be outside expert examples or group members modeling skills for one another in a live group. Group members can then watch the videos to learn effective ways of mastering the skills, such as social interactions or even how to take feedback effectively. Another variation is self-modeling, where the leader provides a group member with a video of that group member mastering a skill, such as confronting a boss. This video can be developed from role plays during the group. The group member then repeatedly watches the video of the successful interaction and, in doing so, models a new strategy for himself or herself. Computer simulations are more advanced forms of videotape behavioral rehearsal, since they add the dimension of active participation. Computer simulations require users to make decisions, and then they confront users with the consequences of those decisions. These types of adjunct structures may be a bit more difficult to set up and lack the intimacy of face-to-face interactions; yet they are interactive and can be tailored to the specific needs of each group member.

In addition to videotaping group members, another way to provide an adjunct structure is to use popular motion pictures to initiate theme-centered discussions on particular topics. Numerous authors have advocated how cinema therapy can provide therapeutic benefit (Lampropoulos, Kazantzis, & Deane, 2004; Sharp, Smith, & Cole, 2002; Wedding, Boyd, & Niemiec, 2010; Wedding & Niemiec, 2003). One of the advantages of using motion pictures is that movies are typically more available, familiar, and accessible, and they often represent easy, quick, and pleasurable activities for many group members. Furthermore, movies represent narratives that transmit the values and ideas of a culture and represent a popular and widespread method of communication and expression. As an adjunct to group treatment, movies can be seen as therapeutic metaphors that introduce group members to material that may be sensitive, be perceived as threatening, or present alternative viewpoints that might usually garner resistance in a group setting (Hesley & Hesley, 2001; Powell & Newgent, 2010).

Lampropoulos et al. (2004) compiled a list of movies that were rank-ordered by therapeutic value. Their top five recommended movies for treatment were *Ordinary People* (multigenerational issues, loss), *Philadelphia* (AIDS, prejudice), *The Great Santini* (father–son issues, abuse), *On Golden Pond* (aging and relationship issues), and *Trip to Bountiful* (age, ageism). The movies chosen for a group would be specifically tailored to the developmental level of the group members and/or to the specific concerns that the group leader wants to access (Powell, Newgent, & Lee, 2006). Adolescent groups, for example, might watch *Mean Creek, Good Will Hunting, The Breakfast Club, Thirteen,* or

Whale Rider; adult groups might view *Parenthood* or *Dad*; a men's group might watch *Into the Wild*; and a women's group might watch *Real Women Have Curves*. Groups exploring themes such as redemption, recognition, and resilience in the face of cultural and economic obstacles might watch *Searching for Sugarman*. Those working through emotional problems might watch *Silver Linings Playbook*. As you can see, there are many movies to choose from; the key is finding a developmental level or theme that relates to the group you are leading.

The dramatic visual stimuli of movies serve to awaken the intensity of emotional responses to issues that are related to group member concerns. With the shared experience of watching the film, participants are able to use it as a platform from which to spring into their own individual concerns. Furthermore, one of the mechanisms for therapeutic benefits is when group members gain insight through conscious identification with the movie characters.

It is also not uncommon for group members to spontaneously talk about a movie that most of the members have seen. For example, Jeffrey remembers an ongoing adult counseling group where, quite by coincidence, six of the nine members had gone to see a movie that had been released the preceding week. They were thus able to speak about their common experiences and their unique perceptions of what they observed, as well as how each one intended to apply the insights to his or her own life.

It is important to remember that the therapeutic viewing of movies is different from simply watching a movie for entertainment. Group members can be asked to focus on the analysis of movie characters, relationships, and behaviors. There are a variety of recommendations for working with movies in a therapeutic setting (Hesley & Hesley, 2001; Norcross et al., 2003; Schulenberg, 2003; Wedding et al., 2010). Here are some basic guidelines:

1. Consider who is and is not a good candidate for the therapeutic use of films.

2. Choose the timing of the intervention and assign a movie that is appropriate for the group's concern.

3. Select movies that group members are familiar with and those recommended by other group leaders.

4. Look for movies that inspire and evoke emotions, show effective problem solving, and present appropriate role models; when possible, find movies with characters who have similar demographics, values, and lifestyles to those of your group members so they can relate.

5. Group leaders should view the movie before assigning it and then normalize the rationale for using a movie as an adjunct to group work. This can include explaining to the group members their expectations from watching the movie, guidance on what the members should look for in the movie, and then a heads-up on any scenes that may be offensive or problematic.

6. The leader should schedule a debriefing time for the group to explore their reactions to the movie, gather insights and benefits from it, explore any negative reactions, and connect the movie to the context of the group and the group members' lives.

Bibliotherapy and Printed Handouts

Bibliotherapy is defined as the therapeutic use of books (Jackson, 2001). Literature has a potential therapeutic effect because readers identify with the literary figures, project on them, and vicariously learn from them (Gladding, 2011a). Bibliotherapy has been known to be, over time, a reliable form of healing. In fact, many religious texts (e.g., the Bible, Tao te Ching, the Koran) have served as resources for guidance and relief (Lampropoulos & Spengler, 2005). Fiction and nonfiction bibliotherapy has been relied on as a successful therapeutic adjunct in group for some time (Dysart-Gale, 2008; Jackson, 2001; Norcross, 2006; Shechtman & Nir-Shfrir, 2008). Short stories, novels, plays, and even self-help books are routinely prescribed by group leaders to augment themes that arise in the course of treatment. In many ways, bibliotherapy shares and operates through the same healing processes as using movies. A benefit of using books is that the book can stand in for a group leader and always be present.

Like guidelines associated with using movies, the group leader needs to be thoughtful and specific when assigning a book to read. Two types of bibliotherapy are generally outlined in the scholarly literature: cognitive and affective (Shechtman & Nir-Shfrir, 2008). Cognitive bibliotherapy is mainly focused on self-help literature used as an intervention to increase self-understanding and problem solving. Literally thousands of self-help books are available, but only a select number are grounded in reliable research and proscribe sound methods (Norcross, 2006). Leaders need to have reviewed the books they recommend to understand the information being presented. One of the most common self-help books is David Burns's *Feeling Good*, though there are many others for any given concern.

Affective bibliotherapy focuses on the exploration of emotion and creating insight. As such, it tends to include more fiction, nonfiction, and poetry.

Memoirs and biographies are also useful books to suggest. For example, a group member struggling with aging and death may be directed to Mitch Albom's *Tuesdays With Morrie* (1997); group members exploring existential issues related to death and dying, illness, and choosing one's attitude in the face of tragedy could read *The Fault in Our Stars* by John Green (2012); a group member exploring women's issues might read Maya Angelou's *The Heart of a Woman* (1997); an adolescent struggling with difficulties related to growing up may be guided to Anne Frank's *The Diary of a Young Girl* (1952), J. D. Salinger's *Catcher in the Rye* (1994), or Stephen Chbosky's *The Perks of Being a Wallflower* (1999); *The Dog Stars* by Peter Heller (2012) can be used to explore issues of loneliness and connection to others; and *The Last Werewolf* by Glen Duncan (2011) can be helpful in focusing on existential issues related to personal and cultural identity. O'Neal (2006) outlined how to use multicultural resources and bibliotherapy to promote the need to identify and employ strengths central to various cultures. Rather than simply reading excerpts, this model looked at creating a guided discussion in the group setting after the reading.

For Reflection

Think about the books you have read that have been therapeutic to you. What did these books teach you? How did they inspire you or lead you to some personal insights? What was so memorable about these books? Now imagine you were going to suggest one of these books to an entire group or to one group member. How would you introduce the book? What guidelines would you give to the reader?

Every group leader has a series of standard mini-lectures that are routinely delivered to groups or specific group members when the need arises. They are sometimes introduced as teaching aids in skill training; more often, they are selected from the leader's repertoire when required. A group member who exhibits confusion between appropriate and inappropriate emotional responses could profit from a mini-lecture on the anatomy of emotions—how they are caused and how they may be altered to fit a situation's natural requirements. A group member who repeatedly speaks of catastrophic failures when expectations are not fulfilled might be exposed to an educational module on the distinction between wants and needs. Many other frequently repeated subjects require the therapist to deliver sermons from time to time.

To save time, minimize repetition, avoid turning a therapeutic group into a classroom, and ensure efficient quality control of crucial educational materials, the mini-lectures can be standardized as handouts for group members to read between sessions. Not only are group members gratified to leave each session with something tangible in their hands, but the handouts ensure that they will think in structured ways about the new ideas to which they have been exposed. Moreover, in many instances the written word carries more weight than the same message spoken aloud. Group members can digest written material at their own speed, mulling over stimulating areas, internalizing new ideas, and rereading confusing or novel passages.

The handouts also help solve the recurring problem of educating loved ones about the nature of the group experience. Most group members feel some frustration in dealing with friends and lovers who have a vested interest in the changes being initiated. Some spouses feel threatened by the increased effectiveness their partners demonstrate as a result of the group. Others may show plain curiosity and interest in progress that can be readily observed. They don't want to be left behind; some may genuinely wish to upgrade the quality of their lives as well, once they see how masterful the group member has become.

Handouts brought home can give everyone in the household a clear idea of what kinds of things the group covers. Loved ones can thus grow along with the group member as they are instructed in new learnings they find intriguing. A common language develops so that seeds planted in the group can begin to sprout in the interaction patterns at home. When the group member laughs at the "approval-seeking behavior" evident in a TV character, for example, family members will "understand where he is coming from."

The content of handouts can be tailored to fit the individual requirements of any group leader's philosophy and goals. Instead of always recommending readings from whoever your favorite theoreticians may be, personally created fare can be prescribed. Even those who regard writing as a chore will find that producing a series of handouts for captive audiences will not only improve their communication capacities but also raise their esteem among their group members. Although specific titles will be determined by individual preference and the unique demands of group members, here are some we find particularly useful with most groups.

- "How You Make Yourself Miserable": An overview of the most common psychological self-torture techniques. Profiles self-defeating behaviors such as worry, guilt, and fear of failure, emphasizing that most internal suffering is self-inflicted.
- "How to Get the Most From Group Experiences": Detailed instructions for capitalizing on the learning opportunities available in therapeutic groups (see the example on the next page.).

How to Get the Most Out of Group: A Worksheet

Please use the following sheet to guide you throughout your time in group. It should help give you some ideas about what you can talk about while in group, particularly if you're feeling stuck. If you're still feeling stuck after using this worksheet, feel free to set up an appointment for an individual discussion with the group leader.

- What I've learned about others/feedback options
- Feedback I'd like to ask for
- What am I learning about myself by how I behave in group?
- What am I noticing as happening in my relationships outside of group?
- What really moved in this session was . . .
- I feel very similar/different from which group members?
- How are relationships in group evolving/developing?
- Who do I make eye contact with? Who do I avoid making eye contact with?
- What members do I feel closest to? Why?
- How am I feeling about the leader?
- Am I able to abide by the group guidelines we agreed to? If not, let's try to understand this. What might be coming in the way of telling the emotionally significant story of my life, for example? Or what might be preventing me from taking my share of talking time?
- Remember that how people talk is as important as what they say. As you listen to others and as you think about what you have been saying, try to think beyond the words to the other messages being sent. Sometimes the meaning of our words doesn't match the tone of voice or the expression on our face.

- "Developing Communication Skills to Help Others": A rationale for learning to be a more effective communicator. Specific guidelines help readers improve their interpersonal skills.
- "Art of Confrontation": Applying knowledge of how groups function and of communication techniques to two very important situations: (1) A discussion of effective and ineffective confrontation styles shows the value of constructive feedback, and (2) readers are also shown how to assert themselves without threatening others and how to accept criticism without feeling attacked.

- "Take a Productive Risk": Motivates the reader to try new things enthusi-astically, experiment with creative behaviors, and become more socially expressive.
- "How to Get Closer to People You Love": Motivates the reader to take risks in relationships by becoming more open and sincere. The reader is helped to initiate more intensity in existing love relationships as well as to find new relationships.
- "Are You Still Alive?": An explanation of how people "kill" their valuable present moments by avoiding living intensely. Sleep is viewed as an exam-ple of practicing for death. Suggestions are offered for sleeping less and living more.
- "What to Do When You Feel Depressed, Frustrated, Anxious, or Angry": Examines the most common negative emotions that upset internal tran-quility—how these emotions arise, why they occur, and how they can be controlled or virtually eliminated.

There is no limit to the titles that could be reserved for use as needed—for further example, "Becoming More Assertive," "Disciplining Children by Teaching Self-Discipline," "Why There Is More Than Your Symptoms," "Moving Into Another Career," "A List of Books to Help You Grow," "Being More Creative," "How You Make Yourself Sick," and "What to Do After the Group Is Over."

Field Trips

Elementary school counselors and child and adolescent counselors have long known that the most important work they do is outside of their offices—on the playgrounds, in the sandboxes, on basketball courts, or during walks through the park.

Group leaders, too, sometimes discover the practical advantages of taking field trips with their group members to help them apply newly learned skills to real-life situations. Under the leaders' supervision and support, group members can receive structured practice, get constructive feedback, and encounter expe-riences similar to those they wish to master.

As a graduation exercise in a weight-loss group, all participants met for supper in an ice cream parlor. There they practiced self-restraint while ordering from the menu, slowed the pace of their eating, and still had a leisurely, delicious, healthful meal. The group leader was present to oversee the "therapeutic

Photo 15.1 Although group field trips are common in schools with young children (these kids from Nepal are dancing outside their school to express themselves), they may be structured in ways to help any group members build collaborative relationships and apply learned skills to their own lives. A group of counseling students visited this school with Jeffrey to learn more about advocacy and social justice issues.

experience," reminding members of concepts they had learned and the weight-loss techniques they had internalized.

A group of young adults working on debilitating shyness were escorted onto a dance floor by their group leader. As the group leader waited behind the scenes, gently prodding his charges to take social risks, the adolescents began to feel a bit more comfortable and less conspicuous. One young lady, rejected by a potential suitor, was quickly surrounded by assigned partners who helped her talk through her feelings and encouraged her to try again. The group leader offered valuable suggestions regarding approach techniques.

Twenty senior citizens, growing more and more dependent in their lives, consistently relied on others to do their bidding and complained of feeling increasingly useless. Group sessions focused on dependency issues, confidence building, and expanding their resources. Finally, they were sent unsupervised to the city's downtown area, each with only $3.50. Each senior had 6 hours for independent entertainment. They had to interpret bus routes and carefully budget the money so they could find meals and keep themselves productively occupied.

There are many possibilities for field trips. A group of unemployed adults can be taken on a tour of various industries, people with drinking problems might be taken to a bar to practice self-restraint, and so on. We like to end our group classes by conducting the last session on the beach, selecting a dramatic location that is likely to have the most impact in cementing their memories of the experience. Members sit in a tight circle within earshot of the crashing waves and then talk about what the group has meant to them and what they intend to do in the future to keep the momentum going. In all these field trips, participants are offered opportunities to move realistically and to apply the insights they have gleaned from their group sessions.

Review of What You Learned

- The goal of therapeutic adjuncts is to intensify any work done within the more traditional latitudes of group practice. Adjuncts support and expand group change mechanisms and provide more opportunities for group members to address their goals.
- Therapeutic writing and journaling are well-established adjuncts to group work. Since actual group time tends to be rather intense and active, time spent outside the group reflecting on the experience can provide insight and direction for group members. There are multiple formats for writing outside of group, which include traditional pen and paper as well as interactive e-journals.
- Homework and questionnaires/logs can be used to monitor progress, strengthen insights and gains from group, and provide useful feedback for group leaders.
- The use of videos, motion pictures, and reading materials (e.g., self-help, fiction) is a creative way to provide new avenues for group members to gain insight, self-reflect, and learn from outside models.
- There are endless other forms of adjunct structures that group leaders can tailor to the needs of the group or individual members.

Group Leadership Applied to Social Justice and Social Action

16

You certainly have your work cut out for you to help those group members within the setting in which you operate. There are more needy group members than you, or all the counselors and group leaders in the world, can possibly assist. Yet your training in group leadership also prepares and qualifies you to make a difference on a far larger scale than you can imagine. You not only have the opportunity to reach out to oppressed and marginalized people, improving their quality of life, but you also have an ethical responsibility to do so (Crethar & Winterowd, 2012; MacNair-Semands, 2007; Singh, Merchant, Skudrzyk, & Ingene, 2012). The codes of every helping profession specifically mandate that each of us has a responsibility to serve not only our own clients but also those who have been most marginalized, oppressed, and neglected, those who would never have the opportunity for mental health services unless we reached out to them.

This chapter talks about the responsibility of group leaders not only to promote constructive change in regard to privilege and oppression in their own groups (Singh & Salazar, 2014) but also to make a difference in the local community, as well as perhaps on a global scale (Kottler, Englar-Carlson, & Carlson, 2013). Many of the most prolific writers in the group work field—beginning with Alfred Adler's work with poor and marginalized families, and

Carl Rogers's commitment to promoting world peace—are devoted to promoting social change. This is, in fact, one of the most significant imperatives of the helping professions (Arredondo, Tovar-Blank, & Parham, 2008; Mays, 2000; Singh & Salazar, 2014). Building on creating social change, group leaders address issues of social justice in their group work, paying particular attention to the influences of both oppression and privilege that impact the health of individuals, groups, communities, and societies (Singh et al., 2012). But in a far clearer and simpler way, your training as a group leader prepares you to understand the dynamics of oppression and privilege, as well as to initiate and support systemic changes that are far more equitable.

Empowered to Make a Difference

Groups comprise myriad individuals drawn from all walks of life and cultural backgrounds. Social justice can be viewed as a dynamic process that occurs when people of different backgrounds come together (Chung & Bemak, 2012). Groups tend to mirror the biases and discrimination found in the greater society (Debiak, 2007). This means that the racism, sexism, and other prejudices your group members experience in their lives will most likely be re-created in other groups in the outside world. After all, group is a social microcosm of individuals of diverse backgrounds and interests (Chen, Kakkad, & Balzano, 2008), and their lives and sociopolitical realities will be present in your groups. Social justice group work is focused on inequities, advocacy, and empowerment strategies for group members of historically marginalized and oppressed populations (Singh & Salazar, 2014). As group leaders, you have continuous opportunities to address issues of prejudice and discrimination as they arise in your groups. When a member uses language disrespectful to others, you can intervene. When you observe someone being devalued, you can draw that person out. When an individual issue is brought up that has larger implications for those who are oppressed, you can make that point clear. When conversations arise related to group members' feeling devalued, links can be made to larger social issues. The main point isn't to hijack or distract the focus from group personal issues but, rather, to help group members realize the ways they sometimes represent larger cultural concerns, and that forces within a group can act in empowering and disempowering ways (Ratts, Anthony, & Santos, 2010; Singh & Salazar, 2014). All your group facilitation skills can be applied to making sure everyone in your groups feels heard, understood, and valued.

Rather than merely hearing about a marginalizing past experience that happened outside the group, group leaders can draw deliberate attention to transform racist, sexist, classist, and other discriminatory dynamics in the group when they occur. This requires intentionality in our interventions to facilitate healing experiences within the group, rather than sitting back and allowing hurtful interactions to perpetuate and repeat. For group leaders, working in this manner means challenging group members to expand their own understanding of culture while advocating for and empowering others to stand up to harmful interactions and experiences (Burnes & Ross, 2010). In one sense, helping group members confront one another about perceived hurts and injustices within the group prepares them to take such action in their outside lives, where it matters most.

For example, during one group session that had reached the working stage, with a fair degree of cohesion and trust, members felt progressively comfortable with one another, sometimes teasing or joking in spontaneous ways.

"You are just so gay when you talk like that," Alan said to Carlos with a hearty laugh. "You just take all this stuff *way* too seriously. What's the big deal if your parents don't accept you? Just screw 'em. That's what I've done with my family."

However well intended this confrontation and suggestion might have been, Carlos was horrified. First of all, he actually *was* gay and had come out in the group. This had been a risk and he had felt vulnerable even though other group members expressed and showed support. Second, his family members were Mexican immigrants, with all the accompanying traditional expectations related to respect for parents and abiding by their wishes and values. Alan's remark had clearly wounded him, as it triggered the many microaggressions he regularly experienced, and it happened in a space he had perceived as safe. He was additionally shocked that other group members did not immediately support him and speak up. This, too, was something he was used to happening outside of group, but he expected better in the group. Carlos began to respond, but then he visibly retreated, moving his chair back from the circle.

This interaction provided an excellent opportunity for the leader not only to process this conflict between the two members but also to talk about the ways insensitivity and impulsive humor can be hurtful and disrespectful to others. And the group did just that in a conversation about power and privilege associated with heteronormativity, and White privilege associated with assuming everyone's families have the same values and expectations. Alan was apologetic and sincerely open to feedback. He liked Carlos and wanted to repair their connection. The group also examined the group process underlying why no one had stood up and denounced the statement but instead had just watched. The group looked at bystander phenomenon, and Carlos was able to talk about what he would have liked from other group members then, and also what he would like in the future. Though intense, this was a powerful group session.

Of course, being a social justice–focused group leader takes additional personal work and effort to provide culturally competent services, as well as to work through one's own biases, prejudices, and cultural assumptions (Fernando & Herlihy, 2010). Singh and Salazar (2014) noted that a social justice perspective in group work requires an ongoing process of exploring how one's own values and cultural worldview influence group members, groups, and larger communities, so that oppressed and marginalized groups can gain access to modes of self-improvement. As group leaders learn to become more sensitive and aware of group members' sensitivities and culturally charged group dynamics, they can be more intentional in facilitating social justice interventions (Ratts et al., 2010). Even more than that, this greater awareness makes each of us far more sensitive to and mindful of the ways we might tolerate or even perpetuate microaggressions in daily life that lead to continued oppression (Sue, 2010).

For Reflection

How aware are you of microaggressions you see? What do you do when you observe microaggressions? Do you say something? Designate an afternoon where you plan to be around plenty of people. Keep track of how many instances of microaggression, or potential microaggression, you encounter, either interpersonally or just around you. Take particular notice of how people respond. Do others stand up, do nothing, or walk away?

Social Justice in Group Leadership

Social justice is often used to describe altruistic efforts in some capacity or another, such as advocating on behalf of those without a voice or for greater equality. Yet, more broadly, it can be viewed as a way of being, a way of walking through the world or daily life fully committed to practicing what we preach toward our clients. This means accessing our compassion and caring, tapping into our respect for others' dignity, and speaking up for those who can't—or won't—defend themselves. One reason why the wealthy become richer and those on the lowest end of the economic ladder become poorer is that we don't take definitive actions to correct this injustice. One reason why racism, gender bias, ageism, homophobia, and prejudice continue to exist is that they aren't more directly challenged whenever they arise. And one reason why inequities still exist is that often those who most need help never have the opportunity to seek such support due to structural barriers (time, cost, transportation, etc.). As multifaceted and broadly applied as the term might be, social justice generally can be described as involving some of the following characteristics or actions (Chung & Bemak, 2012; Lewis, 2011; Ratts, 2009; Singh & Salazar, 2014):

1. *Challenging systemic inequities within an organization or community.* This involves first recognizing that some individuals or groups are marginalized in some way, and then doing something to change the status quo. Specifically, concepts of privilege and oppression are examined and deconstructed. Social justice group work acknowledges that the notion of meritocracy (e.g., those who work the hardest get the most rewards) is simply a myth. Social justice perspectives highlight how systems of privilege and oppression create opportunities for some individuals, groups, and communities, and not for others.

2. *Transforming social institutions.* Once inequities are identified, steps are taken to change the ways schools, agencies, government departments, and other organizations operate.

3. *Inviting fuller access to resources and full participation on the part of excluded people.* Again, this involves constructive action (rather than mere talk) to advocate on behalf of those without equal rights because of their race, age, religion, gender, disability, sexual orientation, education, socioeconomic status, or group membership.

4. *Bringing attention to issues of oppression, prejudice, and social inequities within an organization or community.*

5. *Combating racism, prejudice, homophobia, ageism, and sexism as it is witnessed, and speaking out and taking action in the face of injustices and oppression.* This elevates multicultural competence for group leaders in having the ability to recognize and act in culturally appropriate ways. Multicultural competency is the foundation for effective social justice work in groups (Singh & Salazar, 2014).

6. *Advocating on behalf of human rights*, especially among those who have minority status or who have been historically denied privileges afforded to those of the majority.

7. *Empowering those who have historically been without a voice.* This may involve personal self-sacrifice, as well as surrendering some of your own privileges and advantages.

8. *Volunteering time and devoting personal resources to make a difference among those most in need.* Whether this is with people who are homeless in your own community or with those who are most at risk across the nation or abroad, you can develop and implement strategies for making a difference in the lives of those who need it the most.

When you combine all the dimensions above, what emerges is a vision of social justice in which professionals in a variety of fields act as advocates, activists, and leaders in the cause of promoting human freedom and equality (Chung & Bemak, 2012). Regardless of where you end up working, and what you end up doing for a living, you will have countless opportunities to stand up for the rights of others. Of course, in a group setting, you will constantly see inequity unfold before you as it becomes clear who has a voice in the group and who does not. Some of that could be chalked up to individual differences, but it is often the case that traditional inequalities play out along the lines of race, class, gender, and sexual orientation. Those holding privilege and power in society tend to enact these dynamics by talking more often and ensuring that their needs are placed high on the group's agenda; likewise, those with less privilege and voice tend to remain in the background. A good guiding question for exploring this in the group is, "Who can say what to whom?" This is where the social justice–minded group leader can intervene to change traditional power dynamics and move toward advocacy, egalitarianism, and empowerment (Singh & Salazar, 2014). In this sense, the group setting becomes a medium for healing cultural divisions and contributing to the creation of a more just society.

Group leaders can also create empowerment groups that specifically focus on group members' networking and helping one another with the process of advocacy. These types of groups promote dialogue and garner support among members. Miley, O'Melia, and DuBois (2012) noted that empowerment groups are useful in moving beyond the sharing of experiences and catharsis to an action stage of helping members learn to think, talk, and behave in a manner that builds up group members' self-efficacy around correcting social injustice and inequity. These groups can also help create collaborative social actions and movements so people can work together to create social change. Other groups with a specific social justice focus have been enacted in post-disaster settings (Bemak & Chung, 2014), with immigrant children in schools (Chen, Budianto, & Wong, 2010), with young mothers experiencing homelessness (Coker, Meyer, Smith, & Price, 2010), with unemployed adults (Bhat, 2010), and with transgender clients (dickey & Loewy, 2010).

Beyond your own groups, for those of you who are more ambitious in this enterprise, there are limitless possibilities for you to visit places where oppression, poverty, and injustice are the norm. In these settings, you can use group methods and structures to support social justice actions. Becoming actively involved in social justice projects not only creates new opportunities to be of service to others but also promotes personal and professional growth on many levels. For example, one group of students spent multiple weekends working and staying in a homeless shelter on Skid Row. Not only can such actions make a difference to those who are most marginalized and would never have the opportunity to seek counseling, but they also represent the most transformative experiences for the volunteers—perhaps the most memorable event in their training because it requires such a high degree of commitment and sparks such high levels of emotional arousal.

A Point and Counterpoint

There are some who feel that group leaders have no place being involved in social action movements. "There is a danger here," some might say, "of political editorializing and promoting one's own agenda." This perspective is referring, of course, to the supposed credo of the helping professions to remain value neutral in practice.

Whereas, in theory, it is certainly important that group leaders honor, respect, and value people's different lifestyles and moral choices, we side with Doherty and Carroll (2007) and others who believe that our profession is suffering a crisis of confidence because of our reluctance to take moral stands for positions we know to be right—*and then to follow through on them with consistent, committed action* (Kottler et al., 2013). In the past, some helping professionals have hidden behind a stance of neutrality, holding that it is not really our job to try to change the community, or the world.

For Reflection or a Class Exercise

The point has been made that group leaders have an ethical and moral responsibility to advocate on behalf of those who have been oppressed and marginalized. Yet this position also compromises our supposed value-free neutrality. Argue both sides of this debate, taking the position that we must stand up for social justice issues in our work, as well as the counter-perspective that doing so can become distracting at best, and possibly self-indulgent.

Reflect on (or discuss) how a consensus might be reached that satisfies both positions.

It is one thing to avoid imposing our particular values on group members with regard to our personal preferences about lifestyle issues; it is quite another to avoid taking a stand on issues related to social injustice, poverty, racism, oppression, and discrimination. We would submit that with our unique training and qualifications, we have a responsibility to make things better not only for the group members in our groups but also for the larger community. Indeed, the ethical codes of our professions share this belief when they include sections on "public responsibility" (American Counseling Association, 2005); "respect for people's rights" and "concern for others' welfare" (American Psychological

Association, 2002); pursuit of "social change, particularly with and on behalf of vulnerable and oppressed individuals and groups of people," paying "particular attention to the needs and empowerment of people who are vulnerable, oppressed, and living in poverty" (National Association of Social Workers, 2008); and "community service" (American Association for Marriage and Family Therapy, 2012).

The Association for Specialists in Group Work's *Multicultural and Social Justice Competence Principles for Group Workers* (Singh et al., 2012) is unequivocal in positioning social justice work as one of the cornerstones of effective group leadership. In particular, this document emphasizes social justice advocacy, explores intervention strategies for leaders, links with other professional competency standards (e.g., work with spiritual and religious issues, transgender concerns, advocacy), and expands on the understanding around intersectionality of multiple identities.

In their book on ethical practice, Sommers-Flanagan and Sommers-Flanagan (2007) advocate that helpers must be more than moral and ethical in their work; they must also be virtuous in the sense that they hold altruism and compassion as their highest values. Brabender (2006) adds that the principle of justice also includes being sensitive to and aware of the particular needs in group for those subjected to oppression and inequity. This means that the choice to be a group leader involves not only doing our best to help the group members in our charge but also using our skills to make the world a better place (Kottler, 2001b). And don't get us wrong, we do believe that social justice work at the micro level (e.g., changing yourself and intervening in your groups) and macro level (e.g., community and worldwide projects) *can* change the world (see Kottler et al., 2013, for examples of domestic and international social justice group work).

For a Group Activity

In small teams, brainstorm all the ways group leadership training prepares you for promoting social action. Make a list of specific things that could be done to address those social issues that you feel are most significant.

You might justifiably wonder how you could possibly change the world. Just consider the ways training as a group leader prepares you for social action.

As an expert in conflict resolution, helping people from diverse backgrounds and identities respect different points of view, you can play a role in mediating disagreements between others. "We can begin to hear what's behind the struggles we encounter," write Dass and Gorman (1985, p. 167). "We're more skillful tacticians, nimbler on our toes, ready for conflict if necessary, but always alert to possibilities for reconciliation—not just an end to conflict but a greater harmony than when it all began" (p. 167).

With skills in effective confrontation, you can effectively challenge people who use racist, discriminatory, oppressive, or insensitive language, without sparking defensiveness. Say you hear a racist joke; rather than just letting it go, or offending others by giving a lecture, you attempt to lead a discussion about the deeper meaning of such ridicule. You follow guidelines that have been described as "diversity competencies" for group leaders, to eliminate biases, prejudices, oppression, and discriminatory practices (D'Andrea, 2014; Singh et al., 2012). Importantly, you can facilitate real interactions about tough or difficult issues in real time. These are often called "difficult dialogues" or "courageous conversations" (Singh & Salazar, 2014), where you can use group to address power and privilege dynamics and social injustices, whether or not the group has been intentionally planned with a specific social justice focus. The unique aspect is that many group members might normally shy away from these conversations or refrain from being truly honest, since it is rare to talk about these issues openly in greater society. But guess what? With your group process and leadership skills (knowledge of group dynamics, ability to distinguish content versus process, ability to help members listen to and hear one another, and skills to acknowledge and validate strong feelings that arise; Sue, Lin, Torino, Capodilupo, & Rivera, 2009), you can coordinate the activities of many people toward some common good and engage in these dialogues. You can help people be heard, group members can speak their truth, others can listen and validate, and before you know it you have created a powerful, impactful group setting. These conversations can take place on a one-time basis or may be ongoing, used in small and large group settings, and may be structured, semistructured, or unstructured. Whether part of a community organization to help people who are homeless, collect food for those who are starving, or work within your local parent–teacher organization, nobody is better qualified than a group leader to harness human resources and engage in respectful and transformative interactions.

As a professional with personal power and status, you can model for others a lifestyle devoted to service and doing good for others. Make no mistake: People are watching you very closely. The public is justifiably skeptical about whether helping professionals really mean what they say, really practice what they preach in their lives. Most group leaders and other helping professionals are able to model in their lives what they ask others to do. We would insist that it is our responsibility to be what we expect of those we wish to help. Of course, as you will see below, getting people involved in social welfare is also an effective therapeutic intervention.

With leadership skills, you are an excellent communicator and influencer of others. These verbal abilities can be used to persuade others to become more involved in altruistic causes. It is not only through leading by example that we can make the most significant difference; we are good talkers. We are highly skilled at convincing people to do things they know are good for them but are nevertheless reluctant to do. All our persuasive abilities can be employed to recruit the assistance of others to help us fight against injustices, against bigotry, and for other social causes.

The Role of Altruism

One of the therapeutic factors we've mentioned frequently within group work is the spirit of altruism—that is, becoming focused not just on one's own issues but also working in the best interests of others. Altruism represents benevolent, charitable actions that are not motivated by personal gain or the expectation of reciprocal favors (Post, 2007). This sort of selfless giving is done without major consideration for how it will pay off in the future and has long been considered a bit of a mystery by evolutionary theorists, who have struggled to make sense of why anyone would make personal sacrifices, give away their resources and time, or commit themselves to help others who are not their biological kin (Harman, 2011; Klein, 2014). It turns out that human beings are programmed to do not only what is best to perpetuate our own gene pool but also what is best for the community so we will all have a better chance of survival. That is why animals will sacrifice themselves to call out warnings about nearby predators. Likewise, it is one reason many of us are drawn to helping professions even though we are not compensated nearly as well as we might deserve.

In groups, you will see altruistic behavior occur in many ways; oftentimes, it is rather subtle. In a 12-step group, the role of sponsors and even those who volunteer to run the meetings are examples of how altruism is part of the format. In almost every session you lead, you will observe members putting themselves on the line, taking risks, and reaching out to others, not for personal gain but because they feel inspired to make a difference in others' lives.

Of course, altruism is not only about helping others, since there is almost always some personal benefit to those who extend themselves. In fact, contributing to social welfare has been viewed as a measure of good mental health (Carlson, Watts, & Maniacci, 2005). When people are really honest with themselves, they will often admit that they receive clear payoffs of a personal nature:

- They feel as though their lives are redeemed; they are doing something that they think matters.
- They are giving their lives greater meaning. Many have left high-paying jobs because they felt empty.

- They are paying back what others have given them. They were wounded or hurt earlier in life and have recovered sufficiently to want to ease others' suffering.
- They are following a spiritual path. This can be either self-serving (a ticket to heaven) or a result of divine inspiration.
- They are developing new areas of expertise and gaining valuable experience. This can range from beefing up one's résumé to developing skills that will be useful in the future.
- They are hiding from things they wish to avoid. Helping others is a good distraction from dealing with issues that may be painful or problems that feel overwhelming.
- They can feel like martyrs, making sacrifices and suffering deprivations, all for the greater good.
- They are feeling useful. One's sense of self-worth and importance can be directly related to one's perceived impact on others.

For Reflection

It is often reported that helping others also transforms your own life for the better. People frequently devote their lives to service, purely for intrinsic satisfaction. Think of a time in the past few years when you have devoted significant time and energy to helping someone (or many others), often making sacrifices as a result. What was the outcome for you? How did that experience affect you?

Expand Your Vision: Social Justice on the Global Stage

We have talked about social justice group work in the groups we commonly lead, but there are other ways to blend social justice principles and group by getting outside of traditional group settings and structures. For those who are thus interested and motivated, there are many opportunities to use your group leadership training to promote social justice on a community and global scale. As much of a need as there is to address issues of poverty, discrimination, and prejudice in developed countries, in other parts of the world, people live on less than a dollar a day. They are literally starving to death. They have no access to clean water. Girls and women have few rights. Minority groups are not just oppressed but murdered. People have no access to education or health care. Most of all, they feel forgotten.

Many organizations offer volunteers (especially those with training) opportunities to work on social justice and service projects abroad—think Peace Corps, Habitat for Humanity, and similar movements. Likewise, literally thousands of groups provide so-called volunteer vacations, in which you can combine adventure activities with relatively short-term service projects (see McMillon, Cutchins, & Geissinger, 2012). Yet there are also limitless ways you can initiate projects on your own.

Throughout our travels doing training in group leadership around the world, we have seen students taking time off from school to work on behalf of a project they find meaningful. Often, their work is not part of any organized effort—they just showed up somewhere and made themselves useful. There was one young Norwegian woman, Marie, who had just graduated from high school and decided to take a "gap year" before university. This is a common practice among young people in Europe, Israel, Australia, and other countries, during which they spend a year traveling or volunteering before continuing their education. Marie had been traveling throughout the Himalayan region when she ended up in a very remote village that had tremendous need for someone who could work with the children to improve their English skills. Even though English was her third language and she did not feel that proficient, Marie decided to spend a year working in the schools and developing support groups. Even more remarkable, Marie was 19 years old and completely on her own. After meeting her and watching her work, we could no longer imagine any possible excuse why someone who is sufficiently motivated cannot find a place in the world to make a difference.

Social Justice in Action: Several Case Examples

We found ourselves in the most difficult environment imaginable to undertake a project promoting social justice among the most marginalized people on Earth. Nepal is a country known primarily as a tourist destination for trekkers and climbers who flock to the Himalayas, but it is also a place with some of the worst health care, lowest life expectancies, and most impoverished standards of living. The average income is about $300 per year. There are only a few dozen mental health professionals in the whole country, and that is with a population of close to 30 million people.

The families are so poor that they often cannot afford to feed all their children; difficult decisions must be made. In a culture where women have few rights and girls are considered a drain on the resources, females are often forced into early marriage if they are lucky; if they are not so fortunate, they end up sold into sex slavery. Thousands of girls are sold each year, some as young as 10 years old. An estimate of more than 100,000 Nepali girls and women are currently being held captive in brothels.

Each year for the past 13 years, Jeffrey has taken teams of students, faculty, educators, and health professionals to Nepal to volunteer their time and initiate a social justice project designed to keep girls in school by providing scholarships, support, and mentorship. In 2000, when we first visited a village, we started out with one girl in our program. We are now supporting more than 300 girls in a dozen villages around the country, all without a paid staff or even an office (www.empowernepaligirls.org). Several students, all of whom had completed training in their group leadership course, volunteered to work with the children—consulting in the local schools, raising money for scholarships, and mentoring the girls. They used their background to teach active listening skills to the teachers in the local schools. They met with the children in informal groups to inspire them about possibilities for the future.

As is so often the case, the students' altruistic efforts paid off for them in ways they could never have anticipated. This study of reciprocal effects that occur during social justice projects—that is, the ways helpers are transformed by their efforts—has been described (Kottler & Marriner, 2009), but we would also like to share some of the experiences of the group leadership students who volunteered their time to travel to Nepal with the team.

Photo 16.1 This career conference brought together all the scholarship girls across Nepal who are supported by Empower Nepali Girls. In addition to workshops, experiential groups were facilitated to connect the girls so they could support one another and learn about the range of experiences encountered.

An elementary school teacher working on her graduate degree in family therapy wrote this in her journal after visiting one of the villages:

> I am inspired and empowered by these brave men, women, and children that I met. I am motivated beyond words to help these noble souls reach their goals of providing quality education to their students. We are so privileged here in America and we have such excesses in material items, I think we can share a little to help others to reach their dreams.
>
> Each person I met reaffirmed my belief in the strength and inherent goodness in humans. I had the privilege of teaching in a variety of classrooms while visiting the schools. As I stood in the front of the classroom, I could feel the teacher watching me, reading me, and I knew that inside we were the same. They understood this as well and strong bonds developed between us in a short time. As I taught these beautiful Nepalese children I felt transformed and renewed, just as I feel when I teach in America. I felt like we are all connected. I have always believed that, but that day teaching fifth grade I GOT IT! I understood on a complete physical, emotional, and intellectual level—it was huge!

This student is describing what it feels like to *know* you've made a difference. For those of us who live and work within middle-class America, we take for granted the privileges and opportunities we enjoy. Our group members, however much they are suffering, are often experiencing adjustment difficulties that are the result of meaninglessness in their lives, frustrations at work or with their families, or self-inflicted problems from addiction and overindulgence. Most of the children who attend this student's class in the United States are first-generation immigrants and nonnative speakers, who certainly struggle with a number of issues. But they have food to eat, have a home to sleep in, and don't live in fear of starvation or enslavement. As important as her work as a teacher has been, she had a breakthrough volunteering in Nepal. She has since returned several more times to continue her efforts.

Another student, Christine, also had a powerful experience during her stint as a volunteer. She had never traveled abroad before, much less encountered the challenges of life in the Third World. Some of the places we visited presented hardships that were overwhelming; yet it was precisely that stimulation that influenced Christine in ways that years of therapy could never have touched:

> I am still searching for a way to accurately describe what it was like to watch the young girls receive their scholarships. When it was my turn to give away one of the scholarships, I cried. The little girl was so proud, yet so overcome with all the

attention. She kept hiding her face in her hands, then smiling, then looking away from me. I felt such a connection to her at that moment that it brought me to tears; she seemed overwhelmed with the ceremony, and in that space I think I knew how she felt.

At that time, I was still adjusting to everything about the country: the people, the language, the food, the time change . . . everything. I was on complete sensory overload at that point. It was that little girl's reaction that snapped me out of some serious culture shock. I could immediately relate to how she acted and felt. In a place so foreign, her reaction was so familiar that it just grounded me. For the first time in my life, I really got a sense of the universality of feelings and emotions.

Christine is describing one of the common outcomes described by those who serve others in cultures different from their own. While this can easily occur within your own community, the more novel the environment, the more likely that you will experience lasting changes from a travel immersion experience (Kottler, 1997, 2001b; Wilson & Harris, 2006).

Ali, a senior psychology student with plans to continue into graduate school, reflected on her experiences several weeks after returning from her adventures abroad. She noted,

After being home for a while, there has not been one day that I haven't thought about Nepal. It seems that everything I experience and learn now is different because Nepal is always in the back of my mind. I feel like I know something more, like I'm in on a secret. Now, it is only a memory. I have so many mixed emotions about that. Some of the time, I cry just thinking about it, because when I was there I felt more alive than I had ever felt before, and it's tough to not have that light anymore. Other times, I smile and experience an overwhelming feeling of happiness. I could not be more grateful for the moments that I had, for the things that took my breath away, and for the people that I met. I experienced the secret, and that was enough for me to never forget. When I experience these emotions, I think about my future. I either become very excited to go out and experience these things again in a new way, or I become upset because I don't believe I will have the chance to do so. What I am certain of for my life right now in this moment is that I have gone through something extremely special. My mind has been opened so big that it can never go back to the way it was.

As illustrated in these student narratives, social justice efforts not only help others who are in great need but also affect the helpers in positive ways, especially if they search for opportunities to expand their tolerance for new experiences. We have mentioned that there is altogether too much talk in our journals, books, and conferences about the importance of social justice and advocacy as part of our professional roles as group leaders, but precious little sustained action. In *Helping Beyond the 50-Minute Hour* (Kottler et al., 2013) we collected the stories of several dozen practitioners who launched projects in their communities or in far-flung regions. In each case, the effort began with one small gesture that grew into something bigger and far more sustainable. These were collaborative efforts through which faculty, students, and practitioners worked together to use their skills to help individuals who were survivors of trauma, poverty, neglect, or catastrophe (see Kottler et al., 2013, for all the stories). Most of the stories involve some type of group work intervention.

As just a few examples, some students described how they got involved in projects while in graduate school, whether working in an orphanage in Ghana or social service organizations in Ecuador. Professionals Fred Bemak and Rita Chung launched an organization called Counseling Across Borders, through which they recruit students to work in parts of the world suffering from natural disasters. They are ready to go at a moment's notice to communities ravaged by natural and man-made disasters. Selma de Leon-Yznaga started a community project to mentor and help immigrant women living in poverty in a Texas border town. Cirecie West-Olatunji worked with students to help survivors of floods in New Orleans. Jamila Codrington and Chante DeLoach each began separate projects to assist with Haiti relief efforts after the hurricane there. Sharon Bethea works with inner-city youth as a volunteer. Loretta Pyles works with issues of domestic violence and to empower female survivors to community-organize around their needs and others in similar circumstances. Father Stan Bosch and Joseph Cervantes work in South Central Los Angeles with at-risk boys and girls who have been targeted by gangs in the community. In each case, these group leaders and so many others devote their time and energy to assist those who would never seek help on their own—and they do so not only to make a difference for others but also to help themselves grow and learn.

I (Jeffrey) just returned from a weekend working on Skid Row in Downtown Los Angeles with a group of students, and I am still reeling from the experience, still trying to recover from the trauma of seeing so many thousands of mentally ill and/or drug-addicted people lying on the streets. We slept on the roof of the homeless shelter together and spent most of the night talking about all the reactions that were triggered by the work. In the span of a few days, we saw numerous drug deals going down, crack pipes being lit up, sexual favors being performed for as little as $5 to buy more drugs, gang violence, and predators and prey everywhere. We were there to serve food, but, perhaps not surprisingly, what seemed to make the biggest difference during our visit was engaging residents of the shelter to share their stories, inviting them to talk about their struggles and also their resources. Equally powerful were the stories that group volunteers shared among themselves, building cohesion and intimacy within a few days that could never have happened in a classroom. Curtis, one first-semester counseling student, talks in the next Student Voice box about the breakthrough that occurred for him.

Student Voice

It is hard to explain, but there is something about doing something novel and making a difference in the lives of others with a group of people that made me feel a deeper connection to the group. I guess I felt more comfortable sharing the emotions I was experiencing with other group members because I am sure they were experiencing similar emotions. I think the novel experience and the group context allowed me to become more vulnerable in sharing my emotions. I remember when I was serving food to some of the homeless residents I could feel myself starting to cry, which is rare for me. In that moment I felt the need to share what I was experiencing and was comfortable sharing it with one of my classmates, not because I was close with him but because he was part of the group experiencing the same things.

Working together as a group also allowed me to connect with others on a much deeper level, which was totally unexpected. This one other classmate and I stayed up talking all night, after everyone else fell asleep. We were in our sleeping bags next to each other on the rooftop of a mission in Skid Row. It was wet and cold outside and we could hear all kinds of brutal arguments coming from the streets. People were fighting, drinking, getting high. Mentally ill people were howling. Yet when I was talking to this other guy through the night I didn't feel fear or discomfort; it was only after he fell asleep that I even became aware of what was really going on around me. It seems that no matter how bad things may feel for an individual, knowing that someone else is going through the same thing mitigates those feelings.

Impromptu group experiences evolved with some of the residents of the homeless shelter, in connection with our support and caring guidance. One resident hadn't seen his daughter in 30 years—since she was an infant—and reached out to her with the support of the group. Another resident joined the group to talk about the tragedies of his life—gang membership, his daughter's murder, drug addiction, criminal enterprises—that led him to live on the streets. Police officers shared with the group their own frustrations and sense of futility trying to keep the residents safe in spite of the political realities that handicap them, because so few care much about what happens to those who live in poverty.

Photo 16.2   These students spent multiple weekends volunteering and staying at a homeless shelter on Skid Row in Los Angeles. Throughout the weekend, they processed their experiences and reactions in small facilitated groups. These groups allowed the students to explore some of their own biases, fears, and expectations about their experiences. Over time, the support of the group helped the students voice future intentions for remaining involved in social action.

Because the students had some basic preparation in counseling and leadership skills, they were able not only to make a difference in this neglected community but also to deepen their own relationships. There's nothing like adversity to pull people together in mutual support and build cohesion and intimacy. One student, Tamy, describes what this felt like for her.

Student Voice

A group of us went together to work in a homeless shelter for the weekend. The best part of the experience for me was the bonding that took place between and among us. We all felt a similar curiosity and openness to the experience, as well as an understanding of the environment that we were in. There was a moment when we were distributing fruit to people on the street when I had forgotten to stay with my group. I believe the reason I went off on my own was that I knew the other group members were right behind me and looking out for me. I did not feel scared or alone, because they were there and we were taking care of one another. The process of the work seemed to have a natural flow, which did not require much communication other than instructions from the staff that worked at the shelter. There was this incredible cohesion and closeness between us, something that could only happen in circumstances like this when we have to work together as a team.

Even though we didn't get a chance to verbally process our experience until the end of the first day, I noticed that we were sharing our feelings transparently. One of the moments when it felt most empowering was when we were listening to the story of one of the homeless residents. Although we haven't had much training yet (we are just in our first semester), listening to the man's story seemed to be so validating for him, just as it was so powerful for us to hear and honor his story.

For a Group Activity

On your own, in collaboration with classmates, or organized by your instructor, spend a few days together (or an overnight!) volunteering to work with a marginalized group that would otherwise not seek mental health services. This could involve working in a shelter for people who are homeless or abused women, a service or outreach organization, or an advocacy group that represents those who are suffering or neglected. Focus on the group dynamics and processes that operate within the organization or agency, your group, and the client population you are serving. Make it a priority to spend time with your peers to talk about your reactions and feelings, as well as what you learned from the experience. Commit to making such volunteer experiences a priority throughout your developing career.

After completing the service trip to work with people who were homeless, we conducted a follow-up group to process the experience and give participants the opportunity to talk about how they integrated what they observed and learned. As you read in the voices of the students, while the field trip increased their commitment and motivation to work with marginalized groups, it also solidified their relationships with one another and built a more collaborative cohort among them.

Shoot for Bigger Goals

Most of us joined this profession because we desire to do the most good for the greatest number of people (among other reasons that are far more personal). As we've mentioned throughout this book, that's why we so love group work, because it is possible to help 10 or 20 times more clients in the same period of time. Also consider that someday you may attain a position of leadership as a supervisor, administrator, or instructor. Imagine now that every professional you help not only experiences improved quality of life but also improves the lives of future group members. Now imagine that you can organize the efforts of a whole organization or community toward some common good. Using your knowledge about the ways groups operate, your leadership skills, and persistence, you may be able to practice what Galston (1993) calls "cosmopolitan altruism," the kind of compassionate spirit that reaches out to the disadvantaged people who most need help.

For a Field Study

Identify in your community half a dozen individuals who have been successful in promoting social action causes or have engaged in altruistic pursuits that influence a large group of people. Consider those who volunteer their time to help the needy, as well as philanthropists, heads of charitable organizations, and social activists who address problems of poverty, racism, discrimination, child abuse, and similar causes.

Remember that, as a student, you have access to a wide assortment of people when you introduce yourself this way: "I'm a student doing research for a class, and I'd like to interview you for a few minutes." You may find that some people are difficult to reach, but you will be surprised at how many will make themselves available. Furthermore, many of them will be very open about their motives and activities.

Interview several people who are actively involved in social action causes. Find out how they see their roles as activists and what skills they view as most crucial to promoting their efforts. Talk to them about your own training as a group leader, and discuss ways you could adapt your preparation to include making a difference on a larger scale.

The Costs and Challenges of Social Justice Leadership

Thus far, we have been extolling the benefits and privileges of working with disadvantaged groups during service or advocacy projects. And, indeed, there is considerable research to support that those involved in altruistic efforts experience lower blood pressure, fewer health complaints, greater longevity, improved mental health, and increased life satisfaction (Brehony, 1999; Kottler, 2000, 2014; Kottler et al., 2013; Kottler & Marriner, 2009; Post, 2007, 2011). In addition, they enjoy what has been described as a kind of "helper's high," a boost in the endocrine system likened to what happens with endurance athletes when they extend themselves beyond their normal capacity.

As you've no doubt learned, informed consent refers to providing consumers of our services with the risks, as well as the rewards, of treatment—along with cautions regarding any potential negative side effects. With that in mind, we would be remiss if we didn't mention that advocacy and social justice projects also come with certain personal consequences—notably, that they take a bite out of our souls. However heroic and courageous such efforts might seem, they are incredibly difficult experiences that are often accompanied by a number of trials and tribulations, discomforts and annoyances. For instance, students who participated in the Skid Row project may tell stories about how rewarding, stimulating, and fun it was, but they are glossing over their complaints about sleeping outside in the cold and rain, not sleeping at all, and the utter terror they sometimes felt facing situations that were way outside their comfort zones. Indeed, this is some of the hardest work possible.

Curtis, a student who had just returned from working with people who are homeless, as part of a volunteer group, shared how it was precisely the discomforts and challenges that resulted in closer connections to others. But such growth did not come without certain costs, as he explained:

> I was very overwhelmed with negative emotions such as sadness, fear, worries, and helplessness. Sometimes I was just overwhelmed with the stench and filthiness of the environment, and I couldn't believe that people could actually survive there. I felt sad and helpless because I wished I could do more for these homeless people. When we were walking on the streets I also felt fear, especially after I had been warned not to make direct eye contact or it could be an invitation for trouble.

Those who are actively and continuously involved in group advocacy projects often pay a dear price for their altruistic efforts, in addition to the benefits they receive (Kottler et al., 2013). They sacrifice their time, resources, and money—all valuable commodities for those of us who are already struggling to pay off debts and earn a decent living. They often find themselves emotionally overwhelmed, flooded with feelings they can neither understand nor handle comfortably. They are subjected to difficult working environments and similar deprivations to those faced by the population they are assisting. Perhaps most disturbing of all, they see and experience aspects of human existence that are shielded from most people, except for what we see in movies and films. It is an altogether different experience to face the realities of poverty, neglect, abuse, and trauma in person, especially working with people who have lost all hope.

Since we are primarily focusing on group leadership, there are even greater burdens when you are the one responsible for the welfare, safety, and progress of those in your care, as well as for your team members. Although adversity may build cohesion and trust in a group, it can also tear a group apart. Team members are operating under difficult circumstances, often with very limited resources and in a challenging work environment. Given that people are often feeling exhausted, dispirited, frustrated, and discouraged by the limits of what can actually be accomplished (often much less than we would prefer), nerves are frayed and deep wounds can result. That is why it is so critical for team members to take care of one another and literally watch one another's backs. The good news is, with training and preparation as group leaders, you have precisely those skills and abilities needed to help any group function optimally.

Review of What You Learned

- There is an increasing need for multicultural-competent group leaders who are able to assess and act to address social justice issues.
- Group settings are unique in the helping professions in that the same discrimination and inequities present in the world will appear in the group. This provides an opportunity to intervene and advocate for marginalized group members to support meaningful change.
- Group leaders can challenge group members to expand their own understanding of cultural identity in advocating for and empowering others to stand up to harmful interactions and experiences in the group and in society.
- Promoting social justice as a leader or group member has the added effect of tapping into feelings of altruism. This can bolster one's mental health, as one feels more connected to the social welfare and making a difference in the world.
- Group leadership skills can be useful in promoting social action movements for the larger community.
- Although all professional organizations strongly encourage their members to become involved in social action, there is also a danger of imposing your values on others.
- Social justice projects can be undertaken on a small scale within your community or initiated in developing countries for yearlong (or lifetime) commitments. It isn't important what you do, as long as you do something to make the world a better place.

The End of Our Journey 17

Where to Go Next?

Throughout this book and semester, you have fully entered the world of groups and their tremendous potential to influence behavior and promote constructive changes on multiple levels. You have not only read and studied the basic theory but also applied the concepts to your life and work. You have learned the basic ideas, theories, models, skills, and interventions of group leadership, as well as those personal attributes that most empower effective, relational leadership that brings out the best in others. Of course, we also hope that this process has motivated you to seek out other group experiences as a group member and leader. After so many decades leading groups and supervising other group leaders, we are no longer surprised how much we learn about our craft, and about ourselves, as a result of almost every session. These are the gifts of our profession and the impetus to encourage our own growth and development as professionals and human beings.

You have surely observed that with our high degree of enthusiasm about this specialty, we find leading groups to be the most exciting aspect of our job. Every group is different and challenging in its own right. Every session pushes us to discover new and better ways to make a difference. Every group we lead, whether on our own or with each other as coleaders, offers us new and different opportunities to reflect on what it means to struggle with life's most difficult and interesting problems, most of which are universal. We love the structures of group experiences and, over time, have learned to embrace the inevitable uncertainty, complexity, energy, and chaos that so often leads to personal transformations that unfold right before our eyes.

Photo 17.1   Closing a group, or ending a book, is challenging, because the gains made and the skills learned are not likely to last without ongoing support. That is why it is so critical that you find and create ways to solidify any progress made and help members commit to making further progress in the future. In this closing exercise, participants are engaging in a ritual in which they declare future goals, as well as express gratitude to one another for what each has contributed and shared. The leader is asking each person to embed in his or her memory an image of this moment, always remembering that although the group sessions will end, the effects will last a lifetime.

The most challenging part of ending any learning experience, whether in a classroom, therapy session, or with a textbook such as this, is keeping the momentum going after the experience is done. You might sell your text, throw away your notes, and move on to the next academic challenge. So it is with group experiences; they end, and people move on with their lives. Though most people leave group work on an incredible high, they fall back into familiar patterns.

Often, the changes they made that once seemed so exciting fade over time. Joining another group might seem difficult because of the work involved to get to a working phase. Without ongoing support and tremendous commitment, what you have learned in this class and book will not last very long, unless you find ways to apply the concepts and skills and make them a part of you (Kottler, 2014). As we end our journey together, you are experiencing for yourself the ways the members of your class group are attempting to stabilize and remember new insights, and incorporate them into their lives. It is also a time for closure, to say goodbye. One thing that is so interesting about group modalities for change is that they never really end. The group lives inside you; you continue your dialogue with group members, your instructor, and with us for the rest of your life.

We are aware that this book was just an introduction to the subject of group leadership. You were certainly exposed to all the basics you will need to get started, but to truly master the skills, you will need lots of good practice and supervision. We would, therefore, like to close by offering you some final guidance on where to seek out new group experiences.

1. *As you gain more interest in the field of group leadership, read the good books in the field.* Ask instructors and supervisors you respect to recommend those books they feel are most significant and impactful, not just books about group leadership but also those about being an effective helper and individual. Also, dig into fictional books that explore characters engaged in a group process, especially those that feature therapeutic-type groups as part of the plotline, such as *Girls Gone Bad, Schopenhauer's Cure, Heartburn, She's Come Undone, Infinite Jest,* and *The Men's Club.*

2. *Go to the library (or Internet) and familiarize yourself with the major journals in group work.* As a beginner, you may initially feel overwhelmed by the jargon, research, and style of scholarly writing. As you gain more experience and training, you will find these journals to be an invaluable resource for finding answers to your most pressing questions. These journals will address the contemporary issues in the field and provide pragmatic ideas for groups you are leading. You may, for example, find yourself struggling with a particular group member manifesting symptoms of resistance or obstructiveness, and find helpful suggestions in the literature that will guide you. Or you may be feeling lost and confused about a particular group dynamic that seems to be operating, and discover alternative ways of viewing this phenomenon. Since confusion and uncertainty are so much a part of the leadership experience,

you had better become *very* familiar with resources you can consult on a regular basis.

3. *There is no substitute for getting experience in a group as a participant.* If you have not yet experienced a variety of groups as a member, it will be that much more difficult for you to understand what your group members are going through. Join a support group. Volunteer to be part of as many other groups as you can. During the years when we were in our own graduate programs, we attended support groups that proved to be among the most valuable learning experiences—in some cases, far more instructive than the formal classes.

4. *Attend professional conferences and watch some of the masters in action.* Most professional organizations in the helping professions sponsor annual conventions where you can attend demonstrations and programs in which master practitioners model their skills in action. If you are feeling very courageous, you can even volunteer to be a participant in the demonstration groups. These opportunities are often rare; so you will have to seek them out and take advantage of these group experiences.

5. *Start keeping a journal.* Get in the habit of thinking and writing critically about your own behavior in groups. Be forgiving of your mistakes, but learn from them.

6. *Get as much feedback as you can from peers and supervisors.* Whenever you find yourself in group situations in which you have experimented with new behaviors, discover the impact you made. People will often be polite and shade the truth, so do your best to get them to tell you things they liked least as well as best. Of course, this is predicated on the idea that you can be nondefensive in hearing feedback. If you can learn to take feedback for what it is worth, it will help you grow rapidly.

7. *Recruit mentors into your life to teach and model what you want to know.* Identify those individuals who have the skills and knowledge you want most. Study with them, volunteer to do research with them, or, even better, co-lead a group together. Do not be shy about this; seek out those who can teach you.

8. *Co-lead groups with as many different people as you can.* Make sure you take the time to schedule debriefing sessions so you have the opportunity to

learn from the experience. Select co-leaders strategically, inviting those who you think might be in the best position to teach you new approaches to helping, as well as those who will be supportive and helpful. It's also important that your choices consider those who would be reasonably compatible with your personality and style.

9. *Take more courses and attend group workshops.* Most universities offer an advanced group course, or even several of them. Professional organizations, both locally and nationally, sponsor advanced training opportunities as well. You can also look for 1-day workshops on group leadership to learn about a specific topic or population. Once you join these groups, you will get lots of mail and updates on trainings.

10. *Last but not least, be sure to have fun with this stuff.* In our humble opinion, there really is no other professional work as fulfilling and fun as leading groups. Even with your initial apprehensions and self-doubts, surely you can already appreciate that.

As we end this book and adventure, we want to say thank you for coming on the journey with us. As you go forward, remember to savor, enjoy, and, above all, trust the process.

Photo 17.2 It has been our pleasure to be with you throughout this book. Goodbye for now, but we do hope to meet you in the future.

References

Adams, G. (2005). The cultural grounding of personal relationship: Enemyship in North American and West African worlds. *Journal of Personality and Social Psychology, 88,* 948–968.

Agazarian, Y. M. (2011). A systems-centered approach for individual and group therapy. In S. P. Gantt & Y. Agazarian (Eds.), *Systems-centered therapy: Clinical practice with individuals, families, and groups* (pp. 1–34). London: Karnac.

Albom, M. (1997). *Tuesdays with Morrie: An old man, a young man, and life's greatest lesson.* New York: Doubleday.

Altman, N. (2013). Psychoanalytic therapy. In J. Frew & M. Spiegler (Eds.), *Contemporary psychotherapies for a diverse world* (Rev. ed., pp. 39–86). New York: Routledge.

American Association for Marriage and Family Therapy. (2012). *AAMFT code of ethics.* Washington, DC: Author.

American Counseling Association. (2005). *Code of ethics and standards of practice.* Alexandria, VA: Author.

American Group Psychotherapy Association. (2002). *AGPA and NRCGP guidelines for ethics.* Retrieved from http://www.agpa.org/group/ethicalguide.html

American Group Psychotherapy Association. (2007). *Practice guidelines for group psychotherapies.* New York: Author.

American Psychiatric Association. (2013). *Diagnostic and statistical manual of mental disorders* (5th ed.). Washington, DC: Author.

American Psychological Association. (2002). *Ethical principles of psychologists and code of conduct.* Washington, DC: Author.

American Psychological Association. (2003). Guidelines on multicultural education, training, research, practice, and organizational change for psychologists. *American Psychologist, 58,* 377–402.

Anderson, D. (2007). Multicultural group work: A force for developing and healing. *Journal for Specialists in Group Work, 32,* 224–244.

Angelou, M. (1997). *The heart of a woman.* New York: Bantam Books.

Appiah-Boateng, A., Evans, M. P., Zambrano, E., & Brooks, M. (2014). Cultural considerations in counseling men of color. In M. Englar-Carlson, M. Evans, & T. Duffey

(Eds.), *A counselor's guide to working with men* (pp. 135–158). Washington, DC: American Counseling Association.

Argyrakouli, E., & Zafiropoulou, M. (2007). Qualitative analysis of experiences of members of a psychoeducational assertiveness group. *Psychological Reports, 100*(2), 531–546.

Armstrong, K. (2011). *Twelve steps to a compassionate life.* New York: Knopf.

Arnd-Caddigan, M. (2012). The therapeutic alliance: Implications for therapeutic process and therapeutic goals. *Journal of Contemporary Psychotherapy, 42*(2), 77–85.

Arredondo, P., Tovar-Blank, Z., & Parham, T. (2008). Challenges and promises of becoming a culturally competent counselor in a sociopolitical era of change and empowerment. *Journal of Counseling and Development, 86,* 261–268.

Asnaani, A., & Hofmann, S. (2012). Collaboration in culturally responsive therapy: Establishing a strong therapeutic alliance across cultural lines. *Journal of Clinical Psychology, 68,* 187–197.

Association for Specialists in Group Work. (1998). *Principles for diversity-competent group workers.* Alexandria, VA: Author.

Association for Specialists in Group Work. (2000). *Professional standards for training of group workers.* Alexandria, VA: Author.

Association for Specialists in Group Work. (2012). *Multicultural and social justice competence principles for group workers.* Alexandria, VA: Author.

Atkinson, R., Hare, T., Merriman, M., & Vogel, A. (2009). Therapeutic benefits of expressive writing in an electronic format. *Nursing Administration Quarterly, 33*(3), 212–215.

Avdi, E., & Georgaca, E. (2007). Narrative research in psychotherapy: A critical review. *Psychology and Psychotherapy: Theory, Research and Practice, 80*(3), 407–419.

Baim, C., Burmeister, J., & Maciel, M. (2007). *Psychodrama: Advances in theory and practice.* New York: Routledge.

Baldwin, S., Wampold, B., & Imel, Z. (2007). Untangling the alliance-outcome correlation: Exploring the relative importance of therapist and patient variability in the alliance. *Journal of Consulting and Clinical Psychology, 75,* 842–852.

Bales, R. F. (1950). *Interaction process analysis: A method for the study of small groups.* Cambridge, MA: Addison-Wesley.

Bandura, A. (1969). *Principles of behavior modification.* New York: Holt, Rinehart, & Winston.

Barlow, S. H. (2012). An application of the competency model to group-specialty practice. *Professional Psychology: Research and Practice, 43,* 442–453.

Barlow, S. H. (2013). *Specialty competencies in group psychology.* New York: Oxford University Press.

Barlow, S. H. (2014). The history of group counseling and psychotherapy. In J. L. DeLucia-Waack, C. R. Kalodner, & M. T. Riva (Eds.), *Handbook of group counseling and psychotherapy* (2nd ed., pp. 3–23). Thousand Oaks, CA: Sage.

Barlow, S. H., Burlingame, G., & Fuhriman, A. (2000). Therapeutic application of groups: From Pratt's "thought control classes" to modern group psychotherapy. *Journal of Group Dynamics, 4,* 115–134.

Becvar, R. J., Canfield, B. S., & Becvar, D. S. (1997). *Group work: Cybernetic, constructivist, and social constructionist perspectives.* Denver, CO: Love.

Beebe, S. A., & Masterson, J. T. (2011). *Communication in small groups: Principles and practices* (10th ed.). Boston: Allyn & Bacon.

Behr, H. (2006). Secrecy and confidentiality in groups. *Group Analysis, 39*(3), 356–365.

Bemak, F., & Chung, R. C. (2014). Post-disaster group counseling: A multicultural perspective. In J. L. DeLucia-Waack, C. R. Kalodner, & M. T. Riva (Eds.), *Handbook of group counseling and psychotherapy* (2nd ed., pp. 571–584). Thousand Oaks, CA: Sage.

Bennis, W. G., & Shepard, H. A. (1956). A theory of group development. *Human Relations, 9,* 415–437.

Beres, L., & Nichols, M. (2010). Narrative therapy group interventions with men who have used abusive behaviors. *Families in Society: The Journal of Contemporary Social Services, 91*(1), 60–66.

Berg, R. C., Landreth, G. L., & Fall, K. A. (2012). *Group counseling: Concepts and procedures* (5th ed.). New York: Brunner-Routledge.

Bergsma, A. (2008). Do self-help books help? *Journal of Happiness Studies, 9*(3), 341–360.

Bernard, H., Burlingame, G., Flores, P., Greene, L., Joyce, A., Kobos, J. C., et al. (2008). Clinical practice guidelines for group psychotherapy. *International Journal of Group Psychotherapy, 58,* 455–542.

Berne, E. (1966). *Principles of group treatment.* New York: Oxford University Press.

Bhat, C. (2010). Assisting unemployed adults find suitable work: A group intervention embedded in community and grounded in social action. *Journal for Specialists in Group Work, 35,* 246–254.

Bieling, P. J., McCabe, R., & Antony, M. M. (2006). *Cognitive-behavioral therapy in groups.* New York: Guilford Press.

Bion, W. (1948). Experience in groups. *Human Relations, 1,* 314–329.

Bion, W. R. (1961). *Experiences in groups.* New York: Basic Books.

Bitter, J. R. (2013). *Theory and practice of family therapy and counseling* (2nd ed.). Belmont, CA: Brooks/Cole.

Blattner, J., & Bacigalupo, A. (2007). Using emotional intelligence to develop executive leadership and team and organizational development. *Consulting Psychology Journal: Practice and Research, 59,* 209–219.

Boutin, D. L. (2007). Effectiveness of cognitive-behavioral and supportive-expressive group therapy for women diagnosed with breast cancer: A review of the literature. *Journal for Specialists in Group Work, 32,* 267–284.

Brabender, V. (2006). The ethical group psychotherapist. *International Journal of Group Psychotherapy, 56,* 395–411.

Brabender, V. (2007). The ethical group psychotherapist: A coda. *International Journal of Group Psychotherapy, 57,* 41–47.

Brabender, V., & Fallon, A. (2009). *Group development in practice: Guidelines for clinicians and researchers.* Washington, DC: American Psychological Association.

Brabender, V., Fallon, A., & Smolar, A. (2004). *Essentials of group therapy.* New York: Wiley.

Brambilla, M., Sacchi, S., Rusconi, P., Cherubini, P., & Yzerbyt, V. Y. (2012). You want to give a good impression? Be honest! Moral traits dominate group impression formation. *British Journal of Social Psychology, 51*, 149–166.

Brazaitis, S. J. (2014). Group relations and conflict resolution. In P. Coleman, M. Deutsch, & E. Marcus (Eds.), *The handbook of conflict resolution: Theory and practice* (3rd ed., pp. 947–970). Hoboken, NJ: Wiley.

Breeskin, J. (2010). The co-therapist model in groups. *The Group Psychologist, 20*, 5–6.

Brehony, K. A. (1999). *Ordinary grace.* New York: Riverhead.

Brew, L., Cervantes, J. M., & Shepard, D. S. (2013). Millennial counselors and the ethical use of Facebook. *The Professional Counselor, 3*, 93–104.

Brew, L., & Kottler, J. (2008). *Applied helping skills: Transforming lives.* Thousand Oaks, CA: Sage.

Bridbord, K., & DeLucia-Waack, J. (2011). Personality, leadership style, and theoretical orientation as predictors of group co-leadership satisfaction. *Journal for Specialists in Group Work, 36*(3), 202–221.

Brinson, J. A., & Lee, C. (2005). Culturally responsive group leadership: An integrative model for experienced practitioners. *Counseling and Human Development, 38*(3), 1–8.

Brown, C., & Augusta-Scott, T. (Eds.). (2007). *Narrative therapy: Making meaning, making lives.* Thousand Oaks, CA: Sage.

Brown, L. (2010). *Feminist therapy.* Washington, DC: American Psychological Association.

Brown, N. W. (2003). Conceptualizing process. *International Journal of Group Psychotherapy, 53*, 225–243.

Brown, N. W. (2006). Reconceptualizing difficult members and difficult groups. *Journal of Contemporary Psychotherapy, 36*, 145–150.

Brown, N. W. (2008). Troubling silences in therapy groups. *Journal of Contemporary Psychotherapy, 38*(2), 81–85.

Brown, N. W. (2009). *Becoming a group leader.* Upper Saddle River, NJ: Pearson.

Brown, N. W. (2011). *Psychoeducational groups: Process and practice* (3rd ed.). New York: Routledge.

Bruneau, L., Bubenzer, D., & McGlothlin, J. (2010). Revisioning the self: A phenomenological investigation into self-help reading. *Journal of Humanistic Counseling, Education and Development, 49*(2), 217–230.

Bugental, J. F. T. (1978). *Psychotherapy and process: The fundamentals of an existential-humanistic approach.* Reading, MA: Addison-Wesley.

Bugental, J. F. T. (1990). *Intimate journeys: Stories from life-changing therapy.* San Francisco: Jossey-Bass.

Bunkers, S. (2013). Silence: A double-edged sword. *Nursing Science Quarterly, 26*(1), 7–11.

Burke, C., Lyons, R., DiazGranados, D., Goodwin, G., Salas, E., Klein, C., et al. (2009). Does team building work? *Small Group Research, 40*(2), 181–222.

Burlingame, G., Cox, J., Davies, D., Layne, C., & Gleave, R. (2011). The group selection questionnaire: Further refinements in group member selection. *Group Dynamics: Theory Research and Practice, 15*(1), 60–74.

Burlingame, G. M., Fuhriman, A., & Johnson, J. E. (2001). Cohesion in group psycho-therapy. *Psychotherapy: Theory, Research, Practice, Training, 38,* 373–379.

Burlingame, G. M., Fuhriman, A., & Johnson, J. E. (2011). Cohesion in group psycho-therapy. In J. C. Norcross (Ed.), *Psychotherapy relationships that work* (2nd ed., pp. 110–131). New York: Oxford University Press.

Burlingame, G. M., Fuhriman, A., & Mosier, J. (2003). The differential effectiveness of group psychotherapy: A meta-analytic perspective. *Group Dynamics: Theory, Research and Practice, 7,* 3–12.

Burlingame, G., & Krogel, J. (2005, October). Relative efficacy of individual versus group psychotherapy. *International Journal of Group Psychotherapy, 55,* 607–611.

Burlingame, G., McClendon, D. T., & Alonso, J. (2011a). Cohesion in group therapy. *Psychotherapy, 48,* 34–42.

Burlingame, G., McClendon, D. T., & Alonso, J. (2011b). Group therapy. In J. C. Norcross (Ed.), *Psychotherapy relationships that work* (2nd ed., pp. 110–131). New York: Oxford University Press.

Burlingame, G. M., Strauss, B., & Joyce, A. S. (2013). Change mechanisms and effective-ness of small group treatments. In M. Lambert (Ed.), *Bergin and Garfield's handbook of psychotherapy and behavior change* (6th ed., pp. 640–689). New York: Wiley.

Burlingame, G. M., Whitcomb, K., & Woodland, S. (2014). Process and outcome in group counseling and psychotherapy: A perspective. In J. L. DeLucia-Waack, C. R. Kalodner, & M. T. Riva (Eds.), *Handbook of group counseling and psychother-apy* (2nd ed., pp. 55–68). Thousand Oaks, CA: Sage.

Burnes, T., & Ross, K. (2010). Applying social justice to oppression and marginalization in group process: Interventions and strategies for group counselors. *Journal for Specialists in Group Work, 35,* 169–176.

Burns, G. (2001). *101 healing stories: Using metaphors in therapy.* New York: Wiley.

Burns, G. (2006). *Healing with stories: Your casebook collection for using therapeutic metaphor.* New York: Wiley.

Burton, C. M., & King, L. A. (2004). The health benefits of writing about intensely positive experiences. *Journal of Research in Personality, 38,* 150–163.

Buss, D. (2011). *Evolutionary psychology: The new science of the mind* (4th ed.). Boston: Allyn & Bacon.

Cain, D. (2010). *Person-centered theory.* Washington, DC: American Psychological Association.

Cain, D. (2013). Person-centered therapy. In J. Few & M. Spiegel (Eds.), *Contemporary psychotherapies for a diverse world* (Rev. ed., pp. 165–214). New York: Routledge.

Caldwell, L., Tarver, D., Iwamoto, D., Herzberg, S., Cerda-Lizarraga, P., & Mack, T. (2008). Definitions of multicultural competence: Frontline human service provid-ers' perspective. *Journal of Multicultural Counseling and Development, 36*(2), 88–10.

Calley, N. (2007). Behavioral scaling as a group-guided approach to self-management. In D. Viers (Ed.), *The group therapist's notebook: Homework, handouts, and activities for use in psychotherapy* (pp. 59–66). New York: Haworth Press.

Caplan, T. (2005). First impressions: Treatment considerations from first contact with a groupworker to first group experience. *Groupwork, 15*(3), 44–57.

Caplan, T. (2006). Seeing the forest for the trees: An integrated approach to formulating group work interventions. *Social Work With Groups, 29*(1), 63–77.

Capuzzi, D. (2010). *Introduction to group work* (5th ed.). Denver, CO: Love.

Carlson, J. D., & Englar-Carlson, M. (2013). Adlerian therapy. In J. Frew & M. Spiegler (Eds.), *Contemporary psychotherapies for a diverse world* (Rev. ed., pp. 87–130). New York: Routledge.

Carlson, J. D., Watts, R. E., & Maniacci, M. (2005). *Adlerian psychotherapy.* Washington, DC: American Psychological Association.

Carter, J. (2006). Theoretical pluralism and technical eclecticism. In C. D. Goodheart, A. E. Kazdin, & R. J. Sternberg (Eds.), *Evidence-based psychotherapy: Where practice and research meet* (pp. 63–79). Washington, DC: American Psychological Association.

Casas, J. M., Raley, J. D., & Vasquez, M. J. T. (2008). Adelante! Counseling the Latina/o from guiding theory to practice. In P. B. Pederson, J. G. Draguns, W. J. Lonner, & J. E. Trimble (Eds.), *Counseling across cultures* (6th ed., pp. 129–146). Thousand Oaks, CA: Sage.

Castronovo, V., Kuo, T., Giarolli, L., Anelli, M., Marelli, S., Zucconi, M., et al. (2011). Clinical outcomes of group cognitive behavioral therapy for insomnia (CBT-I). *Sleep Medicine, 12,* S96.

Cavell, T. A., & Malcolm, K. T. (Eds.). (2007). *Anger, aggression and interventions for interpersonal violence.* Mahwah, NJ: Lawrence Erlbaum.

Chan, K. M., & Horneffer, K. (2006). Emotional expression and psychological symptoms: A comparison of writing and drawing. *Arts in Psychotherapy, 33,* 26–36.

Chang, A., Duck, J., & Bordia, P. (2006). Understanding the multidimensionality of group development. *Small Group Research, 37,* 327–350.

Chang, T. (2005). Online counseling: Prioritizing psychoeducation, self-help, and mutual help for counseling psychology research and practice. *The Counseling Psychologist, 33,* 881–890.

Charles, J. (2010). Journaling: Creating space for "I." *Creative Nursing, 16*(4), 180–184.

Chbosky, S. (1999). *The perks of being a wallflower.* New York: MTV Books.

Chen, E., Budianto, L., & Wong, K. (2010). Professional school counselors as social justice advocates for undocumented immigrant students in group work. *Journal for Specialists in Group Work, 35,* 255–261.

Chen, E., Kakkad, D., & Balzano, J. (2008). Multicultural competence and evidence-based practice in group therapy. *Journal of Clinical Psychology, 64*(11), 1261–1278.

Cheung, S., & Sun, S. Y. (2001). Helping processes in mutual aid organization for persons with emotional disturbance. *International Journal of Group Psychotherapy, 51,* 295–308.

Christner, R. W., Stewart, J. L., & Freeman, A. (Eds.). (2007). *Handbook of cognitive-behavior group therapy with children and adolescents: Specific settings and presenting problems.* New York: Routledge.

Chung, R. C., & Bemak, F. (2012). *Social justice counseling: The next steps beyond multiculturalism.* Thousand Oaks, CA: Sage.

Chung, R. C., & Bemak, F. (2014). Group counseling with Asians. In J. L. DeLucia-Waack, C. R. Kalodner, & M. T. Riva (Eds.), *Handbook of group counseling and psychotherapy* (2nd ed., pp. 231–241). Thousand Oaks, CA: Sage.

Chung, Y., Yoon, K., Park, T., Yang, J., & Oh, K. (2013). Group cognitive-behavioral therapy for early psychosis. *Cognitive Therapy and Research, 37*(2), 403–411.

Clarkin, J. (2005). Differential therapeutics. In J. C. Norcross & M. R. Goldfried (Eds.), *Handbook of psychotherapy integration* (2nd ed., pp. 343–361). New York: Oxford University Press.

Cohen, B. D., Ettin, M. F., & Fidler, J. W. (2002). *Group psychotherapy and political reality: A two-way mirror.* Madison, CT: International Universities Press.

Cohen, M., & Fried, G. (2007). Comparing relaxation training and cognitive-behavioral group therapy for women with breast cancer. *Research on Social Work Practice, 17*(3), 313–323.

Cohen, M. B., & DeLois, K. (2001). Training in tandem: Co-facilitation and role modeling in a group work course. *Social Work With Groups, 24,* 21–36.

Cohn, J., & Ekman, P. (2005). Measuring facial action. The new handbook of methods in nonverbal behavior research. In J. A. Harrigan, R. Rosenthal, & K. Scherer (Eds.), *The new handbook of methods in nonverbal behavior research* (pp. 9–64). New York: Oxford University Press.

Coker, A., Meyer, D., Smith, R., & Price, A. (2010). Using social justice group work with young mothers who experience homelessness. *Journal for Specialists in Group Work, 35,* 220–229.

Comas-Díaz, L. (2006). Cultural variation in the therapeutic relationship. In C. D. Goodheart, A. E. Kazdin, & R. J. Sternberg (Eds.), *Evidence-based psychotherapy: Where practice and research meet* (pp. 81–105). Washington, DC: American Psychological Association.

Comstock, D. L., Duffey, T., & St. George, H. (2002). The relational-cultural model: A framework for group process. *Journal for Specialists in Group Work, 27,* 254–272.

Comstock, D. L., Hammer, T., Strentzsch, J., Cannon, K., Parsons, J., & Salazar, G. (2008). Relational-cultural theory: A framework for bridging relational, multicultural, and social justice competencies. *Journal of Counseling and Development, 86,* 279–287.

Connors, J., & Caple, R. (2005). A review of group systems theory. *Journal for Specialists in Group Work, 30,* 93–110.

Conyne, R. K. (1998). What to look for in groups: Helping trainees become more sensitive to multicultural issues. *Journal for Specialists in Group Work, 23,* 22–32.

Conyne, R. K., Crowell, J. L., & Newmeyer, M. D. (2008). *Group techniques: How to use them more purposefully.* Upper Saddle River, NJ: Pearson Education.

Cook, J., & Tedeschi, R. (2007). Systems of care and the integrative clinician: A look into the future of psychotherapy. *Journal of Psychotherapy Integration, 17*(2), 139–158.

Corey, G. (2013). *Theory and practice of group counseling* (9th ed.). Belmont, CA: Brooks/Cole.

Corey, G., Corey, M. S., Callanan, P., & Russell, J. (2015). *Group techniques* (4th ed.). Belmont, CA: Brooks/Cole.

Corey, G., Corey, M. S., Corey, C., & Callanan, P. (2015). *Issues and ethics in the helping professions* (9th ed.). Belmont, CA: Brooks/Cole.

Corey, G., Corey, M. S., & Haynes, R. (2000). *Evolution of a group: Student video and workbook.* Belmont, CA: Brooks/Cole.

Corey, M. S., Corey, G., & Corey, C. (2014). *Groups: Process and practice* (9th ed.). Belmont, CA: Brooks/Cole.

Cottone, R., & Tarvydas, V. M. (2006). *Counseling ethics and decision making* (3rd ed.). Upper Saddle River, NJ: Prentice Hall.

Cox, J., Burlingame, G. N., Davies, R., Gleave, R., & Barlow, S. (2004, February). *The group selection questionnaire: Further refinements in group member selection.* Paper presented at the annual meeting of the American Group Psychotherapy Association, New York.

Craske, M. (2010). *Cognitive-behavioral therapy.* Washington, DC: American Psychological Association.

Crethar, H., & Winterowd, C. (2012). Values and social justice in counseling. *Counseling and Values, 57*(1), 3–9.

Cummings, A. L. (2001). Teaching group process to counseling students through the exchange of journal letters. *Journal for Specialists in Group Work, 26*(1), 7–16.

D'Andrea, M. (2014). Understanding racial/cultural identity development theories to promote effective multicultural group counseling. In J. L. DeLucia-Waack, C. R. Kalodner, & M. T. Riva (Eds.), *Handbook of group counseling and psychotherapy* (2nd ed., pp. 196–208). Thousand Oaks, CA: Sage.

Dass, R., & Gorman, P. (1985). *How can I help?* New York: Knopf.

Davies, E. (2013). Warriors, authors and baseball coaches: The meaning of metaphor in theories of family therapy. *Journal of Family Therapy, 35*(1), 66–88.

Day, S. X. (2014). A unifying theory for group counseling and psychotherapy. In J. L. DeLucia-Waack, C. R. Kalodner, & M. T. Riva (Eds.), *Handbook of group counseling and psychotherapy* (2nd ed., pp. 24–33). Thousand Oaks, CA: Sage.

De Dreu, C. K. W., & Weingart, L. R. (2003). A contingency theory of task conflict and performance in groups and organizational teams. In M. A. West, D. Tjosvold, & K. G. Smith (Eds.), *International handbook of teamwork and cooperative working* (pp. 151–166). Chichester, UK: Wiley.

Debiak, D. (2007). Attending to diversity in group psychotherapy: An ethical imperative. *International Journal of Group Psychotherapy, 57*(1), 1–12.

DeChurch, L., Hamilton, K., & Haas, C. (2007). Effects of conflict management strategies on perceptions of intragroup conflict. *Group Dynamics: Theory, Research, and Practice, 11*(1), 66–78.

DeLucia-Waack, J. L., & Donigian, J. (2004). *The practice of multicultural group work.* Belmont, CA: Brooks.

DeLucia-Waack, J. L., & Fauth, J. (2004). Effective supervision of group leaders. In J. L. DeLucia-Waack, D. A. Gerrity, C. R. Kalodner, & M. T. Riva (Eds.), *Handbook of group counseling and psychotherapy* (pp. 136–150). Thousand Oaks, CA: Sage.

Dickerson, V. C. (2007). Remembering the future: Situating oneself in a constantly evolving field. *Journal of Systemic Therapies, 26,* 23–37.

dickey, l. m., & Loewy, M. I. (2010). Group work with transgender clients. *Journal for Specialists in Group Work, 35,* 236–245.

Doherty, W. J., & Carroll, J. S. (2007). Families and therapists as citizens: The Families and Democracy Project. In E. Aldarondo (Ed.), *Advancing social justice through clinical practice* (pp. 223–244). Mahwah, NJ: Lawrence Erlbaum.

Donigian, J., & Malnati, R. (2005). *Systemic group therapy: A triadic model.* Belmont, CA: Wadsworth.

Dovidio, J. F., Gaertner, S. L., Kawakami, K., & Hodson, G. (2002). Why can't we just get along? Interpersonal biases and interracial distrust. *Cultural Diversity & Ethnic Minority Psychology, 8,* 88–102.

Dryden, W., & Neenan, M. (2002). *Rational emotive behaviour group therapy.* Philadelphia: Whurr.

Duba, J., Kindsvatter, A., & Priddy, C. (2010). Deconstructing the mirror's reflection: Narrative therapy groups for women dissatisfied with their body. *ADULTSPAN Journal, 9*(2), 103–116.

Duffey, T., & Haberstroh, S. (2014). Female counselors working with male clients using relational-cultural theory. In M. Englar-Carlson, M. Evans, & T. Duffey (Eds.), *A counselor's guide to working with men* (pp. 307–324). Washington, DC: American Counseling Association.

Duffey, T., & Somody, C. (2011). The role of relational-cultural theory in mental health counseling. *Journal of Mental Health Counseling, 33*(3), 223–244.

Dugatkin, L. (1999). *Cheating monkeys and citizen bees: The nature of cooperation in animals and humans.* New York: Free Press.

Duncan, B. L., Hubble, M. A., & Miller, S. D. (1997). *Psychotherapy with "impossible" cases.* New York: Norton.

Duncan, G. (2011). *The last werewolf.* New York: Knopf.

Dysart-Gale, D. (2008). Lost in translation: Bibliotherapy and evidence-based medicine. *Journal of Medical Humanities, 29,* 33–43.

D'Zurilla, T. J., & Nezu, A. M. (2007). *Problem-solving therapy: A positive approach to clinical intervention* (3rd ed.). New York: Spring.

Edelwich, J., & Brodsky, A. (1992). *Group counseling for the resistant client.* New York: Lexington.

Egan, G. (2013). *The skilled helper* (10th ed.). Belmont, CA: Cengage Learning.

Ekman, P. (2007). *Emotions revealed: Recognizing faces and feelings to improve communication and emotional life* (2nd ed.). New York: Holt.

Ellis, A., & Ellis, D. J. (2011). *Rational emotive behavior therapy.* Washington, DC: American Psychological Association.

Ellis, S. K., Simpson, C. G., Rose, C. A., & Plotner, A. J. (2014). Group counseling services for persons with disabilities. In J. L. DeLucia-Waack, C. R. Kalodner, & M. T. Riva (Eds.), *Handbook of group counseling and psychotherapy* (2nd ed., pp. 264–275). Thousand Oaks, CA: Sage.

Emer, D. (2004). The use of groups in inpatient facilities: Needs, focus, successes, and remaining dilemmas. In J. L. DeLucia-Waack, D. A. Gerrity, C. R. Kalodner, & M. T. Riva (Eds.), *Handbook of group counseling and psychotherapy* (pp. 351–365). Thousand Oaks, CA: Sage.

Emond, S., & Rasmussen, B. (2012). The status of psychiatric inpatient group therapy: Past, present, and future. *Social Work With Groups, 35*(1), 68–91.

Englar-Carlson, M. (2014). Introduction: A primer on counseling men. In M. Englar-Carlson, M. Evans, & T. Duffey (Eds.), *A counselor's guide to working with men* (pp. 1–31). Washington, DC: American Counseling Association.

Englar-Carlson, M., & Stevens, M. A. (Eds.). (2006). *In the room with men: A casebook of therapeutic change.* Washington, DC: American Psychological Association.

Evans, D. R., Hearn, M. T., Uhlemann, M. R., & Ivey, A. E. (2011). *Essential interviewing: A programmed approach to effective communication* (8th ed.). Belmont, CA: Wadsworth.

Falco, L. D., & Bauman, S. (2004). The use of process notes in the experiential component of training group workers. *Journal for Specialists in Group Work, 29,* 185–192.

Falco, L. D., & Bauman, S. (2014). Group work in schools. In J. L. DeLucia-Waack, C. R. Kalodner, & M. T. Riva (Eds.), *Handbook of group counseling and psychotherapy* (2nd ed., pp. 318–328). Thousand Oaks, CA: Sage.

Fall, K. A., & Menendez, M. (2002). Seventy years of co-leadership: Where do we go from here? *Texas Counseling Association Journal, 30,* 24–33.

Fall, K. A., & Wejnert, T. (2005). Co-leader stages of development: An application of Tuckman and Jensen (1977). *Journal for Specialists in Group Work, 30,* 309–327.

Fallon, A. (2006). Informed consent in the practice of group psychotherapy. *International Journal of Group Psychotherapy, 56*(4), 431–453.

Feder, B., Frew, J., & Burley, T. (2006). A survey of the practice of Gestalt group therapy: A second encore presentation. *Gestalt Review, 10*(3), 242–248.

Fernando, D., & Herlihy, B. (2010). Supervision of group work: Infusing the spirit of social justice. *Journal for Specialists in Group Work, 35,* 281–289.

Fisher, B. A. (1970). Decision emergence: Phases in group decision making. *Speech Monographs, 37,* 53–66.

Fleckenstein, L. B., & Horne, A. H. (2004). Anger management groups. In J. L. DeLucia-Waack, D. A. Gerrity, C. R. Kalodner, & M. T. Riva (Eds.), *Handbook of group counseling and psychotherapy* (pp. 547–562). Thousand Oaks, CA: Sage.

Forsyth, D. R. (2013). *Group dynamics* (6th ed.). Belmont, CA: Wadsworth.

Forsyth, D. R., & Diederich, L. T. (2014). Group dynamics and development. In J. L. DeLucia-Waack, C. R. Kalodner, & M. T. Riva (Eds.), *Handbook of group counseling and psychotherapy* (2nd ed., pp. 34–45). Thousand Oaks, CA: Sage.

Fouad, N. A., & Arredondo, P. (2007). *Becoming culturally oriented: Practical advice for psychologists and educators.* Washington, DC: American Psychological Association.

Frank, A. (1952). *Anne Frank: The diary of a young girl.* New York: Doubleday.

Frank, J. (1991). *Persuasion and healing* (3rd ed.). Baltimore, MD: Johns Hopkins Press.

Frank, J., & Ascher, E. (1951). The corrective emotional experience in group therapy. *American Journal of Psychiatry, 108,* 126–131.

Frankl, V. (1963). *Man's search for meaning.* New York: Washington Square.

Frattaroli, J. (2006). Experimental disclosure and its moderators: A meta-analysis. *Psychological Bulletin, 132,* 823–865.

Freedman, J., & Combs, G. (2012). Narrative, poststructuralism, and social justice: Current practices in narrative therapy. *The Counseling Psychologist, 40*(7), 1033–1060.

Freud, S. (1926). Inhibitions, symptoms, and anxiety. *Standard Edition, 20, 77*–175.

Frew, J., & Spiegler, M. D. (2013). *Contemporary psychotherapies for a diverse world* (Rev. ed.). New York: Routledge.

Frey, L. (2013). Relational-cultural therapy: Theory, research, and application to counseling competencies. *Professional Psychology: Research and Practice, 44*(3), 177–185.

Furukawa, E., & Hunt, D. J. (2011). Therapy with refugees and other immigrants experiencing shame: A multicultural perspective. In R. L. Dearing, & J. P. Tangney (Eds.), *Shame in the therapy hour* (pp. 195–215). Washington, DC: American Psychological Association.

Galanes, G. J. (2003). In their own words: An exploratory study of bona fide group leaders. *Small Group Research, 34*(6), 741–770.

Galston, W. A. (1993). Cosmopolitan altruism. In E. Paul, F. Miller, & J. Paul (Eds.), *Altruism* (pp. 118–134). New York: Cambridge University Press.

Gans, J. S., & Alonso, A. (1998). Difficult patients: Their construction in group therapy. *International Journal of Group Psychotherapy, 48,* 311–326.

Gantt, S. P., & Agazarian, Y. (Eds.). (2011). *Systems-centered therapy: Clinical practice with individuals, families, and groups.* London: Karnac.

Ganzarain, R. (2008). Introduction to object relations group psychotherapy. In G. M. Saiger, S. Rubenfield, & M. D. Dluhy (Eds.), *Windows into today's group therapy: The National Group Psychotherapy Institute of the Washington School of Psychiatry* (pp. 97–111). New York: Routledge.

Garrett, M. (2004). Sounds of the drum: Group counseling with Native Americans. In J. L. DeLucia-Waack, D. A. Gerrity, C. R. Kalodner, & M. T. Riva (Eds.), *Handbook of group counseling and psychotherapy* (pp. 169–182). Thousand Oaks, CA: Sage.

Garte-Wolf, S. (2011). Narrative therapy group work for chemically dependent clients with HIV/AIDS. *Social Work With Groups, 34*(3–4), 330–338.

Gilliam, C., Norberg, M., Villavicencio, A., Morrison, S., Hannan, S., & Tolin, G. F. (2011). Group cognitive-behavioral therapy for hoarding disorder: An open trial. *Behaviour Research and Therapy, 49*(11), 802–807.

Gillies, R., & Haynes, M. (2011). Increasing explanatory behaviour, problem-solving, and reasoning within classes using cooperative group work. *Instructional Science, 39*(3), 349–366.

Gillis, H. L., Gass, M. A., & Russell, K. C. (2014). Adventure therapy with groups. In J. L. DeLucia-Waack, C. R. Kalodner, & M. T. Riva (Eds.), *Handbook of group counseling and psychotherapy* (2nd ed., pp. 560–570). Thousand Oaks, CA: Sage.

Gladding, S. T. (2011a). *The creative arts in counseling* (4th ed.). Alexandria, VA: American Counseling Association.

Gladding, S. T. (2011b). Play and humor in counseling. In S. T. Gladding (Ed.), *The creative arts in counseling* (4th ed., pp. 163–190). Alexandria, VA: American Counseling Association.

Gladding, S. T. (2012). *Groups: A counseling specialty* (6th ed.). Boston: Pearson.

Glantz, K., & Pearce, J. K. (1989). *Exiles from Eden: Psychotherapy from an evolutionary perspective*. New York: Norton.

Glasser, W. (1965). *Reality therapy: A new approach to psychiatry*. New York: Harper & Row.

Glasser, W. (1985). *Control theory: A new explanation of how we control our lives*. New York: Harper & Row.

Glasser, W. (1998). *Choice theory*. New York: HarperCollins.

Gold, J., & Stricker, G. (Eds.). (2006). *A casebook of psychotherapy integration*. Washington, DC: American Psychological Association.

Goldenberg, I., & Goldenberg, H. (2013). *Family therapy: An overview* (8th ed.). Pacific Grove, CA: Brooks.

Goldin, E., Bordan, T., Araoz, D., Gladding, S., Kaplan, D., Krumboltz, J., et al. (2006). Humor in counseling: Leader perspectives. *Journal of Counseling & Development, 84,* 397–404.

Goodrich, K., & Luke, M. (2012). Problematic student in the experiential group: Professional and ethical challenges for counselor educators. *Journal for Specialists in Group Work, 37*(4), 326–346.

Goulding, R. L., & Goulding, M. M. (1991). An intimate model for co-therapy. In B. Roller & V. Nelson (Eds.), *The art of co-therapy: How therapists work together* (pp. 189–209). London: Guilford Press.

Graybeal, A., Sexton, J. D., & Pennebaker, J. W. (2002). The role of story-making in disclosure writing: The psychometrics of narrative. *Psychology and Health, 17,* 571–581.

Green, J. (2012). *The fault in our stars*. New York: Dutton.

Green, S., Haber, E., McCabe, R., & Soares, C. (2013). Cognitive-behavioral group treatment for menopausal symptoms: A pilot study. *Archives of Women's Mental Health, 16*(4), 325–332.

Greenberg, M. A., Wortman, C. B., & Stone, A. A. (1996). Emotional expression and physical health: Revisiting traumatic memories or fostering self-regulation? *Journal of Personality and Social Psychology, 71,* 588–602.

Greer, T., & White, A. (2008). Women of color groups: Group counseling with African American college women. In L. VandeCreek & J. Allen (Eds.), *Innovations in clinical practice: Focus on group, couples, & family therapy* (pp. 253–264). Sarasota, FL: Professional Resource Press.

Guimón, J. (2004). Evidence-based research studies on the results of group therapy: A critical review. *European Journal of Psychiatry, 18,* 49–60.

Gullette, M. M. (2003). From life storytelling to age autobiography. *Journal of Aging Studies, 17,* 101–111.

Haberstroh, S., Parr, G., Gee, R., & Trepal, H. (2006). Interactive E-journaling in group work: Perspectives from counselor trainees. *Journal for Specialists in Group Work, 31*(4), 327–337.

Hadden, S. B. (1947). The utilization of a therapy group in teaching psychotherapy. *American Journal of Psychiatry, 103,* 644–648.

Hajek, K. (2007). Interpersonal group therapy on acute inpatient wards. *Groupwork, 17*(1), 7–19.

Hall, E. T. (1966). *The hidden dimension.* New York: Anchor Books.

Hall, J., & Hawley, L. D. (2004). Interactive process notes: An innovative tool in counseling groups. *Journal for Specialists in Group Work, 29*(2), 193–205.

Harel, Y., Shechtman, Z., & Cutrona, C. (2012). Exploration of support behavior in counseling groups with counseling trainees. *Journal for Specialists in Group Work, 37*(3), 202–217.

Harman, O. (2011). *The price of altruism.* New York: W. W. Norton.

Hays, D. G., Arredondo, P., Gladding, S. T., & Toporek, R. L. (2010). Integrating social justice in group work: The next decade. *Journal for Specialists in Group Work, 35*(2), 177–206.

Hays, D. G., Chang, C., & Havice, P. (2008). White racial identity statuses as predictors of White privilege awareness. *Journal of Humanistic Counseling, Education and Development, 47*(2), 234–246.

Heimes, S. (2011). State of poetry therapy research. *Arts in Psychotherapy, 38*(1), 1–8.

Heller, P. (2012). *The dog stars.* New York: Knopf.

Hendrix, C. C., Fournier, D. G., & Briggs, K. (2001). Impact of co-therapy teams on client outcomes and therapist training in marriage and family therapy. *Contemporary Family Therapy, 23,* 63–82.

Hepworth, D. H., Rooney, R. H., Rooney, G., Strom-Gottfried, K., & Larsen, J. A. (2010). *Direct social work practice: Theory and skills* (8th ed.). Belmont, CA: Brooks/Cole.

Hesley, J. W., & Hesley, J. G. (2001). *Rent two films and let's talk in the morning: Using popular movies in psychotherapy* (2nd ed.). New York: Wiley.

Hoffman, E. (1994). *The drive for self: Alfred Adler and the founding of individual psychology.* New York: Perseus Books.

Hoffman, S., & Rosman, L. (2003). "Procrustean psychotherapy" or differential therapeutics: Teaching treatment selection to trainees. *Journal of Contemporary Psychotherapy, 33*(4), 341–347.

Hogh-Olesen, H. (2008). Human spatial behaviour: The spacing of people, objects and animals in six cross-cultural samples. *Journal of Cognition and Culture, 8*(3–4), 245.

Holmes, S. E., & Kivlighan, D. M. J. (2000). Comparison of therapeutic factors in group and individual treatment processes. *Journal of Counseling Psychology, 47,* 478–484.

Hope, D., Burns, J., Hayes, S., Herbert, J., & Warner, M. (2010). Automatic thoughts and cognitive restructuring in cognitive behavioral group therapy for social anxiety disorder. *Cognitive Therapy and Research, 34*(1), 1–12.

Hopper, E. (2006). Theoretical and conceptual notes concerning transference and countertransference processes in groups and by groups, and the social unconscious: Part I. *Group Analysis, 39,* 549–559.

Hopper, E. (2007). Theoretical and conceptual notes concerning transference and countertransference processes in groups and by groups, and the social unconscious: Part II. *Group Analysis, 40,* 29–42.

Horne, S. G., Levitt, H. M., Reeves, T., & Wheeler, E. E. (2014). Group work with gay, lesbian, bisexual, transgender, queer, and questioning clients. In J. L. DeLucia-Waack, C. R. Kalodner, & M. T. Riva (Eds.), *Handbook of group counseling and psychotherapy* (2nd ed., pp. 253–263). Thousand Oaks, CA: Sage.

Horney, K. (1945). *Our inner conflicts.* New York: Norton.

Hornsey, M. J., Dwyer, L., & Oei, T. P. S. (2007). Beyond cohesiveness: Reconceptualizing the link between group processes and outcomes in group psychotherapy. *Small Group Research, 38,* 567–592.

Hoyt, C. L., Murphy, S. E., Halverson, S. K., & Watson, C. B. (2003). Group leadership: Efficacy and effectiveness. *Group Dynamics: Theory, Research, and Practice, 7,* 259–274.

Huffman, D., & Fernando, D. (2012). Adapting the interpersonal process model of intimacy to enhance the co-leader relationship during training. *Journal for Specialists in Group Work, 37*(2), 152–167.

Hunter, L. B. (2006). Group sand-tray play therapy. In H. G. Kaduson & C. E. Schaefer (Eds.), *Short-term play therapy for children* (2nd ed., pp. 273–303). New York: Guilford Press.

Hunter, S., Witkiewitz, K., Watkins, K., Paddock, S., & Hepner, K. (2012). The moderating effects of group cognitive-behavioral therapy for depression among substance users. *Psychology of Addictive Behaviors: Journal of the Society of Psychologists in Addictive Behaviors, 26*(4), 906–916.

Huppert, J., Fabbro, A., & Barlow, D. (2006). Evidence-based practice and psychological treatments. In C. D. Goodheart, A. E. Kazdin, & R. J. Sternberg (Eds.), *Evidence-based psychotherapy: Where practice and research meet* (pp. 131–152). Washington, DC: American Psychological Association.

Ibrahim, F. (2010). Social justice and cultural responsiveness: Innovative teaching strategies for group work. *Journal for Specialists in Group Work, 35,* 271–280.

Inman, A., & Tummala-Narra, P. (2010). Clinical competencies in working with immigrant communities. In J. Cornish, B. Schreier, L. Nadkarni, L. Metzger, & E. Rodolfa (Eds.), *Handbook of multicultural competencies* (pp. 117–152). New York: Wiley.

Ivey, A. E., Ivey, M. B., & Zalaquett. (2014). *Intentional interviewing and counseling: Facilitating client development in a multicultural society* (8th ed.). Belmont, CA: Wadsworth.

Jackson, S. A. (2001). Using bibliotherapy with clients. *Journal of Individual Psychology, 57,* 289–297.

Jacobs, E. E., Masson, R. L., & Harvill, R. L. (2012). *Group counseling: Strategies and skills* (7th ed.). Pacific Grove, CA: Brooks.

Jacobs, M. (2010). *Psychodynamic counselling in action* (4th ed.). Thousand Oaks, CA: Sage.

Jacobson, M., & Rugeley, C. (2007). Community-based participatory research: Group work for social justice and community change. *Social Work With Groups, 30*(4), 21–39.

Jennings, A. (2007). Time limited group therapy: Losses and gains. *Psychoanalytic Psychotherapy, 21,* 90–106.

Jensen, D., Abbott, M., Beecher, M., Griner, D., Golightly, T., & Cannon, J. (2012). Taking the pulse of the group: The utilization of practice-based evidence in group psychotherapy. *Professional Psychology: Research and Practice, 43*(4), 388–394.

Johnson, D. W., & Johnson, F. (2012). *Joining together: Group theory and group skills* (11th ed.). Boston: Allyn & Bacon.

Johnson, J. E., Burlingame, G. M., Davies, D. R., & Olsen, J. A. (2002, August). *Clarifying therapeutic relationships in group psychotherapy.* Paper presented at the 110th annual convention of the American Psychological Association, Chicago.

Johnson, J. E., Burlingame, G. M., Olsen, J. A., Davies, D. R., & Gleave, R. L. (2005). Group climate, cohesion, alliance, and empathy in group psychotherapy: Multilevel structural equation models. *Journal of Counseling Psychology, 52,* 310–321.

Jolly, M. (2011). What I never wanted to tell you: Therapeutic letter writing in cultural context. *Journal of Medical Humanities, 32*(1), 47–59.

Jordan, J. (2010). *Relational–cultural theory.* Washington, DC: American Psychological Association.

Jordan, K. (2000). Programmed distance writing: Divorce adjustment for children—a case study. *Family Therapy, 27,* 102–109.

Joyce, A. S., Piper, W. E., & Ogrodniczuk, J. S. (2007). Therapeutic alliance and cohesion variables as predictors of outcome in short-term group psychotherapy. *International Journal of Group Psychotherapy, 57,* 269–296.

Kane, T. D., Zaccaro, S. J., Tremble, T. R. J., & Masuda, A. D. (2002). An examination of the leaders' regulation of groups. *Small Group Research, 33*(1), 65–120.

Kaplan, D., Rupley, W., Sparks, J., & Holcomb, A. (2007). Comparing traditional journal writing with journal writing shared over e-mail list serves as tools for facilitating reflective thinking: A study of preservice teachers. *Journal of Literacy Research, 39*(3), 357–387.

Kazantsis, N., Deane, F. P., & Ronan, K. R. (2000). Homework assignments in cognitive and behavioral therapy: A meta-analysis. *Clinical Psychology Science and Practice, 7,* 189–202.

Keats, P., & Sabharwal, V. (2008). Time-limited service alternatives: Using therapeutic enactment in open group therapy. *Journal for Specialists in Group Work, 33*(4), 297–316.

Keeney, B., & Connor, N. (Eds.). (2008). *Shamans of the world.* Boulder, CO: Sounds True.

Kees, N., & Leech, N. (2014). Women's groups: Research and practice trends. In J. L. DeLucia-Waack, C. R. Kalodner, & M. T. Riva (Eds.), *Handbook of group counseling and psychotherapy* (2nd ed., pp. 506–520). Thousand Oaks, CA: Sage.

Kelly, J., Magill, M., & Stout, R. (2009). How do people recover from alcohol dependence? A systematic review of the research on mechanisms of behavior change in Alcoholics Anonymous. *Addiction Research & Theory, 17*(3), 236–259.

Kempler, N. Z. (2003). Finding our voice through poetry and psychotherapy. *Journal of Poetry Therapy, 16,* 217–220.

Kernberg, O. (1975). *Borderline conditions and pathological narcissism*. New York: Jason Aronson.

Kerner, E., & Fitzpatrick, M. (2007). Integrating writing into psychotherapy practice: A matrix of change processes and structural dimensions. *Psychotherapy: Theory, Research, Practice, Training, 44*(3), 333–346.

Kim, D., Wampold, B., & Bolt, D. (2006). Therapist effects in psychotherapy: A random-effects modeling of the National Institute of Mental Health Treatment of Depression Collaborative Research Program data. *Psychotherapy Research, 16,* 161–172.

Kim, J. (2007). A reality therapy group counseling program as an Internet addiction recovery method for college students in Korea. *International Journal of Reality Therapy, 26*(2), 3–9.

King, L. (2001). The health benefits of writing about life goals. *Personality and Social Psychology Bulletin, 27,* 798–807.

Kiselica, A. M., & Kiselica, M. S. (2014). Gender-sensitive group counseling and psychotherapy with men. In J. L. DeLucia-Waack, C. R. Kalodner, & M. T. Riva (Eds.), *Handbook of group counseling and psychotherapy* (2nd ed., pp. 521–530). Thousand Oaks, CA: Sage.

Kivlighan, D. M., Jr., & Holmes, S. (2004). The importance of therapeutic factors: A typology of therapeutic factors studies. In J. L. DeLucia-Waack, D. A. Gerrity, C. R. Kalodner, & M. T. Riva (Eds.), *Handbook of group counseling and psychotherapy* (pp. 23–36). Thousand Oaks, CA: Sage.

Kivlighan, D. M., Jr., & Kivlighan, D. M., III. (2014). Therapeutic factors: Current theory and research. In J. L. DeLucia-Waack, C. R. Kalodner, & M. T. Riva (Eds.), *Handbook of group counseling and psychotherapy* (2nd ed., pp. 46–54). Thousand Oaks, CA: Sage.

Kivlighan, D. M., Jr., London, K., & Miles, J. R. (2012). Are two heads better than one? The relationship between number of group leaders and group members, and group climate and group member benefit from therapy. *Group Dynamics: Theory, Research, and Practice, 16,* 1–13.

Kivlighan, D. M., Jr., Paquin, J., & Miles, J. (2011). Predicting group attendance using in-session behaviors. *Small Group Research, 42*(2), 177–198.

Klaw, E., & Humphreys, K. (2004). The role of peer-led mutual help groups in promoting health and well-being. In J. L. DeLucia-Waack, D. A. Gerrity, C. R. Kalodner, & M. T. Riva (Eds.), *Handbook of group counseling and psychotherapy* (pp. 630–640). Thousand Oaks, CA: Sage.

Klein, K., & Boals, A. (2010). Coherence and narrative structure in personal accounts of stressful experiences. *Journal of Social and Clinical Psychology, 29,* 256–280.

Klein, R., & Schermer, V. L. (2000). *Group therapy for psychological trauma*. New York: Guilford Press.

Klein, S. (2014). *Survival of the nicest: How altruism made us human and why it pays to get along*. New York: Experiment.

Kline, W. B. (2003). *Interactive group counseling and therapy*. Upper Saddle River, NJ: Prentice Hall.

Kohut, H. (1971). *The analysis of the self.* Madison, CT: International Universities Press.

Komives, S., Lucas, N., & McMahon, T. (2013). *Exploring leadership: For college students who want to make a difference* (3rd ed.). San Francisco: Jossey-Bass.

Kösters, M., Burlingame, G., Nachtigall, C., & Strauss, B. (2006). A meta-analytic review of the effectiveness of inpatient group psychotherapy. *Group Dynamics: Theory, Research, and Practice, 10*(2), 146–163.

Kottler, J. A. (1992). *Compassionate therapy: Working with difficult clients.* San Francisco: Jossey-Bass.

Kottler, J. A. (1994). *Advanced group leadership.* Pacific Grove, CA: Brooks.

Kottler, J. A. (1997). *Travel that can change your life.* San Francisco: Jossey-Bass.

Kottler, J. A. (2000). *Doing good: Passion and commitment for helping others.* New York: Routledge.

Kottler, J. A. (2001a). *Doing good: Passion and commitment helping others.* Philadelphia: Accelerated Development.

Kottler, J. A. (2001b). *Making changes last.* New York: Routledge.

Kottler, J. A. (2008). *A brief primer of helping skills.* Thousand Oaks, CA: Sage.

Kottler, J. A. (2010). *On being a therapist* (4th ed.). San Francisco: Jossey-Bass.

Kottler, J. A. (2014). *Change: What really leads to lasting personal transformations.* New York: Oxford.

Kottler, J. A., & Blau, D. (1989). *The imperfect therapist: Learning from failure in therapeutic practice.* San Francisco: Jossey-Bass.

Kottler, J. A., & Carlson, J. D. (2003). *Bad therapy: Master therapists share their worst failures.* New York: Brunner-Routledge.

Kottler, J. A., & Carlson, J. D. (2005). *The client that changed me.* New York: Routledge.

Kottler, J. A., & Carlson, J. D. (2008). *Their finest hour: Master therapists share their greatest success stories* (2nd ed.). Boston: Allyn & Bacon.

Kottler, J. A., & Carlson, J. D. (2009). *Creative breakthroughs in therapy.* New York: Wiley.

Kottler, J. A., & Carlson, J. D. (2014). *On being a master therapist: Practicing what you preach.* New York: Wiley.

Kottler, J. A., Carlson, J. D., & Keeney, B. (2004). *An American shaman: An odyssey of ancient healing traditions.* New York: Brunner-Routledge.

Kottler, J. A., Englar-Carlson, M., & Carlson, J. D. (2013). *Helping beyond the 50-minute hour: Therapists involved in meaningful social action.* New York: Routledge.

Kottler, J. A., & Kottler, E. (2006). *Counseling skills for teachers* (2nd ed.). Thousand Oaks, CA: Corwin.

Kottler, J. A., & Kottler, E. (2009). *Students who drive you crazy: Succeeding with resistant, unmotivated, and otherwise difficult young people* (2nd ed.). Thousand Oaks, CA: Corwin.

Kottler, J. A., & Marriner, M. (2009). *Changing people's lives while transforming your own: Paths to social justice and global human rights.* New York: Wiley.

Kottler, J. A., & Shepard, D. S. (2011). *Introduction to counseling: Voices in the field* (7th ed.). Belmont, CA: Wadsworth.

Koudenburg, N., Postmes, T., & Gordijn, E. (2011). Disrupting the flow: How brief silences in group conversations affect social needs. *Journal of Experimental Social Psychology, 47*(2), 512–515.

Kouzes, J. M., & Posner, B. Z. (2013). *The leadership challenge: How to make extraordinary things happen in organizations* (5th ed.). San Francisco: Jossey-Bass.

Kulp, L., Ladany, N., & Klinger, R. (2012). It's too late to apologize: Therapist embarrassment and shame. *The Counseling Psychologist, 40*(4), 554–574.

Kurzon, D. (2007). Towards a typology of silence. *Journal of Pragmatics, 39,* 1673–1688.

La Coursiere, R. (1980). *The life-cycle of groups: Group development and stage theory.* New York: Human Sciences.

Lampropoulos, G., Kazantzis, N., & Deane, F. (2004). Psychologists' use of motion pictures in clinical practice. *Professional Psychology: Research and Practice, 35*(5), 535–541.

Lampropoulos, G., & Spengler, P. (2005). Helping and change without traditional therapy: Commonalities and opportunities. *Counselling Psychology Quarterly, 18*(1), 47–59.

Lanza, M. (2007). Modeling conflict resolution in group psychotherapy. *Journal of Group Psychotherapy, Psychodrama & Sociometry, 59,* 147–158.

Lau, M. A., Ogrodniczuk, J., Joyce, A. S., & Sochting, I. (2010). Bridging the practitioner-scientist gap in group psychotherapy research. *International Journal of Group Psychotherapy, 60,* 177–196.

Leddick, G. R. (2011). Distinguishing group member roles. In B. R. Erford (Ed.), *Group work: Processes and application* (pp. 52–60). Upper Saddle River, NJ: Pearson Education.

Lemmens, G. D., Eisler, I., Dierick, P., Lietaer, G., & Demyttenaere, K. (2009). Therapeutic factors in a systemic multi-family group treatment for major depression: Patients' and partners' perspectives. *Journal of Family Therapy, 31,* 250–269.

Lent, J. (2009). Journaling enters the 21st century: The use of therapeutic blogs in counseling. *Journal of Creativity in Mental Health, 4*(1), 67–73.

Lepore, S. J. (1997). Expressive writing moderates the relation between intrusive thoughts and depressive symptoms. *Journal of Personality and Social Psychology, 73,* 1030–1037.

Lepore, S. J., & Smyth, J. M. (Eds.). (2002). *The writing cure: How expressive writing promotes health and emotional well-being.* Washington, DC: American Psychological Association.

Lepper, G., & Mergenthaler, E. (2005). Exploring group process. *Psychotherapy Research, 15,* 433–444.

Levi, D. (2011). *Group dynamics for teams* (3rd ed.). Thousand Oaks, CA: Sage.

Lewis, J. (2011). Operationalizing social justice counseling: Paradigm to practice. *Journal of Humanistic Counseling, 50*(2), 183–191.

Lieberman, M. A., & Golant, M. (2002). Leader behavior as perceived by cancer patients in professionally directed support groups and outcomes. *Group Dynamics: Theory, Research, and Practice, 6,* 267–276.

Linehan, M., Ward-Ciesielski, E., & Neacsiu, A. (2012). Emerging approaches to counseling intervention: Dialectical behavior therapy. *The Counseling Psychologist, 40*(7), 1003–1032.

Liu, Y., Tsong, Y., & Hayashino, D. (2007). Group counseling with Asian American women: Reflections and effective practices. *Women & Therapy, 30*(3), 193–208.

Logan, D., King, J., & Fischer-Wright, H. (2011). *Tribal leadership: Levering natural groups to build a striving organization.* New York: Collins.

London, M. (2007). Performance appraisal for groups: Models and methods for assessing group processes and outcomes for development and evaluation. *Consulting Psychology Journal: Practice and Research, 59*(3), 175–188.

Lubin, H., & Johnson, D. (2008). *Trauma centered group psychotherapy with women.* New York: Haworth Press.

Luke, M. (2014). Effective group leader skills. In J. L. DeLucia-Waack, C. R. Kalodner, & M. T. Riva (Eds.), *Handbook of group counseling and psychotherapy* (2nd ed., pp. 107–119). Thousand Oaks, CA: Sage.

Luke, M., & Hackney, H. (2007). Group co-leadership: A critical review. *Counselor Education and Supervision, 46,* 280–293.

Lumley, M. A., & Provenzano, K. M. (2003). Stress management through written emotional disclosure improves academic performance among college students with physical symptoms. *Journal of Educational Psychology, 95*(3), 641–649.

Lyubomirsky, S., Sousa, L., & Dickerhoof, R. (2006). The costs and benefits of writing, talking, and thinking about life's triumphs and defeats. *Journal of Personality and Social Psychology, 90,* 692–708.

MacNair-Semands, R. (2002). Predicting attendance and expectations for group therapy. *Group Dynamics: Theory, Research, and Practice, 6,* 219–228.

MacNair-Semands, R. (2007). Attending to the spirit of social justice as an ethical approach in group therapy. *International Journal of Group Psychotherapy, 57*(1), 61–66.

Madigan, S. (2011). *Narrative therapy.* Washington, DC: American Psychological Association.

Mangione, L., Forti, R., & Iacuzzi, C. M. (2007). Ethics and endings in group psychotherapy: Saying good-bye and saying it well. *International Journal of Group Psychotherapy, 57*(1), 25–40.

Maples, M., Dupey, P., Torres-Rivera, E., Phan, L., Vereen, L., & Garrett, M. (2001). Ethnic diversity and the use of humor in counseling appropriate or inappropriate? *Journal of Counseling & Development, 79*(1), 53–60.

Markin, R. (2009). Exploring a method for transference assessment in group therapy using the social relations model: Suggestions for future research. *Journal for Specialists in Group Work, 34*(4), 307–325.

Markin, R., & Kivlighan, D. M. (2007). Bias in psychotherapist ratings of patient transference and insight. *Psychotherapy: Theory, Research, Practice, and Training, 44,* 300–315.

Markin, R., & Marmarosh, C. (2010). Application of adult attachment theory to group member transference and the group therapy process. *Psychotherapy, 47,* 111–121.

Markus, H. E., & King, D. A. (2003). A survey of group psychotherapy training during predoctoral psychology internship. *Professional Psychology: Research and Practice, 34,* 203–209.

Mays, V. (2000). A social justice agenda. *American Psychologist, 55,* 326–327.

McArdle, S., & Byrt, R. (2001). Fiction, poetry and mental health: Expressive and therapeutic uses of literature. *Journal of Psychiatric and Mental Health Nursing, 8,* 517–524.

McClure, B. (2005). *Putting a new spin on groups: The science of chaos* (2nd ed.). Mahwah, NJ: Lawrence Erlbaum.

McConnell, C. R., & Brue, S. L. (2011). *Economics* (19th ed.). New York: McGraw-Hill.

McDermut, W., Miller, I., & Brown, R. (2001). The efficacy of group psychotherapy for depression: A meta-analysis and review of the empirical research. *Clinical Psychology: Science and Practice, 8,* 98–116.

McDougall, C. (2002). Rogers's person-centered approach: Consideration for use in multicultural counseling. *Journal of Humanistic Psychology, 42*(2), 48–65.

McEvoy, P. (2007). Effectiveness of cognitive behavioural group therapy for social phobia in a community clinic: A benchmarking study. *Behaviour Research and Therapy, 45*(12), 3030–3040.

McEvoy, P., Nathan, P., Rapee, R., & Campbell, B. (2012). Cognitive behavioural group therapy for social phobia: Evidence of transportability to community clinics. *Behaviour Research and Therapy, 50*(4), 258–265.

McGoldrick, M., Gerson, R., & Petry, S. (2008). *Genograms in family assessment* (3rd ed.). New York: Norton.

McMillon, B., Cutchins, D., & Geissinger, A. (2012). *Volunteer vacations: Short-term adventures that will benefit you and others* (11th ed.). Chicago: Chicago Review Press.

McRoberts, C., Burlingame, G. M., & Hoag, M. J. (1998). Comparative efficacy of individual and group psychotherapy: A meta-analytic perspective. *Group Dynamics, 2,* 101–117.

McWhirter, P., & Robbins, R. (2014). Group therapy with native people. In J. L. DeLucia-Waack, C. R. Kalodner, & M. T. Riva (Eds.), *Handbook of group counseling and psychotherapy* (2nd ed., pp. 209–219). Thousand Oaks, CA: Sage.

Mearns, D., Thorne, B., & McLeod, J. (2013). *Person-centered counselling in action* (4th ed.). London: Sage.

Meier, A., & Comer, E. (2011). Using evidence-based practice and intervention research with treatment groups for populations at risk. In G. L. Greif & P. H. Ephross (Eds.), *Group work with populations at risk* (3rd ed., pp. 459–488). New York: Oxford University Press.

Metzger, L., Nadkarni, L., & Cornish, J. (2010). An overview of multicultural competencies. In J. Cornish, B. Schreier, L. Nadkarni, L. Metzger, & E. Rodolfa (Eds.), *Handbook of multicultural competencies* (pp. 1–22). New York: Wiley.

Midura, D., & Glover, D. (2005). *Essentials of team building: Principles and practices.* Champaign, IL: Human Kinetics.

Miles, J., & Kivlighan, D. M. (2008). Team cognition in group interventions: The relation between coleaders' shared mental models and group climate. *Group Dynamics: Theory, Research, and Practice, 12*(3), 191–209.

Miles, J., & Kivlighan, D. M. (2010). Co-leader similarity and group climate in group interventions: Testing the co-leadership, team cognition–team diversity model. *Group Dynamics: Theory, Research, and Practice, 14*(2), 114–122.

Miles, J. R., & Paquin, J. D. (2014). Best practices in group counseling and psychotherapy research. In J. L. DeLucia-Waack, C. R. Kalodner, & M. T. Riva (Eds.), *Handbook of group counseling and psychotherapy* (2nd ed., pp. 178–192). Thousand Oaks, CA: Sage.

Miley, K. K., O'Melia, M. W., & DuBois, B. L. (2012). *Generalist social work practice: An empowering approach* (7th ed.). Engelwood Cliffs, NJ: Pearson.

Miller, J. B., & Stiver, I. (1997). *The healing connection: How women form relationships in therapy and in life.* Boston: Beacon Press.

Miller, S. D., Hubble, M., & Duncan, B. (2008). Supershrinks: What's the secret to their success? *Psychotherapy in Australia, 14,* 14–27.

Mitchell, C. W. (2007). *Effective techniques for dealing with highly resistant clients* (2nd ed.). Johnson City, TN: Author.

Monk, G., Drewery, W., & Winslade, J. (2005). Using narrative ideas in group work: A new perspective. *Counseling and Human Development, 38*(1), 1–16.

Moreno, J. K. (2007). Scapegoating in group psychotherapy. *International Journal of Group Psychotherapy, 57,* 93–104.

Morgan, R. D., & Flora, D. B. (2002). Group psychotherapy with incarcerated offenders: A research synthesis. *Group Dynamics: Theory, Research, and Practice, 6,* 203–218.

Morgan, R. D., Romani, C. J., & Gross, N. R. (2014). Group work with offenders and mandated clients. In J. L. DeLucia-Waack, C. R. Kalodner, & M. T. Riva (Eds.), *Handbook of group counseling and psychotherapy* (2nd ed., pp. 441–449). Thousand Oaks, CA: Sage.

Morran, D. K., Stockton, R., & Whittingham, M. H. (2004). Effective leader interventions for counseling and psychotherapy groups. In J. L. DeLucia-Waack, D. A. Gerrity, C. R. Kalodner, & M. T. Riva (Eds.), *Handbook of group counseling and psychotherapy* (pp. 91–103). Thousand Oaks, CA: Sage.

Morrison, J. (2014). *Diagnosis made easier: Principles and techniques for mental health clinicians* (2nd ed.). New York: Guilford Press.

Motherwell, L., & Shay, J. (2014). *Complex dilemmas in group therapy: Pathways to resolution* (2nd ed.). New York: Routledge.

Nadeau, J. W. (2006). Metaphorically speaking: The use of metaphors in grief therapy. *Illness, Crisis, & Loss, 14*(3), 201–221.

Napier, A. Y., & Whitaker, C. A. (1988). *The family crucible.* New York: Harper & Row.

Napier, R. W., & Gershenfeld, M. K. (2004). *Groups: Theory and experience* (7th ed.). Boston: Houghton Mifflin.

National Association of Social Workers. (2008). *Code of ethics.* Washington, DC: Author.

National Center for Health Statistics. (2014). *International classification of diseases* (10th ed., clinical modification). Hyattsville, MD: Author. Retrieved from http://www.cdc.gov/nchs/icd/icd10cm.htm#icd2014

Nelson-Jones, R. (2012). *Basic counseling skills: A helper's manual* (3rd ed.). London: Sage.

Nichols, M. P., & Schwartz, R. C. (2012). *Family therapy concepts and methods* (10th ed.). Needham Heights, MA: Allyn & Bacon.

Nitza, A. (2014). Selecting and using activities in groups. In J. L. DeLucia-Waack, C. R. Kalodner, & M. T. Riva (Eds.), *Handbook of group counseling and psychotherapy* (2nd ed., pp. 95–106). Thousand Oaks, CA: Sage.

Norcross, J. C. (2006). Integrating self-help into psychotherapy: 16 "practical" suggestions. *Professional Psychology: Research and Practice, 37*(6), 683–693.

Norcross, J. C. (Ed.). (2011). *Psychotherapy relationships that work* (2nd ed.). New York: Oxford University Press.

Norcross, J. C., Santrock, J. W., Campbell, L. F., Smith, T. P., Sommer, R., & Zuckerman, E. L. (2003). *Authoritative guide to self-help resources in mental health* (Rev. ed.). New York: Guilford Press.

Norsworthy, K. L., & Khuankaew, O. (2013). Feminist border crossings: Our transnational partnership in peace and justice work. In J. A. Kottler, M. Englar-Carlson, & J. D. Carlson (Eds.), *Helping beyond the 50-minute hour: Therapists involved in meaningful social action* (pp. 222–233). New York: Routledge.

Northouse, P. G. (2013). *Leadership: Theory and practice* (6th ed.). Thousand Oaks, CA: Sage.

Nova, N. (2005). A review of how space affords socio-cognitive processes during collaboration. *Psychology Journal, 3,* 118–148.

Ogrodniczuk, J. S., & Piper, W. E. (2003). The effect of group climate on outcome in two forms of short-term group therapy. *Group Dynamics: Theory, Research, and Practice, 7,* 64–76.

Okech, J. E. A., & Kline, W. B. (2005). A qualitative exploration of group co-leader relationships. *Journal for Specialists in Group Work, 30,* 173–190.

Okech, J. E. A., & Kline, W. B. (2006). Competency concerns in group co-leader relationships. *Journal for Specialists in Group Work, 31,* 165–180.

O'Neal, G. (2006). Using multicultural resources in groups. *Groupwork, 16*(1), 48–68.

Ormont, L. R. (2004). Group analysis: Drawing the isolate into the group flow. *Group Analytic Society, 37,* 65–76.

Owen, J., Imel, Z., Tao, K., Wampold, B., Smith, A., & Rodolfa, E. (2011). Cultural ruptures in short-term therapy: Working alliance as a mediator between clients' perceptions of microaggressions and therapy outcomes. *Counselling and Psychotherapy Research, 11*(3), 204–212.

Pack-Brown, S. P., Whittington-Clark, L. E., & Parker, W. M. (1998). *Images of me: A guide to group work with African-American women.* Boston: Allyn & Bacon.

Page, B. J. (2003). Introduction to using technology in group work. *Journal for Specialists in Group Work, 28,* 7–8.

Page, B. J., Jenicus, M. J., Rehfuss, M. C., Foss, L. L., Dean, E. P., Petruzzi, M. L., et al. (2003). PalTalk online groups: Process and reflections on students' experience. *Journal for Specialists in Group Work, 28,* 35–41.

Paquin, J., Kivlighan, D., & Drogosz, L. (2013). If you get better, will I? An actor-partner analysis of the mutual influence of group therapy outcomes. *Journal of Counseling Psychology, 60*(2), 171–179.

Parikh, S., Janson, C., & Singleton, T. (2012). Video journaling as a method of reflective practice. *Counselor Education and Supervision, 51*(1), 33–49.

Parr, G., Haberstroh, S., & Kottler, J. (2000). Interactive journal writing as an adjunct in group work. *Journal for Specialists in Group Work, 25*(3), 229–242.

Pedersen, P., Crethar, H., & Carlson, J. (2008). *Inclusive cultural empathy: Making relationships central in counseling and psychotherapy.* Washington, DC: American Psychological Association.

Pennebaker, J. W. (2002). Somatisation in private care: Solitary disclosure allows people to determine their own dose. *British Medical Journal, 324,* 544.

Pennebaker, J. W. (2004). *Writing to heal: A guided journal for recovering from trauma and emotional upheaval.* Oakland, CA: New Harbinger.

Pennebaker, J. W., & Chung, C. K. (2011). Expressive writing and its links to mental and physical health. In H. S. Friedman (Ed.), *The Oxford handbook of health psychology* (pp. 417–437). New York: Oxford University Press.

Pennebaker, J. W., & Francis, M. E. (1996). Cognitive, emotional, and language processes in disclosure. *Cognition and Emotion, 10,* 601–626.

Pennebaker, J. W., Mayne, T. J., & Francis, M. E. (1997). Linguistic predictors of adaptive bereavement. *Journal of Personality and Social Psychology, 72,* 863–871.

Pinterits, E., Poteat, V., & Spanierman, L. (2009). The White privilege attitudes scale: Development and initial validation. *Journal of Counseling Psychology, 56*(3), 417–429.

Piper, W. E. (2008). Underutilization of short-term group therapy: Enigmatic or understandable? *Psychotherapy Research, 18*(2), 127–138.

Piper, W. E., & Ogrodniczuk, J. S. (2004). Brief group therapy. In J. L. DeLucia-Waack, D. A. Gerrity, C. R. Kalodner, & M. T. Riva (Eds.), *Handbook of group counseling and psychotherapy* (pp. 641–650). Thousand Oaks, CA: Sage.

Piper, W. E., Ogrodniczuk, J. S., Lamarche, C., Hilscher, T., & Joyce, A. S. (2005). Level of alliance, pattern of alliance, and outcome in short-term group therapy. *International Journal of Group Psychotherapy, 4,* 527–550.

Piper, W. E., Ogrodniczuk, J. S., & Sierra-Hernandez, C. A. (2014). Group psychotherapies for complicated grief. In J. L. DeLucia-Waack, C. R. Kalodner, & M. T. Riva (Eds.), *Handbook of group counseling and psychotherapy* (2nd ed., pp. 398–409). Thousand Oaks, CA: Sage.

Poole, J., Gardner, P., Flower, M., & Cooper, C. (2009). Narrative therapy, older adults, and group work? Practice, research, and recommendations. *Social Work With Groups, 32*(4), 288–302.

Pope, K., & Vasquez, M. (2011). *Ethics in psychotherapy and counseling: A practical guide for psychologists* (4th ed.). San Francisco: Jossey-Bass.

Post, S. G. (Ed.). (2007). *Altruism and health: Perspectives from empirical research.* New York: Oxford University Press.

Post, S. G. (2011). *The hidden gifts of helping: How the power of giving, compassion, and hope can get us through hard times.* San Francisco: Jossey-Bass.

Posthuma, B. W. (2001). *Small groups in therapy settings: Process and leadership* (4th ed.). Boston: Little, Brown.

Powell, M., & Newgent, R. (2010). Improving the empirical credibility of cinematherapy: A single-subject interrupted time-series design. *Counseling Outcome Research and Evaluation, 1*(2), 40–49.

Powell, M., Newgent, R., & Lee, S. (2006). Group cinematherapy: Using metaphor to enhance adolescent self-esteem. *Arts in Psychotherapy, 33*(3), 247–253.

Prochaska, J. O., & Norcross, J. C. (2010). *Systems of psychotherapy* (7th ed.). Belmont, CA: Brooks/Cole.

Rabinowitz, F. (2014). Counseling men in groups. In M. Englar-Carlson, M. Evans, & T. Duffey (Eds.), *A counselor's guide to working with men* (pp. 55–60). Washington, DC: American Counseling Association.

Rapin, L. S. (2014). Guidelines for ethical and legal practice in counseling and psychotherapy groups. In J. L. DeLucia-Waack, C. R. Kalodner, & M. T. Riva (Eds.), *Handbook of group counseling and psychotherapy* (2nd ed., pp. 71–83). Thousand Oaks, CA: Sage.

Raskin, J., & Bridges, S. (2008). *Studies in meaning 3: Constructivist psychotherapy in the real world.* New York: Pace University Press.

Rath, J. F., Bertisch, H., & Elliot, T. R. (2014). Groups in behavioral health settings. In J. L. DeLucia-Waack, C. R. Kalodner, & M. T. Riva (Eds.), *Handbook of group counseling and psychotherapy* (2nd ed., pp. 340–350). Thousand Oaks, CA: Sage.

Ratts, M. (2009). Social justice counseling: Toward the development of a fifth force among counseling paradigms. *Journal of Humanistic Counseling, Education and Development, 48*(2), 160–172.

Ratts, M., Anthony, L., & Santos, K. (2010). The dimensions of social justice model: Transforming traditional group work into a socially just framework. *Journal for Specialists in Group Work, 35,* 160–168.

Ray, R. G., & Raiche, A. (2006). *The facilitative leader: Behaviors that enable success* (2nd ed.). Little Hocking, OH: Raycom Learning.

Rayle, A., Sand, J., Brucato, T., & Ortega, J. (2006). The "Comadre" group approach: A wellness-based group model for monolingual Mexican women. *Journal for Specialists in Group Work, 31*(1), 5–24.

Ridley, C. R., Mollen, D., & Kelly, S. M. (2011). Beyond microskills: Toward a model of counseling competence. *Counseling Psychologist, 39,* 825–864.

Ringel, S. (2005). Group work with Asian-American immigrants: A cross-cultural perspective. In G. Greif & P. Ephross (Eds.), *Group work with populations at risk* (2nd ed., pp. 181–194). New York: Oxford University Press.

Riva, M. T. (2014). Supervision of group leaders. In J. L. DeLucia-Waack, C. R. Kalodner, & M. T. Riva (Eds.), *Handbook of group counseling and psychotherapy* (2nd ed., pp. 146–158). Thousand Oaks, CA: Sage.

Riva, M. T., Wachtel, M., & Lasky, G. (2004). Effective leadership in group counseling and psychotherapy: Research and practice. In J. L. DeLucia-Waack, D. A. Gerrity, C. R. Kalodner, & M. T. Riva (Eds.), *Handbook of group counseling and psychotherapy* (pp. 37–48). Thousand Oaks, CA: Sage.

Rivera, E. T., Fernandez, I. T., & Hendricks, W. A. (2014). Psychoeducational and counseling groups with Latinos/as. In J. L. DeLucia-Waack, C. R. Kalodner, & M. T. Riva (Eds.), *Handbook of group counseling and psychotherapy* (2nd ed., pp. 242–252). Thousand Oaks, CA: Sage.

Rivera, E. T., Garrett, M. T., & Crutchfield, L. B. (2004). Multicultural interventions in groups: The use of indigenous methods. In J. L. DeLucia-Waack, D. Gerrity, C. Kalodner, & M. T. Riva (Eds.), *Handbook of group counseling and psychotherapy* (pp. 295–306). Thousand Oaks, CA: Sage.

Rizvi, S., Steffel, L., & Carson-Wong, A. (2013). An overview of dialectical behavior therapy for professional psychologists. *Professional Psychology: Research and Practice, 44*(2), 73–80.

Robbins, R. N. (2003). Developing cohesion in court-mandated group treatment of male spouse abusers. *International Journal of Group Psychotherapy, 53,* 261–285.

Robertson, J., & Shepard, D. S. (2008). The psychological development of boys. In M. Kiselica, M. Englar-Carlson, & A. Horne (Eds.), *Counseling troubled boys* (pp. 3–30). New York: Routledge.

Rogers, C. R. (1970). *On encounter groups.* New York: Harper & Row.

Rogers, C. R. (1980). *A way of being.* Boston: Houghton Mifflin.

Roller, B., & Nelson, V. (1991). *The art of co-therapy: How therapists work together.* London: Guilford Press.

Romero, C. (2008). Writing wrongs: Promoting forgiveness through expressive writing. *Journal of Social and Personal Relationships, 25*(4), 625–642.

Rosenthal, H. (2011). *Favorite counseling and therapy homework assignments* (2nd ed.). New York: Routledge.

Roth, B., Stone, W., & Kibel, H. (1990). *The difficult patient in group.* Madison, CT: International Universities Press.

Ruiz, E. (2012). Understanding Latina immigrants using relational cultural theory. *Women & Therapy, 35*(1–2), 68–79.

Rutan, J. S., Stone, W. N., & Shay, J. (2007). *Psychodynamic group psychotherapy* (4th ed.). New York: Guilford Press.

Sadr, A. (2006). How Hollywood's myths about group psychotherapy can benefit beginning group therapists. *International Journal of Group Psychotherapy, 56,* 383–391.

Safran, J. D. (2012). *Psychoanalysis and psychoanalytic therapies.* Washington, DC: American Psychological Association.

Salinger, J. D. (1994). *Catcher in the rye.* London: Penguin Books.

Sarason, I. G., & Sarason, B. R. (2009). Social support: Mapping the construct. *Journal of Social and Personal Relationships, 26,* 113–120.

Satir, V. (1972). *Peoplemaking.* Palo Alto, CA: Science and Behavior Books.

Satir, V., & Baldwin, M. (1983). *Satir step by step: A guide to creating change in families.* Palo Alto, CA: Science & Behavior Books.

Schiller, L. Y. (2007). Not for women only: Applying the relational model of group development with vulnerable populations. *Social Work With Groups, 30,* 11–26.

Schimmel, C. J., & Jacobs, E. E. (2011). When leaders are challenged: Dealing with involuntary members in groups. *Journal for Specialists in Group Work, 36,* 144–158.

Schneider, K., & Krug, O. (2010). *Existential therapy.* Washington, DC: American Psychological Association.

Schoenberg, P., Feder, B., Frew, J., & Gadol, I. (2005). Gestalt therapy in groups. In A. Woldt & S. Toman (Eds.), *Gestalt therapy: History, theory, and practice* (pp. 219–236). Thousand Oaks, CA: Sage.

Schoenwolf, G. (1998). The scapegoat and the holy cow in group therapy. *Journal of Contemporary Psychotherapy, 28,* 277–287.

Schulenberg, S. E. (2003). Psychotherapy and movies: On using films in clinical practice. *Journal of Contemporary Psychotherapy, 33,* 35–48.

Schutz, W. C. (1958). *FIRO: A three dimensional theory of interpersonal behavior.* New York: Rinehart.

Schwartz, S., Unger, J., Zamboanga, B., & Szapocznik, J. (2010). Rethinking the concept of acculturation: Implications for theory and research. *American Psychologist, 65*(4), 237–251.

Scott, M. J., & Stradling, S. G. (1998). *Brief group counseling: Integrating individual and group cognitive-behavioural approaches.* Chichester, UK: Wiley.

Sehgal, R., Saules, K., Young, A., Grey, M., Gillem, A., Nabors, N. A., et al. (2011). Practicing what we know: Multicultural counseling competence among clinical psychology trainees and experienced multicultural psychologists. *Cultural Diversity and Ethnic Minority Psychology, 17*(1), 1–10.

Shakoor, M. (2010). *On becoming a group member: Personal growth and effectiveness in group counseling.* New York: Routledge.

Sharp, C., Smith, J. V., & Cole, A. (2002). Cinematherapy: Metaphorically promoting therapeutic change. *Counselling Psychology Quarterly, 15,* 269–276.

Shechtman, Z., & Gluk, O. (2005). Therapeutic factors in group psychotherapy with children. *Group Dynamics: Theory, Research, and Practice, 9,* 127–134.

Shechtman, Z., & Nir-Shfrir, R. (2008). The effect of affective bibliotherapy on clients' functioning in group therapy. *International Journal of Group Psychotherapy, 58*(1), 103–117.

Shechtman, Z., & Toren, Z. (2010). The association of personal, process, and outcome variables in group counseling: Testing an exploratory model. *Group Dynamics: Theory, Research and Practice, 14,* 292–303.

Shorrock, A. (2008). *The transpersonal in psychology, psychotherapy and counselling.* New York: Palgrave Macmillan.

Shulman, L. (2011). *The skills of helping individuals, families, groups, and communities* (7th ed.). Belmont, CA: Wadsworth.

Singh, A. A., & Hays, D. (2008). Feminist group counseling with South Asian women who have survived intimate partner violence. *Journal for Specialists in Group Work, 33*(1), 84–102.

Singh, A. A., Merchant, N., Skudrzyk, B., & Ingene, D. (2012). Association for Specialists in Group Work: Multicultural and social justice competence principles for group workers. *Journal for Specialists in Group Work, 37*, 312–325.

Singh, A. A., & Salazar, C. F. (2014). Using groups to facilitate social justice change: Addressing issues of privilege and oppression. In J. L. DeLucia-Waack, C. R. Kalodner, & M. T. Riva (Eds.), *Handbook of group counseling and psychotherapy* (2nd ed., pp. 288–300). Thousand Oaks, CA: Sage.

Sloan, D., Bovin, M., & Schnurr, P. (2012). Review of group treatment for PTSD. *Journal of Rehabilitation Research and Development, 49*(5), 689–701.

Smith, T. B., Rodríguez, M. D., & Bernal, G. (2011). Culture. In J. C. Norcross (Ed.), *Psychotherapy relationships that work* (2nd ed., pp. 316–335). New York: Oxford University Press.

Smokowski, P. R. (2003). Beyond role-playing: Using technology to enhance modeling and behavioral rehearsal in groupwork practice. *Journal of Specialists in Group Work, 28*, 9–22.

Smyth, J., & Helm, R. (2003). Focused expressive writing as self-help for stress and trauma. *JCLP/In Session: Psychotherapy in Practice, 59*, 227–235.

Smyth, J., Nazarian, D., & Arigo, D. (2008). Expressive writing in the clinical context. In A. Vingerhoets, I. Nyklícek, & J. Denollet (Eds.), *Emotion regulation: Conceptual and clinical issues* (pp. 215–233). New York: Springer.

Sole, K. (2006). Eight suggestions from the small-group conflict trenches. In M. Deutsch, P. Coleman, & E. Marcus (Eds.), *The handbook of conflict resolution: Theory and practice* (2nd ed., pp. 805–821). Hoboken, NJ: Wiley.

Sommers-Flanagan, R., & Sommers-Flanagan, J. (2007). *Becoming an ethical helping professional: Cultural and philosophical foundations*. Hoboken, NJ: Wiley.

Sonstegard, M., Bitter, J., & Pelonis, P. (2004). *Adlerian group counseling and therapy: Step by step*. New York: Routledge.

Spanierman, L., Todd, N., & Anderson, C. (2009). Psychosocial costs of racism to Whites: Understanding patterns among university students. *Journal of Counseling Psychology, 56*(2), 239–252.

Spiegler, M. D. (2013). Behavior therapy I: Traditional behavior therapy. In J. Frew & M. Spiegler (Eds.), *Contemporary psychotherapies for a diverse world* (Rev. ed., pp. 259–300). Boston: Lahaska Press.

Spiegler, M. D., & Guevremont, D. C. (2010). *Contemporary behavior therapy* (5th ed.). Belmont, CA: Wadsworth.

Stanger, T., & Harris, R. (2005). Marathon group therapy: Potential for university counseling centers and beyond. *Journal for Specialists in Group Work, 30*, 145–157.

Steen, S., Shi, Q., & Hockersmith, W. (2014). Group counseling for African Americans: Research and practice considerations. In J. L. DeLucia-Waack, C. R. Kalodner, & M. T. Riva (Eds.), *Handbook of group counseling and psychotherapy* (2nd ed., pp. 220–230). Thousand Oaks, CA: Sage.

Stockton, R., Morran, K., & Chang, S.-H. (2014). An overview of current research and best practices for training beginning group leaders. In J. L. DeLucia-Waack,

C. R. Kalodner, & M. T. Riva (Eds.), *Handbook of group counseling and psychotherapy* (2nd ed., pp. 133–145). Thousand Oaks, CA: Sage.

Stone, M. (1998). Journaling with clients. *Journal of Individual Psychology, 54,* 535–545.

Stout, C., & Hayes, R. (2005). *The evidence-based practice: Methods, models, and tools for mental health professionals.* Hoboken, NJ: Wiley.

Stricker, G. (2010). *Psychotherapy integration.* Washington, DC: American Psychological Association.

Sudak, D. (2012). Cognitive behavioral therapy for depression. *Psychiatric Clinics of North America, 35*(1), 99–110.

Sue, D. W. (2010). *Microaggressions in everyday life: Race, gender, and sexual orientations.* New York: Wiley.

Sue, D. W., Capodilupo, C., & Holder, A. (2008). Racial microaggressions in the life experience of Black Americans. *Professional Psychology: Research and Practice, 39*(3), 329–336.

Sue, D. W., Capodilupo, C., Torino, G., Bucceri, J., Holder, A., Nadal, K., et al. (2007). Racial microaggressions in everyday life: Implications for clinical practice. *American Psychologist, 62*(4), 271–286.

Sue, D. W., Lin, A., Torino, G., Capodilupo, C., & Rivera, D. (2009). Racial microaggressions and difficult dialogues on race in the classroom. *Cultural Diversity and Ethnic Minority Psychology, 15*(2), 183–190.

Sue, D. W., & Sue, S. (2013). *Counseling the culturally diverse* (6th ed.). Hoboken, NJ: Wiley.

Sue, S., & Zane, N. (2009). The role of culture and cultural techniques in psychotherapy: A critique and reformulation. *Asian American Journal of Psychology, 1,* 3–14.

Suh, S., & Lee, M. (2006). Group work for Korean expatriate women in the United States: An exploratory study. *Journal for Specialists in Group Work, 31*(4), 353–369.

Sullivan, H. S. (1947). *Conceptions of modern psychiatry.* New York: Norton.

Sullivan, H. S. (1953). *The interpersonal theory of psychiatry.* New York: Norton.

Taber, B. J., Leibert, T. W., & Agaskar, V. R. (2011). Relationships among client-therapist personality congruence, working alliance, and therapeutic outcome. *Psychotherapy, 48,* 376–380.

Taha, M., Mahfouz, R., & Arafa, M. (2008). Socio-cultural influence on group psychotherapy leadership style. *Group Analysis, 41,* 391–406.

Teyber, E., & Faith, H. (2011). *Interpersonal process in therapy: An integrated model* (6th ed.). Belmont, CA: Brooks.

Thomas, R. V., & Pender, D. A. (2008). Association for Specialists in Group Work: Best Practice Guidelines 2007 revisions. *Journal for Specialists in Group Work, 33,* 111–117.

Thompson, K. (2011). *Therapeutic journal writing: An introduction for professionals.* London: Jessica Kingsley.

Tomlinson, B. (2009). *Family assessment handbook: An introductory practice to guide family assessment and intervention* (3rd ed.). Belmont, CA: Wadsworth.

Toseland, R. W., Jones, L. V., & Gellis, Z. D. (2004). Group dynamics. In C. D. Garvin, L. M. Gutierrez, & M. J. Galinsky (Eds.), *Handbook of social work in groups* (pp. 13–31). New York: Guilford.

Troop, N., Chilcot, J., Hutchings, L., & Varnaite, G. (2013). Expressive writing, self-criticism, and self-reassurance. *Psychology and Psychotherapy: Theory, Research and Practice, 86*(4), 374–386.

Tschushke, V., Anbeh, T., & Kiencke, P. (2007). Evaluation of long-term analytic outpatient group therapies. *Group Analysis, 40,* 140–159.

Tuckman, B. W. (1965). Developmental sequence in small groups. *Psychological Bulletin, 63,* 384–399.

Tuckman, B. W., & Jensen, M. A. (1977). Stages of small-group development revisited. *Group and Organizational Studies, 2,* 419–427.

Tyson, E. H., & Baffour, T. D. (2004). Arts-based strengths: A solution-focused intervention with adolescents in an acute-care psychiatric setting. *Arts in Psychotherapy, 31,* 213–227.

Ullrich, P. M., & Lutgendorf, S. K. (2002). Journaling about stressful events: Effects of cognitive processing and emotional expression. *Annals of Behavioral Medicine, 24,* 244–250.

Urlić, I. (2010). The phenomenon of silence: A group-analytic exploration of meanings in psychotherapy and in everyday life. *Group Analysis, 43*(3), 337–353.

Vacha-Haase, T. (2014). Group work with those in later life. In J. L. DeLucia-Waack, C. R. Kalodner, & M. T. Riva (Eds.), *Handbook of group counseling and psychotherapy* (2nd ed., pp. 276–287). Thousand Oaks, CA: Sage.

Vander Kolk, C. J. (1985). *Introduction to group counseling and psychotherapy.* Columbus, OH: Merrill.

Vasquez, M. (2007). Cultural difference and the therapeutic alliance: An evidence-based analysis. *American Psychologist, 62*(8), 878–885.

Vereen, L., Butler, S., Williams, F., Darg, J., & Downing, T. (2006). The use of humor when counseling African American college students. *Journal of Counseling & Development, 84,* 10–15.

Vereen, L., Hill, N., & Butler, S. (2013). The use of humor and storytelling with African American men: Innovative therapeutic strategies for success in counseling. *International Journal for the Advancement of Counselling, 35*(1), 57–63.

Viers, D. (Ed.). (2007). *The group therapist's notebook: Homework, handouts, and activities for use in psychotherapy.* New York: Haworth Press.

Von Bertalanffy, L. (1968). *General systems theory: Foundations, development, application.* New York: Braziller.

Wageman, R., Nunes, D. A., Burruss, J. A., & Hackman, J. R. (2008). *Senior leadership teams: What it takes to make them great.* Cambridge, MA: Harvard Business School Press.

Wampold, B. E. (2007). Psychotherapy: "The" humanistic (and effective) treatment. *American Psychologist, 62,* 857–875.

Wampold, B. E. (2010). *The basics of psychotherapy.* Washington, DC: American Psychological Association.

Wang, C., & Leung, A. (2010). The cultural dynamics of rewarding honesty and punishing deception. *Personality and Social Psychology Bulletin, 36*(11), 1529–1542.

Wang, J., Leu, J., & Shoda, Y. (2011). When the seemingly innocuous "stings": Racial microaggressions and their emotional consequences. *Personality & Social Psychology Bulletin, 37*(12), 1666–1678.

Ward, D. E. (2004). The evidence mounts: Group work is effective. *Journal for Specialists in Group Work, 29*(2), 155–157.

Ward, D. E. (2014). Effective processing in groups. In J. L. DeLucia-Waack, C. R. Kalodner, & M. T. Riva (Eds.), *Handbook of group counseling and psychotherapy* (2nd ed., pp. 84–94). Thousand Oaks, CA: Sage.

Ward, D. E., & Litchy, M. (2004). The effective use of processing in groups. In J. L. DeLucia-Waack, C. R. Kalodner, & M. T. Riva (Eds.), *Handbook of group counseling and psychotherapy* (pp. 104–119). Thousand Oaks, CA: Sage.

Wedding, D., Boyd, M., & Niemiec, R. (2010). *Movies and mental illness: Using films to understand psychopathology* (3rd ed.). Ashland, OH: Hogrefe & Huber.

Wedding, D., & Niemiec, R. (2003). The clinical use of films in psychotherapy. *Journal of Clinical Psychology, 59*(2), 207–215.

Weigel, R. G. (2002). The marathon encounter group—vision and reality: Exhuming the body for a last look. *Consulting Psychology Journal: Practice and Research, 54,* 186–198.

Weinberg, H., & Schneider, S. (2007). Ethical considerations in the large group. *Group, 31,* 215–228.

Welfel, E. R. (2013). *Ethics in counseling and psychotherapy: Standards, research, and emerging issues* (5th ed.). Belmont, CA: Brooks/Cole.

Wesner, A., Gomes, J., Detzel, T., Blaya, C., Manfro, G., & Heldt, E. (2014). Effect of cognitive-behavioral group therapy for panic disorder in changing coping strategies. *Comprehensive Psychiatry, 55*(1), 87–92.

Wheelan, S. A. (2004a). *Group processes: A developmental perspective* (2nd ed.). Boston: Allyn & Bacon.

Wheelan, S. A. (2004b). Groups in the workplace. In J. L. DeLucia-Waack, D. A. Gerrity, C. R. Kalodner, & M. T. Riva (Eds.), *Handbook of group counseling and psychotherapy* (pp. 401–413). Thousand Oaks, CA: Sage.

Wheelan, S. A. (2009). Group size, group development, and group productivity. *Small Group Research, 40,* 247–262.

Wheeler, G., & Axelsson, L. (2015). *Gestalt theory.* Washington, DC: American Psychological Association.

Wheeler, N., & Bertram, B. (2012). *The counseling and the law: A guide to legal and ethical practice* (6th ed.). Alexandria, VA: American Counseling Association.

White, M., & Epston, D. (1990). *Narrative means to therapeutic ends.* New York: Norton.

White, N., & Rayle, A. (2007). Strong teens: A school-based small group experience for African American males. *Journal for Specialists in Group Work, 32*(2), 178–189.

White, V. E., & Murray, M. A. (2002). Passing notes: The use of therapeutic letter writing in counseling adolescents. *Journal of Mental Health Counseling, 24,* 166–176.

Wiitala, W. L., & Dansereau, D. F. (2004). Using popular quotations to enhance therapeutic writing. *Journal of College Counseling, 7,* 187–191.

Wilson, E., & Harris, C. (2006). Meaningful travel: Women, independent travel and the search for self and meaning. *Tourism, 54*(2), 161–172.

Wilz, G., & Barskova, T. (2007). Evaluation of a cognitive behavioral group intervention program for spouses of stroke patients. *Behaviour Research and Therapy, 45*(10), 2508–2517.

Wofford, M. (2012). *Making difficult people disappear: How to deal with stressful behavior and eliminate conflict.* New York: Wiley.

Wojciszke, B. (2005). Morality and competence in person- and self-perception. *European Review of Social Psychology, 16*, 155–188.

World Health Organization. (1992). *The ICD-10 classification system of mental and behavioral disorder: Clinical descriptions and diagnostic guidelines.* Geneva, Switzerland: Author.

Wright, R. (1994). *The moral animal: The new science of evolutionary psychology.* New York: Pantheon Books.

Wubbolding, R. (2007). Glasser quality school. *Group Dynamics: Theory, Research, and Practice, 11*(4), 253–261.

Wubbolding, R. (2011). *Reality therapy.* Washington, DC: American Psychological Association.

Yalom, I. D. (1980). *Existential psychotherapy.* New York: Basic Books.

Yalom, I. D. (2008). *Staring into the sun: Overcoming the dread of death.* San Francisco: Jossey-Bass.

Yalom, I. D., & Leszcz, M. (2005). *The theory and practice of group psychotherapy* (5th ed.). New York: Basic Books.

Zane, N., Hall, G. C. N., Sue, S., Young, K., & Nunez, J. (2004). Research on psychotherapy with culturally diverse populations. In M. J. Lambert (Ed.), *Bergin and Garfield's handbook of psychotherapy and behavior change* (5th ed., pp. 767–804). New York: Wiley.

Index

About the Authors

Jeffrey A. Kottler is a professor of counseling at California State University, Fullerton, where he teaches group process and leadership, as well as courses in social justice and advocacy. He is also president of Empower Nepali Girls (www.empower-nepaligirls.org), which provides educational scholarships for marginalized and at-risk girls in rural Nepal. He served as a Fulbright Scholar and a senior lecturer in Peru and Iceland, and also worked as a visiting professor in New Zealand, Australia, Hong Kong, Singapore, and Nepal. He has written more than 80 books in the fields of counseling, psychology, and education, including several about group leadership. Some of his most recent works include *On Being a Therapist, Creative Breakthroughs in Therapy, Change: What Leads to Personal Transformation, On Being a Master Therapist, Helping Beyond the 50-Minute Hour,* and *The Therapist's Workbook.* Jeffrey has led and supervised groups in clinics, hospitals, schools, universities, agencies, and private practice. He has also taught beginning and advanced group classes more than 100 times in North America and in countries throughout the world.

Matt Englar-Carlson is a professor of counseling at California State University, Fullerton, where he teaches courses in group process, counseling theory, and qualitative research. He is also the codirector of the Center for Boys and Men (boysandmencenter.fullerton.edu) at California State University, Fullerton. A former school counselor in Pennsylvania and California, he has taught group counseling and process to hundreds of students across the United States, and has facilitated groups in schools, community settings, work sites, and university settings. He is also a teacher at Esalen Institute in Big Sur, California, where he facilitates experiential workshops for men. Matt coedited *In the Room With Men: A Casebook of Therapeutic Change, Counseling Troubled Boys: A Guidebook for Professionals, Helping Beyond the 50-Minute Hour, A Counselor's Guide to Working With Men*, and the 24-volume American Psychological Association's *Theories of Psychotherapy* book series. Matt lives in Huntington Beach, California, with his wife, Alison, and his two children, Jackson and Beatrix.

⑤SAGE research**methods**

The essential online tool for researchers from the world's leading methods publisher

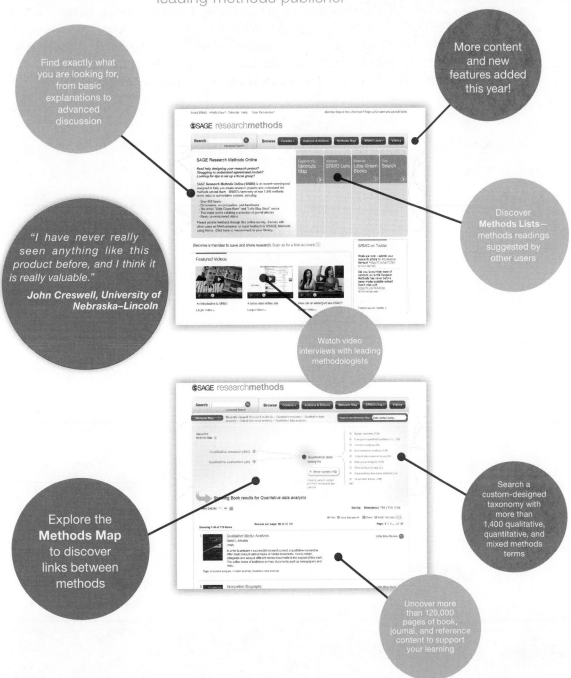

Find exactly what you are looking for, from basic explanations to advanced discussion

More content and new features added this year!

"I have never really seen anything like this product before, and I think it is really valuable."

John Creswell, University of Nebraska–Lincoln

Discover **Methods Lists**—methods readings suggested by other users

Watch video interviews with leading methodologists

Explore the **Methods Map** to discover links between methods

Search a custom-designed taxonomy with more than 1,400 qualitative, quantitative, and mixed methods terms

Uncover more than 120,000 pages of book, journal, and reference content to support your learning

Find out more at
www.sageresearchmethods.com